Behavior Analysis
and Learning

Behavior Analysis and Learning

Fourth Edition

W. David Pierce
University of Alberta

Carl D. Cheney
Utah State University

Ψ Psychology Press
Taylor & Francis Group
NEW YORK AND HOVE

Published in 2008
by Psychology Press
270 Madison Avenue
New York, NY 10016
www.psypress.com

Published in Great Britain
by Psychology Press
27 Church Road
Hove, East Sussex BN3 2FA

Psychology Press is an imprint of the Taylor & Francis Group, an Informa business

Typeset by RefineCatch Limited, Bungay, Suffolk, UK
Printed and bound by Edwards Brothers, Inc. in the USA on acid-free paper
Cover design by Lisa Dynan
Cover illustration by Terry E. Smith

10 9 8 7 6 5 4 3 2 1

Library of Congress Cataloging in Publication Data
A catalog record for this book is available from the Library of Congress

ISBN: 978-0-8058-6260-7 (hbk)

To B. F. Skinner

When an organism acts upon the environment in which it lives, it changes that environment in ways that often affect the organism itself. Some of these changes are what the layman calls rewards, or what are generally referred to technically as reinforcers: when they follow behavior in this way they increase the likelihood that the organism will behave in the same way again.

(Ferster & Skinner, 1957, p. 1)

Contents

Foreword by Philip N. Hineline   xi
Preface   xiii

1 A Science of Behavior: Perspective, History, and Assumptions   1
Science and behavior 2
New directions: Behavior analysis and neuroscience 5
Focus on: B. F. Skinner 9
A brief history of behavior analysis 11
Science and behavior: Some assumptions 18
Chapter summary 21

2 The Experimental Analysis of Behavior   23
Functional analysis of behavior 23
Functional analysis of the environment 25
Tactics of behavioral research 28
Focus on: Operant baselines and behavioral neuroscience 32
Single-subject research 33
Focus on: Assessment of behavior change 34
Advanced section: Perceiving as behavior 36
Chapter summary 39

3 Reflexive Behavior and Respondent Conditioning   41
Phylogenetic behavior 41
Ontogenetic behavior 46
Temporal relations and conditioning 51
Second-order respondent conditioning 53
On the applied side: Drug use, abuse, and complexities of respondent conditioning 53
Note on: Physiology and the control of preparatory responses by conditioned stimuli 54
Advanced section: Complex conditioning 56
Aspects of complex conditioning 56
The Rescorla–Wagner model of conditioning 58
Focus on: The Rescorla–Wagner equation 59
Chapter summary 62

4 Reinforcement and Extinction of Operant Behavior   65
Operant behavior 65
Focus on: Rewards and intrinsic motivation 69
Operant conditioning 72
Focus on: Behavioral neuroscience and operant conditioning of the neuron 74
Focus on: Reinforcement and problem solving 81
Extinction 82
Note on: Remembering and recalling 87
On the applied side: Extinction of temper tantrums 89
Chapter summary 90

5 Schedules of Reinforcement   **93**

Importance of schedules of reinforcement 93
C. B. Ferster: Schedules of reinforcement 94
Focus on: Science and behavior analysis 96
Comment on: Inner causes, schedules, and response patterns 97
Focus on: A system of notation 99
Schedules of positive reinforcement 101
Ratio and interval schedules of reinforcement 103
Focus on: Generality of schedule effects 106
Note on: VI schedules, reinforcement rate, and behavioral momentum 109
Schedule performance in transition 110
On the applied side: Schedules and cigarettes 112
Advanced section: Schedule performance 114
Chapter summary 119

6 Aversive Control of Behavior   **121**

Contingencies of punishment 122
Quick tip: Procedures to reduce rate of response 122
Focus on: Use of punishment in treatment 126
Contingencies of negative reinforcement 129
Focus on: An analysis of avoidance behavior 134
Side effects of aversive procedures 135
Focus on: Social defeat, aversion to social contact, and behavioral neuroscience 139
On the applied side: Coercion and its fallout 144
Note on: The definition of coercion 145
Chapter summary 146

**7 Operant–Respondent Interrelationships and the Biological Context of
    Conditioning**   **149**

Analysis of operant–respondent contingencies 150
Note on: Operants and respondents 157
The biological context of conditioning 158
Focus on: Behavioral neuroscience, taste aversion, and urges for addictive behavior 160
On the applied side: Activity anorexia and interrelations between eating
    and physical activity 164
Advanced section: The nature of autoshaped responses 167
Chapter summary 169

8 Stimulus Control   **171**

Differential reinforcement and discrimination 172
Focus on: Stimulus control, neuroscience, and what birds see 173
Stimulus control and multiple schedules 173
Focus on: Discrimination and the "bird-brained" pigeon 175
Focus on: Determinants of behavioral contrast 178
Generalization 179
Errorless discrimination and fading 182
Complex stimulus control 185
Focus on: Concept formation by pigeons 188
On the applied side: The pigeon as a quality control inspector 190
Chapter summary 191

9 Choice and Preference   **193**
Experimental analysis of choice and preference 193
The matching law 198
Choice, foraging, and behavioral economics 204
Focus on: Activity anorexia and substitutability of food and wheel running 206
Matching and single-operant schedules of reinforcement 208
On the applied side: Application of the quantitative law of effect 210
Advanced section: Quantification of choice and generalized matching 212
Focus on behavioral neuroscience, matching, and sensitivity 218
Chapter summary 219

10 Conditioned Reinforcement   **221**
Note on: Clicker training 222
Chain schedules and conditioned reinforcement 222
Focus on: Backward chaining 224
Determinants of conditioned reinforcement 225
Focus on: Behavioral neuroscience and conditioned reinforcement 227
Delay reduction and conditioned reinforcement 230
Generalized conditioned reinforcement 232
On the applied side: The token economy 236
Advanced section: Quantification and delay reduction 237
Chapter summary 239

11 Correspondence Relations: Imitation and Rule-Governed Behavior   **241**
Correspondence and observational learning 243
Focus on: Behavioral neuroscience, mirror neurons, and imitation 249
On the applied side: Training generalized imitation 253
Focus on: Rules, observational learning, and self-efficacy 257
Rule-governed behavior 257
Focus on: Instructions and contingencies 261
Focus on: Following rules and joint control 264
Chapter summary 265

12 Verbal Behavior   **267**
Language and verbal behavior 267
Focus on: Speaking and evolution of the vocal tract 268
Verbal behavior: Some basic distinctions 269
Operant functions of verbal behavior 271
Research on verbal behavior 273
Additional verbal relations: Intraverbals, echoics, and textuals 276
Analysis of complex behavior in the laboratory 278
Focus on: Reports of private events by pigeons 281
Symbolic behavior and stimulus equivalence 283
Focus on: Behavioral neuroscience and derived conceptual relations 287
On the applied side: Three-term contingencies and natural speech 289
Advanced section: A formal analysis of manding and tacting 290
Chapter summary 292

13 Applied Behavior Analysis   **295**
Characteristics of applied behavior analysis 296
Research in applied behavior analysis 300

Focus on: Personalized system of instruction and precision teaching 305
Applications of behavior principles 310
Focus on: Autism, mirror neurons, and applied behavior analysis 312
The causes and prevention of behavior problems 314
Focus on: Conditioned overeating and childhood obesity 316
On the applied side: MammaCare—detection and prevention of breast cancer 318
Chapter summary 320

14 Three Levels of Selection: Biology, Behavior, and Culture   **323**
Level 1: Evolution and natural selection 323
Focus on: Genetic control of a fixed action pattern 326
Level 2: Selection by reinforcement 329
Level 3: The selection and evolution of culture 335
Focus on: Metacontingencies 336
Chapter summary 338

Glossary   339

References   369

Author index   407

Subject index   419

Foreword

Some three score years ago, behavior analysis emerged as a distinct and coherent viewpoint through a book, *Behavior of Organisms*, along with a handful of seminal papers, all by B. F. Skinner. Over the ensuing decades that systematic account of behavior, *in general* and *as such* (rather than as index or symptom of underlying mental or physiological process), has required remarkably few changes in its core network of concepts. The approach *has*, however, been systematically augmented and elaborated in the manner of cumulative science, and its practical applications have become increasingly important. The early additions and innovations were provided mainly by Skinner himself—for example, clearly delineating how behavior analysis differs from other psychological viewpoints, addressing verbal behavior in terms of its functions instead of its syntactical forms, and providing an account of what is at issue when traditional psychological terms such as awareness and perception are invoked.

Early empirical developments of the approach were firmly based in laboratory work that addressed some key issues that, prior to Skinner, had been largely unrecognized by psychologists. For example, a concept resembling reinforcement had been around since the Greek hedonists, and early in the 20th century was saliently placed within psychology by Thorndike as the "Law of Effect." However, it was only with the systematic program of experimental research initiated by Skinner and his colleagues that a key question was addressed in detail: *What if it doesn't happen every time?* The resulting schedules of reinforcement, while systematically studied in the laboratory and ubiquitous in everyday life, are of a subtlety that to this day often remains unappreciated—as when pathological gambling is attributed to defective characteristics of a person, rather than to the person's history of intermittent reinforcement, and as when theorists fail to distinguish how the relations embedded in "reinforcement" extend powerfully beyond what is understood in use of the more conventional but tenuously related term, "reward." But I digress.

As Skinner's career progressed, his writing shifted increasingly toward the conceptual and cultural implications of the system, offering contributions that ranged widely from book-length argument (*Beyond Freedom and Dignity*) to succinct and pertinent essays ("The Ethics of Helping People"). Meanwhile, the agenda of experimentally-based developments was carried forward by numerous others. Thus, even during Skinner's lifetime the contributory base of behavior analysis broadened rapidly. Some additions to the network of concepts emerged through particular individuals' careful thinking and argument—as in Jack Michael's clarification of *establishing operations*, which elaborated behavior analysis within the domain traditionally addressed with motivational terms that obscure the historical origins of an individual's actions. In another, Zettle and Hayes extended Skinner's account of verbal behavior by introducing terms that apply specifically to the listener's behavior in reciprocal relation to the behavior of the speaker—Skinner had characterized the listener's role in less differentiated fashion, as the "verbal community" that contributes to the individual's aggregate verbal history. The cumulative nature of behavior-analytic developments is especially evident in the more quantitative domains, where Herrnstein's matching law was transformed to accommodate apparent exceptions, in Baum's Generalized Matching Law, which was then integrated into a conceptual synthesis with Signal Detection Theory by Tustin and Davison, and elaborated further by Davison and Nevin, among others.

The result that emerges from all this is contemporary behavior analysis—clusters of research, researchers, and practitioners, related like a loose confederacy of tribes thriving in distinct niches while allied by a common conceptual identity: Home-based interventions for children with autism, system-scale remedies for schools in difficulty, verbal and rule-governed behavior, foraging theory, choice, temporal discounting, safety programs in the workplace, relational frame theory, and, most recently, linkages with contemporary neuroscience. Some readers may be surprised at the last of these, but one does not know what the brain is doing unless one knows what the organism is doing, and behavior analysis is a thoroughgoing, systematic attempt at accounting for the latter.

Making sense of all this presents a daunting challenge to anyone with the temerity to represent the whole field with a single volume, as one must do in writing a textbook. Effective textbooks are crucial, however. While Skinner's *Science and Human Behavior* was his attempt at a systematic text, it was Keller and Schoenfeld's *Principles of Psychology* that initially gained a foothold for behavior analysis within psychology. Subsequently, at any given time the field has been represented by at least two or three alternatives, and in recent years these have become differentiated in their degrees of complexity and sophistication. Now into its fourth edition, this volume by Pierce and Cheney occupies a middle ground, adroitly portraying foundational principles along with indications of contemporary application, contemporary research with sketches of contemporary researchers, concisely defined concepts along with their subtle possibilities—all of this pitched at a level to engage teachers and students alike, and all of which bodes well for its future.

Philip N. Hineline
Temple University
12 November 2007

Preface

We again dedicate this book to the memory of W. Frank Epling who was coauthor of the first two editions of *Behavior Analysis and Learning*. He was a great personal friend of ours, an excellent teacher, and a productive colleague. We have tried to make this fourth edition as good as Frank would accept.

We received a great deal of positive feedback from readers and users of the third edition, which we greatly appreciate. This fourth edition retains much of the major organization, information, and features of the previous editions, yet, as with any revision, we made several alterations in topics and presentation. We tried to respond to user and reviewer comments and to the availability of new information from the literature. Reviewers report that although this is a basic experimental analysis text, they liked the inclusion of applied human and nonhuman examples, and we continue this feature. Most readers indicated that they appreciate the use of Mechner notation as a clear depiction of the experimental contingencies, the independent variables that control behavior. Users and reviewers also encouraged us to include more biobehavioral findings, which we have done. For example, recent reports of "mirror" neurons and their possible involvement in imitation are discussed. We also outline the role of the nucleus accumbens in choice behavior, and the involvement of the amygdala in conditioned reinforcement. An added treatment of the vocal apparatus and verbal behavior contributes, we feel, to the synthesis of biology and behavior. Although we remain dedicated to behavior analysis we appreciate the movement toward a synthesis of a science of behavior with neuroscience.

The pedagogical features remaining in the fourth edition include the *Focus On* inserts, the *Advanced Sections*, and *On The Applied Side* presentations: all considered important and helpful. The *Advanced Sections* have been moved to the end of chapters to permit instructors to address basic material without discussion of more complicated issues. We have added a *New Directions* component and *Chapter Summaries* which we expect will improve student progress.

In this edition we have updated nearly all areas, topics, and coverage as required by new findings, and we have incorporated several different study features. For readers/users we have collected all study questions that had been at the end of each chapter, PowerPoint presentations we have developed, video vignettes illustrating specific points, and other material considered helpful, on a dedicated website at: www.psypress.com/pierceandcheney. Using this system, the authors can add, delete, or alter material as considered appropriate. Many additional websites are indicated, and will be added, which can guide the reader to current items of interest. We consider websites to be a major resource for students and we encourage the instructor to incorporate web assignments whenever appropriate. Although a thorough reading of the text is sufficient to excel, most students nowadays have access to computers, are fluent with using the web, and actually expect to access information via this medium.

Although this is primarily a book about the way the world works with respect to operant behavior and operant conditioning, we maintain a detailed chapter on respondent conditioning but with an abbreviated and less demanding *Advanced Section*. We also continue to address respondent conditioning in the use of drugs and concepts of tolerance and withdrawal. In other chapters, the section on behavior analysis and education has been extensively expanded, and the discussion of genetic and operant control of behavior has continued with updated references, illustrating selection by consequences at different levels. We have also expanded the emphasis on principles of selection and the biological context of conditioning. Behavior analysts recognize the essential nature of biological contributions and constraints while simultaneously emphasizing what can be done with arbitrary selective procedures (contingency management) to alter socially important behavior.

The organization of the book has not changed because we consider the way it is now to be a systematic and reasonable progression of behavior science as a book format requires. We recommend assigning and treating the material in the order in which it is presented; of course individual adjustments and adaptations are possible for personal considerations best left to the instructor. Chapters 1 and 2 set the boundaries of behavior science and introduce many of the critical historical features and individuals relevant to placing behavior analysis in a context familiar to the reader. At this point, the basic behavior paradigm and the three-term operant contingencies of positive reinforcement and extinction are described in detail. The reinforcement and extinction chapter is followed by schedules of reinforcement, the major independent variable of behavior analysis. A new section on C. B. Ferster and reinforcement schedules shows that all operant behavior varies in rate and form with the programmed contingencies, both in the laboratory and the everyday world of people. Next, we introduce the control of behavior using aversive procedures, and the by-products of aversive control are detailed and emphasized. This particular order of the material allows us to more fully address the contingencies of positive and negative punishment, and negative reinforcement (escape and avoidance). By this point in the book all the basic contingencies have been covered.

Next, we focus on the interrelationship of operant and respondent contingencies and the biological context of behavior, showing that operant and respondent processes often (if not always) work together, or in opposition, in complex interacting relations. At this point, we more directly consider issues of antecedent stimulus control and the regulation of higher order behavioral processes such as conditional discrimination, remembering, and concept formation. Choice and preference based on concurrent schedules of reinforcement are the next logical step; in this fourth edition we retain a treatment of the matching law, address research on optimal foraging, behavioral economics, and self-control, and try to clarify the breadth and application of these areas of investigation. As the natural science of behavior matures, there will be an even greater expansion of these areas of analysis to more complex behavior involving multifaceted contingencies. One example of this is conditioned reinforcement and the regulation of behavior by concurrent-chain schedules of reinforcement. In this edition, we have expanded the coverage of concurrent-chain procedures and how these contingencies are used to evaluate the delay-reduction hypothesis and other accounts of conditioned reinforcement.

Imitation and rule-governed behavior are important issues in the analysis of human behavior and we have updated the chapter devoted to these topics, adding a neuroscience dimension to imitation learning. The analysis of the rule-governed behavior of the listener sets up the subsequent chapter on verbal behavior and analysis of the behavior of the speaker. We tried to compress the discussion of verbal behavior into a useful summary for students at this level, reducing some older material but adding new issues. Although we have not devoted as much space as this critical topic deserves, we considered the basic rationale and fundamental components of Skinner's analysis as well as more current analyses. The issues of private events and equivalence relations are discussed, as are some current reports from the *Journal of Verbal Behavior*.

We updated the chapter on applied behavior analysis with more examples, new issues, and recent material. It is nearly impossible or unnecessary to separate basic from applied behavior analysis but, due to its social importance and interest to students, a separate applied chapter is warranted. Behavior principles are so compelling that students often invent new applications when they first encounter the concepts of reinforcement and extinction. Our discipline has become more recognized and appreciated from the visible effects on human behavior in applied situations than from the possibly more important, but clearly more esoteric, findings from the lab. Applied behavior analysis is part and parcel of the experimental analysis of behavior and we include it wherever possible.

We end the book with a discussion of three levels of selection: natural selection, selection by reinforcement, and selection at the cultural level. The three levels of selection are described and the commonalities among them are elaborated as principles of nature. This issue bears careful and repeated mention, in our classes at least. It seems to require some repetition and time for many students to grasp the breadth and significance of what the point here is exactly. The utilization of virtually the same process (selection by consequences) to generate functional relations and explanations at vastly different levels of resolution should be impressive. Selection by consequences is the way the world works with few hard-wired actions but an ability to benefit (i.e., change behavior), depending upon the consequences of any action. The consequences of behaving, whether by a salivary gland, a child, or a political group, are what influence the likelihood of repetition of those actions.

Behavior analysis has always been an exciting scientific field and we hope that we have communicated our own enthusiasm for the discipline described in this book. By its very nature, the study of why we do the things we do appeals to nearly everyone very quickly. The formal aspects of behavior analysis and learning are having an impact on education, industry, therapy, animal training, medicine, clinical psychology, and environmental protection, to name only a few areas of successful application. There is an explicit technology available to those who master the principles of behavior and readers can use these principles to change their own and others' behavior. However, our major focus has remained to present the fundamental principles and procedures that form the foundation of a science of behavior.

Of course, many people have directly and indirectly contributed to this text and we thank them all. Our current world view began to take shape during our upbringing and was formed and promoted by family, friends, personal experience, and our teachers and students. We thank them all for what we are and for what we have produced.

W. David Pierce
Carl D. Cheney

A Science of Behavior: Perspective, History, and Assumptions

1

- Find out about *learning*, a science of behavior and behavior analysis.
- Discover how selection by consequences extends from evolution to the behavior of organisms.
- Focus on behavior analysis and neuroscience.
- Delve into the early beginnings of behavior analysis and learning.
- Investigate some of the basic assumptions of a science of behavior analysis and learning.

Learning refers to the acquisition, maintenance, and change of an organism's *behavior* as a result of lifetime events. The **behavior** of an organism is everything it does, including private and covert actions like thinking and feeling (see section on assumptions in this chapter). An important aspect of human learning concerns the experiences arranged by other people. From earliest history, people have acted to influence the behavior of other individuals. Rational argument, rewards, bribes, threats, and force are used in attempts to promote learning or change the behavior of people. Within society, people are required to learn socially appropriate ways of doing things. As long as a person does what is expected, no one pays much attention. As soon as a person's conduct substantially departs from cultural norms, other people get upset and try to force conformity. All societies have codes of conduct and laws that their people have to learn; people who break moral codes or civil laws face penalties ranging from minor fines to capital punishment. Clearly, all cultures are concerned with human learning and the regulation of human conduct.

Theories of learning and behavior have ranged from philosophy to natural science. When Socrates was told that new discoveries in anatomy proved that bodily movement was caused by the arrangement of muscles, bones, and joints, he replied, "That hardly explains why I am sitting here in a curved position talking to you" (Millenson, 1967, p. 3). About 2300 years later, the philosopher Alfred North Whitehead asked the famous behaviorist B. F. Skinner a similar question. He said, "Let me see you account for my behavior as I sit here saying, 'No black scorpion is falling upon this table'" (Skinner, 1957, p. 457). Although there was no satisfactory account of behavior in the time of Socrates, the science of behavior is currently addressing such puzzling questions.

Human behavior has been attributed to a great variety of causes. The causes of behavior have been located both within and outside of people. Internal causes have ranged from metaphysical entities like the soul to hypothetical structures of the nervous system. Suggested external causes of behavior have included the effect of the moon and tides, the arrangement of stars, and the whims of gods. Some of these theories of behavior remain popular today. For example, the use of astrological forecasts is even found in modern corporations, as demonstrated in the following passage taken from *The Economist*:

> Is astrology the ultimate key to competitive advantage? That is what Divinitel, a French company specializing in celestial consulting, claims. For FFr350 ($70) a session, the firm's astrologers offer

advice on anything from the timing of takeovers to exorcisms. For the busy executive, Divinitel's galaxy of services can be reached via Minitel, France's teletext system. The firm is even planning a flotation on France's over-the-counter stock market in March 1991.

So who is daft enough to pay for such mystical mumbo-jumbo? About 10% of French businesses are, according to a study by HEC, a French business school. A typical client is the boss of a small or medium-sized company who wants a second, astrological opinion on job applicants. The boss of one plastics company even uses Divinitel's advice on star signs to team up salesmen.

("Twinkle, twinkle," p. 91, January 1991)

The trouble with astrology and other such primitive and mystical accounts of behavior is that they are not scientific. That is, these theories do not hold up to testing by scientific methods. Over the last century, a scientific theory of learning and behavior has developed. Behavior theory states that all behavior is due to a complex interaction between genetic influence and environmental experience. The theory is based on observation and controlled experimentation, and it provides a natural-science account of the learning and behavior of organisms, including humans. This book is concerned with such an account.

SCIENCE AND BEHAVIOR

The **experimental analysis of behavior** is a natural-science approach to understanding behavior regulation. Experimental analysis is concerned with controlling and changing the factors affecting the behavior of humans and other animals. For example, a behavioral researcher in a classroom may use a computer to arrange corrective feedback for a student's mathematical performance. The relevant condition that is manipulated or changed by the experimenter may involve presenting corrective feedback on some days and withholding it on others. In this case, the researcher would probably observe more accurate mathematical performance on days when feedback was presented. This simple experiment illustrates one of the most basic principles of behavior—the principle of reinforcement.

The principle of reinforcement (and other behavior principles) provides a scientific account of how people and animals learn complex actions. When a researcher identifies a basic principle that governs behavior, this is called an analysis of behavior. Thus, the experimental analysis of behavior involves specifying the basic processes and principles that regulate the behavior of organisms. Experiments are then used to test the adequacy of the analysis.

Experimental analysis occurs when, for example, a researcher notices that more seagulls fly around a shoreline when people are on the beach than when the beach is deserted. After checking that changes in climate, temperature, time of day, and other conditions do not affect the behavior of the seagulls, the researcher offers the following analysis: People feed the birds and this reinforces flocking to the beach. When the beach is abandoned, the seagulls are no longer fed for congregating on the shoreline. This is a reasonable guess, but it can only be tested by an experiment. Pretend that the behavior analyst owns the beach and has complete control over it. The experiment involves changing the usual relationship between the presence of people and food. Simply stated, people are not allowed to feed the birds, and food is placed on the beach when people are not around. Over time, the behavior analyst notes that there are fewer and fewer seagulls on the beach when people are present, and more and more gulls when the shoreline is deserted. The behaviorist concludes that people regulated coming to the beach because the birds were fed, or reinforced, for this behavior only when people were present. This is one example of an experimental analysis of behavior.

Behavior Analysis: A Science of Behavior

Although experimental analysis is the fundamental method for a **science of behavior**, contemporary researchers prefer to describe their discipline as behavior analysis. This term implies a more general scientific approach that includes assumptions about how to study behavior, techniques to carry out the analysis, a systematic body of knowledge, and practical implications for society and culture (Ishaq, 1991).

Behavior analysis is a comprehensive approach to the study of the behavior of organisms. Primary objectives are the discovery of principles and laws that govern behavior, the extension of these principles across species, and the development of an applied technology for the management of behavior. In the seagull example, the underlying principle is called *discrimination*. The principle of discrimination states that an organism will respond differently to two situations (e.g., presence or absence of people) if its behavior is reinforced in one setting but not in the other.

The principle of discrimination may be extended to human behavior and social reinforcement. You may discuss dating with Carmen, but not Tracey, because Carmen is interested in such conversation while Tracey is not. In a classroom, the principle of discrimination can be used to improve teaching and learning. The use of behavior principles to solve practical problems is called **applied behavior analysis** and is discussed at some length in Chapter 13.

As you can see, behavior analysis has a strong focus on environment–behavior relationships. The focus is on how organisms alter their behavior to meet the ever-changing demands of the environment. When an organism learns new ways of behaving in reaction to the changes that occur in its environment, this is called *conditioning*. The two basic kinds of conditioning are called respondent and operant.

Two Types of Conditioning

Respondent conditioning

A **reflex** is behavior that is *elicited* by a biologically relevant stimulus. When a stimulus (S) automatically elicits (→) a stereotypical response (R), the S → R *relationship* is called a reflex. This behavior and the reflex relationship had survival value in the sense that those animals that quickly and reliably responded to particular stimuli were more likely than other organisms to survive and reproduce. To illustrate, animals that startle and run to a sudden noise may escape a predator, and the startle reflex may provide an adaptive advantage over organisms that do not run, or run less quickly to the noise. Thus, reflexes are selected across the history of the species. Of course, different species of organisms exhibit different sets of reflexes.

Respondent conditioning occurs when a neutral or meaningless stimulus is paired with an unconditioned stimulus. For example, the buzz of a bee (neutral stimulus) is *paired* with the pain of a sting (unconditioned stimulus). After this conditioning experience, a buzzing bee usually causes people to escape it. The Russian physiologist *Ivan Petrovich Pavlov* made explicit this form of conditioning at the turn of the 20th century. He observed that dogs salivated when food was placed in their mouths. This relation between the food stimulus and salivation is an unconditioned reflex, and it occurs because of the animals' biological history. However, when Pavlov rang a bell just before feeding the dogs, they began to salivate at the sound of the bell. In this way, a new feature (sound of the bell) came to control the dogs' respondent behavior (salivation). As shown in Figure 1.1, a **respondent** is behavior that is elicited by the new conditioned stimulus.

Respondent conditioning is one way that organisms meet the challenges of change in their environments. A grazing animal that becomes conditioned to the sound of rustling grass and runs away is less likely to become a meal than one that waits to see the predator. All species that have been

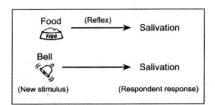

FIG. 1.1 Simple respondent conditioning. In a reflex for a dog, food in the mouth produces salivation. Next, a bell rings (new stimulus) just before feeding the dog; after several pairings of bell and food the dog begins to salivate at the sound of the bell.

tested, including humans, show this kind of conditioning. In terms of human behavior, many of what we call our likes and dislikes are based on respondent conditioning. When good or bad things happen to us, we usually have an emotional reaction. These emotional responses can be conditioned to other people who are present when the positive or negative events occur (Byrne, 1971). Thus, respondent conditioning plays an important role in our social relationships—determining, to a great extent, how we feel about our friends as well as our enemies.

Operant conditioning

Operant conditioning involves the *regulation of behavior by its consequences*. B. F. Skinner called this kind of behavior regulation **operant conditioning** because, in a given situation or setting (S^D), behavior (R) operates on the environment to produce effects or consequences (S^r). Any behavior that operates on the environment to produce an effect is called an **operant**. During operant conditioning, an organism emits behavior that produces an effect that increases (or decreases) the frequency of the operant in a given situation (Skinner, 1938, p. 20). In the laboratory, a hungry rat in a chamber may receive food if it presses a lever when a light is on. If lever pressing increases in the presence of the light, then operant conditioning has occurred (see Figure 1.2).

Most of what we commonly call voluntary, willful, or purposive action is analyzed as operant behavior. *Operant conditioning* occurs when a baby smiles to a human face and is picked up. If smiling to faces increases in frequency because of social attention, then smiling is an operant and the effect is a result of conditioning. In a more complex example, pressing a sequence of buttons while playing a video game will increase in frequency if this response pattern results in hitting a target. Other examples of operant behavior include driving a car, talking on the phone, taking notes in class, walking to the corner store, reading a book, writing a term paper, and conducting an experiment. In each case, the operant is said to be *selected by its consequences*.

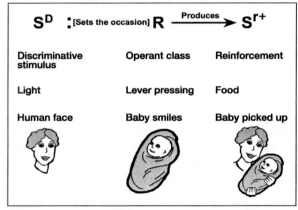

FIG. 1.2 Simple operant conditioning. In an operant chamber, lever pressing produces food for a hungry rat. The consequences of lever pressing (presentation of food) increase its frequency in that setting. In another example, a baby smiles to a human face and is picked up. The consequence of smiling (social attention) increases the frequency of this behavior in the presence of human faces.

Selection as a Causal Process

B. F. Skinner (1938) viewed psychology as the study of the behavior of organisms. From this point of view, psychology is a subfield of biology. The main organizing principle of contemporary biology is evolution through natural selection (Dawkins, 1996). Skinner generalized this concept to a broader principle of **selection by consequences**. Selection by consequences applies at three levels: (1) the selection of characteristics of a species (natural or Darwinian selection); (2) the selection of behavior within the lifetime of an individual organism (selection by operant conditioning); and (3) the selection of behavior patterns (practices, traditions, rituals) of groups of human beings that endure beyond the lifetime of a single individual (cultural selection). In all three cases, it is the consequences arranged by the environment that select for (or against) the frequency of genetic, behavioral, and cultural forms (see Chapter 14).

Selection by consequences is a form of causal explanation. In science we talk about two kinds of causation: immediate and remote. **Immediate causation** is the kind of mechanism studied by physics and chemistry: the "billiard ball" sort of process where we try to isolate a chain of events that directly result in some effect. For example, chemical reactions are explained by describing molecular interactions. In the study of behavior, an immediate causal explanation might refer to the physiology and biochemistry of the organism. For example, the bar pressing of a rat for food or a gambler playing roulette each could involve the release of endogenous opiates and dopamine in the hypothalamus (Shizgal & Arvanitogiannis, 2003).

In contrast, **remote causation** is typical of sciences like evolutionary biology, geology, and astronomy. In this case, we explain some phenomenon by pointing to remote events that made it likely. Thus, the causal explanation of a species characteristic (e.g., size, coloration, exceptional vision, etc.) involves the working of natural selection on the gene pool of the parent population. An evolutionary account of species coloration, for example, would involve showing how this characteristic improved the reproductive success of organisms in a given ecological environment. That is, natural selection for coloration explains the current frequency of the characteristic in the population.

On the behavioral level, the principle of selection by consequences is a form of explanation by remote causation called *functional analysis*. When a rat learns to press a lever for food, we explain the rat's behavior by pointing to its past consequences (the function of behavior). Thus, the current frequency of bar pressing is explained by the contingency between bar pressing and food in the past. The rat's behavior has been *selected by its history of reinforcement*.

Both immediate and remote causal explanations are acceptable in science. Behavior analysts have emphasized functional analysis and selection by consequences (remote causation), but are also interested in direct analysis of physiological and neurochemical processes (immediate causation). Ultimately, both types of causal explanation will provide a more complete account of learning and behavior.

NEW DIRECTIONS: Behavior analysis and neuroscience

Behavior analysis is becoming more involved with the scientific analysis of the brain and nervous system (neuroscience). That is, researchers who primarily study the behavior of organisms are often interested in the brain processes that participate in the regulation of behavior (see special issue on Relation of Behavior and Neuroscience (2005) in *Journal of the Experimental Analysis of Behavior*, *84*, 305–667). For example, brain mechanisms (neurons or groups of neurons) obviously participate in the regulation of behavior (bar pressing) by its consequences (food). Describing how neurons code for, and respond to, reinforcement is an important and exciting addition to a behavior analysis— telling us more about what happens when behavior is shaped by its effects or consequences (Fiorillo, Tobler, & Schultz, 2003).

At the practical level, knowing the reinforcement contingencies (arrangements of the environment) for lever pressing is sufficient to allow us to predict and control the rat's behavior. That is, we can get the rat to increase or decrease its lever pressing by providing or denying food reinforcement for this behavior—there is no need to look at neural systems. But, we gain a more complete account of how a rat's behavior increases when the action of neurons (and neural systems) is combined with the analysis of behavior. For example, in some cases, it may be possible to "sensitize" or "desensitize" a rat to the behavioral contingencies by drugs that activate or block the action of specialized neurons (e.g., Bratcher, Farmer-Dougan, Dougan, Heidenreich, & Garris, 2005). Research at the neural level could, in this way, add to the practical control or regulation of behavior by its consequences (Hollerman & Schultz, 1998).

Neural processes also may participate as immediate consequences (local contingencies) for behavior that had long-range benefits for organisms (distal contingencies, as in evolution and natural selection) (Tobler, Fiorillo, & Schultz, 2005). The so-called *neural basis of reward* involves the inter-relationship of the endogenous opiate and dopamine systems (as well as other neural processes) (Fiorillo et al., 2003). For example, rats that are food restricted and allowed to run in wheels increase running over days—up to 20,000 wheel turns. Wheel running leads to the release of neural opiates that reinforce this behavior (Pierce, 2001). If wheel running is viewed as food-related travel, one function of neural reinforcement is to promote locomotion under conditions of food scarcity. The long-range or distal contingency (travel produces food: travel → food) is proximally supported by the release of endogenous opiates (physical activity → release of endogenous opiates) that "keep the rat going" under conditions of food scarcity (e.g., famine, drought, etc.). We shall see that this process also plays a key role in human anorexia in later chapters.

The integration of the science of behavior with neuroscience (**behavioral neuroscience**) is a growing field of inquiry. Areas of interest include the effects of drugs on behavior (behavioral pharmacology), neural imaging and complex stimulus relations, choice and neural activity, and the brain circuitry of learning and addiction. We will examine some of this research in subsequent chapters in sections that focus on behavior analysis and neuroscience (FOCUS ON sections) or in sections that emphasize applications (ON THE APPLIED SIDE sections).

The Evolution of Learning

When organisms were faced with unpredictable and changing environments in their evolutionary past, natural selection favored those individuals whose behavior could be conditioned. Organisms who condition are more flexible, in the sense that they can learn new requirements and relationships in the environment. Such behavioral flexibility must reflect an underlying structural change of the organism. Genes code for the anatomical and physiological characteristics of the individual. Such structural physical changes allow for different degrees of functional behavioral flexibility. Thus, differences in the structure of organisms based on genetic variation give rise to differences in the regulation of behavior. Processes of learning, like operant and respondent conditioning, lead to greater (or lesser) reproductive success. Presumably, those organisms that changed their behavior as a result of experience during their lives survived and had offspring—those that were less flexible did not. Simply stated, this means that *the capacity for learning is inherited.*

The evolution of learning processes had an important consequence. Behavior that was closely tied to survival and reproduction could be influenced by experience. Specific physiological processes typically regulate behavior related to survival and reproduction. However, for behaviorally flexible organisms, this control by physiology may be modified by experiences during the lifetime of the individual. The extent of such modification depends on the amount and scope of behavioral flexibility (Baum, 1983). For example, sexual behavior is closely tied to reproductive success and is regulated by distinct physiological processes. For many species, sexual behavior is rigidly controlled by genetically driven mechanisms. In humans, however, sexual behavior is also influenced by socially mediated experiences. It is these experiences, not genes, that come to dictate when sexual intercourse will occur, how it is performed, and who can be a sexual partner. Powerful religious or social controls can make people abstain from sex. This example illustrates that even the biologically relevant behavior of humans is partly determined by life experience.

Biological Context of Behavior

Behavior analysts recognize and promote the importance of biology and evolution but focus more on the interplay of the organism and its environment. To maintain this focus, the evolutionary history and biological status of an organism are examined as part of the *context of behavior* (see

Morris, 1988, 1992). This contextualist view is seen in B. F. Skinner's analysis of imprinting in a duckling:

> Operant conditioning and natural selection are combined in the so-called imprinting of a newly hatched duckling. In its natural environment the young duckling moves towards its mother and follows her as she moves about. The behavior has obvious survival value. When no duck is present, the duckling behaves in much the same way with respect to other objects. Recently it has been shown that a young duckling will come to approach and follow any moving object, particularly if it is the same size as a duck—for example, a shoebox. Evidently survival is sufficiently well served even if the behavior is not under the control of the specific visual features of a duck. Merely approaching and following is enough.
>
> Even so, that is not a correct statement of what happens. What the duckling inherits is the *capacity to be reinforced by maintaining or reducing the distance between itself and a moving object* [italics added]. In the natural environment, and in the laboratory in which imprinting is studied, approaching and following have these consequences, but the contingencies can be changed. A mechanical system can be constructed in which movement *toward* an object causes the object to move rapidly away, while movement *away from* the object causes it to come closer. Under these conditions, the duckling will move away from the object rather than approach or follow it. A duckling will learn to peck a spot on the wall if pecking brings the object closer. Only by knowing what and how the duckling learns during its lifetime can we be sure of what it is equipped to do at birth.
>
> (Skinner, 1974, pp. 40–41)

The duckling's biological history, in terms of providing the capacity for reinforcement by proximity to a duck-sized object, is the context for the regulation of its behavior. Of course, the anatomy and physiology of the duck allow for this capacity. However, the way the environment is arranged determines the behavior of the individual organism. Laboratory experiments in behavior analysis identify the general principles that govern the behavior of organisms, the specific events that regulate the behavior of different species, and the arrangement of these events during the lifetime of an individual.

The Selection of Operant Behavior

Early behaviorists like John Watson (1903) used the terminology of stimulus–response (S–R) psychology. From this perspective, stimuli force responses much like meat in a dog's mouth elicits (or forces) salivation. In fact, Watson based his stimulus–response theory of behavior on Pavlov's conditioning experiments. Stimulus–response theories are mechanistic in the sense that an organism is compelled to respond when a stimulus is presented. This is similar to a physical account of the motion of billiard balls. The impact of the cue ball (stimulus) determines the motion and trajectory (response) of the target ball. Although stimulus–response conceptions are useful for analyzing reflexive behavior and other rigid response patterns (i.e., Newtonion mechanics), the push–pull model is not as useful when applied to voluntary actions or operants. To be fair, Watson talked about "habits" in a way that sounds like operant behavior, but he lacked the experimental evidence and vocabulary to distinguish between respondent and operant conditioning.

It was B. F. Skinner (1935, 1937) who made the distinction between two types of conditioned reflex, corresponding to the difference between operant and respondent behavior. In 1938, Skinner introduced the term operant in his classic book, *The Behavior of Organisms*. Eventually, Skinner rejected the mechanistic (S–R) model of Watson and based operant conditioning on Darwin's principle of selection. The basic idea is that an individual *emits* behavior that produces effects, consequences, or outcomes. Based on these consequences, those performances that are appropriate increase—becoming more frequent in the population or class of responses for the situation; at the same time, inappropriate forms of response decline or become extinct. Julie Vargas is the daughter of B. F. Skinner and a professor of behavior analysis. She has commented on her father's model of causation:

> Skinner's paradigm is a *selectionist* paradigm not unlike Darwin's selectionist theory of the evolution of species. Where Darwin found an explanation for the evolution of species, Skinner looked for variables functionally related to changes in behavior over the lifetime of an individual. Both explanations assumed variation; Darwin in inherited characteristics, Skinner in individual acts. Skinner, in other words, does not concern himself with why behavior varies, only with how patterns of behavior are drawn out from the variations that already exist. In looking at the functional relationships between acts and their effects on the world, Skinner broke with the S-R, input-output transformation model.
>
> (Vargas, 1990, p. 9)

Skinner recognized that operants are selected by their consequences. He also noted that operant behavior naturally varies in form and frequency. Even something as simple as opening the door to your house is not done exactly the same way each time. Pressure on the doorknob, strength of pull, and the hand that is used change from one occasion to the next. If the door sticks and becomes difficult to open, a forceful response will eventually occur. This response may succeed in opening the door and become the most likely performance for the situation. Other forms of response will occur at different frequencies depending on how often they succeed in opening the door. Thus, *operants are selected by their consequences*.

Similarly, it is well known that babies produce a variety of sounds called "babbling." These natural variations in sound production are important for language learning. When sounds occur, parents usually react to them. When the infant produces a familiar sound, parents often repeat it more precisely. Unfamiliar sounds are usually ignored. Eventually, the baby begins to produce sounds (we say talk) like other people in their culture or verbal community. Selection of verbal behavior by its social consequences is an important process underlying human communication (Skinner, 1957).

Culture and Behavior Analysis

Although much of the basic research in the experimental analysis of behavior is based on laboratory animals, contemporary behavior analysts are increasingly concerned with human behavior. The behavior of people occurs in a social environment. Society and culture refer to aspects of the social environment, the context, that regulate human conduct. One of the primary tasks of behavior analysis is to show how individual behavior is acquired, maintained, and changed through inter-action with others. An additional task is to account for the practices of the group, community, or society that affect an individual's behavior (Lamal, 1997).

Culture is usually defined in terms of the ideas and values of a society. However, behavior analysts define **culture** as all the conditions, events, and stimuli arranged by other people that regulate human action (Glenn, 1988; Skinner, 1953). The principles and laws of behavior analysis provide an account of how culture regulates an individual's behavior. A person in an English-speaking culture learns to speak in accord with the verbal practices of that community. People in the community provide reinforcement for a certain way of speaking. In this manner, a person comes to talk like and share the language of other members of the public and, in doing so, contributes to the perpetuation of the culture. The customs or practices of a culture are therefore maintained through the social conditioning of individual behavior.

Another objective is to account for the evolution of cultural practices. Behavior analysts suggest that the principle of selection (by consequences) also occurs at the cultural level. Cultural practices therefore increase (or decrease) based on consequences produced in the past. A cultural practice of making containers to hold water is an advantage to the group because it allows for the transportation and storage of water. This practice may include making and using shells, hollow leaves, or fired-clay containers. The cultural form that is selected (e.g., clay jars) is the one that proves most efficient. In other words, the community values those containers that last the longest, hold the most, and are easily stored. Thus, people manufacture clay pots and the manufacture of less efficient containers declines.

Behavior analysts are interested in cultural evolution because cultural changes alter the social conditioning of individual behavior. Analysis of cultural evolution suggests how the social environment is arranged and rearranged to support specific forms of human behavior. On a more practical level, behavior analysts suggest that the solution to many social problems requires a technology of cultural design. B. F. Skinner (1948) addressed this possibility in his utopian book, *Walden Two*. Although this idealistic novel was written some five decades ago, contemporary behavior analysts are conducting small-scale social experiments based on Skinner's ideas (Komar, 1983). For example, behavioral technology has been used to manage environmental pollution, encourage energy conservation, and regulate overpopulation (Glenwick & Jason, 1980).

FOCUS ON: B. F. Skinner

B. F. Skinner (1904–1990) was the intellectual force behind behavior analysis. He was born Burrhus Frederic Skinner on 20 March 1904 in Susquehanna, Pennsylvania. When he was a boy, Skinner spent much of his time exploring the countryside with his younger brother. He had a passion for English literature and mechanical inventions. His hobbies included writing stories and designing perpetual-motion machines. He wanted to be a novelist and went to Hamilton College in Clinton, New York, where he graduated with a degree in English. After graduating from college in 1926, Skinner reported that he was not a great writer because he had nothing to say. He began reading about behaviorism, a new intellectual movement, and as a result went to Harvard in 1928 to learn more about a science of behavior. Skinner earned his master's degree in 1930 and his PhD the following year.

Skinner (Figure 1.3) began writing about the behavior of organisms in the 1930s when the discipline was in its infancy, and he continued to publish papers until his death in 1990. During his long career, Skinner wrote about and researched topics ranging from utopian societies, the philosophy of science, teaching machines, pigeons that controlled the direction of missiles, air cribs for infants, and techniques for improving education. Many people considered him a genius, while some were upset by his theories.

Skinner was always a controversial figure. He proposed a natural-science approach to human behavior. According to Skinner, the behavior of organisms, including humans, was determined. Although common sense suggests that we do things because of our feelings, thoughts, and intentions, Skinner stated that behavior resulted from genes and environment. This position bothered many people who believed that humans have some degree of self-determination. Even though he was constantly confronted with arguments against his position, Skinner maintained that the scientific facts required the rejection of feelings, thoughts, and intentions as causes of behavior. He said that these internal events were not explanations of behavior; rather, these events were additional activities of people that needed to be explained:

FIG. 1.3 B. F. Skinner. © B. F. Skinner Foundation, Cambridge, MA. Published with permission.

The practice of looking inside the organism for an explanation of behavior has tended to obscure the variables which are immediately available for a scientific analysis. These variables lie outside the organism in its immediate environment and in its environmental history. They have a physical status to which the usual techniques of science are adapted, and they make it possible to explain behavior as other subjects are explained in science. These independent variables [causes] are of many sorts and their relations to behavior are often subtle and complex, but we cannot hope to give an adequate account of behavior without analyzing them.

(Skinner, 1953, p. 31)

One of Skinner's most important achievements was his theory of operant behavior. The implications of behavior theory were outlined in his book, *Science and Human Behavior* (1953). In this book, Skinner discussed basic operant principles and their application to human behavior. Topics include self-control, thinking, the self, social behavior, government, religion, and culture. Skinner advocated the principle of positive reinforcement and argued against the use of punishment. He noted how governments and other social agencies often resort to punishment for behavior control. Although punishment works in the short run, he noted that it has many negative side effects. Positive reinforcement, Skinner believed, is a more effective means of behavior change—people act well and are happy when behavior is maintained by positive reinforcement.

People have misunderstood many of the things that Skinner has said and done (Catania & Harnard, 1988; Wheeler, 1973). One popular misconception is that he raised his children in an experimental chamber—the so-called baby in a box. People claimed that Skinner used his daughter as an experimental subject to test his theories. A popular myth is that this experience drove his child crazy. His daughter, Julie, was confronted with this myth and recalls the following:

I took a class called "Theories of Learning" taught by a nice elderly gentleman. He started with Hull and Spence, and then reached Skinner. At that time I had read little of Skinner and I could not judge the accuracy of what was being said about Skinner's theories. But when a student asked whether Skinner had any children, the professor thought Skinner had children. "Did he condition his children?" asked another student. "I heard that one of the children was crazy." "What happened to his children?" The questions came thick and fast.

What was I to do? I had a friend in the class, and she looked over at me, clearly expecting action. I did not want to demolish the professor's confidence by telling who I was, but I couldn't just sit there. Finally, I raised my hand and stood up. "Dr. Skinner has two daughters and I believe they turned out relatively normal," I said, and sat down.

(Vargas, 1990, pp. 8–9)

In truth, the "box" that Skinner designed for his children had nothing to do with an experiment. The air crib was an enclosed cot that allowed air temperature to be adjusted. In addition, the mattress cover could be easily changed when soiled. The air crib was designed so the child was warm, dry, and free to move about. Most importantly, the infant spent no more time in the air crib than other children do in ordinary beds (Skinner, 1945).

Although Skinner did not experiment with his children, he was always interested in the application of conditioning principles to human issues. His many books and papers on applied behavioral technology led to the field of applied behavior analysis. Applied behavior analysis is concerned with the extension of behavior principles to socially important problems. In the first issue of the *Journal of Applied Behavior Analysis*, Baer, Wolf, and Risley (1968) outlined a program of research based on Skinner's views:

The statement [of behavior principles] establishes the possibility of their application to problem behavior. A society willing to consider a technology of its own behavior apparently is likely to support that application when it deals with socially important behaviors, such as retardation, crime, mental illness, or education. Better applications, it is hoped, will lead to a better state of society, to whatever extent the behavior of its members can contribute to the goodness of a society. The differences between applied and basic research are not differences between that which "discovers" and that which merely "applies" what is already known. Both endeavors ask what controls the behavior under study. . . . [Basic] research is likely to look at any behavior, and at any variable which may conceivably relate to it. Applied research is constrained to look at variables which can be effective in improving the behavior under study.

(p. 91)

One area of application that Skinner wrote about extensively was teaching and learning. Although Skinner recognized the importance of behavior principles for teaching people with learning disabilities, he claimed that the same technology could be used to improve our general educational system. In his book, *The Technology of Teaching*, Skinner (1968) offered a personalized system of positive reinforcement for the academic performance of students. In this system, teaching involves arranging materials, designing the classroom, and programming lessons to shape and maintain the performance of students. Learning is defined objectively in terms of answering questions, solving problems, using grammatically correct forms of the language, and writing about the subject matter.

An aspect of Skinner's history that is not generally known is his humor and rejection of formal titles. He preferred to be called "Fred" rather than Burrhus and the only person who called him Burrhus was his close friend and colleague Fred Keller, who felt that he had prior claim on the name Fred (he was a few years older than Skinner). One of Skinner's earliest students, C. B. Ferster, tells about a time early in his acquaintance when Skinner tried to get Ferster to call him "Fred." The story goes (Ferster, personal communication to Paul Brandon) that one day Ferster walked into the living room of Skinner's house to see Skinner seated on the sofa with a large sign around his neck saying "FRED."

In the later part of his life, Skinner worked with Margaret Vaughan (Skinner & Vaughan, 1983) on positive approaches to the problems of old age. Their book, *Enjoy Old Age: A Program of Self-Management*, is written for the elderly reader and provides practical advice on how to deal with daily life. For example, the names of people are easy to forget and even more so in old age. Skinner and Vaughan suggest that you can improve your chances of recalling a name by reading a list of people you are likely to meet before going to an important occasion. If all else fails "you can always appeal to your age. You can please the friend whose name you have forgotten by saying that the names you forget are always the names you most want to remember" (p. 52).

Skinner, who held the A. E. Pierce Chair in Psychology, officially retired in 1974 from Harvard University. Following his retirement, Skinner continued an active program of research and writing. Each day he walked 2 miles to William James Hall, where he lectured, supervised graduate students, and conducted experiments. Eight days before his death on 18 August 1990, B. F. Skinner received the first (and only) citation given for outstanding lifetime contribution to psychology from the American Psychological Association. Skinner's contributions to psychology and a science of behavior are documented in a recent film *B. F. Skinner: A Fresh Appraisal* (1999). Murray Sidman, a renowned researcher in the experimental analysis of behavior, narrated the film (available from the bookstore of the Cambridge Center for Behavioral Studies, www.behavior.org).

A BRIEF HISTORY OF BEHAVIOR ANALYSIS

Contemporary behavior analysis is based on ideas and research that became prominent at the turn of the 20th century. The Russian scientist Ivan Petrovich Pavlov discovered the conditional reflex (a reflex that only occurs under a particular set of conditions such as the pairing of stimuli), and this was a significant step toward a scientific understanding of behavior.

Ivan Petrovich Pavlov (1849–1936)

FIG. 1.4 Ivan Petrovich Pavlov. Reprinted with permission from the Archives of the History of American Psychology, The University of Akron.

Pavlov (Figure 1.4) was born the son of a village priest in 1849. He attended seminary school in order to follow his father into the priesthood. However, after studying physiology he decided on a career in the biological sciences. Although his family protested, Pavlov entered the University of St. Petersburg, where he graduated in 1875 with a degree in physiology. After completing his studies in physiology, Pavlov was accepted as an advanced student of medicine. He distinguished himself and obtained a scholarship to continue his studies of physiology in Germany. In 1890, Pavlov was appointed to two prominent research positions in Russia. He was Professor of Pharmacology at the St. Petersburg Medical Academy and Director of the Physiology Department. For the next 20 years, Pavlov studied the physiology of digestion, and in 1904 he won the Nobel Prize for this work, the year that B. F. Skinner was born.

Ivan Pavlov worked on the salivary reflex and its role in digestion. Pavlov had dogs surgically prepared to expose the salivary glands in the dogs' mouths. The animals were brought into the laboratory and put in restraining harnesses. As shown in Figure 1.5, food was then placed in the dogs' mouths and the action of the salivary glands was observed.

The analysis of the salivary reflex was based on prevailing notions of animal behavior. At this time, many people thought that animals, with the exception of humans, were complex biological machines. The idea was that a specific stimulus evoked a particular response in much the same way that turning a key starts an engine. In other words, animals reacted to the environment in a simple cause–effect manner. Humans, on the other hand, were seen as different from other animals in that their actions were purposive. Humans were said to anticipate future events. Pavlov noticed that his dogs began to salivate at the sight of an experimenter's lab coat *before* food was placed in the animal's mouth. This suggested that the dogs anticipated food. Pavlov recognized that such a result challenged conventional wisdom.

Pavlov made an important observation in terms of the study of behavior. He reasoned that anticipatory reflexes were learned or conditioned. Further, Pavlov concluded that these conditioned reflexes were an essential part of the behavior of organisms. Although some behaviors were described as innate reflexes, other actions were based on conditioning that occurred during the

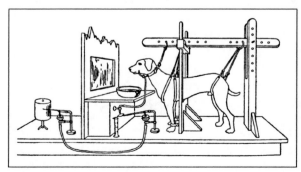

FIG. 1.5 A dog in the experimental apparatus used by Pavlov.

animal's life. These **conditioned reflexes** (termed conditional reflexes in Pavlov, 1960) were present to some degree in all animals but were most prominent in humans.

The question was how to study conditioned reflexes systematically. Pavlov's answer to this question represents a major advance in the experimental analysis of behavior. If dogs reliably salivate at the sight of a lab coat, Pavlov reasoned, then any arbitrary stimulus that preceded food might also be conditioned and evoke salivation. Pavlov replaced the experimenter's lab coat with a stimulus that he could systematically manipulate and reliably control. In some experiments, a metronome (a device used to keep the beat while playing the piano) was presented to a dog just before it was fed. This procedure resulted in the dog eventually salivating to the sound of the metronome. If a particular beat preceded feeding while other rhythms did not, the dog salivated most to the sound associated with food.

Although Pavlov was a physiologist and believed in mental associations, his research was directed at observable responses and stimuli. He discovered many principles of the conditioned reflex. These principles included spontaneous recovery, discrimination, generalization, and extinction. The later part of his career involved an experimental analysis of neurosis in animals. He continued these investigations until his death in 1936.

John Broadus Watson (1878–1958)

Pavlov's research became prominent in North America, and the conditioned reflex was incorporated into a more general theory of behavior by the famous behaviorist John B. Watson (Figure 1.6). Watson acknowledged Pavlov's influence:

> I had worked the thing out [conditioning] in terms of *Habit* formation. It was only later, when I began to dig into the vague word *Habit* that I saw the enormous contribution Pavlov had made, and how easily the conditioned response could be looked upon as the unit of what we had been calling *Habit*. I certainly, from that point on, gave the master his due credit.
>
> (Watson, personal communication to Hilgard & Marquis, 1961, p. 24)

Watson went on to argue that there was no need to make up unobservable mental associations to account for human and animal behavior. He proposed that psychology should be a science based on observable behavior. Thoughts, feelings, and intentions had no place in a scientific account and researchers should direct their attention to muscle movements and neural activity. Although this was an extreme position, Watson succeeded in directing the attention of psychologists to behavior–environment relationships.

Watson was a rebellious young man who failed his last year at Furman University because he handed in a final-exam paper "backwards."[1] He graduated in 1899, when he was 21 years old. After spending a year as a public-school teacher, Watson decided to further his education and was admitted to graduate studies at the University of Chicago. There he studied philosophy with John Dewey, the famous educator. He never really appreciated Dewey's ideas and later in his life commented, "I never knew what he was talking about then, and, unfortunately for me, I still don't know" (Watson, 1936, p. 274). While a graduate student at Chicago, he also studied psychology with James Angell and biology and physiology with Henry Donaldson and Jacques Loeb (Pauley, 1987). In 1903, he obtained his doctorate for research with laboratory rats. The experiments concerned learning and correlated changes in the brains of these animals.

Watson (1903) published a book called *Animal Education: An Experimental Study on the Psychical Development of the*

FIG. 1.6   John Watson. Reprinted with permission from the Archives of the History of American Psychology, The University of Akron.

---

[1] This description of John Watson is partially based on a paper by James Todd and Edward Morris (1986) on "The Early Research of John B. Watson: Before the Behavioral Revolution."

White Rat, Correlated with the Growth of Its Nervous System that was based on his doctoral research. The book demonstrated that Watson was a capable scientist who could clearly present his ideas. Ten years later, Watson (1913) published his most influential work in *Psychological Review*, "Psychology as the Behaviorist Views It." This paper outlined Watson's views on **behaviorism** and argued that objectivity was the only way to build a science of psychology:

> I feel that *behaviorism* is the only consistent logical functionalism. In it one avoids [the problem of mind-body dualism]. These time-honored relics of philosophical speculation need trouble the student of behavior as little as they trouble the student of physics. The consideration of the mind-body problem affects neither the type of problem selected nor the formulation of the solution of that problem. I can state my position here no better than by saying that I should like to bring my students up in ignorance of such hypotheses as one finds among other branches of science.
>
> (Watson, 1913, p. 166)

In this paper, Watson also rejected as scientific data what people said about their thoughts and feelings. Further, he pointed to the unreliability of psychological inferences about another person's mind. Finally, Watson noted that the psychology of mind had little practical value for behavior control and public affairs.

Perhaps Watson's most famous experiment was the study of fear conditioning with Little Albert (Watson & Rayner, 1920). Little Albert was a normal, healthy infant who attended a day-care center. Watson and his assistant used classical-conditioning procedures to condition fear of a white rat. At first Little Albert looked at the rat and tried to touch it. The unconditioned stimulus was the sound of a hammer hitting an iron rail. This sound made Little Albert jump, cry, and fall over. After only six presentations of the noise and rat, the furry animal also produced the fear responses. The next phase of the experiment involved a series of tests to see if the child's fear reaction transferred to similar stimuli. Albert was also afraid when presented with a white rabbit, a dog, and a fur coat.

At this point, Watson and Rayner discussed a number of techniques that could be used to eliminate the child's fear. Unfortunately, Little Albert was removed from the day-care center before counter-conditioning could be carried out. In his characteristic manner, Watson later used the disappearance of Little Albert to poke fun at Freud's method of psychoanalysis. He suggested that as Albert got older, he might go to an analyst because of his strange fears. The analyst would probably convince Albert that his problem was the result of an unresolved Oedipal complex. But, Watson remarked, we would know that Albert's fears were actually caused by conditioning—so much for Freudian analysis.

Watson had many interests and he investigated and wrote about ethology, comparative animal behavior, neural function, physiology, and philosophy of science. Based on his controversial views and charisma, Watson was elected president of the American Psychological Association in 1915 when he was only 37 years old. After leaving Johns Hopkins University, he became successful in industry by applying conditioning principles to advertising and public relations (Buckley, 1989). Watson implemented the use of subliminal suggestion and the pairing of hidden symbols in advertising—techniques still used today.

Edward Lee Thorndike (1874–1949)

Watson's behaviorism emphasized the conditioned reflex. This analysis focuses on the events that precede action and is usually called a stimulus–response approach. Another American psychologist, Edward Lee Thorndike (Figure 1.7), was more concerned with how success and failure affect the behavior of organisms. His research emphasized the events and consequences that follow behavior. In other words, Thorndike was the first scientist to systematically study operant behavior, although he called the changes that occurred **trial-and-error learning** (Thorndike, 1898).

Edward L. Thorndike was born in 1874 in Williamsburg, Massachusetts. He was the son of a Methodist minister and had no knowledge of psychology until he attended Wesleyan University. There he read William James's (1890) book, *Principles of Psychology*, which had a major impact on him. After reading the book, Thorndike was accepted as a student at Harvard, where he studied with William James. It is important to note that James's psychology focused on the mind and used the method of introspection (people's reports of feeling and thoughts). Thus, in contrast to John Watson, Thorndike was concerned with states of mind. In terms of contemporary behavior analysis, Thorndike's contribution was his systematic study of the behavior of organisms rather than his mental interpretations of animal and human behavior.

FIG. 1.7   Edward Thorndike. Reprinted with permission from the Archives of the History of American Psychology, The University of Akron.

Thorndike was always intrigued with animal behavior. While at Harvard, his landlady became upset because he was raising chickens in his bedroom. By this time, James and Thorndike were good friends, and Thorndike moved his experiments to the basement of James's house when he could not get laboratory space at Harvard. He continued his research and supported himself by tutoring students for 2 years at Harvard. Then Thorndike moved to Columbia University where he studied with James McKeen Cattell, the famous expert on intelligence testing. Thorndike took two of his "smartest" chickens with him to Columbia, but soon switched to investigating the behavior of cats.

At Columbia University, Thorndike began his famous experiments on trial-and-error learning in cats. Animals were placed in what Thorndike called a "puzzle box" and food was placed outside the box (Chance, 1999). A cat that struggled to get out of the box would accidentally step on a treadle, pull a string, and lift a latch. These responses resulted in opening the puzzle-box door. Thorndike found that most cats took less and less time to solve the problem after they were repeatedly returned to the box (i.e., repeated trials). From these and additional observations, Thorndike made the first formulation of the **law of effect**:

> The cat that is clawing all over the box in her impulsive struggle will probably claw the string or loop or button so as to open the door. And gradually all the other *non-successful impulses will be stamped out and the particular impulse leading to the successful act will be stamped in by the resulting pleasure* [italics added], until after many trials, the cat will, when put in the box, immediately claw the button or loop in a definite way.
>
> (Thorndike, 1911, p. 40)

Today, Thorndike's law of effect is restated as the principle of reinforcement. This principle states that all operants may be followed by consequences that increase or decrease the probability of response in the same situation. Notice that references to "stamping in" and "pleasure" are not necessary and that nothing is lost by this modern restatement of the law of effect.

Thorndike was appointed to the Teachers College, Columbia University as a professor in 1899, and he spent his entire career there. He studied and wrote about education, language, intelligence testing, comparison of animal species, the nature–nurture problem, transfer of training, sociology of the quality of life, and, most importantly, animal and human learning. Thorndike published more than 500 books and journal articles. His son (Robert Ladd Thorndike, 1911–1990) became a well-known educational psychologist in his own right and in 1937 joined the same department of psychology as his father. Edward Lee Thorndike died in 1949.

B. F. Skinner and the Rise of Behavior Analysis

The works of Pavlov, Watson, Thorndike, and many others have influenced contemporary behavior analysis. Although the ideas of many scientists and philosophers have had an impact, Burrhus Fredrick Skinner (1904–1990) is largely responsible for the development of modern behavior analysis. In the "Focus on: B. F. Skinner" section above, we described some details of his life and some of his accomplishments. An excellent biography is available (Bjork, 1993), and Skinner himself wrote a three-volume autobiography (1976, 1979, 1983). Here we will outline his contribution to contemporary behavior analysis.

Skinner was studying at Harvard during a time of intellectual change. He wanted to extend the work of Pavlov to more complicated instances of the conditioned reflex. Rudolph Magnus was a contemporary of Ivan Pavlov, and he had been working on the conditioning of physical movement. Skinner had read his book *Korperstellung* in the original German and was impressed with it. Skinner said, "I began to think of reflexes as behavior rather than with Pavlov as 'the activity of the cerebral cortex' or, with Sherrington, as 'the integrative action of the nervous system'" (Skinner, 1979, p. 46).

The idea that reflexes could be studied as behavior (rather than as a reflection of the nervous system or the mind) was fully developed in Skinner's (1938) book, *The Behavior of Organisms*. In this text, Skinner distinguishes between Pavlov's reflexive conditioning and the kind of learning reported by Thorndike. Skinner proposed that respondent and operant conditioning regulated behavior. These terms were carefully selected to emphasize the study of behavior for its own sake. Pavlov interpreted reflexive conditioning as the study of the central nervous system, and Skinner's respondent conditioning directed attention to environmental events and responses. Thorndike's trial-and-error learning was based on unobservable states of mind, and Skinner's operant conditioning focused on the functional relations between behavior and its consequences. Both operant and respondent conditioning required the study of observable correlations among objective events and behavior.

Skinner soon talked about a "science of behavior" rather than one of physiology or mental life. Once stated, the study of behavior for its own sake seems obvious, but consider that most of us say that we do something because we have made up our mind to do it or, in more scientific terms, because of a neural connection in our brain. Most people accept explanations of behavior that rely on descriptions of brain, mind, intelligence, cognitive function, neural activity, thinking, or personality. Because these factors are taken as the cause(s) of behavior, they become the focus of investigation. Skinner, however, suggested that remembering, thinking, feeling, the action of neurons, etc. are more behaviors of the organism that require explanation. He further proposed that the action of organisms could be investigated by focusing on behavior and the environmental events that precede and follow it.

Skinner's behavioral focus was partially maintained and influenced by his lifelong friend, Fred Simmons Keller. Skinner and Keller attended Harvard graduate school together, and Keller encouraged Skinner to pursue a behavioral view of psychology. By 1946, Skinner had formed a small group of behaviorists at Indiana University. At this same time, Fred Keller and his friend Nat Schoenfeld organized another group at Columbia University (Keller, 1977, Chapters 2 and 6).

Although the number of **behavior analysts** was growing, there were no sessions on behavioral issues at the American Psychological Association annual meetings. Because of this, Skinner, Keller, Schoenfeld, and others organized their own conference at Indiana University. This was the first conference on the experimental analysis of behavior (see Figure 1.8). These new-style behaviorists rejected the extreme views of John B. Watson and offered an alternative formulation. Unlike Watson, they did not reject genetic influences on behavior; they extended the analysis of behavior to operant conditioning, and they studied behavior for its own sake.

These new behavior analysts found it difficult to get their research published in the major journals of psychology. This was because they used a small number of subjects in their experiments, did not use statistical analysis, and their graphs of response rate were not appreciated. By 1958, the group was large enough to start its own journal, and the first volume of the *Journal of the Experimental Analysis of Behavior* (JEAB) was published. As research accumulated, the practical implications of behavior principles became more and more evident, and applications to mental illness, retardation, rehabilitation, and education increased. In 1968, the *Journal of Applied Behavior Analysis* (JABA) was published for the first time.

By 1964, the number of behavior analysts had grown so much that the American Psychological Association established a special division. Division 25 is called The Experimental Analysis of Behavior and has several thousand members. Subsequently, the Association for Behavior Analysis (ABA) was founded in the late 1970s. This association holds an annual international conference that is attended by behavior analysts from many countries. The association publishes a journal of general issues called *The Behavior Analyst*.

FIG. 1.8   Photograph taken at the first conference on the experimental analysis of behavior held in 1946 at Indiana University. From left to right in front row: Dinsmoor, Musgrave, Skinner, Keller, Schoenfeld, Lloyd. Middle row: Ellson, Daniel, Klein, Jenkins, Wyckoff, Hefferline, Wolin. Back row: Estes, Frick, Anderson, Verplanck, Beire, Hill, Craig. From the *Journal of the Experimental Analysis of Behavior, 5,* 456. Copyright 1958, by the Society for the Experimental Analysis of Behavior, Inc. Reprinted with permission.

In addition to ABA, Robert Epstein, one of B. F. Skinner's last students, and past editor of the well-known magazine *Psychology Today*, founded the Cambridge Center for Behavioral Studies in 1981. The Cambridge Center is devoted to helping people find effective solutions to behavior problems (e.g., in education, business, and other applied settings). As part of this mission, the Center maintains an information web site (www.behavior.org) for the public, publishes books and journals, and sponsors seminars and conferences on effective behavior management in applied settings (e.g., the annual conference *Behavioral Safety Now* in the field of industrial safety).

A continuing issue in the field of behavior analysis is the separation between applied behavior analysis and basic research. During the 1950s and 1960s, no clear distinction existed between applied and basic investigations. This was because applied behavior analysts were trained as basic researchers. That is, the first applications of behavior principles came from the same people who were conducting laboratory experiments. [As an aside, Skinner's second book, after his basic text called *The Behavior of Organisms (1938)*, was a novel describing the application of behavior principles in a Utopian community, *Walden Two* (1948).] The applications of behavior principles were highly successful, and this led to a greater demand for people trained in applied behavior analysis. Soon applied researchers were no longer working in the laboratory or reading the basic journals.

This separation between basic and applied research was first described by Sam Deitz (1978), who noted the changing emphasis from science to technology among applied behavior analysts (see also Hayes, Rincover, & Solnick, 1980; Michael, 1980; Pierce & Epling, 1980). Donald Baer (1981) acknowledged the technical drift of applied behavior analysis, but suggested that this was a natural progression of the field that may have positive effects.

Today the separation issue is not entirely resolved although much progress is apparent. Applied researchers are more in contact with basic research through the *Journal of Applied Behavior Analysis*. In addition to application research, this journal publishes applied articles based on modern behavior principles (e.g., Ducharme & Worling, 1994) as well as reviews of basic research areas (e.g., Mace,

1996). We have written this book assuming that an acquaintance with basic research is important, even for those who are primarily concerned with behavioral applications. Students can study this text for a basic grounding in behavioral science, or for a solid foundation in human behavior and application.

SCIENCE AND BEHAVIOR: SOME ASSUMPTIONS

All scientists make assumptions about their subject matter. These assumptions are based on prevailing views in the discipline and guide scientific research. In terms of behavior analysis, researchers assume that the behavior of organisms is lawful. This means that it is possible to study the interactions between an organism and its environment in an objective manner. To carry out the analysis, it is necessary to isolate behavior–environment relationships. The scientist must identify events that reliably precede the onset of some action and the specific consequences that follow behavior. If behavior systematically changes with variation in the environmental conditions, then behavior analysts assume that they have explained the action of the organism. There are other assumptions that behavior analysts make about their science.

The Private World

Contemporary behavior analysts include internal events as part of an organism's environment. This point is often misunderstood; internal functioning like an upset stomach, full bladder, and low blood sugar are part of a person's environment. Internal physical events have the same status as external stimuli such as light, noise, odor, and heat. Both external and internal events regulate behavior. Although this is so, behavior analysts usually emphasize the external environment. This is because external events are the only stimuli available for behavior change. The objective procedures of psychological experiments are giving instructions and observing how the person acts. From a behavioral view, the instructions are external stimuli that regulate both verbal and nonverbal behavior. Even when a drug is given to a person and the chemical alters internal biochemistry, the direct injection of the drug is an external event that subsequently regulates behavior. To make this clear, without the drug injection neither the biochemistry nor the behavior of the person would change.

Many psychological studies involve giving information to a person in order to change or activate cognitive processes. Thus, cognitive psychologists ". . . invent internal surrogates which become the subject matter of their science" (Skinner, 1978, p. 97); and cognitive psychology has been defined as ". . . an approach to scientific psychology—that encourages psychologists to infer unobservable constructs on the basis of observable phenomena" (Baars, 1986, p. ix). In the cognitive view, thoughts are used to *explain* behavior. The problem is that the existence of thoughts (or feelings) is often inferred from the behavior to be explained, leading to circular reasoning. For example, a child who peers out of the window about the time her mother usually comes home from work is said to do this because of an "expectation." The expectation of the child is said to explain why the child peers from the window. In fact, there is no explanation because the cognition (expectation) is inferred from the behavior it is said to explain. Cognitions could explain behavior if the existence of thought processes were based on some evidence other than behavior. In most cases, however, there is no independent evidence that cognitions caused behavior and the explanation is not scientifically valid. One way out of this problem of logic is not to use thinking and feeling as causes of behavior. That is, thinking and feeling are treated as more behavior to be explained.

Feelings and Behavior

Most people assume that their feelings and thoughts explain why they act as they do. Contemporary behavior analysts agree that people feel and think, but they do not consider these events as causes of behavior. They note that these terms are more correctly used as verbs rather than nouns. Instead of talking about thoughts, behavior analysts point to the action word "thinking." And instead of analyzing feelings as things we possess, the behavioral scientist focuses on the action of feeling or sensing. In other words, thinking and feeling are activities of the organism that require explanation.

Feelings: Real but not causes

Because feelings occur at the same time that we act, they are often taken as causes of behavior. Although feelings and behavior necessarily go together, it is the environment that determines how we act, and at the same time how we feel. Feelings are real, but they are the result of the environmental events that regulate behavior. Thus, a behavioral approach requires the researcher to trace feelings back to the interaction between behavior and environment.

Pretend that you are in an elevator between the 15th and 16th floors when the elevator suddenly stops, and the lights go out. You hear a sound that appears to be the snapping of elevator cables. Suddenly, the elevator lurches and then drops 2 feet. You call out, but nobody comes to your rescue. After about an hour, the elevator starts up again, and you get off on the 16th floor. Six months later, a good friend invites you to dinner. You meet downtown, and you discover that your friend has made reservations at a restaurant called The Room at the Top, which is located on the 20th floor of a skyscraper. Standing in front of the elevator, a sudden feeling of panic overwhelms you. You make a socially appropriate excuse like, "I don't feel well," and you leave. What is the reason for your behavior and the accompanying feeling?

There is no question that you feel anxious, but this feeling is not why you decide to go home. Both the anxious feeling and your decision to leave are easily traced to the negative experience in the elevator that occurred 6 months ago. It is this prior conditioning that behavior analysts emphasize. Notice that the behavioral position does not deny your feelings. These are real events. However, it is your previous interaction with the broken elevator that changed both how you feel and how you act.

Reports of feelings

You may still wonder why behavior analysts study overt behavior instead of feelings—given that both are changed by experience. The answer concerns the accessibility of feelings and overt behavior. Much of the behavior of organisms is directly accessible to the observer or scientist. This public behavior provides a relatively straightforward subject matter for scientific analysis. In contrast, feelings are largely inaccessible to the scientific community. Of course, the person who feels has access to this private information, but the problem is that reports of feelings are highly unreliable.

This unreliability occurs because we learn to talk about our feelings (and other internal events) as others have trained us to do. During socialization, people teach us how to describe ourselves, but when they do this they have no way of accurately knowing what is going on inside us. Parents and teachers rely on public cues to train self-descriptions. They do this by commenting on and correcting verbal reports when behavior or events suggest a feeling. A preschooler is taught to say, "I feel happy" when the parents guess that the child is happy. The parents may base their judgment on smiling, excitement, and affectionate responses from the child. Another way this training is done is that the child may be asked, "Are you happy?" in a circumstance where the parents expect the child to feel this way (e.g., on Christmas morning). When the child appears to be sad, or circumstances suggest that this should be so, saying "I am happy" is not reinforced by the parents. Eventually, the child says, "I am happy" in some situations and not in others.

Perhaps you have already noticed why reports of feelings are not good scientific evidence. Reports are only as good as the training of correspondence between public conditions and private events. In addition to inadequate training, there are other problems with accurate descriptions of feelings. Many of our internal functions are poorly correlated (or uncorrelated) with public conditions, and this means that we cannot be taught to describe such events accurately. Although a doctor may ask for the general location of a pain (e.g., abdomen), he or she is unlikely to ask whether the hurt is in the liver or the spleen. This report is simply inaccessible to the patient because there is no way to teach the correspondence between exact location of damage and public conditions. Generally, we are able to report in a limited way on private events, but the unreliability of such reports makes them questionable as scientific observations. Based on this realization, behavior analysts focus on the study of behavior rather than feelings.

Thinking as Behavior

Behavior analysts have also considered thinking and its role in a science of behavior. In contrast to views that claim a special inner world of thought, behavior analysts suggest that human thought is human behavior. Skinner (1974) stated that:

> The history of human thought is what people have said and done. Symbols are the products of written and spoken verbal behavior, and the concepts and relationships of which they are symbols are in the environment. Thinking has the dimensions of behavior, not a fancied inner process which finds expression in behavior.
>
> (pp. 117–118)

A number of behavioral processes, like generalization, discrimination, matching to sample, and stimulus equivalence (see later chapters), give rise to behavior that, in a particular situation, may be attributed to higher mental functions. From this perspective, thinking is treated as private behavior (see Moore, 2003, and Tourinho, 2006, on private events).

Thinking as private behavior

One of the more interesting examples of thinking involves **private behavior** or behavior only accessible to the person doing it. Thinking as private behavior is observed in a game of chess. We may ask another person, "What is the player thinking about?" A response like "She is probably thinking of moving the castle" refers to thinking that precedes the move itself. Sometimes this prior behavior is observable—the player may place a hand on the castle in anticipation of the move. At other times, behavior is private and cannot be observed by others. An experienced chess player may think about the game, imagining the consequences of moving a particular piece.

Presumably, this private behavior is overt when a person learns to play chess. For example, first the basic rules of the game are explained and a novice player is shown how the pieces move and capture. In moving the pieces from place to place, the player is asked to describe the relationships between the opposing chess pieces. This establishes the behavior of visualizing the layout of the board. As the player receives additional corrective feedback, visualizing the layout becomes more skillful. The person begins to see relationships and moves that were not previously apparent. During the first few games, new players are often given instructions like "Don't move your knight there, or you'll lose it." Additionally, the player may be told, "A better move would have been . . . ," and a demonstration of the superior move is usually given. After some experience, the student is asked to explain why a particular move was made, and the explanation is discussed and evaluated. Eventually, the teacher stops prompting the player and encourages the person to play chess in silence. At this point, visualizing the layout of the board (e.g., white controls the center of the board) and describing the possible consequences of moves (e.g., moving the knight to this square will split the two rooks) becomes covert.

The function of thinking, as private behavior, is to increase the effectiveness of practical action. People can act at the covert level without committing themselves publicly. An advantage is that an action can be revoked if the imagined consequences are not reinforcing. In our example, the chess player considers the possible moves and the consequences that may follow given her/his past experience. Based on the covert evaluation, a player makes the move that appears to be best. Thus, the covert performance functions to prompt and guide overt action. Once the move is made, the player faces the objective consequences. If the move produces an advantage that results in checkmate, then thinking about such a move in similar circumstances is strengthened. On the other hand, a bad move weakens the consideration of such moves in the future. Overall, thinking is operant behavior controlled by its consequences. Thinking about a move that guides effective action is likely to occur again, while thinking that prompts ineffective performance declines.

In this section, we have discussed thinking as covert and private behavior. There are many other ways that the term thinking is used. When a person remembers, we sometimes talk about thinking in the sense of searching and recalling. Solving problems often involves private behavior that furthers a solution. In making a decision, people are said to think about the alternatives before a choice is made. The creative artist is said to think of novel ideas. In each of these instances, it is possible to analyze thinking as private behavior that is regulated by specific features of the environment. The remainder of this book discusses the behavioral processes that underlie all behavior, including thinking.

CHAPTER SUMMARY

This chapter has introduced the idea that behavior often is acquired during one's lifetime as a result of experience. At birth we emit behavior with very little organized activity. However, as our behaviors cause consequences, some responses are strengthened while others are weakened. The consequences of behavior function to select and establish a behavior repertoire. Several prominent persons were introduced to illustrate the history of the science of behavior analysis. In particular B. F. Skinner was described as the major force behind the experimental and applied analyses of behavior, which is the topic of this book. This approach is related to biology in that behavior is considered to be a product of genes interacting with the organism's environment. Behavior analysis can be extended to the understanding of feelings and to complex behavior involving problem solving and thinking.

Key Words

Applied behavior analysis
Behavior
Behavior analysis
Behavior analyst
Behavioral neuroscience
Behaviorism
Conditioned reflex
Culture

Experimental analysis of
  behavior
Immediate causation
Law of effect
Learning
Operant
Operant conditioning
Private behavior

Reflex
Remote causation
Respondent
Respondent conditioning
Science of behavior
Selection by consequences
Trial-and-error learning

The Experimental Analysis of Behavior

2

- Learn about a *functional* analysis of behavior.
- Inquire about the method of experimental analysis of behavior.
- Focus on drugs and behavioral baselines.
- Learn about how to design behavioral experiments.
- Discover how perception is analyzed with behavior principles.

The experimental analysis of behavior (EAB) refers to a method of analyzing behavior–environment relationships. This method is called functional analysis. **Functional analysis** involves classifying *behavior* according to its response functions and analyzing the *environment* in terms of stimulus functions. The term *function* refers to the characteristic effect *produced* by either a behavioral or an environmental event. Once a reliable classification has been established, the researcher uses experimental methods to show a causal relationship between the environmental event and a specified response. Because of this objective method, behavior analysts need not restrict their findings to one or a few species. The principles of behavior–environment relationships hold for all animals. Based on this assumption, and for convenience, researchers often use nonhuman subjects as their "tools" for discovering principles of behavior.

FUNCTIONAL ANALYSIS OF BEHAVIOR

There are two ways to classify the behavior of organisms: structurally and functionally. In the **structural approach**, behavior is analyzed in terms of its form. For example, many developmental psychologists are interested in the intellectual growth of children. These researchers often investigate what a person does at a given stage of development. Children may be said to show "object permanence" when they look for a familiar object that has just been hidden. In this case, the form of response, or what the child does (e.g., looks for and finds the hidden object), is the important aspect of behavior. The structure of behavior is emphasized because it is said to reveal the underlying "stage" of intellectual development. Notice that, in this example, the structural approach studies behavior to draw inferences about hypothetical internal cognitive abilities.

In the previous chapter, we noted that behavior analysts study behavior for its own sake and at its own level. To keep attention focused on behavior, both structure and function are interrelated. That is, a particular form of response is traced to its characteristic effects, outcomes, or consequences. For example, a person presses a light switch with the left hand, the thumb and index finger, and a particular force. This form, structure, or **topography** of response occurs because it has been highly efficient, relative to other ways of operating the light switch. Thus, the topography (structure) of a response is determined by the function (effects or consequences) of this behavior. Functionally, grasping the switch in a particular way produces light in an efficient manner.

In the more complex example of a child who finds a hidden object, a *functional analysis* suggests that this behavior also produces some specific consequence—the child gets the hidden toy. Rather than infer the existence of some intellectual stage of development or internal ability (like object permanence), the behavior analyst suggests that a particular **history of reinforcement** is responsible for the child's capability. Presumably, from a behavioral perspective, a child who demonstrates object permanence (searching for objects when they are not in sight) has had numerous opportunities to search for and find missing or hidden objects. One advantage of this functional account is that it is testable.

A mother who breastfeeds her newborn often removes some of her clothing just before feeding the baby. After some experience, the baby may tug at the mother's blouse when he or she is hungry. This is one potential instance of the early conditioning of searching for hidden objects. A few months later, the infant may inadvertently cover up a favorite rattle. In this situation, getting the toy reinforces pulling back the cover when things are hidden. As children get older, they are directly taught to find hidden objects. This occurs when children are given presents to open at birthdays and when they hunt for Easter eggs. A functional analysis of object permanence accounts for the behavior by pointing to its usual effects or consequences. That is, object permanence occurs because searching for out-of-sight objects usually results in finding them. Also, children who do not have these or similar experiences (playing peek-a-boo) will perform poorly on a test of object permanence.

Response Functions

Behavior is not always composed of discrete responses. In fact, it is better to consider behavior as a performance that follows a specific stimulus and at some point results in a particular consequence. (One memorable three-term notation system used to denote this arrangement is A–B–C, which stands for antecedent, behavior, and consequence, as detailed in Chapter 13.) Although we will use the term *response* throughout this book, the term does not always refer to a discrete movement like a muscle twitch or a lever press. A response is an integrated set of movements, or a behavioral performance, that is functionally related to environmental events. In fact, some writers have referred to a behavioral stream into which antecedent and consequence events are inserted.

Functionally, we speak of two basic types of behavior: respondent and operant. These behavioral classes were briefly discussed in Chapter 1 and will be throughout the book, but here we will emphasize the functional classification of behavior. The term **respondent** is used to refer to behavior that increases or decreases by the presentation of a stimulus (or event) that *precedes* the response. We say that the *presentation of the stimulus regulates or controls the response*. Respondent behavior is **elicited**, in the sense that it reliably occurs when the stimulus is presented. The notation system used with elicited behavior is S → R. The stimulus S causes (arrow) the response R. The constriction (and dilation) of the eye pupil is respondent behavior. It occurs when a bright light is directed into (away from) the eye. Salivation is another respondent that is elicited by food in the mouth. The stimulus S (light or food) elicits the response R (constriction of pupil or salivation). For the moment you may consider respondents to be the activity of smooth muscles or glands.

There is another large class of behavior that does not depend on an eliciting stimulus. This behavior is **emitted** and may (or may not) occur at some frequency. For example, human infants emit a random pattern of vocal sounds usually referred to as "babbling." These sounds contain the basic elements of all human languages. English-speaking parents attend to and repeat back babbling that sounds like English, and the baby soon begins to emit more English sounds. When emitted behavior is strengthened or weakened by the events that follow the response, it is called **operant** behavior. Thus, operants are emitted responses that occur more or less often depending on the consequences they produce. To make clear the subtle distinction between emitted behavior and operants, consider the action word *walking* versus the phrase *walking to the store*. Walking is emitted behavior, but it has no specified function. In contrast, walking to the store is an operant that is defined by getting food at the store. Pecking a disk is emitted behavior by a pigeon, but it is an operant when pecking the disk has resulted in food. Generally, operants are responses that occur in the absence of an obvious antecedent stimulus; these responses are altered in frequency by their effects or consequences.

Operant and respondent behaviors often occur at the same time when dealing with a single organism. A person who steps out of a movie theater in the middle of a bright afternoon may show both types of responses. The change from dark to bright light will elicit pupil contraction. This smooth-muscle activity is a reflexive response that decreases the amount of light entering the eye. At the same time, the person may shade their eyes with a hand or put on a pair of sunglasses. This latter behavior is operant because it is strengthened by the removal of the brightness—the aversive stimulus. In another example, you find that you have failed an important exam. The bad news may elicit a number of conditioned emotional responses like heart palpitations, changes in blood pressure, and perspiration. These physiological responses are probably interpreted as dread or anxiety. The person standing next to you as you read the results of the exam asks, "How did you do on the test?" You say, "Oh, not too bad" and walk down the hall. Your reply is operant behavior that avoids the embarrassment of discussing your poor performance. Although operant and respondent behaviors often occur at the same moment, we will usually analyze them separately in order to simplify and clarify the factors that regulate such behavior.

Response Classes

When a person emits a relatively simple operant like putting on a coat, the performance changes from one occasion to the next. The coat may be put on using either the left or right hand; it may be grasped at the collar or held up by a sleeve. Sometimes one arm is inserted first, while in other circumstances both arms may be used. Careful observation of this everyday action will reveal an almost infinite variety of responses. The important point is that each variation of response has the common effect of staying warm by putting on a coat. To simplify the analysis, it is useful to introduce the concept of a class of responses. A **response class** refers to all the topographic forms of the performance that have a similar function (e.g., putting on a coat to keep warm). In some cases, the responses in a class have close physical resemblance, but this is not always the case. A response class for "convincing an opponent" may include dramatic gestures, giving sound reasons, and paying attention to points of agreement. To get service from a restaurant server, you may call out as he or she passes, wave your hand in the air, or ask the bus-person to send the server to your table.

FUNCTIONAL ANALYSIS OF THE ENVIRONMENT

In Chapter 1, we noted that behavior analysts use the term **environment** to refer to events and stimuli that change behavior. These events may be external to the organism or may arise from internal physiology. The sound of a jet aircraft passing closely overhead or an upset stomach may both be classified as aversive by their common effects on behavior. That is, both events strengthen any behavior that removes them. In the case of a passing jet, people may cover their ears; a stomachache may be removed by taking antacid medication.

The location of the source of stimulation, internal versus external, is not a critical distinction for a functional analysis. There are, however, methodological problems with stomach pains that are not raised by external events like loud sounds. Internal sources of stimulation must be indirectly observed with the aid of instruments or inferred from observable behavior–environment inter-actions. Evidence for stomach pain, beyond the verbal report, may include the kinds of foods recently eaten, the health of the person when the food was ingested, and current external signs of discomfort.

Stimulus Functions

All events and stimuli, whether internal or external, may *acquire* the capacity to affect behavior. When the occurrence of an event changes the behavior of an organism, we may say that the event has a **stimulus function**. Both respondent and operant conditioning are ways to create stimulus functions. During respondent conditioning, an arbitrary event like a tone when paired with food comes to elicit a particular response, like salivation. Once the tone is effective, it is said to have a **conditioned-stimulus function** for salivation. In the absence of a conditioning history, the tone may have no specified function and does not affect behavior.

Similarly, operant conditioning generally results in establishing or changing the functions of stimuli. Any stimulus (or event) that follows a response and increases its frequency is said to have a **reinforcement function** (see Chapter 1). When an organism's behavior is reinforced, those events that reliably precede responses come to have a **discriminative function**. These events *set the occasion* for behavior and are called **discriminative stimuli**. Discriminative stimuli acquire this function because they predict (have been followed by) reinforcement. In the laboratory, a pigeon's key pecks may be followed by food when the key is illuminated red, but not reinforced when the key is blue. After some time, the red key color is said to set the occasion for the response. In everyday language, the red key "tells" the bird when pecking will be reinforced. More technically, the red key is a discriminative stimulus since the probability of reinforcement (and pecking) is higher when the key is red than when it is blue. That is, the bird discriminates or makes a differential response to red and blue.

The concept of stimulus function is an important development in the analysis of behavior. Humans and other animals have evolved in such a way that they can sense those aspects of the environment that have been important for survival. Of all the stimuli that can be physically measured and sensed by an organism, at any one moment, only some affect behavior (have a stimulus func-tion). Imagine you are sitting on a park bench with a friend on a nice sunny day. The physical stimuli include heat, wind current, sounds and smells from traffic, birds, insects, rustling leaves, tactile pressure from sitting, and the sight of kids playing ball, people walking in the park, color of flowers, grass, and trees. Although all of these (and many more) stimuli are present, only some will affect your behavior—in the sense that you will turn your face into the sun, comment on the beauty of the flowers, wrinkle your nose to the odor of exhaust, and look in the direction of a passing fire truck. The remaining stimuli, at this moment in time, either have no function or serve as the context for those events that do.

Stimulus Classes

In a preceding section, we noted that responses that produce similar effects might be many and varied. To encompass response variation in form, behavior analysts use the term *response class*. Stimuli that regulate operant and respondent behavior also vary from one time to the next. When stimuli vary across physical dimension but have a common effect on behavior, they are said to be part of the same **stimulus class**. Bijou and Baer (1978) have used the concept of stimulus class in an analysis of child development and have made the point that:

> A mother's face has a fair consistency to it, we may think, in that we know our mother's face from anyone else's face. But careful observations show that it is sometimes shiny, sometimes dusty,

sometimes wet; occasionally creased into its facial lines, but sometimes smooth; the eyes range between fully open and fully closed, and assume a wide range of angles of regard; sometimes hairs fall in front of the face, sometimes not. Then let us remember that whenever we speak of a stimulus, we will almost surely mean a class of stimuli.

(p. 25)

It is important to note that a stimulus class is defined entirely by its common effect on behavior. That is, a stimulus class cannot be defined by the apparent similarity of the stimuli. Consider the words *boring* and *uninteresting*. In common English, we say they have the same meaning. In behavior analysis, since these words have a similar effect on the person who reads or hears them, they belong to the same stimulus class even though they have completely different physical dimensions. Other stimuli may appear physically similar but belong to different stimulus classes. For example, mushrooms and toadstools look somewhat similar, but for an experienced woods person these stimuli have different functions—you pick and eat mushrooms but avoid toadstools.

Classes of reinforcing stimuli

The concept of stimulus class may also be used to categorize the consequences of behavior. When behavior operates on the environment to produce effects, it is an operant; the effects that increase the frequency of response are a class of reinforcing stimuli. Some consequences strengthen behavior when they are presented, like money for a job well done, and others strengthen it when they are removed, like scratching an itch. In this case, we can divide the general class of reinforcing stimuli into two subsets. Those events that increase behavior when presented are called **positive reinforcers**, and those that increase behavior when removed are **negative reinforcers**. For example, a smile and a pat on the back may increase the probability that a child will complete his or her homework; thus, the smile and pat are positive reinforcers. The same child may stop dawdling and start working on a school project when a parent scolds the child for wasting time and the nagging stops when he gets going. In this case, reinforcement for working is based on the removal of scolding, and the reprimand is a negative reinforcer.

Establishing Operations as Motivation

The relations between stimulus and response classes depend on the broader **context of behavior**. That is, environment–behavior relationships are always conditional—depending on other circumstances. One of the most common ways to change environment–behavior relationships is to have the person (or other organism) experience a period of deprivation or satiation. For example, a pigeon will peck a key for food only if it is deprived of food for some period of time. More specifically, the peck-for-food contingency depends on level of food deprivation.

Michael (1982a) made an important distinction between the discriminative and motivational functions of stimuli. In that paper, he introduced the term **establishing operation** to refer to any environmental change that had two major effects: the change increased the momentary effectiveness of reinforcement supporting operant behavior; and the change increased momentarily the responses that had in the past produced such reinforcement (see also Michael, 1993, 2000). For example, the most common establishing operation is deprivation for primary reinforcement. The procedure involves withholding reinforcement for some period of time or, in the case of food, until the organism reaches 80% of free-feeding body weight (see Chapter 5). This establishing operation of deprivation has two effects. First, food becomes an effective reinforcer for any operant that produces it. That is, the deprivation procedure establishes the reinforcement function of food. Second, behavior that has previously resulted in getting food becomes more likely—in the wild, a bird may start to forage in places where it has previously found food. Formally, an establishing operation is defined as "any change in the environment which alters the effectiveness of some object or event as reinforcement and simultaneously alters the momentary frequency of the behavior that has been followed by that reinforcement" (Michael, 1982a, pp. 150–151).

Establishing operations regularly occur in everyday life and depend on a person's conditioning history. For example, television commercials are said to influence a person's attitude toward a product. One way to understand the effects of TV commercials is to analyze them as establishing operations (technically, *conditioned establishing operations* or CEOs). In this case, an effective commercial alters the reinforcement value of the product and increases the likelihood of purchasing the item or using it if available. For example, dairy farmers advertise the goodness of ice-cold milk. Those who are influenced by the commercial are likely to go to the fridge and have a glass of milk. Of course, this immediate effect of the commercial depletes the amount of milk you have on hand, and eventually you buy more milk.

TACTICS OF BEHAVIORAL RESEARCH

To discover elementary relationships between functional stimuli, responses, and consequences, behavior analysts have relied on experimental methods developed in biology, medicine, and behavior analysis (Bernard, 1927; Bushell & Burgess, 1969; Johnston & Pennypacker, 1993; Sidman, 1960). In 1865, the French physician Claude Bernard outlined the central objectives for experimental analysis. He stated that:

> We can reach knowledge of definite elementary conditions of phenomena only by one road, viz., by *experimental analysis*. Analysis dissociates all the complex phenomena successively into more simple phenomena, until they are reduced, if possible, to just two elementary conditions. Experimental science, in fact, considers in a phenomenon only the definite conditions necessary to produce it.
>
> (Bernard, 1927, p. 72)

In his book, *An Introduction to the Study of Experimental Medicine*, Bernard (1927) provided a classic example of experimental analysis:

> One day, rabbits from the market were brought into my laboratory. They were put on the table where they urinated, and I happened to observe that their urine was clear and acid. This fact struck me, because rabbits, which are herbivora, generally have turbid and alkaline urine; while on the other hand carnivora, as we know, have clear and acid urine. This observation of acidity in the rabbits' urine gave me an idea that these animals must be in the nutritional condition of carnivora. I assumed that they had probably not eaten for a long time, and that they had been transformed by fasting, into veritable carnivorous animals, living on their own blood. Nothing was easier than to verify this preconceived idea or hypothesis by experiment. I gave the rabbits grass to eat; and a few hours later, their urine became turbid and alkaline. I then subjected them to fasting and after twenty-four hours, or thirty-six hours at most, their urine again became clear and strongly acid; then after eating grass their urine became alkaline again, etc. I repeated this very simple experiment a great many times, and always with the same result. I then repeated it on a horse, an herbivorous animal that also has turbid and alkaline urine. I found that fasting, as in rabbits, produced prompt acidity of the urine, with such an increase in urea that it spontaneously crystallizes at times in the cooled urine. As a result of my experiments, I thus reached the general proposition which then was still unknown, to wit, that all fasting animals feed on meat, so that herbivora then have urine like that of carnivora.
>
> But to prove that my fasting rabbits were really carnivorous, a counter proof was required. A

carnivorous rabbit had to be experimentally produced by feeding it with meat, so as to see if its urine would then be clear, as it was during fasting. So I had rabbits fed on cold boiled beef (which they eat very nicely when they are given nothing else). My expectation was again verified, and as long as the animal diet was continued, the rabbits kept their clear and acid urine.

(pp. 152–153)

Bushell and Burgess (1969) provided an outline of the basic tactics of experimental analysis used by Bernard in the rabbit experiment. The following account is loosely based on their outline. Notice that Bernard made an observation that, as a physiologist, seemed unusual and puzzling— namely, that the rabbits from the market had urine that was characteristic of carnivores. Only a trained physiologist familiar with carnivores and herbivores would notice the anomaly of the urine. Most of us would run and get a cloth to wipe it up. The point is that a researcher must have a thorough familiarity with the subject matter to find a significant problem.

Once Bernard identified the *problem*, he stated it in terms of a conjecture. The problem statement related type of diet to the chemistry of the urine. That is, fasting results in the animal living off its own body stores, and this produces acidity of the urine. On the other hand, when herbivores eat their usual diet of grass, their urine is alkaline. Thus, there is a clear relationship between type of diet and the nature of the animal's urine.

Experimentally, Bernard's statement suggests that we change, manipulate, or control the type of diet and measure the chemistry of the urine. The condition that is changed by the experimenter (i.e., type of diet) is called the **independent variable** (variable X) because it is free to vary at the discretion of the researcher. Bernard changed the animal's diet and measured the effect on the urine. The measured effect in an experiment is called the **dependent variable** (variable Y), because a change in it depends on a change in the independent variable. Whether the urine was acid or alkaline (dependent variable) depended on the nature of the diet (independent variable). Figure 2.1 explains the terms used in this section.

The purpose of any experiment is to establish a cause-and-effect relationship between the independent (X) and dependent (Y) variables. To establish such a relationship, the researcher must show that changes in the independent variable are functionally related to changes in the dependent variable. This is called showing covariation of the X and Y variables. In addition, the experimenter must show that the changes in the independent variable preceded changes in the dependent variable. Both of these conditions are seen in Bernard's experiment (Figure 2.2).

In Figure 2.2, you can see that changes between fasting and grass diet reliably alter the chemistry of the rabbits' urine. Thus, changes in type of diet (the X variable) may be said to covary with degree of acidity of urine (the Y variable of Figure 2.2). Recall that Bernard changed the type of diet and then measured its effects on the urine. This procedure of manipulating the independent variable ensures that a change in X (type of diet) precedes the change in Y (chemistry of urine). At this point,

Independent Variable	Dependent Variable
• What is changed in an experiment	• What is measured in an experiment
• X variable	• Y variable
• Commonly called a *cause*	• Commonly called an *effect*
• In Bernard's experiment, type of diet	• In Bernard's experiment, chemistry of urine
• In behavioral experiments, environmental change	• In behavioral experiments, behavior of the organism

FIG. 2.1   A table of scientific terms used to discuss cause-and-effect relationships.

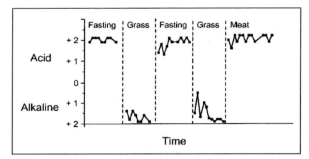

FIG. 2.2 The results of Bernard's experiment. Notice that the change in diet (independent variable) reliably changes the chemistry of the urine (dependent variable). Each time the diet is changed, the urine changes from acid to alkaline or vice versa. From *Behavioral Sociology* by R. L. Burgess and D. Bushell, Jr., 1969, p. 153. Copyright 1969 Columbia University Press. Reprinted with permission.

Bernard has shown two of the three important conditions for causation: (1) covariation of X and Y; and (2) the independent variable precedes a change in the dependent variable.

The central question in all experiments is whether the changes in the dependent variable are uniquely *caused* by changes in the independent variable. The problem is that many other factors may produce changes in the dependent variable, and the researcher must rule out this possibility. In the Bernard experiment, the initial change from fasting to grass diet may have been accompanied by an illness caused by contaminated grass. Suppose that the illness changed the chemistry of the animals' urine. In this case, changes from fasting to grass, or grass to fasting, will change the chemistry of the urine, but the changes are caused by the unknown illness rather than the type of diet. That is, the unknown illness *confounds* the effects of type of diet on the acidity of the urine. At this point, stop reading and look again at Bernard's description of his experiment and at Figure 2.2. Try to determine how Bernard eliminated this rival hypothesis.

One procedure for eliminating rival explanations is the systematic introduction and elimination of the grass diet. Notice that Bernard withholds and gives the grass diet and then repeats this sequence. Each time he introduces and removes the grass, a rapid change occurs from alkaline to acid (and vice versa). This rapid and systematic change makes it unlikely that illness accounts for the results. How can an animal recover from and contract an illness so quickly? Another procedure would be to use different batches of grass, because it is unlikely that they would all be contaminated. However, the most convincing feature of Bernard's experiment, in terms of eliminating rival explanations, is his final procedure of introducing a meat diet. The meat diet is totally consistent with Bernard's claim that the animals were living off their body stores and counteracts the rival explanation that the animals were ill. More generally, the reversal of conditions and the addition of the meat diet help to eliminate most other explanations.

The Reversal Design and Behavior Analysis

Bernard's experimental design for physiology is commonly used to study behavior–environment relationships. It is called an **A–B–A–B reversal design**, and is a powerful tool used to show causal relationships among stimuli, responses, and consequences. The reversal design is ideally suited to show that specific features of the environment control the behavior of a single organism. This kind of research is often called a *single-subject experiment* and involves several distinct phases. The A-phase, or **baseline**, measures behavior before the researcher introduces an environmental change. During baseline, the experimenter takes repeated measures of the behavior under study, and this establishes a criterion against which any changes (caused by the independent variable) may be assessed. Following the baseline phase, an environmental condition is changed (B-phase) and behavior is repeatedly measured. If the independent variable, or environmental condition, has an effect, then the behavioral measure (dependent variable) will change (increase or decrease).

At the same time, as we have indicated, the researcher must rule out rival explanations for the change in behavior, such as simple coincidence. To do this, the baseline phase is reintroduced (A) and behavior is repeatedly measured. When the treatment is removed, behavior should return to pretreatment or baseline levels. Finally, the independent variable is changed again and the behavior is carefully measured (B). According to the logic of the design, behavior should return to a level observed in the initial B-phase of the experiment. This second application of the independent variable helps to ensure that the behavioral effect is caused by the manipulated condition.

An example of the reversal design, as used in behavior analysis, is seen in an experiment conducted by Goetz and Baer (1973). The researchers were interested in the creative play of children and the role of reinforcement for such operant behavior. Several 4-year-old girls in a preschool were said to lack "creative skill" at block building. One measure of creative behavior is the number of different forms that a child builds with blocks during a play session (form diversity). The researchers wondered if positive attention from the teacher could function as reinforcement for building new block constructions (the experimental problem).

During the baseline phase, the teacher watched the child closely but said nothing about the child's use of the blocks. After baseline measures of form diversity were taken, the teacher then socially reinforced novel block constructions. The teacher remarked with "interest, enthusiasm, and delight every time the child placed and/or rearranged blocks so as to create a form that had not appeared previously" (Goetz & Baer, 1973, p. 212). Form diversity was assessed for several sessions with this procedure in effect.

To be certain that the reinforcement procedure was responsible for the increase in diversity, Goetz and Baer altered the contingency between teacher attention and block building. During this phase, the child was reinforced for repeating a form that had previously been built. Thus, similarity of form was reinforced in this phase. Finally, reinforcement of diverse forms was reinstated. The results of this experiment are portrayed for one of the three children (Sally) in Figure 2.3.

The experimental design is a modified A–B–A–B reversal. The baseline phase (A) provides a measure of block-building diversity before any intervention by the teacher. Next, a reinforcement contingency was arranged for novel forms of construction (B). During the third phase (C) of the experiment, the contingency of reinforcement was changed to support repetitive forms. Finally, reinforcement for novel constructions was reinstated (B). The independent variable in this experiment is the contingency of reinforcement— contingent reinforcement of novelty versus contingent reinforcement of repetition. The dependent variable is the number of different forms that the child produced during each phase of the experiment. As you can see, the dependent variable reliably changes in the expected direction with changes in the contingency of reinforcement (i.e., teacher attention for diversity or repetition).

The A–B–A–B reversal design is the most fundamental research design used in the experimental analysis of behavior. There are, however, difficulties that may make this design inappropriate for a given research question. One major problem is that behavior, once changed, may not return to baseline levels. Consider what might happen if you used a reinforcement technique to teach an illiterate adult to read. You could measure reading level, introduce your teaching technique, and after some time withdraw reinforcement for reading. It is very unlikely that the student will again become illiterate.

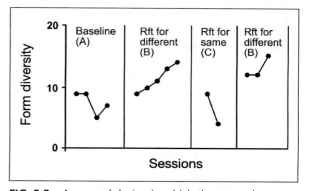

FIG. 2.3 A reversal design in which the researchers altered the contingency between teacher attention and block building. First, a baseline measure of behavior (A) was taken for several days. During the second phase of the experiment (B), the child was reinforced (Rft) for varying a form (diversity) that had been previously built. Next, the child was reinforced for building similar block forms (C), and finally the B-phase was reinstated. Adapted from "Social Control of Form Diversity and the Emergence of New Forms in Children's Blockbuilding," by E. M. Goetz and D. M. Baer, 1973, *Journal of Applied Behavior Analysis, 6,* 209–217. Copyright 1973 held by the Society for the Experimental Analysis of Behavior, Inc. Reprinted with permission.

In behavioral terms, the student's reading is maintained by other sources of reinforcement such as getting information that enables the student to behave effectively (e.g., reading a menu, traffic signs, etc.).

Another difficulty is that it is sometimes unethical to reverse the effects of a behavioral procedure. Suppose that a behavioral program to eliminate the use of crack cocaine works, but the doctors who run the program are not absolutely certain that the decline in drug use is caused by reinforcement procedures. It would be highly unethical to remove and reinsert the reinforcement therapy to be certain about causation. This is because removing the reinforcement procedure could lead to an increase in drug use. Nonetheless, when this and other difficulties are not encountered, the A–B–A–B reversal design is a preferable mode of analysis.

Throughout this book, we address research that uses the reversal design, modified-reversal designs (e.g., adding other control conditions), and other forms of experimental analysis. We have concentrated on the reversal design because it demonstrates the basic logic of behavioral experimentation. The task of all behavioral experiments is to establish with high certainty the cause-and-effect relationships that govern the behavior of organisms. Based on these causal relationships, behavior analysts search for general principles that organize experimental findings (e.g., principle of reinforcement).

FOCUS ON: Operant baselines and behavioral neuroscience

In a given setting, behavior that is reinforced in a particular way (e.g., every 10 responses produce food) becomes very stable (low variability) over repeated experimental sessions. An animal might show a run of responses followed by a break (or time without responding) and then another run. This pattern might be repeated over and over again after long exposure to the reinforcement procedure (called **steady-state performance**). Stable performance under a contingency of reinforcement can be used as a baseline for the effects of other independent variables. That is, when behavior is very stable under a given arrangement of the environment, it is possible to investigate other conditions that disrupt, increase, or decrease the steady-state performance of animals (Sidman, 1960). Recognizing this advantage, behavioral neuroscientists often use steady-state operant behavior as baselines (control conditions) to investigate the effects of drugs on the brain and behavior.

Regarding drugs and baselines, the more stable the baseline the easier it is to detect the effects of small doses of the drug. If an animal's average number of responses for 20 experimental sessions is 10 per minute with a range of ±1 response per minute (more stable baseline), a smaller dose of a drug would show an effect than if the baseline had the same average with a range of ±5 responses per minute (less stable baseline). Notice that the same drug dose that produces a detectable effect for the stable baseline is claimed to be ineffective when inserted on the less stable baseline. The point is that we can detect small effects of drugs (and other variables) if the operant baseline is very stable during steady-state performance.

Operant baselines are said to show sensitivity to drugs. **Baseline sensitivity** means that a low dose of a drug such as amphetamine (a dopamine agonist) can cause substantial changes in baseline behavior. In contrast, the same operant baseline may not show sensitivity to doses of morphine (an opioid agonist). One implication of this kind of finding is that the effectiveness of the reinforcement contingency on behavior may involve the dopamine system more than the endogenous opiates. Based on this inference, the behavioral neuroscientist can further explore how the dopamine system participates in the control of the behavior and what neural structures are involved. Subsequent research could involve anatomical and physiological studies as well as further experiments using behavioral baselines.

Behavioral neuroscientists have used operant baselines to investigate the role of drugs on punished behavior (reviewed by Sepinwall & Cook, 1978). In a series of classic experiments, rats in an operant chamber were trained to respond for presentations of sweetened condensed milk (Geller & Seifter, 1960; Geller, Kulak, & Seifter, 1962). Next, when a clicker sounded, each lever press resulted in the milk and also an electric shock to the floor grid. Data (cumulative records, see Chapter 4) of typical performance by the rats showed that responding was greatly reduced during periods of punishment. A series of sedative or tranquilizing drugs were then administered, and the most interesting findings were that the tranquilizers did not affect overall responding for milk, but they increased responding during the clicker/shock periods. The clicker period is when there is a conflict between responding for milk (positive reinforcement) and receiving the electric shock (punishment). Apparently, the class of drugs called tranquilizers prevented the usual effects of punishment while other classes of drugs used by the researchers did not have this effect.

SINGLE-SUBJECT RESEARCH

Generalizing from **single-subject research** is a well-founded scientific strategy. A single individual (rat, pigeon, or human) is exposed to the values of the independent variable, and the experiment may be conducted with several subjects. Each subject replicates the experiment; if there are four subjects, the investigation is repeated four separate times. Thus, every additional individual in a single-subject experiment constitutes a **direct replication** of the research and adds to the **generality** of the research findings. Direct replication involves manipulating the independent variable in the same way for each subject in the experiment.

Another way to increase the generality of a finding is by **systematic replication** of the experiment. Systematic replication uses procedures that are different but are logically related to the original research question (see Sidman, 1960, for a detailed discussion of direct and systematic replication). For example, in Bernard's research with the rabbits, changing the diet from fasting to grass altered the chemistry of the urine and may be considered an experiment in its own right. Feeding the animals meat may be viewed as a second experiment—systematically replicating the initial research using a grass diet. Given Bernard's hypothesis that all fasting animals become carnivores, it logically follows that meat should change the chemistry of the urine from alkaline to acid.

In a behavioral experiment, such as the creativity experiment by Goetz and Baer (1973), the researchers could have established generality by using a different task and a different kind of reinforcement (e.g., tactile contact like hugging). Here the central idea is that the **contingency of reinforcement** is the critical factor that produced the increase in creative block design. That is, the observed change in behavior does not depend on the type of activity (block building) or the nature of the reinforcer (positive attention). In fact, many behavioral experiments have shown that contingencies of reinforcement generalize across species, type of reinforcement, diverse settings, and different operants.

Generality and Single-Subject Research

A common misunderstanding about single-subject experiments is that generalizations are not possible because a few individuals do not represent the larger population. Some social scientists believe that experiments must include a large group of individuals to make general statements (called the *statistical groups design*). This position is valid if the social scientist is interested in descriptions of what the average individual does. For example, single-subject research is inappropriate for questions like, "What sort of advertising campaign is most effective for getting people in Los Angeles to recycle garbage?" In this case, the independent variable might be the type of advertising and the dependent variable the number of citizens in Los Angeles who recycle their waste. The central question is concerned with how many people recycle, and a group experiment is the appropriate way to approach the problem.

Behavior analysts are less interested in aggregate or group effects. Instead the analysis focuses on the behavior of the individual. These researchers are concerned with predicting, controlling, and interpreting the behavior of single organisms. The generality of the effect in a behavioral experiment is established by *replication*. A similar strategy is sometimes used in chemistry. The process of electrolysis can be observed in an unrepresentative sample of water from Logan, Utah. A researcher who follows the procedures for electrolysis will observe the same result in all samples of water, whether from Logan or from the Ganges. Importantly, the researcher may claim—on the basis of a single experiment—that electrolysis occurs in all water, at all times, and in all places. Of course, only replication of the experiment will increase confidence in this empirical generalization.

FOCUS ON: Assessment of behavior change

Single-subject experiments require a pre-intervention baseline period of measurement. This baseline serves as a comparison or reference for any subsequent change in behavior produced by the independent variable. This baseline is essential to know if your independent variable has any effect. To construct an appropriate baseline, it is necessary to define the response class objectively and clearly. In the animal laboratory, the response class of pressing a lever is most often defined by the closure of an electrical switch. There is no dispute about the state of the switch; it is either on or off. An animal may press the lever in many different ways. The left or right paw may be used as well as the hind foot, nose, and mouth. The point is that no matter how the response is made, all actions that result in a switch closure define the operant class. Once the response class is defined, the number of times the response occurs can be counted and a baseline constructed.

Outside of the laboratory, response classes are usually more difficult to define. Consider that you are asked to help manage the behavior of a troublesome child in a classroom setting. The teacher complains that the child is disruptive and interferes with his teaching. On the surface, measuring the disruptive behavior of the child seems easy. Further reflection, however, suggests that it is not easy to define the operant class. What exactly does the teacher mean when she says "the child is disruptive"? After talking to the teacher and observing the child in the classroom, several "disruptive" responses may be identified: The child is often *out of her seat* without permission and at times when a lesson is being taught. Another behavior that occurs is *talking loudly* to other children during study periods. Both of these responses are more clearly defined than the label "disruptive," but objective measurement may still be difficult. Notice that each response is partially defined by prior events (permission) and the current situation (study periods). In addition, terms like *loud* and *out of seat* are somewhat subjective. How loud is loud, and is sitting on the edge of the desk out of seat? The answer is to keep refining the response definition until it is highly objective. When two observers can agree most of the time on whether a response has occurred, then a baseline can be established.

In addition to defining the response class, assessment of behavior change requires some measure of response variability. During the baseline, repeated measures are taken and the number of responses is plotted. Figure 2.4 is a graph of an idealized experiment to modify the out-of-seat behavior of the child in the foregoing classroom example. Pretend that the teacher is requested to pay attention and give tokens to the child only when she is sitting quietly in her seat. At the end of the school day, the tokens may be exchanged for small prizes. Does this procedure alter the child's behavior? The graphs in Figures 2.4A and 2.4B show two possible baselines and the results of the intervention.

Compare your assessment of the treatment effect in Figures 2.4A and 2.4B. You probably judge that the reinforcement procedure was effective in graph A but possibly not in graph B. What do you suppose led to your conclusion? Notice that the range of values in the baseline of graph A is quite small when compared to graph B. The number of times the child is out of her seat does not change much from day to day, as shown in graph A, but there is substantial variation in the baseline of graph B. The effect of the modification can only be evaluated against a departure from the baseline. Because the baseline of graph B is so variable, it is difficult to judge whether the reinforcement procedure had an effect. If you have had a course in statistics, it may occur to you that the difficulty in graph B could be solved by a statistical test. While this is possible, behavior analysts would try different tactics.

One approach is to reduce the variability of the baseline. This might involve a more precise definition of the out-of-seat response. This would reduce variation introduced by imprecise measurement of the response class. Another reasonable strategy would be to increase the power of the intervention. In this case, the attempt is to produce a larger shift in behavior, relative to the baseline. For example, the small prizes earned at the end of the school day may be changed to more valuable items. Notice that these strategies lead to refinement in measures and procedures used in the experiment. This increases the experimenter's control over the subject matter, and this is a primary objective of the experimental analysis of behavior.

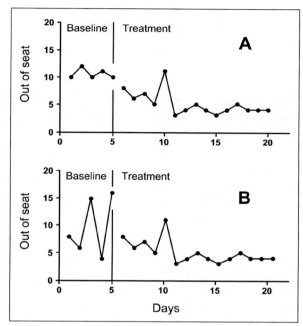

FIG. 2.4 Compare your assessment of the treatment effect in graphs A and B. Notice that the range of values in the baseline of graph A is quite small when compared to graph B. The effect of an experimental manipulation can only be evaluated against a departure from baseline. Because the baseline of graph B is so variable, it is difficult to judge whether the reinforcement procedure had an effect.

Assessment of behavior change may be more difficult if there is a trend in the baseline measures. A **trend** is a systematic decline or rise in the baseline values. A drift in baseline measures can be problematic when the treatment is expected to produce a change in the same direction as the trend. Figure 2.5 is a graph of the loud-talking behavior by the child in our hypothetical experiment. Notice that the number of loud-talking episodes during baseline starts at a moderately high level and

drifts downward over days. Perhaps the child's parents are getting more complaints from the school, and as the complaints mount they put more pressure on the child to "shut up." Regardless of why the trend is occurring, the modification procedure is expected to decrease loud talking. As you can see in Figure 2.5, the trend continues throughout the experiment and the decline in talking cannot be attributed to the treatment.

A downward (or upward) drift in baseline may be acceptable if the treatment is expected to produce an opposite trend. For example, a shy child may show a declining trend in talking to other students. In this case, an intervention could involve reinforcing the

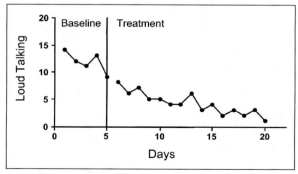

FIG. 2.5 A drift in baseline measures can make interpreting results difficult when the treatment is expected to produce a change in the same direction as the baseline drift.

initiation of conversation by the child. Because the treatment is expected to increase talking, the downward trend in baseline is acceptable. Generally, single-subject research requires a large shift in level or direction of behavior relative to baseline. This shift must be clearly observed when the independent variable is introduced and withdrawn.

ADVANCED SECTION: Perceiving as behavior

Even if you do your best to put down everything you see, will it really be everything? What about the singing of birds? And the freshness of the morning? And your own feeling of somehow being cleansed by it all? After all, as you paint, you perceive these things—they are inseparable from what you see. But how can you capture them in the painting so they are not lost for anyone who looks at it? Obviously they must be suggested by your composition and the color you use—since you have no other means of conveying them.

(Solzhenitsyn, 1973, p. 395)

The concept of stimulus function raises some interesting issues. Most of us believe that we accurately perceive the world around us and are able to report on this with some reliability. In everyday language and in psychology, perception is an inferred, underlying cognitive process that determines behavior. In contrast, behavior analysis suggests that perceiving is behavior that must be accounted for by environment–behavior relationships. The typical account of perception is seen in the following descriptions taken from two introductory psychology textbooks:

The view of perception that has been more or less dominant in psychology over the last 100 years holds that our experiences teach us how to draw broad inferences about the world from very limited sensory information; and that most perceptions are transformed constructions, or synthesizations, from combinations of more elementary sensations. It also maintains that these perceptual inferences are usually so accurate, highly practiced, and nearly automatic that you are almost totally unaware of making them.

(Darley, Glucksberg, & Kinchla, 1991, p. 109)

Perception is the process by which we organize and make meaningful the mass of sensations we receive. Our past experience and our current state of mind influence the intricate series of steps between sensation and perception.

(Martin, 1991, p. 126)

Generally, these passages reflect a view of human experience that has been popular for centuries. The basic idea is that receptors like eyes, ears, and tongue are constantly receiving and processing sensory input that is a disorganized array of raw data. The person is said to transform the sensations by mentally organizing the input into a meaningful representation of the situation.

From a behavioral perspective, the difficulty with this view of perception is that the mental organization and representation of sensory input is not directly observable. That is, there is no objective way of getting information about such hypothetical events except by observing the behavior of the organism. Such **hypothetical constructs** are not always undesirable in science, but when used to account for behavior these terms usually lack explanatory power because they are grounded in the very behavior that they are used to explain. This problem of explanatory power is seen in the perception account of the Stroop effect (Stroop, 1935).

Figure 2.6 gives an example of the Stroop effect that you can try for yourself. First, look at the dots about the line at the top of the figure. Now, as fast as you can, say out loud whether each dot is positioned above or below the line—go! How many errors did you make and about how long did it take? OK, now look at the words ABOVE or BELOW about the line at the bottom of the figure. As fast as you can, say whether each word is positioned above or below the line—go! How many errors

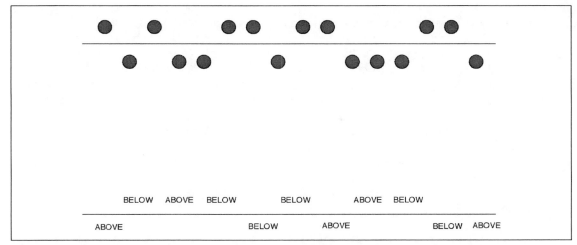

FIG. 2.6   The Stroop effect using dots above and below a line (top) and words for position (bottom). The bottom problem is more difficult in the sense that the position and the word (ABOVE vs. BELOW) compete for the response, "saying the position of the word."

did you make this time and how long did it take? Most people do pretty well when the problem involves dots (top) but poorly when they have to say the position of the words (bottom). Why do you think it is harder to do the problem with the words? Read on to find out.

One account involves perception and cognition as in the following: ". . . the highly practiced and almost automatic perception of word meaning [ABOVE or BELOW] facilitates reading. However, this same perception automatically makes it difficult to ignore meaning and pay attention only to [the position of the word] stimulus. Thus, the Stroop effect is a failure of selective perception" (Darley et al., 1991, p. 112).

From a behavior analysis perspective, the foregoing account restates the fact that your performance is better with the dots than with the words. The meanings and attention referred to in the passage are inferences from behavior with no independent evidence for their occurrence. Without evidence, the selective-perception explanation is not satisfying to the behavior analyst. The question is: How do environment–behavior relationships regulate performance on this task?

The first thing to notice is that all of us have extensive experience in identifying the position of objects as above or below some reference point (the line in Figure 2.6). That is, the position of the object comes to set the occasion for the response of saying "above" or "below." We also have a long history of reinforcement for reading the words ABOVE and BELOW; in books these words correspond to the position of objects in pictures, as in "the airplane is above the ground" or "the sun is below the horizon." Because of this learning, the physical position (location of object X) and written words for position ("above/below") come to control the response class ("object X is above [or below] the reference point"). When written words for location are presented in positions that do not correspond to the word (Word=ABOVE; Position=below), the two properties of the complex stimulus (word/position) compete for the respective responses. Based on the simultaneous control of behavior by two aspects of the blended stimulus, the time to complete the task increases and errors occur. Consider what you might do if you were driving and came to an intersection with a red-hexagon sign that had the word PROCEED painted on it. You would probably wonder what to do and show "brake and go" responses. Instead of using an account based on selective perception, the behavior analysts would point to *response competition* and *reinforcement history* as reasons for your hesitation.

There are other interesting implications of a functional analysis of perceiving. For example, you walk into a room and look around, believing that you are taking in reality. But what do you see?

Seeing itself is something an organism is prepared to do based on its genetic endowment, but seeing a particular object on a given occasion may be analyzed as respondent or operant behavior. That is, observing an object or event is behavior that is elicited by the event, has a high probability due to past consequences, or becomes likely due to motivating conditions (e.g., hunger, thirst, etc.).

Imagine that you have gone camping with several friends. After supper you decide to entertain your friends by telling a horror story about an axe murder that took place in the same area a few years ago. One of your companions is finishing supper, and the fried egg on her plate begins to look like a giant dead eye that is about to explode with yellow "glop." As the night gets darker, another camper hears ominous sounds and begins to see figures moving in the brush. In everyday words, your friends are imagining these events. Behaviorally, the frightening story may be analyzed as a motivating condition that momentarily increases the probability of seeing things that appear to be threatening.

B. F. Skinner (1953) has described other conditions that affect seeing as a conditioned response. He stated that:

> Conditioned seeing explains why one tends to see the world according to one's previous history. Certain properties of the world are responded to so commonly that "laws of perception" have been drawn up to describe the behavior thus conditioned. For example, we generally see completed circles, squares, and other figures. An incomplete figure presented under deficient or ambiguous circumstances may evoke seeing a completed figure as a conditioned response. For example, a ring with a small segment missing when very briefly exposed may be seen as a completed ring. Seeing a completed ring would presumably not be inevitable in an individual whose daily life was concerned with handling incomplete rings.
>
> (pp. 267–268)

Skinner (1953) later points out that operant conditioning can also affect what is seen:

> Suppose we strongly reinforce a person when he finds a four-leaf clover. The increased strength of "seeing a four-leaf clover" will be evident in many ways. The person will be more inclined to look at four-leaf clovers than before. He will look in places where he has found four-leaf clovers. Stimuli that resemble four-leaf clovers will evoke an immediate response. Under slightly ambiguous circumstances he will mistakenly reach for a three-leaf clover. If our reinforcement is effective enough, he may even see four-leaf clovers in ambiguous patterns in textiles, wallpaper, and so on. He may also "see four-leaf clovers" when there is no similar visual stimulation—for example, when his eyes are closed or when he is in a dark room. If he has acquired an adequate vocabulary for self-description, he may report this by saying four-leaf clovers "flash into his mind" or he "is thinking about" four-leaf clovers.
>
> (p. 271)

You must realize that no one knows what a person "sees." What we know is what the perceiver says she sees. The person tells us she sees (or does not see) something and this statement is itself an operant; as an operant the verbal statement of seeing "X" is regulated by its past history of consequences (including the social consequences provided by other people).

Epling and Cameron (1994) reported an interesting instance of operant seeing that appeared in Euell Gibbons's book *Stalking the Wild Asparagus*. Gibbons was enthusiastic about eating wild asparagus and on a fishing trip he spotted some fine young asparagus shoots. Spying these shoots was reinforcement for looking for, seeing, and discovering other clumps of asparagus:

> . . . I was walking along the bank of an irrigation ditch, headed for a reservoir where I hoped to catch some fish. Happening to look down, I spied a clump of asparagus growing on the ditch bank, with half a dozen fat, little spears that were just the right size to be at their best. . . . Even when cutting this cluster, I saw another with several more perfect little sprouts. Alerted, I kept my eyes open and soon found another cluster and then another. . . . About this time I noticed that an old, dry, last-year's stalk

stood above every clump of new asparagus tips. . . . I sat down on the ditch bank and for five minutes I did nothing but just *look* at one old dry asparagus stalk. It looked very much like the dead weeds and plants that surrounded it, and yet there were differences. The old asparagus plant stood about three feet high and had a central stem or "trunk" about a half inch in diameter that easily distinguished it from weeds with forking stems. . . . After getting the size, color and form thoroughly in my mind, I stood up and looked back along the ditch bank. Instantly, I saw a dozen old dead asparagus stalks that I had missed. I went back to where I had found the first clump and worked my way down the ditch again, and this time I really reaped a harvest. . . . That five minutes I spent [many years] ago, concentrating on one dead asparagus plant, has lead me to many pounds of this most delicious of early vegetables. The eye training it gave me has lasted until now. Whenever I drive, in late winter or early spring, my eye automatically picks up the dead asparagus stalks by the roadside, and I make an almost unconscious mental note of the places where the green spears will be plentiful when warm weather arrives.

(pp. 28–32)

Psychologists have called these conditioned seeing effects "perceptual set" or "search image." In fact, many psychologists do not consider seeing as operant or respondent behavior. These researchers prefer to study perception as a cognitive process that underlies behavior. Although the issue is not resolved here, Skinner makes it clear that analyzing seeing as behavior is one way to understand such processes. That is, perceiving may be treated like *signal detection* rather than mental states and processes (Green & Swets, 1966). The behavior analysis of seeing (or, more generally, perceiving) also applies to other sensory dimensions such as hearing, feeling, and smelling. Notice that such an analysis accounts for perceiving without reference to mental events.

CHAPTER SUMMARY

In summary this chapter has introduced the science of behavior analysis. In particular, it is the assessment of the antecedents and consequences of behavior as aspects of the environment that can be manipulated and affect the behavior in question. Innumerable formal and informal studies have determined that the events that follow a specific response will influence whether that response is likely to occur again. If a response has a destructive, obnoxious, painful, or otherwise unpleasant outcome an animal will not repeat it. They are either killed, as by eating toxic plants, or injured, as by touching a leaf with sharp spines, and the behavior is gone. The point is that behaviors have functions in the sense that something happens as a result. We are built by natural evolutionary processes to behave, to walk, to pick up things, to vocalize, etc. We look around and we see different sights; our head turning has a function—it moves our eyes so that we see in different directions. Behavior analysts work to discover the functions of behavior and also to provide functions that end up creating novel behaviors.

A functional analysis is conducted in several uniform and proven effective sets of procedures. A major tactic is the A–B–A–B reversal process whereby the researcher determines if a certain functional outcome (an applied consequence) does indeed control the appearance of a behavior. If a rat gets a pellet for lever pressing, the rat presses the lever and when pellets stop coming he stops pressing. The behavior of organisms can be studied objectively and scientifically and that is why several issues are described concerning replication, validity, generalization, and assessment. The experimental analysis of behavior is a systematic set of tactics for the exploration of the controlling variables of behavior.

Key Words

A–B–A–B reversal design
Baseline
Baseline sensitivity
Conditioned-stimulus
   function
Context of behavior
Contingency of reinforcement
Dependent variable
Direct replication
Discriminative function
Discriminative stimuli
Elicited

Emitted
Environment
Establishing operation
Functional analysis
Generality
History of reinforcement
Hypothetical construct
Independent variable
Negative reinforcer
Operant
Positive reinforcer
Reinforcement function

Respondent
Response class
Single-subject research
Steady-state performance
Stimulus class
Stimulus function
Structural approach
   (to classifying behavior)
Systematic replication
Topography
Trend (as in baseline)

Reflexive Behavior and Respondent Conditioning

3

- Learn about *fixed action patterns* (*FAPs*) and reaction chains.
- Find out about the primary laws of the reflex and the phenomenon of habituation.
- Study *Pavlov's* experiments on respondent conditioning of salivation.
- Learn about the complexities of second-order and compound conditioning.
- Discover the basis of drug tolerance and the effects of context on drug overdose.

A biological imperative, faced by all creatures, is to survive long enough to reproduce. Because of this, behavior related to survival and reproduction often appears to be built into the organism. That is, organisms come into the world with a range of behavior that aids survival and reproduction. Creatures that fly to avoid predators are likely born with the ability to fly. Thus, flying does not need to be learned; it results from the organism's species history. The complex array of motor movement and coordination involved in flying could be learned, but it is much more dependable when this behavior is based on genetic endowment.

For most animals, survival at birth depends on being able to breathe, digest food, and move about. When a worm is dangled over a young robin's head, this stimulus elicits opening the mouth and chirping. The behavior of the chick is the result of biological mechanisms and is elicited by the sight of the dangling worm. The relationship between the dangling worm (stimulus) and the open mouth (response) is a reflex. Presumably, in the evolutionary history of robins, chicks that presented a gaping mouth and chirped were fed and those that did not may have been ignored. That does not mean that there are no learned modifications of such initial behaviors (Walker, 1987, pp. 21–26). For example, Tinbergen and Kuenen (1957) observed that if feeding did not follow gaping to a realistic artificial stimulus thrush chicks stopped responding. In humans, reflexive crying to discomfort or hunger by an infant insures more effective care from the child's parents. Parents engage in a variety of caretaking behaviors in attempts to stop crying. Usually, parental responses such as changing a wet diaper, feeding, or burping the infant will stop the fussing.

PHYLOGENETIC BEHAVIOR

Behavior relations that are based on the genetic endowment of an organism are called **phylogenetic** and are present on the basis of species history. Behavior that aids survival or procreation is often (but not always) unlearned. This is because past generations of organisms that engaged in such behavior survived and reproduced. These animals passed (to the next generation) the characteristics, in terms of genes, that allowed similar behavior. Thus, species history provides the organism with a basic repertoire of responses that are elicited by environmental conditions. Darwin said that these characteristics were naturally selected since they occurred through no action or intervention by man.

Sequences of Behavior

Fixed action patterns or **FAPs** are sequences of behavior (a series of connected movements) that are phylogenetic in origin. All members of a particular species (often all males or all females) engage in the FAP when the appropriate releasing stimuli are presented. Fixed action patterns have been observed and documented in a wide range of animals and over a large number of behaviors related to survival and reproduction. To illustrate, Tinbergen (1951) noted that the male stickleback fish responds with a stereotyped sequence of aggressive displays and movements when other male sticklebacks intrude on its territory during mating season. The female spider *Cupiennius salei* constructs a cocoon and deposits her eggs in it by engaging in a fixed sequence of responses (Eibl-Eibesfeldt, 1975). A greylag goose presented with an egg outside its nest will automatically roll the egg into the nest by reaching over the egg (with its bill) and pulling it carefully toward the nest. If the egg is removed, the bird continues with the fixed sequence of egg-retrieval actions. That is, the bird continues behaving as though the egg is present even though it has been removed. The following passage describes the FAP that the squirrel *Sciurus vulgaris* L. engages in while putting nuts away for the winter:

> The squirrel ... buries nuts in the ground each fall, employing a quite stereotyped sequence of movement. It picks a nut, climbs down to the ground, and searches for a place at the bottom of a tree trunk or a large boulder. At the base of such a conspicuous landmark it will scratch a hole by means of alternating movements of the forelimbs and place the nut in it. Then the nut is rammed into place with rapid thrusts of the snout, covered with dirt with sweeping motions and tamped down with the forepaws.
>
> (Eibl-Eibesfeldt, 1975, p. 23)

Ethologists refer to such predictable and stereotypic behaviors as FAPs to imply that these behaviors are built-in and immutable. They are looking for heritable genetic-based factors with which to account for behavior. On the other hand the behavior science model prefers to consider all behaviors as flexible and adaptable, at least to some degree. So, given the adaptive ability of most animals, we refer to this behavior as *flexible action patterns*. Although the major topographic features of these types of reflex combinations may appear very similar across individuals and situations, there are numerous idiosyncratic differences that show flexibility. For example, all robins (*Turdus americanis*) build nests that appear very similar in construction. But, it is clear they do not all build in the same location, or use the same materials. There is great individual variation in all phases of nest construction, suggesting modification by the environment (ontogeny).

    Reaction chains are similar to FAPs with one major difference—each response in a reaction chain requires an appropriate stimulus to set it off. Recall that once a FAP begins, the animal will continue the sequence even when the stimuli that set off the behavior are removed. In the previous squirrel example, if the nut is taken away from the squirrel, the animal will continue to dig a hole and bury a nonexistent nut. In contrast, a reaction chain requires the presence of a specific stimulus to evoke each link in a patterned sequence of behavior. An organism's performance produces stimuli that set off the next set of responses in the sequence; these behaviors produce the next set of stimuli followed by another set of responses. Presenting stimuli that prompt responses ordinarily occurring in the middle part of the sequence will start the chain at that point rather than at the beginning. Also, unlike FAPs, if the stimuli that evoke behavior are removed, the sequence is disrupted.

    Reaction chains are like consecutive sets of reflexes where the stimulus that elicits the next response in the sequence is produced by the previous reflex. The nursing reaction chain of newborn babies is diagrammed in Figure 3.1. This sequence of reflexive responses may be initiated by tactile stimulation of the infant's cheek. This stimulation elicits the unconditioned rooting response, which involves turning the head towards the stimulation, opening the mouth, etc. Rooting results in mouth contact with the nipple; this oral stimulation in turn elicits sucking. Sucking produces breast milk in the infant's mouth, leading to further sucking. Eventually, internal stimuli arising from a full stomach, changes in blood chemistry, and endocrinology end the sequence and the baby stops feeding. (*Note*: When we discuss operant behavior and operant conditioning in a later chapter we also speak of response chains but in this case the sequences are learned and are described as interlocking three-term contingencies.)

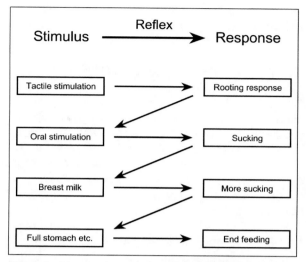

FIG. 3.1 The nursing reaction chain of newborn babies is diagrammed. This sequence of reflexive responses is initiated by tactile stimulation of the infant's cheek. Stimulation of the cheek elicits the unconditioned rooting response that involves turning the head towards the nipple (rooting), opening the mouth, and sucking.

Reflexive Behavior

The principles that describe the reflex (and its conditioning) are similar for many different kinds of reflexes. For example, the laws that govern pupil contraction when a light is shined in the eye or principles describing the relationship between a sudden loud noise and a startle response also hold for the salivation produced when you eat a meal. Early work by Sherrington (1906) focused on the reflex, and the relationships that he discovered, almost a century ago, generalize to a remarkable variety of stimulus–response relationships. When food is placed in a dog's mouth, the salivary glands produce saliva. This relationship between food in the mouth and salivation is a reflex that is based on the genetic endowment of the organism and is not learned. Many reflexes serve defensive, protective or survival functions. Frequently such reflexes are not learned because they have to function before adequate experience is provided.

All organisms are born with a built-in set of reflexes, but many are particular to a species. Thus, humans are born with an array of responses that are elicited by specific stimuli. As illustrated above, tactile stimulation of the human infant's cheek evokes the rooting response—turning toward the stimulation with mouth open, which then receives the nipple. Also, as we have noted, in young robins, the so-called "begging" reflex (open mouth and chirping) serves a similar function—getting fed. Because these relationships are relatively invariant and biologically based, we refer to the eliciting event as the **unconditioned stimulus (US)**. The related behavior following the stimulus is called the **unconditioned response (UR)**. The term *unconditioned* is used because the reflex does not depend on an organism's experience or conditioning during its lifetime (i.e., learning).

When an unconditioned stimulus elicits an unconditioned response (US → UR), the relationship is called a **reflex**. Reflexive behavior is automatic in the sense that a physically healthy organism will always produce the unconditioned response when presented with an unconditioned stimulus. You do not choose to salivate or not when you have food in your mouth; the US (which is "food in the mouth") draws out or **elicits** the UR of salivation. This is the way the animal (you) is built. However, there are times and conditions described below where the US does not elicit the UR.

When repeated presentations of the US lead to a reduction of the UR we call that process *habituation*.

Laws of the Reflex

Aristotle about 350 BC developed principles of association that were rediscovered by psychologists and Pavlov (a physiologist) in the 1900s (Hothersall, 1990, p. 22). Sherrington (1906) studied many different types of reflexes, and formulated the laws of reflex action. Because reflexive behavior occurs across most or all animal species from protozoa (Wawrzyncyck, 1937) to humans (Watson & Rayner, 1920), and because associative or respondent conditioning builds on reflexive behavior, it is important to describe the laws of the reflex. The laws are general in that they hold for all eliciting or unconditioned stimuli (e.g., food in the mouth, a touch of a hot surface, a sharp blow just below the knee, a light shining in the eye) and the corresponding unconditioned responses (salivation, quick finger withdrawal, an outward kick of the leg, pupil contraction).

The unconditioned stimuli that elicit unconditioned responses may vary in intensity. For example, light that is shining in the eye may be bright enough to hurt or so faint that it is difficult to detect. A tap below the knee, causing a kick, may vary from a modest to a heavy blow, etc. The intensity of the eliciting US has direct effects on the elicited reflex. Three **primary laws of the reflex** describe these effects:

1. The **law of the threshold** is based on the observation that at very weak intensities a stimulus will not elicit a response, but as the intensity of the eliciting stimulus increases there is a point at which the response is elicited. That is, *there is a point below which no response is elicited and above which a response always occurs.* The uncertainty region, where roughly 50% of the stimuli that are presented produce a response, is called the threshold.
2. The **law of intensity–magnitude** describes the relationship between the intensity of the eliciting stimulus and the size or magnitude of the elicited response. *As the intensity of the US increases so does the magnitude of the elicited UR.* A light tap on the patella tendon (just below the kneecap) will evoke a slight jerk of the lower leg; a stronger tap will produce a more vigorous kick of the leg (the patella reflex). Of course, there are upper limits to the magnitude of the tap. If a hammer is used to smash into the knee, the result is a broken kneecap and no movement for a long time.
3. The **law of latency** concerns the time between the onset of the eliciting stimulus and the appearance of the reflexive response. Latency is a measure of the amount of time that passes between these two events. *As the intensity of the US increases, the latency to the appearance of the elicited UR decreases.* Thus, a strong puff of air will elicit a quick blink of the eye. A weaker puff will also elicit an eye blink, but the onset of the response will be delayed.

These three laws of the reflex are basic properties of all reflexes. They are called primary laws because, taken together, they define the relationship between the intensity of the eliciting stimulus (US) and the unconditioned response (UR). Reflexes, however, have other characteristics and one of these, habituation, has been shown in animals as simple as protozoa and as complex as humans.

Habituation

One of the more documented secondary properties of the reflex is called **habituation**. Habituation is observed to occur when an unconditioned stimulus repeatedly elicits an unconditioned response and the response gradually declines in magnitude. When the UR is repeatedly elicited it may eventually fail to occur at all. For example, Wawrzyncyck (1937) repeatedly dropped a 4-g weight onto a slide that the protozoa *Spirostomum ambiguum* were mounted on. The weight drop initially elicited a contraction or startle response that steadily declined to near zero with repeated stimulation.

An interesting report of human habituation, in a dangerous setting, appeared in the July 1997 issue of *National Geographic*. The small island of Montserrat has been home to settlers since 1632. Unfortunately, the relatively silent volcano on the island reawakened in July 1995. Suddenly the quiet life that characterized living on Montserrat was rudely interrupted. Before the major eruption of the volcano, a large group of inhabitants refused to evacuate the island and these people suffered through several small volcanic explosions:

> ... Gerard Dyer and his wife, Judith, [have] been staying with friends in St. John's, about as far north of the volcano as you can get.... People could get passes to visit the unsafe zone, which is how Gerard came to be working on the flanks of Soufriere Hills that bright morning.
>
> "If you have animals and crops, you can't just leave them" said Gerard as we walked back to his truck. "You have to come look after them and hope nothing happen." As he spoke, the volcano made a crackling sound like distant thunder—blocks of solid lava rolling down the side of the dome. Gerard didn't even look up.
>
> Montserratians have become so used to the volcano's huffing and puffing that the initial terror has gone. As one woman said, "At first when there was an ashfall, everybody run. Now when the ash falls, everybody look."
>
> (Williams, 1997, p. 66)

In this example, Gerard has been repeatedly exposed to the sound (US) of minor volcanic explosions. At first, this sound elicited a startle/panic response, accompanied by running, but these URs habituated to near zero with repeated eruptions of the volcano. A similar process is observed when people live under an airport flight path; initially the sound of a jet taking off or landing is bothersome, but after some time the sound is barely noticed.

There are a number of general properties that characterize habituation (Thompson & Spencer, 1966). Some of the more important principles of habituation are: (1) the decrease in the habituated response is large at first but this decrement gets progressively smaller as habituation is continued; (2) if the unconditioned stimulus is withheld for some time, the habituated response recovers; and (3) when habituation is repeatedly produced, each series of stimulus presentations generates progressively more rapid habituation. In other words, habituation occurs more quickly on a second series of unconditioned stimulus presentations than on the first, and then even faster on a third set. This may represent the simplest form of learning and also a rudimentary form of memory (Tighe & Leaton, 1976).

Habituation is a behavioral process that has come about because of phylogenetic history. Those animals that habituated were more likely to survive and produce offspring. A herbivore that runs away each time the grass rustles gets less to eat than one that stands its ground. A rustling grass sound may indicate the presence of a predator, or simply the wind blowing. Repeated activation of respondent mechanisms, when unnecessary, stresses the animal as well, which is not good in terms of health and physiology.

At the physiological level, habituation is possible because of the way the reflex arc is constructed. To explain, a sensory neuron with a sensory transducer enters the spinal cord and synapses onto a motor neuron. When activated by a touch, for example, the sensory neuron generates an action potential in an effector neuron across a synapse that in turn causes muscle or gland activity. Synapses have many inputs, some of which are excitatory and some that are inhibitory. The presence of the synapse between sensory and motor neurons allows for the presence of inhibitory input and habituation of the UR (Thompson & Glanzman, 1976).

ONTOGENETIC BEHAVIOR

In addition to phylogenetic history, the behavior of an organism is affected by environmental experience. Each organism has a unique **ontogenetic** history or lifetime of conditioning. Change in behavior as a result of such experience is called *learning* and consists of organism–environment interactions. Events in the physical and social world impact the behavior of organisims. Learning builds on species or *phylogenetic* history to determine when, where, and what kind of behavior will occur at a given moment.

For example, salivation is involved with the digestion of food. People do not learn to salivate to the taste of food; this is a phylogenetic characteristic of the species. After some experience where you learn that McDonald's goes with food, you may salivate to the sight of the golden arches of McDonald's, especially if you are hungry and like hamburgers. Salivating at the sight of McDonald's arches occurs because of respondent conditioning—you were not born that way. It is, however, important to note that respondent conditioning and other learning processes themselves evolved because they provided some sort of reproductive advantage. Those organisms whose behavior came under the control of arbitrary (but important) environmental events presumably gained an advantage over those that did not. Through Darwinian evolution and selection, respondent conditioning became a means of behavioral adaptation. In other words, *organisms with a capacity for respondent learning were more likely to survive and reproduce*—increasing their genes in the population.

Respondent Conditioning

Respondent conditioning involves the transfer of the control of behavior from one stimulus to another by S–S pairing. In Chapter 1, we saw that the sound of a bell could come to elicit salivation after the bell had been associated with food. This kind of conditioning occurs in all species, including humans, and is common in everyday life. Imagine you are out for an early morning walk and pass a bakery where you smell fresh doughnuts. When this happens, your mouth begins to water and your stomach starts to growl. These conditioned responses occur because, in the past, the smell has been associated (paired) with food in the mouth (doughnuts).

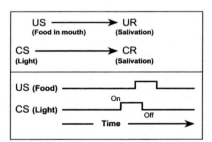

FIG. 3.2 Simple respondent conditioning. An arbitrary stimulus such as a light (CS) is presented just before food is placed in a dog's mouth (US). After several pairings of light and food, the light is presented alone. If the light now elicits salivation, it is called a conditioned stimulus (CS), and salivation to the light is a conditioned response (CR).

Figure 3.2 shows the classical conditioning of salivation described by Pavlov (1960). The upper panel indicates that an arbitrary stimulus such as a light (CS) is presented just before food (US) is placed in a dog's mouth. After several pairings of the light with the food, the light is presented alone. If the light now elicits salivation (test phase), it is called a **conditioned stimulus** (CS), and salivation to the light is called the **conditioned response** (CR).

Notice that a new feature of the environment (a light) has come to regulate the behavior (salivation) of the organism. Thus, classical (Pavlovian or respondent) conditioning involves the transfer of behavior control to new and often arbitrary aspects of the environment. To experience this sort of conditioning, try the following: Read the word *lemon* and consider the last time you ate a slice of lemon. Many people salivate at this CS because the word has been contiguously (near in time) paired with the sour taste of the fruit. This shift in controlling stimulus from food to word is possible because of the anatomy described above involving the critical synapse onto the final common neural pathway. In this case, input to the visual system ends up activating the neuron that innervates the salivary gland.

Because the CR is a response elicited by the CS, it is often called a **respondent**. The terms *conditioned response* and *respondent* are interchangeable throughout this text. The process of presenting stimuli together in time (pairing or associating stimuli) so that a CS comes to regulate the occurrence of the conditioned response is called **respondent conditioning**. Technically, respondent conditioning involves establishing a conditional probability between the CS and US (the occurrence of the US is conditional on the presence of the CS).

Note that the association is between the CS and US (i.e., the word *lemon* and the real fruit in the mouth) because they have been paired together at some time in the past—not because of some cognitive (internal mental) association of events. This is an important point: The word "association" is sometimes taken to mean an internal mental process that a person or other animal performs. We hear people say, "the dog salivates when the bell is sounded because it has associated the sound with the food." In contrast, a behavior analyst points to the physical association of stimuli (CS and US) that occurred in the past. In other words, the association is between events—it does not refer to mental associations. The word *lemon* (CS) elicits salivation (CR) because the word has occurred at a time and place when the chemistry of a lemon (US) produced salivation (UR).

The usual *measures* of behavior for respondent conditioning are magnitude (amount of salivation) and latency (time to salivation) of response following presentation of the US or CS. Magnitude and latency make sense as behavioral measures because respondent conditioning often involves the actions of smooth muscles and glands or responses such as eye-blinks and skin resistance (the UR or CR) that vary on these two dimensions.

Respondent acquisition

When a conditioned stimulus (CS) is repeatedly paired with an unconditioned stimulus (US), the CS comes to produce the conditioned response (CR). The increase in the CR to the presentation of the CS is called **respondent acquisition**. In one experiment, Anrep (1920) demonstrated the conditioning of the salivary reflex to a tone stimulus. The acquisition procedure involved turning on the tone for a brief period, and then placing food in a dog's mouth. Anrep measured the conditioned response as the number of drops of saliva during 30-s intervals wherein the tone occurred without food. Figure 3.3A (acquisition) shows that the amount of salivation to the tone increases rapidly during the first 25 trials and then levels off, or reaches its maximum called the *asymptote*. In other words, with repeated pairings of the CS and US, the magnitude of the conditioned response increases. Once the conditioned reflex reaches asymptote, however, further CS–US pairings have no additional effects.

It is important to note that the asymptote for the conditioned response depends on the intensity of the unconditioned stimulus. As the intensity of the US increases, the magnitude of the UR also increases up to a point. The magnitude of the UR limits the maximum strength of the CR. Thus, the more food a dog is given, the greater the amount of salivation. If a dog is given 2 oz of meat, there will be more salivation than if it is presented with 1 oz. A tone that is

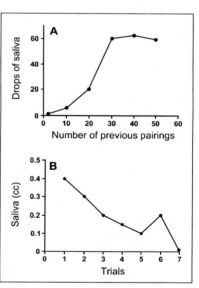

FIG. 3.3 The acquisition and extinction of salivation. The acquisition curve (A) is taken from an experiment by Anrep (1920), who paired a tone (CS) with food placed in a dog's mouth (US). The extinction curve (B) is from Pavlov (1960, p. 53), who presented the CS (sight of food) in the absence of the US (food in the mouth). Results are portrayed as a single experiment.

associated with 2 oz of food will elicit salivation as a CR at a higher level (at asymptote) than a tone associated with 1 oz of food. It is clear that these relationships are limited by an organism's physiology. If a dog is given 1 lb of steak it will probably salivate at maximum strength, and a change to 2 lb will have no further effect. Similar limits are observed for reflexes such as variation in pupil size in response to light, magnitude of the knee jerk in response to a tap, and the degree of startle in response to noise.

Conditioned and unconditioned responses

Notice that the conditioned response of salivation appears to be identical to the unconditioned response. That is, when conditioning to the tone has occurred, turning it on will elicit salivation. This response to the tone seems the same as the salivation produced by food in the dog's mouth. In fact, early theories of learning held that the tone substituted for the food stimulus. This implies that the CS–CR relationship is the same as the US–UR relation. If the CS–CR and the US–UR relationships are the same, then both should follow similar laws and principles. And the *laws of the reflex* govern the US–UR relationship, as you have seen.

If the CS–CR and US–UR relationships are the same, then the law of intensity–magnitude should hold for conditioned stimuli and responses. That is, a rise in the intensity of the CS should increase the magnitude of the CR. In addition, the CS–CR relation should follow the law of latency. An increase in the intensity of the CS should decrease the latency between the CS onset and the conditioned response. Research has shown that these, and other laws of the reflex, typically do *not* hold for the CS–CR relation (Millenson, 1967). Generally, a change in the intensity of the conditioned stimulus decreases the strength of the conditioned response. In Anrep's (1920) experiment, the tone occurred at a particular intensity, and after conditioning it elicited a given magnitude and latency of salivation. If Anrep had increased the sound, there would have been less salivation and it would have taken longer to occur. Thus, the CS–CR relation is specific to the original conditioning and does not follow the laws of the reflex. One reason is that the CS–CR relationship involves processes such as respondent discrimination (see below).

Respondent extinction

Pavlov (1960) reported a very simple experimental procedure that he called **respondent extinction**. The procedure involves repeatedly presenting the CS and not presenting the US. Figure 3.3B (extinction) shows the decline in salivation when Pavlov's assistant, Dr. Babkin, repeatedly presented the CS but no longer fed the dog. As you can see, the amount of salivation declines and reaches a minimal value by the seventh trial. This minimum level of the CR is often similar to the value obtained during the first trial of acquisition and probably reflects the **respondent level** of this behavior. Respondent level, or baseline, refers to the strength of the target response (e.g., salivation) before any known conditioning has occurred.

A distinction should be made between extinction as a procedure and extinction as a behavioral process. The procedure involves presenting the CS but not the US after conditioning has occurred. As a behavioral process, extinction refers to the decline in the strength of the conditioned response when an extinction procedure is in effect. In both instances, the term *extinction* is used correctly. Extinction is the procedure of breaking the CS–US association, resulting in the decline of the CR.

The decline in the strength of the CR is often rapid. This statement is true for the conditioning of salivation, but other types of conditioned responses may vary in resistance to extinction. Even with salivation, Pavlov noted that as the time between trials increased, the CR declined more slowly. A test trial is any instance in which the CS is given in the absence of the unconditioned stimulus. Of course, repeated test trials are the same as extinction. The slower extinction of salivation with longer intervals between test trials may reflect what is called spontaneous recovery.

Spontaneous recovery

Spontaneous recovery is the observation of an increase in the conditioned response after respondent extinction has occurred. Recall that after repeated presentations of the CS without the US, the conditioned response declines to respondent level. Following extinction of the response to respondent level, after some time passes, the CS will again elicit the CR and the more time that passes between the first and second extinction sessions the more the spontaneous recovery (Brooks & Bouton, 1993).

The typical effect is seen in Figure 3.4, which shows the course of extinction and spontaneous recovery from another experiment by Pavlov (1960). In this experiment, the CS was the sight of meat powder, and the US was food in the dog's mouth. As you would expect, the sight of meat powder eventually elicited a conditioned response of salivation. When extinction began, the dog responded with 1 cc of salivation at the sight of the CS. By the fifth extinction trial, the animal showed almost no salivation to the sight of food powder, but after 20 minutes of rest without stimulus presentations, the CS again elicited a conditioned response. Note, however, that the amount of salivation on the spontaneous-recovery trial is much less than the amount elicited on the first extinction trial.

Pavlov (1960) argued that spontaneous recovery shows little weakening of the CS–CR relationship during extinction. He went on to suggest that "internal inhibition" came to block the connection between stimuli and responses. Pavlov viewed conditioning phenomena as an index of brain processes, and in this regard saw behavior as a reflection of central nervous system functioning. In this sense, spontaneous recovery reflected underlying physiological processes, and one of these was an active but temporary "dampening" of associative connections between the CS and the conditioned response. Pavlov called this apparent physiological blocking of the CS–CR relationship "internal inhibition."

In contrast to Pavlov's hypothetical physiological account (he did not actually observe any neural activity), a behavioral analysis of spontaneous recovery suggests that the CS–CR relation is weakened by extinction, but the context or features of the situation in general maintain some level of control over the conditioned response. During respondent conditioning, many stimuli not specified by the researcher as the CS, but present in the experimental situation, come to regulate behavior. For example, background odors, general illumination of the room, the presence of particular researchers, the passage of time, and all the events that signal the start of a conditioning series come to exert some control over the conditioned response. Each time a recovery test is made, some part of the situation that has not yet been extinguished evokes the CR. This gradual decline in contextual stimulus control through repeated extinction also accounts for progressively less recovery of the conditioned response.

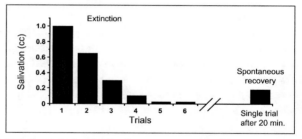

FIG. 3.4 Extinction and spontaneous recovery of salivation elicited by the sight of meat powder (Pavlov, 1960), with data replotted from Bower and Hilgard (1981, p. 51).

Respondent Generalization and Discrimination

Generalization

Pavlov conducted a large number of conditioning experiments and discovered many principles that remain useful today. One of his important findings concerned the principle of respondent generalization. **Respondent generalization** occurs when an organism shows a conditioned response to values

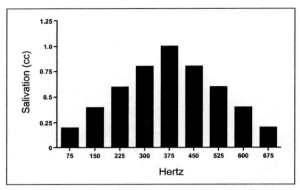

FIG. 3.5 A hypothetical generalization gradient for the salivary response. In this idealized experiment, training would occur at 375 Hz and then CSs ranging from 75 to 675 Hz would be presented.

of the CS that were not trained during acquisition. For example, respondent acquisition will occur when a specific stimulus, such as a 60-dB tone at a known frequency (e.g., 375 Hz), is associated with a US (e.g., food). After several pairings, the CS elicits a conditioned response, in this case salivation. If a 60-dB tone of 375 Hz is now presented without the US (a test trial), the animal will salivate at maximum level. To show generalization, the researcher varies some property of the conditioned stimulus. For example, a 60-dB tone of 75, 150, 225, 300, 375, 450, 525, 600, and 675 Hz is presented on test trials, and the magnitude of the conditioned response is measured. Figure 3.5 shows possible results of such an experiment. As you can see, the amount of salivation declines as the test stimulus departs in both directions from the value used in training. This graph, which plots stimulus value against magnitude of response, is called a **generalization gradient**.

Interestingly, a similar generalization gradient may not occur if the intensity rather than the tonal quality of the CS is varied. That is, if decibels rather than cycles per second (Hertz) are varied in the generalization test, a different result might occur. A few studies have shown that as the intensity of the CS increases, so does the magnitude of the conditioned response (Heinemann & Chase, 1970; Razran, 1949). Heinemann and Chase (1970) found that proportionally more conditioned responses were elicited as the sound intensity of the CS increased. Based on this finding, Heinemann and Chase suggest that there may be consistent increases in the strength of the CR as the intensity of the CS increases, although not all research has supported this finding (Ernst, Engberg, & Thomas, 1971). A conservative conclusion is that as the CS greatly departs from the value that was originally established, the conditioned response becomes weaker (see also Thomas & Setzer, 1972).

Generalization is an adaptive process that allows the organism to respond similarly even when conditions do not remain exactly the same from trial to trial. Consider a situation in which a predator's approach (US) is associated with the sound of snapping twigs, rustling grass, and waving shrubs (CS). An organism that runs away (CR) only in the presence of these exact stimulus conditions would probably not last long. This is because the events that occurred during conditioning are never precisely repeated—each approach of a predator produces variations in sounds, sights, and smells. Even in the laboratory where many features of the environment are controlled, there is some variation in stimuli from one trial to the next. When a bell is paired with food, the dog may change its orientation to the bell and thereby alter the sound; room humidity and other factors may also produce slight variations in tonal quality. Because of generalization, a CS–CR relationship can be strengthened even though the stimulus conditions are never exactly the same from trial to trial. Thus, generalization was likely an adaptive process, allowing organisms to respond to the vagaries of life.

Discrimination

Another conditioning principle that Pavlov discovered is called differentiation or discrimination. **Respondent discrimination** occurs when an organism shows a conditioned response to one stimulus but not to other similar events. This is a process at the other end of the continuum from generalization. A discrimination-training procedure involves presenting both positive and negative conditioning trials. For example, a positive trial occurs when a CS^+ such as a 60-dB tone is associated with an unconditioned stimulus like food. On negative trials, a 40-dB tone is presented (CS^-) but never paired with food. Because of stimulus generalization, the dog may salivate to both the 60-dB (CS⁺) and 40-dB (CS⁻) tones on the early trials. However, if the procedure is continued, the animal will no longer salivate to the CS⁻ (40-dB tone), but will show a response to the CS⁺ (60-dB tone). Once such a differential response occurs, we may say that the dog discriminates between the tones.

Respondent discrimination is another adaptive process. It would be a chaotic world if an animal spent its day running away from most sounds, sights, and smells, generalizing to everything. Such an animal would not survive and reproduce because there would be no time for other essential activities, like eating, drinking, and procreating. Discrimination allows an organism to budget its time and responses in accord with the requirements of the environment. In the predator example, noises that are reliably associated with an animal that considers you a main course should become CS⁺ for flight or fight. Similar noises made by the wind or harmless animals are CS⁻ for such behavior. Notice, however, that there is a fine line between discrimination and generalization in terms of survival.

TEMPORAL RELATIONS AND CONDITIONING

Delayed Conditioning

There are several ways of arranging the temporal relationship between the presentation of a CS and the unconditioned stimulus (US). So far we have described a procedure in which the CS is presented a few seconds before the US occurs. This procedure is called **delayed conditioning** (the presentation of the US is slightly delayed relative to the CS) and is shown in Figure 3.6A).

Delayed conditioning is considered the most effective way to condition simple autonomic reflexes like salivation. In the diagram, the CS is turned on, and 3 s later the US is presented. The interval between the onset of the CS and the onset of the US (called the CS–US interval) determines the effectiveness of conditioning. For autonomic responses like salivation, blood pressure, skin temperature, hormone levels, and sweat secretion, a CS–US interval of 5–30 s appears to be most effective. A brief CS–US interval of about 0.5 s seems to be optimal for the conditioning of quick skeletal responses such as a knee jerk, eye blinks, and retraction of a limb from a hot surface. In human eyeblink conditioning, a delay of 0.4 s between CS and US produces the fastest conditioning in young adults but a longer delay of about 1 s is more effective with older people (Solomon, Blanchard, Levine, Velazquez, & Groccia-Ellison, 1991).

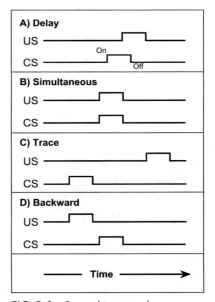

FIG. 3.6 Several temporal arrangements between CS and US commonly used for simple respondent conditioning. Time is shown in the bottom panel of the figure and moves from left to right. The other panels depict the temporal arrangement between US and CS for four basic respondent conditioning arrangements. For example, delayed conditioning is shown in panel A, where the CS is turned on and, a few seconds later, the US is presented.

Simultaneous Conditioning

Another temporal arrangement is called **simultaneous conditioning**, where the CS and US are presented at the same time. This procedure is shown in Figure 3.6B, where the CS and US are presented at the same moment. For example, at the same time that the bell rings (CS), food is placed in the dog's mouth (US). Compared with delayed conditioning, where the CS precedes the US briefly, simultaneous conditioning produces a weaker conditioned response (Smith & Gormezano, 1965; White & Schlosberg, 1952). One way to understand this weaker effect is to note that the CS does not signal the impending occurrence of the US in simultaneous conditioning. Based on this observation, many researchers have emphasized the predictiveness of the CS as a central feature of classical conditioning (see Rescorla, 1966). That is, the CS works because it provides information that "tells" the organism a US will follow. In simultaneous conditioning, however, there can be no predictive information given by the CS and yet some conditioning occurs. This suggests that predictiveness may facilitate conditioning, but is not necessary for it (Papini & Bitterman, 1990).

Trace Conditioning

The procedure for trace conditioning is shown in Figure 3.6C. The CS is presented for a brief period, on and off, and after some time the US occurs. For example, a light is flashed for 2 s and 20 s later food is placed in a dog's mouth. The term **trace conditioning** comes from the idea of a "memory trace" and refers to the fact that the organism must remember the presentation of the CS. Generally, as the time between the CS and US increases, the conditioned response becomes weaker (Ellison, 1964; Lucas, Deich, & Wasserman, 1981). For eyeblink conditioning (a puff of air in the eye US → an eye blink UR), the response to the CS does not occur when the CS and US are separated by as little as 2 s (Schneiderman, 1966). When compared to delay conditioning with the same interval, between the onset of the CS followed by the US, trace conditioning is not as effective—producing a weaker conditioned response. Recent research has extended trace conditioning to taste aversion learning (see Chapter 7) and to biochemical changes that help to bridge stimulus associations over the trace interval (Misanin, Goodhart, Anderson, & Hinderliter, 2002).

Backward Conditioning

As shown in Figure 3.6D, **backward conditioning** stipulates that the US comes on and goes off before the CS comes on. The general consensus has been that backward conditioning is unreliable, and many researchers question whether it occurs at all (but see Barnet & Miller, 1976, and Heth, 1976, for supportive views). It is true that backward conditioning usually does not produce a conditioned response. That is, if you place food in a dog's mouth and then ring a bell, the bell will not elicit the response of salivation when presented later. Most conditioning experiments have used arbitrary stimuli such as lights, tones, and shapes as the conditioned stimulus. However, Keith-Lucas and Guttman (1975) found backward conditioning when they used a biologically significant CS.

These researchers reasoned that following an unsuccessful attack by a predator, the sights, sounds, and smells of the attacker would be associated with pain from the attack. Consider a situation in which a grazing animal is unaware of the approach of a leopard. The attack (US) comes swiftly and without warning (no CS). The animal survives the onslaught and manages to run away. In this case, the pain inflicted by the attack is a US for flight that precedes the sight of the predator (CS). For such a situation, backward conditioning would have adaptive value since the animal would learn to avoid leopards.

Keith-Lucas and Guttman (1975) designed an experiment to test this adaptive-value hypothesis. Rats were placed in an experimental chamber and fed a sugar pellet in a particular location. While eating the pellet, the rats were given a one-trial presentation of electric shock (US). After the shock, the chamber was made completely dark for 1, 5, 10, or 40 s. When the light in the chamber came back on, a toy hedgehog (CS) was presented to the rat. To make this experiment clear, eating sugar pellets was viewed as the laboratory equivalent of grazing, the shock represented an attack, and the appearance of the toy hedgehog substituted for the predator. Two control groups were run under identical conditions, except that one group saw the hedgehog but did not get shocked and the other group got the shock but did not see a hedgehog.

On the next day, each animal was returned to the situation and a number of responses were measured. Compared with the control groups, backward conditioning was found after a delay of 1, 5, and 10 s but not after 40 s. Relative to control animals, experimental subjects showed greater avoidance (fear) of the hedgehog, spent less time in the presence of the hedgehog, and ate less food. Presumably, the shock (US) elicited a fear–flight reaction (UR), and backward conditioning transferred this reaction to the toy hedgehog (CS). The fear induced by the hedgehog (CR) interfered with eating and produced avoidance of the toy animal. This experiment shows that with a biologically relevant CS, backward conditioning is possible. Despite this outcome, most researchers suggest that the backward arrangement of US and then CS does not result in reliable conditioning (but see Cole & Miller, 1999; Siegel & Domjan, 1971; Tait & Saladin, 1986, for backward inhibitory conditioning; also Arcediano & Miller, 2002, for timing and backward conditioning).

SECOND-ORDER RESPONDENT CONDITIONING

So far we have considered only first-order conditioning. To briefly review, in **first-order conditioning**, an apparently neutral stimulus is paired with an unconditioned stimulus. After several such pairings, the control of the response to the US is transferred to the neutral stimulus, which is now called a conditioned stimulus (CS). Second-order conditioning extends this transfer of control to events that have not been directly associated with the unconditioned stimulus. These events gain control over the response because of their pairing with an established conditioned stimulus. Thus, **second-order conditioning** involves pairing a second CS_2 with an already functional CS_1, rather than pairing a CS and US (Rizley & Rescorla, 1972). Such higher order conditioning is important because it extends the range of behavioral effects produced by respondent conditioning, especially with regard to learning word meanings (Staats, 1975) and evaluative conditioning in humans (De Houwer, Thomas, & Baeyens, 2001, for a review).

Some phobic reactions (i.e., an intense and seemingly irrational fear) that people have may be caused by higher order conditioning. Consider a person who refuses to sit with friends in the backyard on a nice summer day. The sight of flowers greatly upsets her and she says that "with so many flowers there are probably bees." A possible interpretation is that the person has been stung (US) by a bee (CS_1), and she has noticed that bees hover around flowers (CS_2). The "phobic" fear of flowers occurs because of the pairing of bees (CS_1) with flowers (CS_2). Thus, phobic reactions and other emotional responses may sometimes involve higher order respondent conditioning (see Martin & Pear, 2006, on systematic desensitization and the fear hierachy).

ON THE APPLIED SIDE: Drug use abuse, and complexities of respondent conditioning

Basic research on simple and complex (i.e., including contextual effects) respondent conditioning has applied importance. Recently, the US government has declared a war on the import and use of illegal drugs. One result of this is that more money is being spent on research to identify the factors that affect drug use and abuse. Several experiments have shown that conditioned stimuli can produce drug-like effects in both humans and other animals, disrupting behavior and producing physiological changes. In addition, stimuli that have been paired with drugs sometimes produce internal conditioned responses that are *opposite* to the unconditioned effects of the drug. For example, when animals are injected with insulin (US), the unconditioned response is a reduction in blood sugar (UR). The response to a stimulus (CS) that has been paired with insulin is exactly the opposite; blood sugar levels increase (Siegel, 1972, 1975).

Similar counteractive effects have been found with drugs other than insulin. For example, amphetamine reduces appetite, but a CS that has been paired with it increases food intake (Poulos, Wilkinson, & Cappell, 1981). Pentobarbital is a sedative, but the response to a conditioned stimulus associated with pentobarbital counteracts the drowsiness ordinarily associated with the drug (Hinson, Poulos, & Cappell, 1982).

Effects such as these suggest that respondent conditioning plays a major role in drug tolerance. Here is how it works. With repeated pairings of a drug (US) and a CS (e.g., injection process), the conditioned response gains in strength and increasingly opposes the unconditioned effects of the drug. This means it will take larger and larger amounts for the user to experience the same degree of effect. In everyday life, conditioned stimuli arise from the time of day that a drug is taken, the way it is administered (e.g., using a needle), the location such as a tavern or home, and social events like a party or dance.

Notice that, in the case of tolerance, the reduction in the effects of the drugs (UR) is not due to habituation; rather, it is the result of the counteractive effects (CR) to the injection process and setting (CS). When more of a drug (US) is needed to obtain the same drug effects (UR), we talk about drug **tolerance** (Baker & Tiffany, 1985). Thus, the counteractive effects of CSs are major components of drug tolerance.

NOTE ON: Physiology and the control of preparatory responses by conditioned stimuli

The concept of homeostasis helps to clarify the control by the CS over conditioned responses opposite to those induced by the US. **Homeostasis** is the tendency for a system to remain stable and to resist change. In terms of a biological system, homeostasis refers to the regulation of the system by negative feedback loops. For example, the body maintains a temperature within a very fine tolerance. If the environment warms up or cools down, physiological mechanisms (sweating or shivering) involving the sympathetic and parasympathetic nervous systems are activated to reduce the drift from normal body temperature. In terms of drug exposure, when a drug (US) is administered it upsets the stability of the system, i.e., it may increase heart rate or reduce respiration (UR). If some aspect of the environment is consistently present when the drug is delivered (e.g., drug paraphenalia, a person, or the room), then that stimulus becomes a conditioned stimulus (CS) capable of eliciting a conditioned response that is often preparatory and compensatory (CR). If the US drug causes heart rate to increase, the conditioned compensatory (homeostatic) response (CR) will be a heart rate decrease; that is, the learned component ($CS_{needle} \rightarrow CR_{heart\ rate\ decrease}$) counteracts the unlearned response to the drug ($US_{drug} \rightarrow UR_{heart\ rate\ increase}$). This counteracting homeostatic effect may be so great that it nullifies the responses to the drug and the user no longer experiences the typical high, a process called *tolerance*. The onset of tolerance can be dangerous for the drug user. If a larger dose of the drug is taken to overcome tolerance and the compensatory counteracting response is not produced, an overdose can occur. Further, if the preparatory stimuli (CSs) elicit their responses and the drug (US) is not delivered, a condition that we call *craving* or *withdrawal* occurs.

Heroin Overdose and Context

To consider drug tolerance as a result of a conditioned response helps to explain instances of drug overdose. Heroin addicts are known to survive a drug dose that would kill a person who did not regularly use the drug. In spite of this high level of tolerance, approximately 1% of heroin addicts die from drug overdose each year. These victims typically die from drug-induced respiratory depression. Surprisingly, many of these addicts die from a dose that is similar to the amount of heroin they usually took each day. Siegel, Hinson, Krank, and McCully (1982) proposed that these deaths resulted from "a failure of tolerance. That is, the opiate addict, who can usually tolerate extraordinarily high doses, is not tolerant on the occasion of the overdose" (p. 436). They suggested that when a drug is administered in the usual context (CS⁺), the CRs that counteract the drug allow for a large dose. When the situation in which the drug is taken is changed, the CSs are not present, the opposing conditioned response does not occur, and the drug is sufficient to kill the user. Siegel and associates designed an animal experiment to test these ideas.

In one study rats were injected with heroin every other day for 30 days. The amount of heroin was gradually increased to a dose level that would produce tolerance to the drug. On nonheroin days, these rats were injected with dextrose solution (i.e., sugar and water). Both heroin and dextrose injections were given in one of two distinctive contexts—the ordinary colony room that the rats lived in, or a different room with constant white noise. A control group of rats was injected only with the dextrose solution in the two situations. The researchers predicted that experimental animals would develop a tolerance to the drug; this tolerance would occur if aspects of the room in which heroin injections were given became CSs that elicited opposing responses (CRs) to the drug.

To test this assumption, Siegel and colleagues (1982) on the test day doubled the amount of heroin given to experimental animals. The same high dose of heroin was given to the control group, who had no history of tolerance. Half of the experimental animals received this larger dose in the room where the drug was usually administered. The other addicted rats were injected with the higher dose in the room where they usually received a dextrose injection.

Figure 3.7 shows the results of this experiment. As you can see, the large dose of heroin killed almost all of the animals in the control group. For the two groups of animals with a history of heroin exposure, one group (same room) received the higher dose in the room where they usually were injected with heroin. Only 32% of the rats died in this condition, presumably because the CSs set off the opposing conditioned responses. This inference is supported by the mortality rate of rats in the different room group. These rats were injected with the double dose of heroin in a room that had never been associated with heroin administration. Twice as many animals in this condition died from the larger dose (64%) when compared to the same room group. It seems the effects of context during this kind of respondent conditioning can be a matter of life or death—tolerance to heroin (and perhaps other drugs) is relative to the situation in which the conditioning has occurred (Siegel, 2001).

What happens when the drug-related CS

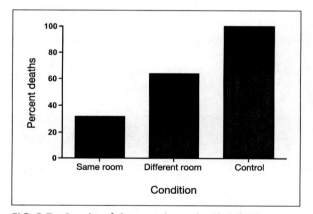

FIG. 3.7   Results of the experiment by Siegel, Hinson, Krank, and McCully (1982). The same room group of rats received the higher dose in the room where they usually were injected with heroin, and only 32% died. Twice as many animals in the different room condition died from the larger dose, presumably because they were injected in a room where heroin had not been given. Heroin killed almost all of the animals in the control group. Adapted from Siegel et al. (1982), *Science, 216*, 436–437.

is presented without the drug US, as in the classical extinction procedure? In this case the elicited respondents are often called "cravings" and the process is known as **conditioned withdrawal**. The CS elicits reactions that are ordinarily countered by the US. However, when the US is not delivered and if those CR reactions occur, the subject experiences what is called withdrawal. A heroin addict can have their withdrawal symptoms immediately terminated by a heroin injection. If you are accustomed to having a cigarette after a meal, the craving you experience can be alleviated with a smoke.

Conditioned Immunosuppression

Conditioned immunosuppression is another example of environmental influences altering what is generally considered to be internal and autonomously controlled processes. In this procedure, a CS (for example a novel flavor) is paired with a US drug that suppresses immune system function, such as the production of antibodies. (Note that drugs like cyclophosphamide are commonly administered to suppress rejection of a transplanted organ.) After several pairings the CS is presented alone and the immune system reaction is measured. Ader and Cohen (1981, 1985, 1993) were the first to systematically investigate and support this phenomenon. Clearly the next question is, can the immune system also be conditioned to increase immune reaction? It appears that it can. In a human study Buske-Kirschbaum, Kirschbaum, Stierle, Jabaij, and Helhammer (1994), after pairing a flavor CS and adrenaline injection US, subsequently raised NK (natural killer) cell production by presentation of the flavor alone.

The issue of conditioned enhancement of the immune system also speaks to the findings of **placebo effects**. How can a neutral substance, a placebo, have any effect on a person's physiological well-being? Many studies have shown that groups receiving a sugar pill do as well as those in the legitimate treatment group (Brody, 2000). How can this be possible when the placebo, by definition, cannot directly cause any change? The obvious conclusion is that there is respondent conditioning occurring. A CS, say the patient's "belief" (resulting from experience with doctors and medication) that they are receiving treatment, is presented and this verbal stimulus acts as a placebo to elicit the CR mechanisms of improvement. Even sham (fake) arthroscopic surgery for arthritis is as functional as actual surgery, and of course with fewer side effects and less cost (Moseley, O'Malley, Petersen, Menke, Brody, Kuykendall, et al., 2002). One thing that these types of studies indicate is that there is much greater two-way interaction between the environment and physiological mechanisms than has been suspected. Organisms are adaptive and they learn. It appears that organs (e.g., salivary glands) and organ systems (e.g., immune system) can also alter their functions as a result of experience. Obviously we need more research to expand and validate these topics.

ADVANCED SECTION: Complex conditioning

ASPECTS OF COMPLEX CONDITIONING

Conditioning and Compound Stimuli

We have so far examined CS and US relationships in isolation, ignoring for the most part the context or background in which these events occur. To investigate the effects of context on respondent behavior, researchers have arranged situations involving **compound stimuli**. In these cases, and to keep things somewhat simple, two conditioned stimuli (e.g., tone and light) are presented together before (delayed) or during (simultaneous) a US. This arrangement of two controllable stimuli (compound CSs) presented together can be shown to acquire the capacity to elicit a single conditioned response.

In an everyday example , the odor of food at a bakery or restaurant probably becomes a CS for salivation, having been paired with donuts or burgers and fries (US). But other related stimuli like the name, the order clerk, the location of the store, and the outdoor signs are also paired with eating. These additional features of the fast-food experience become conditioned stimuli that function as the context (compound CS) that evokes salivation. Differences in conditioning procedures related to compound stimuli result in the behavioral processes called sensory preconditioning, blocking, and overshadowing.

Overshadowing

Pavlov (1960) first described **overshadowing**. A compound stimulus consisting of two or more simple stimuli are presented at the same time. For example, a faint light and loud tone (compound CS) may be turned on at the same time and paired with an unconditioned stimulus such as food. Pavlov found that the most salient element of the compound stimulus came to regulate exclusively the conditioned response. In this case the loud tone and not the faint light will become a CS and elicit salivation. The tone is said to overshadow conditioning to the light. This happens even though the weak light could function as a CS if it were originally presented by itself and was paired with a US.

Blocking

Kamin (1969) reported an effect related to overshadowing that also involved compound stimuli. This effect is called **blocking** and describes a situation in which one CS paired with a US blocks a subsequent CS–US association. In blocking, a CS is paired with a US until the conditioned response reaches maximum strength. Following this conditioning, a second stimulus is presented at the same time as the original CS, and both are paired with the unconditioned stimulus. On test trials, the original CS evokes the CR but the second stimulus does not. For example, a tone (CS) may be associated with food (US) until the tone reliably evokes salivation. Next, the tone plus a light are presented together as a compound CS and both are associated with food (US). On test trials, the tone will elicit salivation but the light will not. The previously conditioned tone blocks conditioning of the light stimulus.

Kamin (1969) used a procedure called **conditioned suppression** (see Estes & Skinner, 1941). In conditioned suppression, a previously neutral stimulus (e.g., tone, light, etc.) is paired with an aversive US such as an electric shock. After several pairings, the originally neutral stimulus becomes a conditioned aversive stimulus (CS^{ave}). The CS^{ave} is said to elicit a conditioned emotional response (CER) that is commonly called anxiety or fear. Once the CS^{ave} has been conditioned, its effects may be observed by changes in an organism's operant behavior. For example, a rat may be trained to press a lever for food. After a stable rate of response is established, the CS^{ave} is introduced. When this occurs, the animal's lever pressing is disrupted, presumably because of the CER elicited by the CS^{ave}. Basically we could say that the CS^{ave} frightens the animal so it stops pressing the bar. Conditioned suppression is a widely used procedure in respondent conditioning, and as you will see later it is important in the study of human emotions.

Using a conditioned-suppression procedure, Kamin (1969) discovered the phenomenon of blocking. Two groups of rats were used: a blocking group and a control group. In the blocking group, rats were presented with a tone (CS^{ave}) that was associated with electric shocks for 16 trials. Following this, the rats received 8 trials during which the compound stimulus of tone and light was followed by shock. The control group did not receive the 16 light-shock conditioning trials but did have the 8 trials of tone and light paired with shock. Both groups were tested for conditioned suppression of lever pressing in the presence of the light. That is, the light was presented alone and suppression of bar pressing for food indicated the occurrence of the CER. Kamin found that the light suppressed bar pressing in the control group but did not affect lever pressing in the blocking group. In other words, prior conditioning with the tone blocked or prevented conditioning to the light. Functionally, the light was a CS^{ave} in the control group but not in the blocking group.

Blocking and overshadowing may also be interpreted as cases of redundant stimuli. If two or more stimuli have been paired with the same US then only one CS element of the compound is required for eliciting the CR. We intentionally generate compound stimuli (actually we can hardly avoid it) so that some aspect or other of the environment will gain eliciting properties. All stimulus manipulations are conducted in some place, be it the lab or elsewhere, and elements of that environment will be paired with the stimuli of interest. It is the repeated, consistent, and predictable nature of the specific CS–US pairing that tends to restrict the connection to only some stimuli.

Sensory Preconditioning

Sensory preconditioning is another example of stimulus control by compound events. In this case, two stimuli such as light and tone are repeatedly presented together without the occurrence of a known US—this is called preconditioning. Later, one of these stimuli is paired with an unconditioned stimulus for several trials and then the other stimulus is tested for conditioning. Even though the second stimulus was never directly associated with the US, it comes to elicit a conditioned response (Brogden, 1939; Pfautz, Donegan, & Wagner, 1978; Prewitt, 1967).

For example, a rat may be repeatedly exposed to 10 s of light with an accompanying 10-s tone. Following this preconditioning phase, the tone is paired with an electric shock. Subsequently, using a conditioned-suppression procedure, it is possible to show that the light will also suppress the animal's operant behavior. Notice that the light has never been paired with the shock but comes to have a CS^{ave} function based on previous association with the tone. Preconditioning is a way that stimuli may acquire corresponding or equivalent functions. It might be said that the light "stands for" the tone and the tone for the light.

THE RESCORLA–WAGNER MODEL OF CONDITIONING

The occurrence of overshadowing, blocking, and sensory preconditioning has led many researchers to the conclusion that cognitive processes underlie conditioning. This is because these effects (and others) seem to imply that an animal learns to expect certain events on the basis of predictive cues. That is, the sight of a predator becomes a predictive cue because the animal expects an attack. The CS is said to provide information about the occurrence of the US, and redundant information, as in blocking, is not processed by the organism.

Although this may be an intuitively satisfying account, inferring cognitive processes is not necessary to describe most of the research in respondent conditioning. Bolles (1979) has commented as follows:

> Are we now in a position to conclude that conditioning is really a cognitive process, that it involves the expectancy of a . . . [US], and that the expectancies reflect predictive relationships the animal perceives between cues and consequences? Some psychologists have come to this conclusion. But others have shown restraint. Indeed, it turns out to be possible to account . . . [for many conditioning effects], all without recourse to any cognitive concepts. It can all be done with the clever application of [temporal pairing of stimuli] and other S-R principles. This remarkable development is the work of Wagner, and

surprisingly, Rescorla himself. They have produced what is widely known as the Rescorla-Wagner model.

(p. 158)

As Bolles (1979) notes, the **Rescorla–Wagner model** (Rescorla & Wagner, 1972; Wagner & Rescorla, 1972) is an S–R pairing theory of respondent conditioning. That is, the Rescorla–Wagner model is a behavioral theory that does not make inferences about underlying cognitive/informational processing.

The basic idea of the Rescorla–Wagner model is that a conditioned stimulus acquires a limited amount of **associative strength** on any trial. We use the term associative strength to *describe* the relation between the CS and the magnitude of the conditioned response (CR). In general, associative strength increases over conditioning trials and reaches some maximum level. It is apparent that a given CS can acquire only so much control over a conditioned response. This is the **maximum associative strength** for the CS. Thus, a tone (CS) that is paired with 1 g of food will have maximum associative strength when salivation (CR) to the tone is about the same as salivation (UR) to the 1 g of food (US). That is, an unconditioned stimulus elicits a given magnitude of the unconditioned response. This magnitude sets the upper limit for the conditioned response. The CS cannot elicit a greater response than the one produced by the unconditioned stimulus.

A conditioned stimulus gains a certain amount of associative strength on any one trial. The amount of gain or increment depends on several factors. One obvious factor is the maximum associative strength that may accrue to the conditioned stimulus. As noted, this maximum is set by the magnitude of the US–UR relationship. An intense US will set a higher maximum value than a weaker one.

Another factor that affects the increment in associative strength on any trial is the **change in associative strength** or the difference between the present strength of the CS and its maximum possible value. As conditioning trials proceed, the CS gains associative strength, and this means that the difference between present and maximum strength decreases; there is less and less to gain on each trial. For example, assume a 10-trial experiment in which 1 g of meat evokes 2 cc of saliva and the meat is paired with a tone. In terms of change in associative strength, the most gain will occur on the 1st trial, there will be less gain by the 5th, and there will be almost no gain in associative strength by the 10th trial.

The change in associative strength of a conditioned stimulus (CS_1) is also affected by the strength of other conditioned stimuli (CS_2, CS_3, etc.) that elicit the conditioned response in that situation. Because there is a maximum associative strength set by the US, it follows that the associative strength of each CS will add together and reduce the difference between the present associative strength and the maximum possible value. Thus, if a tone has been frequently paired with meat, it will evoke almost maximum salivation. If a light is now introduced and presented along with the tone, it will show little control over salivation since most of the possible associative strength has accrued to the tone (blocking).

The Rescorla–Wagner model of respondent conditioning describes a large number of findings and has stimulated a good deal of research. The model makes counterintuitive predictions that have been confirmed in a variety of experimental settings. Since the early 1970s, scores of experiments have been conducted to test some of the implications of the model.

FOCUS ON: The Rescorla–Wagner equation

The three limiting conditions of maximum associative strength, difference between the current strength and maximum, and the number of additional CSs in the situation are represented by an equation suggested by Rescorla and Wagner (1972; see also Wagner & Rescorla, 1972) but simplified here for presentation:

$$\Delta V = S(V_{MAX} - V - V_{SUM})$$

(3.1)

The symbol ΔV stands for the amount of *change in associative strength* (or change in value of the stimulus, V) of any CS that occurs on any one trial. The symbol S is a constant that varies between 0 and 1, and may be interpreted as the **salience** (e.g., dim light versus bright light) of the CS based on the sensory capacities of the organism. The constant S (salience) is estimated after conditioning and determines how quickly the associative strength of the CS rises to a maximum. That is, a larger salience coefficient makes the associative strength of the CS rise more quickly to its maximum. The value V_{MAX} represents the maximum associative strength as measured by the magnitude of the unconditioned response (UR). The symbol V represents the associative strength already accrued to the CS_1 and V_{SUM} is any associative strength gained by any other stimuli in the situation ($V_{SUM} = CS_2 + CS_3 + \ldots CS_N$).

Acquisition

Trial	ΔV	V
1	2.5	2.5
2	1.9	4.4
3	1.4	5.8
4	1.1	6.9
5	0.8	7.7
6	0.6	8.3
7	0.4	8.7
8	0.3	9.0
9	0.25	9.3
10	0.18	9.4

V = associate strength or value
$S = 0.25$
$V_{MAX} = 10$
$V_{SUM} = 0$

FIG. 3.8   A table of values for a 10-trial acquistion experiment based on solving the Rescorla–Wagner equation (our Equation 3.1). The symbols V and ΔV refer to associative strength and change in associative strength for a given trial. The values of V_{MAX}, V_{SUM} and S are also given in the table. See text for details.

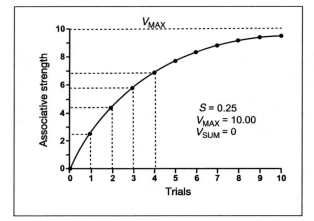

FIG. 3.9   The acquisition curve predicted by the Rescorla–Wagner equation (our Equation 3.1). Gain in associative strength, from trial to trial, declines as the CR comes closer to the asymptote. The asymptote or upper-flat portion of the curve is set in the equation by the value V_{MAX}. The curve is based on the data in Figure 3.8.

Figure 3.8 is a table of values for an idealized experiment on the acquisition of a conditioned response based on Equation (3.1). Figure 3.9 is the graph of the associative strength V based on the data in the table. In this hypothetical experiment, a tone CS is repeatedly paired with an unconditioned stimulus such as food. In the figure, S is set at 0.25 and the asymptote (or maximum possible strength) is 10 arbitrary units of the conditioned response (e.g., salivation). The value of V_{SUM} is assumed to be zero, so that all associative strength accrues to the CS. The value of ΔV is given by the equation when we substitute $S = 0.25$, $V_{MAX} = 10$, and the value of V is zero ($V = 0$) before conditioning begins. Based on Equation (3.1), the increase in associative strength from no conditioning to the first trial is

$$\Delta V = 0.25\,(10 - 0) = 2.50$$

Notice that the value of V has changed from 0 to 2.50 (check this with the tabled values of Figure 3.8).

On each subsequent trial, the associative strength of the CS is 0.25 (salience) of the remaining distance to the asymptote or maximum. Thus for trial 2 we substitute the value 2.50 for V and obtain an increase of 1.88 for ΔV:

$$\Delta V = 0.25\,(10 - 2.50) = 1.88$$

The associative strength of the CS (V), after the second trial is 2.50 + 1.88, or 4.38. This means that roughly half of the maximum associative strength ($V_{MAX} = 10$) of the CS has been acquired by trial 2.

The change in associative strength for trial 3 uses $V = 4.38$ from the second trial and obtains the value:

$$\Delta V = 0.25\,(10 - 4.38) = 1.40$$

And the new estimate of V is $4.38 + 1.40$, or 5.78 (used to obtain ΔV on the 4th trial). Estimates of ΔV and V for all 10 trials of the experiment are obtained in the same way, using Equation (3.1).

As you can see in Figure 3.9, the equation yields a negatively accelerating curve for the associative strength V, which approaches but never quite reaches maximum associative strength. You can see from the horizontal and perpendicular lines that the largest increase in associative strength is on the first trial, and this change corresponds to the difference in associative strength between trial 0 and trial 1 (2.5-unit increase). The change in associative strength (ΔV) becomes smaller and smaller over trials (check this out in the table of Figure 3.8). Notice how the values of ΔV and V depend on the salience, S, of the CS (tone). If the salience of the tone were different, say $S = 0.50$ rather than $S = 0.25$, a new set of estimates would be given by Equation (3.1) for ΔV and V.

Blocking Reconsidered

As Bolles (1979) noted, the Rescorla–Wagner equation accounts for many respondent conditioning effects without making assumptions about cognitive processes. One important effect that we have already discussed is blocking. Equation (3.1) provides a behavioral account of this phenomenon. Consider what will happen when V is almost equivalent to the value V_{MAX}, and a second conditioned stimulus (CS_2) is introduced. For example, a tone (CS_1) is paired with shock until the tone evokes close to maximum response suppression. At this point, a light (CS_2) is presented at the same time as the tone and conditioning continues. In Equation (3.1), the light is represented as V_{SUM} and the tone as V. After the tone acquires close to maximum strength, little is left over for the light (V_{SUM}) and the light has almost no suppressive effect on bar pressing. That is, the previous conditioning to the tone blocks conditioning to the light. Notice that it makes a big difference when the CS_2 is introduced. If CS_1 and CS_2 are paired from the start, then (all things being equal) both stimuli will gain half of the increase in associative strength (ΔV).

Extinction

Equation (3.1) can also be used to account for respondent extinction. In this case, the decline in associative strength (ΔV) is determined by the values of S, V_{MAX}, V, and V_{SUM}. As before, assume that a tone is paired with food until the tone (CS) elicits a conditioned response that is close to maximum; there are no other relevant stimuli, so $V_{SUM} = 0$ and cancels out of the equation. Since the procedure is respondent extinction, the curve must decline toward no associative strength, which means that V_{MAX} must be zero. If $S = 0.25$ and $V_{MAX} = 0$ then the decline in associative strength on the first extinction trial is:

$$\Delta V = 0.25\,(0 - 10) = -2.50$$

Thus, the value of the tone (CS) after the first extinction trial is $10.00 - 2.50$, or 7.50 ($V = 7.50$). Other values of the CS during extinction are determined in a similar fashion (compare with respondent acquisition). Figure 3.10 shows that the predicted extinction curve is the *exact opposite of the acquisition curve* of Figure 3.9. It is important to note that the actual associative strength of the tone before extinction is never exactly equal to the V_{MAX}, but for simplicity we have assumed that it is in Figure 3.10.

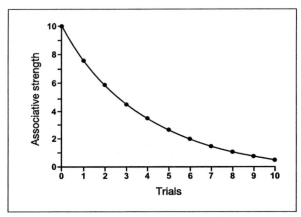

FIG. 3.10 The extinction curve predicted by the Rescorla–Wagner model. Notice that V_{MAX}, or the asymptote, is zero because extinction is in effect.

As you can see, the Rescorla–Wagner equation describes many of the basic aspects of respondent conditioning (acquistion, extinction, and blocking) as well as others not discussed here (e.g., latent inhibition). The equation is usually said to describe processes of associative learning but, as Pear (2001, p. 427) notes, it is also possible to derive equations for operant choice (Chapter 9) from the Rescorla–Wagner model, and vice versa. Thus, both respondent and operant behavior could be related at the most fundamental levels. Advances in neurophysiology may help to show how this is possible in terms of the reward circuitry of the brain (e.g., Zink, Pagnoni, Martin-Skursky, Chappelow & Berns, 2004).

CHAPTER SUMMARY

This chapter has introduced reflexive behavior, which is based on species history or phylogeny. It has explored reflexive sequences or fixed action patterns set off by a releasing stimulus and reaction chains where each response requires an appropriate stimulus to keep the sequence going. Reflexive behavior obeys the three laws of the reflex (threshold, magnitude, and latency) and secondary principles such as reflex habituation. Next, the discussion turned to the ontogeny of behavior and respondent conditioning, which involved pairing a CS (tone) with a US (food in mouth). Respondent behavior is elicited by the US and this function is established for the CS through conditioning. Two major processes of respondent acquisition and extinction were described and research examples were provided. It was also pointed out that respondent behavior shows spontaneous recovery even after an extinction procedure has occurred.

Organisms show generalization of respondent behavior over a stimulus gradient but also show discrimination (a differential response) when the US is presented with one stimulus and withheld to other values of the stimulus array. In addition to simple conditioning effects, temporal relationships between the CS and US are important, as in delayed, simultaneous, trace, and backward conditioning—and second-order conditioning. The implications of respondent conditioning were extended to an analysis of drug use and abuse, with some attention to context and drug tolerance. Finally, more advanced issues of complex conditioning and compound stimulus effects such as overshadowing, blocking, and sensory preconditioning were introduced. The Rescorla–Wagner model of conditioning was described and how the model could be expressed as an equation. This equation predicts the increase in the respondent over time (acquisition) and the decrease during extinction. The equation can also describe the process known as blocking.

Key Words

Associative strength
Backward conditioning
Blocking
Change in associative strength
Compound stimuli
Conditioned response
Conditioned stimulus
Conditioned suppression
Conditioned withdrawal
Delayed conditioning
Elicited
Fixed action pattern
Generalization gradient
Habituation
Homeostasis

Law of intensity–magnitude
Law of latency
Law of the threshold
Maximum associative strength
Ontogenetic
Overshadowing
Phylogenetic
Placebo effect
Primary laws of the reflex
Reaction chain
Reflex
Rescorla–Wagner model
Respondent
Respondent acquisition
Respondent conditioning

Respondent discrimination
Respondent extinction
Respondent generalization
Respondent level
Salience
Second-order conditioning
Sensory preconditioning
Simultaneous conditioning
Spontaneous recovery
Tolerance
Trace conditioning
Unconditioned response
Unconditioned stimulus

Reinforcement and Extinction of Operant Behavior

4

- Find out about operant behavior and the basic contingencies of reinforcement.
- Discover whether reinforcement undermines intrinsic motivation.
- Inquire about the Premack principle and response deprivation hypothesis.
- Learn how to carry out experiments on operant conditioning.
- Find out about operant conditioning of neural responses.
- Delve into reinforcement of variability, problem solving, and creativity.
- Investigate operant extinction and resistance to extinction.
- Learn about extinction and the partial reinforcement effect.

A hungry lion returns to the waterhole where it has successfully ambushed antelope and other prey. A person who plays a slot machine and wins a large jackpot is more likely to play again than a person who does not win. Students who ask questions and are told, "That is an interesting point worth discussing" are prone to ask more questions. When a professor ignores questions or gives fuzzy answers, students eventually stop asking questions. In these cases (and many others), the consequences that follow behavior determine whether it will be repeated in the future.

Recall that operant behavior is said to be emitted (Chapter 2). When operant behavior is followed by reinforcing consequences it is selected, in the sense that it increases in frequency. Behavior that is not followed by reinforcing consequences decreases in frequency. This process, called **operant conditioning**, is a major way that the behavior of organisms is changed on the basis of *ontogeny* or life experience (i.e., learning). It is important, however, to recognize that operant conditioning, as a process, has evolved over species history and is based on genetic endowment. That is, operant (and respondent) conditioning as a *general behavior-change process* is based on phylogeny or species history. In other words, those organisms whose behavior changed on the basis of consequences were more likely to survive and reproduce than animals that did not.

OPERANT BEHAVIOR

Operant behavior is commonly described as intentional, free, voluntary, or willful. Examples of operant behavior include conversations with others, driving a car, taking notes, reading a book, and painting a picture. From a scientific perspective, operant behavior is lawful and may be analyzed in terms of its relationship to environmental events. Formally, responses that produce a change in the environment and an increase in frequency due to that change are called operants. The term **operant** comes from the verb *to operate* and refers to behavior that operates on the environment to produce consequences that in turn strengthen the behavior. The consequences of operant behavior are many and varied and occur across all sensory dimensions. When you turn on a light, dial a telephone, drive a car, or open a door, these operants result in visual clarity, conversation, reaching a destination, and entering a room. A **positive reinforcer** is defined as any consequence that increases the probability of the operant that produced it. For example, pretend that your car will not start, but when you jiggle the ignition key it fires right up. Based on past reinforcement, the operant—jiggling the key—is likely to be repeated the next time the car will not start.

Operants are defined by the consequences they produce. Opening the door to reach the other side is the operant, not the physical movement of manipulating the door. Operants are a class of responses that may vary in **topography**. Topography refers to the physical form or characteristics of the response. Consider the number of different ways you could open a door—you may turn the handle, push it with your foot, or (if your arms are full of books) ask someone to open it for you. All of these responses vary in form or topography and result in reaching the other side of the door. Because these responses result in the same consequence, they are members of the same **operant class**. Thus, the term *operant* refers to a class of related responses that may vary in topography but produce a common environmental consequence (Catania, 1973).

Discriminative Stimuli

Operant behavior is **emitted** in the sense that it often occurs without an observable stimulus preceding it. This is in contrast to reflexive responses, which are **elicited** by a preceding stimulus. Reflexes are tied to the physiology of an organism and, under appropriate conditions, always occur when the eliciting stimulus is presented. For example, Pavlov showed that dogs automatically salivated when food was placed in their mouths. Dogs do not learn the relationship between food and salivation; this reflex is a characteristic of the species. Stimuli may also precede operant behavior. However, these events do not force the occurrence of the response that follows them. A stimulus that precedes an operant, and *sets the occasion for behavior*, is called a **discriminative stimulus**, or S^D (pronounced esse-dee).

Discriminative stimuli change the probability that an operant will be emitted based on a history of differential reinforcement. **Differential reinforcement** involves reinforcing an operant in one situation (S^D) but not in another (S^Δ). The probability of emitting an operant in the presence of an S^D may be very high, but these stimuli do not have a one-to-one relationship with the response that follows them. For example, a telephone ring increases the chances that you will emit the operant, answering the telephone, but it does not force you to do so. Similarly, a nudge under the table may set the occasion for changing the conversation or just shutting up. The events that occasion operant behavior may be private as well as public. Thus, a private event like a headache may set the occasion for taking an aspirin.

Discriminative stimuli are defined by setting the occasion for specific behavior. The probability of raising your hand in class is much greater when the instructor is present than when he or she is absent. Thus, the presence of an instructor is an S^D for asking questions in class. The teacher functions as an S^D only when his or her presence changes the student's behavior. The student who is having difficulty with a math problem may ask questions when the teacher enters the room. However, a student who is easily mastering the material is unlikely to do this. Based on the contingencies, the teacher functions as an S^D (for asking questions) for the first student but not the second. This discussion should make it clear that a stimulus is defined as an S^D only when it changes the probability of operant behavior. You may typically stop when you pull up to a traffic sign that reads STOP; the sign is a discriminative stimulus. If, however, you are driving a badly injured friend to the hospital, the same sign may not function as an S^D. Thus, discriminative stimuli are not defined by physical measures (e.g., color, size, tone); rather, they are defined as stimuli that precede and alter the probability of operant responses.

The consequences that follow operant behavior establish the control exerted by discriminative stimuli. When an S^D is followed by an operant that produces positive reinforcement, the operant is more likely to occur the next time the stimulus is present. For example, a student may ask a particular teaching assistant questions because in the past that teaching assistant has provided clear and concise answers. In this example, the assistant is an S^D and asking questions is the operant that increases in his or her presence. When an operant does not produce reinforcement, the stimulus that precedes the response is called an **S-delta** (S^Δ or esse-delta). In the presence of an S^Δ, the probability of emitting an operant declines. For example, if a second teaching assistant answers questions in a confused and muddled fashion, the student will be less likely to ask that person questions. In this case the second teaching assistant becomes an S^Δ and the probability of asking questions declines in his or her presence.

Contingencies of Reinforcement

A **contingency of reinforcement** defines the relationship between the events that set the occasion for behavior, the operant class, and the consequences that follow this behavior. In a dark room (S^D), when you flip on a light switch (R), the light usually comes on (S^r). This behavior does not guarantee that the room will light up, the bulb may be burned out, or the switch broken. It is likely that the light will come on, but it is not certain. In behavioral terms, the probability of reinforcement is high, but it is not absolute. This probability may vary between 0 and 100%. A high probability of reinforcement for turning the switch to the "on" position will establish and maintain a high likelihood of this behavior.

Discriminative stimuli that precede behavior have an important role in the regulation of operant responses (Skinner, 1969). Signs that read OPEN, RESUME SPEED, or RESTAURANT, green traffic lights, and a smile from across the room are examples of simple discriminative stimuli that may set the occasion for specific operants. These events regulate behavior because of a history of reinforcement in their presence. A smile from across a room may set the occasion for approaching and talking to the person who smiled. This is because, in the past, people who smiled reinforced social interaction.

Each of these events—the occasion, the operant, and the consequences of behavior—make up the contingency of reinforcement. Consider the example of this three-part contingency shown in Figure 4.1. The telephone ring is a discriminative stimulus that sets the occasion for the operant class of answering the phone. This behavior occurs because, in the past, talking to the other party reinforced the operant. The probability of response is very high in the presence of the ring, but it is not inevitable. Perhaps you are in the process of leaving for an important meeting, or you are in the bathtub.

Discriminative stimuli regulate behavior, but they do not stand alone. The consequences that follow behavior determine the probability of response in the presence of the discriminative stimulus. For example, most people show a high probability of answering the telephone when it rings. However, if the phone is faulty so that it rings but you cannot hear the other party when you answer it, the probability of answering the phone decreases as a function of no reinforcement. In other words, you stop answering a phone that does not work.

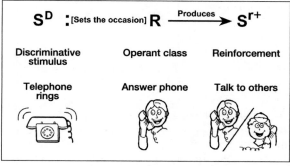

FIG. 4.1   The three-term contingency of reinforcement is illustrated. A discriminative stimulus (S^D) sets the occasion for operant behavior (R) that is followed by a reinforcing consequence (S^r).

Four Basic Contingencies

There are four basic contingencies of reinforcement. Events that follow behavior may be either presented or removed (environmental operation). These events can increase or decrease behavior (effect on behavior). The cells of the matrix in Figure 4.2 define the basic contingencies of reinforcement.

Positive reinforcement

Positive reinforcement is one of the four basic contingencies of operant behavior. **Positive reinforcement** is portrayed in Figure 4.2 (cell 1), where a stimulus follows behavior and, as a result, the rate of that behavior increases. For example, a child is praised for sharing a toy (operant behavior), and the child begins to share toys more regularly (increase in response strength). Positive reinforcers usually include consequences such as food, praise, and money. *These events, however, cannot be called positive reinforcers until they have been shown to increase behavior.*

Negative reinforcement

When an operant results in the removal of an event, and this procedure increases the rate of response, the contingency is called **negative reinforcement**. This contingency is shown in cell 3 of the matrix in Figure 4.2. Negative reinforcement is commonly misunderstood as punishment. However, the matrix makes it clear that negative reinforcement involves completely different procedures and effects than positive or negative punishment.

Negative reinforcement plays a major role in the regulation of everyday human behavior. For example, you put on sunglasses because in the past this behavior *removed* the glare of the sun. You open your umbrella when it is raining because doing so has prevented you from getting wet. You leave the room when someone is rude or critical because this behavior has ended other similar conversations. Consider that you live in a place with a very sensitive smoke detector. Each time you are cooking, the smoke detector goes off. You might remove the sound by tripping the breaker or fuse that controls the alarm. In fact, you will probably learn to do this each time before cooking. As a final example, a mother may pick up and rock her crying baby because, in the past, comforting the child has stopped the crying. In each of these instances, removing an aversive event strengthens an operant.

Stimulus following behavior	Effect on behavior	
	Increase	Decrease
On/presented	1 Positive reinforcement	2 Positive punishment
Off/removed	3 Negative reinforcement	4 Negative punishment

FIG. 4.2 This figure shows the four basic contingencies of reinforcement. The stimulus following a response (consequence) can be either presented (turned on) or removed (turned off). The effect of these procedures is to increase or decrease the rate of response. The cells of the matrix in this figure define the contingencies of reinforcement. A particular contingency of reinforcement depends on whether the stimulus following behavior is presented or removed and whether behavior increases or decreases in frequency.

Positive punishment

Cell 2 of the matrix in Figure 4.2 depicts a situation in which an operant produces an event and the rate of operant behavior decreases. This contingency is called **positive punishment**. For example, spanking a child for running onto a busy road is positive punishment if the child now stops (or turns) before reaching the road. In everyday life, people often talk about punishment (and reinforcement) without reference to behavior. For example, a mother scolds her child for playing with matches. The child continues to play with matches, and the parents may comment, "punishment doesn't work with Nathan." In behavior analysis, positive punishment is defined functionally (i.e., by its effects). When behavior is not changed by apparently aversive events, punishment has not occurred. In other words, the parents are arranging an ineffective contingency. The parents could identify an aversive event that reliably decreases behavior; however, this strategy may backfire. For example, as you will see in Chapter 9, punishment may produce serious emotional and aggressive behavior. Because of this, punishment should be used only as a last resort for the modification of severe behavior problems.

Negative punishment

Punishment can also be arranged by removing stimuli contingent on behavior (cell 4 in Figure 4.2). This contingency is called **negative punishment**. In this case, the removal of an event or stimulus decreases operant behavior. Two children are watching a favorite television program and begin to fight with one another. The parent says, "that's enough fighting" and turns off the television. You tell a sexist joke and people stop talking to you. At school, a student who is passing notes is required to leave the room for a short period of time. In these examples, watching television, talking to others, and participating in classroom activities are assumed to be reinforcing events. When removal of these events contingent on fighting, telling sexist jokes, and passing notes decreases such behavior, negative punishment has occurred.

FOCUS ON: Rewards and intrinsic motivation

Over the past 30 years, many social psychologists and educators have been critical of the practice of using rewards in business, education, and behavior modification programs. The concern is that rewards (reward and reinforcement are often used similarly in this literature) are experienced as controlling, thereby leading to a reduction in an individual's self-determination, intrinsic motivation, and creative performance (e.g., see Deci, Koestner, & Ryan, 1999). Thus, when a child who enjoys drawing is rewarded for drawing, with praise or with tangible rewards like points or money, the child's motivation to draw is said to decrease. From this perspective, the child will come to draw less and enjoy it less once the reward is discontinued. In other words, the contention is that reinforcement reduces people's intrinsic motivation. This view has been enormously influential and has led to a decline in the use of rewards and incentive systems in many applied settings.

In an article published in 1996 in *American Psychologist*, Robert Eisenberger and Judy Cameron (Figure 4.3) provided an objective and comprehensive analysis of the literature concerned with the effects of reinforcement/reward on people's intrinsic motivation. Contrary to the belief of many psychologists, their findings indicated no inherent negative property of reward. Instead, their research demonstrates that reward has a much more favorable effect on interest in activities than is generally supposed.

Analysis of Rewards and Intrinsic Motivation

Those who oppose the use of rewards support their position by citing experimental studies on reward and intrinsic motivation and claiming that rewards have pervasive negative effects (Deci et al., 1999). A cursory examination of these experiments reveals a mixed set of findings. That is, in some studies rewards reduce performance or interest; other studies find positive effects of reward; still others show no effect.

To make sense of these diverse findings, Judy Cameron, Robert Eisenberger, and the author of this textbook, David Pierce (Cameron & Pierce, 1994, 2002; Cameron, Banko, & Pierce, 2001;

FIG. 4.3   (A) Dr. Judy Cameron. (B) Dr. Robert Eisenberger. Published with permission.

Eisenberger & Cameron, 1996; Pierce & Cameron, 2002), conducted quantitative analyses of this literature to determine whether rewards really do negatively affect people's performance and interest. Using a statistical procedure known as meta-analysis, Cameron et al. (2001) analyzed the results from 145 experiments on rewards and intrinsic motivation.

The findings indicated that rewards could be used effectively to enhance or maintain an individual's intrinsic interest in activities. Specifically, verbal rewards (praise, positive feedback) were found to increase people's performance and interest on tasks. In terms of tangible rewards, the results showed that these consequences increased performance and interest for activities that were initially boring or uninteresting. For activities that people find initially interesting, the results from the meta-analysis point to the importance of *reward contingency* as a major determinant of intrinsic motivation. Cameron et al. (2001) found that tangible rewards produced a slight decrease in intrinsic motivation when these rewards were offered simply for doing an activity, regardless of level or quality of performance. When tangible rewards were offered for meeting a level of performance or exceeding the performance of others, people's intrinsic interest was maintained or enhanced (see McGinnis, Firman, & Carlyon, 1999, for an operant design of token reinforcement and intrinsic interest in mathematics). Overall, rewards tied to level or quality of performance increase the intrinsic motivation or leave intrinsic interest the same as it was before rewards were introduced.

Identifying a Reinforcing Stimulus

As you have seen, there are four basic contingencies of reinforcement. In each case, a stimulus consequence is presented or removed contingent on operant behavior. But how do we know if a given event or stimulus will function as reinforcement?

To identify a *positive reinforcer*, you devise a test. The test is to find out whether a particular consequence *increases* behavior. If it does, the consequence is defined as a positive reinforcer. Such tests are common in science. For example, a litmus test in chemistry tells us whether the solution is acid or base. One hundred dollars is defined as a positive reinforcer because it increases the frequency of betting 25 cents and pulling the handle on the slot machine. Notice that the test for a reinforcer is not the same as explaining the behavior. We explain behavior by pointing to the contingencies of reinforcement ($S^D: R \rightarrow S^r$) and basic principles, not by merely identifying a reinforcing stimulus. For example, we can explain a person's betting in a casino by pointing to the schedule of monetary reinforcement (involving large intermittent payoffs) that has strengthened and maintained this behavior.

The Premack principle

Another way to identify a positive reinforcer is based on the **Premack principle**. This principle states that *a higher frequency behavior will function as reinforcement for a lower frequency behavior*. For example, for a person who spends little time practicing piano but lots of time playing basketball, the Premack principle means that playing basketball (high frequency behavior) will reinforce practicing the piano. Generally, David Premack (1959) proposed that reinforcement involved a contingency between two sets of behaviors, operant behavior and reinforcing behavior (behavior^{operant} → behavior^{Sr}), rather than between an operant (behavior) and a stimulus (R → S^r). That is, Premack suggests that it is possible to describe reinforcing events as actions of the organism rather than as discrete stimuli. Thus, reinforcement involves eating rather than the presentation of food; drinking rather than provision of water; and reading rather than the effects of textual stimuli.

In his 1962 experiment, Premack deprived rats of water for 23 h and then measured their behavior in a setting in which they could run on an activity wheel or drink water. Of course, the animals spent more time drinking than running. Next, Premack arranged a contingency between running and drinking. The rats received a few seconds of access to drinking tubes when they ran on the wheels. Running on the wheel increased when it produced the opportunity to drink water—showing that drinking reinforced running. In other words, the rats ran on the wheel to get a drink of water. At this point in the experiment, Premack (1962) gave the rats free access to water. Now, when the rats were allowed to choose between drinking and running, they did little drinking and a lot more running. Premack reasoned that running would reinforce drinking because running occurred at a higher frequency than drinking. The running wheel was locked and the brake was removed if the rats licked the water tube for a few seconds. Based on this contingency, Premack showed that drinking water increased when it produced running. That is, the animals drank water for opportunities to run on the wheels. Overall, this experiment shows that drinking reinforces running when rats are motivated to drink. On the other hand, running reinforces drinking when running is the preferred activity. Thus, when behavior is measured in a situation that allows a choice among different activities, those responses that occur at a higher frequency may be used to reinforce those that occur at a lower frequency.

Premack's principle has obvious applied implications and it provides another way to identify reinforcement in everyday settings. Behavior is measured in a situation where all relevant operants can occur without restriction; any behavior of relatively higher frequency will reinforce an operant of lower frequency. To illustrate, a child is observed in a situation where doing homework, watching television, playing with toys, and recreational reading may all freely occur. Once baseline measures of behavior have been taken, the Premack principle holds that any higher frequency (or longer duration) behavior may serve as reinforcement for any behavior of lower frequency. If television watching is longer in duration than doing homework, watching television may be made contingent on completing homework assignments. This contingency will usually increase the number of homework assignments completed.

Reinforcement and response deprivation

The Premack principle states that a higher frequency behavior can reinforce a lower frequency operant. In a free-choice setting, several behaviors will occur at different frequencies—yielding a **response hierarchy**. Any response in the hierarchy may be used to reinforce any behavior below it; also, a response may be reinforced by any behavior above it.

An important observation is that depriving an animal of opportunity to engage in a given

FIG. 4.4   Dr. William Timberlake.
Published with permission.

behavior changes the response frequencies and hierarchy. By depriving a rat of drinking water, we insure that drinking occurs at a higher frequency than wheel running, and drinking will reinforce running (or behavior such as lever pressing); on the other hand, restriction of running increases its frequency relative to drinking, and running will now reinforce drinking. Thus, deprivation leads to a reordering of the response hierarchy and determines which behaviors will function as reinforcement at a given moment.

Bill Timberlake (Figure 4.4), Professor of Psychological and Brain Sciences at Indiana University, has maintained an interest in behavior regulation using an evolutionary ecological perspective (Timberlake, 1993). His work with James Allison (Timberlake & Allison, 1974) shows that organisms attempt to maintain equilibrium or homeostasis in terms of their responses. That is, rats, humans, and other animals will work to gain access to activities that are restricted (deprivation); they do this to reinstate equilibrium or free-choice levels of the behavior.

Equilibrium analysis makes a distinction between the instrumental and contingent responses. The **instrumental response** is the behavior that produces the opportunity to engage in some activity; the **contingent response** is the activity obtained by making the instrumental response. When a contingency is set between the instrumental and contingent responses, equilibrium is disturbed—the animal is deprived of the contingent response. One implication is that the animal will perform the instrumental response to get back to free-choice or baseline levels of the contingent response.

This analysis can be illustrated with an everyday episode of parent–child interaction. After receiving a poor report from school, Johnny is told, "from now on you can watch television only after you do your homework." In this example, doing homework is the instrumental response and watching TV is the contingent response. Viewing TV will increase doing homework (reinforcement) only if the contingency set by Johnny's parents imposes deprivation on the contingent response. Generally, *response deprivation occurs when access to the contingent behavior is restricted and falls below its baseline (or free-choice) level of occurrence.* Thus, Johnny usually watches about 2 h of TV each night before bedtime (baseline level or equilibrium). The contingency to do homework before watching television imposes a restriction on the contingent activity and pushes it below baseline level, assuming that bedtime does not change. Johnny will now do homework to gain access to television at baseline level (2 h).

Timberlake and Allison (1974) showed that the reason for a reinforcement effect is not the relative frequencies of behavior as stated in the Premack principle; rather, it is due to response deprivation and the disequilibrium imposed by the contingency (e.g., do homework before watching TV). In fact, it is possible to obtain a reinforcement effect with a low-frequency behavior if the person is deprived of the activity by setting a behavioral contingency. That is, equilibrium analysis and response deprivation have a wider range of application than the Premack principle.

OPERANT CONDITIONING

Operant conditioning refers to an increase or decrease in operant behavior as a function of a contingency of reinforcement. In a simple demonstration of operant conditioning, an experimenter may alter the consequences that follow operant behavior. The effects of environmental consequences on behavior were first described in 1911 by the American psychologist E. L. Thorndike, who reported results from a series of animal experiments that eventually formed the basis of operant conditioning. Cats, dogs, and chicks were placed in situations in which they could obtain food by performing complex sequences of behavior. For example, hungry cats were confined to an apparatus that Thorndike called a puzzle box, shown in Figure 4.5. Food was placed outside the box, and if the cat managed to pull out a bolt, step on a lever, or emit some other behavior, the door would open and the animal could eat the food.

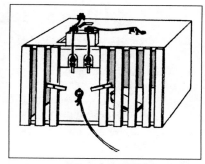

FIG. 4.5   Thorndike's puzzle box for cats. Food was placed outside the box, and if the cat managed to pull out a bolt or step on a lever, the door would open and the animal could get out of the box and eat the food. When the cats were given repeated trials in the box, they became faster and faster at getting out. From Rachlin, 1976. Based on Thorndike, 1911. Reprinted with permission.

After some time in the box, the cat would accidentally pull the bolt or step on the lever and the door would open. Thorndike measured the time from closing the trap door until the cat managed to get it open. This measure, called **latency**, tended to decrease with repeated exposures to the box. In other words, the cats took less and less time to escape from the apparatus as they were given more trials. According to Thorndike, the puzzle-box experiment demonstrated learning by trial and error. That is, the cats repeatedly tried to get out of the box and made fewer and fewer errors. Thorndike made similar observations with dogs and chicks and, on the basis of these observations, formulated the **law of effect**. A modern paraphrase of this law is the principle of reinforcement: Operants may be followed by the presentation of contingent consequences that increase the rate (frequency of response divided by time) of this behavior. Skinner (1988) has commented on Thorndike's analysis of trial-and-error learning:

> Thorndike thought he solved his problem by saying that the successful cat used trial-and-error learning. The expression is unfortunate. "Try" [from trial] implies that a response has already been affected by relevant consequences. A cat is "trying to escape" if it engages in behavior which either has been selected in the evolution of the species because it has brought escape from comparable situations or has been reinforced by escape from aversive stimulation during the life of the cat. The term "error" does not describe behavior; it passes judgment on it. The curves for trial-and-error learning plotted by Thorndike and many others do not represent any useful property of behavior—certainly not a single process called problem solving. The changes which contribute to such a curve include the adaptation and extinction of emotional responses, the conditioning of reinforcers, and the extinction of unrelated responses. Any contribution made by an increase in the probability of the reinforced response is hopelessly obscured.
>
> (p. 219)

In other words, Skinner suggests that simply measuring the time (or latency) taken to complete a task misses changes that occur across several operant classes. Responses that resulted in escape and food were selected while other behavior decreased in frequency. Eventually those operants that produced reinforcing consequences came to predominate the cat's behavior, allowing the cat to get out of the box in less and less time. Thus, latency was an indirect measure of a change in the animal's operant behavior. Today, **rate of response** or operant rate (the number of responses in a specified interval) is considered a better measure of operant behavior. Operant rate provides a direct measure of the selection of behavior by its consequences (i.e., **selection by consequences**).

FOCUS ON: Behavioral neuroscience and operant conditioning of the neuron

When the behavior of an organism acts upon the environment in which it lives, it changes that environment in ways that *often affect the organism itself* [emphasis added]. Some of these changes . . . are generally referred to technically as reinforcers: when they follow behavior in this way they increase the likelihood that the organism will behave in the same way again.

(Ferster & Skinner, 1957, p. 1)

How does the environment "affect the organism itself" during the process of operant conditioning? One possibility is that reinforcement and operant conditioning occur at the level of brain units or elements. Skinner (1953, pp. 93–95) addressed brain units when he stated that ". . .the element rather than the response [is] the unit of behavior. It is a sort of behavioral atom, which may never appear by itself upon any single occasion but is the essential ingredient or component of all observed instances [of behavior]." At the time Skinner made this claim he had no way of knowing the basic element or "behavioral atom" of operant conditioning. Today, the evidence is mounting that the basic units of reinforcement are not complex brain structures of whole responses but elements as small as the neuron itself.

It is possible to investigate the neuron and reinforcement by the method of **in vitro reinforcement** or IVR (Stein, Xue, & Belluzzi, 1994). The idea is that calcium bursts or firings (L-type Ca^{2+}) of a neuron are reinforced by dopamine (a neurotransmitter) binding to specialized receptors. Furthermore, the process of neuronal conditioning can be investigated "in vitro" using brain-slice preparations and drug injections that stimulate the dopamine receptor (dopamine agonists).

In these IVR experiments, a small injector tube (micropipette) is aimed at cells of the brain slice (hyppocampal cells from pyramidal cell layer of CA1). During operant conditioning, micropressure injections of a dopamine drug (agonist) are applied to the cell for 50 ms following bursts of activity (amplified action potentials). When the computer identifies a predefined burst of activity for the target neuron, the pressure-injection pump delivers a minute droplet of the drug to the cell. Drug-induced increases in bursting indicate operant conditioning if the *contingency* between neuron bursts and drug presentation is critical. To be sure that the drug is not just stimulating burst activity, the same drug is given independently of bursting on a *noncontingent* basis.

The results showed that the bursting responses of individual neurons increase in a dose-related manner by response-contingent injections of dopamine agonists. Also, noncontingent presentation of the same drug injections did not increase the bursting responses of the neurons. The findings indicate that reinforcement occurs at the level of individual neural units (Skinner's atoms of behavior) and suggest that subtypes of dopamine neurons (D1, D2, or D3 types) are involved in cellular and behavioral operant conditioning.

Additional IVR experiments indicate that bursting responses of CA1 pyramidal neurons also increase with injections of cannabinoid drugs, whereas the firings of CA3 neurons increase with drugs that stimulate the opiate receptors (Stein & Belluzzi, 1988; Xue, Belluzzi, & Stein, 1993). When these drug injections are administered independent of cellular activity, bursting responses do not increase and often are suppressed. Furthermore, contingent and noncontingent glutamate injections to the CA1 neurons over a range of doses fail to increase bursting or decrease this response. Thus, drug agonists that target specific receptors implicated in reward and addiction (e.g., dopamine, cannabinoid, and opioid) act as reinforcement for neural bursting while glutamate, an excitatory transmitter not associated with behavioral reinforcement, does not augment cellular activity or even suppresses it.

Operant conditioning is a major adaptive mechanism for animals that change behavior on the basis of lifetime experiences (ontogeny). That is, operant conditioning allows for behavioral flexibility, survival, and reproduction. Evidence is accumulating that behavioral flexibility is based on neural plasticity—alterations of the brain units that affect the regulation of behavior by environmental contingencies. In vitro reinforcement experiments show that endogenous brain chemicals binding to particular types of receptors increase the likelihood of neuronal activity. These molecular neural processes presumably underlie the large-scale changes in operant behavior that occur as humans and other animals interact with the world in which they live, moment to moment over a life span.

Procedures in Operant Conditioning

Operant rate and probability of response

Rate of response refers to the number of operant responses that occur in some defined unit of time. For example, if you ask 5 questions during a 2-h class, your rate is 2.5 questions per hour. An animal that presses a lever 1000 times in a 1-h session generates a rate of 1000 bar presses per hour (or 16.7 responses per minute). Skinner (1938) proposed that rate of response is the basic datum (or measure) for operant analysis. **Operant rate** is a measure of the probability of behavior (the **probability of response**). In other words, an operant that occurs at a high rate in one situation has a high probability of being emitted in a similar situation in the future. This increased probability of response is observed as a change in operant rate. Of course, probability of response may decrease and in this case is seen as a decline in rate.

The free operant method

In the **free operant method**, an animal may repeatedly respond over an extensive period of time (see Perone, 1991). The organism is free to emit many responses or none at all. That is, responses can be made without interference from the experimenter. For example, a laboratory rat may press a lever for food pellets. Lever pressing is under the control of the animal, which may press the bar rapidly, slowly, or quit pressing. Importantly, this method allows the researcher to observe changes in rate of response. This is important because rate of response is used as a measure of response probability. Rate of response must be free to vary if it is used to index the future probability of operant behavior.

The analysis of operant rate and probability of response is not easily accomplished when an organism is given a series of trials (as in the Thorndike experiments). This is because the experimenter largely controls the animal's rate of behavior. For example, a rat that runs down a T-maze for food reward is picked up at the goal box and returned to the starting point. Because the experimenter sets the number of trials and response opportunities, changes in rate of response cannot be directly observed and measured. Comparing the T-maze trial procedure with the free operant method, it is clear that the free operant method is more suitable to study the probability of response in a given situation. The free operant method is clearly demonstrated by the procedures used in operant conditioning.

The operant chamber

To study operant conditioning in a laboratory, a device called an **operant chamber** is used (see Ator, 1991). Of course, operant conditioning is also investigated outside laboratories. Nonetheless, investigating the behavior of animals in operant chambers has resulted in the discovery of many principles of behavior. Figure 4.6 shows a student setup of an operant chamber designed to accommodate a laboratory rat (note that a research setup would involve much more experimental control, such as a sound attenuating enclosure and "white noise" to mask sounds from outside). The chamber is a small enclosed box that contains a lever with a light above it and a food magazine or cup connected to an external feeder. The feeder delivers a small food pellet (typically 45 mg) when

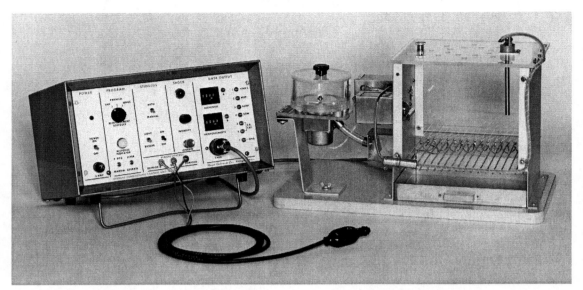

FIG. 4.6   A student setup of an operant chamber for a rat. The chamber is a small box that has a lever that the animal can press. There is a light above the lever that can be turned on or off. A food magazine or cup is connected to an electronically activated feeder. The feeder delivers a small, 45-mg food pellet to the cup. In this situation, the food pellet serves as reinforcement for lever pressing. Reprinted with permission of Gerbrands Corporation, Arlington, MA.

electronically activated. In this situation, the food pellet serves as reinforcement for lever pressing. The operant chamber structures the situation so that the desired behavior will occur and incompatible behavior is reduced. Thus, lever pressing is highly likely, while behavior like running away is minimized. A school classroom also attempts to structure the behavior of students with regard to learning. The classroom, unlike the operant chamber, often contains many distractions (e.g., looking out the window) that interfere with on-task behavior and concentrating on the material being presented.

Deprivation

Because the delivery of food is used as reinforcement, an animal must be motivated to obtain food. An objective and quantifiable measure of motivation for food is percentage of free-feeding body weight. (*Note:* Another way of quantifying deprivation is a timed cycle that specifies the time since the rat last consumed the reinforcer.) Prior to a typical experiment, an animal is brought from a commercial (or research) colony into a laboratory, placed in a cage, given free access to food, and weighed on a daily basis. The average weight is calculated, and this value is used as a baseline. Next, the daily food ration is reduced until the animal reaches 85% of its free-feeding weight. The procedure of restricting access to food (the potentially reinforcing stimulus) is called a **deprivation operation** (see Establishing operations, Chapter 2). At this point, the experimenter assumes, but does not know, that food is a reinforcing stimulus. This is because food delivery must increase the frequency of an operant before it can be defined as a reinforcer.

The weight-loss or deprivation criterion is less severe than it first appears. Laboratory animals typically have food freely available 24 h a day while animals in the wild must forage for their food. The result is that lab animals tend to be heavier than their free-ranging counterparts. Alan Poling and colleagues (Poling, Nickel, & Alling, 1990) nicely demonstrated this point by showing that captured free-range pigeons gained an average 17% body weight when housed under laboratory conditions. Notice that weight gain, for these birds, is roughly equal to the weight loss typically imposed on laboratory animals.

Magazine training

After deprivation for food is established, **magazine training** starts. For example, a rat is placed in an operant chamber and a microcomputer periodically turns on the feeder. When the feeder is turned on, it makes a click and a small 45-mg food pellet falls into the food magazine. Because the click and the appearance of food are associated in time, you would, after training, observe a typical rat staying close to the food magazine; also, the animal would move quickly toward the magazine when the feeder operated and the click occurred. Because the click of the feeder reliably precedes the appearance of food, it becomes a conditioned positive reinforcer (see Chapter 11 for a more complete discussion of conditioned reinforcement). A **conditioned reinforcer** is an event or stimulus that acquires its reinforcing function over the lifetime of the organism (ontogeny). In this case, following the click of the feeder by the presentation of food establishes the sound of the feeder as a conditioned reinforcer for the rat.

The operant class

Staying close to the food cup and moving toward it are operants that have been selected by their reinforcing consequences. In other words, these responses have been reliably followed by food presentation, and as a result they increase in frequency. However, hovering around a food cup and moving toward it are operants that are difficult to measure objectively. In contrast, a lever press may be easily defined as a switch closure that makes an electrical connection. Any behavior emitted by the rat that results in a switch closure defines the operant class. A lever press with the left or right paw produces an identical electrical connection. Another advantage of lever pressing as an operant is that it may be emitted at high or low rates of response. This is an advantage because the primary focus of operant research is on the conditions that affect the rate (probability) of operant behavior.

Operant level and continuous reinforcement

After magazine training, the food-deprived rat is again placed in the operant chamber. The researcher may first want to measure the rate of lever pressing before these responses produce food pellets. Rats emit many exploratory and manipulative responses and as a result may press the lever at some low frequency, even when this behavior is not reinforced with food. This baseline rate of response is called the **operant level** or the rate of response before any known conditioning. Next, the environment is arranged so that each lever press results in the click of the feeder (conditioned reinforcement) and the delivery of a food pellet (primary reinforcement). When each response produces food, the schedule of reinforcement is called **continuous reinforcement (CRF)**. The food pellets are contingent on lever pressing. This contingency between the operant behavior and food reinforcement increases the frequency of lever pressing above operant level.

Shaping: The method of successive approximation

In the preceding example, we took advantage of a rat's behavioral repertoire. The animal's **repertoire** refers to the behavior it is capable of naturally emitting on the basis of species and environmental history. Suppose you want to train some response that the animal does not emit. For example, you may want the rat to activate the switch by an upward thrust of its nose. A baseline period of observation shows that the animal fails to emit this response (in other words, the *operant level is zero*). In this case, the researcher could use **shaping** or the method of **successive approximation** to establish the response (see Gleeson, 1991). This method involves reinforcing closer and closer approximations to the final performance (i.e., nosing the lever).

At first, the rat is reinforced for standing in the vicinity of the lever. It is important to note that the most immediate consequence is the sound of the pellet feeder, and this conditioned reinforcer

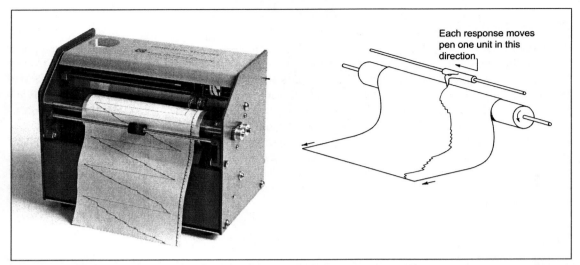

FIG. 4.7   A laboratory instrument used to record operant responses, called a cumulative recorder. The recorder gives a real-time measure of the rate of operant behavior. The faster the lever presses, the steeper the slope or rise of the cumulative record. This occurs because paper is drawn across the roller at a constant speed and the pen steps up a defined distance for each response. Reprinted with permission of Gerbrands Corporation, Arlington, MA.

may be used to shape the desired response. Once the animal is reliably facing the lever, a movement of the head toward the bar is reinforced with a click of the feeder and presentation of food. Next, closer and closer approximations to lifting the lever with the nose are reinforced. Each step of the procedure involves reinforcing closer approximations and no reinforcement (extinction) of more distant responses. Eventually, the rat emits a response that activates the electrical switch. Many novel forms of behavior may be established by the method of successive approximation or shaping (Pryor, 1999).

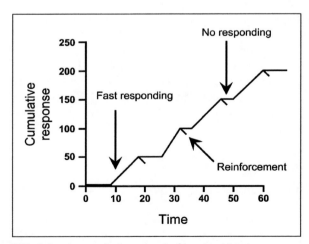

FIG. 4.8   A cumulative record of key pecking by a pigeon. In this illustration, a bird responded 50 times to produce one food delivery. Notice that 50 pecks are followed by reinforcement and that this is indicated by a downward deflection of the pen. Following reinforcement, the rate of response is zero, as indicated by the plateaus or flat portions of the record.

Recording Operant Behavior

A commonly used laboratory instrument that records the frequency of operant behavior in time is called a **cumulative recorder**. Figure 4.7 illustrates this device; each time a lever press occurs, the pen steps up one increment. When reinforcement occurs, this same pen makes a downward deflection. Once the pen reaches the top of the paper, it resets to the bottom and starts to step up again. Since the paper is drawn across the roller at a constant speed, the *cumulative recorder depicts a real-time measure of the rate of operant behavior.* The faster the lever presses, the steeper the slope or rise of the cumulative record.

A **cumulative record** of key pecking by a pigeon is shown in Figure 4.8. In this illustration, a bird responded 50 times to produce one food delivery. Notice that periods of responding are followed by reinforcement (indicated by the deflection of the pen). After reinforcement, the rate of response is zero, as indicated by the plateaus or flat portions of the cumulative record.

In a modern operant laboratory, the cumulative record is used to provide the experimenter with an immediate report of the animal's behavior. Researchers have discovered many basic principles of behavior by examining cumulative records (e.g., Ferster & Skinner, 1957). Today, microcomputers allow researchers to collect, display, and record measures of behavior (e.g., rate of response) that are later submitted to complex numerical analyses (see Gollub, 1991). In this book, we present examples of cumulative records and numerical analyses that have been important to the experimental analysis of behavior.

A Model Experiment

In the previous discussion of operant behavior, some basic principles were illustrated using the laboratory rat. It is important to realize that these same principles can be extended to a variety of species (later chapters will focus more on human behavior). In the following demonstration of operant conditioning, pigeons are used as the experimental subjects. Pigeons are placed in an operant chamber and required to peck a small plastic disk or *key* that is illuminated by a white light. A peck at the key activates a microswitch and makes an electrical connection that controls a food hopper. Presentation of food functions as reinforcement for pecking. A food hopper filled with grain swings forward and remains available for a few seconds. The bird can eat the grain by sticking its head through an opening. Figure 4.9 shows an operant chamber designed for birds. Note that the chamber is very similar to the one used to study the operant behavior of rats.

Before an experiment, the bird is taken from its home colony and is placed alone in a cage. Each pigeon is given free access to food and water. The bird is weighed each day for about a week and its

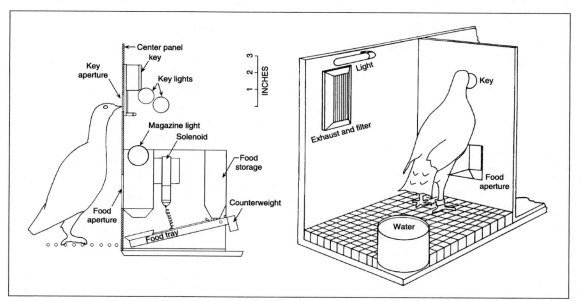

FIG. 4.9   An operant chamber for birds. The chamber contains a small plastic disk illuminated by a light. A peck at the disk activates a microswitch and makes an electrical connection. When reinforcement is scheduled to occur, the food hopper swings forward and remains available for a few seconds. The bird can eat grain from the hopper by sticking its head through the opening in the chamber wall. In principle, the chamber is similar to the one used to study the operant behavior of rats. Adapted from Ferster and Skinner, 1957, Appleton-Century-Crofts, New York.

baseline weight is calculated. Next, the daily food ration is reduced until the bird reaches approximately 80% of free-feeding or **ad libitum weight**. After the deprivation procedure, the pigeon is placed in the operant chamber for magazine training.

When the bird is placed in the chamber for the first time, it may show a variety of emotional responses, including wing flapping and defecating. This is because the chamber presents a number of novel features that initially function as aversive stimuli. For example, the operation of the feeder makes a loud sound that may startle the bird. Eventually, these emotional responses are extinguished by repeated exposure to the apparatus. As the emotional responses dissipate, the bird explores the environment and begins to eat from the food magazine. Since the sound of the hopper is paired with food, the sound becomes a conditioned positive reinforcer. At this point, the bird is said to be magazine trained.

The purpose of this demonstration is to train the pigeon to peck the key for food reinforcement. To show that the behavior occurs because of the contingency between pecking and food, an operant level or baseline of pecking the key must be measured. This is accomplished by placing the bird in the operant chamber and recording pecks on the key before a peck–food contingency is established. In other words, pecking the key does not produce food during this phase of the experiment. The operant level serves as a baseline or control period for assessing a change in behavior.

A bird's operant level of key pecking is typically very low, and it is convenient to train these responses by the method of successive approximation. Shaping key pecking in pigeons is similar to shaping lever pressing in rats; in both cases, shaping involves reinforcing closer and closer approximations to the final performance (i.e., pecking the key hard enough to operate the microswitch). As each approximation occurs, it is reinforced with the presentation of the food hopper. Earlier approximations are no longer reinforced and reduce in frequency. This process of reinforcing closer approximations, and withholding reinforcement for earlier approximations, eventually results in the pigeon pecking the key with sufficient force to operate the microswitch.   The key peck that operates the microswitch to produce food is the *first definable response*. The switch closure and electrical connection define the operant class of pecking for food. At this point, a microcomputer is programmed so that each key peck results in the presentation of food for a few seconds. Because each response produces reinforcement, the schedule is called continuous reinforcement, or CRF.

Figure 4.10 shows the acquisition of key pecking on continuous reinforcement (the bird has presumably been shaped to peck the key for food). Notice that the rate of response is low when the pigeon is initially placed in the chamber. This period is called the warm-up and probably occurs because of the abrupt change from home cage to the operant chamber. After the brief warm-up period, the rate of response is high and stable.

Finally, the record shows that rate of response declines and the plateau indicates that the bird stops pecking the key. This latter effect is called **satiation**, and it occurs because the bird has eaten enough food. More technically, *rate of response declines because repeated presentations of the reinforcer weaken its effectiveness*. A satiation operation decreases the effectiveness of reinforcement. This effect is opposite to deprivation, in which withholding the reinforcer increases its effectiveness.

To be sure that an increase in rate of response is caused by the contingency of reinforcement, it is necessary to withdraw

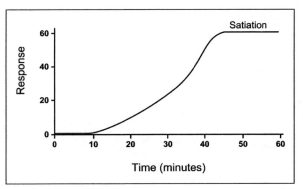

FIG. 4.10   Typical acquisition of key pecking on CRF or continuous reinforcement. Because every response is reinforced, downward deflections indicating reinforcement are omitted. Rate of response is low when the animal is initially placed in the chamber. After this brief period, rate of response is high and stable. Finally, rate of response declines and then levels off. This latter effect is caused by satiation.

that contingency. In other words, if food is no longer presented, the pigeon should give up pecking the key. If the peck–food contingency caused key pecking, then withdrawal of the contingency will result in a decline in key pecking toward the operant level.

Figure 4.11 presents cumulative records for periods in which pecking produces, or does not produce, food. The initial peck–food contingency produces a steady rate of response. When pecking no longer produces food, the rate of response declines and eventually key pecking stops. Thus, key pecking clearly depends upon the contingency of reinforcement.

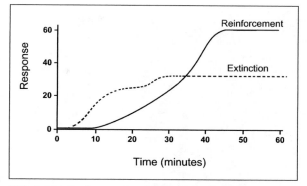

FIG. 4.11 Performance on CRF and extinction. Responses are maintained when they are reinforced. However, when responding is no longer reinforced, rate of response declines and eventually stops.

FOCUS ON: Reinforcement and problem solving

Barry Schwartz (1980, 1982a; Figure 4.12) carried out a series of experiments with pigeons to show that reinforcement produced response stereotypy. In these experiments, reinforcement produced a set pattern of responding that occurred over and over. Once he established this result in pigeons, Schwartz (1982b) used similar procedures with college students to demonstrate the presumed negative effects of reinforcement for human problem solving.

College students were given points on a counter when they completed a complex sequence of responses. The responses were left and right key presses that moved a light on a checkerboard-like matrix of 25 illuminated squares. Figure 4.13 shows the matrix, with the light in the top left square. The task required that the subject press the keys to move the light from the top left corner to the bottom right square. A press on the right key moved the light one square to the right. When the left-hand key was pressed, the light moved one square down. Schwartz required exactly four left (L) and four right (R) presses in any order (e.g., LRLRLRLR, LLLLRRRR, etc.). There were 70 different orders of left and right key presses that would move the light to the bottom right corner. When the light reached the bottom right corner, a point registered on the counter. The points were later exchanged for money. If the subject pressed any key a fifth time (e.g., RRRRR), all matrix lights were turned off and the trial ended without reinforcement.

In a series of experiments, Schwartz found that students developed a stereotyped pattern of responding. The point is that as soon as a student hit on a correct sequence, he or she repeated it and rarely tried another pattern. In other experiments (Schwartz, 1982b), participants were explicitly reinforced for varying their response pattern. When this was done, the students developed higher order stereotypes. From these

FIG. 4.12 Dr. Barry Schwartz. Published with permission.

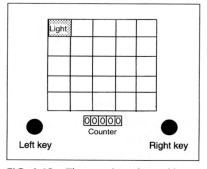

FIG. 4.13 The matrix task used by Schwartz (1982b). A right key press moved the light one square to the right; a left key press moved the light down one square.

FIG. 4.14   Dr. Allen Neuringer. Published with permission.

experiments, Schwartz concluded that reinforcement interfered with problem solving, because it produced stereotyped response patterns.

Allen Neuringer (Figure 4.14) is a behavior analyst who investigates variability, randomness, and behavior. He suggested that the contingencies of the Schwartz experiments produced response stereotypy and that this was not an inevitable outcome of reinforcement. The requirement to emit exactly four left and four right responses was arbitrary and may have resulted in response stereotypy. In several experiments, Page and Neuringer (1985) showed that pigeons doing the light matrix task could generate highly variable response patterns when the contingencies of reinforcement required this behavior. Other experiments demonstrated that behavioral variability and stereotypy are acquired responses. Pigeons learned to respond with a variable pattern in the presence of one key color and to respond with a stereotyped response pattern when another color was presented. A subsequent study by Neuringer (1986) extended the findings on response variability to humans.

In two experiments, Neuringer demonstrated that college students could learn to generate random sequences of two numbers on the keyboard of a computer. Neuringer concluded, "randomlike behaviors are learned and controlled by environmental feedback, as are other highly skilled activities" (p. 72).

The evidence indicates that variability is an operant that increases with reinforcement of behavioral variation. To date, the reinforcement of variability has been shown in a number of species, including dolphins, rats, and human adults and children (Goetz & Baer, 1973; Pryor, Haag, & O'Reilly, 1969; Stokes, Mechner, & Balsam, 1999; van Hess, van Haaren, & van de Poll, 1989). In addition, different experimental procedures have been used to produce variability with a number of different response forms (Blough, 1966; Goetz & Baer, 1973; Machado, 1989; Morgan & Neuringer, 1990; Odum, Ward, Barnes, & Burke, 2006; Pryor et al., 1969).

In summary, Barry Schwartz argues that reinforcement produces behavioral inflexibility and rigidity. In contrast, the research of Allen Neuringer suggests that response stereotypy is not an inevitable outcome of reinforcement. If the contingencies of reinforcement support stereotyped behavior, then this will occur. On the other hand, contingencies may generate novel sequences of behavior if these patterns result in reinforcement (see also Neuringer, 2002, 2004; Machado, 1989, 1992, 1997). Generally, a close analysis of the contingencies is required in problem-solving situations because "what you reinforce is what you get" (stereotypy or variability).

EXTINCTION

The procedure of *withholding reinforcement for a previously reinforced response* is called **extinction**. Skinner (1938) conducted the first extensive study of extinction and its related principles. To produce extinction, you would disconnect the food hopper after the bird had been reinforced for key pecking. It is important to note that the procedure of extinction is a contingency of reinforcement. The contingency is defined as zero probability of reinforcement for the operant response. *Extinction is also a behavioral process and, in this case, refers to a decline in rate of response caused by withdrawal of reinforcement.* For example, you may raise your hand to ask a question and find that a certain professor ignores you. Asking questions may decline because the professor no longer reinforces this behavior.

Behavioral Effects of Extinction

Extinction produces several behavioral effects in addition to a decline in rate of response. In the section that follows, we consider the range of effects generated by the cessation of reinforcement. Many of the responses of organisms to the cessation of reinforcement make sense from an evolutionary perspective. Presumably, when things no longer worked (extinction), natural selection favored organisms that repeated behavior that "worked" in the past, made a greater range of responses in the situation (behavioral variability), emitted more forceful responses to the circumstances, and attacked other members of the species associated with the cessation of reinforcement.

Extinction burst

When extinction is started, operant behavior tends to increase in frequency. That is, organisms repeat behavior that has been reinforced. A pigeon will initially increase the rate of key pecking, and you may raise your hand more often than you did in the past. You may explain your increased tendency to raise your hand by telling a friend, "The instructor doesn't see me; I have an important point to make." If the bird could talk it might also "explain" why it was pecking at an increased rate. The point is that an initial increase in rate of response, or **extinction burst**, occurs when reinforcement is first withdrawn.

Operant variability

In addition to extinction bursts, operant behavior becomes increasingly variable as extinction proceeds (**operant variability**). Behavioral variation increases the chances that the organisms will reinstate reinforcement or contact other sources of reinforcement. You may wave your hand about in an attempt to catch the professor's eye; the bird may strike the key in different locations and with different amounts of force. A classic experiment by Antonitis (1951) demonstrated this effect. Rats were taught to poke their noses through a 50-cm-long slot for food reinforcement. When this occurred, a photocell was triggered and a photograph of the animal was taken. The position of the rat and the angle of its body were recorded at the moment of reinforcement. After the rat reliably poked its nose through the slot, it was placed on extinction. Following this, reinforcement was reinstated, then extinguished, and in a final phase the operant was again reinforced.

Antonitis reported that reinforcement produced a stereotyped pattern of response. The rat repeatedly poked its nose through the slot at approximately the same location, and the position of its body was held at a particular angle. When extinction occurred, the nose poking and position of the body varied. During extinction, the animal poked its nose over the entire length of the slot. Reinforcing the operant after extinction produced even more stereotyped behavior than the original conditioning.

Pear (1985) found a similar effect with pigeons. When birds were reinforced for pecking a key after an average of only 15 s, they stayed close to the key and emitted routine patterns of head and body movements. When these animals were reinforced on a similar schedule, but one that required an average wait of 5 min, they strayed further from the key. Both of these patterns developed during extinction, but as extinction continued their behavior became much more variable.

Force of response

Reinforcement may be made contingent on the force of response (or other properties) resulting in **response differentiation**. Notterman (1959) measured the force that rats used to press a lever during periods of reinforcement and extinction. During reinforcement sessions, animals came to press the lever with a force that varied within a relatively narrow range. When extinction occurred, the force of lever pressing became more variable. Interestingly, some responses were more forceful than any emitted during reinforcement or during operant level. This increase in response force may be due to emotional behavior generated by extinction procedures.

For example, imagine that you have pushed a button for an elevator but the elevator does not arrive, and you have an important appointment on the 28th floor. At first you increase the frequency of pressing the elevator button; you also change the way you hit the button. You probably feel angry and frustrated and you may smash the button. These responses and accompanying feelings occur because of the change from reinforcement to extinction.

Emotional responses

Consider what happens when someone puts money in a vending machine and is not reinforced with an item (e.g., a beverage). The person who is placed on extinction may hit the machine, curse, and engage in other emotional behavior. Soda machines once killed several US soldiers: Young soldiers at the peak of physical fitness are capable of emitting forceful operants and when some of the soldiers put money in soda machines that failed to operate, extinction-induced emotional behavior became so powerful that the men pulled over the 2-ton machines. Thus, their deaths were an indirect outcome of emotional behavior produced by extinction.

A variety of **emotional responses** occur under conditions of extinction. Birds flap their wings, rats bite the response lever, and humans may swear and kick at a vending machine. One important kind of emotional behavior that occurs during extinction is aggression. Azrin, Hutchinson, and Hake (1966) trained pigeons to peck a key for food. After training, a second immobilized pigeon was placed in the operant chamber. The "target" bird was restrained and placed on an apparatus that caused a switch to close whenever the bird was attacked. Attacks to the target reliably occurred when the contingencies of reinforcement were changed from CRF to extinction. Many of the attacks were vicious and unrelenting, lasting up to 10 min.

Discriminated extinction

Suppose that a pigeon was reinforced for pecking a key in the presence of a green light. However, when a red light came on, pecking was not reinforced. During the course of training, the animal would emit emotional responses and extinction bursts when the red light was turned on. Following training, the bird would not emit this behavior and it would simply stop responding when the light changed from green to red. The red light became a *discriminative stimulus (S^Δ) that signaled a period of extinction*. This effect is called **discriminated extinction** and is commonly observed in human behavior. A sign on a vending machine that reads OUT OF ORDER is an S^Δ that signals extinction for putting money in the machine.

Discriminative extinction involves signaling extinction periods with an extroceptive stimulus, such as a change in key color from green to red. When the key is green, a pigeon is trained to peck it for food. Every once in a while the key color changes to red, and reinforcement for pecking no longer occurs. During these extinction periods, rate of response should decline. This decline would occur more rapidly when extinction is signaled by a change in color than when the key color remains the same. Finally, since the red key is consistently associated with extinction, it acquires a discriminative function (S^{Δ}), suppressing responding when it is presented.

Resistance to Extinction

As extinction proceeds, emotional behavior subsides and rate of response declines. When extinction has been in effect long enough, behavior may return to operant level. In practice, however, a return to operant level is rarely accomplished. This is because many extinction sessions are usually required before operant level is attained. Extinction is typically measured as the number of responses emitted in some amount of time. For example, a bird may be reinforced on CRF for 10 consecutive daily sessions; following this, extinction is initiated. The pigeon's responses are recorded over three extinction sessions. The number of responses emitted by the bird or the rate of response during the last session may be used to index resistance to extinction. Operants are rapidly extinguished after a few reinforced responses, but when operants are reinforced many times, resistance to extinction increases. Several experiments (Hearst, 1961; Perin, 1942) have shown that resistance to extinction reaches a maximum after 50–80 reinforced responses.

Partial reinforcement effect (PRE)

Resistance to extinction is substantially increased when a partial or **intermittent reinforcement schedule** has been used to maintain behavior. On an intermittent reinforcement schedule, only some responses are reinforced. For example, instead of reinforcing each response (CRF), the experimenter may program reinforcement after 100 key pecks have been emitted. In this situation, the bird must emit 100 pecks before food is presented. This intermittent schedule will generate many more responses during extinction than continuous reinforcement. When people are described as having a persistent or tenacious personality, their behavior may reflect the effects of intermittent reinforcement.

Nevin (1988a) indicates that the **partial reinforcement effect (PRE)** is the result of two basic processes: reinforcement and discrimination. According to Nevin's analysis, reinforcement has the single effect of increasing resistance to change. That is, *the higher the rate of reinforcement for an operant, the greater the resistance to change.* The implication is that behavior maintained by a CRF schedule is more resistant to change than behavior controlled by an intermittent reinforcement schedule.

But extinction occurs more rapidly on CRF compared to intermittent reinforcement. A reason for the discrepancy is that *discrimination* between reinforcement and extinction is more rapid on CRF than on intermittent reinforcement. That is, an organism discriminates the difference between a high and steady rate of reinforcement (CRF) and no reinforcement (extinction) more easily than between a low and intermittent rate of reinforcement and no reinforcement. In tests for resistance to extinction, the discrimination factor overrides the rate of reinforcement variable and animals show greater resistance on intermittent than CRF schedules. If the effects of discrimination (between reinforcement and extinction) are controlled, behavior maintained by CRF is in fact more resistant to extinction than on intermittent reinforcement schedules.

An additional reason for increased resistance to extinction following intermittent reinforcement involves *contact with the contingencies.* A rat reinforced for every 100 responses must emit 100 responses before contacting the change from reinforcement to extinction. In contrast, an animal that is reinforced for each response contacts the extinction contingency immediately. Since each response is a nonreinforced occurrence, the animal repeatedly encounters the change to extinction. If an animal on CRF emits 50 responses during extinction, it has contacted the extinction contingency 50 times. A rat on intermittent reinforcement may have to emit 5000 responses to have equal experience with the change in contingencies.

Discriminative stimuli and extinction

Intermittent reinforcement is not the only factor that determines the return to operant level during extinction. Resistance to extinction is also affected by discriminative stimuli that are conditioned during sessions of reinforcement. Skinner (1950) showed that "maximal responding during extinction is obtained only when the conditions under which the response was reinforced are precisely reproduced" (p. 204).

Pigeons were trained to peck a yellow triangle on an intermittent schedule of food reinforcement. After training, a red triangle was substituted for the yellow one and extinction was started. During 15 min of extinction in the presence of the red triangle, the rate of response substantially declined. At this point, the yellow triangle replaced the red but extinction was continued. The effect of introducing the yellow triangle was that rapid responding began immediately, and the usual extinction curve followed. This effect is portrayed in Figure 4.15, in which responding in the presence of the yellow triangle is at a high rate during the first 30 min of intermittent reinforcement. When the red triangle and extinction were introduced, the rate of response declined. Finally, extinction was continued and the yellow triangle was reinstated. Notice that rate of response immediately recovers and then declines toward extinction.

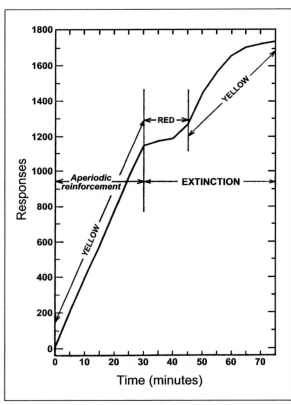

FIG. 4.15 Responding during extinction as a function of discrimination. Responding in the presence of the yellow triangle is high during the first 30 min of intermittent reinforcement. When the red triangle and extinction are introduced, the rate of response declines. Extinction is continued and the yellow triangle is reinstated. When the yellow triangle is presented, the rate of response recovers and then declines toward extinction. From "Are Theories of Learning Necessary?," by B. F. Skinner, 1950, *Psychological Review, 57*, 193–216. Reprinted with permission from APA.

Spontaneous recovery

An interesting phenomenon that occurs during extinction is **spontaneous recovery**. After a session of extinction, the rate of response may be close to operant level. At this point, the animal is taken out of the operant chamber and returned to a holding cage. The next day, the organism is again placed in the operant chamber and extinction is continued. Surprisingly, the animal begins to respond above operant level, and this defines spontaneous recovery. Over repeated sessions of extinction, the amount of recovery decreases. If many sessions of extinction are provided, the rate of response will no longer recover.

Spontaneous recovery is really not spontaneous. Stimuli that have accompanied reinforced responding are usually presented at the beginning of extinction sessions (habituation may also be involved; see Pear, 2001, p. 63). Skinner (1950) has noted that handling procedures and the stimulation arising from being placed in an operant chamber set the occasion for responding at the beginning of each extinction session. Skinner (1950) states:

> No matter how carefully an animal is handled, the stimulation coincident with the beginning of an experiment must be extensive and unlike anything occurring in the latter part of an experimental period. Responses have been reinforced in the presence of, or shortly following, this stimulation. In extinction it is present for only a few moments. When the organism is again placed in the experimental situation the stimulation is restored; further responses are emitted as in the case of the yellow triangle [see aforementioned experiment]. The only way to achieve full extinction in the presence of the stimulation of starting an experiment is to start the experiment repeatedly.
>
> (pp. 199–200)

Human behavior also shows spontaneous recovery. Imagine that you are stranded in a secluded mountain cabin during a week-long snowstorm. The telephone rings, you answer, but all you get is the dial tone. You shout at the dial tone and bang the disconnect button repeatedly. Next, you try to contact the telephone company and discover that you are not able to dial out. Over the course of the first day the phone rings many times, you answer, but it does not work. By the end of the day, you may not be inclined to answer the telephone; you just let it keep on ringing. The next morning you are having breakfast and the phone rings. What do you do? The best guess is that you will again answer the phone. You may say to yourself, "Perhaps they have fixed the line." On this second day of extinction, you answer the phone but give up more quickly. On day 3, the phone rings at 10:00 a.m. and even though you doubt that it will work, you answer it "just to check it out." By day 4, you have had it with the "damn phone and the stupid telephone company" and extinction is complete.

Extinction and Forgetting

During extinction, operant behavior decreases over time. People often talk about the weakening of behavior as loss of memory or forgetting. An important question concerns the procedural differences between forgetting and extinction. Extinction is a procedure in which a previously reinforced response no longer produces reinforcement. The opportunity to emit the operant remains available during extinction. Thus, the pigeon may still peck the illuminated key, or the rat may continue to press the response lever. In contrast, forgetting is said to occur after the mere passage of time. An organism that has learned a response is tested for retention after some amount of time has passed. In this case, there is no apparent opportunity to emit the behavior.

NOTE ON: Remembering and recalling

In much of psychology people and other organisms are said to store information about events in memory. The use of the noun *memory* is an example of reification or treating an action as if it were a thing. In behavior analysis and learning, we use the verb *remembering* (or forgetting) to refer to the effect of some event on behavior after the passage of time (see Donahoe & Palmer, 1994, pp. 324–353; Palmer, 1991). For example, a pigeon that has been reinforced for pecking a green illuminated key, but not for pecking a red one, is removed from the operant chamber and kept in a home cage for 1 year. After 1 year, the pigeon is placed back in the operant chamber and tested for remembering by alternating presentations of the red and green keys. If the pigeon pecks when the key is green, but not when it is red, the pigeon demonstrates remembering of the green/red discrimination. You can see that remembering involves behavior (pecking in the presence of green and red keys) that occurred in the past and now reoccurs after a period of time (see White & Wixted, 1999, for experimental evidence).

For humans, we may say that a person recalls her trip to Costa Rica when a picture of the trip occasions a verbal description of the vacation. From a behavioral perspective, *recalling* "X" (i.e., recalling my trip to Costa Rica) is behavior (mostly verbal) emitted now with respect to events that occurred in the past. That is, remembering and recalling are treated as behavioral processes rather than some mysterious thing (memory) within us. Behavior analysts assume that the event recalled is one that was described (if only to oneself) when it first occurred. Recalling (like remembering) refers to the *reoccurrence* of behavior (mostly verbal) that has already occurred at least once.

Skinner (1938) designed an experiment to assess the behavioral loss that occurs after the passage of time. In this experiment, four rats were trained to press a lever, and each animal received 100 reinforced responses. After 45 days of rest, each animal was placed in the operant chamber and responding was extinguished. The number of responses emitted during extinction was compared with the performance of four other rats selected from an earlier experiment. These animals were similar in age, training, and number of reinforced responses to the experimental subjects. The comparison animals had received extinction 1 day after reinforced bar pressing.

Figure 4.16 shows the results of Skinner's experiment. Results are presented as the cumulative-average number of responses emitted by each group of animals. The group that received extinction 1 day after response strengthening emitted an average of 86 responses in 1 h. The group that was extinguished after 45 days made an average of 69 responses in 1 h. Notice that both groups of animals show a similar number of responses during the first few minutes of extinction. In other words, animals in both groups immediately began to press the lever when placed in the operant chamber. This shows that the rats that received extinction after 45 days had not forgotten what to do to get food (Skinner, 1938).

Following the first few minutes of extinction, there is a difference in the cumulative-average number of responses for the two groups. Resistance to extinction is apparently reduced by the passage of time. Rats that were required to wait 45 days before extinction generated fewer responses per hour than those given extinction 1 day after reinforcement. Although the curves rise at different rates, animals in both groups appear to stop responding after approximately 90 nonreinforced lever presses. Overall, the results suggest that the passage of time affects resistance to extinction, but a well-established performance is not forgotten.

As a further illustration of this point, Markowitz and colleagues in an article titled "Do elephants ever forget?" indicated that they retested three elephants after an 8-year period between training and retest (Markowitz, Schmidt, Nadal, & Squier, 1975). One of the three animals showed near-perfect performance within 6 min of doing a task not experienced for 8 years; it was determined that the other two elephants were suffering from visual impairments.

In a later experiment on forgetting, Skinner (1950) trained 20 pigeons to strike a key with a complex pattern. The pigeons had been used for a World War II naval research project involving missile guidance systems (Project Pigeon; see Skinner, 1960). Skinner had taught the birds to peck at a complex visual image. A particular feature of the New Jersey coastline was projected onto a translucent key. The pigeons were required to strike the specified target to obtain food on an intermittent schedule of reinforcement. Reinforcement was contingent on a high and steady rate of pecking at the specified visual feature.

In a personal conversation on Project Pigeon in 1989, Skinner indicated that he kept some of the birds when funding was

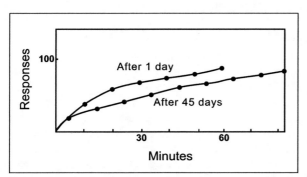

FIG. 4.16 Average extinction curves of four rats 1 day after training and 45 days after training. Curves are from Skinner, 1938, Appleton-Century-Crofts, New York.

discontinued. The birds were housed in a coop in his garden. Skinner said that over a period of 6 years he tested the birds for retention. The birds were food deprived and placed in the original apparatus after 6 months, 1 year, 2 years, 4 years, and 6 years.

Unfortunately, Skinner said that most of the data were unavailable. However, he was impressed that the birds responded immediately to the target image at a high and steady rate. All subjects produced extensive extinction curves even after several years had passed since the initial training. One remarkable observation was that "the extinction curves became smaller" with greater passage of time. Again, passage of time does not seem to affect forgetting, since the birds immediately pecked the target. However, as with the rats, resistance to extinction declined as a function of the retention interval.

ON THE APPLIED SIDE: Extinction of temper tantrums

C. D. Williams (1959) has shown how extinction effects play an important role in the modification of human behavior. In this study, a 20-month-old child was making life miserable for his parents by having temper tantrums when put to bed. If the parents stayed up with the child, he did not scream and cry and eventually went to sleep. A well-known source of reinforcement for children is parental attention, and Williams reasoned that this was probably maintaining the bedtime behavior. That is, when the parents left the bedroom, the child began screaming and crying. These tantrums were reinforced by the return of the parents to the bedroom. The parental behavior stopped the tantrum and withdrawal of screaming by the child reinforced the parental behavior of returning to the bedroom. Base on these contingencies, the parents were spending a good part of each evening in the child's room waiting for him to go to sleep. At this point, the parents were advised to implement extinction by leaving the room and closing the door after the child was put to bed. Figure 4.17 demonstrates the rapid decline in duration of crying when this was done (first extinction).

When extinction was first attempted, the child screamed and cried for 45 min. However, on the next night he did not cry at all. On the third night, the child emitted tantrums for 10 min. By the end of 10 days, the boy was smiling at his parents when they left the room. Unfortunately, his aunt reinforced crying by staying in the room with him when she put him to bed and the temper tantrums reoccurred. A second extinction procedure was then implemented. Duration of crying was longer for the second than for the first period of extinction. The higher probability of response during the second extinction phase is presumably caused by the intermittent reinforcement of tantrums. Recall that intermittent reinforcement increases resistance to extinction. Fortunately, the boy was not reinforced again and tantrums eventually declined to a zero rate. At a 2-year follow-up, the parents reported that bedtime tantrums had been completely eliminated.

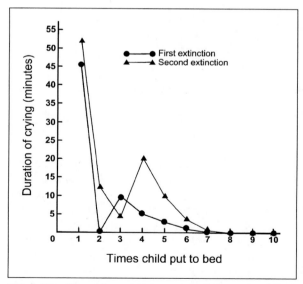

FIG 4.17 First and second extinction procedures for a child's temper tantrums. Adapted from "The Elimination of Tantrum Behavior by Extinction Procedures," by C. D. Williams, 1959, *Journal of Abnormal and Social Psychology, 59*, 269. Adapted with permission from APA.

CHAPTER SUMMARY

In this important chapter, we have addressed the concept that behavior is a function of its consequences. Operants are responses that operate on the environment to produce changes and as a result have an increased (or decreased) probability of occurrence. The measure of the probability of response is most often the rate of operant behavior. If the rate of the particular behavior (or class of behaviors) increases as a result of some specific consequence, then that consequence is defined as a positive reinforcer. The exact definition of a positive reinforcer as a stimulus or event that increases or maintains the rate of the response upon which it is contingent, is fundamental to the science of behavior. The reinforcer is contingent (dependent) upon (delivered after) the response, and no matter what the stimulus, it increases the frequency of operant behavior.

Other situations exist that require formal definitions. For example, when you encounter a disturbing event you may turn away or cover your ears; these behaviors are strengthened by the removal or reduction in occurrence of the event. This is a type of response strengthening called negative (subtracts the event) reinforcement (increases the escape response). Other consequences reduce the rate of the response that produces them and are called punishers. The procedure of making a punisher contingent on a response and the response decreases is called punishment.

If some behavior has a low probability of occurrence, the response can be shaped by reinforcement of successive approximations. In this way new behavior is generated from the variability existing in the response repertoire. When reinforcement is no longer delivered the rate of the response declines back to baseline. This is the process of extinction. For example, if a rat presses a lever and food pellets are delivered it will continue to press the lever as long as some responses are followed by food. When no pellets are delivered, however, the rate of lever pressing eventually declines to zero. This simple demonstration of reinforcement followed by extinction illustrates the central point of the chapter: behavior is a function of its consequences.

Behavior analysis is a formal discipline based on manipulating consequences and thereby shaping, directing, and altering the behavior of organisms. Precise procedures and apparatus have been invented in order to systematize this analysis.

Key Words

Ad libitum weight
Conditioned reinforcer
Contingency of reinforcement
Contingent response
Continuous reinforcement
  (CRF)
Cumulative record
Cumulative recorder
Deprivation operation
Differential reinforcement
Discriminated extinction
Discriminative stimulus (S^D)
Elicited
Emitted
Emotional response

Extinction
Extinction burst
Free operant method
Instrumental response
Intermittent reinforcement
  schedule
In vitro reinforcement
Latency
Law of effect
Magazine training
Negative punishment
Negative reinforcement
Operant
Operant chamber
Operant class

Operant conditioning
Operant level
Operant rate
Operant variability
Partial reinforcement effect
  (PRE)
Positive punishment
Positive reinforcement
Positive reinforcer
Premack principle
Probability of response
Rate of response
Repertoire (of behavior)
Resistance to extinction
Response deprivation

Response differentiation
Response hierarchy
Satiation

S-delta (S^Δ)
Selection of behavior
Shaping

Spontaneous recovery
Successive approximation
Topography

Schedules of Reinforcement

5

- Learn about *schedules of reinforcement* and why they are important.
- Discover how schedules of reinforcement generate characteristic patterns of behavior.
- Find out about the Mechner system of notation and its application to an analysis of schedules of reinforcement.
- Investigate rates of reinforcement and how behavior is made resistant to change.
- Inquire about behavior during transition between schedules of reinforcement and the application to human behavior.
- Discover how schedules of reinforcement are involved when people want to stop smoking.
- Learn about the molecular and molar accounts of performance on schedules of reinforcement.

The stimuli that precede operants and the consequences that follow them may be arranged in many different ways. A **schedule of reinforcement** describes this arrangement. In other words, a schedule of reinforcement is a prescription that states how and when discriminative stimuli and behavioral consequences will be presented (Morse, 1966). In the laboratory, sounding a buzzer in an operant chamber may be a signal (S^D) that sets the occasion for each lever press (operant) to produce food (consequence). A similar schedule operates when a dark room sets the occasion for a person to turn on a lamp that is followed by light in the room.

At first glance, a rat pressing a lever for food and a person turning on a light seem to have little in common. Humans are very complex organisms: They build cities, write books, go to college, go to war, conduct experiments, and do many other things that rats cannot do. In addition, pressing a bar for food appears to be very different from switching on a light. Nonetheless, performances controlled by schedules of reinforcement have been found to be remarkably similar for different organisms, many types of behavior, and a variety of reinforcers. When the schedule of reinforcement is the same, a child solving math problems for teacher approval may generate a pattern of behavior that is comparable to a bird pecking a key for water.

IMPORTANCE OF SCHEDULES OF REINFORCEMENT

Schedules of reinforcement have been investigated over the last five decades. They were first described by B. F. Skinner in the 1930s and were a major discovery. Charles Ferster and B. F. Skinner reported (Ferster & Skinner, 1957) the first and most comprehensive study of schedules ever conducted. Their work on this topic is unsurpassed and represents the most extensive study of this critical independent variable in behavior science. Today, few studies focus directly on simple schedules of reinforcement. However, the lawful relations that have emerged from the analysis of schedules remain an important part of the science of behavior and are used in virtually every study reported in the *Journal of the Experimental Analysis of Behavior*.

C. B. FERSTER: Schedules of reinforcement

In 1957, Charles Bohris Ferster (Figure 5.1) together with B. F. Skinner published *Schedules of Reinforcement*, the most comprehensive description of the behavior (performance) generated by different contingencies of reinforcement. Charles was born in Feehold, New Jersey on 1 November 1922 in the Depression years and, even though life was difficult for the Ferster family, he completed high school and entered Rutgers University in 1940. After receiving his BS degree at Rutgers and doing military service from 1943 to 1946, Charles went on to Columbia University where he studied the reinforcing effects of stimuli (conditioned reinforcers) presented during intermittent reinforcement. He obtained his PhD in 1950 and took a Research Fellowship at Harvard in the behavioral laboratory of B. F. Skinner.

At the Harvard laboratory, Charlie (as he was called) impressed Skinner by vastly improving the design of the equipment used to study the performance of pigeons on a variety of schedules of reinforcement. For example, Charlie made several improvements in the cumulative recorder that eventually resulted in the design by Ralph Gerbrands of the first modern-style instrument, as shown in Chapter 4. In the laboratory, Charlie worked night and day and together with Skinner made Grand Rounds each morning, inspecting cumulative records of pigeons' rates of response and making changes in the programmed schedules. Often there were suprises as Ferster and Skinner tried to predict the performance of the birds under complex schedules; they would then add a new piece of control equipment such as a clock or timer to see what would happen—and again the researchers found the results surprising and dramatic. Charlie said that over a year he stopped predicting the outcomes of experiments as the prediction was often incorrect and "the pigeon really did know best what it was he was likely to do and the conditions under which he would do it" (Ferster, 2000, p. 306).

Ferster and Skinner noted that the only contact that the pigeons had with the programming equipment was at the *moment of reinforcement* but that many stimuli could be involved at this moment, determining the current rate of response and changes in response rates. Stimuli arising from the passage of time and from the number of responses made on the schedule were obvious sources of stimulus control; Ferster and Skinner designed experiments to enhance these stimuli so as to observe the effects in the cumulative records. In recalling these experiments and interactions with Skinner, Ferster (2000) states:

There were many personal and natural consequences of completing a successful experiment [other than the results from the actual behavior of the birds]. A successful experiment lead to conversations about the data, the new devices we could build, the new experiments that had to be started, and the new ways we could organize our past experience from the laboratory.

When we discovered a new degree of orderliness or an unexpected but rewarding result on morning rounds, there was always much excitement and talk about where the experiment might go next and how to manage the equipment for the next experiment that was burning to be done because of the new result.

When new discoveries accumulated too fast . . . there were planning sessions which were always great fun and very exciting. . . . I learned the value of large sheets of paper which we used to aid our thought and to chart our progress. . . . The theoretical structures [organized by the charts] and programmatic aspects of our work appeared as [headings . . .] to appear as chapter and subchapter titles in *Schedules of Reinforcement*. Each entry prompted rearrangements of the theoretical pattern and suggested new experiments and programs which in turn prompted further rearrangements of the data. The interactions between these theoretical exercises and changes in ongoing experiments in the laboratory were continuous and constituted an important reinforcer.

(p. 307)

Most of the experiments for *Schedules of Reinforcement* were completed by 1953 and the writing of the book continued slowly until Ferster received an appointment at the Yerkes Laboratories to begin in 1955. This led Ferster and Skinner to redesign the working environment for high rates of writing and to develop several ways of self-management. They did the work in a room dedicated only to writing and did not take phone calls, to reduce interruptions. When people came to the door, Ferster or Skinner would step into the hallway to speak with them briefly. They began at nine and stopped at lunchtime but did not work in the afternoon, even if they had been productive in the morning or were interested in the data. Their research on fixed-ratio performance convinced them not to work in the afternoon to insure that productivity was at maximum frequency for the morning period of writing.

Ferster and Skinner's program for self-management increased their rate of writing and resulted in the book on schedules of reinforcement that was published in 1957 by Appleton-Century-Crofts. By the publication date, Charlie Ferster had taken an appointment at Indiana University Medical Center where he used his behavior analysis skills with autistic children—subsequently writing *An Introduction to the Science of Human Behavior* with John I. Nurnberger and John Paul Brady in 1963 (Nurnberger, Ferster, & Brady, 1963). Ferster had a distinguished and influential career that is detailed by Fred Keller in an appreciation for his work published in 1981, following Ferster's death. Looking back on his own experience of writing *Schedules of Reinforcement* and what he had learned, Charlie Ferster stated that "a potential reinforcing environment exists for every individual, however, if he will only emit the required performances on the proper occasion. One has merely to paint the picture, write the symphony, produce the machine, tell the funny story, give affection artfully or manipulate the environment and observe the behavior of the animal, and the world will respond in kind with prestige, money, social response, love, and recognition for scientific achievement" (2000, p. 311).

*   *   *

The knowledge that has accumulated about the effects of schedules is central to understanding behavior regulation. G. S. Reynolds (1966b) underscored this point and wrote:

Schedules of reinforcement have regular, orderly, and profound effects on the organism's rate of responding. The importance of schedules of reinforcement cannot be overestimated. No description, account, or explanation of any operant behavior of any organism is complete unless the schedule of reinforcement is specified. Schedules are the mainsprings of behavioral control, and thus the study of schedules is central to the study of behavior. . . . Behavior that has been attributed to the supposed drives, needs, expectations, ruminations, or insights of the organism can often be related much more exactly to regularities produced by schedules of reinforcement.

(p. 60)

Modern technology has made it possible to analyze performance on schedules of reinforcement in increasing detail. Nonetheless, early experiments on schedules remain important. The experimental analysis of behavior is a progressive science in which observations and experiments build on one another. In this chapter, we will present early and later research on schedules of reinforcement. The analysis of schedule performance will range from a global consideration of cumulative records to a detailed consideration of the time between responses.

FOCUS ON: Science and behavior analysis

The experimental analysis of behavior is a progressive enterprise. Research findings are accumulated and integrated to provide a general account of the behavior of organisms. Often, simple animals in highly controlled settings are studied. The strategy is to build a comprehensive theory of behavior that rests on direct observation and experimentation.

The field emphasizes a descriptive approach and discourages speculations that go beyond the data. Such speculations include reference to the organism's memory, thought processes, expectations, and undocumented accounts based on presumed physiological states. For example, a behavioral account of schedules of reinforcement provides a description of how behavior is altered by contingencies of reinforcement. One such account is based on evidence that a particular schedule sets up differential reinforcement of the time between responses (interresponse times, or IRT; see later in this chapter). This sort of analysis provides an understanding of an organism's performance in terms of specific environment–behavior relationships.

Behavior analysts study the behavior of organisms, including people, for its own sake. Behavior is not studied to make inferences about hypothetical mental states or real physiological processes. Although most behaviorists emphasize the importance of biology and physiological processes, they focus on the interplay of behavior and environment.

To maintain this focus, the evolutionary history and biological status of an organism are examined as part of the context for specific environment–behavior interactions. For example, some people seem more influenced by sexual stimuli than others. Natural selection may have resulted in a distribution of susceptibility to sexual reinforcement (of course, cultural conditioning will also contribute). People who are strongly affected by sexual consequences may develop a broad repertoire of behavior that leads to sexual gratification. When given a choice between sexual and nonsexual reinforcement, the person will often select the sexual alternative. In extreme cases, behavior regulated by sexual stimuli may be so exaggerated that the person is called a criminal and is subjected to legal sanctions. A man who makes obscene phone calls is strongly reinforced by a woman's reaction to his words. The woman's reaction is a conditioned reinforcer for his call. Although he has learned the relationship between obscene talk and listener reaction, his biological history plays a role in the effectiveness of the reinforcement contingency.

Accumulating information about environment–behavior relations has, in recent years, led to the formulation of several principles of behavior. For example, animals and people are much more persistent on a task when they have been reinforced on a schedule that only pays off occasionally. This persistence is especially pronounced during extinction and is called the *partial reinforcement effect* (as discussed in Chapter 4). One can observe this phenomenon by contrasting behavior at a vending machine that delivers products on a regular basis and a slot machine that delivers payouts intermittently. If the vending machine does not work, the operater stops inserting coins; but the same person may persist for hours at operating a slot machine that provides highly intermittent payouts. Other principles of behavior (e.g., discrimination, motivation, and conditioned reinforcement) also have been identified through the experimental analysis of schedule effects.

As more information becomes available, the goal of a comprehensive behavior theory comes closer. Chapter 9 presents work on concurrent schedules of reinforcement. This research has been prominent over the recent past and today is used to formulate theories and models of behavioral choice and preference. These theories draw on earlier work and become more complete and sophisticated as data accumulate.

Contemporary behavior analysis continues to build on previous research. The extension of behavior principles to more complex processes and especially to human behavior is of primary importance. The analysis remains focused on the environmental conditions that regulate the behavior of organisms. Schedules of reinforcement concern the arrangement of environmental events that support behavior. The analysis of schedule effects is currently viewed within a biological context. In this analysis, biological factors play several roles. One way biology affects behavior is through specific physiological events that function as reinforcement and discriminative stimuli (see Chapter 1). Biological variables may also constrain or enhance environment–behavior relationships, as we have noted. As behavior analysis and the other biological sciences progress, an understanding of biological factors becomes increasingly important for a comprehensive theory of behavior.

Schedules and Patterns of Response

Patterns of response develop as a result of the organism interacting with a schedule of reinforcement (Ferster & Skinner, 1957). These patterns come about after an animal has experience with the *contingency of reinforcement* ($S^D : R \rightarrow S^r$ arrangement) defined by a particular schedule. Subjects are exposed to a schedule of reinforcement and, following an acquisition period, behavior typically settles into a consistent or **steady-state performance** (Sidman, 1960). It may take many experimental sessions before a particular pattern emerges, but once it does the orderliness of behavior is remarkable.

The first description of schedule performance was provided by B. F. Skinner (1938) in his book, *The Behavior of Organisms*. In the preface to the seventh printing of that book, Skinner writes that "the cumulative records . . . purporting to show orderly changes in the behavior of individual organisms, occasioned some surprise and possibly, in some quarters suspicion" (p. xii). Any suspicion was put to rest when Skinner's observations were replicated in many other experiments (see Morse, 1966, for a review of early work on schedules of reinforcement).

The steady-state behavior generated when a fixed number of responses is reinforced illustrates one of these patterns. For example, a hungry rat might be required to press a lever 10 times to get a food pellet. Following reinforcement, the animal has to make another 10 responses to produce the next bit of food, and then 10 more responses. In industry this requirement is referred to as piece rate.

When organisms (rat, pigeon, or humans) are reinforced after a fixed number of responses, a pause-and-run pattern of behavior develops. Responses required by the schedule are made rapidly and result in reinforcement. Following each reinforcement, there is a pause in responding and then another quick burst of responses (see the section on the fixed ratio later in this chapter for more detail). This pattern repeats over and over and occurs even when the size of the schedule is changed. A pause-and-run pattern has been found for many species, including horses (Myers & Mesker, 1960), chickens (Lane, 1961), a vulture (Witoslawski, Anderson, & Hanson, 1963), and children (Orlando & Bijou, 1960).

COMMENT ON: Inner causes, schedules, and response patterns

We sometimes speak of people being "highly motivated" when we observe them investing energy or time into a project. Motivation seems to explain why people behave as they do. Schoolchildren are said to be unmotivated when they put off or fail to do assignments; in contrast, children are highly motivated when they study hard and overachieve. From a behavioral perspective, there is no need to infer a hypothetical internal process of motivation to understand this kind of behavior. Schedules of reinforcement generate unique and predictable patterns of behavior that are often taken as signs of high motivation; other schedules produce pausing and low rates of response, used as indicators of low motivation. In both cases, behavior is due to environmental contingencies rather than the inferred inner cause of motivation.

Similarly, habits or personality traits are said to be "response dispositions that are activated automatically by context cues that co-occurred with responses during past performance" (Neal,

Wood, & Quinn, 2006). Here reference is made to internal dispositions that account for regular and frequent actions. Instead of inferring dispositions as internal causes, one might say that habits or traits are patterns of steady-state responding; these regularities of behavior are maintained by the consistency of the schedule of reinforcement. That is, a consistent or reliable schedule of reinforcement generates stable rates and patterns of responding. It is these characteristics of behavior that often are used to infer dispositional causes. A behavior analysis indicates that the real causes are the behavioral contingencies rather than dispositional states within us.

Schedules and Natural Contingencies

In the everyday environment, behavior is often reinforced on an intermittent basis. That is, operants are reinforced occasionally rather than each time they are emitted. Every time a child cries, she is not reinforced with attention. Each time a predator hunts, it is not successful. When you dial the number for airport information, you get through sometimes, but often the exchange is busy. Buses do not immediately arrive when you go to a bus stop. It is clear that persistence is often essential for survival and therefore being able to account for such behavior on the basis of the schedule that maintains it is a major discovery. In concluding his review of schedule research, Dr. Michael Zeiler (1977) states:

> It is impossible to study behavior either in or outside the laboratory without encountering a schedule of reinforcement: whenever behavior is maintained by a reinforcing stimulus, some schedule is in effect and is exerting its characteristic influences. Only when there is a clear understanding of how schedules operate will it be possible to understand the effects of reinforcing stimuli on behavior.
>
> (p. 229)

Consider a bird foraging for food. The bird turns over sticks or leaves and once in a while finds a seed or insect. These bits of food occur only every now and then, and the distribution of reinforcement is the schedule that maintains the animal's foraging behavior. If you were watching this bird hunt for food, you would probably see the animal's head bobbing up and down. You might also see the bird pause and look around, change direction, and move to a new spot. This sort of activity is often attributed to the animal's instinctive behavior patterns. However, labeling the behavior as instinctive does not explain it. Although biology certainly plays a role in this episode, perhaps as importantly so does the schedule of food reinforcement.

Dr. Carl Cheney and colleagues created a laboratory analog of foraging that allowed pigeons to choose between two food patches by pecking keys (Cheney, Bonem, & Bonem, 1985). The density of food available from pecking either key was based on two concurrent **progressive ratio schedules** of reinforcement that increased or decreased the ratio requirement with the amount of foraging. As reinforcers were removed from one patch, they became more scarce and required more responses to produce them; this was a progressively increasing ratio schedule (or depleting patch of food). Concurrently, the number of responses for each reinforcement decreased in the other patch (or a repleting patch of food)—a progressively decreasing ratio schedule. As would be expected, this change in reinforcement density up and down generated switching back and forth between the two patches. However, to change patches the center key had to be pecked, which simulated travel time and effort between patches (the side keys). Cheney and colleagues found that the cost of hunting (the schedule of reinforcement for pecking) in a patch, the effort (number of responses) required to change patches, and the rate of food replacement in the alternative patch all contributed to the likelihood that an animal would change patches. This research is an interesting example of an animal model of foraging that uses schedules of reinforcement to simulate natural contingencies in the wild.

Schedules of intermittent reinforcement play an important role in the regulation of human social interaction. In this case, the behavior of one person affects what another individual does, and vice versa. For example, Paul asks his friend Erin, who is looking out of the window, if the pizza delivery person has arrived yet. The operant is Paul's question, "Is the pizza here?" Reinforcement for the question is the reply from Erin. Importantly, Erin's reply is not certain and depends on many factors. Erin may not hear the question; she may be preoccupied with other things; she may have just had an argument with Paul and refuse to talk. No matter what the reason, Paul's question may not be reinforced on a particular occasion. Of course, most of the time Erin answers when asked a question. This means that Paul's verbal behavior is on an intermittent schedule of social reinforcement. Thus, one reason why schedules are important is that they approximate some of the complex contingencies that operate with humans in the everyday environment. This type of interactive verbal conversation is cleverly simulated with pigeons in the video *Cognition, Creativity and Behavior* (Baxley, 1982).

Ongoing Behavior and Schedule Effects

Zeiler's (1977) point that schedules of reinforcement typically affect operant behavior is well taken. Experimenters risk misinterpreting results when they ignore possible schedule effects. This is because schedules of reinforcement may interact with a variety of other independent variables and produce characteristic effects. For example, Azrin (1959) found that when every response on a fixed-ratio schedule of reinforcement (reinforcement occurs after a fixed number of responses) was punished, the pause length after reinforcement increased. However, once the animal emitted the first response, the operant rate to finish the run was unaffected. In other words, the pause increased but otherwise behavior on the schedule remained the same. A possible conclusion is that punishment reduces the tendency to begin responding; however, once started, behavior is not suppressed by contingent aversive stimulation.

This conclusion is not completely correct because further experiments have shown that punishment has other effects when behavior is maintained on a different schedule of reinforcement (Azrin, 1958; Azrin & Holz, 1961). When behavior is reinforced after a fixed amount of time (rather than responses), an entirely different result occurs. On this kind of schedule, when each operant is punished, the pattern of behavior remains the same and the rate of response declines. It is obvious that conclusions concerning the effects of punishment on pattern and rate of response cannot be made without considering the schedule of reinforcement maintaining the behavior.

In summary, schedules of reinforcement produce reliable patterns of response, and these patterns are consistent for different reinforcers, organisms, and a variety of different operants. In our everyday environment, schedules of reinforcement are so common that we take such effects for granted. We wait for a taxi to arrive, line up at a bank to negotiate a transaction, and solve 10 math problems for homework. All of these behavior–environment interactions illustrate schedules of reinforcement in our everyday lives.

FOCUS ON: A system of notation

We have found that using a notation system greatly improves the understanding of contingencies between antecedents, behavior, and consequences. This notation system is based on Mechner's (1959) description of reinforcement contingencies. We have simplified the notation and relabeled some of the symbols. The system of notation only describes independent variables and is similar to a flow chart sometimes used in computer programming. That is, **Mechner notation** describes what the experimenter (instrumentation or computer) does, not the behavior of organisms. In other words, Mechner notation represents the way (sequence of events, the requirements, etc.) that schedules of reinforcement are arranged. Cumulative records or other data collected by computers describe what a subject does (i.e., the dependent variable) on those schedules.

Event	Symbols
S	Stimulus or event
S^r	Reinforcer
S^{r+}	Positive reinforcer
S^{r-}	Negative reinforcer (aversive stimulus)
S^D	Discriminative stimulus (event signaling reinforcement)
S^Δ	S-delta (a discriminative stimulus that signals extinction)
S^{ave}	Conditioned aversive stimulus (an event that has signaled punishment)
R	Response (operant class)
R_a	Response of type a (i.e., a response on lever a)

Time and number symbols

F	Fixed
V	Variable
T	Time
N	Number

Relationships

The horizontal arrow connecting two events (i.e., A → B) indicates that one event follows another. When the arrow leads to a consequence, as in R → S^r, the arrow is read as *produces*. In this case, a response (R) *produces* a consequence (S^r). If the arrow leads to a response, as in R_a → R_b, it is read as *produces a condition where*. In other words, response R_a "sets up" or allows response R_b to produce an effect. For example, a press on lever "a" creates a situation where a press on lever "b" results in food.

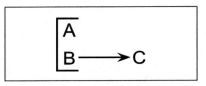

FIG. 5.2 Relations within brackets in Mechner notation. A and B occur and B produces event C.

Brackets

All conditions listed vertically inside a bracket go into effect simultaneously (Figure 5.2). For example, A and B are conditions that occur at the same time, and the occurrence of B leads to event C.

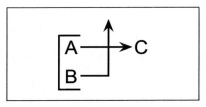

FIG. 5.3 Relations within brackets in Mechner notation. A and B occur; A produces event C but not if B occurs.

When a vertical arrow cuts across a horizontal arrow (Figure 5.3) , it means that the diagrammed event is prevented. In the following example, A and B occur at the same time. Event A leads to condition C, but event B blocks the A → C relationship. In other words, A leads to C but not if A and B occur together.

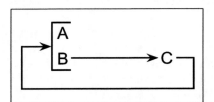

FIG. 5.4 Relations within brackets in Mechner notation. A and B occur and B produces event C. After C occurs the sequence repeats.

When events repeat (Figure 5.4), this may be shown by a horizontal arrow that starts at the end of a sequence and goes back to the beginning. In the presence of A, the event B produces C; and after C occurs, the sequence repeats.

Mechner notation is especially helpful when complex contingencies are involved and the experimenter has to program a computer or other instrumentation for contingencies arranged in an operant chamber. Using this notation system also aids students in specifying exactly what the events, requirements, and their interactions are in an experiment. Finally, the notation makes explicit the programmed contingencies that control the behavior of organisms.

SCHEDULES OF POSITIVE REINFORCEMENT

Continuous Reinforcement

Continuous reinforcement, or **CRF**, is probably the simplest schedule of reinforcement. On this schedule, every operant required by the contingency is reinforced. For example, every time a hungry pigeon pecks a key, food is presented. When every operant is followed by a reinforcer, responses are emitted relatively quickly depending upon the consumatory time for the reinforcer. The organism continues to respond until it is satiated. Simply put, when the bird is hungry (food deprived), it rapidly pecks the key and eats the food until it is full (satiated). If the animal is again deprived of the reinforcer and exposed to a CRF schedule, this pattern of responding followed by satiation occurs again. Figure 5.5 is a typical cumulative record of performance on continuous reinforcement. As mentioned previously in this chapter, the typical vending machine delivers products on a continuous (CRF) schedule.

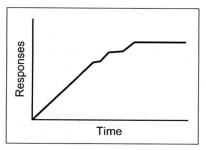

FIG. 5.5 Performance on a continuous reinforcement schedule. Hatch marks indicating reinforcement are omitted since each response is reinforced. The flat portion of the record occurs when the animal stops making the response because of satiation.

CRF and resistance to extinction

Continuous reinforcement generates little resistance to extinction compared with intermittent reinforcement (Harper & McLean, 1992; Jenkins & Stanley, 1950). Recall from Chapter 4 that *resistance to extinction* is a measure of persistence when reinforcement is discontinued. This perseverance can be measured in several ways. The most obvious way to measure resistance to extinction is to count the number of responses and measure the length of time until *operant level* is reached. Again, remember from Chapter 4 that operant level refers to the rate of a response before behavior is reinforced. For example, a laboratory rat could be placed in an operant chamber with no explicit contingency of reinforcement in effect. The number of times the animal pressed the response bar during a 2-h exploration of the chamber is a measure of operant level, or in this case baseline. Once extinction is in effect, measuring the time taken and number of responses made until operant level is attained is the best gauge of resistance to extinction.

Although continuing extinction until operant level is obtained provides the best measure of behavioral persistence, this method requires considerable time and effort. Therefore, arbitrary measures that take less time are usually used. Resistance to extinction may be estimated by counting the number of responses emitted over a fixed number of sessions. For example, after exposure to CRF, reinforcement could be discontinued and the number of responses made in three daily 1-h sessions counted. Another index of resistance to extinction is based on how fast the rate of response declines during nonreinforced sessions. The point at which no response occurs for 5 min may be used to index resistance. The number of responses and time taken to that point are used as an estimate of behavioral persistence. These measures and others may be used to indicate resistance to extinction. The important criterion is that the method must be quantitatively related to extinction responding.

Hearst (1961) investigated the resistance to extinction produced by CRF and intermittent schedules. In this experiment, birds were trained on CRF and two intermittent schedules that provided reinforcement for pecking a key. The number of extinction responses that the animals made during three daily sessions of nonreinforcement were then counted. Basically, Hearst found that the birds made many more extinction responses after training on an intermittent schedule than after exposure to continuous reinforcement.

Response stereotypy on CRF

On continuous reinforcement schedules, the form or topography of response becomes stereotypical. In a classic study, Antonitis (1951) found that on CRF operants were repeated with very little change or variability in topography. In this study, rats were required to poke their noses anywhere along a 50-cm horizontal slot to get a food pellet (see Figure 5.6). Although not required by the contingency, the animals frequently responded at the same position on the slot. Only when the rats were placed on extinction did responses become more variable. These findings are not limited to laboratory rats and may reflect a principle of behavior.

Further research with pigeons suggests that response variability may be inversely related to the rate of reinforcement. In other words, as more and more responses are reinforced, less and less variation occurs in the members of the operant class. Herrnstein (1961a) reinforced pigeons for pecking on an intermittent schedule. The birds pecked at a horizontal strip and were occasionally reinforced with food. When some responses were reinforced, most of the birds pecked at the center of the strip—although they were not required to do so. During extinction, the animals made fewer responses to the center and more to other positions on the strip. Eckerman and Lanson (1969) replicated this finding in a subsequent study also with pigeons. They varied the rate of reinforcement and compared response variability under CRF, intermittent reinforcement, and extinction. Responses were stereotypical on CRF and became more variable when the birds were on extinction or on an intermittent schedule.

One interpretation of these findings is that organisms become more variable in their responding as reinforcement becomes less frequent or predictable. When a schedule of reinforcement is changed from CRF to intermittent reinforcement, the rate of reinforcement declines and response variability increases. A further change in rate of reinforcement occurs when extinction is started. In this case, operants are no longer reinforced and response variation is maximum. The general principle appears to be, "When things no longer work, try new ways of behaving." Or, as the saying goes, "If at first you don't succeed, try, try again."

In solving a problem, people usually employ a solution that has worked in the past. When the usual solution does not work, people try novel approaches to solving the problem. Pretend that you are a camper who is trying to start a fire. Most of the time, you gather leaves and sticks, place them in a heap, strike a match, and start the fire. This time the fire does not start. What do you do? If you are like most of us, you try different ways to get the fire going, many of which may have worked in the past. You may change the kindling, add newspaper, use lighter fluid, swear at the fire pit, or even build a shelter. Clearly, your behavior becomes more variable when reinforcement is withheld after a period of success. This increase in topographic variability during extinction after a period of reinforcement has been refered to as **resurgence** (Epstein, 1983, 1985) and can contribute to the development of creative or original behavior.

In summary, CRF is the simplest schedule of positive reinforcement. On this schedule, every response produces a reinforcer. Continuous reinforcement produces little resistance to extinction. This schedule also generates stereotypical response topographies. Both resistance to extinction and variation in form of response increase on intermittent schedules.

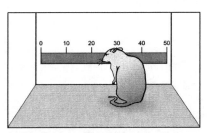

FIG. 5.6 The apparatus used by Antonitis (1951). Rats could poke their noses anywhere along the 50-cm horizontal slot to obtain reinforcement.

RATIO AND INTERVAL SCHEDULES OF REINFORCEMENT

On intermittent schedules of reinforcement, some rather than all responses are reinforced. **Ratio schedules** are response based; that is, these schedules are set to deliver reinforcement following a prescribed number of responses; the ratio specifies the number of responses for each reinforcer. **Interval schedules** pay off when one response is made after some amount of time has passed. Interval and ratio schedules may be fixed or variable. Fixed schedules set up reinforcement after a fixed number of responses, or a constant amount of time, has passed. On variable schedules, response and time requirements vary from one reinforcer to the next. Thus, there are four basic schedules: fixed ratio, variable ratio, fixed interval, and variable interval. In this section, we describe these

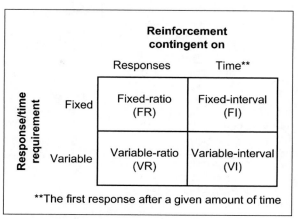

FIG. 5.7   A table of the four basic schedules of positive reinforcement. Adapted from *Behavior Principles*, by C. B. Ferster, S. Culbertson, and M. C. P. Boren, 1975, Prentice-Hall, Englewood Cliffs, NJ.

four basic schedules of reinforcement (shown in Figure 5.7) and illustrate the typical effects they produce. Following this discussion, some of the reasons for these effects are analyzed.

Ratio Schedules

Fixed ratio

A **fixed-ratio (FR)** schedule is programmed to deliver reinforcement after a fixed number of responses is made. Continuous reinforcement (CRF) is FR 1; that is, the ratio is one reinforcer for one response. Figure 5.8 presents a fixed-ratio schedule diagrammed in Mechner notation. The notation is read, "In the presence of a discriminative stimulus (S^D), a fixed number (N) of responses (R) produces an unconditioned reinforcer (S^{R+})." In a simple animal experiment, the S^D is sensory stimulation arising from the operant chamber, the response is a lever press, and food functions as reinforcement. On fixed-ratio 25 (FR 25), 25 lever presses must be made before food is presented. After reinforcement, the returning arrow indicates that another 25 responses will again produce the reinforcer.

The symbol N is used to indicate that fixed-ratio schedules can assume any value. Of course, it is unlikely that very high values (say, FR 100,000,000) would ever be completed. Nonetheless, this should remind you that Mechner notation describes independent variables, not what the organism does. Indeed, FR 100,000,000 could be easily programmed, but this schedule is essentially an extinction contingency because the animal will never complete the response requirement for reinforcement.

In 1957, Ferster and Skinner described the FR schedule and the characteristic effects, patterns, and rates, along with cumulative records of performance on about 15 other sched-

FIG. 5.8   A fixed-ratio schedule of positive reinforcement diagrammed in Mechner notation. In the presence of an S^D, a fixed number of responses results in reinforcement (S^{r+}). As indicated by the returning arrow, the sequence repeats such that another fixed number of responses will again produce reinforcement.

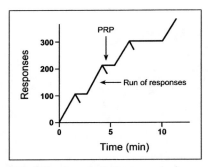

FIG. 5.9   A cumulative record of well-developed performance on FR 100. The typical pause-and-run pattern is presented. Reinforcement is indicated by the hatch marks. This is an idealized record that is typical of performance on many fixed-ratio schedules.

ules of reinforcement (see section on C. B. Ferster in this chapter). Their observations remain valid after literally thousands of replications: FR schedules produce a rapid run of responses, followed by reinforcement, and then a pause in responding (Ferster & Skinner, 1957; Weissman & Crossman, 1966). An idealized cumulative record of behavior on fixed ratio is presented in Figure 5.9. The record looks somewhat like a set of stairs (except at very small FR values, as shown by Crossman, Trapp, Bonem, & Bonem, 1985). There is a steep period of responding (the run), followed by reinforcement (oblique line), and finally a flat portion (the pause). The flat part of the cumulative record is called the **postreinforcement pause**, or **PRP**, to indicate where it occurred.

The pause in responding after the reinforcer is delivered does not occur because the organism is consuming the reinforcer. Research shows that the length of the PRP generated in FR schedules is due to the *upcoming ratio requirement*. Mixed FR schedules described later in this chapter also illustrate the influence of to-be-completed response requirements on FR pausing. The number of responses required and the size of the reinforcer have both been shown to influence PRP (Inman & Cheney, 1974). Calling this pause a "post" reinforcement event accurately locates the pause but the upcoming requirements are what control it. Hence, researchers often refer to the PRP as a **preratio pause** (e.g., Derenne & Baron, 2002; Derenne, Richardson, & Baron, 2006).

Conditioned reinforcers like money, praise, and successful completion of a task also produce a pause when they are scheduled on fixed ratio. Consider what you might do if you had 5 sets of 10 math problems to complete for a homework assignment. A good bet is that you would solve 10 problems and then take a break before starting on the next set. When constructing a sun deck, one of the authors bundled nails into lots of 50 each. This had an effect on the "nailing behavior" of friends who were helping to build the deck. The pattern that developed was to put in 50 nails, then stop, drink some beer, look over what was accomplished, have a chat, and finally start nailing again. In other words, a pause-and-run pattern typical of FR was generated by this simple scheduling of the nails.

Variable ratio

FIG. 5.10   A variable-ratio schedule of positive reinforcement. The symbol V indicates that the number of responses required for reinforcement is varied from one sequence to the next. The schedule is indexed by the average number of responses required for reinforcement. That is, a VR 10 requires an average of 10 responses before reinforcement is presented.

Variable-ratio (VR) schedules are similar to FRs except that the number of responses required for reinforcement changes after each reinforcer is presented. A VR schedule is literally a series of FRs with each FR of a different size. The average number of responses is used to define the schedule. A subject may press a lever for reinforcement 5 times, then 15, 7, 3, and 20. Adding these response requirements for a total of 50 and then dividing by the number of separate response runs (5) yields the schedule value, VR 10. The symbol V in Figure 5.10 indicates that the number of responses required for any one reinforcer is variable. Other than this change, the contingency is identical to fixed ratio (see Figure 5.8).

In general, ratio schedules produce a high rate of response. When VR and FR schedules are compared, responding is typically faster on VR. One reason for this is that pausing after reinforcement (PRP) is reduced or eliminated when the ratio contingency is changed from fixed to variable. This provides further evidence that the PRP does not occur because the animal is tired or is consuming the reinforcer (i.e., eating food). A rat or pigeon responding for food on VR does not pause as many times or for as long after reinforcement. When VR schedules are not excessive, postreinforcement pauses do occur (Kintsch, 1965; Webbe, DeWeese, & Malagodi, 1978) although these pauses are typically smaller than those generated by FR schedules (Mazur, 1983). Figure 5.11 portrays a typical pattern of response on a VR schedule of positive reinforcement.

A VR schedule with a low mean ratio can contain some very small ratio requirements. For example, on a VR 10 schedule there cannot be many ratios requirements above 20 because, to offset those high ratios and average 10, there will have to be many very low ratios. It is the *occasional occurrence of a reinforcer right after another reinforcer (the short runs to reinforcement) that reduces the likelihood of pausing on a VR schedule of reinforcement.* Variable-ratio schedules with high mean ratios (e.g., VR 100) have fewer short ratios following one another and typically generate longer PRPs.

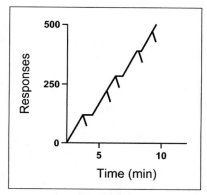

FIG. 5.11   A cumulative graph of typical responding on a variable-ratio schedule of reinforcement. Reinforcement is indicated by the hatch marks. Notice that PRPs are reduced or eliminated when compared with fixed-ratio performance.

In everyday life, variability and probability are routine; thus, ratio schedules involving probabilistic payoffs are more common than strict VR or FR contingencies from the laboratory. You may have to hit one nail three times to drive it in, and the next may take six swings of the hammer. It may, on the average, take 70 casts with a fly rod to catch a trout, but any one strike is probabilistic. In baseball, the batting average reflects the player's schedule of reinforcement. A batter with a .300 average gets 3 hits for 10 times at bat on average, but nothing guarantees a hit for any particular time at bat. The schedule depends on a complex interplay among conditions set by the pitcher and the skill of the batter.

Interval Schedules

Fixed interval

On **fixed-interval (FI)** schedules, an operant is reinforced after a fixed amount of time has passed. For example, on a fixed-interval 90-s schedule (FI 90 s), one bar press after 90 s results in reinforcement. Following reinforcement, another 90-s period goes into effect, and after this time has passed another response will produce reinforcement. It is important to note that responses made before the time period has elapsed have no effect. Notice that in Figure 5.12, one response (R) produces reinforcement (S^{r+}) after the fixed time period (FT) has passed. (*Note*: There is a schedule called *fixed time (FT)* in which reinforcement is delivered without a response following a set, or fixed, length of time. This is also referred to as a *response-independent schedule.* Unless otherwise specified, one should always assume that a response is required on whatever schedule is in effect.)

When organisms are exposed to interval contingencies and they have no way of telling time, they typically produce many more responses than the schedule requires. Fixed-interval

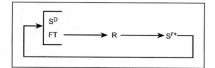

FIG. 5.12   A fixed-interval schedule. In the presence of an S^D, one response is reinforced after a fixed amount of time. Following reinforcement, the returning arrow states that the sequence starts again. This means that the fixed-time interval starts over and, after it has elapsed, one response will again be reinforced.

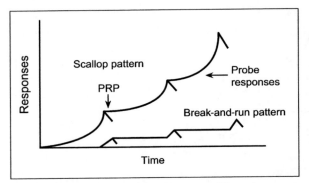

FIG. 5.13 Fixed-interval schedules usually produce a pattern that is called scalloping. There is a PRP following reinforcement and then a gradual increase in rate of response to the moment of reinforcement. Less common is the break-and-run pattern. Break and run occasionally develops after organisms have considerable experience on FI schedules. There is a long pause (break) after reinforcement, followed by a rapid burst (run) of responses.

schedules produce a characteristic steady-state pattern of responding. There is a pause after reinforcement (PRP), then a few probe responses, followed by more and more rapid responding to a constant high rate as the interval times out. This pattern of response is called **scalloping**. Figure 5.13 is an idealized cumulative record of FI performance. Each interreinforcement interval can be broken into three distinct classes: the PRP, followed by a period of gradually increasing rate, and finally a high terminal rate of responding.

Pretend that you have volunteered to be in an operant experiment. You are brought into a small room, and on one wall there is a lever with a cup under it. Other than those objects, the room is empty. You are not allowed to keep your watch while in the room, and you are told, "Do anything you want." After some time, you press the lever to see what it does. Ten dollars falls into the cup. A good prediction is that you will press the lever again. You are not told this, but the schedule is FI 5 min. You have 1 h per day to work on the schedule. If you collect all 12 (60 min ÷ 5 min = 12) of the scheduled reinforcers, you can make $120 a day.

Assume you have been in this experiment for 3 months. Immediately after collecting a $10 reinforcer, there is no chance that a response will pay off (discriminated extinction). However, as you are standing around, or doing anything else, the interval is timing out. You check out the contingency by making a probe response (you guess the time might be up). The next response occurs more quickly because even more time has gone by. As the interval continues to time out, the probability of reinforcement increases and your responses are made faster and faster. This pattern of responding is described by the scallop given in Figure 5.13 and is typical of FI schedules (Dews, 1969; Ferster & Skinner, 1957).

Following considerable experience with FI 5 min, you may get very good at judging the time period. In this case, you would wait out the interval and then emit a burst of responses. Perhaps you begin to pace back and forth during the session, and you find out that after 250 steps the interval has almost elapsed. This kind of mediating behavior may develop after experience with FI schedules (Muller, Crow, & Cheney, 1979). Other animals behave in a similar way and occasionally produce a **break-and-run** pattern of responding (Ferster & Skinner, 1957).

FOCUS ON: Generality of schedule effects

The **assumption of generality** implies that the effects of contingencies of reinforcement extend over species, reinforcement, and behavior (Morse, 1966, p. 59; Skinner, 1969, p. 101). For example, a fixed-interval schedule is expected to produce the scalloping pattern for a pigeon pecking a key for food, as well as for a child solving math problems for teacher approval.

Fergus Lowe (Figure 5.14) is a professor of psychology at the University College of North Wales who has questioned the generality of schedule effects. He states that "the question which provides the main focus of my research is one which should be central to all behavior analysis, namely, how do the principles of behavior derived from animal experiments apply to human behavior?" (personal communication, 20 March 1989).

Lowe (1979) has conducted numerous studies of fixed-interval performance with humans, who press a button to obtain points that are later exchanged for money. Figure 5.15 shows typical performances on fixed-interval schedules by a rat and two human subjects. Building on research by Harold Weiner (1969), Lowe argues that animals show the characteristic scalloping pattern, and humans generally do not. Humans often produce one of two patterns—an inefficient high, steady rate of response, or an efficient low-rate, break-and-run performance. Experiments by Lowe and colleagues have focused on the conditions that produce the high- or low-rate patterns in humans.

The basic idea is that schedule performance in humans reflects the influence of language (see Chapter 12 on verbal behavior). In conditioning experiments, people generate some verbal rule and proceed to behave according to the rule rather than the experimentally arranged contingencies. Lowe, Beasty, and Bentall (1983) commented that:

FIG. 5.14 Fergus Lowe. Published with permission.

> Verbal behavior can, and does, serve a discriminative function that alters the effects of other variables such as scheduled reinforcement. Unlike animals, most humans are capable of describing to themselves, whether accurately or inaccurately, environmental events and the ways in which those events impinge upon them; such descriptions may greatly affect the rest of their behavior.

(p. 162)

In most cases, people who follow self-generated rules satisfy the requirements of the schedule, obtain reinforcement, and continue to follow the rule. For example, one person may say "I should press the button fast" while another says "I should count to 50 and then press the button." Only when the contingencies are arranged so that self-generated rules conflict with programmed reinforcement do people reluctantly abandon the rule and behave in accord with the contingencies (Baron & Galizio, 1983).

One implication of Lowe's analysis is that humans without language skills will show characteristic effects of schedules. Lowe et al. (1983) designed an experiment to show typical fixed-interval performance by children less than 1 year old. The infants sat in a high chair and were able to touch a round metal cylinder. When the cylinder was touched, one infant (John) received a small bit of food (pieces of fruit, bread, or candy) on fixed-interval schedules of reinforcement. A second infant, Ann, was given 4 s of music played from a variety of music boxes on the same schedules. Both infants produced response patterns similar to the rat's performance in Figure 5.15. Thus, infants who are not verbally skilled behave in accord with the fixed-interval contingencies and are substantially different from adult humans.

Based on this finding and other research, Lowe argues that "these studies have shown that 1) the operant behavior of verbally-able humans differs very markedly from nonverbal organisms (i.e., animals and human infants) and 2) verbal behavior plays a major role in bringing about these differences" (personal communication, 1989).

Although the effects of verbal behavior

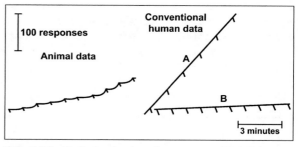

FIG. 5.15 Typical animal performance on FI and the high- and low-rate performance usually seen with adult humans. Adapted from Lowe (1979). © John Wiley & Sons, Ltd. Reproduced with permission.

and self-instruction may account for adult human performance on fixed-interval schedules, there are alternative possibilities. Michael Perone and his colleagues Mark Galizio and Alan Baron in an article concerning the relevance of animal-based principles for human behavior noted:

> When comparisons are made between the performances of humans and animals, discrepancies . . . are not difficult to find and, in themselves, provided little basis for satisfaction. The challenge for the student of human operant conditioning is to identify the similarities in the variables underlying the discrepant performances and ultimately to bring them under experimental control.
>
> (Perone, Galizio, & Baron, 1988, p. 80)

There is no doubt that humans become more verbal as they grow up. However, there are many other changes that occur from infancy to adulthood. An important consideration is the greater experience that adults have with ratio-type contingencies of reinforcement. Infants rely on the caregiving of other people. This means that most of the infant's reinforcement is delivered on the basis of time and behavior (interval schedules). A baby is fed when the mother has time to do so, although fussing may decrease the interval. As children get older, they begin to crawl and walk and reinforcement is delivered more and more on the basis of their behavior (ratio schedules). When this happens, many of the contingencies of reinforcement change from interval to ratio schedules. The amount of experience with ratio schedules of reinforcement may contribute to the differences between adult human and animal/infant performance on fixed-interval schedules.

Research by Wanchisen, Tatham, and Mooney (1989) has shown that rats perform like adult humans on fixed-interval schedules after a history of ratio reinforcement. The animals were exposed to variable-ratio reinforcement and then were given 120 sessions on a fixed-interval 30-s schedule (FI 30 s). Two patterns of response developed on the FI schedule—a high-rate pattern with little pausing and a low-rate pattern with some break-and-run performance. These patterns of performance are remarkably similar to the schedule performance of adult humans (see Figure 5.15). One implication is that human performance on schedules may be explained by a special history of ratio reinforcement rather than self-generated verbal rules. At this time, it is reasonable to conclude that both reinforcement history and verbal ability contribute to fixed-interval performance of adult humans.

Variable interval

On a **variable-interval (VI)**, schedule responses are reinforced after a variable amount of time has passed (see Figure 5.16). For example, on a VI 30 s schedule, the time to each reinforcement changes but the average time is 30 s. The symbol V indicates that the time requirement varies from one reinforcer to the next. The average amount of time required for reinforcement is used to index the schedule.

Interval contingencies are common in the ordinary world of people and other animals. People line up, sit in traffic jams, wait for elevators, time a boiling egg, and are put on hold. In everyday life, variable time periods occur more frequently than fixed ones. Waiting in line to get to a bank teller may take 5 min one day and half an hour the next time you go to the bank. A wolf pack may run down prey following a long or short hunt. A baby may cry for 5 s, 2 min, or a quarter of an hour before a parent picks up the child. A cat waits varying amounts of time in ambush before a bird becomes a meal. Waiting for a bus is rarely reinforced on a fixed schedule, despite the efforts of transportation officials. The bus arrives around an average specified time and waits only a given time before leaving. A carpool is an example of a VI contingency with a limited hold. The car arrives more or less at a specified time but waits for a rider only a limited (usually brief) time. In the laboratory, this **limited-hold** contingency—

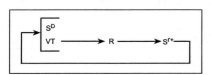

FIG. 5.16 A variable-interval schedule. The symbol V stands for variable and indicates that the schedule is indexed by the average time requirement for reinforcement.

where the reinforcer is available for a set time after a variable interval—when added to a VI schedule increases the rate of responding by reinforcing short interresponse times (IRTs). In the case of the carpool, people on the VI schedule with limited hold are ready for pick-up and rush out of the door when the car arrives.

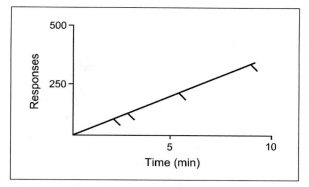

Figure 5.17 portrays the pattern of response generated on a VI schedule. On this schedule, rate of response is moderate and steady. The pause after reinforcement that occurs on FI usually does not appear in the VI record. Because rate of response is steady and moderate, VI performance is often used as a *baseline for evaluating other independent*

FIG. 5.17   Idealized cumulative pattern of response produced by a variable-interval schedule of reinforcement.

variables. Rate of response on VI schedules may increase or decrease as a result of experimental manipulations. For example, tranquilizing drugs such as chlorpromazine decrease the rate of response on VI schedules (Waller, 1961), while stimulants increase VI performance (Segal, 1962). Murray Sidman (1960) has commented on the usefulness of VI performance as a baseline:

> An ideal baseline would be one in which there is as little interference as possible from other variables. There should be a minimal number of factors tending to oppose any shift in behavior that might result from experimental manipulation. A variable-interval schedule, if skillfully programmed, comes close to meeting this requirement.
>
> (p. 320)

In summary, VI contingencies are common in everyday life. These schedules generate a moderate steady rate of response. Because of this pattern, VI performance is frequently used as a baseline.

NOTE ON: VI schedules, reinforcement rate, and behavioral momentum

Behavioral momentum refers to behavior that persists or continues in the presence of a stimulus for reinforcement despite disruptive factors (Nevin, 1992; Nevin & Grace, 2000; see PRE effect and behavioral momentum in Chapter 4). Thus, response rate declines more slowly (relative to its baseline level) in the presence of a stimulus for high-density reinforcement than a stimulus for low-density reinforcement (Shull, Gaynor, & Grimer, 2002). If you are working at the computer, and you keep working even though you are called to dinner, that is an example of behavioral momentum. Also, if you have a tendency to do some specific activity, despite alternative sources of reinforcement, that too shows behavioral momentum.

The analysis of behavioral momentum emerged when it was observed that behavior associated with a higher rate of response and reinforcement was less disrupted than behavior associated with lower rates, when challenged with some distraction. The procedure employed by Nevin (1974) involved a multiple schedule of reinforcement with two separate VI reinforcement conditions, each with a discriminative stimulus (S^D) and separated by a third dark component. Rates of responding were naturally higher in the richer VI component. Then, when free food was provided in the third component (disruption), responding decreased less in the VI condition with the higher rate of reinforcement. That is, behavior in the component with the richer VI schedule (higher rate of reinforcement) showed greater momentum. It continued to keep going in spite of the disruption by free food (see also Cohn, 1998; Lattal, Reilly, & Kohn, 1998).

Many researchers have investigated predictions and analyses based on momentum theory (e.g., Harper & McLean, 1992) and suggestions for applying the theory have also appeared (Brandon & Houlihan, 1997). In one applied study, two individuals with severe mental retardation performed self-paced discriminations on a computer using a touch-sensitive screen and food reinforcement (Dube and McIlvane, 2001). Responses on two separate problems were differentially reinforced. The researchers found that on-task behavior with the higher reinforcement rate was more resistant to change due to prefeeding, free snacks, or alternative activities. Thus, the disruptive factors reduced task performance depending on the prior rates of reinforcement. That is, when performance on a task received a high rate of reinforcement it was relatively impervious to distraction compared with performance maintained on a lower rate schedule.

SCHEDULE PERFORMANCE IN TRANSITION

We have described typical performances generated by different schedules of reinforcement. The patterns of response on these schedules take a relatively long time to develop. Once behavior has stabilized, showing little change from day to day, the organism's behavior is said to have reached a *steady state*. The pause-and-run pattern that develops on FR schedules is a steady-state performance and is only observed after an animal has considerable exposure to the contingencies. Similarly, the steady-state performance generated on other intermittent schedules takes time to evolve. When an organism is initially placed on any schedule of reinforcement, typically behavior patterns are not consistent or regular. This early performance on a schedule is called a **transition-state performance**. Transition states are the periods between initial steady state performance and the next steady state (see Sidman, 1960, for steady-state and transition-state analysis).

Behavior analysts rarely study transitions but one might argue that when behavior is in transition is exactly when most learning is taking place. One problem with an experimental analysis of behavior in transitions is clearly defining what constitutes the boundary between transition- and steady-state performances. How to characterize operant performance as stable has been a point of serious consideration for many decades (e.g., Cumming & Schoenfeld, 1960; Mclean & Blampied, 1995). Most often, stability is determined by some combination of inspection of cumulative records or other rate indicators, and number of sessions. Until the "boundary problem" of transition to steady states is solved, the experimental analysis of behavior in transition is likely to remain a less investigated area of learning. There are, however, interesting patterns of behavior in transition that can be addressed here.

Consider how you might get an animal to press a lever 100 times for each presentation of food (FR 100). First, you shape the animal to press the bar on continuous reinforcement (see Chapter 4). After some arbitrary steady-state performance is established on CRF, you are faced with the problem of how to program the steps from CRF to FR 100. Notice that in this transition there is a large shift in the ratio of reinforcement to bar pressing. This problem has been studied with the use of a *progressive ratio schedule* (Findley, 1958). The ratio of responses following each run to reinforcement is programmed to increase in steps. Stafford and Branch (1998) employed this schedule to investigate the behavioral effects of step size and criteria for stability. If you simply move from CRF to the large FR value, the animal will probably show **ratio strain** in the sense that it pauses longer and longer after reinforcement. One reason is that the time between successive reinforcements contributes to the postreinforcement pause. The pause gets longer as the **interreinforcement interval (IRI**, or time between reinforcement) increases. Because the PRP makes up part of the IRI and is controlled by it, the animal eventually stops responding. Thus, there is a negative-feedback loop between increasing PRP length and the time between reinforcements in the shift from CRF to the large FR schedule.

Large and sudden increases in schedule values also produce extinction. A slow progression to higher schedule values is typically programmed to reduce extinction effects. Even when a small change in the fixed ratio is made, an animal is momentarily exposed to a period of extinction. Recall that during the early phase of extinction, behavior becomes more variable and a burst of responses is likely to occur. This eruption of responses may actually be used to support the transition to a higher ratio requirement. In other words, when continuous reinforcement (FR 1) is changed to FR 5, the animal makes several rapid responses, a burst, and the fifth response is reinforced. Following several reinforced sequences of five responses, the ratio requirement may be raised again. The transition to the next FR requirement also produces an extinction burst and enables the animal to contact the next scheduled value. Notice that extinction effects do not occur with interval schedules. If pausing occurs on VI or FI, the time runs out, the next response is reinforced, and responding is strengthened. These schedules are said to be self-perpetuating—maintaining at least a minimum level of responding.

Extinction bursts and increased behavioral variability allow for adaptation to changing environmental contingencies. When an organism changes its behavior on the basis of life experience, this is called **ontogenetic selection**. In this ontogenetic form of adaptation, the topography and frequency of behavior increase when reinforcement is withheld. These behavioral changes during extinction allow for the selection of behavior by new contingencies of reinforcement. Thus, a wild rat exploiting a compost heap may find that the home owner has covered it over. Faced with this predicament, the rat emits various operants that may eventually uncover the food. The animal digs under the cover, gnaws a hole in the sheathing, or searches for some other means of entry. A similar effect occurs when food in the compost heap is depleted and the animal emits behavior (locomotion and travel) that contacts a new food patch. In the laboratory, the effects of food depletion are measured as increases in the topography and frequency of bar pressing as the progressive ratio is changed.

Transitions from one reinforcement schedule to another play an important role in human development. Developmental psychologists have described periods of life in which major changes in behavior typically occur. One of the most important life stages in Western society is the transition from childhood to adolescence. Although this phase involves many biological and behavioral processes, one of the most basic changes involves schedules of reinforcement.

When a youngster reaches puberty, parents, teachers, peers, and others require more behavior and more skillful performance than they did during childhood. A young child's reinforcement schedules are usually simple, regular, and immediate. In childhood, food is given when the child says "Mom, I'm hungry" after playing a game of tag, or is scheduled at regular times throughout the day. On the other hand, a teenager is told to fix his or her own food and clean up the mess. Notice that the schedule requirement for getting food has significantly increased. The teenager may search through the refrigerator, open packages and cans, sometimes cook, get out plates, eat the food, and clean up. Of course, any part of this sequence may or may not occur depending on the disciplinary practices of the parents. Although most adolescents adapt to this transition state, others may show signs of ratio strain and extinction. Poor eating habits by teenagers may reflect the change from regular to intermittent reinforcement.

Many other behavioral changes may occur during the transition from childhood to adolescence. Ferster, Culbertson, and Boren (1975) have noted the transition to intermittent reinforcement that occurs in adolescence:

> With adolescence, the picture may change quite drastically and sometimes even suddenly. Now money becomes a reinforcer on a fixed-ratio schedule instead of continuous reinforcement as before. The adolescent may have to take a job demanding a substantial amount of work for the money which heretofore he received as a free allowance. Furthermore, he now needs more money than when he was

younger to interact with people he deals with. A car or a motorcycle takes the place of the bicycle. Even the price of services such as movies and buses is higher. Money, particularly for boys, frequently becomes a necessary condition for dealing with the opposite sex. The amount of work required in school increases. Instead of simple arithmetic problems, the adolescent may now have to write a long term paper, cover more subjects, or puzzle through a difficult algebra problem which will require much trial and error.

(pp. 416–417)

There are other periods of life in which our culture demands large shifts in schedules of reinforcement. A current problem involves a rapidly aging population and the difficulties generated by forced retirement. In terms of schedules, retirement is a large and rapid change in the contingencies of reinforcement. Retired people face significant alterations in social, monetary, and work-related consequences. For example, a person who has enjoyed his or her academic career as a professor is no longer reinforced for research and teaching by the university community. Social consequences for these activities may have included approval by colleagues, academic advancement, interest of students, and intellectual discussions. Upon retirement, these social reinforcers are reduced in frequency or completely eliminated. It is not surprising, therefore, that retirement is an unhappy time of life for many people. Although retirement is commonly viewed as a problem of old age, a behavior analysis points to the abrupt change in rates and sources of reinforcement (Skinner & Vaughn, 1983).

ON THE APPLIED SIDE: Schedules and cigarettes

The use of drugs is operant behavior maintained in part by the reinforcing effects of the drug. One implication of this analysis is that reinforcement of an incompatible response (i.e., abstinence) can reduce the probability of taking drugs. The effectiveness of an abstinence contingency depends on the magnitude and schedule of reinforcement for nondrug use (e.g., Higgins, Bickel, & Hughes, 1994).

In a recent investigation of cigarette smoking, Roll, Higgins, and Badger (1996) assessed the effectiveness of three different schedules of reinforcement for promoting and sustaining drug abstinence. These researchers conducted an experimental analysis of cigarette smoking because cigarettes can function as reinforcers, smoking can be reduced by reinforcement of alternative responses, and it is relatively more convenient to study cigarette smoking than illicit drugs. Furthermore, cigarette smokers usually relapse within several days following abstinence. This suggests that reinforcement factors regulating abstinence exert their effects shortly after the person stops smoking and it is possible to study these factors in a short-duration experiment.

Sixty adults, who smoked between 10 and 50 cigarettes a day, took part in the experiment. The smokers were not currently trying to give up cigarettes. Participants were randomly assigned to one of three groups: progressive reinforcement, fixed rate of reinforcement, and a control group. They were told to begin abstaining from cigarettes on Friday evening so that they could pass a carbon monoxide (CO) test for abstinence on Monday morning. Each person in the study went at least 2 days without smoking before reinforcement for abstinence began. On Monday through Friday, participants agreed to take three daily CO tests. These tests could detect prior smoking.

Twenty participants were randomly assigned to the progressive reinforcement group. The progressive schedule involved increasing the magnitude of reinforcement for remaining drug free. Participants earned $3.00 for passing the first CO test for abstinence. Each subsequent consecutive CO sample that indicated abstinence increased the amount of money participants received by $0.50. The third consecutive CO test passed earned a bonus of $10.00. That is, passing the first CO test yielded $3.00, passing the second $3.50, the third $14.00 ($4.00 and bonus of $10.00), and the fourth $4.50. In addition, a substantial response cost was added for failing a CO test. If the person failed the test, the payment for that test was withheld and the value of payment for the next test was reset to $3.00. Three consecutive CO tests indicating abstinence following a reset returned the payment schedule to the value at which the reset occurred (Roll et al., 1996, p. 497), supporting efforts to achieve abstinence.

Participants in the fixed reinforcement group ($N = 20$) were paid $9.80 for passing each CO test. There were no bonus points for consecutive abstinences and no resets. The total amount of money available for the progressive and fixed groups was the same. Smokers in both the progressive and fixed groups were informed in advance of the schedule of payment and the criterion for reinforcement. The schedule of payment for the control group was the same as the average payment obtained by the first 10 participants assigned to the progressive condition. For these people, the payment was given no matter what their CO levels were. The control group was, however, asked to try and cut their cigarette consumption, reduce CO levels, and maintain abstinence.

Smokers in the progressive and fixed reinforcement groups passed more than 80% of the abstinence tests while the control group only passed about 40% of the tests. The effects of the schedule of reinforcement are shown in Figure 5.18A. The figure indicates the percentage of participants who passed three consecutive tests for abstinence and then resumed smoking over the 5 days of the experiment. Only 22% of those on the progressive schedule resumed smoking, compared with 60% and 82% in the fixed and control groups. Thus, the progressive schedule of reinforcement was superior at preventing the resumption of smoking (after a period of abstinence).

Figure 5.18B shows the percentage of smokers who gave up cigarettes throughout the experiment. Again, a strong effect of schedule of reinforcement is apparent. Fifty percent of those on the progressive reinforcement schedule remained abstinent for the 5 days of the experiment. This compares with 30% and 5% of the fixed and control participants.

Overall, these results indicate that a progressive reinforcement schedule, combined with an escalating response cost, is an effective short-term intervention for abstinence from smoking. Further research is necessary to see whether a progressive schedule maintains abstinence after the schedule is withdrawn. Long-term follow-up studies of progressive and other schedules are necessary to assess the lasting effects of reinforcement schedules on abstinence. What is clear, at this point, is that schedules of reinforcement may be an important component of stop-smoking programs.

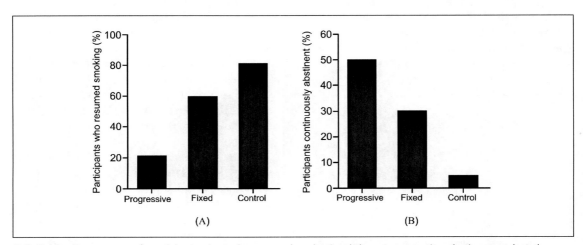

FIG. 5.18 Percentage of participants in each group who obtained three consecutive abstinences, but then resumed smoking (A). Percentage of smokers in each group who were abstinent on all trials during the entire experiment (B). From "An Experimental Comparison of Three Different Schedules of Reinforcement of Drug Abstinence Using Cigarette Smoking as an Exemplar," by J. M. Roll, S. T. Higgins, and G. J. Badger, 1996, *Journal of Applied Behavior Analysis*, *29*, 495–505. Copyright 1996 held by the Society for the Experimental Analysis of Behavior, Inc. Republished with permission.

ADVANCED SECTION: Schedule performance

Each of the basic schedules of reinforcement (FR, FI, VR, VI) generates a unique pattern of responding. Ratio schedules produce a higher rate of response than interval schedules. A reliable pause after reinforcement (PRP) occurs on fixed-ratio and fixed-interval schedules but not on variable-ratio or variable-interval schedules.

Rate of Response on Schedules

The issue about what produces rapid responding on ratio schedules and moderate rates on interval schedules has not been resolved. The two major views concern molecular versus molar conceptions of schedule control. **Molecular accounts of schedule performance** focus on small moment-to-moment relationships between behavior and its consequences. **Molar accounts of schedule performance** are concerned with large-scale factors that may occur over the length of an entire session.

Molecular account of rate of response

The time between any two responses, or what is called the **interresponse time (IRT)**, may be treated as an operant. Consider Figure 5.19 in which 30-s segments of performance on VR and VI schedules are presented. Responses are portrayed by the vertical marks, and the occurrence of reinforcement is given with the familiar symbol S^{r+}. As you can see, IRTs are much longer on VI than on VR. On the VR segment, 23 responses occur in 30 s, which gives an average time between responses of 1.3 s. The VI schedule generates longer IRTs, with a mean of 2.3 s.

Generally, ratio schedules produce shorter IRTs and consequently higher rates of response than interval schedules. Skinner (1938) suggested that this came about because ratio and interval schedules reinforce short or long interresponse times, respectively. To understand this, consider the definition of an operant class. It is a class of behavior that may increase or decrease in frequency on the basis of contingencies of reinforcement. In other words, if it could be shown that the time between responses changes as a function of selective reinforcement then the IRT is, by definition, an operant in its own right. To demonstrate that the IRT is an operant, it is necessary to identify an IRT of specific length (e.g., 2 s between any two responses) and then reinforce that interresponse time, showing that it increases in frequency.

Computers and other electronic equipment have been used to measure the IRTs generated on various schedules of reinforcement. A response is made and the computer starts timing until the next response is emitted. Typically, these interresponse times are slotted into time bins. For example, all IRTs between 0 and 2 s are counted, followed by those that fall in the 2–4-s range, and then number of 4–6-s IRTs. This method results in a distribution of interresponse times. Several experiments have shown that the distribution of IRTs may in fact be changed by selectively reinforcing interresponse times of a particular duration (for a review, see Morse, 1966). Figure 5.20 shows the results of a hypothetical experiment in which IRTs of different duration are reinforced on a VI schedule. On the standard

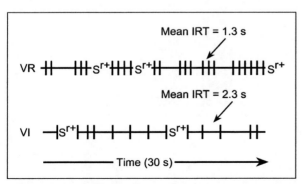

FIG. 5.19   Idealized distributions of response on VR and VI schedules of reinforcement. Responses are represented by the vertical marks, and S^{r+} stands for reinforcement.

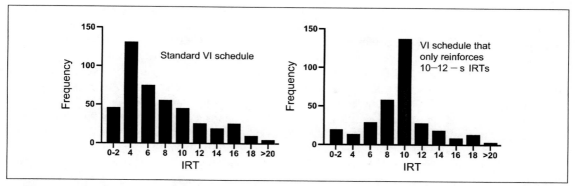

FIG. 5.20   Hypothetical distributions of interresponse times (IRTs) for an animal responding on a standard VI schedule of reinforcement and on a VI that only reinforces IRTs that fall between 10 and 12 s.

VI, most of the IRTs are 2–4 s long. When an additional contingency is added to the VI schedule that requires IRTs of 10–12 s, the IRTs increase in this category. Also, a new distribution of IRTs is generated. Whereas on a VR the next response may be reinforced regardless of the IRT, on VI the combination of pause plus response is required for reinforcement.

Anger (1956) conducted a complex experiment demonstrating that IRTs are a conditionable property of behavior. In this experiment, the IRT also was considered to be a stimulus that set the occasion for the next response (S^D). Reynolds (1966a) subsequently showed that the IRT controlled performance that followed it. In other words, IRTs seem to function as discriminative stimuli for behavior. The difficulty with this conception is that stimulus properties are inferred from performance. Zeiler (1977) has pointed out:

> If the IRT is treated as a differentiated response unit [an operant], unobservable stimuli need not be postulated as controlling observable performance. Given the one-to-one correspondence between response and inferred stimulus properties, however, the two treatments appear to be equivalent.
>
> (p. 223)

We treat the IRT as an operant rather than as a discriminative stimulus. As an operant, the IRT is considered to be a conditionable property of the response that ends the time interval between any two responses. For example, a rat may press a lever R_1, R_2, R_3, R_4, and R_5 times. The time between lever presses R_1 and R_2 is the interresponse time associated with R_2. In a similar fashion, the IRT for R_5 is the elapsed time between R_4 and R_5. This series can be said to constitute a homogenous chain that is divisible into discrete three-term-contingency links.

As part of Anger's (1956) experiment, animals were placed on a VI 300-s schedule of reinforcement. On this schedule, the response that resulted in reinforcement had to occur 40 s or more after the previous response. If the animal made many fast responses with IRTs of less than 40 s, the schedule requirements would not be met. In other words, IRTs of more than 40 s were the operant that was reinforced. Anger found that this procedure shifted the distribution of IRTs toward 40 s. Thus, the IRT that is reinforced is more likely to be emitted than other interresponse times. Additional experiments have demonstrated a similar effect (Dews, 1963; Ferster & Skinner, 1957; Kelleher, Fry, & Cook, 1959; Platt, 1979; Shimp, 1969), and Morse (1966) provides a formal analysis supporting the conclusion that IRTs are a conditionable property of operant behavior. Lattal and colleagues at West Virginia University have extended these findings. Their research on delay of reinforcement suggests that basic behavioral units, like IRTs, are conditioned even when the contingencies of reinforcement do not directly require it (Arbuckle & Lattal, 1988; Lattal, 1984; Lattal & Ziegler, 1982).

Ratio schedules generate rapid sequences of responses with short interresponse times (Gott &

Weiss, 1972; Weiss & Gott, 1972). On a ratio schedule, consider what the probability of obtaining reinforcement is following a burst of very fast responses (short IRTs) or a series of responses with long IRTs. Recall that ratio schedules are based on the number of responses that are emitted. Bursts of responses with short IRTs rapidly count down the ratio requirement and are more likely reinforced than sets of long IRT responses (slow responding). Thus, ratio schedules, because of the way they are constructed, differentially reinforce short IRTs. According to the molecular IRT view of schedule control, this is why the rate of response is high on ratio schedules.

When compared to ratio schedules, interval contingencies generate longer IRTs and consequently a lower rate of response. Interval schedules pay off after some amount of time has passed and a response is made. As the IRTs become longer, more and more of the time requirement on the schedule elapses and the probability of reinforcement increases. In other words, longer IRTs are differentially reinforced on interval schedules (Morse, 1966). In keeping with the molecular view, interval contingencies differentially reinforce long IRTs, and the rate of response is moderate on these schedules.

Molar accounts of rate differences

There are several problems with the IRT account of rate differences on ratio and interval schedules. One problem is that experiments on selective reinforcement of IRTs do not prove that IRTs are controlled in this way on interval or ratio schedules. Also, there is evidence that when long IRTs are reinforced, organisms continue to emit short bursts of rapid responses. Animals typically produce these bursts even on schedules that never reinforce a fast series of responses (differential reinforcement of low rate, DRL). For these reasons, molar hypotheses have been advanced about the rate of response differences on reinforcment schedules.

Molar explanations of rate differences are concerned with the overall relationship between responses and reinforcement. In molar terms, the *correlation between responses and reinforcement* produces the difference in rate on interval and ratio schedules. Generally, if a high rate of response is associated with a higher rate of reinforcement in the long run, animals will respond rapidly. When an increased rate of response does not affect the rate of reinforcement, organisms do not respond faster (Baum, 1993).

Consider a VR 100 schedule of reinforcement. On this schedule, a subject could respond 50 times per minute and in a 1-h session obtain 30 reinforcers. On the other hand, if the rate of response was 300 per minute (not outside the range of pigeons or humans), the number of reinforcers earned would increase to 180 an hour. According to supporters of the molar view, this correlation between increasing rate of response and increased frequency of reinforcement is responsible for rapid responding on ratio schedules.

A different correlation between rate of response and rate of reinforcement is set up on interval schedules. Recall that interval schedules program a reinforcer after time has passed and one response is made. Suppose you are responding on a VI 3-min schedule for $5 reinforcers. You have 1 h a day to work on the schedule. If you respond at a reasonable rate, say 30 lever presses per minute, you will get most or all of the 20 scheduled reinforcers. Now pretend that you increase your rate of response to 300 a minute. The only consequence is a sore wrist, and rate of reinforcement stays at 20 per hour. In other words, after some moderate value, it does not pay to increase the rate of response on interval schedules, hence lower rates are maintained on interval schedules.

Postreinforcement Pause on Fixed Schedules

Fixed-ratio and fixed-interval schedules generate a pause that follows reinforcement. Accounts of pausing on fixed schedules also may be classified as molecular or molar. Molecular accounts of pausing are concerned with the moment-to-moment relationships that immediately precede reinforcement. Such accounts are concerned with the relationship between the number of bar presses that produce reinforcement and the subsequent postreinforcement pause. In contrast, molar accounts of pausing focus on the overall rate of reinforcement for a session and the average pause length.

Research shows that the postreinforcement pause (PRP) is a function of the *interreinforcement interval (IRI)*. As the IRI becomes longer, the PRP increases. On fixed-interval schedules, in which the time between reinforcement is controlled by the experimenter, the PRP is approximately half of the IRI. For example, on a FI 300-s schedule (in which the time between reinforcements is 300 s), the average PRP will be 150 s. On fixed ratio, the evidence suggests similar control by the IRI (Powell, 1968)—as the ratio requirement increases, the PRP becomes longer.

There is, however, a difficulty with analyzing the PRP on FR schedules. On ratio schedules, the IRI is partly determined by what the animal does. That is, the animal's rate of pressing the lever affects the time between reinforcements. Another problem with ratio schedules, for an analysis of pausing, is that the rate of response goes up as the size of the ratio is increased (Boren, 1961). Unless the rate of response exactly coincides with changes in the size of the ratio, adjustments in ratio size alter the IRI. For example, on FR 10 a rate of five responses per minute produces an IRI of 2 min. This same rate of response produces an IRI of 4 min on a FR 20 schedule. Thus, changes in postreinforcement pause as ratio size is increased may be caused by the ratio size, the IRI, or both.

Molar interpretation of pausing

We have noted that the average PRP is half of the interreinforcement interval. Another finding is that the PRPs are normally distributed (bell-shaped curve) over the time between reinforcements. In other words, on a FI 320-s schedule, pauses will range from 0 to 320 s, with an average pause of around 160 s. As shown in Figure 5.21, these results can be accounted for by considering what would happen if the normal curve moved upward so that the mean pause was 225 s. In this case, many of the pauses would exceed the FI interval and the animal would get fewer reinforcements for the session. An animal that was sensitive to *overall rate of reinforcement* (maximization) should come to emit pauses that are on average half of the FI interval, assuming a normal distribution. Thus, maximization of reinforcement provides a molar account of the postreinforcement pause (Baum, 2002).

Molecular interpretations of pausing

There are two molecular accounts of pausing on fixed schedules that have some amount of research support. One account is based on the observation that animals often emit other behavior during the PRP (Staddon & Simmelhag, 1971). For example, rats may engage in grooming, sniffing, scratching, and stretching after the presentation of a food pellet. Because this other behavior reliably follows reinforcement, it is said to be induced by the schedule. *Schedule-induced* behaviors (see Chapter 6) may be viewed as operants that automatically produce reinforcement. For example, stretching may relieve muscle

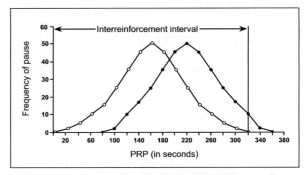

FIG. 5.21 Two possible distributions of PRPs on a fixed-interval 320-s schedule. The distribution given by the open circles has a mean of 160 s and does not exceed the interreinforcement interval set on the FI schedule. The bell curve for the distribution with the dark circles has an average value at 225 s, and many pauses are longer than the IRI.

tension and scratching may eliminate an itch. One interpretation is that pausing occurs because the animal is maximizing local rates of reinforcement. That is, the rat gets food for bar pressing as well as the automatic reinforcement from the induced activities (see Shull, 1979). The average pause should therefore reflect the allocation of time to induced behavior and to the operant that produces scheduled reinforcement (food). At present, experiments have not ruled out or clearly demonstrated the induced-behavior interpretation of pausing (e.g., Derenne & Baron, 2002).

A second molecular account of pausing is based on the **run of responses** or amount of work that precedes reinforcement (Shull, 1979, pp. 217–218). This "work-time" interpretation holds that the previously experienced run of responses regulates the length of the postreinforcement pause. Work time affects the PRP by altering the value of the next scheduled reinforcement. In other words, the more effort or time expended for the previous reinforcer, the lower the value of the next reinforcer and the longer it takes for the animal to initiate responding (pause length). Interestingly, Skinner made a similar interpretation in 1938 when he stated that pausing on fixed-ratio schedules occurred because "the preceding run which occurs under reinforcement at a fixed ratio places the [reflex] reserve in a state of strain which acts with the temporal discrimination of reinforcement to produce a pause of some length" (p. 298). Skinner's use of the strained reserve seems equivalent to the more current emphasis on work time. Overall, this view suggests that the harder one works for reinforcement, the less valuable the next reinforcement and therefore the longer it takes to start working again.

Neither the induced behavior nor the work-time accounts of pausing are sufficient to handle all that is known about patterning on schedules of reinforcement. A schedule of reinforcement is a procedure for combining a large number of different conditions that regulate behavior. Some of the controlling factors arise from the animal's behavior, and others are set by the experimenter. This means that it is exceedingly difficult to unravel the exact processes that produce characteristic schedule performance. Nonetheless, the current interpretations of pausing point to some of the more relevant factors that play a role in the regulation of behavior on fixed schedules.

The Dynamics of Schedule Performance

There are reasons for detailed research on the PRP and interresponse time. The hope is to analyze schedule effects in terms of a few basic processes. This area of research, called **behavioral dynamics**, is an important endeavor because the environment of people and other animals can be arranged in an infinite number of ways. If performance on schedules can be reduced to a small number of fundamental principles, then reasonable interpretations may be made about any particular arrangement of the environment. Also, it should be possible to predict behavior more precisely from knowledge of the operating contingencies and the axioms that govern reinforcement schedules.

Behavioral dynamics is at the leading edge of behavior analysis and, like most scientific research, it requires a high level of mathematical sophistication. Both linear and nonlinear calculus are used to model the behavioral impact of schedules of reinforcement. In the 1990s, an issue of the *Journal of the Experimental Analysis of Behavior* was devoted to this important subject and included topics like chaos theory and performance on fixed-interval schedules, dynamics of behavioral structure, behavioral momentum, resistance to behavior change, and feedback functions for variable-interval schedules (see Baum, 1992; Galbicka, 1992; Gibbon & Church, 1992; Harper & McLean, 1992; Hoyert, 1992; Killeen, 1992; Marr, 1992; McDowell, Bass, & Kessel, 1992; Nevin, 1992; Palya, 1992; Rachlin, 1992; Shimp, 1992; Zeiler, 1992). In this same issue, Peter Killeen, a professor at Arizona State University, builds on his previous work and suggests that "behavior may be treated as basic physics" with responses viewed as movement through behavioral space (Killeen, 1974, 1975, 1985, 1992). Although these issues are beyond the scope of this book, the student of behavior analysis should be aware that the physics of schedule performance is an advanced area of the science of behavior.

CHAPTER SUMMARY

A schedule of reinforcement describes the arrangement of stimuli, operants, and consequences. Such contingencies were outlined by Ferster and Skinner (1957) and are central to the understanding of behavior regulation in humans and other animals. The research on schedules and performance patterns is a major component of the science of behavior, a science that progressively builds on previous experiments and theoretical analysis. Schedules of reinforcement generate consistent, steady-state performances involving runs of responses and pausing that are characteristic of the specific schedule (ratio or interval). In the laboratory, the arrangement of progressive ratio schedules can serve as an animal model of foraging in the wild and intermittent reinforcement plays a role in most human behavior, especially social interaction.

To improve the description of schedules as contingencies of reinforcement, we introduced the Mechner system of notation. The notation is useful for programming contingencies in the laboratory or analyzing complex enviroment–behavior relations. In this chapter, we outlined continuous reinforcement (CRF) and resistence to extinction on this schedule. CRF also results in response stereotypy based on the high rate of reinforcement. Fixed-ratio (FR) and fixed-interval (FI) schedules were introduced, as well as the postreinforcement pausing (PRP) on these contingencies. Adult humans have not shown classic scalloping or break-and-run patterns on FI schedules and the performance differences of humans relate to language or verbal behavior as well as histories of ratio reinforcement. Variable-ratio (VR) and variable-interval (VI) schedules produce less pausing and higher overall rates of response. Adding a limited hold to a VI schedule increases the response rate by reinforcing short interresponse times (IRT). When rates of reinforcement are varied on VI schedules, the higher the rate of reinforcement the greater the behavioral momentum.

The study of behavior during the transition between schedules of reinforcement has not been well researched due to the boundary problem of steady-state behavior. Transition states, however, play an important role in human behavior—as in the shift in the reinforcement contingencies from childhood to adolescence, or the change in schedules from employment to retirement. Reinforcement schedules also have applied importance and research shows that cigarette smoking can be regulated by a progressive schedule combined with an escalating response–cost contingency. Finally, in the advanced section of this chapter, we addressed molecular and molar accounts of response rate and rate differences on schedules of reinforcement. We emphasized the analysis of IRTs for molecular accounts and the correlation of overall rates of response and reinforcement for molar explanations.

Key Words

Assumption of generality	Interval schedules	Ratio strain
Behavioral dynamics	Limited hold	Resurgence
Break and run	Mechner notation	Run of responses
Continuous reinforcement (CRF)	Molar perspective	Scalloping
Fixed interval (FI)	Molecular perspective	Schedule of reinforcement
Fixed ratio (FR)	Ontogenetic selection	Steady-state performance
Interreinforcement interval (IRI)	Postreinforcement pause (PRP)	Transition-state performance
Interresponse time (IRT)	Preratio pause	Variable interval (VI)
	Progressive ratio schedule	Variable ratio (VR)
	Ratio schedule	

Aversive Control of Behavior

6

- Learn the difference between positive and negative punishment.
- Investigate negative reinforcement as the basis of escape and avoidance.
- Learn about reduction in shock frequency as a determinant of avoidance.
- Delve into the phenomenon of learned helplessness induced by inescapable aversive stimuli.
- Differentiate between respondent and operant aggression.
- Learn about the use of coercion and its negative side effects in our society.

Aversive stimuli are those events that organisms evade, avoid, or escape from. Stings, attacks, foul odors, bright light, and very loud noises are events that organisms are prepared to evade on the basis of phylogeny. Escaping or avoiding these **primary aversive stimuli** was adaptive, presumably because those animals that emitted this behavior in the presence of these kinds of events survived and reproduced. In other words, organisms do not learn that these are aversive stimuli; they are biologically prepared to avoid or escape such events.

Other stimuli acquire aversive properties when associated with primary aversive events during an animal's lifetime. For people, **conditioned aversive stimuli (S^{ave})** include threats, public criticism, a failing grade, a frown, and verbal disapproval. To affect behavior, these events usually depend on a history of punishment. A 1-week-old infant is not affected by a reprimand such as, "Don't do that!" However, by the time the child is 2 years old, the command may stop the toddler from tearing pages out of your favorite book. Animals also learn responses to conditioned stimuli as aversive events. People commonly shout "No!" when pets misbehave, and this auditory stimulus eventually reduces the probability of the response it follows (e.g., chewing on your new chair). A wolf may snap at a yellow-jacket wasp, but following a sting or two the animal will avoid yellow-and-black striped insects.

There are good reasons for not using aversive contingencies in the regulation of behavior, and these reasons will be discussed later in this chapter. Nonetheless, a large amount of human (and animal) behavior is regulated by contingent and non-contingent aversive stimuli, and the extensive use of aversive control makes the analysis necessary. Azrin and Holz (1966), pioneers in the analysis of punishment, stated:

> We have seen that several methods other than punishment are available for eliminating behavior. For whatever the reasons, we may wish to use methods other than punishment. To what extent is this objective practicable? At the institutional level, it would seem to be quite possible to eliminate the use of physical punishment. Conceivably, administrative regulations could be altered such that public punishment in the form of flogging, spankings, or other physical abuse would be excluded. At the level of individual behavior, it seems somewhat more difficult but still not impossible to eliminate the use of physical punishment. *One type of punishment, however, seems to be virtually impossible to eliminate, and that is the punishing contingencies that are arranged by the physical world.* Whenever we interact with the physical world, there are many punishing contingencies awaiting us. A good example of this would be any behavior that moves us through space such as walking, running, or reaching. It is only necessary to shut one's eyes while running to realize the extent to which punishing contingencies surround

our movement. The degree to which these punishing contingencies are actually applied can be seen in the initial efforts of the young child in learning to walk and to run. So powerful are these potential punishing contingencies that they exist even when we sleep. The response of rolling off a bed is punished immediately and severely by collision with the floor below. Elimination of punishing contingencies by the physical world would appear to require elimination of all behavior that involves interaction with the physical world.

(p. 438, emphasis added)

This passage makes it clear that, at least in the physical world, punishment is a fact of life. Sidman (2001) points out that we use coercion almost exclusively to control human behavior. Yet, we do precious little research on aversive control and how best to minimize its side effects and reduce its prevalence.

CONTINGENCIES OF PUNISHMENT

When a behavioral contingency results in a *decrease* in rate of response the contingency is called **punishment**. Any event or stimulus that decreases the rate of operant behavior is called a **punisher**. Figure 6.1 makes it clear that it is the relationship between the consequence and its effects on behavior that defines the contingency. At this point, we discuss contingencies of punishment; negative reinforcement is addressed later in this chapter.

QUICK TIP: Procedures to reduce rate of response

Many operations other than a punishment contingency reduce the rate of response. These include satiation, extinction, behavioral contrast, restraint, precommittment, and richer alternative schedules of reinforcement. Each of these procedures is discussed throughout this textbook. Punishment is defined when an event is contingent on the occurrence of a specified response and the probability of response is reduced. If shock is contingent on lever pressing and lever pressing repeatedly has produced shocks, the rat is less likely to press the lever. The effect and the contingency are called punishment.

Stimulus following behavior	Effect on behavior	
	Increase	Decrease
On/presented		2 Positive punishment
Off/removed	3 Negative reinforcement	4 Negative punishment

FIG. 6.1 Aversive contingencies of reinforcement and punishment (adapted from Figure 4.2 in Chapter 4). When a stimulus or event follows operant behavior, then the behavior increases or decreases in frequency. It is this relationship between behavior and consequence that defines the contingency.

Positive Punishment

Positive punishment occurs when a stimulus is *presented* following an operant and the operant *decreases* in rate of response. The contingency of positive punishment is shown in cell 2 of Figure 6.1. When a parent spanks a child for running into the street and the child stops doing it, this is positive punishment (see Gershoff, 2002, on corporal punishment by parents; also, Park, 2002, on the difficulty of isolating the effects of parental punishment from a "package" of disciplinary tactics). Of course, spanking is functioning as punishment only if it decreases the probability of running into the street. This is an important point because in usual language people talk about punishment without considering its effects on behavior. For example, you may shout and argue with another person when he or she expresses a particular political position. Your shouting is positive punishment only if the other individual stops (or decreases) talking about politics. In fact, the person may increase his or her rate of political conversation (as often happens in arguments). In this case, you have reinforced rather than punished arguing with you. Thus, positive punishment is defined as a decrease in operant behavior produced by the presentation of a stimulus that follows it. By this functional definition, punishment always works.

Negative Punishment

Negative punishment is portrayed in cell 4 of Figure 6.1. When an ongoing stimulus is *removed* contingent on a response and this removal results in a decrease in rate of behavior, the contingency is called **negative punishment** (or omission). In other words, if the organism responds, the stimulus is taken away and behavior decreases. A hungry bird is given continuous access to food, but if it pecks the key, food is removed. A child is watching TV, but if the child runs around, the television is turned off. A person has earned money and is fined for speeding. In these cases, positive reinforcement (i.e., provision of food, TV is turned on, or earned money) is removed contingent on behavior and the behavior decreases.

Negative punishment is often confused with extinction. *Extinction occurs when a previously reinforced response no longer produces reinforcement.* In this case, a response has produced reinforcement; extinction for that response is in effect when the response → reinforcer contingency is discontinued. A pigeon may peck a key for food, but when extinction is programmed, pecking no longer produces the food reinforcer. Similarly, a child may be allowed to watch a favorite television show after completing homework assignments. When the TV is broken the contingency is no longer in effect and doing homework is on extinction.

In Figure 6.2, ongoing reinforcement could be eating a meal with the family, and responses R_2 ... R_N may involve talking to a sister, passing food around the table, or turning on a compact disk player. Licking your plate is represented by R_1 and results in father telling you to leave the table for a period of time (negative punishment). Forcing you to leave your supper reduces your tendency to engage in this nasty habit when you next have a meal with your family (in applied behavior analysis this procedure is called *time out* from reinforcement).

Relativity of Punishment: The Premack Principle

In Chapter 4, we discussed the principle of reinforcement and the Premack (1959, 1962) principle. The principle states that the opportunity to engage in a higher frequency behavior will reinforce a lower frequency response. That is, *reinforcement is relative not absolute.* Premack (1971) extended this principle to the **relativity of punishment**. Consider a rat that can run in an activity wheel and drink water from a tube. The wheel apparatus is modified so that a break can be activated, locking the wheel and preventing the rat from running. In addition, a motor is installed that permits the wheel to rotate at a set speed, forcing the rat to run. In this modified apparatus, withholding running while giving free access to water makes running the higher frequency behavior. On the other hand,

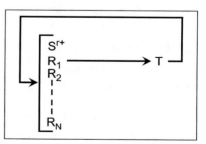

FIG. 6.2 Negative punishment occurs when operant responses R_2 through R_N do not affect ongoing reinforcement (S^{r+}). If the response R_1 is emitted, however, reinforcement is removed for some period of time (T). After that time period has passed, reinforcement is reinstated.

depriving the rat of water while giving it access to running makes drinking the more probable behavior.

At this point, forced running (motorized wheel) is made the consequence of drinking. That is, the rat's drinking is followed by bouts of forced running. What do you think happens? The answer is that it depends on the relative frequency of running and drinking. When running is more probable than drinking (deprivation for running), bouts of forced running reinforce drinking (drinking increases). In contrast, when running is less probable than drinking (deprivation for water), bouts of forced running punish drinking (drinking decreases).

Notice that the same consequence (forced bouts of running) can function as either reinforcement or punishment for behavior, depending on the relative frequencies of the respective behaviors. More generally, Premack's analysis indicates that, like reinforcement, *punishment is relative not absolute*. Even electric shock, usually viewed as an aversive stimulus or punisher, can function as reinforcement under appropriate conditions—as when a fixed-interval schedule of shock is superimposed on a schedule of food reinforcement for lever pressing or on a schedule of brain stimulation reinforcement in humans and other animals (Heath, 1963; Sidman, Brady, Boren, Conrad, & Schulman, 1955).

How to Make Punishment Most Effective

Note that punishment does not teach or condition new behavior. Contingencies of punishment eliminate or, more often, temporarily suppress the rate of operant behavior. In this section, we describe some of the conditions that increase the effectiveness of punishment. Experimental investigations of punishment are important. In the everyday world of people (and other animals), many consequences of behavior involve punishment. Parents scold and spank children, people fall off bicycles, individuals are forced to pay fines, and school kids are made to stand in a corner. All modern cultures use legal sanctions to control their citizens' conduct, and these contingencies are usually punitive. Experiments on punishment have shown how to make punishment most effective. Other research has suggested strong reasons to avoid the use of punishment whenever possible (Sidman, 2001).

The study of punishment is complicated by the fact that punished responses are typically maintained on some schedule of positive reinforcement. In other words, a schedule of punishment is superimposed on a baseline of positive reinforcement. This means that we are really investigating the effects of punishment on behavior maintained by some schedule of positive reinforcement, and results may reflect both of these contingencies. Nonetheless, there are reasonably clear findings that suggest how to make punishment most effective.

Abrupt introduction of punishment

Azrin, Holz, and Hake (1963) found that birds would continue to respond even when intense levels of electric shock (130 V) were delivered for key pecks. This effect occurred when the punisher was introduced at 60 V or less and gradually increased. On the other hand, pigeons that suddenly received moderate-intensity shocks, at 80 V, completely quit responding (see also Azrin, 1959; Miller, 1960). Behavior that produced sudden shock of sufficient intensity was irreversibly suppressed.

Consider the following scenario: Mike has bought a new stereo system and his friend Joe and Joe's 2-year-old daughter drop in for a visit. The child is eating a glob of peanut butter and makes a beeline for the new equipment. Nervously, Mike looks at his friend, who says, "Emily, don't touch—that's Mike's new disk player." The child continues to fondle the knobs on Mike's $900 music system and Joe says, "Please leave that alone!" Emily is still smearing peanut butter on Mike's investment, so Joe glowers at his child and loudly says, "I said stop that!" Emily does not stop and is now threatened with, "If you don't stop, Dad will give you a spanking!" Emily still plays with the stereo.

In desperation, Joe gives Emily a light tap on the bottom, which she ignores. In this circumstance, presumed punishers are introduced at low intensity and gradually increased. Laboratory research suggests that this is a formula for creating a masochist. Of course, the best solution for the stereo problem would be to wipe the child's hands off, or place the equipment out of reach.

Intensity of punishment

The preceding discussion should make it clear that if punishment is going to be used, it should be introduced at a moderate intensity on the first occasion. Generally, higher intensity of punishment results in greater response suppression. Low-intensity positive punishment may leave behavior relatively unaffected, while severe values of the punisher may permanently change behavior (Appel & Peterson, 1965; Azrin, 1960). Several experiments have shown that intense punishment can completely eliminate responding (Appel, 1961; Storms, Boroczi, & Broen, 1962). One interesting implication is that once complete suppression of responding occurs, behavior is unlikely to recover for some time even when the punishment contingency is withdrawn. This is because the organism stops responding and never contacts the changed environment.

If an animal does respond again after punishment is withdrawn, behavior eventually recovers to prepunishment levels. These observations lead Skinner (1953) and others to suggest that punishment only produces a temporary suppression of behavior:

> Recently, the suspicion has . . . arisen that punishment does not in fact do what it is supposed to do. An immediate effect in reducing a tendency to behave is clear enough, but this may be misleading. The reduction in strength may not be permanent.
>
> (p. 183)

This passage reflects Skinner's lifelong objection to the use of punishment for behavior regulation. That is, Skinner argued against the use of punishment and for the use of positive reinforcement in human affairs.

Nonetheless, research shows that high-intensity positive punishment can permanently eliminate responding. This elimination of responses does not seem to be affected by time away from the experimental situation (Azrin, 1959, 1960). For example, Masserman (1946) placed cats in a situation in which they had been punished 20 months earlier. The animals did not emit the punished response, even though the punishment contingency was discontinued. Thus, high-intensity punishment can reduce the rate of response to absolute zero, and this appears to be an enduring effect.

Immediacy of punishment

Punishment is most effective at reducing responses when it closely follows behavior (Azrin, 1956; Cohen, 1968). This effect can be missed easily because punishment generates emotional behavior that may disrupt operant responses. In other words, when first introduced, *positive punishment elicits reflexive behavior that prevents the occurrence of operant behavior*. Watch a child (or adult) who has just been chastised severely for making rude noises. You will probably see the child sit quietly, possibly cry, or look away from others. In common language, we may say that the child is pouting but, in fact, what is happening is that reflexive emotional behavior is disrupting all operant behavior. If punishment follows immediately for making rude noises (the target behavior), those noises (as well as many other operants) would decrease in frequency. Making noises, however, would be relatively unaffected if punishment did not closely follow the target response.

Estes (1944) punished some rats immediately after they made a response, while another group received *delayed* punishment. Both groups of animals showed a similar reduction in bar pressing. This finding was replicated 11 years later by Hunt and Brady (1955) and suggests that positive punishment reduces operant responses because it elicits competing respondent behavior. Later research by Azrin (1956) found that after the first hour of exposure to positive punishment, immediate versus delayed punishment makes a large difference. Responses that were punished after a time delay recovered substantially, but when the punisher was delivered immediately, responses were often completely eliminated. Thus, it appears that the introduction of punishment generates conditioned emotional responses that may at first disrupt operant behavior. However, the contingency is eventually contacted and, in the long run, makes a large difference. To make punishment most effective, it should be delivered immediately after the response.

Schedule of punishment

In general, positive punishment is most effective when it is delivered after each response or continuously (Zimmerman & Ferster, 1963) rather than intermittently (Filby & Appel, 1966). Azrin, Holz, and Hake (1963) trained pigeons to peck a key on a VI 3-min schedule of food reinforcement. Once responding was stable, shocks were presented after 100, 200, 300, 500, or 1000 key pecks. Rate of response substantially declined even when punishment was delivered after 1000 responses. As rate of punishment increased, the number of responses per hour declined. In other words, as more responses were punished, operant rate decreased. Continuous punishment (FR 1) produced the greatest response suppression. The effect is similar to increasing the intensity of the punisher—to maximize suppression of responses, deliver the punisher as frequently as possible and increase its intensity.

Rate of response patterns on various schedules of punishment (FR, FI, VI, and VR) are usually *opposite* to the patterns produced on similar schedules of positive reinforcement. For example, an FI schedule of punishment when superimposed on a VI schedule of reinforcement for key pecking by pigeons produces an *inverse scallop* (recall that FI reinforcement often yields a scalloping pattern). That is, the occurrence of each punisher is followed by an immediately high rate of pecking that gradually declines as the time to the next punishment approaches (Azrin, 1956).

In summary, to make punishment most effective one should abruptly deliver an intense aversive stimulus immediately following the response and do this every time the response occurs.

FOCUS ON: Use of punishment in treatment

There are behaviorally deficient and psychotic people who, for a variety of reasons, engage in self-destructive behavior. This behavior may escalate to the point at which the person is hitting, scratching, biting, or gouging himself or herself most of the day. In some cases, self-destructive acts are so frequent and intense that the person is hospitalized. Occasionally physical injury is irreversible, as when a child bangs his or her head on a wall until brain damage occurs. Although positive-reinforcement programs have been used to alleviate severe behavior problems, these contingencies are not always successful. Because of this, behavior therapists have resorted to punishment as a way of reducing self-destructive behavior.

One seemingly benign type of punishment used to suppress self-injurious behavior is water misting (Osborne, 2002). The literature indicates that contingent misting in the face reduces self-injurious behavior by 30–90% depending upon alternative sources of reinforcement. However, the use of water misting as an effective—if not completely effective—punishment procedure has not been formally used for several years.

Misting and other techniques of positive punishment have been controversial (Feldman, 1990). Opponents of punishment argue that such procedures are morally wrong and they advocate a total ban on its use (e.g., Guess, Helmstetter, Turnbull, & Knowlton, 1986; Sobsey, 1990). These researchers also suggest that punishment is not necessary because many positive methods are available to treat severe behavior problems. They further propose that positive techniques are as effective as punishment for eliminating self-destructive responses. On the other side of the issue are therapists and parents of self-abusive children who advocate the individual's right to effective treatment (e.g., Matson & Taras, 1989; Van Houten, Axelrod, Bailey, Favell, Foxx, Iwata, et al., 1988). The proponents of effective treatment claim that a combination of positive reinforcement and punishment is the best way to manage severely self-injurious behavior.

One reason given for not using punishment in applied settings is that aversive techniques may generate emotional distress and aggression (LaVigna & Donnellan, 1986; Lohrman-O'Rourke & Zirkel, 1998; Meyer & Evans, 1989). Opponents of positive punishment often support this view by pointing to research with animals concerning electric shock and pain-elicited aggression (see the section "Side Effects of Aversive Procedures" later in this chapter). Essentially, when animals are given noncontingent electric shock, they attack other animals or inanimate objects. Murray Sidman (2001) has advanced broad opposition to punishment in his book, *Coercion and Its Fallout*. Sidman argues that most of the world's problems both individually and socially are the product and by-products of coercive contingencies (punishment and negative reinforcement). In a treatment setting, these effects and side effects of punishment imply that aversive therapy may produce as many problems as it alleviates. Nonetheless, Kushner (1970) presents a review of the effective and justified use of electric shock with humans in a clinical context. And other applied researchers currently are investigating the use of less intrusive conditioned punishers for the regulation of severe problem behavior in people with developmental disabilities (Salvy, Mulick, Butter, Bartlett, & Linscheid, 2004; Vorndran & Lerman, 2006).

Some time ago, Solomon (1969) recognized that there must be explicit conditions that lead to the side effects of punishment—under specific conditions punishment has devastating and debilitating effects, whereas under other conditions punishment may not. Solomon (1969) stated:

> When punishments are asserted to be ineffective controllers of [operant] behavior, they are in contrast, often asserted to be devastating controllers of emotional reactions, leading to neurotic and psychotic symptoms, and to general pessimism, depressiveness, constriction of thinking, horrible psychosomatic diseases, and even death! This is somewhat of a paradox, I think. The convincing part of such generalizations is only their face validity. There are experiments, many of them carefully done, in which these neurotic outcomes were clearly observed. . . . The side effects are frightening, indeed, and should not be ignored! But there *must be* some rules, some principles, governing the appearance of such side effects, for they *do not* appear in all experiments involving the use of strong punishment or the elicitation of terror.
>
> (p. 89)

Solomon believes that an in-depth scientific analysis of punishment will solve the value question of whether or not to use punishment in a given situation. Although we agree with Solomon's hopes, current research on punishment is not sufficient to answer value questions. That is, research evidence suggests that complex interactions may occur between the reinforcement schedule maintaining behavior and punishment (Epling & Pierce, 1990; Linscheid & Meinhold, 1990). Most of these interactions, however, have not been sufficiently studied or replicated to draw any firm conclusions.

One reason for the lack of modern research is that many people think that it is not right to expose animals to punishment procedures. On the basis of animal ethics, investigations of punishment have almost been eliminated at the basic level. Until our society finds it more important to understand punishment and its use, questions about the coercive control of behavior cannot be well informed by scientific analysis.

Reduce the effectiveness of positive reinforcement

Punishment suppresses behavior more when positive reinforcement for the response is reduced in effectiveness (Dinsmoor, 1952). Azrin, Holz, and Hake (1963) trained pigeons to peck a key on a VI 3-min schedule of food reinforcement. After responding was stable, they introduced an intense

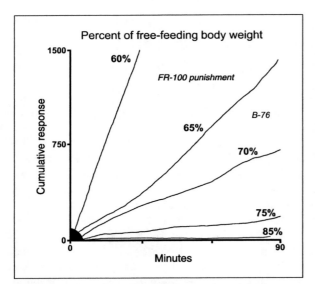

Percent of free-feeding body weight

FIG. 6.3 Level of food deprivation and punished responding maintained by a VI food reinforcement schedule. Adapted from "Fixed-Ratio Punishment" by N. H. Azrin, W. C. Holz, and D. Hake, 1963, *Journal of the Experimental Analysis of Behavior, 6*, 141–148. Copyright 1963 by the Society for the Experimental Analysis of Behavior, Inc.

160-V shock for every 100th response. Birds were exposed to the schedule of reinforcement plus punishment at several levels of food deprivation. Recall that deprivation for food is an *establishing operation* that should increase pecking the key for food (and increase the reinforcement effectiveness of food). The animals were punished for responding at 60, 65, 70, 75, and 85% of free-feeding body weight. At 85% weight, punishment virtually stopped the birds' responding. However, at 60% weight the pigeons maintained a high, stable rate of response. As shown in Figure 6.3, rate of response was ordered by level of deprivation—the less the deprivation for food (satiation), the more effective punishment was. Thus, behavior that is punished may be completely suppressed when the positive reinforcement contingency is made less effective through satiation. Interestingly, there is evidence that once complete suppression has occurred, the behavior does not recover even when the probability to respond for reinforcement is increased (Masserman, 1946; Storms et al., 1962). For example, a rat may be punished when it responds for food and its behavior completely eliminated. Next, the level of food deprivation is increased but responding remains at a zero rate.

These findings may have practical implications. Punishment is sometimes used to reduce the frequency of human behavior (see the preceding section). And there are side effects of punitive regulation, suggesting that these techniques should be used with caution. Nonetheless, when people behave in ways that hurt themselves or others, punishment can be used to quickly suppress this behavior. Children who severely hurt themselves by banging their heads, hitting themselves, and chewing on their flesh may benefit when positive punishment is used to rapidly reduce self-injury.

Self-injurious behavior may be maintained by unintentional attention from caretakers. Lovaas and Simmons (1969) treated three severely self-destructive children who were placed on extinction (adult attention was withdrawn) for hitting themselves. During extinction, one child (John) hit himself 9000 times before stopping. The other child who was treated with extinction demonstrated similar behavior, emitting many self-injurious responses before extinction was complete. Lovaas and Simmons (1969) commented that:

> This procedure of withdrawing or making potential reinforcers unavailable has an undesirable attribute, in that it is not immediately effective and temporarily exposes the child to the danger of severe damage from his own self-destruction, which is particularly intense during the early stages of the extinction run. In some cases of severe self-destruction, it is ill advised to place the child on extinction. Marilyn, . . . for example, could have inflicted serious self-injury or possibly even killed herself during an extinction run.
>
> (p. 155)

In contrast, when positive punishment was used to reduce self-injury, all three children hit themselves a few times and then quit. In cases like these, punishment seems warranted both in terms of effectiveness and ethical considerations.

Temporary use of punishment can save a child from years of self-injury. Even so, animal research suggests further ways to make punishment even more humane. The children treated by Lovaas and Simmons (1969) were apparently engaging in self-injurious behavior due to social attention from adult caretakers. One way to refine the punishment procedure would involve satiation for caretaker attention. Adults would provide lots of noncontingent attention to a child before using punishment of self-injury. This would be easy to implement; staff would hold, cuddle, and talk to the child for a few days before punishment is used. Once satiation for attention has occurred, even mild punishment may eliminate the self-injurious responses. Basic research, as we have seen, also suggests that when deprivation for attention increases again, self-destructive responding will not recover.

Response alternatives

A straightforward way to make punishment more effective is to give a person another way to obtain reinforcement. When a reinforced response alternative is available, even moderate levels of punishment suppress behavior. To use a response alternative procedure, it is essential to identify the consequences maintaining the target behavior. Next, motivation may be reduced and the person given another way to obtain the same reinforcer. Herman and Azrin (1964) had people lever press on a VI schedule of reinforcement. Each lever press then produced an annoying buzzing sound, but the procedure only slightly reduced the rate of response. When people were given another response option that did not produce the buzzer, they quickly changed to that alternative and punished responses were eliminated (see also Azrin & Holz, 1966, p. 405).

Pretend that there is a convenience store in the middle of the block directly behind your house. You often walk to the store, but if you turn left to go around the block you pass a chained pit bulldog that lunges and growls at you. On the other hand, if you turn right you do not pass the dog. It is obvious that most of us will choose the unpunished route to the store. If, however, turning right leads to a path that does not get you to the store, you may continue walking past the dog. In reality, of course, you could walk on the other side of the street or drive to the store—these are also unpunished alternative responses.

CONTINGENCIES OF NEGATIVE REINFORCEMENT

When an organism emits an alternative unpunished response, the behavior may be viewed as escape or avoidance. If the response is made while the punishing stimulus is occurring, it is an **escape** response. The pit bulldog is growling at you, and you escape by crossing to the other side of the street. When the operant prevents the punishing stimulus, the behavior is **avoidance**. You turn right to go around the block and do not walk by the dog. In both cases, the removal or prevention of an event or stimulus *increases* operant behavior and the contingency is defined as **negative reinforcement** (cell 3 of Figure 6.1).

Any event or stimulus that increases operant rate by its removal (or prevention) is called a **negative reinforcer**. Notice that the same event (e.g., delivery of electric shock) is a punisher in a punishment procedure and a negative reinforcer in a negative reinforcement procedure. When neither punishment nor negative reinforcement is well defined, we refer to the event as an *aversive stimulus*—a stimulus that the organism evades, escapes, or avoids.

In everyday life, the distinction between negative and positive reinforcement is occasionally uncertain (Michael, 1975) and continues as a major topic of debate in behavior analysis (Baron & Galizio, 2005, 2006). For example, do you open a window on a hot day to get a cool breeze or to escape the heat? Putting on glasses clarifies vision but also removes a blurry view of the world. Hineline (1984) made this point when he stated:

The addition of one event is the removal of another, and vice versa: Adding heat is removing cold; adding food is decreasing deprivation; adding a smile removes a frown. However, there is a fundamental asymmetry, for if a stimulus or situation is to be reducible or removable by some response, that response must occur in its presence. In contrast, positively reinforced responses necessarily occur in the absence of the stimuli upon which reinforcement is based.

(pp. 496–497)

One issue is that physics tells us that there is no such thing as cold—there is only an increase or a decreases in heat. Thus, a person who places logs on a fire is adding heat and the behavior is controlled by positive reinforcement not negative reinforcement (removing cold). On the other hand, there are many other instances where it may be difficult to tell the difference in everyday life. In the operant laboratory, however, the distinction between positive and negative reinforcement is reasonably easy to arrange, and experimental investigations of negative reinforcement are relatively clear-cut (Khalili, Daley, & Cheney, 1969). When a response results in the removal or postponement of a stimulus and the rate of response increases, negative reinforcement has occurred (see also Catania, 1973).

The distinction between escape and avoidance is somewhat artificial. Consider an experiment on escape, in which an animal makes a response that turns off a continuous electric shock. Hineline (1977) has suggested that in experiments like this:

Electric shock continuously delivered may not be continuously received. For example, if it is grid shock the animal may produce intermittency by jumping up and down. Nevertheless the escape procedure is treated as a clear case of negative reinforcement by removal of shock. The experimenter may even arrange an escape procedure by explicitly presenting intermittent pulses of shock several times per second, rather than presenting it continuously. But if shock is presented several times per second, why not just twice per second, or once per second, or even less frequently? At some point we tend to stop labeling it continuous shock, and call it a stream of shocks. Responses are reinforced by interruption of (escape from) a stream of shocks. But as the pulses of shocks are spaced out still further, to one every five, ten, or twenty seconds, we tend to characterize suspension of this situation not as removal of shock . . . but as reduction in shock frequency [avoidance].

(p. 369)

To make this clear, when an animal presses a lever to turn off a stream of shocks that are occurring every 0.2 s, we call this escape. If, however, the same animal makes a response that interrupts shocks that are scheduled every 20 s, then shocks are postponed and the procedure is usually called avoidance.

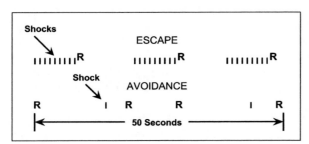

FIG. 6.4 In the escape contingency, shocks (indicated by the vertical lines) are scheduled once every second and a response (R) delays the aversive stimulus for 10 s. The amount of time that a response delays shock onset is called the response–shock interval. During avoidance, shocks occur once every 10 s and a response produces a 10-s delay. Notice that the only difference in the two procedures is the time between shock deliveries, called the shock–shock interval.

The only difference between escape and avoidance, presented in Figure 6.4, is the time between shocks, or the **shock–shock interval (S–S)**. In both procedures, the time away from shock produced by responses is the same; the **response–shock interval (R–S)** is 10 s in both cases. Thus, *escape and avoidance represent endpoints on a continuum of negative reinforcement.*

In this chapter, however, we make the traditional distinction between escape and avoidance. In avoidance, an organism evades, prevents, or postpones some event; in escape, it removes the stimulus (or itself) from the situation. A person escapes a boring party by leaving it, or the party is avoided by never going to it. That is, a person who avoids going to the party presumably has a history of boring parties and so evades them by staying at home. Thus, the person who escapes the party and the one who avoids it are both showing the effects of negative reinforcement.

Escape

In escape learning, an operant changes the situation from one in which a negative reinforcer is present to one in which it is absent, for some period of time. A pigeon is exposed to continuous loud white noise, and when the bird pecks a key the noise is turned off. If pecking the key increases, then this defines the procedure as negative reinforcement. A person hangs up the telephone to cut off an obscene caller. Children may run home after school because a bully picked on them. A dog jumps across a barrier (leaves the situation) to escape electric shock. Figure 6.5 is a diagram of a shuttle-box apparatus that is used to train escape in dogs. The figure also shows the notation for an escape contingency. Notice that there are many responses that may be emitted, but only R_1 removes the negative reinforcer.

In general, organisms acquire escape responses more readily than avoidance responses. This is easy to understand. In escape (but not avoidance), there is an *immediate change* from the presence to absence of the negative reinforcer.

Another factor that affects how quickly an escape response occurs is its compatibility with reflexive behavior elicited by the negative reinforcer. Evolution has ensured that organisms respond to aversive stimuli. In the everyday world, animals may only get one chance to save their lives in the presence of an aversive event. Running like crazy makes good sense (in many cases) when a predator appears. Those animals that "ponder over" the situation are likely to have contributed calories to the predator but not genes to the next generation. Thus, natural selection has insured that species-specific reflexes often are elicited by aversive stimuli that also function as negative reinforcers. When rats are presented with intense electric shock, they typically freeze—emitting a response that interferes with escape conditioning. That is, depressing and releasing a lever is incompatible with freezing, the species-typical response to shock. If the animal is simply required to press the lever and hold it down, the escape response is more readily acquired; this is because holding the lever down is compatible with freezing. Generally, *negative reinforcement frequently elicits reflexive behavior that interferes with the acquisition of operant behavior supported by the removal of the negative reinforcer.* Khalili and Cheney (1969), however, developed a program of shock-off titration that reduced interference by reflexive behavior. With this procedure, rats were trained to lever press for shock removal on fixed-ratio (FR) schedules as high as 80 responses.

Conditioning escape behavior is easier when the *operant is similar to reflexive behavior elicited by the aversive stimulus.* A rat can be readily trained to run on a wheel to escape electric shocks, but conditioning the animal to stand up is much more difficult (Bolles, 1970). Running is a species-typical response to electric shock but standing is not. Although respondent and operant conditioning interact during escape training, behavior eventually comes under the control of the operant contingency. For example, rats that are trained to run on a wheel (or hold down a lever) to escape shock will stop running (or bar holding) if this response does not terminate the negative reinforcer. The species-specific response does not predominate over behavior required by the contingencies of reinforcement.

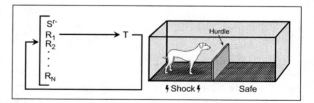

FIG. 6.5 (Left) An escape contingency: In the presence of a negative reinforcer (S^{r-}), an operant (R) produces a period of time (T) in which the aversive stimulus is absent. The increase in the operant is the process of negative reinforcement. (Right) A shuttle box that may be used to condition escape responses in dogs. The animal is placed in the left compartment at the start of a trial. Electric shock is turned on, and the dog can escape the aversive stimulus by jumping the hurdle and going to the safe area, on the right side of the box.

Avoidance

When an operant prevents the occurrence of an aversive stimulus, the contingency is called avoidance. You typically walk the shortest distance to the university, but recently an acquaintance has joined you at the halfway mark, blabbing on and on about boring topics. Now you walk a longer distance than needed to the university because that route does not take you by the boring person's house. During their annual migration, young wildebeests stop to drink at a river infested with large crocodiles. The crocodiles wait each year for this gourmet lunch and "pig out" on rare wildebeest. Survivors of the crocodile picnic choose a different watering spot the next year.

Discriminated avoidance

Avoidance may involve responding when a warning signal precedes an aversive stimulus. Because the organism only responds when the warning signal occurs, the procedure is called **discriminated avoidance**. A parent may say to a child, "Nathan, keep the noise down or else you will have to go to bed." An antelope may smell a lion and change the direction it is traveling. In these cases, the child is told what not to do and the antelope detects what direction to avoid. Pretend that you are all set to go to a party but are told that Dr. Hannibal Sloat will be attending. Dr. Sloat is an unusually obnoxious professor, and you have just flunked his human sexuality class. In this case, the warning that he will be at the bash may result in you avoiding the party. Figure 6.6 is a diagram of discriminated avoidance in an experimental situation. In the presence of a warning stimulus (S^{ave}), a response postpones for some time (T) the onset of a negative reinforcer (S^{r-}). If the response does not occur, the negative reinforcer is presented and after some time the warning stimulus comes on again.

In the operant laboratory, discriminated avoidance is typically acquired only after many hours of training. Rats will quickly learn to lever press for food, but take a surprisingly long time to acquire lever pressing to avoid electric shock (Solomon & Brush, 1956). Pigeons are also slow at acquiring avoidance behavior when they are required to peck a key to avoid an aversive event. A major reason for this is that in the discriminated avoidance procedure, the warning stimulus (S^{ave}) is also a CS that elicits respondent behavior (like freezing) that interferes with operant behavior (Meyer, Cho, & Wesemann, 1960). As stated in the section on escape conditioning, other responses like running and jumping are elicited by shock and are acquired much more readily than lever pressing. For example, Macphail (1968) reported that pigeons required 120 trials of signaled avoidance to run down a straight alley to avoid shock. Notice that running to a warning stimulus for shock is not species-typical behavior for pigeons—birds usually fly away. Rats, on the other hand, required only two or three trials to learn to jump onto a platform when a warning stimulus occurred (Baum, 1965, 1969). For rats, jumping to safety is respondent behavior to the warning stimulus; this behavior also was compatible with the operant avoidance contingency.

In an interesting series of experiments, Modaresi (1990) found that lever pressing to avoid shock was acquired more readily if the lever was high on the wall and if lever pressing not only avoided the shocks but also resulted in access to a platform to stand on. Additional experiments showed that these two aspects of the situation were in accord with the rats' species-specific behavior. That is, rats naturally stretch upward and seek a safe area when faced with painful aversive stimuli. Thus, to produce rapid acquisition of avoidance responses, choose behavior that is naturally elicited by the negative reinforcer.

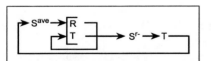

FIG. 6.6 Discriminated avoidance occurs when a warning stimulus (S^{ave}) leads to a condition in which, after some time (T), a negative reinforcer (S^{r-}) is presented. If a response (R) is made, the negative reinforcer is delayed and further responses continue to prevent the onset of the aversive stimulus. Once the negative reinforcer is presented, some amount of time passes and the warning stimulus again comes on.

Nondiscriminated (Sidman) avoidance

In the laboratory, a rat may press a lever to avoid the delivery of an electric shock. Shocks are scheduled every 60 s, and each lever press prevents the shock and starts another 1-min cycle (a postponement schedule of negative reinforcement). The shocks are simply programmed to occur on the basis of time, and there is *no warning signal* that they are about to be presented. When there is no warning stimulus, the contingency is called **nondiscriminated avoidance**. There are people who compulsively wash their hands to get rid of unseen germs. In this case, hand washing is the operant and reduction in the rate of sickness negatively reinforces washing. As you will see in later chapters,

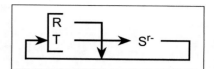

FIG. 6.7   A Mechner diagram of nondiscriminated avoidance. A response (R) produces some time (T) in which negative reinforcers (S^{r-}) are not presented.

negative reinforcement appears to underlie many so-called abnormal behavior patterns. Figure 6.7 illustrates simple nondiscriminated avoidance in which the aversive event is presented without a warning signal.

This book was written on a computer and an unexpected power failure could result in many hours of lost work. To prevent this event, the authors regularly emit the behavior of *hitting the save key*. This avoidance response saves the text to a disk or hard drive and is maintained because it has prevented computer crashes from costing the authors a day's work. Over time, however, pressing the save key is so effective that loss of work rarely occurs and the rate of response begins to decline—we say we forgot to save or were careless. At this point, a computer crash or equivalent "shock" happens and reinstates the avoidance behavior. Thus, avoidance is inherently cyclical. It is a paradox: the more effective the avoidance response, the less shocks received; but the less shocks, the weaker the avoidance behavior. Like all operant behavior, avoidance responses must be reinforced at least occasionally for the behavior to be maintained at high strength. In *Coercion and Its Fallout*, Murray Sidman (2001) pointed to the avoidance paradox when he compared contingencies of avoidance and positive reinforcement. He stated:

> The avoidance paradox reveals a critical difference between positive reinforcement and negative reinforcement by avoidance. With avoidance, success breeds failure; the behavior weakens and will stop unless another shock brings it back. With positive reinforcement, success breeds more of the same; the behavior continues. If the only reason a student studies is to keep from failing, an occasional failure or near-failure will be necessary to keep the studying going. A student who studies because of the options that new learning makes available will stop only if the products of learning become irrelevant. If citizens keep within the law only because that keeps them out of jail, they will eventually exceed the speed limit, cheat on their income taxes, give or accept bribes, or worse. Citizens who keep within the law because of the benefits from participating in an orderly community will not face cyclic temptations to break the law.
>
> (p. 145)

The use of check stops by police and audits by the tax department insure that drivers and taxpayers encounter or are threatened with occasional negative reinforcers. Without these occasional "shocks" there would be far fewer honest people in our society. More generally, moral behavior that is learned as avoidance will weaken and stop without socially arranged negative reinforcement backing it up.

Murray Sidman (1953) was the first to investigate nondiscriminated avoidance and the procedure is often called **Sidman avoidance** or free operant avoidance. Periodic shocks were given to a rat unless the animal emitted an operant response. The time between shocks was (and still is) called the *shock–shock* (S–S) interval. When a response occurred, it delayed the onset of shock for some specified period of time called the *response–shock* (R–S) interval (see Figure 6.4 again). *Avoidance responding is learned more rapidly when the R–S interval is longer than the S–S interval* (Leaf, 1965;

Sidman, 1962). In other words, when the operant delays the negative reinforcer (R–S) for a period greater than the time between shocks (S–S), conditioning is enhanced (see Baron, 1991, p. 191).

FOCUS ON: An analysis of avoidance behavior

Pretend that you live in a world in which evil professors have absolute authority over students. One day you walk into class and your professor says, "Class, from today until the end of term you are subjects in a shocking experiment." You notice the straps attached to your desk and the two large electrodes embedded in your chair. Although you protest vigorously, the teaching assistant straps you to the chair and says, "Press the button on your desk, if you want to." You look at the button and wish you had taken another course. A powerful (but your professor says harmless) electric shock is delivered every 20 s (S–S = 20 s). In desperation, you press your button and notice that the frequency of shocks declines (you get fewer shocks). Each press of the button delays shock for 30 s (R–S = 30 s), and after some experience you regularly press your button and avoid most or all of the shocks. Consider, however, what would happen if the S–S interval remained at 20 s but the R–S interval changed to 5 s. Pressing the button would increase the frequency of shocks unless you maintained a high rate of response. This occurs because a response brings the next shock closer than not responding does (5 s versus 20 s). Animal research suggests that under these conditions avoidance behavior is poorly maintained.

Shock Frequency and Avoidance Behavior

Avoidance behavior is poorly maintained when responses do not reduce the frequency of aversive stimulation (Sidman, 1962). In a classic experiment, Herrnstein and Hineline (1966) exposed 18 rats to a random sequence of electric shocks. The animals could press a lever to reduce the frequency of shocks, but some responses were still followed by the negative reinforcer. That is, bar pressing reduced the number of shocks per second but did not completely eliminate them. Seventeen of the 18 rats in this experiment showed avoidance responding—they reliably pressed the lever.

This finding has generated a debate over the critical factors that regulate avoidance behavior. Essentially, the issue concerns molar versus molecular control of behavior in avoidance. From a **molecular perspective**, the moment-to-moment time between shocks (S–S) and the time from response to shock (R–S) represent the essential variables regulating avoidance responses (Dinsmoor, 1977, 2001a, 2001b). Nonetheless, the bulk of the evidence supports a **molar perspective** (Baum, 2001), suggesting that the molar variable, *overall reduction in shock frequency* (or sensitivity to rates of shock), establishes and maintains operant avoidance (Gardner & Lewis, 1976; Hineline, 1970; Lewis, Gardner, & Hutton, 1976; Mellitz, Hineline, Whitehouse, & Laurence, 1983).

Consider what happens when your friend persistently nags you to stop watching television and start working on your term paper. You may tell the person, "Leave me alone, I'll get to it after the movie is over." This will likely reduce the frequency of nagging but not eliminate it. In fact, your reply sometimes may be followed by, "I can't understand how you can just sit there glued to the idiot box, when you have so much to do." Assuming that the nagging is a negative reinforcer, how can your vocal operant ("leave me alone . . .") be maintained? The answer, of course, is that it has reduced the overall number of nagging episodes while you are engrossed in *Return of the Killer Tomatoes*.

Although reduction in shock frequency can establish and maintain avoidance behavior, Hineline (personal communication, May 1989) has stated that "rather than trying to establish either the molar or molecular view as correct, the point [is] to discover what determines the scale of process. That is, under what circumstances is behavior sensitive to its more remote consequences, as contrasted with its more immediate ones?" (see also Hineline, 2001, for a more detailed assessment). Philip Hineline is a professor of psychology at Temple University in Philadelphia. He has been interested in negative reinforcement and the regulation of operant behavior over short and long timescales. In his work with Timothy Hackenberg, he has drawn these two interests together.

Long-Term Effects of Negative Reinforcement

Hackenberg and Hineline (1987) used a conditioned-suppression paradigm to show the interrelations between avoidance and behavior maintained by positive reinforcement. *Conditioned suppression* is a procedure in which a conditioned aversive stimulus (a tone that has signaled shock) is presented when an animal is responding for food reinforcement. The tone usually suppresses the operant behavior regulated by food. Hackenberg and Hineline (1987) introduced an interesting twist to show that a similar effect could be obtained when a period of avoidance either preceded or followed entire sessions of food reinforcement.

In their experiment, eight rats were trained to press a lever for food on a fixed-interval 3-min schedule (FI 3 min). After response rates were stable on the FI schedule, animals were exposed to 100 min of unsignaled shock avoidance. During this period, shocks occurred every 5 s (S–S = 5 s) unless the rat pressed a lever that postponed the shocks for 20 seconds (R–S = 20 s). These avoidance periods were presented to four rats just before the food reinforcement s. The other four animals were given the avoidance period immediately after they responded for food. The question was whether the avoidance periods would suppress responding during food reinforcement sessions.

Results indicated that operant responding for positive reinforcement was disrupted when avoidance periods either preceded or followed the food sessions. This suppression occurred even though the response rates of the rats remained high enough to obtain most of the available food. The avoidance periods had an effect that did not depend on interference with behavior maintained by positive reinforcement. When avoidance periods came after food reinforcement sessions, there was more disruption of food-related behavior than when avoidance periods preceded fixed-interval responding for food. In addition, when avoidance was discontinued, operant responses for food took longer to recover if the avoidance periods came after the sessions of positive reinforcement.

In everyday language, the rats seemed worried about their appointment with doom (remember the animals had experienced these appointments in the past). This is not unlike a student who has difficulty studying because she is scheduled to have a wisdom tooth extracted a few hours later. People, and apparently rats, respond to *long-term aversive consequences in their environment*. This disruption of responding is severe when long-term aversive consequences are impending. Immediately delivered aversive events can also suppress operant behavior but, all things being equal, do not appear to affect responses as strongly as long-term aversive consequences. By implication, a child who receives reprimands from a teacher for talking out of turn will show little disruption of play and school work. In contrast, a student who is regularly harassed by a bully after school is over may show *general disruption* of school activities throughout the day.

SIDE EFFECTS OF AVERSIVE PROCEDURES

There are obvious ethical reasons for not using punishment contingencies to change behavior. In addition to ethical concerns, there are serious side effects that often arise when contingencies of punishment and negative reinforcement are employed. Skinner (1953, 1971) has consistently argued against the use of punishment techniques:

The commonnest technique of control in modern life is punishment. The pattern is familiar: if a man does not behave as you wish, knock him down; if a child misbehaves, spank him; if the people of a country misbehave, bomb them. Legal and police systems are based on such punishments as fines, flogging, incarceration, and hard labor. Religious control is exerted through penances, threats of excommunication, and consignment to hell-fire. Education has not wholly abandoned the birch rod. In everyday personal contact we control through censure, snubbing, disapproval, or banishment. In short, the degree to which we use punishment as a technique of control seems to be limited only by the degree to which we can gain the necessary power. All of this is done with the intention of reducing tendencies to behave in certain ways. Reinforcement builds up these tendencies; punishment is designed to tear them down.

The technique [punishment] has often been analyzed, and many familiar questions continue to be asked. Must punishment be closely contingent upon the behavior punished? Must the individual know what he is being punished for? What forms of punishment are most effective and under what circumstances? This concern may be due to the realization that the technique has unfortunate by-products. In the long run, punishment, unlike reinforcement, works to the disadvantage of both the punished organism and the punishing agency. The aversive stimuli which are needed generate emotions, including predispositions to escape or retaliate, and disabling anxieties. For thousands of years men have asked whether the method could not be improved or whether some alternative practice would not be better.

(Skinner, 1953, pp. 182–183)

Behavioral Persistence

As we have seen, punishment may under some circumstances produce a rapid decline in behavior. Consider that when positive punishment is used, it is almost always in a circumstance in which one person is attempting to reduce the aversive behavior of another. A teacher punishes a child who talks loudly out of turn in class; a wife shouts at her husband for making sexist comments at a party; and a boss threatens to fire an employee who is insubordinate. In each of these examples, the responses of the teacher, wife, and boss are *negatively reinforced* by a reduction in talking out of turn, sexist jokes, and insubordinate comments. Thus, individuals who effectively use punishment are more likely to use aversive regulation on future occasions. This is an important point: The "successful" use of punishment leads to further use of the technique, which produces the other side effects of aversive control.

Operant–respondent interactions and persistence

Consider a person who has received a painful wasp sting. The sight and buzz of the insect precede the sting and (for some people) become powerful conditioned stimuli (CS) that elicit anxiety. The CS^- that is established will likely generalize to similar sights and sounds (i.e., the sight of other flying insects, the buzz of a harmless fly). The CS^- also has a dual function: In terms of Pavlovian conditioning, it elicits anxiety; in an operant sense, it functions as a conditioned aversive stimulus (S^{ave}) and will strengthen behavior that removes it (negative reinforcement). To extinguish the effects of the CS^-, it must be presented in the absence of the unconditioned stimulus (respondent extinction). Under ordinary circumstances the CS^- would rapidly extinguish since buzzing sounds and flying insects (CS^-) are rarely accompanied by pain (US). However, people who are afraid of wasps and bees avoid places in which they may be found and leave locations in which they encounter buzzing sounds and flying insects. That is, *avoidance behavior maintained by operant conditioning prevents respondent extinction.*

One way to place avoidance behavior on extinction is to expose the organism to aversive stimulation while preventing effective escape responses. A rat may be trained to press a lever to turn off electric shock, but during extinction bar presses have no effect. Extinction occurs most rapidly when it is clearly signaled—a buzzer could be turned on during extinction and turned off when responses prevented shock. However, in many everyday settings, escape and avoidance responses are resistant to extinction. This *persistence occurs when the difference between the acquisition and extinction setting is low* (extinction is not clearly signaled). When the difference between the extinction setting and conditions under which the contingency is in effect is slight, extinction is not discriminated and avoidance responding continues. In everyday life, a particular dentist's office smells and looks similar to one in which pain was experienced or flying insects and buzzing sounds were accompanied by a sting.

The famous psychiatrist who survived the Nazi concentration camps, Bruno Bettelheim, provided a moving account of behavioral persistence and aversive control:

> Often an SS man would for a while enforce some nonsensical rule, originating in a whim of the moment. Usually it was quickly forgotten, but there were always some old prisoners who continued to observe it and tried to enforce it on others long after the SS had lost interest. Once, for example, an SS man was inspecting the prisoners' apparel and found that some of their shoes were dirty on the inside. He ordered all prisoners to wash their shoes inside and out with soap and water. Treated this way, the heavy shoes became hard as stone. The order was never repeated, and many prisoners did not even try to carry it out the first time, since the SS, as was often the case, gave the order, stood around for a few minutes and then left. Until he was gone, every prisoner busied himself with carrying out the order, after which they promptly quit. Nevertheless there were some old prisoners who not only continued to wash the insides of their shoes every day but cursed all who failed to do so as being negligent and dirty. These prisoners believed firmly that all rules set down by the SS were desirable standards of behavior, at least in the camp.

> (in Scott, 1971, p. 206)

The prisoners were, of course, washing their shoes to escape the negative reinforcers that the SS would administer if the prisoners did not obey the order. Some of the men became very persistent and continued washing their shoes even when the SS did not require them to do so. Generally, it was the older prisoners who had more experience with the aversive contingencies of the SS who were likely to persist in washing their shoes. For these men, the concentration camp experience generated escape and avoidance behavior. The older prisoners in the concentration camp also accepted the rules of the SS and preached these standards to their fellow inmates. These responses are more complex than simple avoidance and may be analyzed as rule-governed behavior (Skinner, 1969; see also Chapter 11).

Learned Helplessness

A similar persistence effect occurs when animals are exposed to inescapable aversive stimulation and then are given an opportunity to escape. In the phenomenon called **learned helplessness**, an animal is first exposed to inescapable and severe aversive stimulation. Eventually the animal gives up and stops attempting to avoid or escape the situation. Next, an escape response, which under ordinary circumstances would be acquired easily, is made available, but the animal does not make the response. In an early experiment, Seligman and Maier (1967) exposed dogs to intense, inescapable electric shock. Following this, they attempted to teach the animals to avoid signaled shocks by jumping across a shuttle-box barrier (see Figure 6.5). The dogs failed to avoid the shocks, and even after the shocks came on (for 50 s) they would not escape by crossing the barrier to safety. The researchers suggested that the dogs had learned to give up and become helpless when presented with inescapable aversive stimulation. Of course, dogs that are not first exposed to inescapable shock learn quickly to escape and avoid shocks in a shuttle box.

Learned helplessness has been found in a large number of experiments and has been documented in other animals (Baker, 1976; Glazer & Weiss, 1976a, 1976b; Maier, 1970; Maier, Albin, &

Testa, 1973; Maier & Seligman, 1976; Maier, Seligman, & Solomon, 1969; Overmier & Seligman, 1967; Seligman & Maier, 1967). For example, Jackson, Alexander, and Maier (1980) found that rats in a maze had difficulty learning to escape electric shocks after exposure to inescapable aversive stimuli.

Similar results have been reported for humans. Hiroto and Seligman (1975) exposed college students to a series of inescapable loud noises. Following this procedure, the students had to solve a number of anagram problems. Students who were exposed to inescapable noise had more difficulty solving problems than students who did not get the loud noise. Most control subjects solved all the anagrams and reached solutions faster and faster. In contrast, students exposed to inescapable noise failed many problems and made slow improvements in performance.

The practical implication of these findings seems obvious. When people are exposed to inescapable "shocks," they may learn to give up and become helpless. A parent who spanks a child on the basis of his or her mood rather than for the child's misbehavior may create a socially withdrawn individual. The child has learned "No matter what I do, I get a spanking." A husband that frequently "blows up" for no apparent reason might produce a similar set of responses in his partner.

Helplessness, punishment, and avoidance

Inescapable social "shocks" are not the only way to learn helplessness. Indiscriminant punishment and avoidance contingencies were brutally arranged by the Nazi guards to instill a kind of helplessness and docility in Jewish prisoners. Many people have questioned how it is that so many people could go to their deaths without resisting the Nazi captors. The answer lies in the power of aversive control that far exceeds what we can imagine.

The jailors often used unpredictable and arbitrary slaughter of prisoners to maintain control only after using death by execution for any minor act of resistance. That is, the Jewish captives learned to avoid death by doing what they were supposed to. Once this helpless avoidance had been set up, the SS guards could keep it going by occasionally selecting a few prisoners to shoot or exterminate on an arbitrary whim. These executions were unrelated to anything that the victims did or did not do—being unavoidable. Sidman (2001) explains that imposing indiscriminate death by execution on learned avoidance of death was the basis of the observed helplessness:

> If the shock had merely been painful [instead of death], the Jews might have resisted, welcoming death as the ultimate escape. With death itself as the shock, however, escape from death was the controlling contingency. That shock, delivered frequently with machinelike ruthlessness, was at first contingent on the prisoners' actions—when they resisted, for example, or failed to obey orders. Later, the shocks bore no relation to anything they actually did or failed to do. Because the original contingencies had generated required avoidance behavior—docility—the subsequent noncontingent shocks [arbitrary shooting of prisoners] kept that form of avoidance going. An outside observer, or a historian, could see that their quiet march to the ovens was futile. The change in the rules had come without notice, however, and those who were about to be murdered were simply doing what the original contingencies [of avoidance] had taught them was necessary for survival. Their deaths served to maintain the docility of those who remained.
>
> (pp. 147–148)

It is important to recognize that helplessness had nothing to do with the Jewish people being unable to resist. Anyone exposed to similar kinds of coercive control would behave in a similar fashion, regardless of race, ethnicity, or religious orientation. Helplessness does not rest within the victims of violence, but with the powerful behavioral effects engendered by the aversive contingencies.

Helplessness and depression

Seligman (1975) argued that the research on learned helplessness with animals provides a model for clinical depression. For example, there is evidence that helplessness is involved in the relationship between alcohol dependence and depression (Sitharthan, Hough, Sitharthan, & Kavanagh, 2001). More generally, thousands of people each year are diagnosed as depressive. These individuals show insomnia, report feeling tired, often say that life is not worth living, have difficulty performing routine tasks, and may be suicidal. Clinical depression is severe, long lasting, and is not easily traced to a recent environmental experience.

Although animal experiments may shed light on human depression, there are differences (Abramson, Seligman, & Teasdale, 1978; Peterson & Seligman, 1984). For the most part, Seligman points to differences that occur because of human verbal behavior. That is, people talk about their problems and attribute them to either internal or external causes. When people attribute their difficulties to personal causes (e.g., "I am a failure"), these responses could function to occasion giving up (as in rule-governed behavior in Chapter 11). In terms of treatment, Seligman suggested that depressed individuals be placed in situations in which they cannot fail. In this manner, the person may eventually learn appropriate responses in the presence of aversive events.

Seligman has also suggested how to prevent learned helplessness and depression. A person who has already learned to escape from punitive control may be "immunized" from the effects of inescapable aversive events. Such an effect is suggested by experiments where animals initially learn some response (e.g., wheel running) to escape electric shocks. That is, the animals first learn an effective escape response to negative reinforcement contingencies. Next, the animals are exposed to the typical learned helplessness procedures of inescapable shocks. Finally, the subjects are tested in a situation where a new response produces escape from shocks (e.g., switching sides in a shuttle box). The typical effect of pre-exposure to escape is that this experience blocks the learned helplessness usually brought on by inescapable aversive stimulation (Maier & Seligman, 1976; Williams & Lierle, 1986).

Helplessness, depression, and neuroscience

In addition to behavioral approaches (i.e., arranging for success or immunization), neuroscience research is currently underway using Seligman's procedures to induce learned helplessness in animals. The basic idea is to examine the interrelationships between brain chemistry and depression with the hope of finding neurochemical regulators of human depression. For example, dopamine (a neurotransmitter) and several brain sites seem to play a role in the depression caused by learned helplessness (Bertaina-Anglade, La Rochelle, & Scheller, 2006; Besson, Privat, Eschalier, & Fialip, 1999; Kram, Kramer, Ronan, & Petty, 2002; Takamori, Yoshida, & Okuyama, 2001). Drugs that target the dompaminergic systems eventually may be helpful in the treatment of clinical depression, especially when combined with behavioral treatments focused on overcoming and preventing learned helplessness.

FOCUS ON: Social defeat, aversion to social contact, and behavioral neuroscience

Psychiatric disorders that include depression, social phobia, and post-traumatic stress disorder (PTSD) have been linked to social withdrawal and to abnormalities of the dopaminergic system. To understand these links, Berton, McClung, DiLeone, Krishnan, and Renthal (2006) used a social defeat procedure that profoundly alters the social interactions of rodents.

In their study, mice were given daily episodes of social defeat, followed by a period of protected exposure to the larger aggressor—both animals were placed in a cage separated by a barrier to allow for sensory contact. The test mice were subjected to defeat by different aggressors over 10 days and measures of social behavior were obtained. The researchers measured social approach to an unfamiliar mouse enclosed in a wire cage using a video-tracking system. Control animals (undefeated) spent most of the time in close proximity to the unfamiliar mouse. Defeated mice displayed intense aversion responses and spent less time near the unfamiliar mouse in the cage, but not when the wire cage was empty. The response was to the social target (unfamiliar mouse) and not the novel wire cage. When tested again after 4 weeks, mice with a history of social defeat still displayed avoidance of the social target. These avoidance responses were greater to the aggressor, but also generalized to unfamiliar mice that were physically distinct from the aggressor.

Next, the researchers showed that antidepressant drugs used with humans improved the social interaction of defeated mice, but anxiety-related drugs did not have this effect. One possibility is that antidepressant drugs operate on the dopaminergic pathways of the brain.

To characterize the neurobiological mechanisms of social aversion induced by defeat, Berton et al. (2006) targeted the dopamine neurons of the mesolimbic brain in the ventral tegmental area (VTA), as well as the projections of these neurons to the nucleus accumbens (NAc). Previous research has shown that these pathways are associated with emotionally salient stimuli and avoidance behavior. The neurotrophic factor BDNF (brain-derived neurotrophic factor) is a major regulator of the mesolimbic dopamine pathway—modulating the release of dopamine. BDNF also is involved with dopamine release in the NAc via the TrkB receptor on the dopamine nerve terminals. The findings showed that BDNF levels in the NAc were increased by social defeat and this effect occurred 24 h and 4 weeks after the episodes of social defeat.

The source of the BDNF protein in the NAc is thought to be the VTA, where the messenger RNA (mRNA) for BDNF is expressed. Berton et al. (2006) deleted the gene encoding for BDNF in the VTA of adult mice and found an *antidepressant-like effect*; the deletion of the gene for BDNF and dopamine release reduced the acquisition of social avoidance behavior in defeated mice. This finding and other control conditions indicated that *BDNF from the VTA neurons is required for a social target to become an aversive stimulus that regulates the avoidance behavior of defeated mice.*

One implication is that humans diagnosed with affective disorders may be showing avoidance responses acquired by a history of social punishment and defeat. These behavioral effects may involve BDNF and the dopaminergic pathways. Behavior therapy when combined with specialized antidepressant drugs could be especially effective at reducing social aversion and increasing socially appropriate behavior.

Aggression

Reflexive aggression

When two rats are placed in the same setting and painful shocks are delivered, the animals may attack one another (Ulrich and Azrin 1962; Ulrich, Wolff, & Azrin, 1964). The fighting generated by these contingencies is called **reflexive aggression** (or pain-elicited aggression) because the attack follows the presentation of aversive events. Attack occurs even though neither animal is responsible for the occurrence of the shocks. Elicited aggression has been documented in several species, including humans (Azrin, Hutchinson, & Hake, 1963; Hutchinson, 1977), and has been found with painful stimuli other than electric shock (Azrin, Hake, & Hutchinson, 1965). Most people recognize that they are more prone to aggression when exposed to painful stimuli. When feeling good you may never shout at your partner, but you may do so if you have a severe toothache.

In these early experiments (O'Kelly and Steckle, 1939), rats were placed in a small enclosure and electric shock occurred periodically, no matter what the animals did (a procedure similar to learned helplessness, but with two rats). When the rats were periodically shocked, they began to fight.

Twenty-three years later, Ulrich and Azrin (1962) systematically investigated the fighting behavior of rats to inescapable and intermittent shocks. These researchers began by testing whether two rats would fight when simply placed in a small operant chamber. They noted that the animals did not usually attack one another when placed in a confined space. However, when random shocks were delivered, the animals would immediately stand up and vigorously strike and bite one another (see Figure 6.8).

Shocks were delivered at increasing frequencies, and the number of attacks increased as more shocks were presented. In addition, Ulrich and Azrin (1962) found that the probability of attack for any single shock increased as the number of shocks went up. When the animals got one shock every 10 min, attack followed approximately 50% of the shocks. When the animals received 38 shocks a minute, fighting followed 85% of the shocks. The probability that a painful event will induce aggressive behavior is greater following high rates of inescapable aversive stimulation.

Painful stimulation also produces attack-like responses in humans and monkeys (Azrin & Holz, 1966; Azrin, Hutchinson, & Sallery, 1964; Hutchinson, 1977). In one experiment, squirrel monkeys were strapped into a small test chamber and electric shock was delivered to the animals' tails (Azrin et al., 1964). As with rats, attack was elicited by electric shocks. The animals attacked other monkeys, rats, mice, and inanimate objects such as a stuffed doll, round ball, and a rubber hose that they could bite. As shock intensity increased, so did the probability and duration of the attacks—a result that parallels the findings with rats.

FIG. 6.8 Two rats in the attack position induced by electric shock. From "Reflexive Fighting in Response to Aversive Stimulation" by R. E. Ulrich and N. H. Azrin, 1962, *Journal of the Experimental Analysis of Behavior*, 5, 511–520. Copyright 1962 by the Society for the Experimental Analysis of Behavior, Inc. Republished with permission.

In a review of the side effects of aversive control, Hutchinson (1977) described bite reactions by humans to aversive stimulation. Subjects were paid volunteers who were given inescapable loud noise at regular intervals. Because the noise was delivered on a predictable basis, the subjects came to discriminate the onset of the aversive stimulus. Unobtrusive measures indicated that humans would show aggressive responses (or, more precisely, bite on a rubber hose) following the presentation of loud noise. The human response to noise parallels the elicited fighting found in monkeys and other animals. However, Hutchinson suggests that the human results should be interpreted with caution. The subjects were told that they would receive aversive stimulation but the intensity would be tolerable. Also, he noted that subjects were paid to stay in the experiment, and most people would leave such a situation in everyday life.

Operant aggression

When one person punishes another's behavior, the punished individual may retaliate. This is not difficult to understand; one way to escape from punishment is to eliminate or neutralize the person who is delivering it (Azrin & Holz, 1966). This strategy is called **operant aggression**, and it is shaped and maintained by negative reinforcement (i.e., removal of the punishment). When two people have a fistfight, the winner of the combat is reinforced by the absence or reduction of punches from the other person. Unfortunately, this analysis suggests that physical aggression will increase in frequency for people who successfully use counteraggression to stop the punishment arranged by others.

Consider a situation in which a husband and wife argue and the husband loses his temper and strikes his spouse—suppressing her yelling and screaming at him. Because men are typically larger and stronger than women, this probably ends the argument and the husband is negatively reinforced (by the wife's submission) for his physical abuse. Although this does not completely explain spouse abuse, it does suggest that negative reinforcement plays a large role in many cases.

Investigating human aggression

Although human aggression is easily recognized, it is difficult to study in the laboratory. This is because aggressive behavior is a dangerous form of human conduct. Realizing the danger, researchers have developed procedures that protect the victim from harm. In the laboratory situation, participants are led to believe that they have an opportunity to hurt another person when in reality they do not (e.g., Baron, Russell, & Arms, 1985; Gustafson, 1989; Zillmann, 1988). In a typical experiment, participants are told that they can deliver a punisher (e.g., loud noise, electric shock, etc.) to another person by pressing a button on a response panel. The other person is, in fact, an accomplice or confederate of the researcher and acts the role of victim but does not receive the aversive stimulus.

There has been a debate about the reality or external validity of these procedures. However, evidence suggests that these methods constitute a reasonable analog of human aggression in everyday life. Participants in aggression experiments are convinced that their actions harmed the confederate (Berkowitz & Donnerstein, 1982). When the accomplice provokes (e.g., with insults) the subjects, they deliver greater amounts of painful stimulation than when they are not provoked (Baron & Richardson, 1993). Finally, people who are known to be violent usually select and deliver stronger levels of aversive stimulation than those without such a history (Gully & Dengerink, 1983; Wolfe & Baron, 1971).

Aggression breeds aggression

Operant and respondent principles suggest that the presentation of an aversive stimulus may elicit or set the occasion for aggressive behavior. Provocation by others is a common form of aversive stimulation that occurs in a variety of social settings. Consider a situation in which you have worked extremely hard on a term paper and you feel it is the best paper you have ever written. Your professor calls you to his office and says, "Your paper is rubbish. It lacks clarity, scholarship, organization, and is riddled with grammatical mistakes. Only an idiot could write and submit such trash!" You probably protest the unfair treatment, but to no avail. You storm out of the office mumbling a few choice words, and once down the hall you kick the elevator door. Later in the term you are asked to fill out a teaching evaluation and, in retaliation, you score the professor as one of the worst teachers you have known. In this example, the professor's insulting remarks generated aggressive responses that ranged from kicking doors to counterattack by negative evaluation. Generally, aggression breeds aggression (Patterson, 1976).

Skinner (1953) described the cycle of aggression in his account of a game played by sailors during the 18th century:

> Sailors would amuse themselves by tying several boys or younger men in a ring to a mast by their left hands, their right hands remaining free. Each boy was given a stick or whip and told to strike the boy in front of him whenever he felt himself being struck by the boy behind. The game began by striking one boy lightly. This boy then struck the boy ahead of him, who in turn struck the boy next ahead, and so on. Even though it was clearly in the interest of the group that all blows be gentle, the inevitable result was a furious lashing. The unstable elements in this interlocking system are easy to identify. We cannot assume that each boy gave precisely the kind of blow he received because this is not an easy comparison to make. It is probable that he underestimated the strength of the blows he gave. The slightest tendency to give a little harder than he received would produce the ultimate effect. Moreover, repeated blows probably generate an emotional disposition in which one naturally strikes harder. A comparable instability is seen when two individuals engage in a casual conversation which leads to a

vituperative quarrel. The aggressive effect of a remark is likely to be underestimated by the man who makes it, and repeated effects generate further aggression. The principle is particularly dangerous when the conversation consists of an exchange of notes between governments.

(p. 309)

Skinner's analysis is confirmed by controlled experiments showing that both physical and verbal provocation produces aggression. In terms of physical provocation, experiments show that people respond to attacks with escalating counterattacks (Borden, Bowen, & Taylor, 1971; O'Leary & Dengerink, 1973; Taylor & Pisano, 1971). In these experiments, participants tried to beat their opponents on a reaction time game in which the loser received an electric shock. In fact, there were no actual opponents, but participants received shocks that were programmed by the researchers. In this game, subjects were made to lose on a number of trials and the shocks from the fictitious opponent increased in magnitude. Faced with increasing physical provocation, subjects retaliated by escalating the intensity of the shocks they gave when the "opponent" lost.

Recent experiments on provocation and aggressive behavior further support and refine Skinner's (1953) analysis of aggression. In one study, people matched their level of aggression to the level of provocation (Juujaevari, Kooistra, Kaartinen, & Pulkkinen, 2001). Also, people retaliated more when they were provoked and subsequently presented with a minor annoyance than when they were only provoked or received no provocation. The minor annoyance became a "trigger" for retaliation when preceded by provocation; by itself it had no effect on aggressive behavior (Pedersen, Gonzales, & Miller, 2000).

Verbal insults also evoke and set the occasion for strong counterattacks. Wilson and Rogers (1975) suggest that verbal provocation can lead to physical retaliation, and they have noted incidents that began with verbal taunts escalating into violent fistfights. In a laboratory study of verbal insults, Geen (1968) found that subjects who were exposed to unprovoked, nasty comments from a confederate would retaliate with physical aggression. The subjects in this study were allowed to deliver shocks to the insulting confederate (in fact, no shocks were actually given). Compared with personal frustration (a confederate prevents them from competing an assigned task) and task frustration (the task did not have a solution), verbal insults produced the highest level of aggression toward the confederate.

In a more recent set of experiments, insults increased aggressive behavior more in people who came from a "culture of honor" (the southern USA) than from those who did not (the northern USA). For those who valued honor, insults diminished the person's reputation and the retaliation was behavior that had previously restored status and respect (Cohen, Nisbett, Bowdle, & Schwarz, 1996). Generally, aggression (both verbal and physical) breeds aggression, and aggressive episodes escalate toward greater levels of violence, especially in cultures that propagate dignity and honor (see Skinner, 1971, on other problems of freedom and dignity).

The dictum that aggression breeds aggression also can be extended to problems of violence in schools and other social situations. One common form of group behavior involves social exclusion of others based on their characteristics and behavior. For example, a student who shows high accomplishments in academic subjects may be excluded from the "in group" whose members call him a "nerd." Can this kind of group behavior instigate aggression in those who receive it? A recent experiment investigated this question in the laboratory (Twinge, Baumeister, Tice, & Stucke, 2001). Human participants were exposed to social exclusion by telling them that other participants had rejected them as part of the group. Social exclusion caused participants to behave more aggressively in various contexts.

When insulted by another person (target), excluded people retaliated by "blasting" the target with higher levels of aversive noise. In another experiment, the target received the same aggressive treatment even though he or she had not insulted the excluded people. This suggests that it is social exclusion itself that instigated the aggressive behavior. A further experiment showed that the effects of social exclusion on aggression could be mitigated if the target provided social praise to the excluded person. That is, provision of social rewards prevented the retaliation induced by exclusion from the group. The researcher indicated that these responses were specific to social exclusion as opposed to other kinds of misfortunes. One implication is that schoolchildren who are excluded or rejected by their classmates may show aggressive behavior directed toward group members—another instance of aggression breeds aggression.

Social Disruption

When punishment is used to decrease behavior, the attempt is usually made to stop a particular response. The hope is that other unpunished behavior is not affected. Two factors work against this: The person who delivers punishment and the setting in which punishment occurs can both become conditioned aversive stimuli (S^{ave}). Because of this conditioning, individuals will attempt to escape from or avoid the punishing person or setting. Azrin and Holz (1966) have called this negative side effect of punishment **social disruption**:

> It is in the area of social disruption that punishment does appear to be capable of producing behavioral changes that are far-reaching in terms of producing an incapacity for an effective life. . . . For example, a teacher may punish a child for talking in class, in which case it is desired that the unauthorized vocalization of the child be eliminated but his other behaviors remain intact. We have seen previously, however, that one side effect of the punishment process was that it reinforced tendencies on the part of the individual to *escape from the punishment situation itself*. In terms of the example we are using, this means that punishment of the vocalization would not only be expected to decrease the vocalization, but also increase the likelihood of the child leaving the classroom situation. Behavior such as tardiness, truancy, and dropping out of school would be strengthened. The end result would be termination of the social relationship, which would make any further social control of the individual's behavior impossible. This side effect of punishment appears to be one of the most undesirable aspects of having punishment delivered by one individual against another individual since the socialization process must necessarily depend upon continued interaction with other individuals.
>
> (pp. 439–440, emphasis added)

It is also worth recalling the general suppressive effects of aversive stimuli. A teacher, parent, or employer (social agent) who frequently uses aversive techniques *becomes a conditioned punishing stimulus*. Once this occurs, the mere presence of the social agent can disrupt all ongoing operant behavior. This means that positive behavior falls to low levels when this person is present (see previous FOCUS ON section).

ON THE APPLIED SIDE: Coercion and its fallout

In a book titled *Coercion and Its Fallout*, Sidman (2001) (Figure 6.9) provides a behavior analysis of coercion and its frequent use in North American society. **Coercion** is defined as the "use of punishment and the threat of punishment to get others to act as we would like, and to our practice of rewarding people just by letting them escape from our punishments and threats" (p. 1). That is, coercion involves the basic contingencies of punishment and negative reinforcement. An interesting part of this book concerns escape and "dropping out" of the family, community, and society.

NOTE ON: The definition of coercion

In this section, we have followed Sidman's usage of the term coercion as the control of behavior through the arrangement of aversive contingencies. Paul Brandon (2005) notes that C. B. Ferster, who worked with Skinner on schedules of reinforcement (Chapter 5), defines coercion in a more general sense, involving control that uses disproportionate consequences (Ferster, 1979). Thus, reinforcement contingencies that use large reinforcers to cause people to do something they would usually not do are coercive. The offer of large sums of money to turn in a poor performance at a track meet would involve coercion and is usually called a bribe. Also, with the broader definition of coercion, negative reinforcement arranged by one person (the controller) to control the behavior of another (the controllee) is coercive when the long-term benefits accrue to the controller (also see Baum, 2005, pp. 185–187, on asymmetry of control in a coercive relationship). A teacher who gives out detentions for noisy talking or being out of seats is using coercive control—compliance by the students provides reinforcement (orderly classroom with peace and quiet) for the teacher's use of detentions but there is little gain for the students. A positive reinforcement contingency set by another

FIG. 6.9   Murray Sidman. Reprinted with permission.

teacher to help students attend to and work on academic material would not be coercive as the benefits in the long run are for the student (learning of academic material), not the teacher. The issues of control and coercion are often confused. From a behavior analysis viewpoint, all contingencies involve control but not all control is coercive (Skinner, 1971).

One kind of escape contingency is dropping out—a major social problem of our time. People drop out of education, family, personal and community responsibility, citizenship, society, and even life. Sidman (2001, p. 101) points out that the common element in all of these forms of conduct is negative reinforcement. Once involved in an aversive system, people can get out by removing themselves from the coercive situation and this strengthens the behavior of dropping out. Sidman notes that society is the loser when people cease to participate; dropping out is nonproductive since dropouts no longer contribute to their own or society's welfare.

An unfortunate, but common, example is the school dropout. Day after day, students are sent to schools where coercion is a predominant way of teaching. That is, often the teacher's job is to "get students to learn" by punishing them when they fail. The pupil who is slow to answer or who errs on obvious questions is subjected to ridicule. Written work is filled with negative comments and classmates observe the low grades on assignments as papers are returned from front to rear. Report cards emphasize failing grades in red ink; poor students are seated at the back of the room as examples of what happens to failures. Students who cannot deal with the normal workload are required to do extra work at school and home, making those who fail social outcasts who are deprived of play and other activities. Children who fail eventually conclude that learning and pleasure are not compatible—the more learning, the less the pleasure.

As the aversive control escalates, escape is inevitable. Students show increasingly severe forms of dropping out. Tardiness, feigned illness, "playing hooky," and never showing up for school are common responses to the escalation of coercion in schools. Sidman summarizes the problem as follows:

The current discipline and dropout crises are the inevitable outcome of a history of educational coercion. One may long for the days when pupils feared their teachers, spoke to them with respect, accepted extra work as punishment, submitted to being kept after school, and even resigned themselves to being beaten. But through the years, all these forms of coercive control were sowing the seeds of the system's destruction. Wherever and whenever coercion is practiced, the end result is loss of support of the system on the part of those who suffered from it. In every coercive environment, the coerced eventually find ways to turn upon the coercers. An adversarial relationship had developed between pupils and teachers, and the former victims, now parents, no longer support the system against their children.

(Sidman, 2001, p. 107)

As Sidman goes on to note, not all teachers (or school systems) use coercion or negative reinforcement as a way to induce students to learn. Some teachers and educators are familiar with and use positive reinforcement effectively. A teacher who uses positive reinforcement looks to reward small steps of success rather than punish instances of failure. Schools who adopt positive reinforcement methods are likely to promote the enjoyment of learning as well as high academic performance (Cameron and Pierce, 2002). Positive reinforcement turns dropping out into "tuning in."

CHAPTER SUMMARY

This chapter highlighted the major contingencies of aversive control. The basic aversive contingencies were outlined in terms of positive and negative punishment and negative reinforcement. Positive punishment involves a decrease in operant behavior that produces or adds an event or stimulus. Negative punishment is a decrease in response that terminates or removes ongoing reinforcement. In both cases, punishment is defined by a reduced probability of response following a punishment procedure. We saw that punishment is relative and is made more effective by abrupt, intense, and immediate delivery of the punisher. The schedule of punishment (continuous is best), reduced effectiveness of positive reinforcement, and the availability of response alternatives also enhance the regulation of behavior by punishment contingencies.

Next, we turned to the control of behavior by negative reinforcement and the increase in operant behavior that removes or prevents the negative reinforcer. Two kinds of negative reinforcement were identified as escape and avoidance, with the only difference being the shock–shock intervals (see Figure 6.4). The FOCUS ON section on avoidance behavior introduced the molecular and molar perspectives in terms of analysis, the conditioned suppression paradigm, and the disruption of ongoing operant behavior by periods of scheduled avoidance.

We then turned to the side effects of aversive control and noted that avoidance behavior is persistent because operant avoidance often prevents respondent extinction. A similar persistence effect was observed with exposure to inescapable punishers and learned helplessness. After a history of inescapable shocks, animals did not learn to escape the shocks; people and other animals fail to emit responses that could remove the punishing events (helplessness). The implications of learned helplessness for clinical depression and its neural basis in social defeat were addressed. Reflexive and operant aggression were analyzed as side effects of aversive control. Analysis showed that aggression breeds aggression and the research on human aggression supported this observation. In fact, people who control behavior by punishment often become conditioned punishers themselves (social disruption).

Finally, we looked briefly at the analysis of coercion and its fallout by Sidman—emphasizing how coercive control may lead people to drop out of society and adolescents to drop out of the school system. The answer to this problem is to reduce coercive control in schools and increase the regulation of academic behavior by positive reinforcement.

Key Words

Aversive stimulus
Avoidance
Coercion
Conditioned aversive stimulus
  (S^{AVE})
Discriminated avoidance
Escape
Learned helplessness
Molar perspective

Molecular perspective
Negative punishment
Negative reinforcement
Negative reinforcer
Nondiscriminated avoidance
Operant aggression
Positive punishment
Primary aversive stimulus
Punisher

Punishment
Reflexive aggression
Relativity of punishment
Response–shock interval
Shock–shock interval
Sidman avoidance
Social disruption

Operant–Respondent Interrelationships and the Biological Context of Conditioning

7

- Find out how operant and respondent contingencies interrelate in complex ways.
- Explore the phenomena of sign tracking, autoshaping, and negative automaintenance.
- Investigate how researchers showed that operant contingencies could regulate behavior usually viewed as respondent.
- Investigate the biological context of conditioning and the phenomenon known as taste aversion learning.
- Learn how adjunctive behavior is induced by interval and fixed-time schedules of reinforcement.
- Discover the interrelationships of eating and physical activity and how this relates to activity anorexia in humans and other animals.

So far, we have considered operant and respondent behavior as separate domains. Respondent behavior is elicited by the events that precede it, and operants are strengthened (or weakened) by stimulus consequences that follow them. Assume that you are teaching a dog to sit and you are using food reinforcement. You might start by saying "sit," push the animal into a sitting position, and follow this posture with food. After training, you present the dog with the discriminative stimulus "sit," and it quickly sits. This sequence nicely fits the operant paradigm—the S^D "sit" sets the occasion for the response of sitting, and food reinforcement strengthens this behavior (Skinner, 1953).

In most circumstances, however, both operant and respondent conditioning occur. If you look closely at what the dog does, it is apparent that the "sit" command also elicits respondent behavior. Specifically, the dog salivates just after you say "sit." This occurs because the "sit" command reliably preceded and was paired with the presentation of food, becoming a conditioned stimulus that elicits respondent salivation. For these reasons, the stimulus "sit" is said to have a dual function: It is an S^D in the sense that it sets the occasion for operant responses, and it is a CS that elicits respondent behavior. Shapiro (1960) demonstrated that respondent salivation was positively correlated with operant lever-pressing for fixed-interval food in dogs.

Similar effects are seen when a warning stimulus (a tone) is turned on that signals imminent shock if a rat does not press a lever. The signal is a discriminative stimulus that increases the probability of bar pressing, but it is also a CS that elicits changes in heart rate, hormone levels, and other physiological responses (all of which can be called fear). Consider that you are out for a before-breakfast walk and you pass a doughnut and coffee shop. The aroma from the shop may be a CS that elicits salivation and also an S^D that sets the occasion for entering the store and ordering a doughnut. These examples should make it clear that in many settings respondent and operant conditioning are intertwined—probably sharing common neural pathways in the brain.

One reason for the interrelationship of operant and respondent conditioning is that whatever happens to an organism is applied to the *whole neurophysiological system*, not just to one set of effectors or the other. That is, we analytically separate respondents (as smooth-muscle and gland activity) from operants (striated skeletal muscle activity) but the contingencies are applied to the entire organism. When operant reinforcement occurs, it is contiguous with everything going on inside the individual. When a CS or US is presented, there will be all kinds of operant behavior going on as well. The separation of operant and respondent models is for analytical convenience and control but the organism's interaction with the environment is more complicated than these basic distinctions.

ANALYSIS OF OPERANT–RESPONDENT CONTINGENCIES

In some circumstances, the distinction between operant and respondent behavior becomes even more difficult. Experimental procedures (contingencies) can be arranged in which responses that are typically considered reflexive increase when followed by reinforcement; that is, respondents are treated as operants. Other research has shown that behavior usually thought to be operant may be elicited by the stimuli that precede it; operants are treated as respondents. People sometimes incorrectly label operant or respondent behavior in terms of its form or topography. That is, pecking a key is automatically called an operant, and salivation, no matter how it comes about, is labeled a reflex. Recall, though, that operants and respondents are defined by the experimental procedures that produce them, not by their topography. When a pigeon pecks a key for food, pecking is an operant. If another bird reliably strikes a key when it is lit up, and does this because the light has been paired with food, pecking is a respondent.

When biologically relevant stimuli like food are contingent on an organism's behavior, species-characteristic behavior is occasionally elicited at the same time. One class of species-characteristic responses that is elicited (when operant behavior is expected) is unconditioned reflexive behavior. This intrusion of reflexive behavior occurs because *respondent procedures are sometimes embedded in operant contingencies of reinforcement*. These respondent procedures cause species-characteristic responses that may interfere with the regulation of behavior by operant contingencies.

At one time, this intrusion of respondent conditioning in operant situations was used to question the generality of operant principles and laws. The claim was that the biology of an organism overrode operant principles (Hinde & Stevenson-Hinde, 1973; Schwartz & Lacey, 1982; Stevenson-Hinde, 1983) and behavior was said to drift toward its biological roots.

Operant (and respondent) conditioning is, however, part of the biology of an organism. Conditioning arose on the basis of species history; organisms that changed their behavior as a result of life experience had an advantage over animals that did not change their behavior. Behavioral flexibility by operant conditioning allowed for rapid adaptation to an altered environment. As a result, organisms that evolved the neural mechanisms for operant learning were more likely to survive and produce offspring.

Both evolution and learning involve selection by consequences. Darwinian evolution has developed species-characteristic behavior (reflexes, fixed action patterns, and reaction chains) and basic mechanisms of learning (operant and respondent conditioning) through natural selection of the best fit. Operant conditioning during an organism's lifetime selects response topographies, rates of response, and repertoires of behavior through the feedback from consequences. A question is whether unconditioned responses (UR) in the basic reflex model (US→UR) also are selected by consequences. In this regard, it is interesting to observe that the salivary glands are activated when food is placed in the mouth; as a result, the food can be tasted, ingested (or rejected), and digested. That is, there are notable physiological effects following reflexive behavior. If the pupil of the eye constricts when a bright light is shown, the result is an escape from retinal pain and the avoidance of retina damage. It seems that reflexes have come to exist and operate because they do something; it is the effects of these responses that maintain the operation of the reflexive behavior. One might predict that if the effects of salivating for food or blinking at a puff of air did not result in improved performance (ease of ingestion or protection of the eye) then neither response would continue, as this behavior would not add to the fitness of the organism.

Respondent Contingencies Predominate Over Operant Regulation

The Breland and Breland demonstration

Marion and Keller Breland worked with B. F. Skinner as students and later established a successful animal training business. They conditioned a variety of animals for circus acts, arcade displays, advertising, and movies. In an important paper (Breland & Breland, 1961), they documented occasional instances in which species-specific behavior interfered with operant responses. For example, when training a raccoon to deposit coins in a box, they noted:

> The response concerned the manipulation of money by the raccoon (who has "hands" rather similar to those of primates). The contingency for reinforcement was picking up the coins and depositing them in a 5-inch metal box.
>
> Raccoons condition readily, have good appetites, and this one was quite tame and an eager subject. We anticipated no trouble. Conditioning him to pick up the first coin was simple. We started out by reinforcing him for picking up a single coin. Then the metal container was introduced, with the requirement that he drop the coin into the container. Here we ran into the first bit of difficulty: he seemed to have a great deal of trouble letting go of the coin. He would rub it up against the inside of the container, pull it back out, and clutch it firmly for several seconds. However, he would finally turn it loose and receive his food reinforcement. Then the final contingency: we put him on a ratio of 2, requiring that he pick up both coins and put them in the container.
>
> Now the raccoon really had problems (and so did we). Not only could he not let go of the coins, but he spent seconds, even minutes rubbing them together (in a most miserly fashion), and dipping them into the container. He carried on the behavior to such an extent that the practical demonstration we had in mind—a display featuring a raccoon putting money in a piggy bank—simply was not feasible. The rubbing behavior became worse and worse as time went on, in spite of non-reinforcement.
>
> (Breland & Breland, 1961, p. 682)

Breland and Breland documented similar instances of what they called instinctive drift in other species. **Instinctive drift** refers to species-characteristic behavior patterns that became progressively more invasive during training. The term instinctive drift is problematic because the concept suggests a conflict between nature (biology) and nurture (environment). Behavior is said to drift toward its biological roots. There is, however, no need to talk about behavior "drifting" toward some end. Behavior is appropriate to the operating contingencies. Recall that respondent procedures may be embedded in an operant contingency and this seems to be the case for the Brelands' raccoon.

In the raccoon example, the coins were presented just before the animal was reinforced with food. For raccoons, food elicits rubbing and manipulating food items. Since the coins preceded food delivery, they became a CS that elicited the respondent behavior of rubbing and manipulating (coins). This interpretation is supported by the observation that the behavior increased as training progressed. As more and more reinforced trials occurred, there were necessarily more pairings of coins and food. Each pairing increased the strength of the $CS_{(coin)} \rightarrow CR_{(rubbing)}$ relationship, and the behavior became more and more prominent.

Respondent processes also occur as by-products of operant procedures with rats and kids. Rats will hold on to marbles longer than you might expect when they receive food pellets for depositing the marble in a hole. Kids will manipulate tokens or coins prior to banking or exchanging them. The point is that what the Brelands found is not that unusual or challenging to an operant account of behavior. Today, we talk about the interrelationship of operant and respondent contingencies rather than label these observations as a conflict between nature and nurture.

Sign tracking

Suppose that you have trained a dog to sit quietly on a mat, and you have reinforced the animal's behavior with food. Once this conditioning is accomplished (the dog sits quietly on the mat), you start a second training phase. During this phase, you turn on a buzzer located on the dog's right side. A few seconds after the sound of the buzzer, a feeder delivers food to a dish that is placed 6 ft in front of the dog. Figure 7.1 is a diagram of this sort of arrangement.

When the buzzer goes off, the dog is free to engage in any behavior it is able to emit. From the perspective of operant conditioning it is clear what should happen. When the buzzer goes off, the dog should stand up, walk over to the dish, and eat. This is because the sound of the buzzer is an S^D that sets the occasion for the operant of going to the dish, and this response has been reinforced by food. In other words, the three-term contingency, SD: R $\rightarrow$ Sr, specifies this outcome and there is little reason to expect any other result. A careful examination of the contingency, however, suggests that the sign (sound) could be either an S^D (operant) that sets the occasion for approaching and eating the reinforcer (food); or a CS^+ (respondent) that is paired with the US (food). In this latter case, the CS would be expected to elicit food-related conditioned responses.

Jenkins, Barrera, Ireland, and Woodside (1978) conducted an experiment very much like the one described here. Dogs were required to sit on a mat and a light/tone stimulus compound was presented either on the left or right side of the animal. When the stimulus was presented on one side it signaled food, and on the other side it signaled extinction. As expected, when the extinction stimulus came on, the dogs did not approach the food tray and for the most part ignored the signal. However, when the food signal was presented, the animals unexpectedly approached the signal (light/speaker) and made, what was judged by the researchers to be, "food-soliciting responses" to the stimulus.

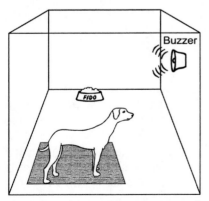

FIG. 7.1 Diagram of apparatus used in sign tracking. When the signal for food is given, the dog approaches the signal and makes "food-soliciting" responses rather than go directly to the food dish.

Some of the dogs physically contacted the signal source, and others seemed to beg at the stimulus by barking and prancing. This behavior is called **sign tracking** because it refers to approaching a sign (or stimulus) that has signaled a biologically relevant event (in this case, food).

The behavior of the dogs is not readily understood in terms of operant contingencies of reinforcement. As stated earlier, the animals should simply trot over to the food and eat it. Instead the dogs' behavior appears to be elicited by the signal that precedes food delivery. Importantly, the ordering of stimulus $\rightarrow$ behavior resembles the CS $\rightarrow$ CR arrangement that characterizes classical conditioning. Of course, S^D: R follows the same time line, but in this case the response should be a direct approach to the food, not to the signal. Additionally, behavior in the presence of the stimulus appears to be food directed. When the tone/light comes on, the dog approaches it, barks, begs, prances, licks the signal source, and so on. Thus, the temporal arrangement of stimulus followed by response, and the form or topography of the animal's behavior, suggests respondent conditioning. Apparently, in this situation the unconditioned stimulus (US) features of the food are stronger (in the sense of regulating behavior) than the operant-reinforcement properties of the food. Because of this, the light/tone gains strength as a CS with each pairing of light/tone and food. A caution is that one cannot entirely dismiss the occurrence of operant behavior in this experiment. If the dog engages in a chain of responses that is followed by food you can expect the sequence to be maintained, and this seems to be the case in such experiments.

Autoshaping

Shaping is the usual way that a pigeon is taught to strike a response key. In the laboratory, a researcher operating the feeder with a hand-switch reinforces closer and closer approximations to the final performance (key pecking). Once the bird makes the first independent peck on the key, electronic programming equipment activates a food hopper and the response is reinforced. The contingency between behavior and reinforcement both during shaping and after the operant is established is clearly operant (R → S^r). This method of differential reinforcement of successive approximation requires considerable patience and a fair amount of skill on the part of the experimenter.

Brown and Jenkins (1968) reported a way to automatically teach pigeons to peck a response key. In one experiment, they first taught birds to approach and eat grain whenever a food hopper was presented. After the birds were magazine trained, automatic programming turned on a key light 8 s before the grain was delivered. Next, the key light went out and the grain hopper was presented. After 10–20 pairings of this key light followed by food procedure, the birds started to orient and move toward the lighted key. Eventually all 36 pigeons in the experiment began to strike the key even though pecking did not produce food. Figure 7.2 shows the arrangement between key light and food presentation. Notice that the light onset precedes the presentation of food and appears to elicit the key peck.

The researchers called this effect **autoshaping**, an automatic way to teach pigeons to key peck. Brown and Jenkins offered several explanations for their results. In their view, the most likely explanation had to do with species characteristics of pigeons. They noted that pigeons have a tendency to peck at things they look at. The bird notices the onset of the light, orients toward it, and "the species-specific look–peck coupling eventually yields a peck to the [key]" (Brown & Jenkins, 1968, p. 7). In their experiment, after the bird made the response, food was presented, and this contiguity could have accidentally reinforced the first peck.

Another possibility was that key pecking resulted from respondent conditioning. The researchers suggested that the lighted key had become a CS that elicited key pecks. This could occur because pigeons make unconditioned pecks (UR) when grain (US) is presented to them. In their experiment, the key light preceded grain presentation and may have elicited a conditioned peck (CR) to the lighted key (CS). Brown and Jenkins comment on this explanation and suggest that although it is possible, it "seem[s] unlikely because the peck appears to grow out of and depend upon the development of other motor responses in the vicinity of the key that do not themselves resemble a peck at grain" (1968, p. 7). In other words, the birds began to turn toward the key, stand close to it, and make thrusting movements with their heads, all of which led eventually to the key peck. It does not seem likely that all these are reflexive responses. They seem more like operant approximations that form a chain culminating in pecking.

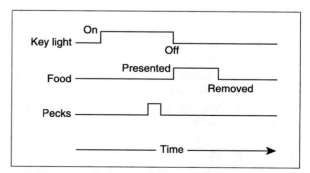

FIG. 7.2 Autoshaping procedures are based on Brown and Jenkins (1968). Notice that the onset of the light precedes the presentation of food and appears to elicit the key peck.

Notice that respondent behavior like salivation, eye blinks, startle, knee jerks, pupil dilation, and other reflexes do not depend on the conditioning of additional behavior. When you touch a hot stove you rapidly and automatically pull your hand away. This response simply occurs when a hot object is contacted. A stove does not elicit approach to it, orientation toward it, movement of the hand and arm, and other responses. All of these additional responses seem to be clearly operant, forming a chain or sequence of behavior that avoids contact with the hot stove.

Autoshaping extends to other species and other types of reinforcement and responses. Chicks have been shown to make autoshaped responses when heat was the reinforcer (Wasserman, 1973). When food delivery is signaled for rats by lighting a lever or by inserting it into the operant chamber, the animals lick and chew on the bar (Peterson, Ackil, Frommer, & Hearst, 1972; Stiers & Silberberg, 1974). These animals also direct social behavior toward another rat that signals the delivery of food (Timberlake & Grant, 1975). Rachlin (1969) showed autoshaped key pecking in pigeons using electric shock as negative reinforcement. The major question that these and other experiments raise is: What is the nature of the behavior that is observed in autoshaping and sign-tracking experiments?

In general, research has shown that autoshaped behavior is at first respondent, but when the contingency is changed so that pecks are followed by food, the pecking becomes operant. Pigeons reflexively peck (UR) at the sight of grain (US). Because the key light reliably precedes grain presentation, it acquires a CS function that elicits the CR of pecking the key. However, when pecking is followed by grain, it comes under the control of contingencies of reinforcement and it is an operant. To make this clear, autoshaping produces respondent behavior that can then be reinforced. Once behavior is reinforced, it is regulated by consequences that follow it and it is considered to be operant.

Contingencies of Sign Tracking, Autoshaping, and Instinctive Drift

In discussing their 1968 experiments on autoshaping, Brown and Jenkins report that:

> Experiments in progress show that location of the key near the food tray is not a critical feature [of autoshaping], although it no doubt hastens the process. Several birds have acquired the peck to a key located on the wall opposite the tray opening or on a side wall.
>
> (p. 7)

This description of autoshaped pecking by pigeons sounds similar to sign tracking by dogs. Both autoshaping and sign tracking involve species-characteristic behavior that is elicited by food presentation. Instinctive drift also appears to be reflexive behavior that is elicited by food. Birds peck at grain and make similar responses to the key light. That is, birds sample or taste items in the environment by the only means available to them, beak or bill contact. Dogs make food-soliciting responses to the signal that precedes food reinforcement. For example, this kind of behavior is clearly seen in pictures of wolf pups licking the mouth of an adult returning from a hunt. Raccoons rub and manipulate food items and make similar responses to coins that precede food delivery. And we have all seen humans rubbing dice together between their hands before throwing them. It is likely that autoshaping, sign tracking, and instinctive drift represent the same (or very similar) processes (for a discussion, see Hearst & Jenkins, 1974).

One proposed possibility is that all of these phenomena (instinctive drift, sign tracking, and autoshaping) are instances of **stimulus substitution**. That is, when a CS (e.g., light) is paired with a US (e.g., food) the conditioned stimulus is said to substitute for, or generalizes from, the unconditioned stimulus. This means that responses elicited by the CS (rubbing, barking and prancing, pecking) are similar to the ones caused by the US. While this is a parsimonious account, there is evidence that it is wrong.

Recall from Chapter 3 that the laws of the reflex (US → UR) do not hold for the CS → CR relationship, suggesting that there is no universal substitution of the CS for the US. Also, in many experiments, the behavior evoked by the US is opposite in direction to the responses elicited by the CS (see Chapter 3, ON THE APPLIED SIDE). Additionally, there are experiments conducted within the autoshaping paradigm that directly refute the stimulus substitution hypothesis.

In an experiment by Wasserman (1973), chicks were placed in a very cool enclosure. In this situation, a key light was occasionally turned on and this was closely followed by the activation of a heat lamp. All the chicks began to peck the key light in an unusual way. The birds moved toward the key light and rubbed their beaks back and forth on it: behavior described as snuggling. These responses resemble the behavior that newborn chicks direct toward their mothers, when soliciting warmth. Chicks peck at their mothers' feathers and rub their beaks from side to side, behavior that results in snuggling up to their mother.

At first glance, the "snuggling to the key light" seems to illustrate an instance of stimulus substitution. The chick behaves to the key light as it does toward its mother. The difficulty is that the chicks in Wasserman's (1973) experiment responded completely differently to the heat lamp than to the key light. In response to heat from the lamp, a chick extended its wings and stood motionless, behavior that it might direct toward intense sunlight. In this experiment, it is clear that the CS does not substitute for the US because these stimuli elicit completely different responses (also see Timberlake & Grant, 1975).

An alternative to stimulus substitution has been proposed by Timberlake (1983, 1993), who suggested that each US (food, water, sexual stimuli, heat lamp, and so on) controls a distinct set of species-specific responses or a behavior system. That is, for each species there is a behavior system related to procurement of food, another related to obtaining water, still another for securing warmth, and so on. For example, the presentation of food to a raccoon activates the **behavior system** that consists of procurement and ingestion of food. One of these behaviors, rubbing and manipulating the item, is evoked. Other behaviors like bringing the food item to the mouth, salivation, chewing, and swallowing of the food are not elicited. Timberlake goes on to propose that the particular responses elicited by the CS depend, in part, on the physical properties of the stimulus. Presumably, in the Wasserman experiment, properties of the key light (a visual stimulus raised above the floor) were more closely related to snuggling than to standing still and extending wings.

At the present time, it is not possible to predict which responses in a behavior system a given CS will elicit. That is, a researcher can predict that the CS will elicit one or more of the responses controlled by the US, but cannot specify which responses will occur. One possibility is that the salience of the US affects which responses are elicited by the CS. For example, as the intensity of the heat source increases (approximating a hot summer day) the chicks' response to the CS key light may change from snuggling to behavior appropriate to standing in the sun (open wings and motionless).

Operant Contingencies Predominate over Respondent Regulation

As you have seen, there are circumstances in which both operant and respondent conditioning occur. Moreover, responses that are typically operant on the basis of topography are occasionally regulated by respondent processes (and, as such, are respondents). There are also occasions in which behavior that, in form or topography, appears to be reflexive is regulated by the consequences that follow it.

Reinforcing reflexive behavior

In the 1960s, a number of researchers attempted to show that involuntary reflexive or autonomic responses could be operantly conditioned (Kimmel & Kimmel, 1963; Miller & Carmona, 1967; Shearn, 1962). Miller and Carmona (1967) deprived dogs of water and monitored their respondent level of salivation. The dogs were separated into two groups. One group was reinforced with water for increasing salivation and the other group was reinforced for a decrease. Both groups of animals showed the expected change in amount of salivation. That is, the dogs that were reinforced for increasing saliva flow showed an increase, and the dogs reinforced for less saliva flow showed a decrease.

At first glance, this result seems to demonstrate the operant conditioning of salivation. However, Miller and Carmona (1967) noticed an associated change in the dogs' behavior that could have produced the alteration in salivation. Dogs that increased saliva flow appeared to be alert, and those that decreased it were described as drowsy. For this reason, the results are suspect—salivary conditioning may have been mediated by a change in the dogs' operant behavior. Perhaps drowsiness was operant behavior that resulted in decreased salivation, and being alert increased the reflex. In other words, the change in salivation could have been part of a larger, more general behavior pattern that was reinforced. Similar problems occurred with other experiments. For example, Shearn (1962) showed operant conditioning of heart rate, but this dependent variable can be affected by a change in pattern of breathing.

The Miller experiments

It is difficult to rule out operant conditioning of other behavior as a mediator of reinforced reflexes. However, Miller and DiCara (1967) conducted a classic experiment in which this explanation was not possible. The researchers reasoned that operant behavior could not mediate conditioning if the subject had its skeletal muscles immobilized. To immobilize their subjects, which were white rats, they used the drug curare. This drug paralyzes the skeletal musculature and interrupts breathing, and the rats were maintained by artificial respiration. When given curare the rats could not swallow food or water; Miller and DiCara solved this problem by using electrical stimulation of the rats' pleasure center in the brain as reinforcement for visceral reflexes.

Before starting the experiment, the rats had electrodes permanently implanted in their hypothalamus. This was done in a way that allowed the experimenters to connect and disconnect the animals from the equipment that stimulated the pleasure center. To make certain that the stimulation was reinforcing, the rats were trained to press a bar in order to turn on a brief microvolt pulse. This procedure demonstrated that the pulse was, in fact, reinforcing since the animals pressed a lever for the stimulation.

At this point, Miller and DiCara administered curare to the rats and reinforced half of them with electrical stimulation for decreasing their heart rate. The other animals were reinforced for an increase in heart rate. Figure 7.3 shows the results of this experiment. Both groups start out with heart rates in the range of 400–425 beats per minute. After 90 min of contingent reinforcement, the groups are widely divergent. The group that was reinforced for slow heart rate is at about 310 beats per minute, and the fast rate group is at approximately 500 beats per minute.

Miller and Banuazizi (1968) extended this finding. They inserted a pressure-sensitive balloon into the large intestine of rats, which allowed them to monitor intestinal contractions. At the same time, the researchers measured the animals' heart rate. As in the previous experiment, the rats were administered curare and reinforced with elec-

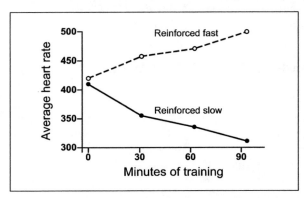

FIG. 7.3   Effects of curare immobilization of skeletal muscles and the operant conditioning of heart rate are shown (Miller & DiCara, 1967). Half of the rats received electrical brain stimulation for increasing heart rate and the other half for decreasing heart rate.

trical brain stimulation. In different conditions, reinforcement was made contingent on increased or decreased intestinal contractions. Also, the rats were reinforced on some occasions for a decrease in heart rate, and at other times for an increase.

The researchers showed that reinforcing intestinal contractions or relaxation changed them in the appropriate direction. The animals also showed an increase or decrease in heart rate when this response was made contingent on brain stimulation. Finally, Miller and Banuazizi (1968) demonstrated that a change in intestinal contractions did not affect heart rate and, conversely, changes in heart rate did not affect contractions.

In these experiments contingent reinforcement modified behavior usually considered to be reflexive, under conditions in which skeletal responses could not affect the outcome. Also, the effects were specific to the response that was reinforced, showing that brain stimulation was not generating general physiological changes that produced the outcomes of the experiment. It seems that responses that are usually elicited can be conditioned using an operant contingency of reinforcement. Greene and Sutor (1971) extended this conclusion to humans, showing that a galvanic skin response (GSR) could be regulated by negative reinforcement (for more on operant autonomic conditioning, see DiCara, 1970; Engle, 1993; Jonas, 1973; Kimmel, 1974; Miller, 1969).

Although this conclusion is probably justified, the operant conditioning of autonomic responses like blood pressure, heart rate, and intestinal contraction has run into difficulties. Miller even had problems replicating the results of his own experiments (Miller & Dworkin, 1974), concluding "that the original visceral learning experiments are not replicable and that the existence of visceral learning remains unproven" (Dworkin & Miller, 1986). The weight of the evidence does suggest that reflexive responses are, at least in some circumstances, affected by the consequences that follow them. This behavior, however, is also subject to control by contiguity or pairing of stimuli. It is relatively easy to change heart rate by pairing a light (CS) with electric shock and then using the light to change heart rate. It should be evident that controlling heart rate with an operant contingency is no easy task. Thus, autonomic behavior may not be exclusively tied to respondent conditioning, but respondent conditioning is particularly effective with these responses.

NOTE ON: Operants and respondents

Clearly, the fundamental distinction between operant and respondent conditioning is operational. The distinction is operational because conditioning is defined by the operations that produce it. Operant conditioning involves a contingency between behavior and its consequences. Respondent conditioning entails the pairing of stimuli.

Autonomic responses are usually respondents and are best modified by respondent procedures. When these responses are changed by the consequences that follow them, they are operants. Similarly, skeletal responses are usually operant and most readily changed by contingencies of reinforcement, but when modified by the pairing of stimuli they are respondents. The whole organism is impacted by contingencies (environmental arrangement of events), whether these contingencies are designed as operant or respondent procedures. That is, most contingencies of reinforcement activate respondent processes and Pavlovian contingencies often involve the reinforcement of operant behavior.

THE BIOLOGICAL CONTEXT OF CONDITIONING

As we stated in Chapter 1, the evolutionary history, ontogenetic history, and current physiological status of an organism is the **context for conditioning**. Edward Morris (1992) has described the way we use the term *context*:

> Context is a funny word. As a non-technical term, it can be vague and imprecise. As a technical term, it can also be vague and imprecise—and has been throughout the history of psychology. In what follows, I mean to use it technically and precisely. . . . First, the historical context—phylogenetic and ontogenetic, biological and behavioral—establishes the current structure and function of biology (anatomy and physiology) and behavior (form and function). Second, the form or structure of the current context, organismic or environmental, affects (or enables) what behavior can physically or formally occur. Third, the current context affects (actualizes) the functional relationships among stimuli and response (i.e., their "meaning" for one another).
>
> (p. 14)

Context is a way of noting that the probability of behavior depends on certain conditions. Thus, the effective contingencies (stimuli, responses, and reinforcing events) may vary from species to species. A hungry dog can be reinforced with meat for jumping a hurdle and a pigeon will fly to a particular location to get grain. These are obvious species differences, but there are more subtle effects of the biological context. The rate of acquisition and level of behavior once established may be influenced by an organism's physiology, as determined by species history. Moreover, within a species, reinforcers, stimuli, and responses can be specific to particular situations.

Behavior that is observed with any one set of responses, stimuli, and reinforcers may change when different sets are used. In addition, different species may show different environment–behavior relationships when the same set of responses and events is investigated. Although the effects of contingencies sometimes depend on the particular events and responses, principles of behavior like extinction, discrimination, and spontaneous recovery show generality across species. The behaviors of schoolchildren working at math problems for teacher attention and of pigeons pecking keys for food are regulated by the principles of reinforcement even though the particular responses and reinforcers vary over species. With regard to generalization of behavior principles, human conduct is probably more sensitive to environmental influence than the behavior of any other species. In this sense, humans may actually be the organisms best described by the principles of behavior.

As early as 1938, Skinner recognized that a comprehensive understanding of the behavior of organisms required the study of more than "arbitrary" stimuli, responses, and reinforcers (Skinner, 1938, pp. 10–11). By using simple stimuli, easy-to-execute and record responses, and precise reinforcers Skinner hoped to identify *general principles* of operant conditioning. By and large, this same strategy is used today in the modern operant laboratory.

Taste Aversion Learning

In an experiment by Wilcoxon, Dragoin, and Kral (1971), quail and rats were given blue salty water. After the animals drank the water, they were made sick. Following recovery, the animals were given a choice between water that was not colored but tasted salty and plain water that was colored blue. The rats avoided the salty-flavored water and the quail would not drink the colored solution. This finding is not difficult to understand—when feeding or drinking, birds rely on visual cues; and rats are sensitive to taste and smell. In the natural habitat, drinking liquids that produce illness should be avoided and this has obvious survival value. Because quail typically select food on the basis of what it looks like they avoided the colored water. Rats on the other hand avoided the taste, as it was what had been associated with sickness.

In the Wilcoxon et al. (1971) experiment, the taste and color of the water was a compound CS that was paired with the US illness. Both species showed **taste aversion learning**. That is, the animals came to avoid one or the other of the CS elements based on biological history. In other words, the biology of the organism dictated which cue became a CS, but the conditioning of the aversion, or CS–US pairing, was the same for both species. Of course, a bird that relied on taste for food selection would be expected to associate taste and illness. This phenomenon has been called **preparedness**— quail are more biologically prepared to discriminate critical stimulus features when sights are associated with illness and rats respond best to a flavor–illness association. Other experiments have shown that within a species the set of stimuli, responses, and reinforcers may be affected by the biology of the organism.

Garcia and colleagues conducted several important experiments that were concerned with the conditions that produce taste aversion in rats.[1] Garcia and Koelling (1966) had thirsty rats drink tasty (saccharin-flavored) water, or unflavored water accompanied by flashing lights and gurgling noises (bright-noisy water). After the rats drank the water half of each group was immediately given an electric shock for drinking. The other animals were made ill by injecting them with lithium chloride or by irradiating them with X-rays. Lithium chloride and high levels of X-rays produce nausea roughly 20 min after administration. Figure 7.4 shows the four conditions of the experiment.

After aversion training and recovery the rats were allowed to drink and their water intake was measured. The major results of this experiment are shown in Figure 7.5. Baseline measures of drinking were compared to fluid intake after shock or lithium or X-rays paired with a visual or flavor stimulus (CS). Both shock and illness induced by X-ray exposure suppressed drinking. Those rats that received shock after drinking the bright-noisy water and the ones that were made sick after ingesting the flavored water substantially reduced their fluid intake. Water intake in the other two groups was virtually unaffected. The animals made sick after drinking the bright-noisy water and those shocked for ingesting the flavored water did not show a conditioned aversion.

These results are unusual for several reasons. During traditional respondent conditioning, the CS and US typically overlap or are separated by only a few seconds. In the Garcia and Koelling (1966) experiment, the taste CS was followed much later by the US— drug or X-ray. Also, it is often assumed that

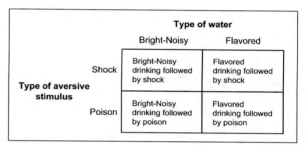

FIG. 7.4   Conditions used to show taste aversion conditioning by rats in an experiment by Garcia and Koelling (1966). From a description given in same study.

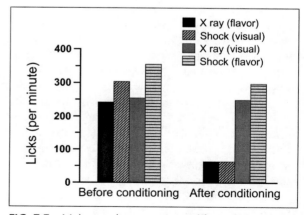

FIG. 7.5   Major results are presented from the taste-aversion experiment by Garcia and Koelling (1966). Based on data from same study.

---

[1] It is worth noting that the rat is an ideal subject in these experiments for generalizing to humans. Like humans the rat is omnivorous—it eats both meats and vegetables. Rats live wherever humans do and are said to consume 20% of the world's human food supply.

the choice of CS and US is irrelevant for respondent conditioning. Pavlov claimed that the choice of CS was arbitrary; he said anything would do. However, taste and grastrointestinal malaise produced aversion, but taste and shock did not. Therefore, it appears that for some stimuli the animal is *prepared* by nature to make a connection and for others they may even be contraprepared (Seligman, 1970). Generally, for other kinds of classical conditioning many CS–US pairings are required, but aversion to taste is conditioned after a single pairing of flavor–illness. In fact, the animal need not even be conscious in order for an aversion to be formed (Provenza, Lynch, & Nolan, 1994). Finally, it appears necessary for the animal to experience nausea in order for taste aversion to condition. Being poisoned by strychnine, which inhibits spinal neurons but does not cause sickness, will not work (Cheney, van der Wall, & Poehlmann, 1987).

These results can be understood by considering the biology of the rat. The animals are omnivorous and as such they eat a wide range of meat and vegetable foods. Rats eat 10–16 small meals each day and frequently ingest novel food items. The animals are sensitive to smell and taste but have relatively poor sight, and they cannot vomit. When contaminated, spoiled, rotten, or naturally toxic food is eaten, it typically has a distinctive smell and taste. For this reason, taste and smell but not visual cues are associated with illness. Conditioning after a long time period between CS and US occurs because there is usually a delay between ingestion of a toxic item and nausea. It would be unusual for a rat to eat and then have this quickly followed by an aversive stimulus (flavor–shock); hence there is little conditioning. The survival value of one-trial conditioning, or quickly avoiding food items that produce illness, is obvious—eat that food again and it may kill you.

FOCUS ON: Behavioral neuroscience, taste aversion, and urges for addictive behavior

Behavior is why the nervous system exists. Those organisms with a nervous system that allowed for behavioral adaptation and reproduction survived. To reveal the neural mechanisms that interrelate brain and behavior, neuroscientists often look for changes in behavior as a result of functional changes in the brain as the organism solves problems posed by its environment. This approach has been used to understand how organisms acquire aversions to food tastes and avoidance of foods with these tastes.

A recent study investigated the sites in the brain responsive to lithium chloride (LiCl), a chemical often used in conditioned taste aversion learning to induce nausea. The researchers used brain imaging to measure the presence of *c*-fos, a protein with a short neural expression that is implicated in the neural reward system (Andre, Albanos, & Reilly, 2007). The gustatory area of the thalamus showed elevated levels of *c*-fos following LiCl treatment, implicating this brain region as central to conditioned taste aversion. Subsequent research by Yamamoto (2007) showed that two regions of the amygdala were also involved in taste aversion conditioning. One region is concerned with detecting the conditioned stimulus (e.g., distinctive taste) and the other is involved with hedonic shift from positive to negative, as a result of taste aversion experience. Thus, brain research is showing that several areas of the brain are involved in the detection of nausea from toxic chemicals and the subsequent aversion to tastes predictive of such nausea.

There are also brain sites that relate to urges, cravings, and excessive behavior. The cortical brain structure called the insula appears to be an area that turns physical reactions into sensations of craving. A recent investigation in *Science* showed that smokers with strokes that injured or destroyed this area lost their craving for cigarettes (Naqvi, Rudrauf, Damasio, & Bechara, 2007). The insula area appears critical for behaviors whose bodily effects are experienced as pleasurable, like cigarette smoking. Specific brain sites seem to code for the physiological reactions to stimuli and "upgrade" the integrated neural responses into awareness, allowing the person to act on the urges of an acquired addiction. Since humans have learned to modulate their own brain activity to reduce the sensation of pain, they also may be able to learn to deactivate the insula and thus reduce cravings associated with excessive use of drugs.

Behavioral neuroscience is progressively relating behavior to the neurological mechanisms of the brain. Eventually, scientists will have a more complete account of how the external environment and the neurophysiology of the organism interrelate to produce specific behavior in a given situation.

*   *   *

Taste aversion learning has been replicated and extended in many different experiments (see Barker, Best, & Domjan, 1977; Rozin & Kalat, 1971). Revusky and Garcia (1970) showed that the interval between a flavor CS and an illness-inducing US could be as much as 12 h. Other findings indicate that a novel taste is more easily conditioned than one with which an animal is familiar (Cheney & Eldred, 1980; Revusky & Bedarf, 1967). A novel setting (as well as taste) has also been shown to increase avoidance of food when a toxin is the unconditioned stimulus. For example, Mitchell, Kirschbaum, and Perry (1975) fed rats in the same container at a particular location for 25 days. Following this, the researchers changed the food cup and made the animals ill. After this experience, the rats avoided eating from the new container (see Parker, 2003, for difference between taste aversion and avoidance). Taste aversion learning also occurs in humans of course (Arwas, Rolnick, & Lubow, 1989; Logue, 1979, 1985, 1988a). Alexandra Logue at the State University of New York, Stony Brook, has concluded:

> Conditioned food aversion learning in humans appears very similar to that in other species. As in other species, aversions can be acquired with long CS–US delays, the aversion most often forms to the taste of food, the CS usually precedes the US, aversions frequently generalized to foods that taste qualitatively similar, and aversions are more likely to be formed to less preferred, less familiar foods. Aversions are frequently strong. They can be acquired even though the subject is convinced that the food did not cause the subject's illness.
>
> (1985, p. 327)

Imagine that on a special occasion you spend an evening at your favorite restaurant. Stimuli at the restaurant include your companion, waiters, candles on the table, china, art on the wall, and many more aspects of the setting. You order several courses, most of them familiar, and "just to try it out" you have *pasta primavera* for the first time. What you do not know is that a flu virus has invaded your body and is percolating away while you eat. Early in the morning, you wake up with a clammy feeling, rumbling stomach, and a hot acid taste in the back of your throat. You spew *primavera* sauce, wine, and several other ugly bits and pieces on the bathroom mirror.

The most salient stimulus at the restaurant was probably your date. Alas, is the relationship finished? Will you get sick at the next sight of your lost love? Is this what the experimental analysis of behavior has to do with romance novels? Of course, the answer to these questions is no. It is very likely that you will develop a strong aversion only to *pasta primavera*. Interestingly, you may clearly be aware that your illness was caused by the flu, not the new food. You may even understand taste aversion learning but, as one of the authors (Cheney) of this book can testify to, it makes no difference. The novel-taste CS, because of its single pairing (delayed by several hours even) with nausea, is likely to be avoided in the future.

Taste aversion conditioning and activity anorexia

Taste aversion learning may be involved in human anorexia. In activity anorexia (Epling & Pierce, 1992, 1996a), food restriction increases physical activity and mounting physical activity reduces food intake (see ON THE APPLIED SIDE in this chapter). Two researchers, Bo Lett and Virginia Grant (Lett & Grant, 1996), at Memorial University in Newfoundland, Canada suggested that human anorexia induced by physical activity could involve taste aversion learning. Basically, it is known that physical activity like wheel running suppresses food intake in rats (e.g., Epling, Pierce & Stefan,

1983; Routtenberg & Kuznesof, 1967). Lett and Grant proposed that suppression of eating could be due to a conditioned taste aversion (CTA) induced by wheel running. According to this view, a distinctive taste becomes a conditioned stimulus (CS) for reduced consumption when followed by the unconditioned stimulus (US) of nausea from wheel running. In support of this hypothesis, rats exposed to a flavored liquid that was paired with wheel running drank less of the liquid than control rats that remained in their home cages (Lett & Grant, 1996; see also Heth, Inglis, Russell, & Pierce, 2001).

Further research by Sarah Salvy, who worked with Pierce (author of textbook) and is now in Pediatrics at the State University of New York (Buffalo), indicates that CTA induced by wheel running involves respondent processes (Salvy, Heth, Pierce, & Russell, 2004; Salvy, Pierce, Heth, & Russell, 2002, 2003), although operant components have not been ruled out. Salvy conducted "bridging experiments" in which a distinctive food rather than a flavored liquid is followed by wheel running (Salvy et al., 2003). Rats that ate novel food snacks (flavored cat treats) followed by bouts of wheel running consumed less of the food compared with control rats receiving the food followed by access to a locked wheel. That is, CTA induced by wheel running was generalized to novel food stimuli. In our laboratory at the University of Alberta we have consistently obtained wheel-running-induced CTA to novel food, but have not yet been able to establish CTA with familiar food (laboratory chow). Familiar laboratory chow, however, is used in the activity anorexia procedure. One possibility is that CTA occurs during activity anorexia but does not explain the suppression of eating during the cycle (see Sparks, Grant, & Lett, 2003). Another possibility is that CTA and other nonassociative processes combine to produce activity anorexia. Further research is necessary to clarify the role of CTA for the onset and maintenance of activity anorexia.

Adjunctive Behavior

On time-based and interval schedules, organisms may emit behavior patterns that are not required by the contingency of reinforcement (Staddon & Simmelhag, 1971). If you received $5 for pressing a lever once every 10 min you might start to pace, twiddle your thumbs, have a sip of soda, or scratch your head between payoffs on a regular basis. Staddon (1977) has noted that during a fixed time between food reinforcers animals engage in three distinct types of behavior. Immediately after food reinforcement **interim behavior** like drinking water may occur; next an organism may engage in **facultative behavior** that is independent of the schedule of reinforcement (e.g., rats may groom themselves); finally, as the time for reinforcement gets close, animals engage in food-related activities called **terminal behavior**, such as orienting toward the lever or food cup. The first of these categories, **interim** or adjunctive behavior,[2] is of most interest for the present discussion as it is behavior not required by the schedule but *induced by reinforcement*. Because the behavior is induced as a side effect of the reinforcement schedule, it is also referred to as **schedule-induced behavior**.

When a hungry animal is placed on an interval schedule of reinforcement, it will ingest an excessive amount of water if allowed to drink. Falk (1961, 1964, 1969) suggested that this **polydipsia** or excessive drinking is adjunctive behavior induced by the time-based delivery of food. A rat that is working for food on an intermittent schedule may drink as much as half its body weight during a single session (Falk, 1961). This drinking occurs even though the animal is not water deprived. The rat may turn toward the lever, press for food, obtain and eat the food pellet, drink excessively, groom itself, and then repeat the sequence. Pressing the lever is required for reinforcement, and grooming may occur in the absence of food delivery, but polydipsia appears to be induced by the schedule.

In general, **adjunctive behavior** refers to any excessive and persistent behavior pattern that occurs

---

[2] Induced behavior that immediately follows reinforcement has been called interim (Staddon, 1997) and adjunctive (Falk 1961, 1964, 1969). The terms are interchangeable in this book.

as a side effect of reinforcement delivery. The schedule may require a response for reinforcement, or it may simply be time based, as when food pellets are given every 30 s no matter what the animal is doing. Additionally, the schedule may deliver reinforcement on a fixed time basis (e.g., every 60 s) or it may be constructed so that the time between reinforcers varies (e.g., 20 s, then 75, 85, 60 s, and so on).

Schedules of food reinforcement have been shown to generate such adjunctive behavior as attack against other animals (Flory, 1969; Hutchinson, Azrin, & Hunt, 1968; Pitts & Malagodi, 1996), licking at an airstream (Mendelson & Chillag, 1970), drinking water (Falk, 1961), chewing on wood blocks (Villareal, 1967), and preference for oral cocaine administration (Falk & Lau, 1997; Falk, D'Mello, & Lau, 2001). Adjunctive behavior has been observed in pigeons, monkeys, rats, and humans; reinforcers have included water, food, shock avoidance, access to a running wheel, money, and for male pigeons the sight of a female (see Falk, 1971, 1977; Staddon, 1977, for reviews). Muller, Crow, and Cheney (1979) induced locomotor activity in college students and retarded adolescents with fixed-interval (FI) and fixed-time (FT) token delivery. Stereotypic and self-injurious behavior of humans with developmental disabilities also has been viewed as adjctive to the schedule of reinforcement (Lerman, Iwata, Zarcone, & Ringdahl, 1994). Thus, adjunctive behavior occurs in different species, is generated by a variety of reinforcement procedures, and extends to a number of induced responses.

A variety of conditions affect adjunctive behavior, but the schedule of reinforcement delivery and the deprivation status of the organism appear to be the most important. As the time between reinforcement deliveries increases from 2 to 180 s, adjunctive behavior increases. After 180 s adjunctive behavior drops off and reaches low levels at 300 s. For example, a rat may receive a food pellet every 10 s and drink only a bit more than a normal amount of water between pellet deliveries. When the schedule is changed to 100 s drinking increases; polydipsia goes up again if the schedule is stretched to 180 s. As the time between pellets is further increased to 200, 250, and then 300 s, water consumption goes down. This increase, peak, and then drop in schedule-induced behavior is illustrated in Figure 7.6 and is called a bitonic function. The function has been observed in species other than the rat and occurs for other adjunctive behavior (see Keehn & Jozsvai, 1989, for contrary evidence).

In addition to the reinforcement schedule, adjunctive behavior becomes more and more excessive as the level of deprivation increases. A rat that is at 80% of its normal body weight and is given food pellets every 20 s will drink more water than an animal at 90% weight and on the same schedule. Experiments have shown that food-schedule-induced drinking (Falk, 1969), airstream licking (Chillag & Mendelson, 1971), and attack (Dove, 1976) go up as an animal's body weight goes down. Thus, a variety of induced activities escalate when deprivation for food is increased and when food is the scheduled reinforcer.

Falk (1977) has noted that "on the surface" adjunctive behavior does not seem to make sense:

[Adjunctive activities] are excessive and persistent. A behavioral phenomenon which encompasses many kinds of activities and is widespread over species and high in predictability ordinarily can be presumed to be a basic mechanism contributing to adaptation and survival. The puzzle of adjunctive behavior is that, while fulfilling the above criteria its adaptive significance has escaped analysis. Indeed, adjunctive activities have appeared not only curiously exaggerated and persistent, but also energetically quite costly.

(p. 326)

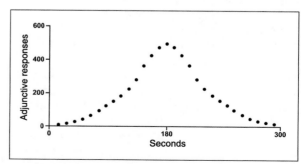

FIG. 7.6   A bitonic relationship is presented, showing time between food pellets and amount of adjunctive water drinking.

In fact, Falk (1977) goes on to argue that induced behavior does make biological sense.

The argument made by Falk is complex and beyond the scope of this book. Simply stated, adjunctive behavior may be related to what ethologists call displacement behavior. **Displacement behavior** is seen in the natural environment and is "characterized as irrelevant, incongruous, or out of context. . . . For example, two skylarks in combat might suddenly cease fighting and peck at the ground with feeding movements" (Falk, 1971, p. 584). The activity of the animal does not make sense given the situation, and the displaced responses do not appear to follow from immediately preceding behavior. Like adjunctive behavior, displacement activities arise when consummatory (i.e., eating, drinking, etc.) activities are interrupted or prevented. In the laboratory, a hungry animal is interrupted from eating when small bits of food are intermittently delivered.

Adjunctive and displacement activities occur at high strength when biologically relevant behavior (i.e., eating or mating) is blocked. Recall that male pigeons engage in adjunctive behavior when reinforced with the sight of (but not access to) female members of the species. These activities may increase the chance that other possibilities in the environment are contacted. A bird that pecks at tree bark when prevented from eating may find a new food source. Armstrong (1950) has suggested that "a species which is able to modify its behavior to suit changed circumstances by means of displacements, rather than by the evolution of ad hoc modifications starting from scratch will have an advantage over other species" (Falk, 1971, p. 587). Falk, however, goes on to make the point that evolution has probably eliminated many animals that engage in nonfunctional displacement activities.

Adjunctive behavior is another example of activity that is best analyzed by considering the biological context. Responses that do not seem to make sense may ultimately prove adaptive. The conditions that generate and maintain adjunctive and displacement behavior are similar. Both types of responses may reflect a common evolutionary origin, and this suggests that principles of adjunctive behavior will be improved by analyzing the biological context.

ON THE APPLIED SIDE: Activity anorexia and interrelations between eating and physical activity

Eating and Physical Activity

In 1967, Carl Cheney (who was then at Eastern Washington State University) ran across a paper (Routtenberg & Kuznesof, 1967) that reported self-starvation in laboratory rats. Cheney (coauthor of this textbook) thought that this was an unusual effect since most animals are reluctant to kill themselves for any reason. Because of this, he decided to replicate the experiment and he recruited W. Frank Epling (former coauthor of this textbook), an undergraduate student at the time, to help run the research. The experiment was relatively simple. Cheney and Epling (1968) placed a few rats in running wheels and fed them for 1 h each day. The researchers recorded the daily number of wheel turns, the weight of the rat, and the amount of food eaten. Surprisingly, the rats increased wheel running to excessive levels, ate less and less, lost weight, and if allowed to continue in the experiment died of starvation. Importantly, the rats were not required to run and they had plenty to eat, but they stopped eating and ran as much as 10 miles a day.

Twelve years later, Frank Epling (who was then an assistant professor of psychology at the University of Alberta) began to do collaborative research with David Pierce (coauthor of this textbook), a professor of sociology at the same university. They wondered if anorexic patients were hyperactive like the animals in the self-starvation experiments. If they were, it might be possible to develop an animal model of anorexia. Clinical reports indicated that indeed many anorexic patients were excessively active. For this reason, Epling and Pierce began to investigate the relationship between wheel running and food intake (Epling & Pierce, 1988; Pierce & Epling, 1991; Pierce, 2001). The basic finding is that physical activity decreases food intake and that decreased food intake increases activity. Epling and Pierce call this feedback loop activity-based anorexia or just **activity anorexia**, and argue that a similar cycle occurs in anorexic patients (see Epling & Pierce, 1992; Epling, Pierce, & Stefan, 1983).

This analysis of eating and exercise suggests that these activities are interrelated. Depriving an animal of food should increase the reinforcing value of exercise. Rats that are required to press a lever in order to run on a wheel should work harder for wheel access when they are deprived of food. Additionally, engaging in exercise should reduce the reinforcing value of food. Rats that are required to press a lever for food pellets should not work as hard for food following a day of exercise. Pierce, Epling, and a graduate student, Doug Boer, designed two experiments to test these ideas (Pierce, Epling, & Boer, 1986).

Reinforcement Effectiveness of Physical Activity

We asked whether food deprivation increased the reinforcing effectiveness of wheel running. If animals worked harder for an opportunity to exercise when deprived of food, this would show that running had increased in its capacity to support behavior. That is, depriving an animal of food should increase the reinforcing effectiveness of running. This is an interesting implication because increased reinforcement effectiveness is usually achieved by withholding the reinforcing event. Thus, to increase the reinforcement effectiveness of water a researcher typically withholds access to water, but (again) in this case food is withheld in order to increase the reinforcing effectiveness of wheel access.

We used nine young rats of both sexes to test the reinforcing effectiveness of wheel running as food deprivation changed. The animals were trained to press a lever to obtain 60 s of wheel running. When the rat pressed the lever, a brake was removed and the running wheel was free to turn. After 60 s, the brake was again activated and the animal had to press the lever to obtain more wheel access for running. The apparatus that we constructed for this experiment is shown in Figure 7.7.

Once lever pressing for wheel running was stable, each animal was tested when it was food deprived (75% of normal weight) and when it was at free-feeding weight. Recall that the animals were expected to work harder for exercise when they were food deprived. To measure the reinforcing effectiveness of wheel running the animals were required to press the lever more and more for each opportunity to run: a *progressive ratio schedule*. Specifically, the rats were required to press 5 times to obtain 60 s of wheel running, and then 10, 15, 20, 25, and so on. The point at which they gave up pressing for wheel running was used as an index of the reinforcing effectiveness of exercise.

The results of this experiment are shown in Figure 7.8. All animals lever pressed for wheel running more when they were food deprived than when at normal weight. In other words, animals worked harder for exercise when they were hungry. Further evidence indicated that the reinforcing effectiveness went up and down when an animal's weight was made to increase and decrease. For example, one rat pressed the bar 1567 times when food deprived, 881 times at normal weight,

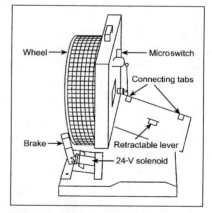

FIG. 7.7 Wheel-running apparatus used in the Pierce, Epling, and Boer (1986) experiment on the reinforcing effectiveness of physical activity as a function of food deprivation. From "Deprivation and Satiation: The Interrelations between Food and Wheel Running," by W. David Pierce, W. Frank Epling, and D. P. Boer, 1986, *Journal of the Experimental Analysis of Behavior*, 46, 199–210. Copyright 1986 held by the Society for the Experimental Analysis of Behavior. Republished with permission.

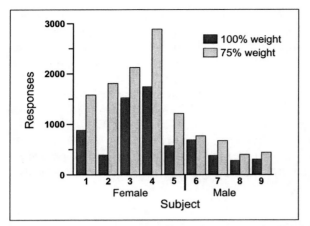

FIG. 7.8   The graph shows the number of bar presses for 60 s of wheel running as a function of food deprivation. From "Deprivation and Satiation: The Interrelations between Food and Wheel Running," by W. David Pierce, W. Frank Epling, and D. P. Boer, 1986, *Journal of the Experimental Analysis of Behavior, 46,* 199–210. Copyright 1986 held by the Society for the Experimental Analysis of Behavior. Republished with permission.

and 1882 times when again food deprived. This indicated that the effect was reversible and was tied to the level of food deprivation (see Belke, Pierce, & Duncan, 2006, on substitutability of food and wheel running).

Reinforcement Effectiveness of Food

In a second experiment, we investigated the effects of exercise on the reinforcing effectiveness of food. Four male rats were trained to press a lever for food pellets. When lever pressing occurred reliably, we tested the effects of exercise on each animal's willingness to work for food. In this case, we expected that a day of exercise would decrease the reinforcement effectiveness of food on the next day.

Test days were arranged to measure the reinforcing effects of food. One day before each test, animals were placed in their wheels without food. On some of the days before a test, the wheel was free to turn, and on other days it was not. Three of the four rats ran moderately in their activity wheels on exercise days. One lazy rat did not run when given the opportunity. This animal was subsequently forced to exercise on a motor-driven wheel. All animals were well rested (3–4 h of rest) before each food test. This ensured that any effects were not caused by fatigue.

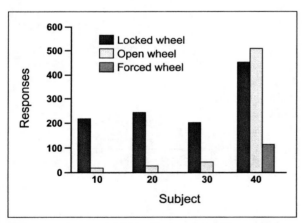

FIG. 7.9   The graph shows the number of bar presses for food when rats were allowed to run on a wheel as compared with no physical activity. From "Deprivation and Satiation: The Interrelations between Food and Wheel Running," by W. David Pierce, W. Frank Epling, and D. P. Boer, 1986, *Journal of the Experimental Analysis of Behavior, 46,* 199–210. Copyright 1986 held by the Society for the Experimental Analysis of Behavior. Republished with permission.

The reinforcement effectiveness of food was assessed by counting the number of lever presses for food as food became more and more difficult to obtain. For example, an animal had to press 5 times for the first food pellet, 10 for the next, then 15, 20, 25, and so on. As in the first experiment, the giving-up point was used to measure reinforcement effectiveness. Presumably, the more effective the reinforcer (i.e., food), the harder the animal would work for it.

Figure 7.9 shows that when test days were preceded by a day of exercise, the reinforcing effectiveness of food decreased sharply. Animals pressed the lever more than 200 times when they were not allowed to run but no more than 38 times when running preceded test sessions. Food no longer supported lever presses following a day of moderate wheel running, even though a lengthy rest period preceded the test. Although wheel running was moderate it represented a large change in physical activity since the animals were previously sedentary.

Prior to each test, the animals spent an entire day without food. Because of this, the reinforcing effectiveness of food should have increased. Exercise, however, seemed to override the effects of food deprivation since responding for food went down rather than up. Other evidence from these experiments suggested that the effects of exercise were similar to feeding the animal. Although exercise reduces the reinforcement effectiveness of food, the effect is probably not because wheel running serves as an economic substitute for food consumption (Belke, Pierce, & Duncan, 2006).

The rat that was forced to run also showed a sharp decline in lever pressing for food (see Figure 7.9). Exercise was again moderate but substantial relative to the animal's sedentary history. Because the reinforcement effectiveness of food decreased with forced exercise, we concluded that both forced and voluntary physical activity produce a decline in the value of food reinforcement. This finding suggests that people who increase their physical activity because of occupational requirements (e.g., ballet dancers) may value food less.

The Biological Context of Eating and Activity

In our view, the motivational interrelations between eating and physical activity have a basis in natural selection. Natural selection favored those animals that increased travel in times of food scarcity. During a famine, organisms can either stay and conserve energy or become mobile and travel to another location. The particular strategy adopted by a species depends on natural selection. If travel led to reinstatement of food supply and staying put resulted in starvation, then those animals that traveled gained reproductive advantage.

A major problem for an evolutionary analysis of activity anorexia is accounting for the decreased appetite of animals that travel to a new food patch. The fact that increasing energy expenditure is accompanied by decreasing caloric intake seems to violate common sense. From a *homeostatic* (i.e., energy balance) perspective, food intake and energy expenditure should be positively related. In fact, this is the case if an animal has the time to adjust to a new level of activity and food supply is not greatly reduced.

When depletion of food is severe, however, travel should not stop when food is infrequently contacted. This is because stopping to eat may be negatively balanced against reaching a more abundant food patch. Frequent contact with food would signal a replenished food supply, and this should reduce the tendency to travel. Recall that a decline in the reinforcing effectiveness of food means that animals will not work hard for nourishment. When food is scarce, considerable effort may be required to obtain it. For this reason, animals ignore food and continue to travel. However, as food becomes more plentiful and the effort to acquire it decreases, the organism begins to eat. Food consumption lowers the reinforcement effectiveness of physical activity and travel stops (see also Belke, Pierce, & Duncan, 2006, on the partial substitution of food for physical activity). On this basis, animals that expend large amounts of energy on a migration or trek become anorexic.

ADVANCED SECTION: The nature of autoshaped responses

Negative Automaintenance

When scientists are confronted with new and challenging data, they are typically loathe to accept the findings. This is because researchers have invested time, money, and effort in experiments that may depend on a particular view of the world. Consider a person who has made a career of investigating the operant behavior of pigeons, with rate of pecking a key as the major dependent variable. The suggestion that key pecking is actually respondent rather than operant behavior would not be well received by such a scientist. If key pecks are reflexive, then conclusions about operant behavior based on these responses are questionable. One possibility is to go to some effort to explain the data within the context of operant conditioning.

In fact, Brown and Jenkins (1968) suggested just this sort of explanation for their results. Recall that these experimenters pointed to the species-specific tendency of pigeons to peck at stimuli they look at. When the light is illuminated, there is a high probability that the birds will look and peck. Some of these responses are followed by food, and pecking increases in frequency. Other investigators noted that when birds are magazine trained they stand in the general area of the feeder and the response key is typically at head height just above the food tray. Anyone who has watched a pigeon knows that they have a high frequency of bobbing their heads. Since they are close to the key and are making pecking (or bobbing) motions, it is possible that a strike at the key is inadvertently followed by food delivery. From this perspective, key pecks are superstitious in the sense that they are accidentally reinforced. The superstitious explanation has an advantage because it does not require postulating a look–peck connection and it is entirely consistent with operant conditioning.

Although these explanations of pecking as an operant are plausible, the possibility remains that autoshaped pecking is respondent behavior. An ingenious experiment by Williams and Williams (1969) was designed to answer this question. In their experiment on **negative automaintenance**, pigeons were placed in an operant chamber and key illumination was repeatedly followed by food. This is, of course, the same procedure that Brown and Jenkins (1968) used to show autoshaping. The twist in the Williams and Williams procedure was that if the bird pecked the key when it was illuminated, food was not presented. This is called *omission training* because if the pigeon pecks the key the reinforcer is omitted, or if the response is omitted the reinforcer is delivered.

The logic of this procedure is that if pecking is respondent, then it is elicited by the key light and the pigeon will reflexively strike the disk. If, on the other hand, pecking is operant, then striking the key prevents reinforcement and responses should not be maintained. Thus, the clear prediction is that pecking is respondent behavior if the bird continues to peck with the **omission procedure** in place. Using the omission procedure, Williams and Williams (1969) found that pigeons frequently pecked the key even though responses prevented reinforcement. This finding suggests that the sight of grain is an unconditioned stimulus for pigeons, eliciting an unconditioned response of pecking at the food. When a key light stimulus precedes grain presentation, it becomes a CS that elicits pecking at the key (CR). Figure 7.10 shows this arrangement between stimulus events and responses. It is also the case that by not presenting the food (US), the key light (CS) is no longer paired with the US and the response (CR) undergoes extinction.

In discussing their results, Williams and Williams state that "the stimulus–reinforcer pairing overrode opposing effects of . . . reinforcement indicat[ing] that the effect was a powerful one, and demonstrat[ing] that a high level of responding does not imply the operation of . . . [operant] reinforcement" (1969, p. 520). The puzzling aspect of this finding is that in most cases pecking to a key is regulated by reinforcement and is clearly operant. Many experiments have shown that key pecks increase or decrease in frequency depending on the consequences that follow behavior.

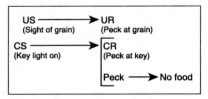

FIG. 7.10   Omission procedures are based on Williams and Williams (1969). The birds pecked the key even though these responses prevented reinforcement.

The Nature of the Autoshaped Response

Because of this apparent contradiction, several experiments were designed to investigate the nature of autoshaped pecking. Schwartz and Williams (1972a) preceded grain reinforcement for pigeons by turning on a red or white light on two separate keys. The birds responded by pecking the illuminated disk (i.e., they were autoshaped). On some trials, the birds were presented with both the red and white keys. Pecks on the red key prevented reinforcement, as in the omission procedure used by Williams and Williams (1969). Pecks to the white key, however, did not prevent reinforcement.

On these choice trials, the pigeons showed a definite preference for the white key that did not stop the delivery of grain. In other words, the birds more frequently pecked the key that was followed by the presentation of grain. Because this is a description of behavior regulated by an operant contingency (peck → food), autoshaped key pecks cannot be exclusively respondent. In concluding their paper, Schwartz and Williams wrote:

> A simple application of respondent principles cannot account for the phenomenon as originally described . . . and it cannot account for the rate and preference results of the present study. An indication of the way operant factors can modulate the performance of automaintained behavior has been given. . . . The analysis suggests that while automaintained behavior departs in important ways from the familiar patterns seen with arbitrary responses, the concepts and procedures developed from the operant framework are, nevertheless, influential in the automaintenance situation.
>
> (Schwartz & Williams, 1972a, p. 356)

Schwartz and Williams (1972b) went on to investigate the nature of key pecking by pigeons in several other experiments. The researchers precisely measured the contact duration of each peck that birds made to a response key. When the omission procedure was in effect, pigeons produced short-duration pecks. If the birds were autoshaped, but key pecks did not prevent the delivery of grain, the duration of the pecks was long. These same long-duration pecks occurred when the pigeons responded for food on a schedule of reinforcement. Generally, it appears that there are two types of key pecks: short-duration pecks evoked (perhaps elicited) by the presentation of grain, and long-duration pecks that occur when the bird's behavior is brought under operant control.

Other evidence also suggests that both operant and respondent conditioning are involved in autoshaping. It is likely that the first autoshaped pecking is respondent behavior elicited by light–food pairings. Once pecking produces food, however, it comes under operant control. Even when the omission procedure is in effect both operant and respondent behavior is conditioned and there is probably no uniform learning process underlying autoshaped responses (Papachristos & Gallistel, 2006). During omission training, a response to the key turns off the key light and food is not delivered. If the bird does not peck the key, the light is eventually turned off and food is presented. Because on these trials turning the light off is associated with reinforcement, a dark key becomes a conditioned reinforcer. Thus, the bird pecks the key and is reinforced when the light goes off. Hursh, Navarick, and Fantino (1974) provided evidence for this view. They showed that birds quit responding during omission training if the key light did not immediately go out when a response was made.

CHAPTER SUMMARY

This chapter has considered several areas of research on respondent–operant interactions. Autoshaping showed that an operant response (key pecking for food) could actually be elicited by respondent procedures. Before this research, operants and respondents had been treated as separate systems subject to independent controlling procedures. The Brelands' animal training demonstrations provided a hint that the two systems were not distinct—with species-specific behavior being elicited by operant contingencies. Their work revealed the biological foundations of conditioning as well as the contributions made by biologically relevant factors. Animals are prepared by evolution to be responsive to specific events and differentially sensitive to various aspects of the environment.

Other experiments indicated that respondent behavior could be controlled by operant contingencies. The Miller studies used curare to immobilize rats, showing that heart rate, an autonomic response, could be reinforced by electrical stimulation of the brain. The implication again is that the neural systems regulating respondent and operant behavior are interrelated, allowing for operant conditioning of behavior (heart rate) often considered to be hard-wired.

Taste aversion is another example of biological factors underlying conditioning procedures. The findings of Garcia and Koelling indicate that interoceptive stimuli are paired with each other (flavor–sickness) better than crossing system stimuli (flavor–shock), illustrating how organisms are prepared for conditioning based on evolution and natural selection. Work in this area contributes to managing toxic plant ingestion by livestock and to predicting and controlling diet selection. Finally, we discussed activity anorexia both as a real-world human problem and as an interesting research question. What neurophysiological–behavioral mechanisms could possibly interact to drive an organism to self-starvation? It turns out that a combination of restricted access to food and the opportunity to exercise are the conditions leading to this deadly spiral.

Key Words

Activity anorexia	Facultative behavior	Preparedness
Adjunctive behavior	Instinctive drift	Schedule-induced behavior
Autoshaping	Interim behavior	Sign tracking
Behavior system	Negative automaintenance	Stimulus substitution
Context for conditioning	Omission procedure (training)	Taste aversion learning
Displacement behavior	Polydipsia	Terminal behavior

Stimulus Control

- Learn about stimulus control of behavior and multiple schedules of reinforcement.
- Delve into stimulus control, behavioral neuroscience, and what birds see.
- Solve the problem of the "bird-brained" pigeon and see what it means for teaching and learning.
- Investigate the behavioral contrast and its determinants.
- Inquire about stimulus generalization, peak shift, errorless discrimination, and fading.
- Investigate delayed matching to sample and an experimental analysis of remembering.

In the everyday world, human behavior is changed by signs, symbols, gestures, and spoken words. Sounds, smells, sights, and other sensory stimuli that do not depend on social conditioning also regulate behavior. When social or nonsocial events precede operant behavior and affect its occurrence, they are called controlling stimuli. A **controlling stimulus (S)** is said to alter the probability of an operant, in the sense that the response is more (or less) likely to occur when the stimulus is present.[1]

One kind of controlling stimulus that we discussed in Chapter 4 is the S^D or *discriminative stimulus*. An S^D is a controlling stimulus that sets the occasion for reinforcement of an operant. In a pigeon experiment, a red light may reliably signal the presentation of food for pecking a key. After some experience, the bird will immediately strike the key when it is illuminated with the red light. Thus, the discriminative stimulus sets the occasion for a high probability of response.

The discriminative stimuli that regulate human behavior may be as simple as in the pigeon experiment or far more complex. A green traffic light and the word WALK set the occasion for pedestrians to cross a street. In a library, the call numbers posted above the stacks and on the books are discriminative stimuli for stopping, turning corners, and so on that result in finding a book. On the football field, a quarterback who is about to pass the ball must decide whether to pick the left or right receiver. Throwing the ball to a receiver is based on the degree of coverage (number and proximity of defensive players). In this example, the degree of coverage is a complex S^D that controls the direction, speed, and elevation of the quarterback's pass.

Another kind of controlling stimulus is called an S^Δ (S-delta) or an *extinction stimulus*. An S^Δ is a stimulus that sets the occasion for nonreinforcement or extinction of an operant (see Chapter 4). A rat may press a lever on a VI schedule of food reinforcement. Every now and then a tone comes on and a period of extinction is in effect. After some time, the rat will stop pressing the bar as soon as the tone is presented. Thus, the tone is defined as an S^Δ because lever pressing has a low probability of occurrence in its presence due to extinction.

Extinction stimuli that regulate human behavior also range from simple to complex. When your

---

[1] In this chapter, we present a classification scheme for stimuli that precede and set the occasion for reinforcement, extinction, or punishment of operant behavior. We introduce the generic term *controlling stimulus* (S) to stand for all events that exert stimulus control over operant behavior. There are three kinds of controlling stimuli: S^D, S^Δ, and S^{ave}. Notice that the controlling stimulus is modified to reflect its function based on the contingencies of reinforcement that have established it (i.e., reinforcement, extinction, or punishment). The notations S^+ and S^- are also commonly used to represent the S^D and S^Δ functions of stimuli.

car is almost out of gas, a service-station sign that says CLOSED is an S^Δ for turning into that station. A tennis opponent who usually wins the match may become an extinction stimulus for playing the game. In this case, you may play tennis with others, but not with the person who always wins. Sometimes breakdown of communication between married couples may be caused by stimuli that signal extinction for conversation. A wife may try to talk to her husband about a variety of issues, and he pretends to read the newspaper. The husband's behavior is an S^Δ for conversation if the wife reliably stops talking when he picks up the paper.

DIFFERENTIAL REINFORCEMENT AND DISCRIMINATION

When an organism makes a response in one situation but not in another, we say that the animal discriminates between the situations. The simplest way to train a **differential response** or **discrimination** is to reinforce an operant in one situation and withhold reinforcement in the other.

Figure 8.1 shows the development of a differential response to a single key that is alternately illuminated red and green for 5 min. The graph shows the cumulative number of responses over a 90-min session. Pecks to the red light by a pigeon are intermittently reinforced with food. Responses emitted in the presence of the green light are extinguished, never reinforced. The procedure of alternating between periods of reinforcement and extinction is termed *differential reinforcement*.

As you can see in this idealized experiment, the pigeon begins by emitting about the same number of responses to the red and green stimuli. After about 20 min, the cumulative response curves start to separate, indicating that the bird is pecking in the presence of red more than green. At about 60 min, the pigeon seldom responds when the key is green, as shown by the leveling off of the curve for this stimulus. Notice, however, that the cumulative curve for pecking the red key continues to rise. Because the bird pecks in the presence of red, but does not respond when the key is green, we may say that the pigeon *discriminates* between these two colors. At this point, it is possible to label the red and green stimuli in terms of their functions. The red light is called a discriminative stimulus (S^D) and the green color is an extinction stimulus (S^Δ).

Suppose the bird is returned to its home cage after 90 min of such *differential reinforcement*. On the next day, the pigeon is again placed in the operant chamber and the key is illuminated with the red light. During the test session, reinforcement is not given for pecking in the presence of either red or green. Because of its previous training, the bird has a high probability of pecking the red key.

Over a 60-s period, the bird may emit many responses when the S^D is present. After 60 s, the key light is changed from red to green. When the green light comes on, the probability of response declines and the bird makes few pecks to the green key. By continuing to alternate between red and green, the researcher can show the stimulus control exerted by the respective colors.

Stimulus control refers to the change in behavior that occurs when either an S^D or S^Δ is presented. When an S^D is presented the probability of response increases; when an S^Δ is presented the probability of response decreases. The stimuli that commonly control human behavior occur across all sensory dimensions. Stopping when you hear a police

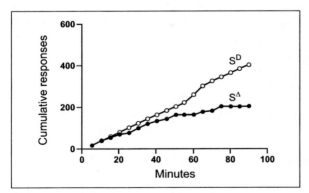

FIG. 8.1 Development of a differential response in the presence of red and green stimuli. Cumulative number of responses over a 90-min session in which responses in the presence of red are reinforced and responses in the presence of green are on extinction.

siren, coming to dinner when you smell food, expressing gratitude following a pat on the back, elaborating an answer because the student looks puzzled, and adding salt to your soup because it tastes bland are instances of stimulus control in human behavior.

FOCUS ON: Stimulus control, neuroscience, and what birds see

What do birds see and how do they see it? We actually do not know what humans "see," let alone birds. We do know a great deal about the structure and physiology of vision but what is actually "seen" can only be speculation. Vision and other sensations are private experiences even though the operation of the physiological system can be observed and analyzed.

The evolution of vision is an example of the natural selection of structures that enhance the organism's reproductive fitness (Dawkins, 1996). Many very primitive biological organisms have light-sensitive structures that contribute to that organism's survival even if it is only a matter of telling light from dark. Darker places are often safer than lighter places and organisms sensitive to the difference produce more offspring. In terms of avian evolution it is apparent that both structure and function have interacted to produce the current forms of vision, making birds more viable (Goldsmith, 2006).

Vision occurs when light enters the eye and is transduced from one form of energy to another by processes in the retina—involving light photons to neural impulses that travel from the eye via the optic nerve to the brain (see Donovan, 1978, on structure and function of pigeon vision). Nothing is actually "seen" at any point. However, identifying the mechanisms in the retina and brain provides the basis for predicting how the organism might behave, as well as advancing our scientific knowledge of visual discrimination.

A direct demonstration of a bird's ability to see color, shape, and movement requires behavioral experiments wherein the subject has to discriminate aspects of these stimuli. D. S. Blough (1957) provided the first thorough behavioral assessment of color vision in pigeons, even though the anatomy of the bird eye predicted such ability long before. Goldsmith and Butler (2005), using a modified Blough procedure, trained parakeets to go to a yellow light for food. Then the researchers presented a light composed of a mix between red and green as a comparison stimulus and showed that with a certain mix (90% red–10% green) the birds could not discriminate the mix from the yellow.

These findings indicated to behavioral neuroscientists that separate retinal receptors (cones) were responsive to different hues and were used by birds to guide their behavior. Four types of cones were identified that contained different pigments and oil droplet filters; one of these receptors is sensitive to ultraviolet wavelengths that allow birds to discriminate colors we cannot even imagine. Subsequently, behavioral experiments using operant contingencies showed that birds could make the visual discriminations predicted from the analysis of retinal receptors. The evidence suggests that ultraviolet wavelengths are seen as separate colors by birds due to the presence of UV receptors. In the everyday world of birds, these receptors allow for differential mate selection (Hausmann, Arnold, Marshall, & Owens, 2003), locating ripe fruit, and detecting vole trails.

STIMULUS CONTROL AND MULTIPLE SCHEDULES

Behavior analysts often use multiple schedules of reinforcement to study stimulus control in the laboratory. On a **multiple schedule**, two or more simple schedules are presented one after the other and each schedule is accompanied by a distinctive controlling stimulus—in some cases two or more

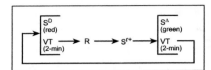

FIG. 8.2 Mechner notation for a MULT VI 2-min EXT 1-min schedule of reinforcement.

reinforcement schedules are presented, neither of which is extinction. The idealized experiment that we have just discussed is one example of a multiple schedule. Pecking was reinforced when a red light appeared on the key and a schedule of extinction was in effect when the green light was on. The schedules and the associated stimuli alternated back and forth every 5 min. As indicated, these procedures result in a *differential response* to the colors.

In an actual experiment, presenting the component schedules for a fixed amount of time or on an FI schedule (e.g., 5 min) would confound the results. Without a test procedure, the researcher would not be sure that the bird discriminates on the basis of color rather than time. That is, time itself may have become a discriminative stimulus. For this reason, variable interval (VI) schedules are often used for discrimination training (Guttman & Kalish, 1956; Harrison, 1991).

Figure 8.2 is one example of a multiple variable-interval extinction schedule of reinforcement (MULT VI EXT). The Mechner notation shows that in the presence of the red S^D the first response after an average of 2 min produces reinforcement. Following reinforcement, the key light changes from red to the green S$^\Delta$ and pecking the key no longer results in reinforcement. After an average of 2 min of extinction, the green light goes out and the red stimulus appears again. Pecking the key is now reinforced on the VI 2-min schedule and the components continue to alternate in this fashion.

A likely result of this multiple schedule is shown in Figure 8.3. The graph portrays the total number of responses during the red and green components for 1-h daily sessions. Notice that the bird begins by pecking equally in the presence of the red and green stimuli. Over sessions the number of pecks to the green extinction stimulus, or S$^\Delta$, declines. By the last session, almost all responses occur in the presence of the red S^D and almost none when the green light is on. At this point, pecking the key can be controlled easily by presenting the red or green stimulus. When red is presented the bird will peck the key at a high rate, and if the color changes to green the pigeon will immediately stop.

One way to measure the stimulus control exerted by the S^D and S$^\Delta$ at any moment is to use a **discrimination index (I_D)**. This index compares the rate of response in the S^D component to the sum of the rates in both S^D and S$^\Delta$ phases (Dinsmoor, 1951):

$$I_D = (S^D \text{ rate})/(S^D \text{ rate} + S^\Delta \text{ rate})$$

Prior to discrimination training, the measure varies between 0.00 and 1.00. When the rates of response are the same in the S^D and S$^\Delta$ components, the value of I_D is 0.50, indicating no discrimination. When all responses occur during the S^D phase and no responses occur during the S$^\Delta$ component, the I_D is 1.00. Thus, a discrimination index of 1.00 indicates a perfect discrimination and maximum stimulus control of behavior. Intermediate values of the index signify more or less control by the discriminative stimulus.

A study by Pierrel, Sherman, Blue, and Hegge (1970) illustrates the use of the discrimination index. The experiment concerned the effects of sound intensity on acquisition of a differential response. The researchers were interested in sound–intensity relationships (measured in decibels) between S^D and

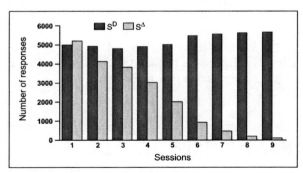

FIG. 8.3 Idealized results for a MULT VI 2-min EXT 1-min schedule of reinforcement. Relative to the red VI component, pecking declines over sessions to almost zero responses per minute in the green extinction phase.

S^Δ. The basic idea was that the more noticeable the difference in sounds, the better the discrimination. For example, some people have doorbells for the front and back entrances to their houses. If the chimes are very close in sound intensity, a ring will be confusing and you may go to the wrong door. One way to correct this problem is to change the intensity of sound for one of the chimes (of course, another is to replace one chime with a buzzer).

In one of many experimental conditions, 16 rats were trained to respond on a MULT VI 2-min EXT schedule. The animals were separated into four equal groups, and for each group the auditory S^D for the VI component was varied while the S^Δ for the extinction phase was held constant. For each group, the S^Δ was a 60-dB tone but the S^D was different, a choice of 70, 80, 90, or 100 dB. Thus, the difference in decibels or sound intensity between the S^D and S^Δ increased over groups (70–60, 80–60, 90–60, and 100–60 dB). The rats lived in operant chambers for 15 days. Two 8-h sessions of the multiple schedules were presented each day with a 4-h break between sessions.

Figure 8.4 shows the average acquisition curves for each experimental group. A mean discrimination index based on the four animals in each group was computed for each 8-h session. As you can see, all groups begin

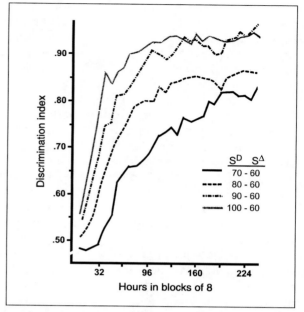

FIG. 8.4   Discrimination index (I_D) curves for different values of S^D and S^Δ. Each curve is a plot of the average I_D values based on a group of four animals, repeatedly exposed to 8-h sessions of discrimination training. From p. 22 of "Auditory Discrimination: A Three-variable Analysis of Intensity Effects," by R. Pierrel, G. J. Sherman, S. Blue, and F. W. Hegge, 1970, *Journal of the Experimental Analysis of Behavior*, *13*, 17–35. Copyright 1970 held by the Society for the Experimental Analysis of Behavior, Inc. Republished with permission. The labels for the X- and Y-axes have been simplified to promote clarity.

with I_D values of approximately 0.50 or no difference in responding between the S^D and S^Δ components. As discrimination training continues, a differential response develops and I_D values rise toward 1.00 or perfect discrimination. The accuracy of the discrimination, as indicated by the maximum value of I_D, is determined by the difference in sound intensity between S^D and S^Δ. In general, more rapid acquisition and a more accurate discrimination occur when the difference between S^D and S^Δ is increased.

FOCUS ON: Discrimination and the "bird-brained" pigeon

Pretend that you are doing a class assignment that involves training a pigeon to discriminate between red and green components of a multiple schedule. The assignment counts for 30% of the course grade, and you must show the final performance of the bird to your instructor. Students are given a pigeon, an operant chamber, and a microcomputer that allows them to control key color and the delivery of food from a hopper. Sessions are scheduled for 1 h a day over a 2-week period that ends with the professor's evaluation of your project. The pigeon has been food deprived, magazine trained, and taught to peck at a white-illuminated key on a VI 60-s schedule.

You and the other students follow the Mechner notation for a MULT VI 60-s EXT 60-s schedule in which you signal the VI component with a red-key light and a minute of extinction by turning the key green. To create the VI schedule and the variable 60 s of extinction you use operant-conditioning software to program your computer. The software program is set up to record the number of key pecks in each component of the multiple schedule. Your program starts a session with the key illuminated red and the first response after an average of 60 s is reinforced with food (VI 60 s). After food is presented, the key color changes to green and extinction is in effect for an average of 60 s.

Day after day, your bird pecks at a similar rate in both the red and green components. You become more and more concerned since other students have trained their birds to peck when the key is red and stop when it is green. By the 11th session you are in a panic because everyone else is finished, but your bird has not made much progress. You complain to your instructor that you were given a dumb or color-blind bird and it is not fair to get a low mark because you tried your best. Your professor is a strict behavior analyst who replies, "The fault is with the program, not with the pigeon; go study your computer program in terms of Mechner notation." You spend the night pondering the program and, somewhat like Kohler's apes (Kohler, 1927), you "have an insight." Pecking in the extinction green-key component has been reinforced with the presentation of the red-key light.

You realize that the red color is always associated with food reinforcement and this suggests that the red stimulus has more than one function. It is obviously an S^D that sets the occasion for reinforced pecking. In addition, the stimulus itself is a conditioned reinforcer because of its association with food. Presumably, during the extinction component the bird sometimes pecked the green key and on the basis of the computer program the color changed to red. This change in color accidentally or adventitiously reinforced pecking in the extinction component. From the bird's point of view, pecking the key during extinction turns on the red light that allows food reinforcement. In fact, the pigeon is displaying **superstitious behavior** because pecking in the green component does not affect the presentation of the red color.

Figure 8.5 shows how to solve the adventitious reinforcement problem in Mechner notation. The first part of the diagram presents the notation for a simple MULT VI 60-s EXT 60-s schedule. Enclosed within the dotted lines is an additional, critical contingency. This contingency prevents the onset of the red stimulus if responding is occurring at the moment that the extinction phase (is supposed to) ends. That is, if the extinction period ends with the bird pecking the key, the onset of the red stimulus is delayed. The added contingency is called **differential reinforcement of other behavior**, or **DRO**. Notice that when extinction ends the DRO contingency requires an additional 2-s period before the red stimulus is presented. During this DRO time, each response or peck resets the 2-s interval. If the bird does anything other than strike the key for 2-s, the red stimulus occurs.

With this insight, you rush to the laboratory and add DRO to your computer program. At the first opportunity, you place your "dumb or color-blind" pigeon in the operant chamber and initiate the program. As you watch the bird's performance on the cumulative recorder, the rate of response during the S^D and S^Δ components begins to separate. After two more sessions, the discrimination index (I_D) is almost 0.90, indicating good discrimination between reinforcement and extinction components. The instructor is impressed with your analytical skills and you get the highest mark possible for the assignment (A+).

This analysis has implications for teaching and learning. When most people learn from instruction but a few do not, educators,

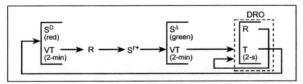

FIG. 8.5 Mechner diagram of how to solve the adventitious reinforcement problem on a multiple schedule of reinforcement. The first part of the diagram presents the notation for a simple MULT VI 60-s EXT 60-s schedule. Notice that when extinction ends, the DRO contingency requires an additional 2-s period before the red stimulus is presented. During this DRO time, each response or peck resets the 2-s interval. If the bird does anything other than strike the key for 2 s, the red stimulus will occur.

psychologists, and parents often blame the poor student, confused client, or stubborn child. They see the failure to learn as a deficiency of the person rather than a problem of contingencies of reinforcement (called blaming the victim; Shaver, 1985). The ones that fail to learn are said to be learning disabled, low in intelligence, and dim-witted. Of course, some people and animals may have neurological and/or sensory impairment (e.g., color blindness, deafness, organic brain damage) that contributes to their poor performance. Nonetheless, defective contingencies of reinforcement also may contribute to, or exclusively produce, problems of discrimination and learning. In the case of the apparently dumb pigeon, the fault was caused entirely by *adventitious reinforcement* of responding during extinction. A small change in the contingencies of reinforcement (adding DRO) made a "bird-brained" pigeon smart.

Behavioral Contrast

Consider an experiment by Guttman (1977) in which rats were exposed to a two-component multiple schedule with a variable-interval 30-s reinforcement schedule in both components (MULT VI 30 s VI 30 s). A sound (white noise) signaled one component and a light the other. The sound and light alternated every 3 min, and the rats made about the same number of responses in both components. Next, in the presence of the sound stimulus the contingencies were changed from VI to extinction (MULT VI EXT). As you might expect, rate of response declined in the extinction component. Surprisingly, rate of response increased on the VI component signaled by the light. The increase in rate occurred even though the reinforcement contingencies for the VI component remained the same. Thus, changing the contingencies of reinforcement on one schedule affected reinforced behavior on another schedule.

This effect is called **behavioral contrast** (Reynolds, 1961a, 1961b, 1963). Contrast refers to a negative correlation between the response rates in the two components of a multiple schedule—as one goes up, the other goes down. There are two forms of behavioral contrast, positive and negative. **Positive contrast** occurs when rate of response in an unchanged setting *increases* with a decline in behavior in another situation. **Negative contrast** occurs when rate of response *decreases* in the unchanged component with increases in behavior in the other.

There are many different explanations of behavioral contrast. For example, when reinforcement is reduced in one component of a multiple schedule habituation to the reinforcer is less—resulting in a more effective reinforcement in the unchanged component (McSweeney & Weatherly, 1998; see also the role of dishabituation, McSweeney, Murphy, & Kowal, 2003). Other explanations include the addition of autoshaped key pecks to responding in the unchanged component, fatigue or rest attributed to the amount of responding on the changed schedule, and compensating for response rate changes on the altered component (de Villiers, 1977; McSweeney, Ettinger, & Norman, 1981; Schwartz & Gamzu, 1977). Although there is some dispute, one account suggests that behavioral contrast results from changes in *relative rates of reinforcement*. On a multiple VI schedule, relative rate of reinforcement for the unchanged component increases when the number of reinforcers goes down on the other schedule. Of course, relative rate of reinforcement for the unchanged component goes down when the number of reinforcers is increased on the other schedule.

For example, if an animal obtains 30 reinforcers each hour on the unchanged component and gets another 30 on the other schedule, then 50% of the reinforcement occurs on both components. If the schedule is changed to MULT VI EXT, then 100% of the reinforcements occur on the unaltered component. As the *relative rate of reinforcement goes up on the unchanged component, so does the rate of response.* Similarly, response rate on the unaltered schedule would go down if relative rate of reinforcement declines because of an increase in reinforcement on the changed component. Relative rates of reinforcement provide an account of performance on multiple schedules that is consistent with a behavioral analysis of choice and preference (see Chapter 9).

FIG. 8.6   Dr. Ben Williams.
Reprinted with permission.

Although relative rates of reinforcement are important for an analysis of behavioral contrast, there is evidence that other conditions also contribute to such effects. Research shows that contrast only occurs in some species and may depend on the type of response required for reinforcement, although the data are inconsistent and sometimes contradictory (e.g., Beninger & Kendall, 1975; Hemmes, 1973; Pear & Wilkie, 1971; Westbrook, 1973).

Francis McSweeney and colleagues (Ettinger & McSweeney, 1981; McSweeney, Melville, & Higa, 1988) examined how different kinds of responses and different types of reinforcement (e.g., food, water, alcohol, etc.) affect behavioral contrast. Her research on food and alcohol reinforcement suggests that the nature of the reinforcers on a multiple schedule may limit the impact of relative rates of reinforcement.

Changes in relative rates of reinforcement produced positive contrast (i.e., rate of response went up on the unchanged schedule) when food reinforcement was continued in one component and extinction for alcohol was introduced in the other. However, behavioral contrast did not occur when alcohol reinforcement was continued and responding for food was placed on extinction. One possibility is that *alcohol is an economic substitute for food* (as rice is for potatoes), but food is not a substitute for alcohol (I'll drink to that!)—called partial substitutes. Anderson, Ferland, and Williams (1992) also reported a dramatic negative contrast wherein rats stopped responding for food and switched exclusively to responding for electrical stimulation of the brain (ESB). Relative rates of reinforcement may produce contrast only when reinforcers are substitutable, based on reinforcement history or biology.

After hundreds of studies of behavioral contrast, it is clear that contrast effects may occur in pigeons, rats, and even humans (Simon, Ayllon, & Milan, 1982). In addition, contrast has been shown with various schedules of reinforcement (both ratio and interval), different kinds of responses (e.g., lever pressing, key pecking, and treadle pressing), and different types of reinforcement (e.g., food, water, and alcohol) in the component schedules. This suggests that behavioral contrast is an important process that may have adaptive value. A bird that forages successively in two patches would be expected to increase searching for food in one patch if the other became depleted (i.e., positive contrast). Similarly, negative contrast would occur when food in one of the patches becomes more abundant than in the other. In this case, the bird would decrease foraging in the less plentiful location (Cheney, DeWulf, & Bonem, 1993).

A problem with the research on behavioral contrast is that some of the findings are puzzling. Many experiments result in contrast but others with apparently similar procedures do not, and it is not clear how this happens. Generally, there are several theories of behavioral contrast, but none of the accounts handle all the data (see Pear, 2001, pp. 154–158 for more on habituation, autoshaping, and following-schedule theories of behavioral contrast).

FOCUS ON: Determinants of behavioral contrast

Behavioral contrast is a topic that has interested many behavior analysts. Although contrast is not difficult to describe as a behavioral process, its analysis has been a puzzle for several decades. One of the more prominent researchers in this area is Ben Williams (Figure 8.6), a professor of psychology at the University of California, San Diego. After obtaining a PhD at Harvard University, Williams pursued a career in basic research. His interests include concurrent schedules of reinforcement, delay of reinforcement, conditioned reinforcement, and stimulus control of operant and respondent behavior. He has been actively involved in an analysis of behavioral contrast for more than 30 years (see Williams, 1974).

As one of his programs of research on behavioral contrast, Williams investigated the sequencing of schedules and stimuli. That is, Williams (1976, 1979, 1981, 1990, 1992) began to investigate how contrast depends on the contingencies that preceded or followed a target schedule. For example, in the schedule sequence A → B → C, the target schedule is component B and response rates for this schedule may be influenced by the contingencies set by A or C.

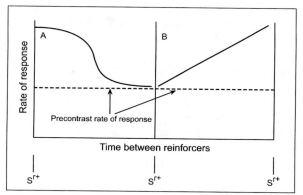

FIG. 8.7 Two patterns of behavioral contrast. The drop-off pattern presented in panel A is often elicited by contingencies that precede the target schedule. The linear pattern presented in panel B is called anticipatory contrast and is a function of the contingencies that follow the target schedule.

Generally, Williams (1981) found that the schedule preceding the target component produced weak, variable, and transitory contrast effects. This transitory effect is shown in Figure 8.7 (panel A) where the rate of response is high following reinforcement and drops off to precontrast levels. The schedule that followed the target component generated strong contrast effects that increased as training progressed (Figure 8.7, panel B). Williams called this strong contrast effect **anticipatory contrast** to distinguish it from the weak elicited responding evoked by the preceding schedule (respondent contingencies).

Today, the causes of behavioral contrast still are not completely understood. What is clear from this research is that performance on a schedule of reinforcement is affected by the contingencies that precede and follow the current schedule. As in other areas of behavior analysis, performance on a multiple schedule is a function of the operating contingencies and the context of reinforcement (Williams, 2002).

GENERALIZATION

An organism that responds in one situation but not in another is said to discriminate between the settings. An organism that behaves similarly in different situations is said to generalize across circumstances. **Generalization** is a common observation in everyday life. A child may call all adult males "daddy," label all small furry animals as dogs, and drink anything that looks like juice (one reason for child-proof caps on dangerous liquids). Some students call all university teachers "profs" even though professors are only the senior academics. Most of us have seen an old friend at a distance only to find out that the person was not who we expected. A rude person is one who tells vulgar jokes no matter who is listening. In these and many more examples, it appears that common properties of the different stimuli set the occasion for operant behavior.

The problem is that an observer cannot be sure of the stimulus properties that regulate a common response. That is, it is difficult to specify the geometry of dad's face, the physical characteristics that differentiate dogs from other animals, the common aspects of different audiences for the joke teller, and so on. In the operant laboratory, however, it is usually possible to specify the exact physical dimensions of stimuli in terms of wavelength, amplitude, size, mass, and other physical properties. On the basis of experiments that use well-defined stimuli, it is possible to account for everyday examples of generalization and discrimination.

Stimulus Generalization

Formally, **stimulus generalization** occurs when an operant that has been reinforced in the presence of a specific discriminative stimulus (S^D) also is emitted in the presence of other stimuli. The process is called stimulus generalization because the operant is emitted to new stimuli that presumably share common properties with the discriminative stimulus. Generalization and discrimination refer to differences in the *precision of stimulus control*. Discrimination refers to the precise control of an operant by a stimulus, and generalization involves less precise regulation of operant behavior.

Generalization gradients

Guttman and Kalish (1956) conducted a classic study of stimulus generalization. Pigeons were trained to peck a key on a VI 1-min schedule of reinforcement. The key was illuminated with a green light of 550 nm, a wavelength of light that is approximately in the middle of the color spectrum.[2] Once the rate of key pecking for food had stabilized in the presence of the green light, the researchers tested for stimulus generalization. To do this, the pigeons were exposed to 10 additional values of wavelength (variations in color) as well as the original green light. All 11 colors were presented in a random order and each wavelength was shown for 30 s. During these test trials, pecking the key was not reinforced (extinction). After the 11 wavelengths were presented (one block of trials), a new random series of the same colors was initiated. A total of 12 blocks of trials were given to the birds. Of course, as the test for generalization continued, key pecking decreased because of extinction, but the decline was equal over the range of stimuli because different wavelengths were presented randomly.

As shown in Figure 8.8, generalization gradients resulted from the experiment. A **generalization gradient** shows the relationship between probability of response and stimulus value. In the experiment by Guttman and Kalish (1956), probability of response is measured as the number of responses emitted by the pigeons, and stimulus value is wavelength of light. As you can see, a symmetrical curve with a peak at 550 nm (yellow-green training stimulus) describes stimulus generalization for pigeons trained at this wavelength. The more the new stimulus differed from the wavelength used in training, the fewer the number of responses. Importantly, these results were typical of the curves for individual birds. In addition, similar generaliza-

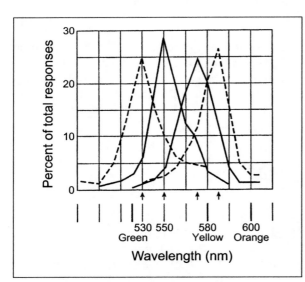

FIG. 8.8   Stimulus generalization gradients of wavelength obtained from four groups of pigeons trained at different wavelengths. Adapted from "Discriminability and Stimulus Generalization," by N. Guttman and H. I. Kalish, 1956, *Journal of Experimental Psychology*, *51*, 79–88. Adapted with permission of APA.

---

[2] The visible color spectrum is seen when white light is projected through a prism. The spectrum ranges from violet (400 nm) on one end to red (700 nm) on the other.

tion gradients were found for three other groups of pigeons using 530, 580, and 600 nm as the training stimuli. Generally, probability of response is highest for a stimulus that has signaled reinforcement (S^D), less for stimuli that are close but not identical to the S^D, and low for stimuli that substantially depart from the discriminative stimulus.

Peak shift

Multiple schedules may be used to study generalization gradients. Hanson (1959) reported an experiment with pigeons that was similar to the Guttman and Kalish (1956) study just discussed. The procedural difference was that four groups of birds were exposed randomly to periods of VI reinforcement and extinction. For the experimental groups, the S^A period was 555, 560, 570, or 590 nm and the S^D phase was always 550 nm. A control group only received training on the VI schedule, with 550 nm of light on the response key. Notice that the S^D for all groups was a key light of 550 nm, replicating one of the stimulus values used by Guttman and Kalish.

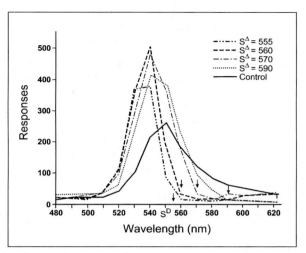

FIG. 8.9   Peak shift of a generalization gradient. The control shows a peak of the distribution at 550 nm and is symmetrical around this value (check this out). In contrast, the experimental groups uniformly show a shift in the peak of the distribution from 550 to 540 nm, moving away from the stimulus value of the S^A, which was always greater than 550 nm. Adapted from "Effects of Discrimination Training on Stimulus Generalization," by H. M. Hanson, 1959, *Journal of Experimental Psychology, 58,* 321–334. Adapted with permission of APA.

Figure 8.9 shows the major results of Hanson's (1959) experiment. The control group that received only VI training produced a generalization gradient that replicates the findings of Guttman and Kalish. The peak of the distribution is at 550 nm and is symmetrical around this value (check this out). In contrast, the experimental groups uniformly showed a shift in the peak of the distribution from 550 to 540 nm, moving away from the stimulus value of the S^A that was always greater than 550 nm. For this reason, **peak shift** refers to the change in the peak of a generalization gradient on the side of the S^D away from the stimulus (S^A) that signals extinction (see Cheng & Spetch, 2002; and Spetch, Cheng, & Clifford, 2004, for peak shifts in human spatial generalization and recognition of faces). Also, the number of responses made at the peak of each distribution is greater for the experimental groups when compared to the control subjects. This latter finding reflects *positive behavioral contrast* that occurs on multiple schedules with S^D and S^A components (see the previous section, Behavioral Contrast).

Absolute and relative stimulus control

Peak shift is an unusual effect from the point of view of absolute control by a stimulus. **Absolute stimulus control** means that the probability of response is highest in the presence of the stimulus value used in training. In fact, this occurs when reinforcement is the only procedure used to establish stimulus control (no extinction training). This is clearly seen in the results of the Guttman and Kalish (1956) study and in the control group of Hanson's (1959) experiment. In both studies, the peak of the generalization gradient is at the exact (or absolute) value of the stimulus presented during training (550 nm). When both S^D and S^A procedures are arranged (reinforcement and extinction), the peak of the distribution shifts away from the absolute value of the training stimulus— often analyzed as the interrelationship of excitatory and inhibitory stimulus gradients (Pear, 2001, pp. 158–162).

The shift in the peak of the generalization gradient may involve relative rather than absolute stimulus control. **Relative stimulus control** means that an organism responds to *differences* among the values of two or more stimuli. For example, a pigeon may be trained to peck the "larger" of two triangles projected on a response key rather than respond to the absolute size of the discriminative stimulus. Similarly, the birds in the peak-shift experiments may have come under the control of the relative value of the wavelengths. That is, the S^D was "greener" than the yellow-green S^Δ used in discrimination training. Because of this, the birds pecked most at stimuli that were relatively "greener," shifting the peak to 540 nm.

There are other ways of showing *relational control* by stimuli. To study generalization gradients and peak shift, researchers usually arrange the presentation of S^D and S^Δ so that one follows the other. This is called **successive discrimination**. An alternative procedure is labeled **simultaneous discrimination**—the S^D and S^Δ are presented at the same time and the organism responds to one or the other. For example, a pigeon may be presented with two keys both illuminated with white lights, but one light is brighter than the other. The bird may be reinforced for pecking the "dimmer" of the two keys. Pecks to the other key are on extinction. After training, the pigeon mostly pecks the darker of the two keys. To test that the bird's performance is caused by the difference between the two stimuli, it is necessary to present new values of luminosity and observe whether the pigeon pecks the dimmer of two keys.

Simultaneous discrimination tasks are often used in education. The television program *Sesame Street* teaches youngsters the relations of "same" and "different" by presenting several objects or pictures at the same time. The jingle "one of these things is just like the others" sets the occasion for the child to identify one of several items. After the child makes a covert response, something like "it's the blue ball," the matching item is shown. In this case, getting the correct answer is reinforcement for the discriminative response.

ERRORLESS DISCRIMINATION AND FADING

When the S^D and S^Δ are alternately presented as in successive discrimination, the organism initially makes many errors. That is, the animal or person continues to respond in the presence of the S^Δ on the basis of generalization. As extinction and reinforcement continue, a differential response occurs to the S^D and S^Δ. A pigeon is taught to peck a green key for food. Once this behavior is well established, the color on the key is changed to blue and pecking is not reinforced. The blue and green colors are alternately presented and the corresponding schedules of extinction or reinforcement are in effect. During the early sessions, the onset of extinction will often generate emotional behavior that interferes with ongoing operant behavior.

Extinction is an aversive procedure. Pigeons flap their wings in an aggressive manner and will work for an opportunity to attack another bird during the presentation of the S^Δ on a multiple schedule. Birds will peck a different key if pecking turns off the extinction stimulus, implying that the stimulus is aversive. There are other problems with successive discrimination procedures. Because emotional behavior is generated, discriminative responding takes a long time to develop. In addition, spontaneous recovery of S^Δ responding from session to session interferes with the acquisition of discrimination. Finally, even after extensive training, birds and other organisms continue to make errors by responding in the presence of the signal for extinction.

Errorless Discrimination

These problems can be eliminated with a discrimination procedure described by Terrace (1963). The method is called **errorless discrimination** because the trainer or teacher does not allow the organism to make mistakes by responding to the extinction stimulus. In his 1963 experiment, Terrace used early progressive training to reduce errors of discrimination. This training began when pigeons were conditioned to peck a red key for food reinforcement. The birds were started on continuous reinforcement and moved gradually to a variable-interval 1-min schedule. Early in this training, the key light was turned off for 5 s and extinction was in effect. Thus, a dark key was the S^Δ in this early phase. It is important to note that pigeons usually do not peck at a dark key, and Terrace made use of this fact.

As discrimination training continued, the dark key was gradually illuminated with a green light. The light became progressively brighter and remained on for longer and longer intervals, until it stayed on the same amount of time as the red key light. At this point, the duration of the S^D (red) was increased to 3 min and the S^Δ (green) was gradually increased from 5 s to 3 min.

Now the birds were responding on a MULT VI 1-min EXT 3-min schedule. On this schedule, the red key was presented for 3 min and the pigeons pecked for food on a VI 1-min schedule for this period. After 3 min in the reinforcement component, the key color was changed from red to green and extinction was in effect for 3 min. With these new contingencies in effect, the pigeons had sufficient time in the S^Δ component to make numerous errors, but they did not respond in the presence of the green light.

When this early progressive training was compared with standard successive discrimination procedures, there were far less mistakes with the errorless technique. Figure 8.10 shows that the three pigeons trained with errorless discrimination procedures made about 25 pecks each to the extinction stimulus (errors). Another three birds had the S^Δ introduced later in the experiment, at full intensity and for 3 min (standard method); these pigeons made between 2000 and 5000 pecks to the S^Δ. Compared with the errorless group, most of the pecks to the S^Δ in the standard condition occurred during the first three sessions. Overall, errorless discrimination procedures result in faster acquisition of a discrimination and substantially less incorrect responding (see Roth, 2002, for training of dolphins on auditory and visual tasks; and Benbasset & Abramson, 2002, for human flight simulation and use of landing flares).

Once discrimination is established with errorless training, it may be difficult to reverse the roles of the S^D and S^Δ. Marsh and Johnson (1968) trained two groups of birds to discriminate between red

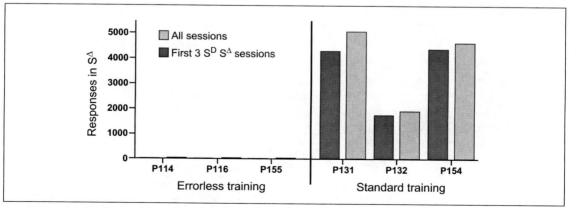

FIG. 8.10   Results of the errorless discrimination procedure used by Terrace. Adapted from Fig. 1 of "Discrimination Learning with and without 'Errors'," by H. S. Terrace, 1963, *Journal of the Experimental Analysis of Behavior, 6,* 1–27.

(S^D) and green (S^Δ) stimuli. One group received errorless training and the other got the standard discrimination procedure. After performance stabilized, the S^D and S^Δ were reversed so that the green stimulus now signaled reinforcement and the red indicated extinction. The birds trained by the errorless method continued responding in terms of their initial training—they would not respond to the S^Δ (the new S^D from the point of view of the researcher) even when explicitly reinforced for such behavior. Birds given standard discrimination training were not as persistent and quickly discriminated the change in contingencies.

These findings suggest that errorless procedures may be most useful in education when there is little chance of a change in the contingencies of reinforcement. For example, students may learn and retain better their multiplication tables, standard word spellings, rules for extracting a square root, and other types of rote learning with the errorless method. Students also enjoy learning, learn very rapidly, and make few errors with errorless teaching procedures (Powers, Cheney, & Agostino, 1970; see Luciano, 1986, for training verbal discriminations in language-delayed children). In problem-solving situations where there are many alternative solutions requiring error elimination or where the contingencies of reinforcement change, the standard method of trial-and-error learning may produce more flexibility in responding and allow better remembering and recall, as when university students prepare for exams (Anderson & Craik, 2006).

Fading

Errorless discrimination involves two basic procedures: early introduction of the S^Δ and gradual transfer of stimulus control. It is the latter procedure, called fading, that has received the most attention by clinicians and educators. **Fading** involves transferring stimulus control from one value of a stimulus to another. This is done by gradually changing a controlling stimulus from an initial value to some designated criterion. When Terrace (1963) gradually changed the dark key toward the green color, this was fading. Cheney and Tam (1972) used fading to transfer control by a color discrimination to control by line angle tilt in pigeons; the procedure involved gradually increasing the intensity of the line segments projected on the key while decreasing the intensity of the colors. Control transferred from color to mirror-image line angles with some, but very few, errors.

Sherman (1965) gave a practical example of fading when he used the procedure to get a mute psychotic to say his first words. He described the patient as:

> . . . a 63-year-old man, diagnosed, in 1916, as dementia praecox, hebephrenic type. He had been in the hospital continuously for 47 years, with a history of mutism for 45 of those years. At the time of this study he was not receiving any medication or participating in psychotherapy. Periodically, when seen on the ward, . . . [he] could be observed walking around mumbling softly to himself. However, all of this mumbling appeared to be nonsensical vocal behavior. In his 45-year history of mutism [he] had not exhibited any recorded instance of appropriate verbal behavior.
>
> (1965, p. 157)

After many sessions of reinforcement and imitation training, Sherman succeeded in getting the patient to say "food"—his first distinct utterance in 45 years. At this point, Sherman used fading to bring this response under appropriate stimulus control—responding "food" to the question, "What is this?" The training was as follows:

> To obtain the word "food" from the subject when the experimenter asked "What is this?" a fading procedure was used. With the fading procedure, the experimenter continued to hold up a bite of food each time and to deliver instructions to the subject. The behavior of the subject—that is saying "food"—was maintained with reinforcement while the instructions to the subject were gradually changed in the following steps: (a) "Say food"; (b) "Say foo_"; (c) "Say f___"; (d) "What is this? Say f___"; (e) "What is this? Say _____"; (f) "What is this?"
>
> (Sherman, 1965, p. 158)

This example shows that the patient initially replied "food" after the experimenter said "say food." The original verbal stimulus for the response "food" was gradually faded and replaced with a new stimulus of "What is this?"

Fading procedures have been regularly used with autistic children, as when the youngsters show resistance to drinking liquids such as milk. Both for health and nutritional benefits it is sometimes necessary for children to drink (or eat) things they usually reject. In one study (Luiselli, Ricciardi, & Gilligan, 2005), the researchers treated milk avoidance by a 4-year-old autistic girl by fading out a beverage she consumed 100% of the time and fading in the milk. That is, the amount of beverage was reduced and the amount of milk was increased over training sessions. Fading allowed rapid acquisition of milk consumption without interruptions to the fading sequence by the child's usual refusal and fussing.

In everyday life, fading is an important aspect of complex human behavior that often goes unrecognized because of its gradual nature. Children learn to identify many objects in the world by the step-by-step transfer of stimulus control. A parent may present a glass of apple juice to a 2-year-old child and state, "Say juice." Eventually, the child says "juice" when a glass of juice is given. Once the response "juice" is established, stimulus control may be gradually transferred from "say juice" to questions such as "What is this?" by fading. In another example, a parent may initially stay at a day-care center in order to make the child comfortable in the new setting. Once the child starts to participate in activities, the parent sneaks out and stimulus control for a variety of behavior is transferred to the new situation and the teacher.

COMPLEX STIMULUS CONTROL

To this point, we have discussed the control of behavior by relatively simple configurations of stimuli, as when a red color signals reinforcement and green signals no reinforcement. There are other procedures that allow for the investigation of performance regulated by more complex stimulus arrays.

Matching to Sample

Discrimination of identity

One procedure that is often used to investigate identity discriminations is called **matching to sample**. In a simple identity procedure, a pigeon may be presented with three keys, as in Figure 8.11. Panel A shows a triangle projected onto the center key. The triangle is the sample stimulus in the sense that it is an instance of a larger set of geometric forms. To ensure that the bird attends to the sample, it is required to peck the sample key. When this observing response happens, two side keys are illuminated with a triangle on one and a square on the other, which are called the comparison stimuli. If the bird pecks the comparison stimulus that corresponds to

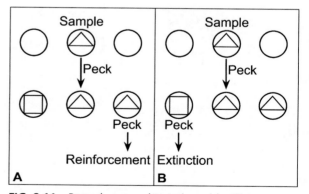

FIG. 8.11   Procedures used to train an identity discrimination by a pigeon. Panel A shows that a peck to the sample key (triangle) results in two shapes on the side keys. A peck to the side key that matches the sample is reinforced. Panel B shows a sequence that is not reinforced.

the sample (a match), this behavior is reinforced and leads to the presentation of a new sample. Panel B shows a non-reinforced sequence in which pecks to the noncorresponding stimulus result in extinction and the next trial. Over a number of trials, the comparison stimuli appear on the left or right keys with equal probability. After some training, pigeons accurately match to sample even with new (never reinforced) samples and comparison stimuli (Blough, 1959, 1982). The evidence suggests that pigeons' behavior can be regulated by the identity or similarity among stimuli.

Delayed matching to sample and remembering

A twist on the standard matching to sample task is called **delayed matching to sample**. This procedure was first described by Blough (1959) and involves adding a delay between the offset of the sample stimulus and the onset of the two comparison stimuli. For example, in Figure 8.12 a pigeon is presented with a center key (sample) that is illuminated with a red light. The red sample turns off and a few seconds later (e.g., 10 s) red and green comparison stimuli are presented on the side keys. A response to the stimulus that matches the sample is reinforced and responses to the other stimulus are not. The basic finding is that the percentage of correct responses decreases as the delay increases (Blough, 1959; Grant, 1975).

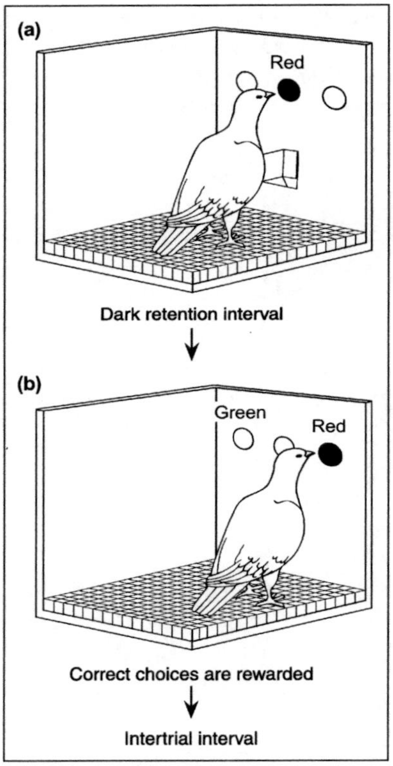

FIG. 8.12 Delayed matching to sample in a pigeon. The sequence begins (a) by the pigeon pecking a red or green sample on the center response key. The response to the sample is followed by the chamber being darkened during a retention interval. Next, the pigeon chooses (b) between red and green side keys; choices that match to the sample are reinforced with food, and after a time interval another trial begins. Adapted from White (2002).

Delayed matching to sample has been used to investigate behavior that is said to reflect cognition and memory. For example, the time between the offset of the sample stimulus and the onset of the comparison stimuli is usually called the **retention interval**. The idea is that during this interval the organism is covertly doing something that helps to retain the information about the sample. Thus, Grant (1981) found that pigeons would "forget" the sample if they were given a sign (a vertical line on the key) that indicated that the comparison stimuli would not appear on that trial. In terms of remembering the sample, Grant reported that the pigeons performed poorly if the forget cue was presented soon after the sample went off (see also Maki & Hegvik, 1980; Stonebraker, Rilling, & Kendrick, 1981). Performance was not as disrupted if the signal was given later in the interval. One interpretation is that the cue to forget interferes with covert rehearsal of the sample stimulus (Grant, 1981; Stonebraker & Rilling, 1981).

The cognitive metaphor of memory processes (encoding, storage, retrieval, rehearsal, etc.) is popular in psychology. Tulving (1983) explained that remembering an event involves mental encoding of the event and subsequent retrieval of the information from memory due to reactivation of the encoding operations. He proposed that encoding results in a memory trace or representation of the past event. The memory trace becomes manifest when combined with retrieval processes. Thus, memory research has emphasized how encoding produces mental representations that in turn aid in retrieval.

An explanation of remembering based on inferred mental processes is unacceptable to behavior analysts. Unless the mental processes have direct evidence, encoding, mental representations, and retrieval from memory are inferences from remembering itself. When mental processes are inferred from remembering (and delays in remembering), they cannot be used to explain it—the explanation is said to be circular. Behavior analysts insist that a scientific analysis of remembering must refer to contingencies of reinforcement and basic behavior principles. Of course, direct observations of brain functions during remembering would be included in a behavioral account, but cognitive theories are not viewed as adding to the explanation of this behavior (see Wixted & Gaitan, 2002, on cognitive theories of memory as surrogates for reinforcement histories).

Geoffrey White in the Department of Psychology at the University of Otago (Dunedin, New Zealand) has developed a behavioral approach to memory using basic operant principles. White (2002) indicates that a behavior analysis of memory points to actions or choices (e.g., choosing between the comparison stimuli) based on current contingencies and how those choices are in part regulated by the reinforcement history for similar choices in the past. In this regard, White (2002) explains:

> **Remembering** is not so much a matter of looking back into the past or forward into the future as it is of *making choices at the time of remembering*. The [behavioral] approach treats remembering as a process of discriminating the relevant events from alternative possibilities. By analogy with the discrimination of objects at a physical distance, objects or events can be discriminated at a temporal distance. . . . That is, the discrimination is not made at the time of encoding, or learning, but at the time of remembering.
>
> (pp. 141–142, emphasis added)

One aspect of White's behavioral approach to memory is that it challenges the well-known finding that remembering gets worse as the retention interval increases. If the discrimination of a past event is made at the time of remembering, White suggests that it is possible to train pigeons to be accurate at a specific delay. In this case, the remembering of a stimulus would be more accurate at a specific delay than with less delay or no delay. That is, remembering would not decline in accord with the retention interval.

Using the delayed matching to sample procedure of Figure 8.12, Sargisson and White (2001) compared the performance of pigeons trained with a 0-s delay and those trained with one specific delay at the outset. Typically, birds are trained to match to sample with a 0-s delay and subsequently the delay or retention interval is gradually lengthened. In the new procedure, pigeons were trained in matching to sample at one specific delay (e.g., 4 s) and then asked to remember the sample at different retention intervals.

Figure 8.13 shows the discriminability of the sample for birds trained with a 0-s delay (circles). Notice that the accuracy of the discrimination decreases with the retention interval, as would be predicted by cognitive theories of memory. For pigeons trained with a 4-s delay, however, their accuracy does not systematically decrease over the retention interval (triangles). Instead, these birds were most accurate at the training delay of 4-s, a finding that argues against the mental

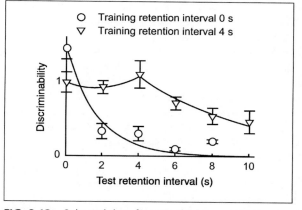

FIG. 8.13   Selected data from Sargisson and White (2001), showing the accuracy of matching to sample in different groups of pigeons trained with either a 0-s retention interval or a 4-s retention interval; pigeons were tested with retention intervals that varied from 0 to 10 s. The discriminability measure is the log of the ratio of correct to error responses, and is not influenced by response bias. From "Psychophysics of Remembering: the Discrimination Hypothesis," by K. G. White, 2002, *Current Directions in Psychological Science, 11*, 141–145. Reprinted with permission of the American Psychological Society. © 2002 by Blackwell Publishing, Ltd.

representation of the sample with a declining memory trace. Notice also that the birds were not trained to perform with less accuracy at brief delays. That is, the discrimination of the "to be remembered color" should have been easier at short delays (e.g., 0 s) because the sample color was observed very recently. The data show, however, that the pigeons were less accurate at delays less than 4 s, again disconfirming a cognitive representational account. Overall, the results of the experiment support a behavioral view that remembering involves discriminative operant behavior specific to the time interval of retrieval (see White & Wixted, 1999, for a discrimination model of remembering; see White, Parkinson, Brown, & Wixted, 2004, on proactive interference and the role of reinforcement).

FOCUS ON: Concept formation by pigeons

Principles of stimulus control are involved in many instances of concept formation and abstract reasoning. People usually assume that conceptual thinking is a defining feature of humans that separates them from other animals. Although this kind of behavior is common in humans, it occurs in a more limited way in other organisms. Herrnstein and Loveland (1964) designed an experiment to teach pigeons to identify humans from other objects (learning the concept—human).

Consider what it means to know that this is a human being and other objects are not. Humans come in a variety of sizes, shapes, colors, postures, and so on. Characteristics of the stimulus "human" are abstract and involve multiple stimulus dimensions rather than a single property such as wavelength of light. For example, human faces differ in terms of presence or absence of hair, geometric form, and several other factors. Defining characteristics of faces include bilateral symmetry, two eyes, a nose, a mouth, and many additional features common to all people.

Although a precise physical description of humans is elusive, Herrnstein and Loveland (1964) asked whether pigeons could respond to the presence or absence of human beings in photographs. If a bird can do this, then its behavior is controlled by the abstract property of humanness. There is no concrete set of attributes that visually equals a human being, but there are relations among such attributes that define the stimulus class. The bird's task is to respond correctly to instances of the stimulus class and by doing so demonstrate concept formation. Herrnstein and Loveland (1964) described the experiment as follows:

> It is well known that animals can use one or a few distinguishing features to discriminate stimuli such as simple visual arrays differing in size, shape, or color. In the experiment described here, however, pigeons were trained to detect human beings in photographs, a class of visual stimuli so diverse that it precludes simple characterization.
>
> [After pigeons were trained to peck at a hinged switch in the presence of a translucent plate] . . . the plate was illuminated throughout each session with projections of 35-m color slides from a projector that housed 81 slides. . . . Over 1200 unselected slides obtained from private and commercial sources were available. Before each session, the projector was loaded with 80 or 81 different photographs of natural settings, including countryside, cities, expanses of water, lawn, meadow, and so on. For any one session, approximately half the photographs contained at least one human being; the remainder contained no human beings—in the experimenter's best judgment. In no other systematic way did the slides appear to differ. Many slides contained human beings partly obscured by intervening objects: trees, automobiles, window frames, and so on. The people were distributed throughout the pictures: in the center or to one side or the other, near the top or the bottom, close up or distant. Some slides contained a single person; others contained groups of various sizes. The people themselves varied in appearance: they were clothed, semi-nude, or nude; adults or children; men or women; sitting, standing or lying; black, white, or yellow. Lighting and coloration varied: some slides were dark, others light; some had either reddish or bluish tints, and so on.
>
>   . . . Pictures containing people . . . meant an opportunity to feed . . . and pictures without people meant no such opportunity. . . . Each day the slides themselves and also the random sequence of

positive (S^D) slides (that is, containing a person) and negative (S^Δ) slides (without people), were changed for each pigeon. Many slides were used again in later sessions, but never in the order with other slides in which they had appeared earlier. The pigeons had no opportunity, therefore, to learn groups of particular slides or sequences of positives and negatives in general.

(pp. 549–550)

The results showed that the pigeons could discriminate between slides with people and ones without them. Within 10 sessions of this training, every bird was responding at a higher rate to slides with humans in them. Over several months, the performance of the birds steadily improved. After extensive training, the birds were given 80 (or 81) slides that they had never seen before. Pigeons pecked at a high rate to new slides with people and at lower rates to slides without them. Generally, this experiment shows that pigeons can differentially respond to the abstract stimulus class of human being.

Additional experiments on concept formation have been conducted with other stimulus classes and different organisms. Pigeons have discriminated trees (Herrnstein, 1979), geometric forms (Towe, 1954), letters of the alphabet (Blough, 1982), fish (Herrnstein & de Villiers, 1980), one person from another (Herrnstein, Loveland, & Cable, 1976), and aerial photographs of human-made objects (Lubow, 1974). Concept formation has also been reported for monkeys (Schrier & Brady, 1987), an African gray parrot (Pepperberg, 1981), and mynah birds (Turney, 1982). And pigeons trained to differentially respond to real objects show these responses to corresponding pictures of the objects—even when the pictures only contain novel views of the stimuli (Spetch & Friedman, 2006).

Overall, this research suggests that animals differentially respond to abstract properties of stimulus classes. These stimulus classes are commonly called categories when humans make similar discriminations. When people describe different categories, they are said to "understand the concept." People can easily identify a computer disk and an automobile as human-made objects. When other animals show similar performances, we are reluctant to attribute the discriminative behavior to the creature's understanding of the concept.

Rather than attribute understanding to complex performances by humans or other animals, it is possible to provide an account based on evolution and the current demands of the environment. Natural selection shapes sensory capacities of organisms that allow for discrimination along abstract dimensions. Birds obtain food, navigate, care for young, find mates, and so on, largely on the basis of visual stimuli (see section on What Birds See in this chapter). Many of these activities require subtle adjustments to a complex and changing visual world. It is not surprising, therefore, that these creatures are readily able to discriminate abstract properties of visual objects, especially when reinforcement contingencies favor such a discrimination.

Conditional Discrimination

In everyday life, stimuli that regulate behavior (S^D and S^Δ) often depend on the context. Consider a matching-to-sample experiment in which a bird has been trained to match to triangles or squares based on the sample stimulus. To turn this experiment into a conditional-discrimination task, a red or green light illuminates the sample stimulus. The bird is required to match to the sample when the background light is green and to choose the noncorresponding stimulus when the light is red. That is, when a green triangle is the sample, the bird must peck the comparison triangle, but when a red triangle is presented, pecks to the circle are reinforced. Of course, if a green circle is the sample, pecks to the circle are reinforced, and when the sample turns red, pecking the triangle is the correct response. Conditional matching to sample involves simultaneous discrimination of three elements in a display. The animal must respond to geometric form depending on the background color of the sample. It also must respond to the correspondence or noncorrespondence of the comparison stimuli.

Conditional discrimination is a common aspect of human behavior. A person who is hurrying to an appointment on the 15th floor of an office building will ordinarily enter the first available elevator. This same person may wait for the next lift if the elevator is full. Thus, getting on the elevator (operant) when the doors open (S^D) is conditional on the number of people in the car. In another example, you will say "eight" when shown 3 + 5 and "fifteen" if the relation is 3 × 5. Your response to the 3 and 5 is conditional on the + and × symbols. In the chapter on verbal behavior (Chapter 12), we will see that conditional discrimination is also important for the emergence of symbolic behavior and communication. When people say that the spoken word cat, the written word CAT, and a picture of a cat are the same, their behavior is a result of such complex discrimination training (see more on conditional discrimination in Chapter 12, Analysis of Complex Behavior in the Laboratory).

ON THE APPLIED SIDE: The pigeon as a quality control inspector

In industrial settings, workers often are hired as quality control inspectors. Quality control usually is a monotonous job of checking samples of a product to identify any defects. The most important skills or attributes needed for such jobs are good visual acuity and color vision. Based on these visual requirements, Thom Verhave (1966) suggested to the management of a drug company that the laboratory pigeon (*Columba livia domestica*) would be a cheap and efficient quality control inspector. Although skeptical, the director of research for the company gave Verhave the go ahead to train pigeons as inspectors.

The procedures were similar to a matching to sample (identity matching) task. Pigeons were trained to inspect a line of drug capsules, accepting those that met a fixed standard and rejecting defective ones. In this procedure (Figure 8.14), a bird compared a drug capsule with a standard sample (a perfect one) and pecked Key 1 if it matched or pecked Key 2 if there was a defect (a skag).

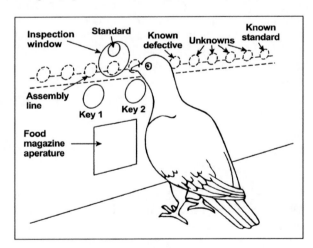

FIG. 8.14   Drawing depicts Verhave's (1966) discrimination procedures as described in the text. Pigeons were trained to inspect a line of drug capsules, accepting those that met a fixed standard and rejecting defective ones. From *Behavior Principles*, p. 558, by C. B. Ferster, S. Culbertson and M. C. P. Boren, 1975, Englewood Cliffs, NJ: Prentice-Hall. Republished with permission. © 1975, Pearson Education, Inc.

The standard capsule was fixed in position behind an inspection window. A line of capsules passed by the same window one at a time; some were perfect and others were defective. In order to initiate an inspection, the pigeon pecked at the inspection window, activating a beam of light that illuminated the sample and the comparison capsules. During training, all capsules on the inspection line were precoded by an electrical switch as either perfect or skags. If a capsule on the line was precoded as perfect, then the pigeon's response to Key 1 (matching response) resulted in food, turned off the beam of light behind the inspection window, and moved a new capsule into place. If a capsule was precoded as a skag, then a response to Key 2 (nonmatching response) turned off the illumination, moved a new capsule into the inspection window, and resulted in presentation of the food hopper. All other responses were false alarms or misses that were not reinforced and resulted in a 30-s blackout.

With these contingencies in effect, the birds were about 99% accurate in identifying perfect capsules and skags.

One practical problem that Verhave faced concerned the persistence of a pigeon's performance on a real-life inspection line. In everyday life, there is no experimenter to designate perfect capsules, skags, misses, and false alarms. Without this monitoring, differential reinforcement for "hits versus misses" cannot be maintained and a bird's performance will deteriorate over time to chance levels. A solution was to introduce capsules "known to be perfect or defective" occasionally onto the inspection line. Reinforcement or punishment was only in effect for "known" instances of matching (or nonmatching) to sample. With this procedure, sufficient differential reinforcement occurred to maintain stimulus control by the sample and comparison capsules.

In addition to Verhave (1966), there have been other attempts to use pigeons for navigation of missiles (Skinner, 1960) or to run assembly lines (Cumming, 1966). More recently, Azar (2002) reports that the US navy in the 1970s and 1980s used pigeons to find people stranded at sea. Navy scientist Jim Simmons, PhD, trained pigeons by operant conditioning for search and rescue missions. The pigeons were trained to recognize objects floating in the water from an aircraft and were 93% accurate, compared with only 38% accuracy for human flight crews. When combined with human searchers, the pigeons' detection rate rose to almost perfect. Today with the threat of terrorism, there is talk of using pigeons to screen baggage at airport terminals, but history suggests that such a project would not work. In each pigeon project, the company's management (or military officers) were at first skeptical and amused by the claim that pigeons could perform such feats. Once it became clear that behavioral researchers could establish and maintain precise performance in pigeons, upper-level management no longer found this research humorous or acceptable, and immediately stopped all funding.

CHAPTER SUMMARY

In summary, this chapter has presented research and discussion of the stimulus conditions that set the occasion for operant behavior—changing its probability of occurrence. Control of the probability of responding is a matter of differential reinforcement in the presence or absence of a stimulus. Such control can be produced in the absence of "errors" by the judicious use of stimulus fading. Generalization across stimuli means that there is a lack of discrimination and responding occurs in the presence of many different stimuli. The process of remembering (memory) is treated as a response probability issue in that the question is, what are the stimulus conditions that enhance the likelihood of a specific response at a specific moment in time? The idea of a "concept" not as something inside the organism but as overt behavior under the control of precise stimuli also was presented. Birds were shown to learn the concept "human" when the contingencies supported responding to (identifying) pictures of humans and rejecting pictures without humans. Procedures such as matching to sample and training with only the S^D were discussed and outcomes such as peak shift and behavioral contrast were highlighted.

Key Words

Absolute stimulus control	Conditional discrimination	Differential reinforcement of
Anticipatory contrast	Controlling stimulus (S)	other behavior (DRO)
Behavioral contrast	Delayed matching to sample	Differential response

Discrimination index (I_D)
Errorless discrimination
Fading
Generalization
Generalization gradient
Matching to sample

Multiple schedule
Negative contrast
Peak shift
Positive contrast
Relative stimulus control
Remembering

Retention interval
Simultaneous discrimination
Stimulus control
Stimulus generalization
Successive discrimination
Superstitious behavior

Choice and Preference

9

- Find out how to study choice and preference in the laboratory.
- Learn about the matching law as a basic principle of behavioral choice.
- Inquire about optimal foraging, behavioral economics, and self-control.
- Investigate matching on a single schedule of reinforcement.
- Discover mathematics and the behavior analysis of choice and preference.
- Focus on behavioral neuroscience and concurrent schedules of reinforcement.

Over the course of a day, an individual makes many decisions that range from ones of great importance to ones of small consequence. A person is said to make a decision when buying a new car, when choosing to spend an evening with one friend rather than another, or when deciding what to eat for supper. Animals also make a variety of decisions; they may choose mates with particular characteristics, select one type of food over another, or decide to leave a territory.

From a behavioral view, the analysis of **choice** is concerned with the distribution of operant behavior among alternative sources of reinforcement (options). When several options are available, one alternative may be selected more frequently than others. When this occurs, it is called **preference** for an alternative source of reinforcement. For example, a person may choose between two food markets (a large supermarket and the corner store) on the basis of price, location, and variety. Each time the individual goes to one store rather than the other, she is said to choose. Eventually, the person may shop more frequently at the supermarket than the local grocery, and when this occurs the person is showing preference for the supermarket alternative.

Many people describe choosing to do something, or a preference for one activity over another, as a subjective experience. For example, you may simply like one person better than others, and based on this you feel good about spending a day with that person. From a behavioral perspective, your likes and feelings are real but they do not provide an objective scientific account of what you decide to do. To provide that account, it is necessary to identify the conditions that affected your attraction to (or preference for) the other person or friend.

EXPERIMENTAL ANALYSIS OF CHOICE AND PREFERENCE

For behavior analysts, the study of choice is based on principles of operant behavior. In previous chapters, operant behavior was analyzed in situations in which one response class was reinforced on a single schedule of reinforcement. For example, a child is reinforced with contingent attention from a teacher for correctly completing a page of arithmetic problems. The teacher provides one source of reinforcement (attention) when the child emits the target operant (math solutions). The single-operant analysis is important for the discovery of basic principles and applications. However, this same situation may be analyzed as a choice among behavioral options. The child may choose to do math problems or emit other behavior (e.g., look out of the window or talk to another child). This

193

analysis of choice extends the operant paradigm or model to more complex environments in which several response and reinforcement alternatives are available.

In the everyday environment, there are many alternatives that schedule reinforcement for operant behavior. A child may distribute time and behavior among parents, peer group, and sport activities. Each alternative may require specific behavior and provide reinforcement at a particular rate and amount. To understand, predict, and change the child's behavior, all of these response–consequence relationships must be taken into account. Thus, the operant analysis of choice and preference begins to contact the complexity of everyday life, offering new principles for application.

The Choice Paradigm

The two-key procedure

In the laboratory, choice and preference are investigated by arranging **concurrent schedules of reinforcement** (Catania, 1966). Figure 9.1 shows a concurrent **two-key procedure** for a pigeon. In the laboratory, two or more simple schedules (i.e., FR, VR, FI, or VI) are simultaneously available on different response keys (Ferster & Skinner, 1957). Each key is programmed with a separate schedule of reinforcement, and the organism is free to distribute behavior between the alternative schedules. The distribution of time and behavior among the response options is the behavioral measure of choice and preference. For example, a food-deprived bird may be exposed to a situation in which the left response key is programmed to deliver 20 presentations of the food hopper each hour, while the right key delivers 60 reinforcers an hour. To obtain reinforcement from either key, the pigeon must respond according to the schedule on that key. If the bird responds exclusively to the right key (and never to the left) and meets the schedule requirement, then 60 reinforcers will be delivered each hour. Because the bird could have responded to either side, we may say that it prefers to spend its time on the right alternative.

Concurrent schedules of reinforcement have received considerable research attention because they may be used as an analytical tool for understanding choice and preference. This selection of an experimental paradigm or model is based on the reasonable assumption that contingencies of reinforcement contribute substantially to choice behavior. Simply stated, all other factors being equal, the more reinforcement (higher rate) provided by an alternative, the more time and energy spent on that alternative. For example, in choosing between spending an evening with two friends, the one who has provided the most social reinforcement will probably be the one selected. Reinforcement may be social approval, affection, interesting conversation, or other aspects of the friend's behavior. The experience of deciding to spend the evening with one friend rather than the other may be something like, "I just feel like spending the evening with Fred." Of course, in everyday life choosing is seldom as uncomplicated as this, and a more common decision might be to spend the evening with both friends. However, to understand how reinforcement processes are working, it is necessary to control the other factors so that the independent effects of reinforcement on choice may be observed.

FIG. 9.1   A two-key operant chamber for birds. Schedules of food reinforcement are arranged simultaneously on each key.

Concurrent ratio schedules

Figure 9.2 shows a two-key concurrent-operant setting for humans. Consider that you are asked to participate in an experiment in which you may earn up to $50 an hour. As an experimental participant, you are taken to a room that has two response keys separated by a distance of 8 ft. Halfway between the two keys is a small opening just big enough for your hand to fit. The room is empty, except for the unusual-looking apparatus. You are told to do anything you want. What do you do? You probably walk about and inspect your surroundings and, feeling somewhat foolish, eventually press one of the response keys. Immediately following this action, $1 is dispensed by a coin machine and is held on a plate inside the small opening. The dollar remains available for about 5 s, and then the plate falls away and the dollar disappears. Assuming that you have retrieved the dollar, will you press one of the keys again? In reality, this depends on several factors: perhaps you are wealthy and the dollar is irrelevant; perhaps you decide to "get the best of the experimenter" and show that you are not a rat; maybe you do not want to appear greedy; and so on. However, assume for the moment that you are a typical poor student and you press the key again. After some time pressing both keys and counting the number of key presses, you discover a rule. The left key pays a dollar for each 100 responses, while the right side pays a dollar for 250 responses. Does it make sense to spend your effort on the right key when you can make money faster on the other alternative? Of course it does not, and you decide to spend all of your work on the key that pays the most. This same result has been found with other organisms. When two ratio schedules (in this case FR 100 and FR 250) are programmed as concurrent schedules, the alternative that produces more rapid reinforcement is chosen exclusively (Herrnstein & Loveland, 1975).

Because ratio schedules result in exclusive responding to the alternative with the highest rate of payoff, these schedules are seldom used to study choice. We have discovered something about choice: Ratio schedules produce exclusive preference (see McDonald, 1988, on how to program concurrent ratio schedules to produce response distributions similar to those that occur on interval schedules). Although this result is interesting, it suggests that other schedules should be used to investigate choice and preference. Once exclusive responding occurs on ratio schedules, it is not possible to study how responses are distributed between the alternatives—the major objective for an experimental analysis of choice.

Concurrent interval schedules

Consider, however, what you might do if interval schedules were programmed on the two response keys. Remember that on an interval schedule a single response must occur after a defined amount of time. If you spend all of your time pressing the same key, you will miss reinforcement that is programmed on the other alternative. For example, if the left key is scheduled to pay a dollar every 2 min and the right key every 6 min, then a reasonable tactic is to spend most of your time responding on the left key but every once in a while check out the other alternative. This behavior will result in obtaining most of the money set up by both schedules. In fact, when exposed to concurrent interval schedules, most animals

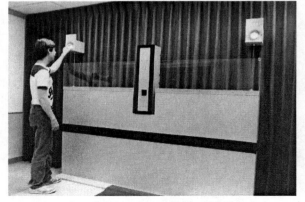

FIG. 9.2 A two-key operant chamber for humans. Pressing the keys results in money from a coin dispenser (middle), depending on the schedules of reinforcement.

distribute their time and behavior between the two alternatives in such a manner (de Villiers, 1977). Thus, the first prerequisite of the choice paradigm is that *interval schedules* must be used to study the distribution of behavior.

Interval schedules are said to be independent of one another when they are presented concurrently. This is because responding on one alternative does not affect the rate of reinforcement programmed for the other schedule. For example, a fixed-interval 6-min schedule (FI 6 min) is programmed to deliver reinforcement every 6 min. Of course, a response must be made after the fixed interval has elapsed. Pretend that you are faced with a situation in which the left key pays a dollar every 2 min (FI 2 min). The right key delivers a dollar when you make a response after 6 min. You have 1 h a day in the experiment. If you just respond to the FI 2-min schedule, you would earn approximately $30. On the other hand, you could increase the number of payoffs an hour by occasionally pressing the FI 6-min key. This occurs because the left key pays a total of $30 each hour and the right key pays an additional $10. After many hours of choosing between the alternatives, you may develop a stable pattern of responding. This *steady-state performance* is predictable. You should respond for approximately 6 min on the FI 2-min alternative and obtain three reinforcers ($3). After the third reinforcer, you may feel like switching to the FI 6-min key, on which a reinforcer is immediately available. You obtain the money on this key and immediately return to the richer schedule (left key). This steady-state pattern of responding may be repeated over and over with little variation.

Concurrent variable-interval schedules

Recall that there are two major types of interval schedules. On variable-interval schedules (VI), the time between each programmed reinforcer changes and the average time to reinforcement defines the specific schedule (VI 60 s). Because the organism is unable to discriminate the time to reinforcement on VI schedules, the regular switching pattern that characterizes concurrent FI FI performance does not occur. This is an advantage for the analysis of choice because the organism must respond on both alternatives as switching does not result always in reinforcement. Thus, operant behavior maintained by concurrent VI VI schedules is sensitive to the rate of reinforcement on each alternative. For this reason, VI schedules are typically used to study choice.

Alternation and the changeover response

At this point, the choice paradigm is almost complete. Again, however, consider what you would do in the following situation. The two keys are separated and you cannot press both at the same time. The left key now pays a dollar on a VI 2-min schedule while responses to the right alternative are reinforced on VI 6 min. The left key pays $30 each hour, and the right one delivers $10 if you respond. Assuming you obtain all programmed reinforcers on both schedules, you earn $40 for each experimental session. What can you do to earn the most per hour? If you stay on the VI 2-min side, you end up missing the 10 reinforcers on the other alternative. However, if you frequently change over from key to key, most of the reinforcers on both schedules will be obtained. This is in fact what most animals do when faced with these contingencies (de Villiers, 1977).

Simple alternation between response alternatives prevents an analysis of choice because the distribution of behavior remains the same (approximately 50/50) no matter what the programmed rates of reinforcement. Frequent switching between alternatives may occur because of the correlation between rate of switching and overall rate of reinforcement (dollars per session). In other words, as the rate of switching increases, so does the hourly payoff. Another way of looking at this alternation is that organisms are accidentally reinforced for the **changeover response**. This alternation is called concurrent superstition (Catania, 1966) and occurs because as time is spent on one alternative, the other schedule is timing out. As the organism spends more time on the left key, the probability of a reinforcer being set up on the right key increases. This means that a changeover to the right alternative will be reinforced even though the contingencies do not require the changeover response. Thus, switching to the other response key is an operant that is inadvertently strengthened.

The changeover delay

The control procedure used to stop rapid switching between alternatives is called a **changeover delay**, or **COD** (Shull & Pliskoff, 1967). The COD contingency stipulates that responses will not have an effect immediately following a change from one schedule to another. After switching to a new alternative, a brief time is required before a response can be reinforced (e.g., 3-s delay). For example, if an organism has just changed to an alternative that is ready to deliver reinforcement, there is a 3-s delay before a response is effective. As soon as the 3-s delay has elapsed, a response is reinforced. Of course, if the schedule has not timed out, the COD is irrelevant because reinforcement is not yet available. The COD contingency operates in both directions whenever a change is made from one alternative to another. The COD prevents frequent switching between alternatives. To obtain reinforcement, an organism must spend a minimal amount of time on an alternative before switching to another schedule. For example, with a 3-s COD, changing over every 2 s will never result in reinforcement. The COD is therefore an important and necessary feature of the operant-choice procedure.

Experimental procedures to study choice

The basic paradigm for investigating choice and preference is now complete. In summary, a researcher interested in behavioral choice should:

1. Arrange two or more concurrently available schedules of reinforcement.
2. Program interval schedules on each alternative.
3. Use variable- rather than fixed-interval schedules.
4. Require a COD in order to stop frequent alternation between or among the schedules.

The Findley procedure

Findley (1958) described an interesting variation on the basic choice procedure. The **Findley procedure** involves a single response key that changes color. Each color is a stimulus that signals a particular schedule of reinforcement. The color and the programmed schedule may be changed by a response to a second key. This key is called the *changeover key*. For example, a pigeon may respond on a VI 30-s schedule that is signaled by red illumination of the response key. When the bird pecks a second changeover key, the color on the response key changes from red to blue and a new schedule is operative. In the presence of the blue light, the pigeon may respond on a VI 90-s schedule of reinforcement. Another response on the changeover key reinstates the red light and the VI 30-second schedule. The advantage of the Findley procedure is that *the response of changing from one alternative to another is explicitly defined and measured.* Figure 9.3 compares the two-key and Findley procedures, showing that the Findley method allows for the measurement and control of the changeover response.

    Current evidence suggests that the same principles of choice account for behavior in

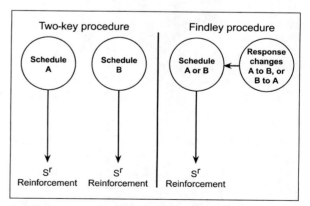

FIG. 9.3   Comparison of two-key and Findley procedures. Notice that the Findley method highlights the changeover response.

both the two-key and changeover procedures. For this reason, researchers have not made a theoretical distinction between them. However, such a distinction may be important for the analysis of human behavior. Sunahara and Pierce (1982) suggested that the two-key procedure provides a model for social interaction. For example, in a group discussion a person may distribute talk and attention to several group members. These members may be viewed as alternative sources of social reinforcement for the person. On the other hand, the changeover-key procedure may model role taking, in which an individual responds differentially to the role of another person. In this case, the individual may change over between the reinforcement schedules provided by the other person as a friend or as a boss. For example, while at work the changeover may be made by saying, "Could I discuss a personal problem with you?" In other words, a person who is both your friend and supervisor at work may sometimes deliver social reinforcement as a friend and at other times as your boss. Your behavior changes when the other person provides differential reinforcement in these two different roles.

THE MATCHING LAW

In 1961, Richard Herrnstein (Figure 9.4) published an influential paper that described the distribution of behavior on concurrent schedules of positive reinforcement. He found that pigeons matched relative rates of behavior to relative rates of reinforcement. For example, when 90% of the total reinforcement was provided by schedule A (and 10% by schedule B), approximately 90% of the bird's key pecks were on the A schedule. This equality or matching between relative rate of reinforcement and relative rate of response is known as the **matching law**. To understand this law, we turn to Herrnstein's (1961b) experiment.

Proportional Matching

Herrnstein's experiment

FIG. 9.4   Richard Herrnstein. Reprinted with permission.

In this study, Herrnstein investigated the behavior of pigeons on a two-key concurrent schedule. Concurrent VI VI schedules of food reinforcement were programmed with a 1.5-s COD. The birds were exposed to different pairs of concurrent variable-interval schedules for several days. Each pair of concurrent schedules was maintained until response rates stabilized. That is, behavior on each schedule did not significantly change from session to session. After several days of stable responding, a new pair of schedule values was presented. Overall rate of reinforcement was held constant at 40 reinforcers per hour for all pairs of schedules. Thus, if the schedule on the left key was programmed to deliver 20 reinforcers an hour (VI 3 min), then the right key also provided 20 reinforcers. If the left key supplied 10 reinforcers, then the right key supplied 30 reinforcers. The schedule values that Herrnstein used are presented in Figure 9.5.

The data in Figure 9.5 show the schedules operating on the two keys, A and B. As previously stated, the total number of scheduled reinforcers is held constant for each pair of VI schedules. This is indicated in the third column, in which the sum of the reinforcements per hour (Rft/h) is equal to 40 for each set of schedules. Because the overall rate of reinforcement remains constant, changes in the distribution of behavior cannot be attributed to this factor. Note that when key A is programmed to deliver 20 reinforcers an hour, so is key B. When this occurs, the responses per hour (Rsp/h) are the same on each key. However, the responses per hour (or absolute rate) are not the critical measure of preference. Recall that choice and preference are measured as the distribution of time or behavior between alternatives. To express the idea of distribution, it is important to direct attention to *relative* measures. Because of this, Herrnstein focused on the relative rates of response. In Figure 9.5, the relative rate of response is expressed as a proportion. That is, the rate of response on key A is the numerator and the sum of the response rates on both keys is the denominator. The proportional rate of response on key A is shown in the final column, labeled "Relative responses."

Key	Schedule	Rft/h	Rsp/h	Relative reinforcement	Relative responses
A	VI 3-min	20.00	2000	0.50	0.50
B	VI 3-min	20.00	2000	0.50	0.50
A	VI 9-min	6.7	250	0.17	0.08
B	VI 1.8-min	33.30	3000	0.83	0.92
A	VI 1.5-min	40.00	4800	1.00	1.00
B	Extinction	0.00	0	0.00	0.00
A	VI 4.5-min	13.30	1750	0.33	0.31
B	VI 2.25-min	26.70	3900	0.66	0.69

FIG. 9.5   A table of schedule values and data. Reinforcement per hour (Rft/h), responses per hour (Rsp/h), relative reinforcement (proportions), and relative responses (proportions) are shown. Adapted from Fig. 1 (bird 231) and text of "Relative and Absolute Strength of Responses as a Function of Frequency of Reinforcement," by R. J. Herrnstein, 1961b, *Journal of the Experimental Analysis of Behavior, 4,* 267–272.

Calculation of proportions

To calculate the proportional rate of responses to key A for the pair of schedules VI 4.5 min VI 2.25 min, the following simple formula is used:

$$B_a/(B_a + B_b)$$

The term B_a is behavior measured as the rate of response on key A, or 1750 pecks per hour. Rate of response on key B is 3900 pecks per hour and is represented by the term B_b term. Thus, the proportional rate of response on key A is

$$1750/(1750 + 3900) = 0.31$$

In a similar fashion, the proportion of reinforcement on key A may be calculated as

$$R_a/(R_a + R_b)$$

The term R_a refers to the scheduled rate of reinforcement on key A, or 13.3 reinforcers per hour. Rate of reinforcement on key B is designated by the term R_b and is 26.7 reinforcers each hour. The proportional rate of reinforcement on key A is calculated as

$$13.3/(13.3 + 26.7) = 0.33$$

These calculations show that the relative rate of response (0.31) is very close to the relative rate of reinforcement (0.33). If you compare these values for the other pairs of schedules, you will see that the proportional rate of response approximates the proportional rate of reinforcement.

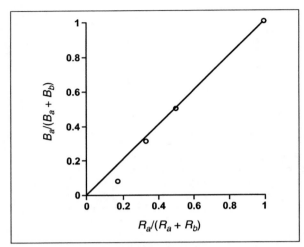

FIG. 9.6 Proportional matching of the response and reinforcement rates for bird 231. Figure is based on results from Herrnstein (1961b) and the data reported in Figure 9.5.

Importance of relative rates

Herrnstein showed that the major dependent variable in choice experiments was **relative rate of response**. He also found that relative rate of reinforcement was the primary independent variable. Thus, in an operant-choice experiment, the researcher manipulates the **relative rate of reinforcement** on each key and observes the relative rate of response to the respective alternatives.

Figure 9.5 shows that Herrnstein manipulated the independent variable, relative rate of reinforcement on key A, over a range of values. Because there are several values of the independent variable and a corresponding set of values for the dependent variable, it is possible to plot the relationship. Figure 9.6 shows the relationship between proportional rate of reinforcement, $R_a/(R_a + R_b)$ and proportional rate of response $B_a/(B_a + B_b)$ for pigeon 231 based on the values in Figure 9.5.

The matching equation

As relative rate of reinforcement increases, so does the relative rate of response. Further, for each increase in relative reinforcement there is about the same increase in relative rate of response. This equality of relative rate of reinforcement and relative rate of response is expressed as a proportion in Equation (9.1):

$$B_a/(B_a + B_b) = R_a/(R_a + R_b) \qquad (9.1)$$

Notice we have simply taken the $B_a/(B_a + B_b)$ and the $R_a/(R_a + R_b)$ expressions, which give the proportion of responses and reinforcers on key A, and mathematically stated that they are equal. In verbal form, we are stating that *relative rate of response matches (or equals) relative rate of reinforcement*. This statement, whether expressed verbally or mathematically, is known as the *matching law*.

In Figure 9.6, **matching** is shown as the solid black line. Notice that this line results when the proportional rate of reinforcement exactly matches the proportional rate of response. The matching law is an ideal representation of choice behavior. The actual data from pigeon 231 approximates the matching relationship. Herrnstein (1961b) also reported the results of two other pigeons that were well described by the matching equation.

Extension of the Matching Law

The generality of matching

The equality of rates of response and reinforcement is called a law of behavior because it describes how a variety of organisms choose among alternatives (de Villiers, 1977). Animals such as pigeons (Davison & Ferguson, 1978), wagtails (Houston, 1986), cows (Matthews & Temple, 1979), and rats (Poling, 1978) have demonstrated matching in choice situations. Interestingly, this same law applies to humans in a number of different settings (Bradshaw & Szabadi, 1988; Pierce & Epling, 1983). Reinforcers have ranged from food (Herrnstein, 1961b) to points that are subsequently exchanged for money (Bradshaw, Ruddle, & Szabadi, 1981). Behavior has been as diverse as lever pressing by rats (Norman & McSweeney, 1978) and conversation in humans (Conger & Killeen, 1974; Pierce, Epling, & Greer, 1981). Environments in which matching has been observed have included T-mazes, operant chambers, and open spaces with free-ranging flocks of birds (Baum, 1974a), as well as discrete-trial and free operant choice by human groups (Madden, Peden, & Yamaguchi, 2002). Also, special education students have been found to spend time on math problems proportional to the relative rate of reinforcement (e.g., Mace, Neef, Shade, & Mauro, 1994). Thus, the matching law describes the distribution of individual (and group) behavior across species, types of response, different reinforcers, and a variety of settings.

Matching and human communication

An interesting test of the matching law was reported by Conger and Killeen (1974). These researchers assessed human performance in a group discussion situation. A group was composed of three experimenters and one experimental participant. The participant was not aware that the other group members were confederates in the experiment and was asked to discuss attitudes toward drug abuse. One of the confederates prompted the participant to talk. The other two confederates were assigned the role of an audience. Each listener reinforced the subject's talk with brief positive words or phrases when a hidden cue light came on. The cue lights were scheduled so that the listeners gave different rates of reinforcement to the speaker. When the results for several participants were combined, relative time spent talking to the listener matched relative rate of agreement from the listener. These results suggest that the matching law operates in everyday social interaction.

Departures from matching

In the laboratory, the matching relationship between relative rate of reinforcement and relative rate of response does not always occur. Figure 9.7 shows idealized patterns of departure from the matching law based on the proportion equation. The matching line is the dashed line going through the middle of the graphs. This line shows that when .5 of the reinforcements are on the left key then .5 of the responses are on this key, and when .75 of the reinforcements are obtained from the left side then .75 of responses are distributed to the left alternative. The first departure from ideal matching is called **undermatching** (Figure 9.7A). Notice that the response proportions are less sensitive to changes in the reinforcement proportions. In the case of undermatching, when relative rate of reinforcement is .75 the relative rate of response is only .55—it takes a large change in relative rate of reinforcement to produce a small change in relative behavior. The opposite of undermatching is called **overmatching** (Figure 9.7B), in which the response proportions are more extreme than reinforcement proportions. Research evidence suggests that undermatching is observed more often than overmatching (deVilliers, 1977). Figure 9.7C portrays a third kind of departure from matching known as response **bias**. In this case, the animal consistently spends more behavior on one alternative than predicted by the matching equation. The graph of response bias illustrates a situation where the pigeon spends more time on the right key than is expected by the matching relationship. Such bias indicates a systematic condition that affects preference other than the relative rate of reinforcement. For example, a pigeon may prefer the green key on the right compared to red on the left if the bird has a history of differential reinforcement in the presence of green.

In the complex world of people and other animals, departures from matching frequently occur (Baum, 1974b). This is because in complex environments, contingencies of positive and negative reinforcement may interact, reinforcers differ in value, and histories of reinforcement are not controlled. In addition, discrimination of alternative sources of reinforcement may be weak or absent. For example, pretend you are talking to two people after class at the local bar and grill. You have a

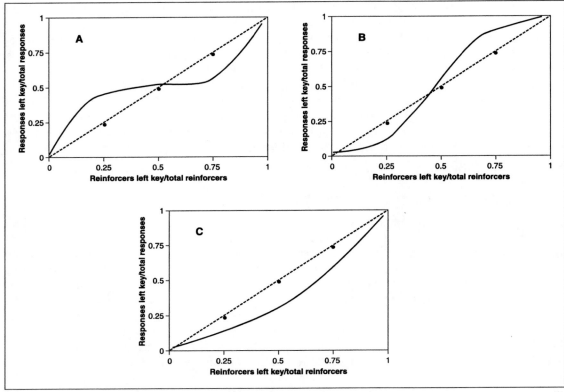

FIG. 9.7 Idealized graphs of undermatching (A), overmatching (B), and response bias (C), as would occur with the proportional matching equation. See text for details.

crush on one of these two and the other you do not really care for. Both of these people attend to your conversation with equal rates of social approval, eye contact, and commentary. You can see that even though the rates of reinforcement are the same, you will probably spend more time talking to the person you like best (response bias). Because this is a common occurrence in the nonlaboratory world, you might ask, "What is the use of matching and how can it be a law of behavior?"

The principle of matching is called a law because it describes the regularity underlying choice. Many scientific laws work in a similar fashion. Anyone who has an elementary understanding of physics can tell you that objects of equal mass fall to the earth at the same rate. Observation, however, tells you that a pound of feathers and a pound of rocks do not fall at the same velocity. We can only see the lawful relations between mass and rate of descent when other conditions are controlled. In a vacuum, a pound of feathers and a pound of rocks fall at equal rates and the law of gravity is observed. Similarly, with appropriate laboratory control, relative rate of response matches relative rate of reinforcement (see ADVANCED SECTION for more on departures from matching).

Matching time on an alternative

Behavioral choice can also be measured as time spent on an alternative (Baum & Rachlin, 1969; Brownstein & Pliskoff, 1968). Time spent is a useful measure of behavior when the response is continuous, as in talking to another person. In the laboratory, rather than measure the number of responses, the time spent on an alternative may be used to describe the distribution of behavior. The matching law can also be expressed in terms of relative time spent on an alternative. Equation (9.2) is similar to Equation (9.1) but states the matching relationship in terms of time:

$$T_a/(T_a + T_b) = R_a/(R_a + R_b) \tag{9.2}$$

In this equation, the time spent on alternative A is represented by T_a and the time spent on alternative B is T_b. Again, R_a and R_b represent the respective rates of reinforcement for these alternatives. The equation states that relative time spent on an alternative equals relative rate of reinforcement from that alternative. This extension of the matching law to continuous responses, such as standing in one place or looking at objects is important. Most behavior outside of the laboratory does not occur as discrete responses. In this case, Equation (9.2) may be used to describe choice and preference.

Matching on More Than Two Alternatives

A consideration of either Equation (9.1) or Equation (9.2) makes it evident that to change behavior the rate of reinforcement for the target response may be adjusted; alternatively, the rate of reinforcement for other concurrent operants may be altered. Both of these procedures manipulate the relative rate of reinforcement for the specified behavior. Equation (9.3) represents relative rate of response as a function of several alternative sources of reinforcement:

$$B_a/(B_a + B_b + \ldots B_n) = R_a/(R_a + R_b + \ldots R_n) \tag{9.3}$$

In the laboratory, most experiments are conducted with only two concurrent schedules of reinforcement. However, the matching law also describes situations in which an organism may choose among several sources of reinforcement (Davison & Hunter, 1976; Elsmore & McBride, 1994; Miller & Loveland, 1974; Pliskoff & Brown, 1976). In Equation (9.3), behavior allocated to alternative A (B_a) is expressed relative to the sum of all behavior directed to the known alternatives ($B_a + B_b + \ldots B_n$). Reinforcement provided by alternative A (R_a) is stated relative to all known sources of reinforcement ($R_a + R_b + \ldots R_n$). Again, notice that an equality of proportions (matching) is stated.

Practical Implications of the Matching Law

The matching law has practical implications. A few researchers have shown that the matching equations are useful in applied settings (Borrero & Vollmer, 2002; Epling & Pierce, 1983; McDowell, 1981, 1982, 1988; Myerson & Hale, 1984; Plaud, 1992). One applied setting where the matching law has practical importance is the classroom, where students' behavior often is maintained on concurrent schedules of social reinforcement.

Matching, modification, and reinforcement schedules

In a classroom, appropriate behavior for students includes working on assignments, following instructions, and attending to the teacher. In contrast, yelling and screaming, talking out of turn, and throwing paper airplanes are usually viewed as undesirable. All of these activities, appropriate or inappropriate, are presumably maintained by teacher attention, peer approval, sensory stimulation, and other sources of reinforcement. However, the schedules of reinforcement maintaining behavior in complex settings like a classroom are usually not known. When the objective is to increase a specific operant and the concurrent schedules are unknown, Myerson and Hale (1984) recommend the use of VI schedules to reinforce target behavior.

Recall that on concurrent ratio schedules, exclusive preference develops for the alternative with the higher rate of reinforcement (Herrnstein & Loveland, 1975). Ratio schedules are in effect when a teacher implements a grading system based on the number of correct solutions for assignments. The teacher's intervention will increase the students' on-task behavior only if the rate of reinforcement by the teacher is higher than another ratio schedule controlling inappropriate behavior. Basically, an intervention is either completely successful or a total failure when ratio schedules are used to modify behavior. In contrast, interval schedules of reinforcement will always redirect behavior to the desired alternative, although such a schedule may not completely eliminate inappropriate responding.

When behavior is maintained by interval contingencies, interval schedules remain the most desirable method for behavior change. Myerson and Hale (1984) used the matching equations to show that behavior-change techniques based on interval schedules are more effective than ratio interventions. They stated that "if the behavior analyst offers a VI schedule of reinforcement for competing responses two times as rich as the VI schedule for inappropriate behavior, the result will be the same as would be obtained with a VR schedule three times as rich as the schedule for inappropriate behavior" (pp. 373–374). Generally, behavior change will be more predictable and successful if interval schedules are used to reinforce appropriate behavior.

CHOICE, FORAGING, AND BEHAVIORAL ECONOMICS

Optimal Foraging, Matching, and Melioration

One of the fundamental problems of evolutionary biology and behavioral ecology concerns the concept of "optimal foraging" of animals (Krebs & Davies, 1978). Foraging involves prey selection where prey can be either animal or vegetable. Thus, a cow taking an occasional mouthful of grass in a field and a redshank wading in the mud and probing with its beak for an occasional worm are examples of foraging behavior. Because the function of foraging is finding food, foraging can be viewed as operant behavior regulated by food reinforcement. The natural contingencies of foraging present animals with alternative sources of food called *patches*. Food patches provide items at various rates (patch density) and in this sense are similar to concurrent schedules of reinforcement arranged in the laboratory.

Optimal foraging is said to occur when animals obtain the highest overall rate of reinforcement from their foraging. That is, over time organisms are expected to select between patches so as to optimize (obtain the most possible value from) their food resources. In this view, animals are like organic computers comparing their behavioral distributions with overall outcomes and stabilizing on a response distribution that ensures **maximization** of the overall rate of reinforcement.

In contrast to the optimal foraging hypothesis, Herrnstein (1982) proposed a process of **melioration** (doing the best at the moment). Organisms, he argued, are sensitive to fluctuations in the momentary rates of reinforcement rather than to long-term changes in overall rates of reinforcement. That is, an organism remains on one schedule until the local rates of reinforcement decline relative to that offered by a second schedule. Herrnstein (1997, pp. 74–99) showed that the steady-state outcome of the process of melioration is the matching law where relative rate of response matches relative rate of reinforcement. Thus, in a foraging situation involving two patches, Herrnstein's melioration analysis predicts matching of the distributions of behavior and reinforcement (e.g., Herrnstein & Prelec, 1997). Optimal foraging theory, on the other hand, predicts maximization of the overall rate of reinforcement (Charnov, 1976; Nonacs, 2001).

It is not possible to examine all the evidence for melioration, matching, and maximizing in this chapter, but Herrnstein (1982) has argued that melioration and matching are the basic processes of choice. That is, when melioration and matching are tested in choice situations that distinguish matching from maximizing, matching theory has usually predicted the actual distributions of the behavior.

One example of the application of matching theory to animal foraging is reported by Baum (1974a; see also Baum, 1983, on foraging) for a flock of free-ranging wild pigeons. The subjects were 20 pigeons that lived in a wooden frame house in Cambridge, Massachusetts. An opening allowed them to freely enter and leave the attic of the house. An operant apparatus with a platform was placed in the living space opposite to the opening to the outside. The front panel of the apparatus contained three translucent response keys and, when available, an opening allowed access to a hopper of mixed grain. Pigeons were autoshaped to peck to the center key and, following this training, a perch replaced the platform so that only one pigeon at a time could operate the keys and obtain food. Pigeons were now shaped to peck the center key on a VI 30-s schedule of food reinforcement. When a stable performance occurred, the center key was no longer illuminated or operative, and the two side keys became active. Responses to the illuminated side keys were reinforced on two concurrent VI VI schedules. Relative rates of reinforcement on the two keys were varied and the relative rate of response was measured.

Although only one bird at a time could respond on the concurrent schedules of reinforcement, Baum (1974b) treated the aggregate pecks of the group as the dependent measure. When the group of 20 pigeons chose between the two side keys, each of which occasionally produced food, the ratio of pecks to these keys approximately equaled the ratio of grain presentations obtained from them. That is, the aggregate behavior of the flock of 20 pigeons was in accord with the generalized matching equation, a form of matching equation based on ratios rather than proportions (see ADVANCED SECTION). This research suggests that the matching law applies to the behavior of wild pigeons in natural environments. Generally, principles of choice based on laboratory experiments can predict the foraging behavior of animals in the wild.

Behavioral Economics, Choice, and Addiction

Choice and concurrent schedules of reinforcement have been analyzed from a microeconomic point of view (Rachlin, Green, Kagel, & Battalio, 1976). **Behavioral economics** involves the use of basic economic concepts and principles (law of demand, price, and substitutability) to analyze, predict, and control behavior in choice situations. One of the more interesting areas of behavioral economics concerns laboratory experiments that allow animals to work for drugs such as alcohol, heroin, and cocaine. For example, Nader and Woolverton (1992) showed that a monkey's choice of cocaine over food was a function of drug dose, but that choosing cocaine decreased as the price (number of responses per infusion) increased. That is, the reinforcing effects of the drug increased with dose but these effects were modified by price, an economic factor. In another experiment, Carroll, Lac, and Nygaard (1989) examined the effects of a substitute commodity on the use of cocaine. Rats nearly doubled their administration of cocaine when water was the other option than when the option was a sweet solution. These effects were not found in a control group that self-administered an inert saline solution, suggesting that cocaine infusion functioned as reinforcement for self-administration and that the sweet solution substituted for cocaine. Again, the reinforcing effects of the drug were altered by an economic factor, in this case the presence of a substitute commodity (see Carroll, 1993, for similar effects with monkeys and the drug PCP).

The concept of substitute commodities (reinforcers) may be useful in understanding the treatment of heroin addicts with methadone. From an economic perspective, methadone is a partial substitute for heroin because it provides only some of the reinforcing effects of the actual drug. Also, methadone is administered in a clinical setting that is less reinforcing than the social context in which heroin is often used (Hursh, 1991). Based on this analysis, it is unlikely that availability of methadone treatment will, by itself, eliminate the use of heroin.

To reduce drug abuse, Vuchinich (1999) suggests a multifaceted approach that (1) increases the cost of using drugs by law enforcement that reduces the supply (i.e., price goes up), (2) provides easy access to other, nondrug activities (e.g., sports, musical entertainment, etc.) and arranges reinforcement from family, friends, and work for staying drug free, and (3) provides reinforcement for nondrug behavior promptly, as delayed reinforcement is ineffective. These principles can be applied to many behavior problems, including smoking, use of alcohol, and compulsive gambling (Bickel & Vuchinich, 2000). It is no longer necessary or sensible to treat people as if they had an underlying illness or disease (e.g., alcoholism). Behavioral economics and learning principles offer direct interventions to modify excessive or addictive behavior.

FOCUS ON: Activity anorexia and substitutability of food and wheel running

Activity anorexia occurs when rats are placed on food restriction and provided with the opportunity to run. The initial effect is that food intake is reduced, body weight declines, and wheel running increases. As running escalates, food intake drops off and body weight plummets downward, further augmenting wheel running and suppressing food intake. The result of this cycle is emaciation and, if allowed to continue, the eventual death of the animal (Epling & Pierce, 1992, 1996b; Epling, Pierce, & Stefan, 1983; Routtenberg & Kuznesof, 1967).

A behavioral economic model can describe the allocation of behavior between commodities such as food and wheel running. For example, the imposed food restriction that initiates activity anorexia can be conceptualized as a substantial increase in the price of food, resulting in reduced food consumption. Low food consumption, in turn, increases consumption of physical activity—suggesting that food and physical activity may be economic substitutes (see Green & Freed, 1993, for a review of behavioral economic concepts).

In two experiments, Belke, Pierce, and Duncan (2006) investigated how animals choose between sucrose (food) and wheel running reinforcement. Rats were exposed to concurrent VI 30-s VI 30-s schedules of wheel running and sucrose reinforcement. Sucrose solutions varied in concentration: 2.5, 7.5, and 12.5%. As concentration increased, more behavior was allocated to sucrose and more reinforcements were obtained from that alternative. Allocation of behavior to wheel running decreased somewhat, but the obtained wheel-running reinforcement did not change. The results suggested that food-deprived rats were sensitive to changes in food supply (sucrose concentration) while continuing to engage in physical activity (wheel running). In the second study, rats were exposed to concurrent variable ratio (VR VR) schedules of sucrose and wheel running, wheel running and wheel running, and sucrose and sucrose reinforcement. For each pair of reinforcers, the researchers assessed substitutability by changing the prices for consumption of the commodities. Results showed that sucrose substituted for sucrose, and wheel running substituted for wheel running, as would be expected. Wheel running, however, did not substitute for sucrose—the commodities were independent; but sucrose partially substituted for wheel running.

The partial substitutability of sucrose for wheel running in the Belke et al. (2006) experiments reflects two energy-balance processes: the initiation and maintenance of travel induced by loss of body weight and energy stores (wheel running does not substitute for food) and the termination of locomotion as food supply increases (food does substitute for wheel running). In terms of activity anorexia, the fact that travel does not substitute for food insures that animals with low energy stores keep going on a food-related trek—even if they eat small bits along the way. As animals contact stable food supplies, the partial substitutability of food for wheel running means that travel would subside as food intake and body stores return to equilibrium. Behavioral economics therefore provides one way to understand the activity anorexia cycle.

Self-Control and Preference Reversal

Students often face the choice of going out to party or staying home and "hitting the books." Often, when given the options, students pick the immediate reward of partying with friends over the delayed benefits of studying, learning the subject matter, and high grades. When a person (or other animal) selects the smaller, immediate payoff over the larger, delayed benefits, we may say that he/she shows **impulsive behavior**. On the other hand, a person who chooses the larger, delayed reward while rejecting the smaller, immediate payoff is said to show **self-control behavior**. In term of a student's choices to party or study, choosing to party with friends is impulsive behavior while choosing to stay home and study is self-control behavior.

One of the interesting things about self-control situations is that our preferences change over time. That is, we may value studying over partying a week before the party, but value partying when the night of the party arrives. Howard Rachlin (1970, 1974) and George Ainslie (1975) independently suggested that these preference reversals could be analyzed as changes in reinforcement

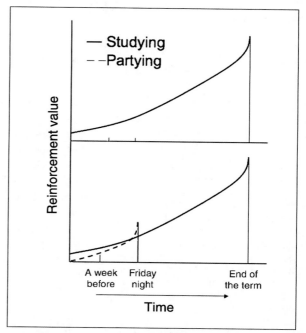

FIG. 9.8   An application of the Ainslie–Rachlin principle. The top panel shows that the reinforcement value of studying declines the farther the student is from the benefits obtained at the end of term. In the lower panel, the value of studying is lower than going to the party at the night of the party. However, the value of going to the party declines below the value of studying a week before the party. That is, the student's preference reverses.

effectiveness with increasing delay. The **Ainslie–Rachlin principle** states that *reinforcement value decreases as the delay between making a choice and obtaining the reinforcer increases* (see top panel of Figure 9.8).

As shown in Figure 9.8 (lower panel), the value of studying on the Friday night of the party (choice point) is lower than having fun with friends (partying) because the payoffs for studying (learning and good grades) are delayed until the end of the term. But if we move back in time from the choice point to a week before the party, the value of studying relative to partying reverses. That is, adding delay to each reinforcement option before a choice is made reverses the value of the alternative reinforcers. More generally, at some time removed from making a choice, the value of the smaller, immediate reinforcer will be less than the value of the larger, delayed reward, indicating a **preference reversal**. When preference reversal occurs, people (and other animals) will make a commitment response to forego the smaller, immediate reward and lock themselves into the larger, delayed payoff (see Chapter 13, section on Training Self-Control). Figure 9.9 shows the commitment procedure for eliminating the choice between studying and partying a week before the party. The **commitment response** is some behavior emitted at a time prior to the choice point that eliminates or reduces the probability of impulsive behavior. A student who has invited a classmate over to study on the Friday night of the party (commitment response) insures that she will "hit the books" and give up partying when the choice arrives.

Preference reversal and commitment occur over extended periods in humans and involve many complexities (e.g., Green, Fry, & Myerson, 1994; Logue, Pena-Correal, Rodriguez, & Kabela, 1986). In animals, delays of reinforcement by a few seconds can change the value of the options, instill

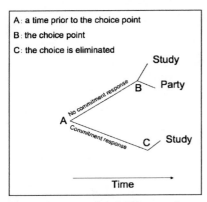

A: a time prior to the choice point
B: the choice point
C: the choice is eliminated

Study

No commitment response

B   Party

A

Commitment response

C   Study

Time

FIG. 9.9   Example of self-control through commitment based on preference reversal, as required by the Ainslie–Rachlin principle (as in Figure 9.8). The student will make a commitment to study at point A (a week before the party) because the value of studying is higher than partying, but not at the choice point B (the night of the party). The commitment response removes going to the party as an option on the night of the party (C).

commitment, and insure self-control over impulsiveness. As an example of preference reversal, consider an experiment by Green, Fisher, Perlow, and Sherman (1981) where pigeons responded on two schedules of reinforcement, using a trials procedure. The birds were given numerous trials each day. On each trial a bird made its choice by pecking one of two keys. A single peck at the red key resulted in 2 s of access to grain, while a peck at the green key delivered 6 s of access to food. The intriguing aspect of the experiment involved adding a brief delay between a peck and the delivery of food. In one condition, there was a 2-s delay for the 2-s reinforcer (red key) and a 6-s delay for 6-s access to food (green key). The data indicated that birds were impulsive, choosing the 2-s reinforcer on nearly every trial and losing about two-thirds of their potential access to food.

In another procedure, 18 additional seconds were added to the delays for each key so that the delays were now 20 s for the 2-s reinforcer and 24-s for the 6-s access to food. When the birds were required to choose this far in advance, they pecked the green key that delivered 6-s of access to food on more than 80% of the trials. In other words, the pigeons showed preference reversal and self-control when both reinforcers were farther away.

Other research by Ainslie (1974) and Rachlin and Green (1972) shows that pigeons can learn to make a commitment response, thereby reducing the probability of impulsive behavior. Generally, animal research supports the Ainslie–Rachlin principle and its predictions. One implication is that changes in reinforcement value over extended periods also regulate self-control and impulsiveness in humans (see Ainslie, 2005; Rachlin, 2000; Rachlin & Laibson, 1997). In this way, behavior principles may help to explain the impulsive use of credit cards in our society and the fact that most people have trouble saving their money (self-control).

MATCHING AND SINGLE-OPERANT SCHEDULES OF REINFORCEMENT

The matching law suggests that operant behavior is determined by rate of reinforcement for one alternative relative to all other known sources of reinforcement. Even in situations in which a contingency exists between a single response and a reinforcement schedule, organisms usually have several reinforced alternatives that are unknown to the researcher. Also, many of the activities that produce reinforcement are beyond experimental control. A rat that is lever pressing for food may gain additional reinforcement from exploring the operant chamber, scratching itself, or grooming. In a similar fashion, rather than work for teacher attention, a pupil may look out of the window, talk to a friend, or even daydream. Thus, even in a single-operant setting, multiple sources of reinforcement are operating. Richard Herrnstein (1970, 1974) argued this point and suggested that all operant behavior must be understood as behavior emitted in the context of other alternative sources of reinforcement.

Based on these ideas, Herrnstein proposed a matching equation that describes the absolute rate of response on a single schedule of reinforcement. This mathematical formulation is called the

quantitative law of effect. The law states that the *absolute rate of response on a schedule of reinforcement is a hyperbolic function of rate of reinforcement on the schedule relative to the total rate of reinforcement*, both scheduled and extraneous reinforcement. That is, as the rate of reinforcement on the schedule increases, the rate of response rapidly rises, but eventually further increases in rate of reinforcement produce less and less of an increase in rate of response (a hyperbolic curve; see Figure 9.10 for examples).

The rapid rise in rate of response with higher rates of reinforcement is modified by extraneous sources of reinforcement. **Extraneous sources of reinforcement** include any unknown contingencies that support the behavior of the organism. For example, a rat that is pressing a lever for food on a particular schedule of reinforcement could receive extraneous reinforcement for scratching, sniffing, and numerous other behaviors. The rate of response for food will be a function of the programmed schedule as well as the extraneous schedules controlling other behavior. In humans, a student's mathematical performance will be a function of the schedule of correct solutions as well as extraneous reinforcement for other behavior from classmates or teachers, internal neurochemical processes, and changes to the physical/chemical environment (e.g., smell of food drifting from the cafeteria).

Extraneous reinforcement slows down the rise in rate of response with higher rates of reinforcement. One implication is that control of behavior by a schedule of reinforcement is reduced as the sources of extraneous reinforcement increase. A student who does math problems for a given rate of teacher attention will do less if extraneous reinforcement is available by looking out of the window of the classroom. Alternatively, the teacher will have to use higher rates of attention for problem solving when "distractions" are available than when there are few additional sources of reinforcement.

Experimental Evidence for the Quantitative Law of Effect

The quantitative law of effect has been investigated in laboratory experiments. In an early investigation, Catania and Reynolds (1968) conducted an exhaustive study of six pigeons that pecked a key for food on different variable-interval (VI) schedules. Rate of reinforcement ranged from 8 to 300 food presentations each hour. Herrnstein (1970) replotted the data on X and Y coordinates. Figure 9.10 shows the plots for the six birds, with reinforcements per hour on the X-axis and responses per minute on the Y-axis.

Herrnstein used a statistical procedure to fit his hyperbolic equation to the data of each pigeon. Figure 9.10 presents the curves that best fit these results. Notice that all of the birds produce rates of response that are described as a hyperbolic function of rate of reinforcement. Some of the curves fit the data almost perfectly while others are less satisfactory. Overall, Herrnstein's quantitative law of effect is well supported by these findings.

The quantitative law of effect has been extended to magnitude of food reinforcement, brain stimulation, quality of reinforcement, delay of positive reinforcement, rate of negative reinforcement, magnitude or intensity of negative reinforcement, and delay of negative reinforcement (see de Villiers, 1977, for a thorough review). In a summary of the evidence, Peter de Villiers (1977) stated:

> The remarkable generality of Herrnstein's equation is apparent from this survey. The behavior of rats, pigeons, monkeys and . . . people is equally well accounted for, whether the behavior is lever pressing, key pecking, running speed, or response latency in a variety of experimental settings. The reinforcers can be as different as food, sugar water, escape from shock or loud noise or cold water, electrical stimulation of a variety of brain loci, or turning a comedy record back on. Out of 53 tests of Equation [9.6] on group data the least-squares fit of the equation accounts for over 90% of the variance in 42 cases and for over 80% in another six cases. Out of 45 tests on individual data, the equation accounts

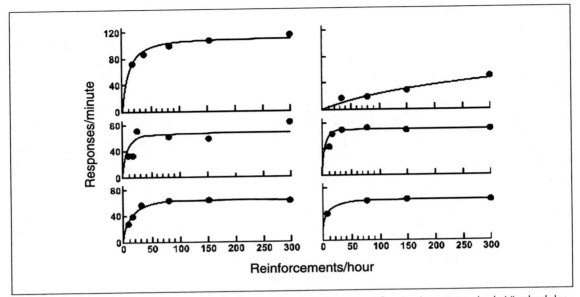

FIG. 9.10   Rate of response as a function of rate of food reinforcement for six pigeons on single VI schedules. From "On the Law of Effect," by R. J. Herrnstein, 1970, *Journal of the Experimental Analysis of Behavior, 13,* 243–266. Copyright 1970 held by the Society for the Experimental Analysis of Behavior, Inc. Republished with permission.

for over 90% of the variance in 32 cases and for over 80% in another seven cases. The literature appears to contain no evidence for a substantially different equation.... This equation therefore provides a powerful but simple framework for the quantification of the relation between response strength and both positive and negative reinforcement.

(p. 262)

ON THE APPLIED SIDE: Application of the quantitative law of effect

FIG. 9.11   Jack McDowell. Reprinted with permission.

Dr. Jack McDowell (Figure 9.11) from Emory University was the first researcher to use Herrnstein's matching equation for a single schedule of reinforcement to describe human behavior in a natural setting. McDowell's expertise in mathematics and behavior modification spurred him to apply Herrnstein's matching equation for a single operant to a clinically relevant problem.

Mathematics and Behavior Modification

Carr and McDowell (1980) were involved in the treatment of a 10-year-old boy who repeatedly and severely scratched himself. Before treatment the boy had a large number of open sores on his scalp, face, back, arms, and legs. In addition, the boy's body was covered with scabs, scars, and skin discoloration, where new wounds could be produced. In their 1980 paper, Carr and McDowell demonstrated that the boy's scratching was operant behavior. Careful observation showed that the scratching occurred predominantly when he and other family members were in the living room watching television. This suggested that the self-injurious behavior was under stimulus control. In other words, the family and setting made scratching more likely to occur.

Next, Carr and McDowell looked for potential reinforcing consequences maintaining the boy's self-injurious behavior. The researchers suspected that the consequences were social because scratching appeared to be under the stimulus control of family members. In any family interaction there are many social exchanges, and the task was to identify those consequences that reliably followed the boy's scratching. Observation showed that family members reliably reprimanded the boy when he engaged in self-injury. Reprimands are seemingly negative events, but the literature makes it clear that both approval and disapproval may serve as reinforcement.

Although social reinforcement by reprimands was a good guess, it was still necessary to show that these consequences in fact functioned as reinforcement. The first step was to take baseline measures of the rate of scratching and the rate of reprimands. Following this, the family members were required to ignore the boy's behavior. That is, the presumed reinforcer was withdrawn (i.e., extinction) and the researchers continued to monitor the rate of scratching. Next, the potential reinforcer was reinstated, with the family members again reprimanding the boy for his misconduct. Relative to baseline, the scratching decreased when reprimands were withdrawn and increased when they were reinstated. This test identified the reprimands as positive reinforcement for scratching. Once the reinforcement for scratching was identified, behavior modification was used to eliminate the self-injurious behavior.

In a subsequent report, McDowell (1981) analyzed the boy's baseline data in terms of the quantitative law of effect. He plotted the reprimands per hour on the X-axis and scratches per hour on the Y-axis. McDowell then fit the matching equation for a single schedule of reinforcement to the points on the graph. Figure 9.12 shows the plot and the curve of best fit. The matching equation provides an excellent description of the boy's behavior. You will notice that most of the points are on, or very close to, the hyperbolic curve. In fact, more than 99% of the variation in rate of scratching is accounted for by the rate of reprimands. McDowell has indicated the significance of this demonstration. He states:

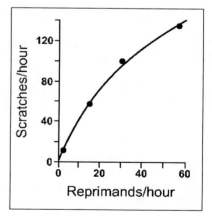

FIG. 9.12 Rate of social reinforcement and self-injurious scratching of a young boy. The data were fitted by Herrnstein's single-operant equation. Adapted from *Quantification of Steady-State Operant Behavior* (pp. 311–324), by J. J. McDowell, 1981, Elsevier/North-Holland, Amsterdam.

> As shown in the figure [9.12] the single-alternative hyperbola accounted for nearly all the variance in the data. This is especially noteworthy because the behavior occurred in an uncontrolled environment where other factors that might have influenced the behavior had ample opportunity to do so. It may be worth emphasizing that the rates of reprimanding ... occurred naturally; that is, they were not experimentally arranged. ... Thus, the data ... demonstrate the relevance of matching theory to the natural ecology of human behavior.
>
> (McDowell, 1988, pp. 103–104)

Overall, the quantitative law of effect or Herrnstein's hyperbolic equation has been an important contribution to the understanding of human behavior and to the modification of human behavior in applied settings (see Fisher & Mazur, 1997; Martens, Lochner, & Kelly, 1992).

ADVANCED SECTION: Quantification of choice and generalized matching

The proportion equations (Equations 9.1–9.3) describe the distribution of behavior when alternatives differ only in rate of reinforcement. However, in complex environments other factors also contribute to choice and preference.

Sources of Error in Matching Experiments

Suppose a pigeon has been trained to peck a yellow key for food on a single VI schedule. This experience establishes the yellow key as a discriminative stimulus that controls pecking. In a subsequent experiment, the animal is presented with concurrent VI VI schedules of reinforcement. The left key is illuminated with a blue light and the right with a yellow one. Both of the variable-interval schedules are programmed to deliver 30 reinforcers each hour. Although the programmed rates of reinforcement are the same, the bird is likely to distribute more of its behavior to the yellow key. In this case, stimulus control exerted by yellow is an additional variable that affects choice.

In this example, the yellow key is a known source of experimental bias that came from the bird's history of reinforcement. However, many unknown variables also affect choice in a concurrent-operant setting. These factors arise from the biology and environmental history of the organism. For example, sources of error may include different amounts of effort for the responses, qualitative differences in reinforcement such as food versus water, a history of punishment, a tendency to respond to the right alternative rather than the left, and sensory capacities.

Matching of Ratios

To include these and other conditions within the matching law, it is useful to express the law in terms of ratios rather than proportions. A simple algebraic transformation of Equation (9.1) gives the matching law in terms of ratios:

1. Proportion equation: $B_a/(B_a + B_b) = R_a/(R_a + R_b)$.
2. Cross-multiplying: $B_a/(R_a + R_b) = R_a/(B_a + B_b)$.
3. Then: $(B_a \times R_a) + (B_a \times R_b) = (R_a \times B_a) + (R_a \times B_b)$.
4. Canceling: $B_a \times R_b = R_a \times B_b$.
5. Ratio equation: $B_a/B_b = R_a/R_b$.

In the ratio equation, B_a and B_b represent rate of response or time spent on the A and B alternatives. The terms R_a and R_b express the rates of reinforcement. When relative rate of response matches relative rate of reinforcement, the ratio equation is simply a restatement of the proportional form of the matching law.

The Power Law

A generalized form of the ratio equation may, however, be used to handle the situation in which unknown factors influence the distribution of behavior. These factors produce systematic departures from ideal matching but may be represented as two constants (parameters) in the generalized matching equation, as suggested by Baum (1974b):

$$B_a/B_b = k(R_a/R_b)^a \qquad (9.4)$$

In this form, the matching equation is represented as a **power law for matching** in which the coefficient k and the exponent a are values that represent two sources of error for a given experiment. When these parameters are equal to 1, Equation (9.4) is the simple ratio form of the matching law.

Bias

Baum suggested that variation in the value of k from 1 reflects preference caused by some factor that has not been identified. For example, consider a pigeon placed in a chamber in which two response keys are available. One of the keys has a small dark speck that is not known to the experimenter. Recall that pigeons have excellent visual acuity and a tendency to peck at stimuli that approximate a piece of grain. Given a choice between the two keys, a pigeon could show a systematic response *bias* for the key with a spot on it. In the generalized matching equation, the presence of such bias is indicated by a value of k other than 1. Generally, bias is some unknown asymmetry between the alternatives that affects preference over and above the relative rates of reinforcement.

Sensitivity

Both undermatching and overmatching were previously described in this chapter for proportional matching. Here we discuss these aspects of sensitivity in term of the generalized matching equation.

When the exponent a takes on a value other than 1, another source of error is present. A value of a greater than 1 indicates that changes in the response ratio (B_a/B_b) are larger than changes in the ratio of reinforcement (R_a/R_b). Baum (1974b) called this outcome *overmatching* because relative behavior increased faster than predicted from relative rate of reinforcement. Although overmatching has been observed, it is not the most common result in behavioral-choice experiments. The typical outcome is that the exponent a takes on a value less than 1 (Baum, 1979; Davison & McCarthy, 1988; Myers & Myers, 1977; Wearden & Burgess, 1982). This result is described as *undermatching*. Undermatching refers to a situation in which changes in the response ratio are less than changes in the reinforcement ratio.

One interpretation of undermatching is that changes in relative rates of reinforcement are not well discriminated by the organism (Baum, 1974b). Sensitivity to the operating schedules is adequate when the value of the a coefficient is close to 1. An organism may not detect subtle changes in the schedules, and its distribution of behavior lags behind the current distribution of reinforcement. This slower change in the distribution of behavior is reflected by a value of a less than 1. For example, if a pigeon is exposed to concurrent VI VI schedules without a COD procedure, then the likely outcome is that the bird will rapidly and repeatedly switch between alternatives. This rapid alternation usually results in the pigeon being less sensitive to changes in the reinforcement ratio, and undermatching is the outcome. However, a COD may be used to prevent the superstitious switching and increase sensitivity to the rates of reinforcement on the alternatives. The COD is therefore a procedure that reduces undermatching, and this is reflected by values of a close to 1.

Although problems of discrimination or sensitivity may account for deviations of a away from 1, some researchers believe that undermatching is so common that it should be regarded as an accurate description of choice and preference (Davison, 1981). If this position is correct, then matching is not the lawful process underlying choice. Most behavior analysts have not adopted this position and view matching as a fundamental process. Nonetheless, the origin of undermatching is currently a focus of debate and is not resolved at this time (Allen, 1981; Baum, 1979; Davison & Jenkins, 1985; Prelec, 1984; Wearden, 1983).

FIG. 9.13   William Baum. Reprinted with permission.

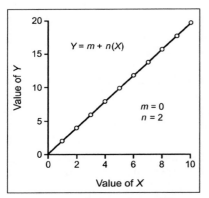

FIG. 9.14   A plot of the algebraic equation for a straight line. Slope is set at 2.0, and intercept is zero.

Estimating Bias and Sensitivity

Dr. William Baum (1974b) (Figure 9.13) formulated the **generalized matching law**, as shown in Equation (9.4). In the same article, he suggested that Equation (9.4) could be represented as a straight line when expressed in logarithmic form. In this form, it is relatively easy to portray and interpret deviations from matching (i.e., bias and sensitivity) on a line graph. Baum suggested that in linear form the value of the slope of the line measured sensitivity to the reinforcement schedules, while the intercept reflected the amount of bias.

Algebra for a straight line

The algebraic equation for a straight line is

$$Y = m + n(X)$$

In this equation, n is the slope and m is the intercept. The value of X (horizontal axis) is varied, and this changes the value of Y (vertical axis). Assume that X takes on values of 1–10, $m = 0$, and $n = 2$. When X is 1, the simple algebraic equation is $Y = 0 + 2\,(1)$ or $Y = 2$. The equation can be solved for the other nine values of X and the (X, Y) pairs plotted on a graph. Figure 9.14 is a plot of the (X, Y) pairs over the range of the X values. The rate at which the line rises, or the slope of the line, is equal to the value of n and has a value of 2 in this example. The intercept m is zero in this case and is the point at which the line crosses the Y-coordinate.

A log-linear matching equation

To write the matching law as a straight line, Baum suggested that Equation (9.4) be expressed as a **log-linear matching equation** (Equation 9.5):

$$\log(B_a/B_b) = \log k + [a \times \log(R_a/R_b)]. \tag{9.5}$$

Notice that in this form, $\log(B_a/B_b)$ is the same as the Y value in the algebraic equation for a straight line. Similarly, $\log(R_a/R_b)$ is the same as the X value. The term a is the same as n and is the slope of the line. Finally, $\log k$ is the intercept, as is the term m in the algebraic equation.

The case of matching

Figure 9.15 shows the application of Equation (9.5) to idealized experimental data. The first and second columns give the number of reinforcers per hour delivered on the A and B alternatives. Notice that the rate of reinforcement on alternative B is held constant at 5 per hour, while the rate of reinforcement for alternative A is varied from 5 to 600 reinforcers. The relative rate of reinforcement is shown in column 3, expressed as a ratio (i.e., R_a/R_b). For example, the first ratio for the data labeled "matching" is 5/5 = 1, and the other ratios may be obtained in a similar manner. The fourth column is the logarithm of the ratio values. Logarithms are obtained from a calculator and are defined as the exponent of base 10 that yields the original number. For example, the number 2 is the logarithm of 100 since 10 raised to the second power is 100. Similarly, in Figure 9.15 the logarithm of the ratio 120 is 2.08 because 10 to the power of 2.08 power equals the original 120 value.

Notice that logarithms are simply a transformation of scale of the original numbers. Such a transformation is suggested because logarithms of ratios plot as a straight line on X, Y coordinates, while the original ratios may not be linear. Actual experiments involve both positive and negative logarithms since ratios may be less than 1. For simplicity, the constructed examples in Figure 9.15 only use values that yield positive logarithms.

Columns 5 and 6 provide values for the slope and intercept for the log-ratio equation. When relative rate of response is assumed to match (or equal) the relative rate of reinforcement, the slope (a) assumes a value of 1.00 and the value of the intercept (log k) is zero. With slope and intercept so defined, the values of Y or $\log(B_a/B_b)$ may be obtained from the values of X or $\log(R_a/R_b)$, by solving Equation (9.5). For example, the first Y value of 0.00 for the final column is obtained by substituting the appropriate values into the log-ratio equation, $\log(B_a/B_b) = 0.00 + [1.00 \times (0.00)]$. The second value of Y is 0.78, or $\log(B_a/B_b) = 0.00 + [1.00 \times (0.78)]$, and so on.

Figure 9.16A plots the "matching" data. The values of X or $\log(R_a/R_b)$ were set for this idealized experiment, and Y or log (B_a/B_b) values were obtained by solving Equation (9.5) when $a = 1$ and log $k = 0$. Notice that the plot is a straight line that rises at 45°. The rate of rise in the line is equal to the value of the slope (i.e., $a = 1$). This value means that a unit change in X (i.e., from 0 to 1) results in an equivalent change in the value of Y. With the intercept (log k) set at 0, the line passes through the origin ($X = 0$, $Y = 0$). The result is a matching line in which log ratio of responses equals log ratio of reinforcement.

Rft/h A	Rft/h B	(R_a/R_b)	X value log (R_a/R_b)	Slope (a)	Intercept (log k)	Y value log (B_a/B_b)
			MATCHING			
5	5	1	0.00	1.00	0.00	0.00
30	5	6	0.78	1.00	0.00	0.78
100	5	20	1.30	1.00	0.00	1.30
600	5	120	2.08	1.00	0.00	2.08
			UNDERMATCHING			
5	5	1	0.00	0.50	0.00	0.00
30	5	6	0.78	0.50	0.00	0.39
100	5	20	1.30	0.50	0.00	0.65
600	5	120	2.08	0.50	0.00	0.14
			BIAS			
5	5	1	0.00	1.00	1.50	1.50
30	5	6	0.78	1.00	1.50	2.28
100	5	20	1.30	1.00	1.50	2.80
600	5	120	2.08	1.00	1.50	3.58

FIG. 9.15   Application of log-linear matching equation (Equation 9.5) to idealized experimental data. Shown are reinforcements per hour (Rft/h) for alternatives A and B, the ratio of the reinforcement rates (R_a/R_b), and the log ratio of the reinforcement rates (X values). The log ratios of the response rates (Y values) were obtained by setting the slope and intercept to values that produce matching, undermatching, or bias.

Undermatching or sensitivity

The data of Figure 9.15 labeled "undermatching" represent the same idealized experiment. The value of the intercept remains the same (log $k = 0$); however, the slope now takes on a value less than 1 ($a = 0.5$). Based on Equation (9.5), this change in slope results in new values of Y or $\log(B_a/B_b)$. Figure 9.16B is a graph of the line resulting from the change in slope. When compared with the matching line ($a = 1$), the new line rises at a slower rate ($a = 0.5$). This situation is known as undermatching and implies that the subject gives less relative behavior to alternative A [$\log(B_a/B_b)$] than expected on the basis of relative rate of reinforcement [$\log(R_a/R_b)$]. For example, if log-ratio reinforcement changes from 0 to 1, the log ratio of behavior will change only from 0 to 0.5. This suggests poor discrimination by the subject of the operating schedules of reinforcement (low sensitivity).

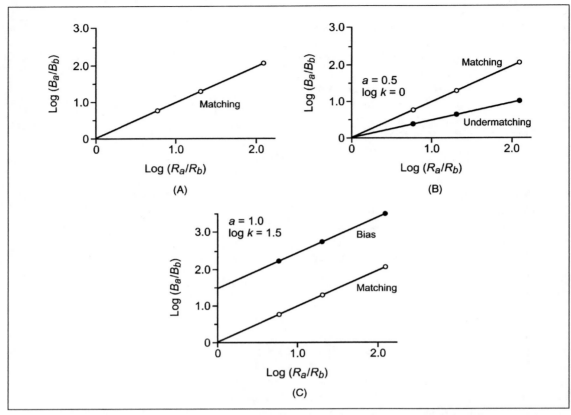

FIG. 9.16 (A) An X–Y plot of the data for "Matching" from Figure 9.15 The value of the slope is set at 1 ($a = 1$), and the intercept is set at zero (log $k = 0$). The matching line means that a unit increase in relative rate of reinforcement [log(R_a/R_b)] produces a unit increase in relative rate of response [log(B_a/B_b)]. (B) An X–Y plot of the data for "Undermatching" from Figure 9.15. The value of the slope is set at less than 1 ($a = 0.5$), and the intercept is set at zero (log $k = 0$). Undermatching with a slope of 0.5 means that a unit increase in relative rate of reinforcement [log(R_a/R_b)] produces a half-unit increase in relative rate of response [log(B_a/B_b)]. (C) An X–Y plot of the data for "Bias" from the data of Figure 9.15 The value of the slope is set at 1 ($a = 1$), and the intercept is more than zero (log $k = 1.5$). A bias of this amount indicates that the new plotted data on X–Y coordinates are deflected 1.5 units from the matching line.

Response bias

It is also possible to have a systematic bias for one of the alternatives. For example, a right-handed person may prefer to press a key on the right side more than to the left. This tendency to respond to the right side may occur even though both keys schedule equal rates of reinforcement. Recall that response bias refers to any systematic preference for one alternative that is not explained by the relative rates of reinforcement. In terms of the idealized experiment, the data labeled "bias" in Figure 9.15 show that the slope of the line is 1 (matching), but the intercept (log k) now assumes a value of 1.5 rather than zero. A plot of the X or log(R_a/R_b) and Y or log(B_a/B_b) values in Figure 9.16C reveals a line that is systematically deflected 1.5 units from the matching line.

Experiments and Log-Linear Estimates

Setting the values of the independent variable

In actual experiments on choice and preference, the values of the slope and intercept are not known until the experiment is conducted. The experimenter sets the values of the independent variable, $\log(R_a/R_b)$, by programming different schedules of reinforcement on the alternatives. For example, one alternative may be VI 30 s and the other VI 60 s. The VI 30-s schedule is set to pay off at 120 reinforcers per hour, and the VI 60-s schedule is set to pay off at 60 reinforcers each hour. The relative rate of reinforcement is expressed as the ratio $120/60 = 2$. To describe the results in terms of Equation (9.5), the reinforcement ratio, 2, is transformed to a logarithm, using a calculator with logarithmic functions. Experiments are designed to span a reasonable range of log-ratio reinforcement values. The minimum number of log-ratio reinforcement values is three, but most experiments program more than three values of the independent variable.

Each experimental subject is exposed to different pairs of concurrent schedules of reinforcement. The subject is maintained on these schedules until rates of response are stable, according to preset criteria. At this point, relative rates of response are calculated (B_a/B_b) and transformed to logarithms. For example, a subject on a concurrent VI 30-s VI 60-s schedule may generate 1000 responses per hour on the VI 30-s alternative and 500 on the VI 60-s schedule. Thus, the response ratio is $1000/500 = 2$, or 2:1. The response ratio, 2, is transformed to a logarithm. For each value of $\log(R_a/R_b)$, the observed value of the dependent variable $\log(B_a/B_b)$ is plotted on X, Y coordinates.

To illustrate the application of Equation (9.5), consider an experiment by White and Davison (1973). In this experiment, several pigeons were exposed to 12 sets of concurrent schedules. Each pair of schedules programmed a different reinforcement ratio. The pigeons were maintained on the schedules until key pecking was stable from day to day. The data for pigeon 22 are plotted in Figure 9.17A on logarithmic coordinates. Plotting the reinforcement and response ratios on logarithmic coordinates is the same as plotting the log ratios on ordinary graph paper. Notice that actual results are not as orderly as the data of the idealized experiment. This is because errors in measurement, inconsistencies of procedure, and random events operate to affect response ratios in actual experiments. The results appear to move upward to the right in a linear manner, but it is not possible to draw a simple line through the plot.

Estimates of slope and intercept

To find the line that best fits the results, a statistical technique (i.e., least-squares regression) is used to estimate values for the slope and intercept of Equation (9.5). The idea is to select slope and intercept values that minimize

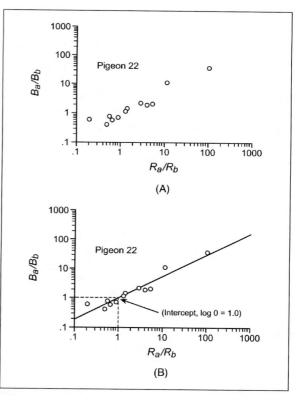

FIG. 9.17   (A) Reinforcement and response ratios for pigeon 22 plotted on logarithmic coordinates. (B) The line of best fit for the data of pigeon 22. Based on Table 1 and Figure 1 from White and Davison (1973).

the errors in prediction. For a given value of the reinforcement ratio (*X*-axis), an error is the difference between the response-ratio value on the line (called the predicted value) and the actual or observed response ratio.

The mathematics that underlie this statistical technique are complicated and beyond the scope of this book. However, most personal computers have programs that will do the calculations for you. For example, you can use a program like Microsoft Excel with a PC to obtain the best-fitting line, using linear regression analysis. The estimate of slope was *a* = 0.77, indicating that pigeon 22 undermatched to the reinforcement ratios. The estimate of the intercept was zero (log *k* = 0), indicating that there was no response bias. With these estimates of slope and intercept, Equation (9.5) may be used to draw the best-fitting line.

In Figure 9.17B, the line of best fit has been drawn. You can obtain the line of best fit by substituting values for $\log(R_a/R_b)$ and finding the predicted $\log(B_a/B_b)$ values. You only need to find two points on the *X*, *Y* coordinates to draw the line. Notice that the data and best-fit line are plotted on a graph with logarithmic coordinates. Because there was no bias (log *k* = 0), the line must pass through the point *X* = 1, *Y* = 1 when *Ra/Rb* and *Ba/Bb* values are plotted on logarithmic paper.

As a final point, you may be interested in how well the matching equation fits the results of pigeon 22. One measure of accuracy is called explained variance. This measure varies between 0 and 1 in value. When the explained variance is 0, it is not possible to predict the response ratios from the reinforcement ratios. When the explained variance is 1, there is perfect prediction from the reinforcement ratios to the response ratios. In this instance, the explained variance is 0.92, indicating 92% accuracy. The log-linear matching equation is a good description of the pigeon's behavior on concurrent schedules of reinforcement.

FOCUS ON: Behavioral neuroscience, matching, and sensitivity

The generalized matching law can be used to study neural events and processes using pharmacological interventions. A recent study by Bratcher, Farmer-Dougan, Dougan, Heidenreich, and Garris (2005) applied the generalized matching equation (Equation 9.5) to investigate how the brain is involved in the regulation of behavior by relative rates of reinforcement. The point was to detect the effects of specific drugs on choice behavior using the estimates of the slope *a* value (sensitivity) of the matching equation.

Dopamine (DA), a neurotransmitter in the brain, is known to be a behavioral activator and different dopamine receptors D1 and D2 appear to be involved in the regulation of different aspects of behavior. Thus, drug activation of D2 receptors was predicted to induce focused search for food, increased behavior directed at lever pressing, and overmatching (or matching) to relative reinforcement with estimates of *a* taking a value greater than 1. In contrast, drug activation of D1 receptors was predicted to elicit nonspecific food-related behavior, increased behavior away from lever pressing, and subsequent undermatching to relative reinforcement with estimates of *a* taking a value less than 1.

In this study, rats were trained to press levers for food on concurrent VI VI schedules and drug or control treatments (saline) were administered 20 min before sessions. When behavior stabilized, response and reinforcement ratios were determined and a fit to the generalized matching law was made, providing estimates of *a* or sensitivity to relative reinforcement. The results showed that the sensitivity value was slightly higher than baseline with quinpirole (a D2 agonist) and was substantially lower than baseline with SKF38393 (a D1 agonist). That is, as predicted, SKF38393 produced considerable undermatching (poor control by relative rate of reinforcement).

Analysis of video recordings of the rats' behavior indicated that quinpirole (D2 agonist) increased chewing and sniffing of the lever and food cup, behaviors compatible with lever pressing.

The D1 agonist SKF38393 increased grooming and sniffing at some distance away from the lever, behavior that was incompatible with lever pressing and the reinforcement contingencies. Bratcher et al. (2005) suggested, ". . . sensitivity to reward may have been due to changes in the value of the scheduled and/or any unscheduled reinforcers. That is, other behaviors elicited by D1 or D2 drug exposure . . . may have taken on greater reinforcement value than operant responding" (pp. 389–390). These alternative behaviors were either compatible or incompatible with lever pressing for food, leading to the observed differences in the estimates of the slope *a* value. The researchers concluded that further study is warranted of the DA receptors in the regulation of operant behavior, and the matching law provides a powerful analytical basis for research on brain and behavior relationships.

CHAPTER SUMMARY

Why do people and other animals choose to do the things that they do? Are they compelled by impulses or is their behavior random? Behavior analysts have proposed a model based on the assumption that consequences influence behavior choices. Richard Herrnstein and William Baum have worked out many of the details of a law that states that relative rates of response to alternatives or options will match the relative rate of reinforcement. The matching law is the outcome of an experimental analysis of concurrent choice performance. This chapter describes the methods by which researchers have investigated this process. It has been determined that we are always confronted with at least two alternatives (take it or leave it) and that the alternative we choose is determined by the probability of reinforcement provided by that choice. This law can be stated in the form of a mathematical equation, and manipulations based on that equation have provided valuable insights into many components of choice behavior. Use of the matching law has been shown to work best in the laboratory with concurrent variable-interval schedules of reinforcement, but it also applies with free-ranging wild pigeons and in human social situations. Other applications of the matching law have proven useful in areas such as behavioral economics, substance addiction, self-control, and preference reversal. The generality of the matching equation is remarkable and it will continue to improve the quantification of the relation between rates of response and rates of reinforcement.

Key Words

Ainslie–Rachlin principle
Behavioral economics
Bias
Changeover delay (COD)
Changeover response
Choice
Commitment response
Concurrent schedules of
    reinforcement
Extraneous sources of
    reinforcement

Findley procedure
Generalized matching law
Impulsive behavior
Log-linear matching equation
Matching law
Maximization
Melioration
Overmatching
Power law for matching

Preference
Preference reversal
Quantitative law of effect
Relative rate of reinforcement
Relative rate of response
Self-control behavior
Two-key procedure
Undermatching

Conditioned Reinforcement

10

- Learn about conditioned reinforcement and chain schedules of reinforcement.
- Inquire about multiple functions of stimuli in homogeneous and heterogenous chains.
- Investigate backward chaining and how it can be used to improve your golf game.
- Learn how to make conditioned reinforcement most effective.
- Inquire about the problems with an informational account of conditioned reinforcement.
- Learn about generalized conditioned reinforcement, human behavior, and the token economy.
- Investigate the delay-reduction hypothesis, concurrent-chain schedules, and conditioned reinforcement.

Human behavior is often regulated by consequences whose effects depend on a history of conditioning. Praise, criticism, good grades, and money are often consequences that may strengthen or weaken behavior. Such events acquire these effects because of the different experiences that people have had throughout their lives. Some people have learned the value of what others say about their actions—others are indifferent. Henry Ford marketed and sold cars because of monetary reinforcement, status, and power, but Mother Teresa took care of the poor for other reasons. In these examples, the effectiveness of a behavioral consequence depends on a personal history of conditioning. A positive reinforcer may be defined as a stimulus or event, the delivery of which will increase or maintain the rate of the response upon which it is contingent. The critical component is the influence on response rate, not what exactly the stimulus or event is.

Conditioned reinforcement occurs when behavior is strengthened by events that have an effect because of a conditioning history. The important aspect of the history involves a correspondence between an arbitrary event and a presently effective reinforcer. Once the arbitrary event becomes able to increase the frequency of an operant, it is called a **conditioned reinforcer**. (It may also be called a secondary reinforcer but conditioned is best.) For example, the sound of the pellet feeder operating becomes a conditioned reinforcer for a rat that presses a lever because the sound is paired with food. The immediate effect of lever pressing or key pecking is the sound of the feeder, not the consumption of food. Food is a biological or **unconditioned reinforcer** that accompanies the sound of the feeder. Magazine training is the procedure of deliberately and contiguously pairing the sound of food delivery with the immediate access to the food. The point in this case is to be able to deliver an auditory reinforcer, the feeder sound, wherever the subject is or whenever you wish. One way to demonstrate the reinforcing effectiveness of the feeder sound is to arrange a contingency between some other operant (e.g., pressing a spot on the wall) and delivering only the sound. If operant rate increases, the process is conditioned reinforcement and the sound is a conditioned reinforcer.

In his book, *The Behavior of Organisms*, Skinner (1938) described a procedure that resulted in conditioned reinforcement. Rats were exposed to a clicking sound and were given food. Later the animals were not fed, but the click was used to train lever pressing. Lever pressing increased although it only produced the clicking sound. Because the click was no longer accompanied by food, each occurrence of the sound was also an extinction trial. For this reason, the sound declined in reinforcing effectiveness and lever pressing for clicks decreased at the same time. It should occur to you that the pairing process of establishing a conditioned reinforcer is similar to the development of a CS in respondent conditioning. A previously neutral stimulus is contiguously presented with a functioning reinforcer and this stimulus becomes capable of maintaing behavior upon which it is contingent. Of course, as in respondent conditioning, presenting the CS without the occasional US leads to the absence of the CR because the CS loses its eliciting ability.

NOTE ON: Clicker training

There is a major industry built around the use of conditioned reinforcement in training animals. Karen Pryor (1999; www.clickertraining.com) has exploited the fact that a click from a little hand-held clicker paired with (usually) a food treat can be used to strengthen behavior. Clicker training is like the old game of "hot and cold" where a person is searching for something and the only help given is in the form of telling the searcher whether she is "hot" (meaning close) or "cold" (meaning further away). Clicks are used as indications of "hot" and no clicks mean "cold" for such behavior shaping (Peterson, 2004). Clicker training has been adopted by many zoo animal keepers (e.g., Lucas, Marr, & Maple, 1998; Wilkes, 1994) and is highly effective in training companion animals of all species (e.g., dogs and horses).

This **new-response method** for studying conditioned reinforcement sometimes results in short-lived effects. Because of extinction (the sound without the food), the conditioned reinforcer quickly loses its effectiveness and is only capable of maintaining a few responses (see Kelleher & Gollub, 1962; Miller, 1951; Myers, 1958; Wike, 1966). On the other hand, Skinner (1938, p. 82 and his Figure 13) reported that ". . . considerable conditioning can be effected before a state of extinction." This conclusion is in accord with Alferink, Crossman, and Cheney (1973). These researchers demonstrated the conditioned reinforcing strength of the hopper light in maintaining pecking even in the presence of free food. Trained pigeons continued to peck on an FR 300 schedule of hopper light presentation even with the hopper propped up so that food was always available. At the present time it is not possible to say when conditioned reinforcement based on the new-response method will be short-lived or enduring. Experience with conditioned reinforcement in everyday life suggests, however, that these events can support a lot of behavior without noticable extinction.

Animals typically engage in long and complex sequences of behavior that are often far removed from unconditioned reinforcement. This is particularly true for humans. People get up in the morning, take buses to work, carry out their jobs, talk to other workers, and so on. These operants occur day after day and are maintained by conditioned reinforcement. Thus, conditioned reinforcement is a durable process, but the new-response method does not always reveal how this occurs. Because of this, behavioral researchers have turned to procedures that clarify the long-lasting effects of conditioned reinforcement.

CHAIN SCHEDULES AND CONDITIONED REINFORCEMENT

One way to investigate conditioned reinforcement is to construct sequences of behavior in the laboratory. A **chain schedule of reinforcement** involves two or more simple schedules (CRF, FI, VI, FR, or VR), each of which is presented sequentially and is signaled by an arbitrary stimulus. Only the final or terminal link of the chain results in unconditioned reinforcement. Figure 10.1 shows the

Mechner notation for a three-component chain schedule of reinforcement. The schedule is a chain VI FR FI, and each link (or component) of the chain is signaled by a red, blue, or green light. For example, in the presence of the red light, a pigeon must emit a key peck after an average of 1 min has elapsed (VI 60 s). When the peck occurs, the light changes from red to blue and the bird must peck the key 50 times (FR 50) to produce the green light. In the presence of the green light, a single peck after 2 min (FI 120 s) produces food and the light changes back to red (i.e., the chain starts over).

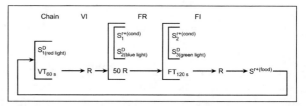

FIG. 10.1   Mechner notation for a three-component chain schedule of reinforcement, VI 60 s FR 50 FI 120 s. Notice that the red light only has a discriminative stimulus function, while the blue and green lights have multiple functions, including S^D and $S^{r(cond)}$.

When the pigeon pecks in the red component, the only consequence is that the light changes to blue. Once the blue condition is in effect, 50 responses turn on the green light. If the bird pecks for the blue and green lights, the change in color is reinforcement. Recall that any stimulus that strengthens behavior is by definition a reinforcing stimulus. Thus, these lights have multiple functions: They are S^Ds that set the occasion for pecking the key in each link and also conditioned reinforcement, $S^{r(cond)}$, for behavior that produces them. The notation in Figure 10.1 indicates that the red light is only a discriminative stimulus. You might suspect that it is a conditioned reinforcer, and it may have this function. However, the chain procedure as outlined does not require a separate response to produce the red light (the last response in the chain produces food and afterward the red light automatically comes on), and for this reason a conditioned reinforcing function is not demonstrated.

Multiple-Stimulus Functions

Consider a sequence of two schedules, FR 50 FI 120 s, in which the components are not signaled. Formally, this is called a **tandem schedule**. A tandem is a schedule of reinforcement in which unconditioned reinforcement is programmed after completing two or more schedules, presented sequentially *without discriminative stimuli*. In other words, a tandem schedule as shown in Figure 10.2 is the same as an unsignaled chain.

Gollub (1958) compared the behavior of pigeons on similar tandem and chain schedules of reinforcement. On a tandem FI 60 s FI 60 s schedule, performance resembled the pattern observed on a simple FI 120-s schedule. The birds produced the typical scallop pattern observed on fixed-interval schedules—pausing after the presentation of food, and accelerating in response rate to the moment of reinforcement. When the tandem schedule was changed to a chain FI 60 s FI 60 s by adding distinctive stimuli to the links, the effect of conditioned reinforcement was apparent. After some experience on the chain schedule, the birds responded faster in the initial link than they had on the tandem. In effect, the birds produced two FI scallops rather than one during the 120 s. This change in behavior may be attributed to the discriminative stimulus in the final link that also reinforced responses in the first component. In other words, the discriminative stimulus signaling the terminal link is also a conditioned reinforcer for responses in the first component of the chain (see also Ferster & Skinner, 1957).

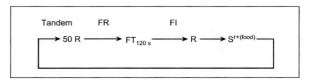

FIG. 10.2   A tandem schedule of reinforcement is the same as an unsignaled chain.

Homogeneous and Heterogeneous Chains

Operant chains are classified as **homogeneous chains** when the topography or form of response is similar in each component. For example, in the chain schedule discussed earlier, the bird pecks the same key in each link. Because a similar response occurs in each component, this is a homogeneous chain. In contrast, a **heterogeneous chain** requires different responses for each link. Dog trainers make use of heterogeneous chains when they teach complex behavioral sequences to their animals. In going for a walk, a seeing-eye dog stops at intersections, moves forward when the traffic is clear, pauses at a curb, avoids potholes, and finds the way home. Each of these different responses is occasioned by specific stimuli and results in conditioned reinforcement. Although heterogeneous chains are common in everyday life and are created easily in the laboratory, they are usually too complex for experimental analysis. For this reason, conditioned reinforcement is typically investigated with homogeneous chains.

Chain schedules show how sequences of behavior are maintained by conditioned reinforcement in everyday life. Conditioned reinforcers in chains remain effective because the terminal link continues to schedule unconditioned reinforcement. Viewed as a heterogeneous chain schedule, going to a restaurant may involve the following links: A person calls and makes a reservation, gets dressed for the occasion, drives to the restaurant, parks the car, enters and is seated, orders dinner, and eats the meal. In this example, the S^Ds are the completion of the response requirements for each link. That is, being dressed for dinner (S^D) sets the occasion for going to the car and driving to the restaurant. Conditioned reinforcement involves the opportunity to engage in the next activity—bringing you closer to unconditioned reinforcement.

Of course, each of these components may be subdivided into finer and finer links in the chained performance. For example, dressing for dinner is comprised of many different responses with identifiable discriminative stimuli (e.g., putting on shoes sets the occasion for tying laces). Even tying shoelaces may be separated into finer and finer links of a heterogeneous chain. The degree of detail in describing a chain performance depends on the analytical problem. An analysis of going out for dinner does not require details about how a person ties his or her shoes. On the other hand, a behavior analyst teaching a retarded child to dress may focus on fine details of the chained performance.

FOCUS ON: Backward chaining

Imagine that you have just been hired as a behavioral technician at a group home for retarded children. One of your first assignments is to use the principle of conditioned reinforcement to teach a child to make his bed. The child is profoundly retarded and cannot easily follow instructions or examples. He does have good motor coordination and is reinforced by potato chips. You and the child are in one of the bedrooms with sheets, blankets, and pillowcases stacked on the bed. You have decided to use potato chips as a reinforcer for bed making.

Many people would start at the beginning of the sequence by unfolding a sheet, shaking it out, and placing it over the mattress. This tactic works for students (or children) who are easily able to follow instructions. However, this is not the case for this child and the initial links of the chain are far removed from unconditioned reinforcement. Also, there are no conditioned reinforcers established along the way for completing the components.

The alternative way of teaching is to use a technique called **backward chaining**. The idea is to begin training at the end of the sequence. That is, you first teach the behavior in the final link of the chain. The child is reinforced with chips when he places the top of the bedspread over the pillow. Once this behavior is well established, the bedspread is pulled down further. Unconditioned reinforcement now occurs when the child pulls covers up to the pillow and then finishes making the bed. In this manner, responses that are more and more remote from the final performance are maintained by conditioned reinforcement (engaging in the next sequence). Of course, you eventually pair chips with social approval (i.e., "Your bed looks great!") and maintain the behavior without direct unconditioned reinforcement.

In everyday life, backward chaining has been used to train athletic skills. O'Brien and Simek (1983) taught golf using principles of backward chaining. In their article they state:

> The teaching of sports has been largely unaffected by the advances in learning other operants. Golf, for example, is still routinely taught by handing the novice a driver and instructing him verbally how to get his body, arms and head to combine to hit a 250 yard drive. The usual result of such instruction is a series of swings that end in wiffs, tops and divots. This is followed by more verbal explanations, some highly complex modeling, and loosely administered feedback. Endless repetitions of this chain then follow.
>
> A behavioral analysis of golf would suggest that the reinforcer for this exercise is putting the ball in the hole. The trip from tee to green represents a complex response chain in which the swing of the club up over the head and back to hit the ball is shortened as one gets closer to the hole. The final shot may be a putt of six inches or less leading to the reinforcement of seeing the ball disappear into the ground. This putt requires a backswing of only a few inches but involves the same basic stroke as the long backswinged shot from the tee. Since the short putt seems to be the simplest response and the one closest to reinforcement, it would seem appropriate to teach the golf chain by starting with the putt and working back to the drive.

(pp. 175–176)

The superiority of the backward-chaining method in athletics or other areas of learning results from the principle of conditioned reinforcement. Behavior that is closest to unconditioned reinforcement is taught first. By doing this, the instructor ensures that operants in the sequence are maintained by effective consequences. With the backward-chaining method, each step in the chain may be added as the previous link is mastered.

DETERMINANTS OF CONDITIONED REINFORCEMENT

Operant chains show how complex sequences of behavior can be maintained by events that have acquired a reinforcement function based on the past experience of an organism. The task for experimental analysis is to identify the critical conditions that contribute to the strength of conditioned reinforcement. It is also important to specify the factors that determine the reinforcing effectiveness of conditioned stimuli.

Strength of Conditioned Reinforcement

Frequency of unconditioned reinforcement

The effectiveness of a conditioned reinforcer depends on the frequency of unconditioned reinforcement correlated with it. Autor (1960) found that preference for a conditioned reinforcer increased with the frequency of unconditioned reinforcement in its presence. The power or effectiveness of a conditioned reinforcer increases with more and more presentations of unconditioned reinforcement, but eventually levels off. As the frequency of unconditioned reinforcement goes up, the strength of a conditioned reinforcer reaches a maximum value. This relationship is strikingly similar to the increase in associative strength of a CS as described by the Rescorla–Wagner model of classical conditioning (see Chapter 3).

Variability of unconditioned reinforcement

Variability of unconditioned reinforcement also affects the strength of a conditioned reinforcer. Fantino (1967) showed that birds preferred a conditioned reinforcer that was correlated with an alternating schedule (FR 1 half of the time and FR 99 for the other half of the trials) to one that was associated with a fixed schedule with the same rate of payoff (FR 50). Thus, variability of unconditioned reinforcement increases the value of a conditioned reinforcer (see also Davison, 1969, 1972; Fantino, 1965; Herrnstein, 1964a). Variable schedules increase the effectiveness of conditioned reinforcement because these schedules occasionally program short intervals to unconditioned reinforcement. Compared with fixed schedules, these short intervals enhance responding and the value of stimuli correlated with them (Herrnstein, 1964b).

Establishing operations

The effectiveness of a conditioned reinforcer is enhanced by events that establish unconditioned reinforcement. A bird will respond for a light correlated with food more when it is hungry than when it is well fed. People attend to signs for washrooms, restaurants, and hospitals when their bladders are full, they have not eaten for some time, or they are sick. Generally, conditioned reinforcement depends on stimuli that establish unconditioned reinforcement (Michael, 1982a).

Delay to unconditioned reinforcement

On a chain schedule, the longer the delay between a discriminative stimulus and unconditioned reinforcement, the less effective it is as a conditioned reinforcer. Gollub (1958) compared the performance of pigeons on three different schedules—FI 5 min, chain FI 1 FI 1 FI 1 FI 1 FI 1 min, and tandem FI 1 FI 1 FI 1 FI 1 FI 1 min. On the simple FI 5-min schedule a blue key light was on throughout the interval. On the chain, a different key color was associated with each of the five links. The components of the tandem schedule were not signaled by separate colored lights, but a blue key light was on throughout the links. Birds responded to the tandem as they did to the simple FI—producing the typical FI scallop. On the extended chain schedule, responding was disrupted in the early components, and some of the birds stopped responding after prolonged exposure to the schedule (see also Fantino, 1969b). Disruption of responding occurs because the S^Ds in the early links (farthest from unconditioned reinforcement) signal a long time to unconditioned reinforcement and are weak conditioned reinforcers. A similar effect occurs when people give up when faced with a long and complex task. Students who drop out of school may do so because the signs of progress are weak conditioned reinforcers—far removed from a diploma or degree.

Establishing Conditioned Reinforcement

Many experiments have used an extinction procedure to investigate conditioned reinforcement. In most of these experiments, a conspicuous stimulus is presented just before the delivery of food. The *new-response method* involves pairing a distinctive stimulus such as a click with unconditioned reinforcement. After several pairings, the stimulus is presented without unconditioned reinforcement and is used to shape a new response. Another extinction technique is called the **established-response method**. An operant that produces unconditioned reinforcement is accompanied by a distinctive stimulus, just prior to reinforcement. When responding is well established, extinction is implemented but half of the subjects continue to get the stimulus that accompanied unconditioned reinforcement.

The other subjects undergo extinction without the distinctive stimulus. Generally, subjects with the stimulus present respond more than the subjects who do not get the stimulus associated with unconditioned reinforcement. This result is interpreted as evidence for the effects of conditioned reinforcement.

Pairing, discrimination, and conditioned reinforcement

Both extinction methods for analyzing conditioned reinforcement involve the presentation of a stimulus that was closely followed by unconditioned reinforcement. This procedure is similar to CS–US pairings used in respondent conditioning. One interpretation, therefore, is that conditioned reinforcement is based on classical conditioning. This interpretation is called the stimulus–stimulus or **S–S account of conditioned reinforcement**. That is, all CSs are also conditioned reinforcers.

Although this is a straightforward account, the experimental procedures allow for an alternative analysis. In both the new-response and established-response methods, the stimulus (e.g., a click) sets the occasion for behavior that produces unconditioned reinforcement. For example, the click of a feeder (S^D) sets the occasion for approaching the food tray (operant) and eating food (S^r). Thus, the **discriminative-stimulus account of conditioned reinforcement** is that an S^D is a conditioned reinforcer only and does not function as a CS associated with food.

There have been many experiments that have attempted to distinguish between the S^D and S–S accounts of conditioned reinforcement (Gollub, 1977; Hendry, 1969). For example, Schoenfeld, Antonitis, and Bersh (1950) presented a light for 1 s as an animal ate food. This procedure paired food and light, but the light could not be a discriminative stimulus since it did not precede the food delivery. Following this training, the animals were placed on extinction and there was no effect of conditioned reinforcement.

Given this finding, it seems reasonable to conclude that a stimulus must be discriminative in order to become a conditioned reinforcer. Unfortunately, current research shows that simultaneous pairing of CS and US results in weak conditioning (see Chapter 3). For this and other reasons, it has not yet been possible to have a definitive test of the S^D and S–S accounts of conditioned reinforcement.

On a practical level, distinguishing between these accounts of conditioned reinforcement makes little difference. In most situations, procedures that establish a stimulus as an S^D also result in that stimulus becoming a conditioned reinforcer. Similarly, when a stimulus is conditioned as a CS it almost always has an operant reinforcement function. In both cases, contemporary research (Fantino, 1977) suggests that the critical factor is the temporal delay between the onset of the stimulus and the later presentation of unconditioned reinforcement.

FOCUS ON: Behavioral neuroscience and conditioned reinforcement

One major issue of behavioral neuroscience has been locating where in the nervous system response consequences are "evaluated" or assigned a hedonic value. That is, how does an event or stimulus such as money take on value and become a strong reinforcer? We know that conditioned reinforcers maintain behavior over long periods of time and often in the absence of unconditioned reinforcers; these conditioned consequences also play a central role in complex social behavior.

Several brain areas (pain/pleasure centers) are known to code for hedonic value of stimuli (Olds & Milner, 1954) and continuing research has refined the brain circuits involved. Thus, Parkinson, Crofts, McGuigan, Tomic, Everitt, and Roberts (2001) reported that the amygdala is critical for the conditioned reinforcement process in primates. They made lesions to the amygdala of marmosets and observed behavioral insensitivity to the absence of conditioned reinforcement for pressing a touch-screen panel. In contrast, responding for unconditioned reinforcement was not disrupted. Control subjects with an intact amygdala nearly ceased responding when conditioned reinforcement stopped, showing sensitivity to the contingencies. An intact and functioning amygdala seems necessary for the control of behavior by conditioned reinforcement.

Other recent evidence suggests that both aversive and rewarding stimuli, conditioned or unconditioned, affect similar brain areas. These areas include the prefrontal cortex and the nucleus accumbens (Ventura, Morrone, & Puglisi-Allegra, 2007). The nucleus accumbens septi (which is near the medial extension of the head of the caudate nucleus) is known to release dopamine in response to salient conditioned stimuli regardless of their hedonic valence (positive or aversive). Nucleus accumbens dopamine depletion slows the rate of operant responding and speeds the rate of acquisition by reducing the effectiveness of the reinforcer, not by impairing motor behavior (Salamone, Mingote, & Weber, 2003). And in vivo microdialysis procedures have shown that high levels of dopamine from the nucleus accumbens are present in rats that learn response–outcome relationships, but not in rats that fail to learn (Cheng & Feenstra, 2006). Clearly, the nucleus accumbens and dopamine are involved in establishing and maintaining control of behavior by contingencies of reinforcement.

Behavioral neuroscience is providing a circuitry map for what goes on inside the brain when overt conditioning and learning are taking place. The interesting issue is how conditioning with arbitrary stimuli is supported by neural activity. Objects or events that were originally neutral can quickly become very attractive and valuable when specific brain activity occurs during conditioning. What goes on in the brain when this happens? Researchers are making progress in synthesizing how the brain and environment work together—providing a more complete understanding of behavior and its regulation.

Information and conditioned reinforcement

Stimuli that provide information about unconditioned reinforcement may become effective conditioned reinforcers. Egger and Miller (1962) used the extinction method to test for conditioned reinforcement. They conditioned rats by pairing two different stimuli (S_1 and S_2) with food. Figure 10.3 describes the procedures and major results. In their experiment (panel A), S_1 came on and S_2 was presented a half-second later. Both stimuli were turned off when the animals were given food. Both S_1 and S_2 were paired with food, but only S_1 became an effective conditioned reinforcer. In another condition (panel B), S_1 and S_2 were presented as before, but S_1 was occasionally presented alone. Food was never given when S_1 occurred by itself. Under these conditions, S_2 became a conditioned reinforcer.

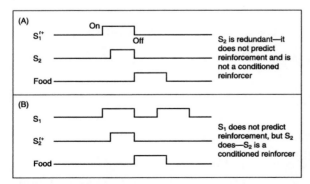

FIG. 10.3 Procedures and major results of an experiment using the extinction method to test for conditioned reinforcement. Based on the description of procedures from Egger and Miller (1962).

To understand this experiment, consider the informativeness of S_2 in each situation. When S_1 and S_2 are equally correlated with food, but S2 always follows S_1, then S_2 is *redundant*—providing no additional information about the occurrence of food. Because it is redundant, S_2 gains little conditioned reinforcement value. In the second situation, S_1 only predicts food in the presence of S_2 and for this reason S_2 is informative and becomes a conditioned reinforcer. These results, along with later experiments (e.g., Egger & Miller, 1963), suggest that a stimulus will become a conditioned reinforcer if it provides information about the occurrence of unconditioned reinforcement.

Good news and bad news

The informativeness of a stimulus should not depend on whether it is correlated with positive or negative events, because bad news is just as informative as good news. Wyckoff (1952, 1969) designed an observing-response procedure to evaluate the strength of a conditioned reinforcer that predicted good or bad news. In this procedure, periods of reinforcement and extinction alternate throughout a session, but the contingencies are not signaled by S^Ds or S^Δs. The contingency is called a **mixed schedule of reinforcement**. A mixed schedule is the same as a multiple schedule, but without discriminative stimuli. Once the animal is responding on the mixed schedule, an observing response is added to the contingencies. The **observing response** is a topographically different operant that functions to produce an S^D or S^Δ depending on whether reinforcement or extinction is in effect. In other words, an observing response changes the mixed to a multiple schedule. Figure 10.4 shows the relationships among mixed, multiple, tandem, and chain schedules of reinforcement.

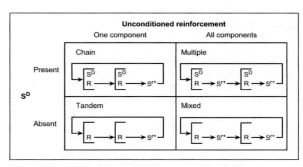

FIG. 10.4 The relationships among mixed, multiple, tandem, and chain schedules of reinforcement. These four schedules depend on whether an S^D is present or absent and whether unconditioned reinforcement occurs in one or all of the compontents.

Wyckoff (1969) showed that pigeons would stand on a pedal in order to observe red and green colors associated with FI 30-s reinforcement or EXT 30 s. Before the birds had an observing response available, they pecked equally in the reinforcement and extinction phases—showing failure to discriminate the schedules. When the observing response was added, the pigeons showed a high rate of pecking in the reinforcement phase and very low rates during extinction. Because the observing response was maintained, the results suggest that stimuli correlated with either reinforcement or extinction (good or bad news) became conditioned reinforcers.

Although Wyckoff's data are consistent with an information view of conditioned reinforcement, it is noteworthy that his pigeons only spent about 50% of the time making the observing response. One possibility is that the birds were observing the stimulus correlated with reinforcement (red color) but not the stimulus that signaled extinction (green color). In other words, the birds may have only responded for good news.

In fact, subsequent experiments by Dinsmoor, Brown, and Lawrence (1972) and Killeen, Wald, and Cheney (1980) supported the good-news interpretation of conditioned reinforcement. In Dinsmoor et al. (1972), pigeons were trained to peck a key on a VI 30-s schedule of food reinforcement that alternated with unpredictable periods of extinction. The birds could peck another key in order to turn on a green light correlated with reinforcement and a red light correlated with extinction. That is, if reinforcement was in effect, an observing response turned on the green light, and if extinction was occurring, the response turned on the red light.

Observing responses were maintained when they produced information about both reinforcement and extinction. In the next part of the experiment, observing responses only produced the green light signaling reinforcement, or the red light associated with extinction. In this case, observing responses produced either good or bad news, but not both. When observing responses resulted in the green light correlated with reinforcement, the birds pecked at a high rate. In contrast, the pigeons would not peck a key that only produced a stimulus (red) signaling extinction. Thus, good news functions as conditioned reinforcement, but bad news does not.

The good-news conclusion is also supported by research using aversive, rather than positive, consequences. Badia, Harsh, Coker, and Abbott (1976) exposed rats to electric shocks. The shocks were delivered on several variable-time schedules, independent of the rats' behavior. During training, a light was always on and a tone occurred just before each shock. In Experiment 2 of their study, the researchers allowed the animals to press a lever that turned on the light for 1 min. During this time, if shocks were scheduled, they were signaled by a tone. In one condition, the light was never accompanied by tone and shocks. That is, when the light was on, the animal was completely safe from shocks. Other conditions presented more and more tones and shocks when the animal turned on the light. In these conditions, the light predicted less and less safety, and responding for the light decreased. In other words, the animals responded for a stimulus correlated with a shock-free period, but not for information about shock given by the tone signals (see also DeFran, 1972; Dinsmoor, Flint, Smith, & Viemeister, 1969; Mueller & Dinsmoor, 1986). Once again, conditioned reinforcement is based on good news but not on bad news.

There are human examples of the good- and bad-news effects (see Case, Ploog, & Fantino, 1990, for good-news effects; and Lieberman, Cathro, Nichol, & Watson, 1997, for bad-news effects). Students who usually do well on mathematics exams quickly look up their marks on posted lists, while those who have done poorly wait for their grades to come in the mail. Seeing a grade is a conditioned reinforcer for students who are skilled at mathematics, but not for those who find the subject difficult. People who have taken care of their teeth find it easy to make a dental appointment, but those with inadequate dental health postpone the visit. Visiting the dentist is a safe period for patients with good teeth, but it signals "pulling and drilling" for those with poor dental hygiene. Unfortunately, the worse things get in such situations, the less likely people are to do anything about them—until it is too late.

Overall, research has shown that stimuli correlated with positive or negative reinforcement maintain an observing response (Dinsmoor et al., 1972; Fantino, 1977), and stimuli that are correlated with extinction or punishment do not (Blanchard, 1975; Jenkins & Boakes, 1973; Katz, 1976). For this reason, the mere informativeness of a stimulus is not the basis of conditioned reinforcement.

DELAY REDUCTION AND CONDITIONED REINFORCEMENT

Fantino and Logan (1979) have reviewed the observing response studies and point out that:

> Only the more positively valued of two stimuli should maintain observing, since the less positive stimulus is correlated with an increase, not a reduction, in time to positive reinforcement (or a reduction, not an increase, in time to an aversive event). . . . Conditioned reinforcers are those stimuli correlated with a reduction in time to reinforcement (or an increase in time to an aversive event).
>
> (p. 207)

This statement is based on Edmund Fantino's (1969a) **delay-reduction hypothesis**. Stimuli closer in time to positive reinforcement, or further in time from an aversive event, are more effective conditioned reinforcers. Stimuli that signal no reduction in time to reinforcement (S^Δ) or no safety from an aversive event (S^{ave}) do not function as conditioned reinforcement. Generally, the value of a conditioned reinforcer is due to its delay reduction—how close it is to reinforcement or how far it is from punishment.

Modern views of conditioned reinforcement are largely based on the concept of delay reduction (Fantino, 1969a; Squires & Fantino, 1971). The idea is to compare the relative value of two (or more) stimuli that are correlated with different amounts of time to reinforcement. To do this, a complex-choice procedure involving concurrent-chain schedules is used. On these schedules, an organism may choose between alternatives that signal different amounts of time to reinforcement.

Concurrent-Chain Schedules of Reinforcement

In Chapter 9, we discussed the analysis of choice based on *concurrent schedules of reinforcement*. We have also noted the importance of chain schedules for the study of conditioned reinforcement. These schedules allow a researcher to change the temporal location of a stimulus in relation to unconditioned reinforcement. For example, the terminal-link discriminative stimulus (S^D_2) on a chain VI 20 s VI 10 s is six times closer to unconditoned reinforcement than it is on a chain VI 20 s VI 60 s. This relation is shown in Figure 10.5. In terms of time, the terminal-link S^D that is

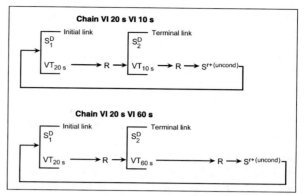

FIG. 10.5 Comparison of chain VI 20 s VI 10 s with chain VI 20 s VI 60 s. Notice that the S^D closer to unconditioned reinforcement should be a more effective conditioned reinforcer.

nearer to unconditioned reinforcement should be a stronger conditioned reinforcer than one associated with a longer delay. Thus, the terminal-link S^D accompanying the VI 10-s schedule ought to be a more effective conditioned reinforcer than a discriminative stimulus correlated with VI 60 s.

To assess the effects of delay, organisms must be able to choose between stimuli associated with different reductions in time to unconditioned reinforcement. For example, using a two-key choice procedure, a chain VI 20 s VI 10 s may be programmed on the left key and a chain VI 20 s VI 60 s on the right key.

This two-key **concurrent-chain schedule** is diagrammed in Figure 10.6. Consider the situation in which responses to the left key are eventually reinforced with food. To start, both left and right keys are illuminated with white lights. A bird makes left- and right-key pecks and, after the left VI 20-s schedule times out, the first peck to the left key has two effects. The light on the right key goes out and the VI 20-s schedule on that key stops timing. That is, the key becomes dark and inoperative. At the same time, the left key changes from white to a diamond pattern. In the presence of this pattern, pecking the left key is reinforced with food on a VI 10-s schedule. After unconditioned reinforcement, both left and right keys are again illuminated white and the bird chooses between the two alternatives.

A similar sequence occurs when the right key times out and the bird pecks this key. The left key becomes dark and inoperative and the right key changes from white to a dotted pattern. In the presence of this pattern, pecking the right key is reinforced with food on a VI 60-s schedule. Following reinforcement, the discriminative stimuli in the initial links of the two chains (left and right white keys) are in effect and the bird again chooses to enter one of the terminal links (left or right).

The patterned stimuli on the left and right keys have two functions. These stimuli are S^Ds that set the occasion for pecking for food in the terminal links of the two chain

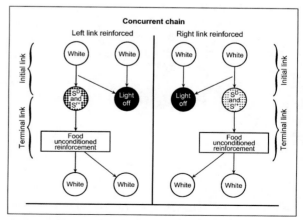

FIG. 10.6 A two-key concurrent-chain schedule of reinforcement. A chain VI 20 s VI 10 s is programmed on the left key, and a chain VI 20 s VI 60 s on the right.

schedules. In addition, the patterned stimuli function as conditioned reinforcement for pecking one or the other white keys in the initial-links or choice phase of the experiment. That is, reinforcement for pecking in the choice phase is the onset of the stimuli (S^D and S^r) associated with unconditioned reinforcement in the terminal links. Because the bird is free to distribute pecks, the distribution of behavior in the initial links is a measure of the relative effectiveness of the two conditioned reinforcers.

Delay Reduction and Concurrent-Chain Schedules

Humans often respond on concurrent-chain schedules of reinforcement. A businessperson who frequently flies from Kansas City to Denver may call either Delta or American Airlines to book a ticket. Many people are trying to book flights, and the telephone lines to both companies are always busy. To contact an agent, the businessperson calls one airline and then the other. Eventually, one of the calls is successful, but both companies have recorded messages that state, "All lines are busy at the moment; please hold until an agent is available." After waiting for some time, an agent answers and the ticket is booked.

In this example, calling the two airlines is the choice phase. The length of time to complete a call and get the hold message (initial-link schedules) is determined by the number of telephone lines at each airline and the number of people phoning the companies. The recorded message is conditioned reinforcement for dialing that company. The amount of time waiting on hold to book a flight (terminal-link schedule) is a function of the number of available agents. Waiting in the terminal link is reinforced by booking the flight. The sequence is repeated the next time the businessperson has a meeting in Denver.

To predict how much more (or less) reinforcing it is to be placed on hold at Delta relative to American Airlines, it is useful to consider a situation in which the initial- and terminal-link schedules are known for each company. Say that, on average, the telephone lines of both companies are busy for 120 s before a call is successful. In other words, the initial links for Delta and American are similar to concurrent VI 120-s schedules. The terminal-link schedules are different for the two airlines. It takes an average of 30 s to talk to a Delta agent after being placed on hold. That is, the terminal link for Delta is similar to a VI 30-s schedule. After being placed on hold at American, it takes an average of 90 s to reach an agent, so that the terminal link for American is similar to a VI 90-s schedule. Thus, the sequence for booking a ticket at Delta is chain VI 120 s VI 30 s, and it is chain VI 120 s VI 90 s at American (see ADVANCED SECTION for quantification of this example).

In this situation, Fantino's delay-reduction hypothesis predicts that the businessperson will prefer Delta more than American. This is because more of the total time to reinforcement has elapsed when the person is placed on hold at Delta when compared to American. The conditioned reinforcement in this situation is getting the message, "All lines are busy at the moment; please hold until an agent is available." After the message occurs, it is faster to book a ticket at Delta compared with American. There has been relatively more reduction in delay to reinforcement when the Delta message occurs.

GENERALIZED CONDITIONED REINFORCEMENT

Formally, a **generalized conditioned reinforcer** is any event or stimulus that is associated with, or exchangeable for, many sources of unconditioned reinforcement. Generalized reinforcement does not depend on deprivation or satiation for any specific reinforcer. Skinner (1953) describes its effects in the following passage:

A conditioned reinforcer is generalized when it is paired with more than one unconditioned reinforcer. The generalized reinforcer is useful because the momentary condition of the organism is not likely to be important. The operant strength generated by a single reinforcement is observed only under an appropriate condition of deprivation—when we reinforce with food, we gain control over the hungry man. But if a conditioned reinforcer has been paired with reinforcers appropriate to many conditions, at least one appropriate state of deprivation is more likely to prevail upon a later occasion. A response is therefore more likely to occur. When we reinforce with money, for example, our subsequent control is relatively independent of momentary deprivations.

(p. 77)

Generalized Social Reinforcement

A major source of generalized reinforcement is mediated by the behavior of other people. Social consequences such as praise, attention, status, and affection are powerful reinforcers for most people. Approval, attention, affection, and praise function as **generalized social reinforcement** for human behavior (Buckleitner, 2006; Kazdin & Klock, 1973; Kirby & Shields, 1972; Ruggles & LeBlanc, 1982; Vollmer & Hackenberg, 2001). In a classroom, a child's misbehavior may be followed regularly by attention, as when the teacher says, "What are you doing out of your seat?" The teacher may complain that the student is an unmanageable child. But the problem may concern the social reinforcement contingency between the student's misbehavior and the teacher attention.

Misbehavior usually captures the teacher's attention because it is highly intense (even aggressive) activity. Attention is reinforcing to most children because it necessarily precedes other types of reinforcement from people. When attention is contingent on misbehavior, then misbehavior increases. The solution to the problem is not to change the child, but to alter the contingency of reinforcement. One possibility is to ignore misbehavior (extinction) and attend to the child at any time other than when he or she is misbehaving (differential reinforcement of other behavior, or DRO). "Catch them being good" is the operative phrase.

The importance of generalized social reinforcement involving approval and affection is recognized in the following passage from Skinner (1953):

Another person is likely to reinforce only that part of one's behavior of which he approves, and any sign of his approval therefore becomes reinforcing in its own right. Behavior which evokes a smile or the verbal response "That's right" or "Good" or any other commendation is strengthened. We use this generalized reinforcer to establish and shape the behavior of others, particularly in education. For example, we teach both children and adults to speak correctly by saying "That's right" when appropriate behavior is emitted.

A still stronger generalized reinforcer is affection. It may be especially connected with sexual contact as an unconditioned reinforcer but when anyone who shows affection supplies other kinds of reinforcement as well, the effect is generalized.

It is difficult to define, observe, and measure attention, approval, and affection. They are not things but aspects of the behavior of others. Their subtle physical dimensions present difficulties not only for the scientist who must study them but also for the individual who is reinforced by them. If we do not easily see that someone is paying attention or that he approves or is affectionate, our behavior will not be consistently reinforced. It may therefore be weak, may tend to occur at the wrong time, and so on. We do not "know what to do to get attention or affection or when to do it." The child struggling for attention, the lover for a sign of affection, and the artist for professional approval show the persevering behavior which . . . results from only intermittent reinforcement.

(pp. 78–79)

Skinner goes on to discuss the submissiveness of others as generalized reinforcement (see also Patterson, 1982, 2002). In an aggressive episode, two people use threats and possibly physical attack to control each other's behavior. Eventually, one of the combatants gives up, and this submissive behavior serves as reinforcement for the aggressive behavior of the other person. Giving up the argument often results in cessation of the attack by the aggressor, and this is reinforcement for the submissive behavior displayed by the other. Unfortunately, the contingencies of aggression and submission arrange for an indefinite escalation of conflict, which may inadvertently result in serious harm that is legally judged as assault or murder.

The contingencies of aggression may account for many instances of abuse involving children, spouses, the elderly, and individuals incarcerated in prisons and mental hospitals. To the extent that these people are dependent on the benevolence of their parents, spouses, or caretakers, they must give in to the demands of their keepers. Consider a woman who is unemployed, has few friends, and is married to a man who physically assaults her. When her husband becomes aggressive, she has little recourse other than submission. If she calls the police or tells a neighbor, she risks losing her home and income, and she may have learned that her husband will only become more angry. For these reasons, the husband's aggressive behavior is shaped to more extreme levels.

Occasionally, victims develop an emotional attachment to the people who mistreat them, sometimes called the Stockholm syndrome. This kind of affectionate behavior may be shaped as part of the aggressive episode. The contingencies could involve negative reinforcement, as when the aggressor's attack is reduced or removed by signs of affection from the victim. After some exposure to these contingencies, victims may even claim to love their abusers.

There are several steps that may be taken to reduce the incidence of victim abuse in our society. One solution involves the issue of control and countercontrol. To prevent abusive control, the victim must be able to arrange consequences that deter the actions of the aggressor. This *countercontrol* by victims is established when society provides agencies or individuals who monitor abusers and take action on behalf of the victims. Countercontrol may also involve passing laws to protect the rights of persons who are in highly dependent situations. Another possibility is to teach alternative behavior in terms of negotiation and conflict resolution. Finally, a society that supports aggression for entertainment in sports, television, and movies should not be surprised at having high levels of violence in daily life.

FIG. 10.7 Token reinforcement and chimpanzee behavior. Reprinted with permission from Yerkes Regional Primate Research Center, Emory University.

Tokens, Money, and Generalized Reinforcement

Other conditioned reinforcers are economic in the sense of being exchangeable for goods and services. Awards, prizes, and scholarships support an enormous range of human activity. Perhaps the most important source of economic reinforcement is money. One way to understand the reinforcing effects of money is to view it as a type of token (coins or bills), exchangeable at a later time for a variety of goods and services.

Token reinforcement has been demonstrated in chimpanzees (Figure 10.7; see also Cowles, 1937). Chimpanzees (*Pan troglodytes*) were trained to exchange poker chips for raisins. After tokens and fruit were paired, the animals learned to select one of several patterns to get poker chips that were later exchanged for raisins. The animals collected several tokens and went to another room, where they inserted the chips in a vending machine for raisins. Because the discriminative operant (pattern selection) was maintained, the chips were by definition conditioned reinforcers.

Another study (Wolfe, 1936) also showed that chimpanzees

would tolerate a delay between getting a token and exchanging it for food. The animals earned white chips, which could be inserted into a vending machine that immediately delivered grapes. Inserting the chip into the machine was shaped by successive approximation. The experimenter placed a token partway in the vending slot, and any push by the chimpanzee caused the chip to drop—resulting in a grape. This procedure continued until the animals started retrieving the chips and inserting them in the slot. Following this training, the animals were taught to pull a lever to get chips. At this point, access to the vending machine was delayed but the chimpanzees continued to work for tokens. Some animals even began saving their tokens much like people save money. When delays occurred after the chimpanzees had inserted the tokens into the vending machine, the reinforcing effectiveness of the tokens declined (the delay to reinforcement was increased, hence the delay-reduction hypothesis was supported). This suggests that the token bridged the interval between earning and spending.

Kelleher (1956, 1958) trained chimpanzees to press a telephone key for poker chips (token) on fixed-ratio (FR) schedules of reinforcement. In addition to varying the FR size, Kelleher also varied the number of poker chips collected before it was possible to exchange them for food. The results for FR schedules of token reinforcement were comparable to those obtained with food reinforcement, showing high stable rates of response. The only notable difference between tokens and food was the occurrence of prolonged pauses at the beginning of sessions with higher FR values for token reinforcement.

Sousa and Matsuzawa (2001) explored the effectiveness of token reinforcement in maintaining chimpanzees' performance on discrimination tasks, and studied the "saving" behavior of the animals. One experiment involved token reinforcement for a matching-to-sample task in which the tokens were exchanged for food by three adult female chimpanzees. Subjects' performances were maintained at constant high levels of accuracy, suggesting that the tokens were almost equivalent to food reinforcement. The results also showed the emergence of saving behavior. Chimpanzees spontaneously saved the tokens during the matching-to-sample task before exchanging them for food. The chimpanzees also learned a new symbolic discrimination task with token reinforcement. During this learning process a rarely reported phenomenon emerged—one of the subjects showed symmetry, a form of stimulus equivalence (see Chapter 12 for more on stimulus equivalence; see Bronsnan, 2005, for tokens and bartering in chimpanzees).

For people, money is a form of token reinforcement that maintains an enormous diversity and amount of behavior. A major difference between the chimpanzees' tokens and money is that money is exchangeable for many different reinforcers. For this reason, money is a *generalized conditioned reinforcer*. Most behavioral experiments involving humans have used money as reinforcement. Money is relatively independent of momentary deprivation, is easily quantified, and is exchangeable for numerous goods and services outside of the laboratory.

Schedules of monetary reinforcement have been used to assess matching (see Chapter 9) and delay reduction with humans. Belke, Pierce, and Powell (1989) created a human-operant chamber, and people were required to pick up tokens from a dispenser and exchange them for 25¢ apiece. At first, a single token was exchanged for 25¢, then two tokens for 50¢, and then four tokens for $1. By extending the delay between earning and exchanging tokens, subjects learned to collect up to 40 tokens before trading them for $10.

In this experiment, there were no instructions and pressing left or right keys was shaped by monetary reinforcement. Various reinforcement schedules were then programmed to test matching, maximizing, and delay-reduction accounts of human choice and preference. Human performance on monetary schedules of reinforcement was better described by matching and maximizing models than by the delay-reduction equation. Relative rate of monetary reinforcement was the most important determinant of behavior in this situation (see Jackson & Hackenberg, 1996, on tokens used as substitutes for food with pigeons).

The applied advantage of money and tokens is that they are tangible objects that are observed easily, and their exchange value can be specified precisely. For this reason, a large amount of research has been conducted on experimental communities in which economic reinforcement is scheduled for effective patterns of behavior.

ON THE APPLIED SIDE: The token economy

One of the most important applications of behavior analysis is based on using tokens as generalized conditioned reinforcement. Tokens are arbitrary items like poker chips, tickets, coins, checkmarks in a daily log, and stars or happy-face symbols given to students. To establish these objects as reinforcement, the applied researcher has a person exchange tokens for a variety of backup reinforcers. A child may exchange five stars for a period of free play, a selection of toys, access to drawing materials, or an opportunity to use a Lego™ set.

A **token economy** is a set of contingencies or a system based on token (conditioned) reinforcement. That is, the contingencies specify when, and under what conditions, particular forms of behavior are reinforced with tokens. It is an economy in the sense that the tokens may be exchanged for goods and services, much like money is in our economy. This exchange of tokens for a variety of backup reinforcers ensures that the tokens become conditioned reinforcers.

Systems of token reinforcement have been used to improve the behavior of psychiatric patients (Ayllon & Azrin, 1968), juvenile delinquents (Fixsen, Phillips, Phillips, & Wolf, 1976), pupils in remedial classrooms (Breyer & Allen, 1975), normal children in the home (Alvord & Cheney, 1994), and medical patients who must follow a plan of treatment (Carton & Schweitzer, 1996; Dapcich-Miura, & Hovell, 1979). Token economies also have been designed for alcoholics, drug addicts, prisoners, nursing-home residents, and retarded persons (see Kazdin, 1977).

One of the first token systems was designed for psychiatric patients who lived in a large mental hospital. Schaefer and Martin (1966) attempted to modify the behavior of 40 female patients who were diagnosed as long-term schizophrenics. A general characteristic of these women was that they seemed disinterested in the activities and happenings on the ward. Additionally, many of the women showed little interest in personal hygiene (i.e., they showed a low probability for washing, grooming, brushing teeth, and so on). In general, Schaefer and Martin referred to this class of behavior as apathetic and designed a token system to increase social and physical involvement by these patients.

The women were randomly assigned to a treatment or control group. Women in the control group received tokens no matter what they did (i.e., noncontingent reinforcement). Patients in the contingent reinforcement group obtained tokens that could be traded for a variety of privileges and luxuries. Tokens were earned for specific classes of behavior. These response classes were personal hygiene, job performance, and social interaction. For example, a patient earned tokens when she spoke pleasantly to others during group therapy. A social response like "Good morning, how are you?" resulted in a ward attendant giving her a token and praising her effort. Other responses that were reinforced included personal hygiene, like attractive use of cosmetics, showering, and generally maintaining a well-groomed appearance. Finally, tokens were earned for specified jobs such as wiping tables and vacuuming carpets and furniture.

Notice that the reinforcement system encouraged behavior that was incompatible with the label "apathetic." A person who is socially responsive, well groomed, and who carries out daily jobs is usually described as being involved with life. To implement the program, general response classes such as personal hygiene had to be specified and instances of each class, such as brushing teeth or combing hair, had to be defined. Once the behavior was well defined, ward staff were trained to identify positive instances and deliver tokens for appropriate responses.

Over a 3-month period of the study, the ward staff counted instances of involved and apathetic behavior. Responses in each class of behavior—hygiene, social interaction, and work—increased for women in the contingent-token system, but not for patients who were simply given the tokens.

Responses that were successful in the token economy apparently were also effective outside the hospital. Only 14% of the patients who were discharged from the token system returned to the hospital, and this compared favorably with an average return rate of 28%.

Although Schaefer and Martin (1966) successfully maintained behavioral gains after patients were discharged, not all token systems are equally effective (see Kazdin, 1983, for a review). Programs that teach social and life skills have lower return rates than those that do not. This presumably occurs because patients taught these skills can take better care of themselves and interact more appropriately with others. Of course, these operants are valued by members of the social community who reinforce and thereby maintain this behavior.

Token economies that gradually introduce the patient to the world outside the hospital also maintain behavior better than those programs with abrupt transitions from hospital to home. A patient on a token-economy ward may successively earn day passes, overnight stays, weekend release, discharge to a group home, and eventually a return to normal living. This gradual transition to everyday life has two major effects. Contrived reinforcement on the token system is slowly reduced or faded and, at the same time, natural consequences outside of the hospital are contacted. Second, the positive responses of patients are shifted from the relatively dense schedules of reinforcement provided by the token system to the more intermittent reinforcement of the ordinary environment. The effectiveness of token systems in managing transitions to settings outside the institution is a topic of considerable ongoing debate (Paul, 2006; Wakefield, 2006).

Because of increasing budget constraints for many mental hospitals in the United States, there has been an alarming increase in the rapid discharge of psychiatric patients. Many of these individuals have been relegated to the ranks of the poor and homeless. According to our analysis of the token economy, this kind of policy is shortsighted. Programs that teach a range of useful skills and that allow for successful entry into work and community settings are more humane and economically productive in the long run. Generally, programs of behavior management and change offer alternative solutions for many social problems (Glenwick & Jason, 1980).

ADVANCED SECTION: Quantification and delay reduction

Going back to businessperson phoning Delta and American Airlines and how long it takes to get placed on hold at the two airlines (section on Delay Reduction and Conditioned Reinforcement), the average time to be placed on hold at both airlines is 120 s. If the person is dialing back and forth between Delta and American, the average time to get through is 120 s divided by the two choices, or 60 s (i.e., 120/2 = 60). This is because the initial-link schedules are simultaneously available and are both timing out.

Next, consider how long it takes to contact an agent once placed on hold at one or the other airlines. In this example, the person is stuck on hold at one airline and can no longer dial the other company. The average time in the terminal links of the two chains is 30 s for Delta plus 90 s for American divided by the two links, or 60 s [i.e., (30 + 90)/2 = 60]. That is, over many bookings the person has sometimes waited 90 s for an American agent and at other times 30 s for a Delta agent. On average, the length of time spent waiting on hold is 60 s.

Based on the average times in the initial and terminal links (60 s + 60 s), the overall average total time, T, to book a flight is 120 s or 2 min. Given that it takes an average of $T = 120$ s to book a flight, how much will the businessperson prefer booking at Delta relative to American Airlines? Recall that it takes an average of 30 s to contact an agent at Delta and 90 s at American, after being placed on hold. This terminal-link time is represented as $t_{2 \text{ DELTA}} = 30$ s, and $t_{2 \text{ AMERICAN}} = 90$ s.

Of the average total time, 90 s has elapsed when the person is placed on hold at Delta ($T - t_{2 \text{ DELTA}} = 120 - 30 = 90$ s). That is, the reduction in delay to reinforcement (booking a flight) is 90 s at Delta. The delay reduction at American is 30 seconds ($T - t_{2 \text{ AMERICAN}} = 120 - 90 = 30$ s).

The greater the delay reduction at Delta relative to American, the more the conditioned reinforcement value of Delta compared with American. This relation may be expressed as:

$$\frac{R_{\text{DELTA}}}{R_{\text{DELTA}} + R_{\text{AMERICAN}}} = \frac{\tilde{T} - t_{2\,\text{DELTA}}}{(T - t_{2\,\text{DELTA}}) - (T - t_{2\,\text{AMERICAN}})}$$

$$= \frac{120 - 30}{(120 - 30) + (120 - 90)}$$

$$= \frac{90}{90 + 30}$$

$$= 0.75$$

The R values represent responses or, in this example, the number of calls to Delta (R_{DELTA}) and American (R_{AMERICAN}), respectively. The relative number of calls made to Delta is equal to the relative reduction in time to book a flight (reinforcement). This time is calculated as the proportion of delay reduction at Delta to the total delay reduction. According to the calculation, 0.75 or 75% of the businessperson's calls will be directed to Delta Airlines.

Experimental Test of Delay Reduction

Edmund Fantino (Figure 10.8), a professor of psychology at the University of California, San Diego, first proposed and tested the delay-reduction analysis of conditioned reinforcement. He was trained in operant conditioning at Harvard University, where he worked in B. F. Skinner's laboratory and graduated with a PhD in 1964. After a brief stay at Yale University, he joined the faculty at San Diego and continued his research on the experimental analysis of choice. Fantino recounts his discovery of the delay-reduction hypothesis in the following passage:

> One of my first experiments at [San Diego], on choice behavior, was producing strange but consistent results in each of four pigeons. I was losing sleep over these results until one morning I awoke with the following hypothesis: Choice responses don't match rates of reinforcement of the outcomes but instead match the relative reduction in delay to reinforcement associated with these outcomes. This delay-reduction hypothesis then served to guide scores of experiments assessing its generality and limitations in areas such as choice, conditioned reinforcement, elicited responding, self-control, observing and experimental analogs of foraging decisions.
>
> (E. Fantino, personal communication, 1992)

Fantino (1969a) proposed a general equation for preference on a concurrent-chain schedule that was based on delay reduction. Equation (10.1) is a generalized statement of the formula used to calculate preference for Delta and American:

$$\frac{R_{\text{L}}}{R_{\text{L}} + R_{\text{R}}} = \frac{T - t_{2}}{(T - t_{2\text{L}}) + (T - t_{2\text{R}})} \tag{10.1}$$

FIG. 10.8 Edmund Fantino. Reprinted with permission.

In this equation, R_{L} and R_{R} represent the rate of response on the left and right initial links of a concurrent-chain schedule of reinforcement. The symbol T is the average time to reinforcement (see the airlines example for calculation). The time required in the left and right terminal links is represented by t_{2L} and t_{2R} in the equation. The equation states that relative rate of response is a function of relative reduction in time to unconditioned reinforcement.

The delay-reduction equation emphasizes conditioned reinforcement as a major determinant of choice. This is because the onset of the terminal-link S^D for each chain is correlated with a reduction in time to unconditioned reinforcement. This reduction is $T - t_{2L}$ for the left alternative and $T - t_{2R}$ for the right. Recall that the greater the reduction in time to unconditioned reinforcement signaled by a stimulus, the greater the conditioned-reinforcement value of that stimulus. The delay-reduction equation is a mathematical expression of this idea.

Fantino (1969a) designed an experiment to test the delay-reduction equation. The subjects were six pigeons who responded for food on concurrent-chain schedules of reinforcement. In this experiment, the terminal links were always set at $t_{2L} = 30$ s and $t_{2R} = 90$ s. Notice that for the left alternative the relative rate of unconditioned reinforcement is 0.75, and according to the matching law the birds should spend 75% of their time on the left key. The situation becomes more complex when initial-link schedules are varied. Fantino's experiment involved adding initial links to the VI 30-s and VI 90-s schedules. That is, he investigated concurrent-chain schedules with 30- and 90-s terminal links. The schedules in the initial links were always the same for both alternatives, but the values of these schedules were varied over the course of the experiment. For example, in one condition the initial links were VI 30 s on the left and VI 30 s on the right. In another condition, the initial-link schedules were both VI 600 s. Other initial-link values between these two extremes were also investigated. The important question is what happens to the pigeons' preference for the shorter (VI 30 s) terminal link as time is increased in the first link of the chains.

Figure 10.9 shows the proportion of responses predicted by Equation (10.1) for the shorter (VI 30 s) terminal link as time is added equally to the initial links of the concurrent-chain schedule. When the schedules were chain VI 30 s VI 30 s on the left and chain VI 30 s VI 90 s on the right, the birds responded almost exclusively to the left alternative. When the chains were VI 120 s VI 30 s on the left and VI 120 s VI 90 s on the right, the pigeons showed response distributions close to matching (0.75 responses on the left). Finally, when time in the initial links was greatly increased to VI 600 s, the birds showed no preference for either alternative. As you can see in Figure 10.9, these results are in accord with the declining preference predicted by the delay-reduction equation.

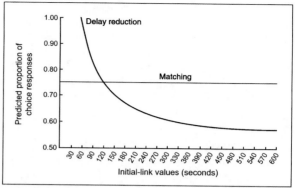

FIG. 10.9 Proportion of responses predicted by the delay-reduction equation for the shorter (VI 30 s) terminal link as time is added equally to the initial links of the concurrent-chain schedule. Adapted from "Conditioned Reinforcement, Choice, and the Psychological Distance to Reward," by E. Fantino, 1969, *Journal of the Experimental Analysis of Behaviour, 12,* 723–730. Copyright 1969 held by the Society for the Experimental Analysis of Behavior, Inc. Adapted with permission.

CHAPTER SUMMARY

This chapter introduced the concept of conditioned reinforcement and some research to demonstrate the variables that determine its effectiveness. There are few unconditioned reinforcers, but when these biologically relevant events are correlated with previously ineffective stmuli, from light flashes to poker chips, these stimuli become capable of reinforcing behavior. Money is perhaps the most common and effective generalized conditioned reinforcer in human culture.

In order to demonstrate how conditioned reinforcers are studied we described the use of chain schedules. Chain schedules involve stimuli that have more than one function (multiple functions). The discriminative stimulus sets the occasion for a response that can sometimes be reinforced and a chain schedule shows that the S^D also may function as a conditioned reinforcer. The nearness in time of the conditioned stimulus to the unconditioned reinforcer is a critical factor in the delay-reduction account of conditioned reinforcement. Brain areas (amygdala and nucleus accumbens) and neurochemicals (dopamine) participate in the regulation of behavior by contingencies of conditioned reinforcement. Organisms select the stimulus in a concurrent-chain procedure that reduces the time to reinforcement. In addition, we saw that using backward chaining to teach skills (building the chain backwards from the terminal reinforcer) is a very effective procedure. Finally, the text described the systematic use of conditioned reinforcers in the form of tokens in primates, including humans. Token systems are microexamples of money economies and these systems help to manage problems of human behavior in a variety of institutional settings.

Key Words

Backward chaining
Chain schedule of
    reinforcement
Concurrent-chain schedule
Conditioned reinforcement
Conditioned reinforcer
Delay-reduction hypothesis
Discriminative-stimulus
    account of conditioned
    reinforcement

Established-response method
Generalized conditioned
    reinforcer
Generalized social
    reinforcement
Heterogeneous chain schedule
Homogeneous chain schedule
Mixed schedule of
    reinforcement

New-response method
Observing response
S–S account of conditioned
    reinforcement
Tandem schedule
Token economy
Unconditioned reinforcer

Correspondence Relations: Imitation and Rule-Governed Behavior

11

- Find out about contingencies of correspondence and human behavior.
- Learn about spontaneous imitation in natural settings and the laboratory.
- Investigate human imitation and mirror neurons.
- Inquire about generalized imitation and observational learning.
- Distinguish between rule-governed and contingency-shaped behavior.
- Learn about instructions and sensitivity of behavior to contingencies.

People often do what others do. A child who observes his brother raid the cookie jar may engage in similar behavior—at least until they are both caught by their parent. Adults sometimes watch their teenagers' dancing and repeat aspects of these performances at a neighborhood party. Both of these examples involve **correspondence relations** between the demonstrated behavior and the replicated performance. Thus, correspondence involves a special type of stimulus control where the discriminative stimulus is behavior of an individual. In the case of social modeling, we may say that the behavior of one person sets the occasion for an equivalent response by the other.

There are other correspondence relations established by our culture. People look for and reinforce the correspondence between saying and doing (e.g., Lovaas, 1961; Matthews, Shimoff, & Catania, 1987; Paniagua & Baer, 1982; Risley & Hart, 1968; also see Lattal & Doepke, 2001, on correspondence as complex conditional discrimination). When a child promises to clean her room and actually does so, parents are pleased; failure to follow through on the promise may make the parents angry. A large part of socialization involves arranging social reinforcement for correspondence between what is said and what is done (see Luciano, Herruzo, & Barnes-Holmes, 2001, on training generalized correspondence in children).

By the time a person is an adult, people expect consistency between spoken words and later performance. A minister who preaches moral conduct and lives a moral life is valued; when moral words and moral deeds do not match, people become upset and act to correct the inconsistency. In such instances, what is said does not correspond adequately with what is done. Cognitive dissonance theory (Festinger, 1957; Gerard, 1994) predicted that people who were confronted with inconsistency (dissonance) between saying and doing would escape from it (dissonance reduction), insuring that attitudes matched behavior. Considerable research has supported this prediction. Behavior analysis helps to explain why people engage in dissonance reduction—pointing to the social contingencies that punish low correspondence between words and actions.

Consistency also is important when people report on private internal events or happenings. In these cases, the correspondence is between the internal stimulation of the body, behavior, and the report. The social community establishes an accurate description of private stimulation (see "Report

241

of Feelings" in Chapter 1). Successful training of such reports involves reinforcing self-descriptive statements such as "I feel angry" or "I am sick" in the presence of presumed private events. Because public cues and private events usually go together, people use external cues from behavior to train correspondence between reports and internal stimulation (see Bem, 1972; see also "FOCUS ON: Reports of Internal Events by Pigeons" in Chapter 12). When a child is taught about being hurt, parents use crying, holding the wounded area, and physical damage to infer that she is in pain. Because the child's behavior and private stimulation of pain are well correlated, she eventually reports, "I am hurt" or other internal happenings solely on the basis of the private stimulation. The private event (painful stimulation) comes to function as a discriminative stimulus for self-descriptive reports.

A problem of privacy also is faced when the community must establish consistency between private social acts and the report of those actions. In this case, correspondence is between doing and saying (Baer & Detrich, 1990; Deacon & Konarski, 1987; Lubinski & Thompson, 1987). During socialization children are asked to report on their behavior in a variety of situations. A child who returns her empty plate to the kitchen may be asked if she ate her carrots. The response "Yes, I ate every last one" can be verified and reinforced for accuracy (see Paniagua, 1989, on lying in children as "do-then-report" correspondence).

This repertoire of doing and saying sometimes has serious implications in adult life. When an employee describes sexual harassment in the workplace, there is some attempt to check on the correspondence between what is said and the actual happenings. This monitoring of doing and saying by the community is necessary to maintain accuracy. The harassed person is questioned for explicit details, the accused is asked to give his or her story, and accounts by other people are used to ensure exactness of the reported events. Based on this inquiry, the community ensures reliable reports by victims and the punishment of sexual misconduct. Many aspects of legal trials involve procedures to check on and maintain correspondence between actions and recall.

There is evidence that expressing one's feelings, saying and doing, and recalling actions and events are aspects of verbal behavior (Skinner, 1957). One important function of verbal behavior involves formulating and following rules, maxims, or instructions (Skinner, 1969). Rules may be analyzed as verbal stimuli that alter the responses of a listener. A doctor may state that, "too much cholesterol increases the risk of heart attack," and the patient may follow this advice by reducing or eliminating foods with high cholesterol. Advice and other instructions regulate behavior because such rules usually guide effective action (i.e., health improves by selecting low-cholesterol foods).

Based on personal experiences, people often describe contingencies (formulate rules) as speakers and then follow them as listeners (rule-governed). Social psychologists have extensively studied the impact of self-rules on thinking and actions but have relied on cognitive explanations (e.g., attribution theory) of this complex behavior (Kunkel, 1997). Behavior analysts insist that following rules, even self-rules, is behavior maintained by contingencies of reinforcement (Galizio, 1979). At the end of this chapter, we analyze the listener's actions as rule-governed behavior. The speaker's behavior in stating rules or describing contingencies is examined as verbal behavior in the next chapter of this book (see Chapter 12).

Initially, we describe the process of observational learning as a correspondence relation. Learning by observation involves doing what others do, in which the performance of an observer or learner is regulated by the actions of a model (correspondence). Although modeling can produce a variety of effects (e.g., social facilitation, stimulus enhancement, and so on), **imitation** requires the learner to produce a novel response that could only occur by observing a model emit a similar response (Thorpe, 1963). This kind of social learning may arise from an innate capacity for spontaneous imitation from an early age (see "FOCUS ON: Behavioral Neuroscience, Mirror Neurons, and Imitation" in this chapter). More complex forms of observational learning involve contingencies that appear to build on this basic repertoire.

CORRESPONDENCE AND OBSERVATIONAL LEARNING

Although doing what others do involves a large amount of social learning, this type of correspondence may have a biological basis. At the beginning of the 20th century, psychologists suggested that social organisms have an innate tendency to imitate the actions they see others perform (Baldwin, 1906; James, 1890; McDougall, 1908; Morgan, 1894). This assumption was largely based on observations that young infants imitate the actions of an adult. McDougall (1908) indicated that, as early as 4 months of age, his child would stick out his tongue when an adult did the same.

Of course, 4-month-old infants already have a considerable history of interaction with their parents and the observed behavior may simply be attributable to social conditioning. That is, people may smile and laugh when a young child imitates some adult movement. Presumably, these social consequences strengthen imitation by the child. Although social conditioning is a possibility, recent research with newborn infants and animals suggests that innate or spontaneous imitation occurs without reinforcement. Furthermore, specialized neurons in the brains of primates seem to allow for more complex forms of imitation and observational learning (see "FOCUS ON: Behavioral Neuroscience, Mirror Neurons, and Imitation" in this chapter).

Spontaneous Imitation in Animals and Humans

Innate or **spontaneous imitation** is based on evolution and natural selection (a characteristic of the species) rather than experiences during the lifetime of the individual. That is, imitation of others may be an important form of adaptive behavior (Davis, 1973; Hutchinson, 1981; Millard, 1979; Porter, 1910; Thorpe, 1963). This behavior may range from a few instinctive actions to a more generalized set of responses, depending on the species. In addition, imitation may occur only when the model is present or it may be delayed for some time after the model has been removed. Such **delayed imitation** is often taken as a more complex form since it involves remembering the modeled stimulus, rather than direct stimulus control (see Courage & Howe, 2002, pp. 257–259, on cognitive development and delayed imitation).

There are ethnological reports of imitation by animals and birds (e.g., Alcock, 1969; Fisher & Hinde, 1949; Kawai, 1965). Fisher and Hinde (1949) described how birds in a southern English village obtained milk by spearing the foil tops of bottles left on doorsteps. Eventually, this behavior spread to several species of birds throughout England, Wales, Scotland, and Ireland. It stretches the imagination to suppose that so many birds learned the same response on their own. One conclusion is that the behavior was acquired and transmitted through observation and imitation (see also Dawson & Foss, 1965, for imitation of removal of container caps by budgerigars).

Japanese monkeys also seem to pass on novel behavior by observational learning. A report by Kawai (1965) describes the social transmission of an innovative way of feeding. The researchers spread grains of wheat on a sandy beach where the troop often visited. Each monkey picked the grains from the sand and ate them one at a time. Then a young monkey learned to separate the sand from the wheat more efficiently by tossing a handful of mixture into the water. When this happened, the sand sank to the bottom and the wheat floated to the top. Using this technique, the monkey obtained more wheat with less effort. Other members of the troop observed this behavior and were soon imitating this new method of feeding. Kawai indicated that observational learning transmitted many other novel behaviors, including washing the sand off sweet potatoes and swimming in the ocean (see Ball, 1938, and Breuggeman, 1973, for imitation by rhesus monkeys; Bering, Bjorklund, & Ragan, 2000, for delayed imitation by rhesus monkeys and orangutans; and Custance, Whiten, Sambrook, & Galdikas, 2001, for a failure to observe imitation in the orangutans).

Although it seems likely that some birds, monkeys, and a few other species (e.g., African Gray parrots: Moore, 1992; dolphins: Tayler & Saayman, 1973; infant rhesus macaques: Ferrari, Visalberghi, Pauker, Fogassi, Ruggiero, & Suomi, 2006) can imitate the novel responses of a model, these naturalistic studies are not sufficient to establish spontaneous imitation or to rule out alternative processes like social facilitation (Zajonc, 1965), stimulus enhancement, or copying (Galef, 1988, pp. 15–16; Galef, 1990; see Zentall, 2006, for a review). Social animals have many experiences that may contribute to doing what others do. Therefore, it is not possible to be sure that the imitation was spontaneous (based on species history) rather than acquired (based on social learning). Only laboratory experiments can distinguish between acquired and spontaneous imitation.

Imitation in the Laboratory

Thorndike (1911) conducted the earliest experiment on spontaneous imitation. The experiment involved getting out of a puzzle box by observing the successful performance of others. A well-trained cat was placed in the box and an inexperienced cat was allowed to watch the performance from an adjacent cage. The experiment was a dismal failure. The cat that observed the successful performance was no better at getting out of the box than a naïve animal. There was no improvement in learning regardless of the number of observational trials. Thorndike obtained similar negative results with chicks, dogs, and monkeys and concluded that animals cannot learn by observation.

This conclusion stalled experiments on animal imitation for some time. Then Herbert and Harsh (1944) reported that cats could learn to solve manipulative problems by observation if they observe mistakes as well as successful performances. Cats that observed both mistakes and correct responses by a model did better at problems than cats that only watched skillful performance. When many alternative responses are available, seeing what does and does not work is necessary for observational learning (see Biederman & Vanayan, 1988, for a similar effect with pigeons).

About this same time, Warden and associates (Warden, Fjeld, & Koch, 1940; Warden & Jackson, 1935) showed imitation in rhesus monkeys. They trained monkeys by reinforcement to solve puzzles that opened doors to reveal hidden raisins. When this performance was well established, a naïve monkey watched a trained animal obtain raisins. Observation of the model produced instantaneous solutions on 76% of the test trials. However, only the first instance of imitation could be described as spontaneous since the discovery of the raisin would reinforce this behavior and increase its likelihood.

Spontaneous and delayed imitation in pigeons

In fact, it is difficult to find an experiment that reliably demonstrates spontaneous imitation. This is because reinforcement of the observer's behavior always confounds the results. Based on this realization, Robert Epstein (Figure 11.1) designed an experiment to show spontaneous imitation with pigeons (Epstein, 1984). The experimental procedures ensured that the observer was naïve, and there were no programmed sources of reinforcement for imitative responses.

Figure 11.2 shows the subjects and apparatus that Epstein used. Some birds served as models, and others were observers. Observers had never been in a laboratory experiment and none had ever eaten from a laboratory feeder. The model and observer pigeons could see one another through a clear partition that separated the chamber into two compartments, left and right. Each side had exactly the same configuration. Models were

FIG. 11.1   Robert Epstein. Published with permission.

always placed in the left side of the chamber, where a feeder was filled with food. Observers were placed in the right side of the chamber, where the feeder never contained food. The modeled performance in various conditions was pecking or pushing a ball, pulling on a rope, or pecking a key. All models were trained by operant conditioning to emit the requisite performance for food reinforcement.

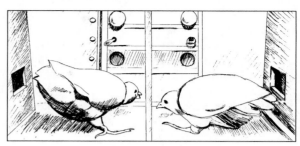

FIG. 11.2   Subjects and apparatus used by Robert Epstein to study spontaneous imitation by pigeons. Adapted from Epstein (1984).

There were five conditions in the first experiment. During adaptation, a naïve-observer bird was placed in the right side of the chamber. One object (a ping-pong ball, rope, or key) was situated in the left compartment but not available to the bird in the right chamber. After three sessions, the same object was added to the right side and the naïve bird was placed alone in the chamber for three sessions of baseline. Next, the object was removed from the right chamber and the model bird was added. During exposure and adaptation to the model, the model engaged in the reinforced performance of pecking the ball, pulling the rope, or pecking the key, and the observer was exposed to this performance without the object for another three sessions. Following this phase, Epstein conducted a test for model-present imitation; he added the object to the observer's chamber while the model continued to demonstrate the performance. If the observer emitted the designated response at a higher rate than during baseline, this was evidence of direct spontaneous imitation. Finally, Epstein designed a test for model-absent imitation. The object remained present but the model was removed. If the observer responded to the object at a higher level than baseline, this was evidence of delayed spontaneous imitation.

Of the four observer pigeons tested, all showed more responses (key, ball, or rope) with the model present than during baseline. Two of the birds demonstrated strong spontaneous imitation, but the effect was weaker for the other two pigeons. Birds that strongly imitated the model were found to continue this imitation even when the model was removed (i.e., model-absent imitation). The data suggested that delayed spontaneous imitation can occur in laboratory pigeons, but the results were inconsistent over subjects.

Epstein (1984) ran a second experiment that specifically focused on delayed spontaneous imitation. In this experiment, he used only "peck the ball" as the imitative response. The same conditions were used as in the first experiment, but the model-present phase was omitted. Thus, the birds never were able to match their responses immediately to those of the model. Results for three new birds were clear. In each case, pecking the ball was higher after exposure to and removal of the model than during baseline. Spontaneous imitation occurred even after 24 h had elapsed between watching the model and the test for imitation.

Analysis of Epstein's experiments

These experiments on direct and delayed spontaneous imitation are important. Experimental procedures ensured that the occurrence of imitation was not attributable to previous experience or current reinforcement. It therefore appears that spontaneous imitation is a real effect and is a form of phylogenetic behavior. That is, imitative behavior occurs because it has been important to the survival and reproduction of the species (i.e., contingencies of survival). In other words, organisms that imitated others were more likely to find food, avoid predators, and eventually produce offspring.

The phylogenetic basis of spontaneous imitation is a reasonable hypothesis. However, as Epstein notes, at least three aspects of the experiments suggest that some environmental experience is also necessary. The birds were raised in a colony and may have had social interactions that contributed to imitative performance. Pigeons who are isolated from birth may show smaller effects of exposure to a model (May & Dorr, 1968). In addition, the effects of food reinforcement may have contributed to the results. Although observers were never directly reinforced with food for imitation, they did see the models eat from the feeder. In fact, Epstein remarked that occasionally the naïve bird would thrust its head into the feeder hole when the model did, even though it did not receive food. Finally, only one object was present in the right and left sides of the chamber. If three objects were available, would the observer peck or pull the one the model did, without training? Each of these aspects opposes a strong conclusion about the biological basis of spontaneous imitation in Epstein's experiments (see Zentall, 2006, for a variety of alternative effects that are mistaken for imitation).

There are other results, however, that point to an evolutionary basis for such behavior. The fact that pigeons showed imitation after a substantial delay is noteworthy and deferred imitation also has been observed in Japanese quail (see also Dorrance & Zentall, 2001). In discrimination experiments, birds often have trouble remembering events delayed by a few seconds. However, the birds in Epstein's second experiment showed imitation 24 h after the model had pecked the ball. And Japanese quail imitated treadle responses up to 30 min after the model's demonstration. The extended retention of such behavior is in accord with a biological account, suggesting the preparedness of these animals to imitate what others have done.

The experimental research by Epstein (1984) on imitation and delayed imitation in pigeons remains controversial and imitation in rats is also in dispute (see Mitchel, Heyes, Gardner, & Dawson, 1999, for effects of odor; see Ray, Gardner, & Heyes, 2000, against odor cues; see Zentall, 2006, for review). Thus, Pear (2001, p. 96) argues on the basis of related research that stimulus enhancement, or pairing of a conspecific (member of a species) with the ping-pong ball, accounts for the apparent direct and delayed imitation by pigeons (recall, however, that Epstein used a ball, rope, and key). On the other hand, research using a two-action method of pecking or pressing a treadle supports Epstein's claim of spontaneous imitation by pigeons (Dorrance & Zentall, 2001; Kaiser, Zentall, & Galef, 1997; Zentall, Sutton, & Sherburne, 1996). Although there is no further research evidence of delayed imitation by pigeons, newer evidence indicates that pigeons can imitate a complex conditional discrimination (Dorrance, 2001), suggesting that delayed imitation is a possible interpretation of Epstein's results.

Spontaneous imitation by human infants

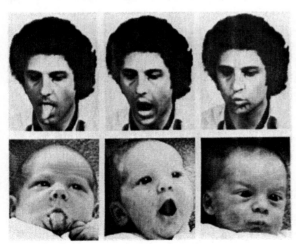

FIG. 11.3 Infants' facial gestures and modeled stimuli are shown. From Meltzoff and Moore (1977), reprinted with permission from AAAS.

There is evidence that spontaneous imitation occurs in human infants, almost from the moment of birth. Meltzoff and Moore (1977) were the first to report that 12- to 21-day-old infants can imitate the facial and hand movements of adult models. In these experiments, the imitative responses were tongue protrusion, mouth opening, lip protrusion, and sequential finger movement. The infants' facial gestures and modeled stimuli are illustrated in Figure 11.3.

Experiment 1 used three male and three female infants who ranged in age from 12 to 17 days. The experimenter presented a passive face for 90 s to the infant. Each infant was then shown four gestures (i.e., the modeled stimulus) in random order. The modeled stimulus was presented four times in a 15-s presentation period. An imitation-test period followed in which the experimenter resumed a passive face and the infant was monitored for imitative responses. Each new gesture was followed by 70 s of passive face.

The researchers made a videotape of the infants' behavior, and the segments were scored in random order by trained adult judges. For each segment, the judges were to order the four gestures from most likely to least likely in terms of imitation of the modeled stimulus. These judgments were collapsed to yes or no ratings of whether a particular gesture was the imitative response. In all cases, more yes judgments occurred when the gesture was imitative than when it was not.

Meltzoff and Moore (1977) designed a second experiment to correct some procedural problems with the first study. Six male and six female infants between 16 and 21 days old were used as subjects. The experiment began with the researcher inserting a pacifier into the infant's mouth and presenting a passive face for 30 s. A baseline period of 150 s followed in which the pacifier was removed, but the passive face continued to be presented. Next, the pacifier was reinserted in the infant's mouth and the researcher presented one of two gestures, mouth opening or lip protrusion. The modeled stimulus was presented until the infant had watched it for 15 s. The experimenter then stopped gesturing and resumed a passive face. At this point, the pacifier was removed and a 150-s response period or imitation test began, during which time the researcher maintained a passive face. Again, the pacifier was reinserted and the second gesture was presented in the same fashion.

The videotapes were scored in random order in terms of the frequency of tongue protrusion and mouth opening. Figure 11.4 shows the frequency of response during baseline and after exposure to the experimenter's gesture. When tongue protrusions were the modeled stimulus, the infant produced this response more frequently than during baseline. On the other hand, when mouth openings were the modeled stimulus, the infant frequently produced this response during the test period, but not tongue protrusions. These results suggest that babies are capable of spontaneous imitation of facial gestures (see Kuhl & Meltzoff, 1996, for imitation of vocal speech sounds).

In subsequent experiments, Meltzoff and Moore (1983) showed imitation of mouth opening and tongue protrusions in newborns that were 0.7–71 hours old. These results are in accord with Field, Woodson, Greenberg, and Cohen (1982), who reported imitation of mouth opening, mouth widening, and lip protrusion in infants who averaged 36 h in age (see also Jacobson, 1979). More recently, human neonates between a few hours to a few days old showed spontaneous imitation of finger movements (Nagy, Compagne, Orvos, Pal, Molnar, Janszky, et al., 2005) and auditory–oral matching of consonant sounds (early vocal imitation), behavior thought to be beyond newborn infants' capabilities (Chen, Striano, & Rakoczy, 2004). Notably, neonatal imitation has been

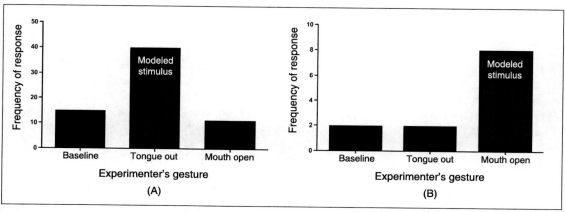

FIG. 11.4 Frequency of response during baseline and after exposure to the experimenter's gesture. In panel A the modeled stimulus is "tongue out" and the frequency response of "tongue out" responses by infants increases relative to baseline and the control response of "mouth open." When the modeled stimulus is "mouth open" (panel B), the frequency of "mouth open" responses by the infant increases relative to the control conditions. Adapted from Meltzoff and Moore (1977).

reported for chimpanzees (*Pan troglodytes*), suggesting that an imitative capacity at birth is not unique to *homo sapiens* (Bard, 2007).

Difficulties with infant imitation research

The results of Meltzoff and Moore's experiments remain controversial (for reviews, see Anisfeld, 1996; Bjorklund, 1987). Hayes and Watson (1981) were unable to produce infant imitation despite careful attempts to follow Meltzoff and Moore's (1977) procedures. In their second experiment, Hayes and Watson found that the pacifier could evoke mouth movements and that this, rather than the experimenter's presentation of the modeled gesture, may have produced the responses. If this is the case, infant imitation may simply be an artifact of the experimental procedures, although recent studies do not appear to have these problems (Chen et al., 2004; Nagy et al., 2005). Jacobson (1979) found that the imitative responses of infants could be elicited by nonspecific events. For example, tongue protrusion occurred when a pen was moved toward the infant's face (see Anisfeld, 1996, on infant behavior and innate releasers; also Provine, 1989, on fixed action patterns). And Jones (2006) found that an auditory stimulus (music) that substituted for the behavioral model increased tongue protrusions, indicating that these responses occur to "interesting distal stimuli."

Other problems concern measurement, restricted range of responses, and infant attention to the modeled stimulus. Meltzoff and Moore (1977) noted that infants' responses are not discrete or well formed each time they occur. This means that the response class is not clearly defined and it is therefore difficult to obtain a reliable measure. Because the response class is unclear, coders who observe the modeled gesture may "see" the imitative response more frequently than other response forms (see Ullstadius, 2000, on variability in judgment of infant imitation).

Additionally, there are few experimentally useful infant behaviors for imitation research (Meltzoff & Moore, 1983), and these responses may have several determinants. Thus, facial movements may be determined by general arousal, be elicited by nonspecific events, or be imitations of a model. Research on finger movements (Nagy et al., 2005) and auditory–vocal imitation of consonants (Chen et al., 2004) suggests that restricted range of behaviors may no longer be a serious problem. Finally, it is difficult to keep the infant focused on the model. Because of this, researchers wait until the infant is "ready" before presenting the modeled stimulus. If experimenters match the model stimulus to infants' behavior, it may be that they are generating correspondence as an artifact (see also Jones, 1996, for oral exploration as an artifact). In other words, the experimenter accidentally imitates the infant instead of the infant imitating the experimenter's gesture (Field et al., 1982; Hayes & Watson, 1981; Jacobson, 1979).

Delayed imitation by human infants

In 1988, Meltzoff reported on delayed imitation in 14-month-old infants (Meltzoff, 1988b). These infants were exposed to six modeled actions using different objects (e.g., an adult bending over and touching his or her head to an orange panel, causing a light to flash). One of the six actions had a zero probability of occurrence in spontaneous play. In the delayed imitation condition, infants observed the modeled behavior but were not permitted to touch the objects, thereby preventing direct imitation of the model. Following a delay of 1 week, infants returned to the experimental setting and their imitation of the model's actions was scored. Infants in the delayed imitation condition emitted more target actions than infants in control groups who were not exposed to the modeled actions. There was also evidence for delayed imitation of the novel action even though the infants had never directly imitated this behavior at the time it was presented, a finding replicated by Barr and Hayne (1996).

A series of studies by Meltzoff (1988a, 1988b, 1988c) indicate that infants ranging in age from 9 to 24 months will imitate significantly more modeled actions than a control group over delays ranging from 24 h in the youngest infants to 4 months in the oldest infants. Additional research indicates that 14-month-old infants will show delayed imitation of behavior modeled on television after a 24-h delay. In the same study, the researchers found delayed imitation by infants of behavior modeled by an "expert" toddler performing a novel response after a 48-h delay and a change in context from the experimental situation to the home setting (Hanna & Meltzoff, 1993). The basic findings of the Meltzoff group have been replicated with 6–30-month-old infants by other researchers (see Courage & Howe, 2002, for a review).

Analysis of spontaneous and delayed imitation by infants

Although spontaneous imitation by newborn infants is still open to question (as is the research with pigeons), the evidence is mounting that this is true imitation and not merely an artifact of experimental procedures or a more simple process such as innate releasers of fixed action patterns.

Spontaneous imitation in human newborns involves the infant observing a modeled gesture and responding with a set of muscle movements that correspond to the visual stimulus. The correspondence between the modeled stimulus and the form of response is a remarkable achievement because the infant is unable to see its own face when it reproduces the facial gestures of the adult model (called opaque imitation by Zentall, 2006). Meltzoff and Moore (1999) refer to this process as "active intermodal mapping" where infants can monitor their facial movements through proprioceptive feedback and compare this felt activity to what they see. At the present time, it is not possible to provide a detailed evolutionary account of active intermodal mapping and spontaneous imitation (see Meltzoff, 1999, for a speculative account). The evidence is growing that mirror neurons in the brains of humans play a role in the capacity for observed goal-related actions of others but this system does not seem well developed in neonates or even 6-month-old infants (Falck-Ytter, Gredeback, & von Hofsten, 2006). Thus, a definitive account of spontaneous imitation in newborn infants is not yet available.

FOCUS ON: Behavioral neuroscience, mirror neurons, and imitation

Some say imitation is the highest form of flattery. Within the last decade, neurons have been detected in the ventral premotor area of the brain that respond when a primate views someone doing something that the monkey has done before. These so-called "mirror neurons" were active in macaque monkeys when the animals watched another monkey perform the same action that they had done themselves (Gallese, Fadiga, Fogassi, & Rizzolatti, 1996; Rizzolatti & Craighero, 2004). When a monkey engages in some action, neurons in its frontal lobe are active during the "doing" and a subset of these same neurons fire when the monkey just *watches* another monkey perform a similar response. The neurons fire as though the observer monkey were mirroring the movements of the model. Located at the merger of the anterior dorsal visual stream into the motor cortex, mirror neurons have both motor and visual functions. But, these neural cells are not directly stimulated by visual input and nor do they initiate motor activity.

Another set of mirror-type cells found in the human anterior cingulate fire when a person is poked with a needle, but surprisingly they also fire when the patient watches someone else getting poked. Some researchers have concluded that mirror neurons dissolve the distinction between "self" and "others," providing humans with the capacity for empathy and the ability to understand others better. Given the probability of mirror neurons existing in human infants, this could support the claims of those reporting infant facial imitation and active intermodal mapping (Meltzoff & Moore, 1999). However, the mirror circuits are largely underdeveloped in early infancy, requiring more interaction with the environment in order to organize into a functional mirror system (Coren, Ward, & Enns, 2004, pp. 453–455). Iriki (2006) suggests that the neural mechanisms for imitation even exist in lower primates, but that training (in tool use) is required for this capacity to become fully operational.

Actually the functions of mirror neurons are not entirely clear, but there are several hypothesized possibilities. Oberman, Hubbard, McCleery, Altschuler, Ramachandran, & Pineda (2005) reported that autistic children show a dysfunctional mirror neuron system that may help to explain some of their behavioral deficit. Children with autism often fail to show empathy (recognizing the feelings of others), age-appropriate language skills (mirror cells are near Broca's language area), or imitation of significant others (Iacobini, Woods, Brass, Bekkering, Mazziota, & Rizzolatti, 1999). These findings suggest that the mirror neuron system plays a central role in children's socialization and language learning. Furthermore, mirror neurons seem to enable observers to form action-understandings from others that do not strictly correspond to their own motor representations (Ferrari, Rozzi, & Fogassi, 2005).

A recent study by Repacholi and Meltzoff (2007) found that 18-month-old youngsters could regulate their imitation of an adult model on the basis of emotions expressed by a third party toward the model (angry or neutral). This kind of emotional eavesdropping by infants is what might be expected if the mirror neuron system allowed for action-understandings based on the emotional reactions of others. In adults, the act of imagining oneself swinging a golf club like Tiger Woods may activate the mirror circuits and improve your own swing (Buccino, Vogt, Ritzl, Fink, Zilles, Freund, et al., 2004), especially when accompanied by corrective feedback from hitting the ball (reinforcement). Observational learning (described later in this chapter) may therefore have its basis in the mirror neuron circuits of the human brain.

Birds, apes, and humans seem to engage in spontaneous imitation. The appearance of similar behavior does not necessarily imply identical functions and mechanisms. That is, the evolution of spontaneous imitation (and delayed) in pigeons and quail, if real, probably resulted from different biological contingencies than those that led to this behavior in humans. For example, spontaneous imitation may be related to care taking in humans and to food gathering in birds. Only a detailed evolutionary analysis of behavior will provide an account that may be tested. Even with such experiments, it will be difficult to be certain about the adaptive advantage of spontaneous imitation for different species. Supplementary studies from behavioral neuroscience, however, should be helpful in unraveling the infant's capacity for innate imitation.

Although imitation by neonates probably has biological origins, later imitation is likely also due to reinforcement and other ontogenetic experiences (see Bering, Bjorklund, & Ragan, 2000, for deferred imitation in chimpanzees and orangutans). Skinner (1984a, p. 220) noted that only the first instance of any behavior is entirely attributable to genetic history. Thus, delayed imitation by older human infants is probably not as much related to biology as to environmental experiences (see Tomasello, Savage-Rumbaugh, & Kruger, 1993, for a similar conclusion for chimpanzees and humans). Even so, there is no conclusive behavioral evidence showing that reinforcement history accounts for delayed imitation by 6-week-old infants. Generalized imitation ("do what I do" correspondence) can be established by reinforcement, but no one has yet shown this in 6-week-old infants. In fact, Horne and Erjavec (2007) could not obtain generalized imitation in 1-year-old infants (see next section on generalized imitation).

Another aspect of delayed imitation by young infants is that they do not have to emit the novel actions of the model during the initial demonstration. That is, they merely observe the modeled stimulus and later show imitation in the absence of the model. Again, it is possible to provide an account of delayed imitation based on generalized imitation (see below), but whether this account can extend to 6-week-old infants is unknown. A good bet is that delayed imitation involves a capacity to reproduce the modeled actions in the absence of the model (see previous FOCUS ON section), as well as a reinforcement history that substantially builds on this biological capacity.

Operant and Generalized Imitation

It is possible to train imitation as an operant in a social contingency of reinforcement. The discriminative stimulus is the behavior of the model (S^D_{model}), the operant is a response that matches the modeled stimulus (R_{match}), and reinforcement is a verbal praise (S^r_{social}). Matching the model is reinforced, while noncorrespondent responses are extinguished. These social contingencies are similar to the discrimination experiments involving matching to sample for primary reinforcement (see Chapter 8).

In fact, Miller and Dollard (1941) proposed that observational learning was simply a special case of operant discrimination. If imitation is reinforced and nonimitation is extinguished, imitation of the model will increase. On the other hand, nonimitation occurs if imitation is extinguished and nonimitation is reinforced. In one study, Miller and Dollard (1941) showed that children who were reinforced for imitation of a leader repeated these actions more than children who did not receive reinforcement. This kind of leader–follower behavior has also been reported for rats and other animals (Hake, Donaldson, & Hyten, 1983).

Although **operant imitation** provides a straightforward account of observational learning, Bandura (1969) noted that the operant account may be limited to situations in which the observer sees the model, an imitative response immediately occurs, and reinforcement follows. In everyday life, there are occasions when imitation does not conform to this sequence. For example, a young child is seated in front of a television set watching *Sesame Street*, and she observes Kermit the Frog sing "It's not easy being green" for the first time. After watching Kermit's performance, the child turns off the television and goes to help her parent in the kitchen. The next day, the girl begins to sing Kermit's song. The child's performance approximates the puppet's song. She may not remember every word, but she has the basic tune. Notice that the girl has never before performed this sequence of responses. Because of this, reinforcement could not have strengthened her performance. Also, the child's imitative sequence occurred in the absence of the model; Kermit was not present when she imitated him. Finally, the girl's imitative performance was delayed; she sang the song the next day, not immediately after Kermit's demonstration.

The Kermit song is typical of observational learning in everyday life, but it seems to defy an S^D: $R \rightarrow S^r$ interpretation. The imitative response is novel and reinforcement for the song is missing. In addition, the girl sings the song 1 day later with the model or S^D absent. Finally, Bandura (1969) noted that there is no account of the long delay between modeled performance and later imitation.

Although Bandura (1969, 1977, 1986) has argued against an operant account based on these difficulties, Donald Baer (Figure 11.5) and associates provided a behavior analysis of imitation that handles each of the apparent challenges to the operant paradigm (Baer, Peterson, & Sherman, 1967; Baer & Sherman, 1964). The approach is called **generalized imitation** and is based on operant principles of discrimination and generalization (see Glossary for complete definition).

The procedures of generalized imitation begin with simple reinforcement of correspondence between the modeled performance (S^D model) and the imitative operant (R_{match}). The contingency requires the observer to perform the same action as the model. Reinforcement increases imitative behavior, while extinction makes it decrease. If a child is reinforced with praise for imitation of nonsense syllables by a puppet, this response will increase. When praise is withheld, imitation of the puppet declines (Baer & Sherman, 1964).

FIG. 11.5 Donald Baer. Reprinted with permission.

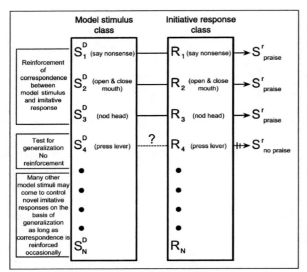

FIG. 11.6 Discrimination procedures used by Baer and Sherman to establish generalized imitation are shown. After training several imitative responses, a test for generalization is given without reinforcement. Generalized stimulus (model) and response (imitation) classes eventually are formed on the basis of training the model-imitation exemplars. Based on a description of the contingencies in "Reinforcement Control of Generalized Imitation in Young Children," by D. M. Baer and J. A. Sherman, 1964, *Journal of Experimental Child Psychology, 1,* 37–49.

The actual discrimination procedures are shown in Figure 11.6 and involve several modeled stimuli (S^D) and multiple operants (R_{match}). The puppet's head nodding is an S^D for the child to nod her head and an S^Δ for saying nonsense syllables or opening and closing her mouth. When the puppet opens and closes its mouth, this is an S^D for similar behavior by the child and an S^Δ for the other two responses. In each case, what the model does sets the occasion for reinforcement of a similar response by the child; all other responses are extinguished. This training results in a stimulus class of modeled actions and an imitative response class. The child now imitates whichever of the three responses that the model performs.

The next step is to test for generalization of the stimulus and response classes. Baer and Sherman (1964) showed that a new-modeled stimulus would set the occasion for a *novel* imitative response, without any further reinforcement. If the puppet began pressing a lever, the child also imitated this performance even though this response was never reinforced with praise. Thus, *generalized imitation* accounted for the appearance of novel imitative acts in children—even when these responses were never reinforced.

What about the absence of the discriminative stimulus and long delays? It is important to note that all instances of modeling and imitation involve the absence of the S^D before the imitative response occurs. That is, the model demonstrates the action (S^D presented), and after the demonstration (S^D removed) the imitative response is emitted. A contingency may be established that requires a delay of some time between the presentation of the discriminative stimuli and the imitative response. This is the same as when a pigeon pecks a key that matches the sample, but reinforcement depends on delaying the matching response by a few seconds. The delay between the offset of the sample stimulus and the occurrence of the matching response may be lengthened by successive approximation. Eventually, the pigeon may be accurate even after 20 s without seeing the sample.

Similarly, children may learn to delay their imitative responses. Adults may reinforce newborn infants when the baby mimics their behavior. As the child gets older, reinforcement of imitation depends on increasing delays between the modeled performance and the imitative response. If you tell a joke to someone, the person seldom repeats it in your presence. Immediate repetition of the joke does not reinforce the listener. Later the joke is told to another audience, whose laughter reinforces the imitative performance. In this way, social contingencies generate extensive delays between the model stimulus and the imitative response.

It is important to account for the maintenance of generalized imitation. One interpretation involves conditioned reinforcement. Baer and Sherman (1964) suggest that similarity becomes a conditioned reinforcer. When a child is taught to imitate, reinforcement occurs only if there is correspondence between the model's actions and the learner's performance. Since reinforcement depends on similarity, imitating others becomes a conditioned reinforcer. Thus, when it occurs, imitation is automatically reinforced.

Alternatively, generalized imitation may be maintained by intermittent reinforcement. Gewirtz (1971) indicated that there was no need to postulate similarity as a conditioned reinforcer. He noted that there is no way of separating similarity from the imitative behavior it is said to explain. Intermittent reinforcement for imitation may account for the persistence of generalized imitation. If there were occasional reinforcement of imitation, this would maintain the stimulus–response relationships. That is, occasionally imitating others pays off, as when a person learns to operate a computer by watching others.

ON THE APPLIED SIDE: Training generalized imitation

Donald Baer conducted the early research on generalized imitation and pioneered its application. Together with Montrose M. Wolf and Todd R. Risley at the University of Kansas (1965–2002), he founded the discipline of applied behavior analysis. He received numerous awards from the American Psychological Association and the Society for the Experimental Analysis of Behavior, served as an international distinguished professor, and was the Roy A. Roberts Distinguished Professor of Human Development at the University of Kansas. Don Baer died on 29 April 2002 while having lunch. He was known for his wit, intellectual brilliance, and advocacy on behalf of individuals with behavioral disabilities. In this section we learn about Baer's use of generalized imitation principles to teach imitation to a child with severe disabilities (Baer et al., 1967).

Marilla was a profoundly retarded child who had never shown signs of imitating others. At 12 years old, she had a limited repertoire of responses that included grunting sounds, following simple commands like "sit down," dressing and feeding herself, going to the washroom, and responses such as turning a knob or opening a door. Although the staff at Firecrest School had tried their best with Marilla, they were now convinced that the child was "just too dumb to learn anything." At this point, Baer and his associates used operant principles to teach generalized imitation to Marilla.

About an hour before lunch, Marilla was brought to a room with a table and chairs in it. The training began when the teacher said, "Do this," and raised his arm (S^D). Marilla simply stared at him and did not imitate the response. The same sequence was tried several times without success. On the next attempt, the teacher raised his arm and assisted Marilla in doing the same. After this sequence, Marilla received a spoonful of her lunch and at the same time the teacher said, "Good." After several assisted trials, Marilla needed less and less help and reinforcement only occurred when she lifted her arm by herself. Sometimes Marilla raised her arm when the performance was not modeled (S^Δ); these responses were not reinforced. With this training, Marilla acquired a simple response of raising her hand when the teacher said, "Do this," and demonstrated the action (direct imitation).

Other imitative responses, such as tapping a table and parts of the body with the left hand, were established by shaping and differential reinforcement. After seven examples were taught, the teacher said, "Do this," and tapped the arm of a chair. Marilla immediately made the same response although she had never been reinforced for doing so. This was the first instance of generalized imitation. A novel modeling stimulus (tapping the arm of the chair) resulted in a new imitative response (Marilla tapping the arm of her chair).

As more instances of reinforced imitation were added to Marilla's repertoire, the percentage of novel imitations increased. Some of the responses were more important in everyday life, such as scribbling on paper, placing geometric forms in order, crawling under a table, and burping a doll. After 120 examples of reinforced imitation, the girl would immediately imitate new examples of modeled performance.

The basic idea of generalized imitation is that reinforcement of some members of the stimulus and response classes maintains the strength of all members—including novel imitations that never have been reinforced. To show the importance of reinforcement for Marilla's novel imitations, the contingency of reinforcement was changed. The teacher continued to model various actions, but Marilla was no longer reinforced for imitating. However, when she did anything except imitate, reinforcement occurred every 30 s. This differential reinforcement of other behavior (DRO) maintains the reinforcer in the setting, places imitation on extinction, and increases behavior that is incompatible with imitation. In less than 20 sessions, both reinforced and novel imitations declined to near-zero responses for each session. Clearly, generalized imitation was maintained by reinforcement.

Next, reinforcement for imitation was reinstated and generalized imitation was acquired again. At this point, the researcher began to teach sequences or chains of imitative performance to Marilla. For example, the teacher would raise his hand and stand up; reinforcement depended on Marilla imitating this two-response sequence. With small steps, the teacher was able to add more and more responses until Marilla could follow a seven-response sequence. Many of the sequences included novel imitative responses that had never been reinforced.

In the final phase of this project, Baer and associates decided to add vocal responses to the imitative sequences. Since Marilla made grunting sounds, the teacher said, "Do this," rose from his chair, walked to the middle of the room, and said, "Ah." Marilla followed the sequence, but when it came to the vocal response she only made mouth movements. The facial expression was, however, a good first approximation and was reinforced. Over time, closer and closer approximations occurred until Marilla completed the sequence with a well expressed, "Ah." Using fading, the teacher was able to get the girl to say, "Ah," whenever he said, "Do this," and demonstrated the vocal response.

Once the imitation of various sounds was well established, the teacher combined the sounds into words and after about 20 h of vocal imitation Marilla could imitate words like "hi," "okay," "Marilla," and the names of familiar objects. When generalized imitation of motor and vocal responses was well established, new male and female experimenters were used to extend the performance to new models. Now, any teacher could work with Marilla to broaden her skills and add to her behavioral repertoire. Once a sizable imitative repertoire is available, further learning occurs much more rapidly. Rather than teach separate responses, a person can be shown what to do. This rapid learning of complex skills is necessary for getting along in the world.

The work of Baer et al. (1967) has important practical implications for learning-delayed people. What is less obvious is the theoretical value of this work. This research shows that complex human behavior may arise from relatively simple behavior principles operating in combination. One implication is that these same principles, when added to a possible cross-modal matching capacity (Meltzoff & Moore, 1999), account for the development of observational learning in everyday life.

Complex Observational Learning

Albert Bandura (Figure 11.7) has worked on complex observational learning and self-regulatory processes for about 50 years and is one of the most cited researchers in psychology. Currently, Dr. Bandura is David Starr Jordan Professor of Social Sciences in Psychology at Stanford University. His work on observational learning, imitation, and aggression is discussed in the following section.

The Bobo doll experiment

Bandura (1965) designed an experiment to show a more complex form of learning by observation than generalized imitation. Children participated in this experiment on the imitation of aggressive behavior. As shown in Figure 11.8, each child watched a short film in which an adult demonstrated four

FIG. 11.7 Albert Bandura.

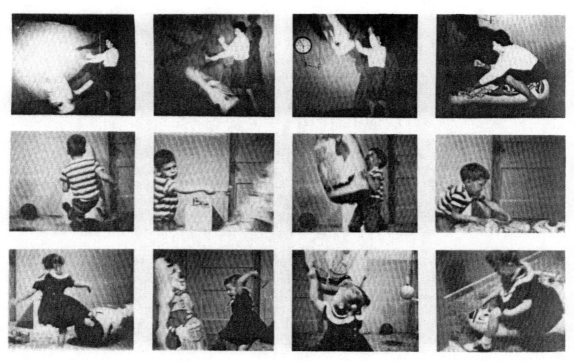

FIG. 11.8   Imitation of modeled aggression against a Bobo doll. After viewing a model hit, jump on, and verbally insult a Bobo doll, male and female children also showed these imitative aggressive responses. Reprinted from "Imitation of Film-Mediated Aggressive Models," by A. Bandura, D. Ross, and S. A. Ross, 1969, *Journal of Abnormal and Social Psychology, 66*, 3–11. Copyright 1969 held by Albert Bandura. Reprinted with permission.

distinctive aggressive actions toward an inflated Bobo doll (cf. Bandura, Ross, & Ross, 1963). Every aggressive action was accompanied by a unique verbal response. While sitting on the Bobo doll, the adult punched it in the face and said, "Pow, right in the nose, boom, boom." In another sequence, the adult hit the doll with a mallet saying, "Sockeroo, stay down." Also, the model kicked the Bobo doll and said, "Fly away," and threw rubber balls at the doll while saying, "Bang."

Some of the children saw the model rewarded by another adult, who supplied soda, snack, and candies while saying, "strong champion." Other children saw the model receive negative consequences. The adult scolded and spanked the model for "picking on that clown" and warned him or her not to act that way again. A third group saw the modeled aggression, but no consequences were portrayed for the aggressive behavior.

When the film ended, a child was taken to a room that contained many toys, including a Bobo doll. The child was encouraged to play with the toys and then was left alone. The researchers watched through a one-way mirror and recorded instances of aggression and imitative aggression directed at the Bobo doll. Generally, there was a high frequency of imitative aggressive behavior toward the Bobo, and boys were more aggressive than girls.

Bandura (1965) also found that reward and punishment of the model's actions affected the imitation of aggression. Children who saw the model punished were less likely to imitate aggression than those who saw the model rewarded. Children who saw the model rewarded did not differ in imitative aggression from those who watched the model perform the actions without receiving social consequences. Importantly, this means that just seeing modeled aggression (no consequences) had about as much impact on imitation as observing violence being rewarded. Finally, Bandura offered an incentive to all the children if they could remember the actions of the model in the film. With this incentive, all three groups recalled the modeled aggression at about the same level. It seemed that all children had learned equally from the modeled aggression, but those who witnessed punishment of the model were less inclined to perform the aggressive sequences.

Social cognitive interpretation

Bandura (1986) argued that the difference between learning and performing modeled aggression requires a cognitive theory of **observational learning**. The observer pays attention to the modeled sequence, noting the arrangement of each action. The general information in the sequence must be coded and rehearsed, as when the child says, "First sit on the Bobo, and then say the word 'pow.'" Once this abstract information is retained in memory, imitation is a matter of reproducing the component responses in the correct sequences.

Complex behavior patterns, however, cannot be learned by observation until the component skills have been mastered. It is impossible to fly a plane or do an inward one-and-a-half dive by mere observation. When the separate skills have been acquired, observing others can provide information on how to sequence complex performances, especially with corrective feedback. The golf instructor may show a person how to stand, hold the golf club, and swing at the ball. This demonstration could produce a sequencing of these responses, but the person may still not hit the ball well. It takes corrective feedback from the instructor and the trajectory of the ball to improve performance. Finally, the anticipated consequences of imitation determine whether an imitative response will occur. People who expect positive outcomes are likely to perform actions they have witnessed, and those who expect negative consequences are less likely to imitate such actions.

Behavioral interpretation

A behavioral interpretation for complex observational learning is that it may build on the processes of generalized imitation. As we have noted, generalized imitation provides an account of novel instances of imitation. From an operant perspective, imitation is most likely to occur in situations in which it was reinforced previously. Such behavior is unlikely in situations in which it was extinguished, or in settings in which it was punished.

Doug witnesses his brother, Barry, raid the cookie jar before dinner. Barry is caught by his mother and sent to his room. Later, Doug steals a cookie, is also caught, and is sent to his room. Over time, such experiences teach the child "what happens to others can happen to me." Based on such a learning history, children show *differential imitation* based on modeled consequences. Doug avoids activities in which Barry has been punished and imitates the rewarded actions of his brother. This kind of conditioning history provides a plausible account of Bandura's results concerning complex observational learning.

The learning and performance differences of the Bobo doll research may also be due to previous conditioning. When Bandura offered an incentive for recalling the modeled action, he presented a discriminative stimulus that increased the probability of this verbal behavior. For most children, it is likely that being promised a reward for recalling some action is a situation that has accompanied reinforcement in the past. That is, a child may be told, "Mommy and Daddy will be proud of you if you can remember the alphabet," and the child is reinforced for reciting the ABCs. Many such instances result in a generalized tendency to recall events and actions when promised a reward. Given such a history and the incentive conditions that Bandura used, children in all three groups would show a high frequency of recalling what they have observed.

FOCUS ON: Rules, observational learning, and self-efficacy

Recently, Bandura has noted that observational learning in humans involves the discovery and use of abstract rules. In a dialogue with Richard Evans (1989), he stated:

> I began to develop the notion of modeling as a broad phenomenon that serves several functions. This conceptualization of modeling is concerned more with the observers' *extracting the rules* and structure of behavior, rather than copying particular examples they had observed. For example, in language learning, children are extracting the rules of how to speak grammatically rather than imitating particular sentences. Once they acquire the structure and the rules, they can use that knowledge to generate new patterns of behavior that go beyond what they've seen or heard. As they acquire the rules of language, they can generate sentences they have never heard. So modeling is a much more complex abstract process than a simple process of response mimicry.
>
> (Evans, 1989, p. 5)

From a behavioral perspective, "extracting the rules" is verbal operant behavior that describes the contingencies of reinforcement (Skinner, 1957, 1969). Both Skinner and Bandura agree about the importance of rules for human behavior, but they differ in terms of interpretation and philosophy.

Bandura (in Evans, 1989) talks about rules as cognitive events, and Skinner (1969) views them as verbal descriptions. For Skinner, following rules is behavior under the control of verbal stimuli. That is, statements of rules, advice, maxims, or laws are discriminative stimuli that set the occasion for behavior. Rules, as verbal descriptions, may affect observational learning. In this regard, Bandura's modeling experiments involve a number of distinct behavioral processes—including generalized imitation, descriptions of contingencies, and rule-governed behavior. Behavior analysts study each of these processes to understand how they may combine in complex forms of human behavior, including observational learning.

One kind of rule or description of contingency involves statements about oneself, such as "I am a competent person who can cope with this situation." This self-description can be contrasted with statements such as "I am an incompetent person who is unable to cope with this situation." Bandura (1997) refers to these kinds of responses as beliefs in self-efficacy, and provides evidence that these "cognitions" have a large impact on human behavior.

From a behavior analysis view, statements of self-efficacy, as a class of verbal stimuli, can affect subsequent behavior (see next section). For example, when confronted with speaking to a large audience, John thinks (or states out loud) that he does not have the verbal skills to succeed and estimates that his chances are only 40% for giving a well-organized, interesting, and clear presentation. Subsequently, John gives the talk and, as expected, performs at a low level. In this example, John's statement of self-efficacy describes a past history of behavior at speaking engagements (a rule). As a rule, the verbal stimulus sets up compliance as reinforcement (e.g., establishing operation). That is, for most people, stating and following rules (compliance) have resulted in generalized social reinforcement from a verbal community. Based on social conditioning for compliance, statements of self-efficacy often predict how a person will act in subsequent (similar) situations.

RULE-GOVERNED BEHAVIOR

A large part of human behavior is regulated by verbal stimuli. Verbal stimuli are the products of speaking, writing, signing, and other forms of verbal behavior (see Chapter 12). Rules, instructions, advice, and laws are verbal stimuli that affect a wide range of human action. The common property of these kinds of stimuli is that they describe the operating contingencies of reinforcement. The instruction "turn on the computer and use the mouse to click the desired program in the menu" is a description of the behavior that must be executed to get a program running. Formally, rules, instructions, advice, and laws are **contingency-specifying stimuli**, describing the S^D: R → S^r relations of everyday life (Skinner, 1969).

The term **rule-governed behavior** is used when the listener's (reader's) performance is regulated by contingency-specifying stimuli. According to this definition, a scientist shows rule-governed behavior when following specified procedures to make observations. People, as listeners, may generate their own rules when they speak. Travelers who read a map to get to their cabin may say to themselves, "Take Interstate 5 and turn left at the first exit." The self-directions are verbal rules that describe the contingencies of reinforcement that result in getting to the cabin. In a classroom, a student may solve a set of mathematical problems by following the square-root rule. Rule-governed behavior is seen when a client follows the advice given by a counselor. When people obey the laws as expressed by posted speed limits, signs that say NO SMOKING, and proscriptions not to steal, the behavior is rule-governed.

Constructing and Following Rules

In solving a problem, people often make up or construct their own discriminative stimuli (response-produced stimuli). A person who has an important, early morning appointment may set an alarm clock for six o'clock a.m. Technically, setting the alarm is **precurrent behavior**, or an operant that precedes some other response. This behavior produces a discriminative stimulus that sets the occasion for getting up and going to the meeting. Thus, a major function of *precurrent behavior* is the **construction of S^Ds** that regulate subsequent action.

As shown in Figure 11.9, people also may construct discriminative stimuli through written words or spoken sounds (verbal stimuli). For example, a person may make a shopping list before going to the supermarket. Making a list is precurrent behavior, and the list is a discriminative stimulus for choosing groceries. Similarly, economical shoppers may say to themselves, "Only buy products that are on sale." This verbal stimulus acts something like the grocery list in the previous example. As a rule, the verbal expression points to the relation between the stimuli, behavior, and reinforcement in the marketplace (see Taylor & O'Reilly, 1997, for use of self-instruction in shopping by people with mild learning disabilities). The words *on sale* identify a property of products that is correlated with saving money (reinforcement). The rule makes it easier to discriminate a good deal from a bad one, is easily recalled, and may be executed in any relevant situation.

Constructing discriminative stimuli and rules is important for a technological society. To improve mail delivery, zip codes are added to letters. When a person puts a zip code on a letter, the code is a verbal S^D that regulates sorting by postal employees. Letters are directed electronically throughout the postal system and arrive at an address specified by the code. Without such codes, mail is sorted at a much slower rate, and many letters get misdirected, lost, or returned.

Folk wisdom represents another example of constructing and following rules. People who constructed the golden rule "Do unto others ..." presumably did better in social relationships. When others transcribed the

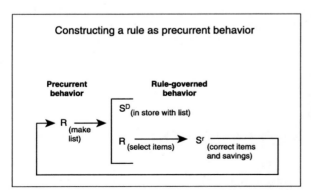

FIG. 11.9 Illustration of how precurrent verbal behavior (or rules) functions as a discriminative stimulus regulating subsequent behavior (rule-governed behavior).

rule, it provided a guideline for successful interpersonal relationships to all who read it. Thus, a statement of wisdom is precurrent behavior that results in a verbal discriminative stimulus. The rule as an S^D regulates the subsequent behavior of the person. Once the rule is made public, it affects others as it did the originator.

Formal laws of government or religion may also involve constructing and following verbal discriminative stimuli (e.g., Norton, 2001). Laws of property rights likely developed from social contingencies. When someone stole another person's property, the victim and family usually retaliated. Eventually, the contingencies were described by rules like, " Thou shall not steal." Descriptions of the contingencies made it easier for people to avoid stealing. Once formulated and codified, the laws were stated by authorities and backed up by religious and legal sanctions. In this way, members of the group or culture conformed to the codified rules without risking exposure to the actual contingencies.

Although much human behavior is based on constructing and following rules, some contingencies seem to defy reliable description. An elite athlete may execute a skillful gold medal performance but be unable to say exactly how it happened. A scientist may make an important discovery and yet be unable to advise others on how to be inventive. Creative artists and musicians produce interesting visual and auditory effects in ways that cannot be stated. In all such cases, the interrelations of stimuli, responses, and reinforcements are so subtle that rules have not yet been described. In these situations, behavior is governed by exposure to the contingencies of reinforcement (contingency shaped) rather than regulated by rules (rule governed).

Rule-Governed and Contingency-Shaped Behavior

People are said to solve problems either by discovery or instruction. From a behavioral perspective, the difference is between the direct effects of contingencies (discovery) and the indirect effects of rules (instruction). When performance is attributed to direct exposure to reinforcement contingencies, it is called **contingency-shaped behavior**. As previously noted, performance set up by constructing and following instructions (and other verbal stimuli) is termed *rule-governed behavior* (Catania, Matthews, & Shimoff, 1990; Hayes, 1989b).

Skinner (1969) illustrated the differences between contingency-shaped and rule-governed behavior in his analysis of a baseball player "catching the ball" and a naval commander "catching a satellite":

> The behavior of a baseball outfielder catching a fly ball bears certain resemblances to the behavior of the commander of a ship taking part in the recovery of a re-entering satellite. Both (the outfielder and commander) move about on a surface in a direction and with a speed designed to bring them, if possible, under a falling object at the moment it reaches the surface. Both respond to recent stimulation from the position, direction, and speed of the object, and they both take into account effects of gravity and friction. The behavior of the baseball player, however, has been almost entirely shaped by contingencies of reinforcement, whereas the commander is simply obeying rules derived from the available information and from analogous situations.
>
> (Skinner, 1969, p. 146)

Although behavior attributed to rules and contingencies occasionally may look the same, the variables that affect performance are in fact quite different. One difference is motivational—reinforcement determines the rate of response (probability) for a given setting, while rules only affect how the response is executed (topography). Recall that a rule is a special kind of discriminative stimulus and that S^Ds affect behavior because they set the occasion for reinforcement. This means that *rule-following itself must arise from contingencies of reinforcement*. The advice of a friend is taken only because such directions have been useful in the past. For example, a friend may have recommended a certain restaurant and you found it enjoyable. Based on these consequences, you are now more likely to follow your friend's advice, especially for dining.

Reinforcement for following the advice of others in various situations may establish a general tendency to do what others recommend. This kind of reinforcement history may underlie a *generalized susceptibility to social influence* (Orne & Evans, 1965). You probably know someone who is a sucker for a sales pitch. Many sales pitches are presented as advice, in the sense that a salesperson describes the benefits of owning a product. Often, however, the purchase results in more benefits to the seller than to the buyer. The television evangelist does not have a material product, but uses advice, promises, and threats of retribution to get people to send in money.

When directions are backed up with social punishment rather than natural consequences, they are called orders and commands (see Zettle & Hayes, 1982, on generalized compliance or *pliance* versus *tracking*). Individuals follow orders, regardless of the particular commands, because they have been punished for disobedience (blind obedience). Of course, a generalized tendency for obedience often results in avoiding many aversive consequences in the world, as when a child is told, "don't play in the street," by a parent who has punished disobedience.

Generalized obedience, however, may be a problem. Governments can induce blind obedience in which a person harms another without regard to the moral consequences. In many countries, Amnesty International has documented the torture of political prisoners by guards and police. In these cases, obedience to authority is unquestioned and obviously results in serious harm or death to the victims (Milgram, 1974). The torture and abuse of Iraqi prisoners by some of the military guards (372nd Military Police Company of the United States) at Abu Ghraib prison probably involved generalized obedience to direct or implied orders from the Pentagon (as well as other behavioral processes). Figure 11.10 shows Dr. Stanley Milgram (left) with a shock panel that human participants in New Haven, Connecticut were ordered to use. The right-hand photograph shows an elderly gentleman who was given the supposed shocks. Participants in the experiment delivered bogus shocks that they considered real. Many participants delivered the shocks even though the man complained of a heart problem. The tendency to obey the commands of the authority (experimenter) outweighed the signs and sounds of distress from the elderly victim. In fact, more than half

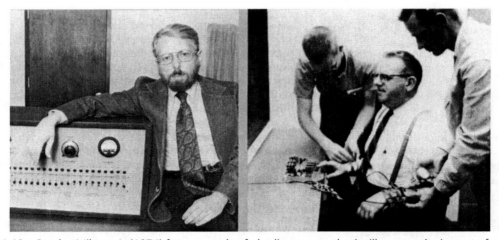

FIG. 11.10 Stanley Milgram's (1974) famous study of obedience to authority illustrates the impact of orders and commands on human behavior. Based on the experimenter's orders, subjects administered what they thought were increasingly severe electric shocks to a 59-year-old man who complained of a heart condition. (Left) Stanley Milgram with the shock generator used in the obedience experiment. (Right) Photograph of learner being strapped into the chair, from the film *Obedience* © 1968 by Stanley Milgram; © renewed 1993 by Alexandra Milgram; and distributed by Penn State Media Sales. Both reproduced with the permission of Alexandra Milgram.

of the participants continued to administer shocks to the highest level on the shock generator and believed that the shocks might injure or kill the victim.

The importance of reinforcement contingencies in establishing and maintaining rule-following behavior is clearly seen with ineffective rules and instructions. One kind of rule that is likely to be weak is based on statistical analysis of contingencies. For example, it is unlikely that a person will give up smoking merely based on the directive, "Stop smoking—smoking causes cancer." The actual consequences are too remote and the statistical chances of getting cancer too unlikely. Of course, smoking usually declines when a person gets cancer, but at this point it is too late. When rules describe delayed and improbable events, it is necessary to find other reasons to follow them.

Recently, government reports of second-hand smoke and its effects have led some communities to classify public smoking as illegal. Towns and cities arrange fines and other penalties for failing to obey the no-smoking bylaw. In this case, smokers follow the anti-smoking rule for reasons unrelated to smoking itself (i.e., social punishment). A similar effect is obtained when smoking is called sinful or shameful and religious sanctions are used to promote compliance. Generally, social contingencies may be used to establish rule-following behavior when natural contingencies are too remote or improbable to be effective.

Baum (1995, 2005, pp. 167–171) emphasizes the importance of rules in terms of long-term contingencies between behavior and biological fitness. As a discriminative stimulus, the rule strengthens listeners' behavior that is reinforced in the short run by social contingencies, but the rule also enters into the long-term contingencies that enhance the listeners' fitness (reproductive success). For example, in following the rule "Do not smoke" the listener is reinforced by the speaker's consequences in the short run, but this behavior is also related to better health and longer reproductive years. When the rule is "internalized," the listener's behavior has switched from short- to long-term control. The fitness-enhancing consequences of long-term contingencies are health, resources, relationships, or reproduction. Baum's analysis of fitness and rule-governed behavior, therefore, integrates behavior analysis explanations of human behavior with evolutionary theory and natural selection.

FOCUS ON: Instructions and contingencies

In his discussion of rule-governed and contingency-shaped behavior, Skinner (1969) speculated that instructions might affect performance differently than the actual contingencies of reinforcement. One way to test this idea is to expose humans to reinforcement procedures that are accurately or inaccurately described by the experimenter's instructions. If behavior varies with the instructions while the actual contingencies remain the same, this would be evidence for Skinner's assertion (see Hackenberg & Joker, 1994, on correspondence between instructions and contingencies).

An early study by Lippman and Meyer (1967) showed that human performance on a fixed-interval schedule varied with instructions. When subjects were told that points (exchanged for money) became available after a specific amount of time, their performance was characterized by a low rate of response, appropriate to the fixed interval. In contrast, subjects told that points depended on a certain number of responses produced a high and steady rate of response. In a similar kind of study, Kaufman, Baron, and Kopp (1966) placed subjects on a variable-interval (VI) schedule of reinforcement and told them that points were available on either a fixed-interval or variable-ratio basis. Performance was more in accord with the experimental instructions than with the actual VI contingencies.

The fact that instructions, in these experiments, seem to override the actual contingencies has been used to argue against a reinforcement analysis of human behavior. Bandura (1971, 1974) linked instructions to modeling. He argued that both of these procedures activate subjects' expectations, which in turn affect subsequent behavior. This means that expected reinforcement, rather than actual

FIG. 11.11   Mark Galizio. Published with permission.

contingencies, is the stronger determinant of human behavior. In addition, Dulany (1968) disputed the claim that instructions were complex discriminative stimuli. He argued that there was no evidence to show that instructions gain (or lose) control over behavior because of selective reinforcement.

Mark Galizio (Figure 11.11) addressed both objections when he showed that following instructions is in fact a discriminative operant (Galizio, 1979). In a series of important experiments, human subjects responded to avoid the loss of money. Subjects received a payment to attend experimental sessions, and they could turn a handle to avoid a loss of five cents from their earnings. When they turned the handle to the right, the onset of a red light and loss of money were postponed. Subjects were exposed to four different contingencies during a session. A change in the contingency was signaled by one of four amber lights. One condition had no losses, but the other three had costs scheduled every 10 s. For the conditions in which costs occurred, each response delayed the next loss for either 10, 30, or 60 s.

To vary instructional control, labels were placed above the amber lights that signaled each condition. When instructions were accurate, there were no discrepancies between labels and the contingencies. Thus, the component in which each response postponed the loss for 10 s was labeled correctly as "10 s," as were the "30 s," "60 s," and "no loss" components.

Galizio (1979) also created conditions of inaccurate instructions in which the labels did not match the actual contingencies. In a no-contact condition, all the components were changed to no losses, but the labels incorrectly described different response requirements. If subjects behaved in accord with the instructions, they made unnecessary responses, but there was no monetary loss. As you might expect, people followed the rules. For example, subjects turned the handle more when the label said "10 s" than when it said "60 s."

At this point, a contact condition was implemented in which losses occurred every 10 s in all components. The signs still read 10, 20, 60 s, and no loss. In this situation, responding to the instructions produced considerable loss of earnings. Consider a person who turned the handle every 60 s but lost money every 10 s. Subjects quickly stopped following the instructions and responded in terms of the actual contingencies of reinforcement. Galizio (1979) explained the significance of these findings as follows:

> [In] the CONTACT condition, when instruction-following led to exposure to the loss contingency, instructional control was rapidly eliminated. The elimination of instruction-following persisted when the NO CONTACT condition was reinstated. This last finding is particularly important, since it shows that subject reactions to the instructions were irreversibly altered after exposure to the CONTACT condition. Subjects now "disbelieve" the instructions and the schedule assumes control of behavior. But contact with schedule-instruction discrepancies is necessary for the elimination of instruction-following, not simply the existence of such a discrepancy. *Instruction-following is controlled by its consequences*
>
> (p. 62)

Overall, the results of Galizio's experiments provide strong support for the view that instructional control is a form of rule-governed behavior (see also Buskist & Miller, 1986; Hayes, Brownstein, Haas, & Greenway, 1986; Horne & Lowe, 1993; Ribes & Martinez, 1998; Ribes & Rodriguez, 2001; see Hayes & Ju, 1997, and Plaud & Newberry, 1996, for applied implications of rule-governed behavior). In accord with numerous other experiments, subjects were found to rapidly acquire appropriate responses to the contingencies when instructed about how to behave. Importantly, the influence of instructions depended on the consequences of following these rules (see

Svartdal, 1992). When the costs of rule-following behavior increased, people no longer followed the rules. Additional evidence showed that following instructions could be brought under stimulus control. Thus, people follow instructions in situations that lead to reinforcement, but not in situations that signal extinction or aversive consequence. Finally, Galizio showed that accurate instructions have reinforcing properties, a characteristic shared by simple discriminative stimuli. People not only respond to instructions but seek out reliable descriptions of the contingencies.

Instructions about interval (or ratio) contingencies often occur in everyday life (see Luciano, 2000; Poppen, 1982). Students are given timetables, calendars, and outlines for lectures, due dates, examination periods, and official holidays. When instructions accurately describe contingencies, behavior is highly efficient. A professor who shows up at the stated time will have students who are punctual. And, as we have noted, reliable instructions are reinforcing; people seek out information about scheduled events, such as television programs and arrival–departure times of airlines.

Inaccurate instructions lead to several different effects. People will continue to follow misleading instructions when there is some benefit and little cost. Buses may never arrive as scheduled, but people continue to follow the listed times because the buses eventually show up. People may continue to follow inaccurate instructions because of social reinforcement. Students follow the rule, "Go to class to get good grades." A few students who get satisfactory grades do not pay attention to the lectures, but they "put in time" in going to class. They follow the rule because their friends go to class, even though it has no effect on their grades. Unreliable instructions, however, are not followed if the rules lead to extinction or aversive consequences. When this occurs, people ignore the rule and act on the basis of the actual contingencies. Instructions to spend during periods of economic recession may be ignored as consumers contact the costs of buying (e.g., increasing debt, threats to basic essentials, etc.). Loss of consumer confidence may reflect the weakening of rule-governed behavior because of contact with the actual contingencies of the market (see Cullen, 1998, on the problems with rules).

Rules as Function-Altering Events

Altering discriminative relations

Although the discriminative function (S^D) of rules is well established, several researchers (Malott, 1988; Michael, 1982a, 1984; Schlinger & Blakely, 1987) have argued that contingency-specifying stimuli have additional, and perhaps even more crucial, effects. Rules can act as **function-altering events**, altering the function of other stimuli and, thereby, the strength of relations among these stimuli and behavior (Schlinger & Blakely, 1987). A passenger on an airplane is instructed to respond to a drop in cabin pressure by "placing the yellow oxygen mask over your mouth and breathing normally." The instruction is a *function-altering event* that sets up the "dangling yellow mask" as a discriminative stimulus for placing the mask on the face. In the absence of the rule, the dangling mask might occasion looking at it or asking for the stewardess (see Schmitt, 2001, for rule following after a delay). The function-altering effect of the airline rule is shown when the passengers put on their masks only at the appropriate moment. Also, the probability of placing masks on faces is higher for those who are given the instruction.

Rules may alter the discriminative functions of stimuli in more complex ways, as when a person is given detailed instructions. A person may be told, "See George about buying the car, but if Craig is there don't make an offer." As a result of this verbal description, the listener emits a conditional discrimination: George is S^D for making an offer and Craig is an S^Δ for this behavior. Notice that without the detailed instruction or rule, George and Craig may have no discriminative functions when buying a car.

FOCUS ON: Following rules and joint control

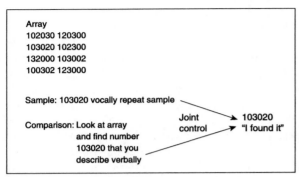

Array
102030 120300
103020 102300
132000 103002
100302 123000

Sample: 103020 vocally repeat sample

Comparison: Look at array
and find number
103020 that you
describe verbally

Joint
control

103020
"I found it"

FIG. 11.12   Joint control is illustrated. The two verbal stimuli—repeating the required number and identifying that number in the array—jointly controlled the terminal verbal response "103020, I found it" (response function). Based on "Joint Control of Rule Following: An Analysis of Purpose," by B. Lowenkron, 1999, *Annual Meeting of the Association for Behavior Analysis*, Chicago (http://www.calstatela.edu/faculty/zlowenk/toc.html).

In 1999, Barry Lowenkron gave a talk on "Joint control of rule following: An analysis of purpose" at the Annual Meetings of the Association for Behavior Analysis in Chicago (available at http://www.calstatela.edu/faculty/zlowenk/toc.html). The talk centered on how rules control behavior. That is, how do verbal statements of contingencies (rules) emitted at one time regulate behavior at a later time? Barry presented three problems for a behavior analysis of rules: (1) memory function or how rules have effects after a delay, (2) recognition function or how the event specified by a rule is known, and (3) response function or how the specified event occasions the specific response. In order to answer these questions without using the language of cognition and mental events, Lowenkron introduced the notion of **joint control** where two verbal stimuli exert stimulus control over a common verbal topography.

Figure 11.12 depicts a task that involves joint control. The problem is for you to locate the number 103020 in the array at the top of the figure. This is a type of matching to sample problem with the array as the comparison. Try to do it now. Finding the correct sequence required joint control by verbal stimuli over the terminal verbal response "103020, I found it." Given the statement of the problem, you probably rehearsed or repeated the sequence to yourself (memory function) as you looked at the array of numbers to verbally identify the correct sequence (recognition function). The two verbal stimuli, repeating the required number and identifying that number in the array, jointly controlled the terminal verbal response "103020, I found it" (response function) (see Chapter 12 for formal analysis of the verbal responses by the speaker).

In another common example, you are getting ready for a birthday party and there is a cake in the oven. Your friend has to go to the store for some soft drinks and states, "When the cake has risen, take it out of the oven" (rule). You are likely to repeat the rule ("better see if the cake is done") and check the cake as it is baking. Notice that the memory function of the rule is fulfilled by repetition or verbal rehearsal of the rule statement over time, not by a mental event or cognition. At some point, you repeat the rule to "check the cake," look in the oven, and verbally identify that "the cake has risen." The verbal stimulus "the cake has risen" fulfills the recognition function without reference to cognitive events. Rehearsal of the rule statement and verbally identifying that the cake has risen exert joint control over the terminal verbal response "the cake is done; take it out of the oven" and removing the cake from the oven.

Notice that the form or topography of the terminal response is completely specified by your friend's statement of the rule—you say that the cake is done and take it out of the oven to comply with your friend's request (rule). Failure to follow the rules often results in social punishment, as people get upset when their instructions are not reinforced with compliance. Also, rules that are ignored usually have additional aversive consequences, such as ruined cakes and spoiled birthday parties (see Cerutti, 1989, on collateral consequences of rule following). As we have seen in this chapter, the contingencies of reinforcement insure that we often follow the rules of others and the rules we give to ourselves (self-generated rules). Thus, rule-governed behavior is operant behavior regulated by contingencies of reinforcement.

CHAPTER SUMMARY

In this chapter we have learned about correspondence relations, focusing on imitation and rule-governed behavior. Spontaneous imitation occurs in several species, including human infants, but the evidence is still controversial. The discovery of mirror neurons suggests that early imitation in infants and other primates is based on neural mechanisms that have been selected during our evolutionary history. It seems that operant imitation, generalized imitation, and complex observational learning build on a basic capacity for imitation. Observational learning seems to integrate imitation with rule-following behavior to produce behavior that is transmitted from one person to another and from one generation to the next. Rule-governed behavior concerns the effects of verbal stimuli on the behavior of the listener. That is, instructions (and other verbal stimuli) are products of the behavior of the speaker that regulate the behavior of the listener. We discovered that rules play a large and important role in the regulation of human behavior, not as mental events but as verbal descriptions of the contingencies. Rule-following behavior is maintained by social and collateral contingencies, but instructed behavior often appears insensitive to contingencies. However, when inaccurate rules generate behavior with high costs, people give up following the rules and respond to the actual contingencies. One way to understand rule-governed behavior is based on joint control, where two verbal stimuli combine to control a common form of verbal response. In the next chapter, we examine contingencies of reinforcement that regulate the behavior of the speaker or, what Skinner (1957) called, the analysis of verbal behavior.

Key Words

Construction of S^Ds

Contingency-shaped behavior

Contingency-specifying stimuli

Correspondence relations

Delayed imitation

Function-altering event

Generalized imitation

Imitation

Joint control

Observational learning

Operant imitation

Precurrent behavior

Rule-governed behavior

Spontaneous imitation

Verbal Behavior

12

- Find out about the difference between language and verbal behavior.
- Discover the operant functions of verbal behavior.
- Investigate complex behavior in the laboratory involving communication between pigeons.
- See how reinforcement contingencies can result in pigeons reporting on their internal states on drugs.
- Learn about why the flag is a symbol of America by investigating the research on stimulus equivalence.

Humans are social animals. Most of the daily life of people takes place in the company of others. An important aspect of human social behavior involves what we do with words, as in speaking, writing, signing, and gesturing. Behavior analysts use the term verbal behavior to refer to this kind of human activity. In this chapter, verbal behavior is analyzed according to the same principles of behavior that have been used throughout this book. The analysis explores the role of contingencies of reinforcement in the regulation of verbal behavior.

In terms of behavior analysis, Lee (1981a) notes that language tends to obscure environment–behavior relationships. Language usually directs research attention to grammar, syntax, and unobservable mental representations and processes (structure), rather than to the objective conditions that influence the behavior of a speaker or writer (function). Catania (1998a) also has noted that the "language of reference" implicitly proceeds from words to objects in the world. The possibility that environmental contingencies regulate our speaking and writing is usually not considered. Catania (1998a) states:

> We also speak of language as if it were directed toward events or objects. We say that words or sentences refer to, deal with, speak of, call attention to, or are about things. The language of reference implicitly includes the direction from verbal behavior to environment. Everyday language doesn't include words that emphasize the opposite direction. What if our everyday language has prejudiced us about the ways in which our verbal behavior works? We hardly ever say that we utter nouns in the presence of relevant objects or that sentences are occasioned by relevant events. Instead, we say that words refer to objects or that sentences are about events. There are good reasons for these usages; . . . [but] they may be misleading in an analysis of the behavior of speakers and listeners or readers and writers.
>
> (pp. 239–240)

LANGUAGE AND VERBAL BEHAVIOR

People usually use the term language when they talk about speaking and other forms of communication. Although some researchers argue that language is behavior (Baer & Guess, 1971), others use the term to refer to a set of linguistic habits (Hockett, 1958, 1968), while still others point to the underlying mental rules that are presumed to organize spoken and written words (e.g., Chomsky, 1957). Some view language as a cultural phenomenon that does not depend on individual behavior and mental rules (Sanders, 1974). Finally, language is said to consist of three main features involving vocabulary, syntax, and meaning (Erlich, 2000, p. 140). As you can see, there is little agreement on the definition of language. The most important implication of this confusion is that language may not be a useful concept for a natural-science approach to speaking (and other forms of verbal behavior).

To rectify these problems, Skinner (1957) introduced the term verbal behavior. The term helps to redirect attention to the operating contingencies. In contrast with the term language, **verbal behavior** deals with the performance of a speaker and the environmental conditions that establish and maintain such performance. That is, verbal behavior concerns the *function* of what we do with words that are spoken, written, or signed. Some of the functions of verbal behavior that have been researched include how we learn to talk about things and events in the world, how we learn to communicate our feelings and emotions, and how the listener's response to what we say shapes what we talk about.

FOCUS ON: Speaking and evolution of the vocal tract

B. F. Skinner (1986) indicated: ". . .verbal behavior does not evolve. It is the product of the verbal environment or what linguists call a language, and it is the verbal environment that evolves" (p. 115). That is, how people of a culture reinforce the verbal behavior of others changes over time and modification of the social contingencies alters what people say. If biological evolution did not lead to mental rules of language, as is usually assumed (Dessalles, 2007, pp. 153–164), it is useful to ask what role did it play in human speech and communication. In his 1986 paper on evolution and verbal behavior, Skinner speculated about the role of natural selection for vocal behavior or speaking. He stated:

> The human species took a crucial step forward when its vocal musculature came under operant control in the production of speech sounds. Indeed, it is possible that all the distinctive achievements of the species can be traced to that one genetic change. Other species behave vocally, of course, and the behavior is sometimes modified slightly during the lifetime of the individual ... but ... the principal contingencies have remained phylogenetic. ... Some of the organs in the production of speech sounds were already subject to operant conditioning. The diaphragm must have participated in controlled breathing, the tongue and jaw in chewing and swallowing, the jaw and teeth in biting and tearing, and the lips in sipping and sucking, all of which could be changed by operant conditioning. Only the vocal cords and pharynx seem to have served no prior operant function. The crucial step in the evolution of verbal behavior appears, then, to have been the genetic change that brought them under the control of operant conditioning and made possible the coordination of all of these systems in the production of speech sounds.
>
> (p. 117)

Skinner's evolutionary analysis of the human anatomy allowing for vocal speech has been confirmed subsequently by research in acoustics, physiology, and anatomy. Although there is much controversy about the evolution of human speech, most scientists now agree on the "principles of physiology and the 'laws' of physical acoustics that determine the capabilities of the anatomy involved in the production of human speech" (Lieberman, Laitman, Reidenberg, & Gannon, 1991, p. 447).

Speech production occurs during the outward flow of air from the lungs. During expiration, normal breathing is substantially modified as speakers take more air into their lungs before producing a long sentence or phrase. This modification of breathing is often attributed to "planning ahead" but is quite consistent with operant control of the breathing system.

The human upper respiratory tract serves as the intersection for the breathing, swallowing, and vocalizing systems. Studies have shown that the position of the larynx in the neck determines the function of these intersecting tracts. In most mammals and nonhuman primates, the larynx is positioned high in the neck, insuring mostly separate respiration and digestive tracts. One result of this location is that the production and variation of audible speech sounds is severely limited in mammals, including the great apes. Human infants retain the nonhuman primate and mammalian location of the larynx (upper neck, C3) and cannot make the vowel sounds [i], [u], and [a] present in adult speech. Over the first 2–3 years, the larynx of the child shows a developmental descent to the adult position (C6) in the neck. This descent is accompanied by other anatomical changes that dramatically alter the way children breathe and swallow. During this developmental period, neuromuscular control is extended within the larynx and pharynx, with changes beginning even before the descent of the larynx has occurred (see Laitman & Reidenberg, 1993).

Phonation, or audible sources of speech sound, is made possible by the activity of the larynx involving the movement of the vocal folds or cords. Complex neuromuscular control insures that the vocal folds are able to move inward before the onset of speech and rapidly in and out for continued speech production. Rates of vocal fold movement can vary between 60 (adult males) to 1500 (children) open–close cycles per second. People can modulate their rate of vocal fold movement and airflow pattern by adjusting the tensions of the muscles in the larynx and the alveolar air pressure; the effect is sustained and prolonged emission of sounds that are the basis of human speech (Lieberman et al., 1991).

Clearly, the vocal apparatus of humans has the capability for fine-grain operant control of sound that can allow for varied vocal forms of verbal behavior (Skinner, 1957). During the course of human evolution, the breathing and digestive regions were modified from the two-tube system of our earliest hominid ancestors to the intersecting upper tracts we have today. These changes would have involved substantial "restructuring in the respiratory, digestive and vocalizing patterns and would have occurred contemporaneously with parallel changes in central and peripheral neural control" (Lieberman et al., 1991, p. 324). It is likely that many minor modifications of morphology had already appeared in the genus *Homo* more than 1 million years ago. These modifications were further elaborated by natural selection and appeared as the integrated respiratory, upper digestive, and vocal tract of *Homo sapiens* approximately 300,000–400,000 years ago. Specification of the selection pressures that favored such changes awaits further research.

VERBAL BEHAVIOR: SOME BASIC DISTINCTIONS

Verbal behavior refers to the vocal, written, and signed behavior of a speaker, writer, or communicator. This behavior operates on the listener, reader, or observer, who arranges for reinforcement of the verbal performance in a particular setting. A woman who is hungry may ask a waiter for "the tossed green salad with the egg sandwich." The speaker's behavior affects the listener, who in turn supplies reinforcement (i.e., placing the meal on the table). A similar effect is produced if the woman writes her order on a piece of paper. In this case, the written words function like the spoken ones; the waiter reads the order and brings the meal. Verbal behavior therefore expands the ways that humans can produce effects on the world.

Verbal behavior allows us to affect the environment *indirectly* (Vargas, 1998). This contrasts with nonverbal behavior, which often results in direct and automatic consequences. When you walk toward an object, you come closer to it. If you lift a glass, there is a direct and automatic change in its position. Verbal behavior, on the other hand, only works through its effects on other people. To change the position of a lamp, the speaker says, "Lift the blue lamp at the back of the room" to a listener who is inclined to respond. Notice that reinforcement of the verbal response is not automatic, since many conditions may affect what the listener does. The listener may not hear you, may be distracted, or may not understand (i.e., picks up the red lamp rather than the blue one). Generally,

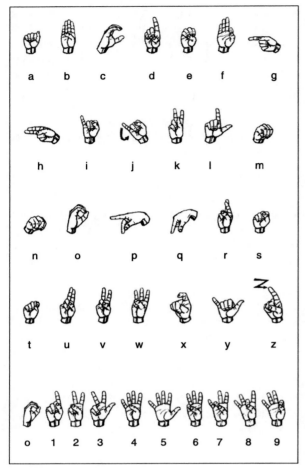

FIG. 12.1   Illustration of American Sign Language (ASL)—finger-spelled letters and numbers.

the social contingencies that regulate verbal behavior are complex, subtle, and highly flexible.

The Range of Verbal Behavior

Although verbal behavior is usually equated with speaking, vocal responses are only one of its forms. In addition to talking, a person emits gestures and body movements (signs) that indirectly operate on the environment through their effects on others. In most cultures, a frown sets the occasion for others to remove some aversive event, while a smile may signal the observer to behave in ways that produce positive reinforcement. In fact, frowns and smiles have such consistent and pervasive effects on others that some researchers have considered these gestures as universal symbols (Ekman & Friesen, 1975; Rosenberg & Ekman, 1995).

Another kind of verbal behavior involves manual signing rather than speech sounds. In American Sign Language (ASL), the speaker produces arm and hand movements that are functionally similar to speech sounds. In this case, regulation of the listener's behavior is along a visual dimension. Deaf speakers may also acquire complex finger movements known as "finger spelling" that function like letters in the English alphabet. Figure 12.1 illustrates some of the basic manual movements of ASL and digital positions for finger spelling.

In the behavioral view, writing is verbal behavior that functions to regulate the behavior of a reader. Although written words and sentences have little formal similarity to spoken ones, the two modes of communication have equivalent functions. Recall that behavior analysts classify behavior in terms of its functions, and for this reason both writing and speaking are commonly categorized as *verbal operants*.

Speaking, Listening, and the Verbal Community

The behavior of the speaker (or writer) is functionally different from the behavior of the listener (or reader). That is, the conditions that regulate speaking are distinct from those that affect listening. In the field of psycholinguistics, the distinction between speaking and listening is often blurred by talking about language encoding and decoding. Since both are treated as aspects of language (i.e., the transmission of meaning), there is little attempt to analyze the separate functions of such behavior. In fact, Skinner (1969) used the term *rule-governed behavior* to describe the behavior of the listener and *verbal behavior* to specify the performance of the speaker. Of course, in any actual communication between two people each person alternates as a speaker and a listener. The repertoires of behavior are, however, analytically distinct from Skinner's perspective.

Rule-governed behavior refers to the effects of words in the form of instructions, advice, maxims, and laws on the listener's behavior (see Chapter 11). In this view, rules are seen as complex discriminative stimuli, and the principles that govern stimulus control also regulate the behavior of the listener. While many behavior analysts have accepted this perspective, others have suggested that rule-governed behavior involves additional processes (see Parrott, 1987, for a discussion of these issues).

Regardless of one's view about the behavior of the listener, verbal behavior requires special attention because the consequences of verbal behavior are *mediated by the actions of others* (Vargas, 1998). The way a person speaks is shaped by the consequences supplied by the listener. A busy mother may not respond to the polite response of "milk, please" by her child. However, a change in form to "Give me milk!" may induce compliance. Inadvertently, the mother is teaching her child to give commands in a loud voice. Subtle contingencies of reinforcement shape the style, dialect, tonal quality, and other properties of speaking.

The contingencies that regulate verbal behavior arise from the practices of people in the **verbal community**. These practices are part of the culture of the group and they have evolved over time (Skinner, 1953). The practices of the verbal community therefore refer to the customary ways that people reinforce the behavior of a speaker. In an English-speaking community, the speaker who substitutes "also" for "in addition" or "besides" is likely to be reinforced, especially if repetition is bothersome to the listener. When linguists analyze the grammar of a language, they state rules that describe the reinforcing practices of the verbal community. For example, the grammatical rule "i before e except after c" describes a requirement for reinforcement set by the community; the written word *recieved* is reinforced while *received* is not. Thus, verbal behavior is established and maintained by the reinforcing practices of the community and these practices change based on cultural evolution. The analysis of cultural change in terms of verbal practices requires the integration of several fields of study, including anthropology, archeology, and linguistics, and is beyond the scope of this textbook.

OPERANT FUNCTIONS OF VERBAL BEHAVIOR

In his book *Verbal Behavior*, Skinner (1957) presented a preliminary analysis of this kind of human activity. Although some linguists have treated Skinner's work as a behavioral theory of language, it is more likely that the book represents a set of testable hypotheses about verbal behavior (MacCorquodale, 1970). Skinner described verbal behavior in terms of the principles found in the operant laboratory. Such an analysis must ultimately be judged in terms of its adequacy. That is, it must deal with the facts of the speaker's behavior in natural settings and the experimental and observational evidence that supports or refutes such an account. In this section, the basic verbal classes are outlined using Skinner's (1957) distinctions as well as clarifications made by others (e.g., Michael, 1982b; Oah & Dickinson, 1989). Remember that the basic units or elements of verbal behavior would be combined, elaborated, and extended in any comprehensive account of speaking, talking, and communicating. How these basic units are integrated into actual complex speech requires continuing analysis and research, as found in the journal *The Analysis of Verbal Behavior* published by the International Association for Behavior Analysis.

Functional Operant Units: Manding and Tacting

Verbal behavior may be separated into two broad operant classes, manding and tacting, based on the regulating conditions. These two operant classes involve the functions of getting what you want from others (manding) and making contact or reference to things and happenings in the world (tacting).

When you say, "Give me the book," "Don't do that," "Stop," and so on, your words are regulated by motivational conditions—deprivation for the book, or another person doing something unpleasant. In behavior analysis, this verbal behavior is called manding. **Manding** refers to a class of verbal operants whose form is regulated by establishing operations (e.g., deprivation, aversive stimulation, etc.). The word manding comes from the common English word *commanding*, but commanding is only a small part of this operant class.

Everyday examples of manding include asking someone for a glass of water when thirsty, or requesting directions from a stranger when lost. Notice that specific reinforcement is made effective for manding by some establishing operation. A glass of water reinforces asking for it when you are deprived of water, and directions are reinforcement for requesting them when you are lost. Common forms of manding include speaking or writing orders, asking questions, requesting objects or things, giving flattering comments to others, and promoting commercial products (i.e., "buy this detergent").

There is another major class of verbal operants. **Tacting** is defined as a class of verbal operants whose form is regulated by nonverbal discriminative stimuli (nonverbal S^D) and maintained by generalized conditioned reinforcement from the verbal community. A child is tacting when she says "The sun is orange" in the presence of the midday sun on a beach with her mother. In this example, the presence of the sun in the sky (and the relevant property of color) is a nonverbal S^D for tacting by the child. The operant class of tacting is maintained by generalized conditioned reinforcement from the verbal community (e.g., mother, father, teacher, and others), usually in the form of corrective feedback such as "yes," "right," and so on. The word tacting comes from the more familiar term *contacting* and refers to verbal behavior that makes contact with events in the world (nonverbal S^Ds). Everyday examples of tacting include describing a scene, identifying objects, providing information about things or issues, and reporting on your own behavior and that of others.

Occasionally, it is difficult to distinguish between manding and tacting. A child who says "juice" in the presence of a glass of apple juice could mean "give juice" or "that is a glass of juice." If the response is equivalent to "give juice" it is functioning as manding (controlled by deprivation and the specific reinforcement of "getting juice"), but it is tacting if the response is controlled by the non-verbal stimulus of the glass of juice. In another example, a person who says, "I believe you have the sports page," may be tacting the nonverbal stimulus (the sports page) or manding specific reinforce-ment (getting the sports page). The issue is often resolved by the listener saying "Yes, I do" and returning to read the paper. If the original response was manding, the listener's reply will not function as reinforcement (the sports page is not given). In this case, the speaker is likely to clarify the disguised manding by stating, "May I please have the sports page!"

In a further example, a man who picks up his girlfriend for a date may say, "Darling, you look beautiful tonight." Again, *the form of response cannot distinguish manding from tacting*. If the man's verbal response is regulated by abstract properties of "beauty" (nonverbal S^D) of the woman, he is tacting. On the other hand, the verbal response could be regulated by deprivation for sexual reinforcement and, if so, the man is manding. Only an analysis and test of the relevant contingencies can distinguish between manding and tacting behavior. Thus, the woman could test the controlling contingencies by withholding sexual reinforcement—testing the veracity of her date's flattering remarks.

Many advertisements and television commercials are disguised manding, in the sense that the verbal responses of an announcer seem to describe the benefits of the product (tacting), but are in fact requests to buy it (manding). A television actor dressed in a doctor's white coat states that "Xprin relieves pain and muscle ache" and is available at your local drug store. The verbal descrip-tion of the product (relieves pain) suggests tacting by the speaker (actor) but there are manding (profit) aspects to the verbal behavior. Given these conflicting contingencies, listeners learn how to reveal the disguised manding of a speaker (testing the controlling variables), and speakers learn to conceal their obvious manding of a listener (making the verbal description of the product appear as tacting its benefits). Persuasion and attitude change may be analyzed therefore in terms of manding, tacting, and the interaction of speakers and listeners (Bem, 1965).

RESEARCH ON VERBAL BEHAVIOR

Training of Verbal Operants

According to Skinner (1957), the basic classes of verbal behavior are functionally independent in the sense that the relations involved in manding are distinct from those that define tacting. This functional independence means that it is possible to teach manding and tacting as separate operant classes. It also implies that there is no basic ordering of the verbal repertoire; that is, it is not necessary to train manding in order to train tacting, or vice versa. In this section, research on basic verbal relations will be outlined and assessed in terms of **functional independence** of the response classes.

Manding relations

Recall that the manding relation is defined by an establishing operation (EO) and specific reinforcement. An establishing procedure regulates the topography or form of manding behavior and sets up a specific consequence as reinforcement. To train manding, the most direct procedure is to manipulate an EO and reinforce the verbal response with the specified consequence. In the laboratory, establishing operations usually involve a history of deprivation for some event that functions as primary reinforcement (e.g., food).

Most human behavior, however, is regulated by conditioned reinforcement. To investigate the manding of conditioned reinforcement, Michael (1988) suggested the use of a **conditioned establishing operation (CEO)**. The procedure is called the blocked-response CEO, in which a response that usually occurs is blocked because of the temporary absence of a specific condition, stimulus, or event. For example, you may leave your seminar notes at home as you rush to the university. Because you cannot complete the behavioral sequence of giving a seminar presentation, obtaining the notes would function as reinforcement for making a telephone call to get them. The notes would not have a reinforcement function during a casual lunch with an old friend, because they are not necessary to this behavioral sequence. Whenever an event or stimulus is required to complete a behavior chain, withholding the event will establish it as reinforcement for operant behavior (see Michael, 2000, for a more extensive analysis).

Hall and Sundberg (1987) used the blocked-response CEO to train manding by deaf subjects. The first step was to teach a sequence or chain of responses. For example, a subject was taught to open a can of fruit with a can opener, to pour the contents into a bowl, and to eat it with a spoon. When the sequence was trained, the subject was given the items to complete the chain, except that one was missing. In this situation, a previously trained verbal response that specified the missing item (manding) was reinforced by the teacher supplying the object. Since subjects came to emit such verbal responses, it appears that CEO and specific reinforcement are regulating conditions for manding behavior (see also Carroll & Hesse, 1987; Yamamoto & Mochizuki, 1988).

There are other studies of manding training that did not manipulate an establishing operation (Hung, 1980; Rogers-Warren & Warren, 1980; Savage-Rumbaugh, 1984; Simic & Bucher, 1980; Sundberg, 1985). In these studies, humans, apes, and pigeons were required to produce a response that specified a particular object (food items or toys). The objects were shown to the subject to evoke an appropriate manding response (EO). When the verbal response occurred, the object was given and this functioned as specific reinforcement.

For example, in the study by Savage-Rumbaugh (1984), chimpanzees were shown a number of food items. If the animal pointed to the corresponding symbol on a communication panel, the item was given as reinforcement. Chimpanzees readily acquired this kind of verbal behavior and even more complex symbolic communication (Savage-Rumbaugh, 1986; Savage-Rumbaugh & Lewin,

1994; Savage-Rumbaugh, Shanker, & Taylor, 1998). However, there is some question as to the exact regulating conditions. The food items may have functioned as discriminative stimuli that set the occasion for selecting the corresponding symbol key, in which case the chimpanzee was tacting rather than manding. Because the sources of control were complex, the behavior is best described as *impure manding* (i.e., it is attributable to the control exerted by the food items as discriminative stimuli and specific reinforcement).

In chimpanzee studies, pointing to a food symbol is taken as manding since it results in getting the item. Pointing at something is a type of manding in which the response topography or form (index finger extended) remains constant but the response is directed at different stimuli (banana, apple, etc.). This contrasts with human speech, in which the topography of the vocal response varies with the establishing operation and specific reinforcement (i.e., "give food" versus "give water"). Vocal manding facilitates discrimination by a listener (the form of response varies) and may therefore produce more rapid and precise compliance to manding. Although pointing to what you want is formally manding, saying what you want is much more effective—especially if the listener is in another room, or the object is out of sight.

Finally, manding can involve control of verbal behavior by contingencies of negative reinforcement. In a recent study, Yi, Christian, Vittimberga, and Lowenkron (2006) developed a program to increase the quality of life for three children with autism. The researchers taught the youngsters manding for the removal of nonpreferred items. This negatively reinforced manding generalized to other untrained items as well.

Tacting relations

To train tacting responses, a speaker must come to emit a verbal operant whose form depends on a nonverbal discriminative stimulus. A second requirement is that the operant class be acquired and maintained by *nonspecific reinforcement*. Reinforcement is nonspecific if the reinforcer for one response exerts no stimulus control over the form of the next response. In animal studies, a response may qualify as tacting even if it is reinforced with food, as long as food reinforcement does not set the occasion for a subsequent verbal response or the selection of the next symbol. For example, a chimpanzee may be offered an apple, and when it selects the symbol key for apple it is given a piece of banana. The presentation of the banana cannot set the occasion for pressing the symbol for apple on the next trial.

Tacting relations have been investigated with chimpanzees. Savage-Rumbaugh (1984) used pointing to symbol keys as the verbal response. When the experimenter displayed an item of food (apple), a response to the corresponding symbol resulted in praise and the delivery of a different item of food (banana). That is, the item of food used as reinforcement always differed from the one on display.

In this situation, the display of an item of food was a nonverbal S^D that set the occasion for a response to the appropriate symbol key (tacting). Since reinforcement was nonspecific, the consequences of behavior could not regulate pointing to a particular symbol. That is, because the chimpanzee points to the apple symbol (in the presence of an apple) and is reinforced with a banana, we can be sure that the verbal response is tacting rather than manding.

Chimpanzees' symbol pointing came under the control of the displayed food items and therefore qualified as tacting. In this experiment, the *topography of the tact was the same* (i.e., pointing with finger), but its location changed. In contrast, vocal tacting in human speech involves *changes in topography depending on the nonverbal stimulus* (i.e., "that's a chair" or "there's a table"). Finally, the delivery of a food item is probably not necessary and generalized conditioned reinforcement (e.g., praise, acceptance, etc.) alone could be used to train tacting in both apes and human children (see Savage-Rumbaugh, Murphy, Sevcik, Brakke, Williams, & Rumbaugh, 1993; Savage-Rumbaugh, Shanker, & Taylor, 1998; see also Sundberg, 1996, for a behavioral analysis).

Researchers also have used pigeons to investigate tacting relations. Michael, Whitley, and Hesse

(1983) attempted to train tacting based on changes in response topography. Pigeons received nonspecific reinforcement (food) that depended on a bird emitting a particular form of response in the presence of a nonverbal discriminative stimulus. For example, a thrust of the head was reinforced when a red ball was presented, and turning in a circle produced reinforcement when a blue ball was the discriminative stimulus. Functionally, this is equivalent to a child who says "That's a red coat" and "This is a brown coat" and is reinforced by acceptance of the description by the listener. Tacting in the pigeons was successfully established even though the contingencies required correspondence between the nonverbal stimulus and the form of the bird's response. A question that is left unanswered by this research is whether pigeons (or chimps) can show generalization of a tacting relation. That is, without further training, would the respective responses for blue and red occur when the objects were triangles or squares rather than balls?

In terms of application, there are behavioral experiments with language-delayed humans that trained tacting as part of a more general program of language acquisition (Carroll & Hesse, 1987; Guess, 1969; Guess & Baer, 1973; Guess, Sailor, Rutherford, & Baer, 1968; Lamarre & Holland, 1985; Lee, 1981a). Carroll and Hesse (1987) investigated the effects of alternating between manding and tacting training. During manding training, a response to an object produced the item. When tacting was trained, the experimenter presented the objects as discriminative stimuli and provided praise as reinforcement for correct responses. Results indicated that subjects responded appropriately to the verbal contingencies, and that *manding training facilitated the acquisition of tacting*. That is, manding "give cup" increased the acquisition of tacting "that's a cup." This latter finding is interesting because it suggests that under some conditions manding and tacting are not independent classes of behavior (e.g., Sigafoos, Doss, & Reichle, 1989; Sigafoos, Reichle, Doss, Hall, & Pettitt, 1990). Apparently, these verbal operant relations may interrelate, as when parts of the response forms are shared (i.e., both involve the word "cup").

Experiments by Lamarre and Holland (1985) and Lee (1981b) also concerned the acquisition of tacting by language-delayed humans (see also Partington, Sundberg, Newhouse, & Spengler, 1994, for tacting training of an autistic child). In these experiments, one object was placed on the left and another on the right. The tact response was saying "on the right" or "on the left" depending on the position of the object. For example, the experimenter would prompt "Where is the dog?" The subject who answered "on the right" when the dog was on the right of a flower was reinforced with social praise. This type of training successfully established verbal responses that contacted the position of an object. In another version of tacting training, Guess (1969), Guess and Baer (1973), and Guess et al. (1968) trained verbal responses that contacted the quantity of an object. Subjects with language deficits were taught to emit the singular form of a noun when a single object was shown, and to emit the plural form if two identical items were presented.

In these experiments, correct responses produced food, rather than praise. Thus, the subject was presented with a single cup, and saying "cup" rather than "cups" was reinforced with food. Food may be defined as nonspecific reinforcement in such studies because it does not exert any stimulus control over the next verbal response "cup." In humans, both generalized conditioned reinforcement (e.g., praise) and nonspecific reinforcement (e.g., food in the preceding example) may be used to establish tacting to various features of the nonverbal environment (e.g., position of objects, quantity, etc.).

Overall, Skinner's (1957) description of the controlling variables for manding and tacting has been verified by research on a variety of animals, including primates, young children, and language-delayed humans. This research shows that manding is verbal behavior under the control of an establishing operation (EO) and specific reinforcement. In contrast, tacting is verbal behavior controlled by nonverbal discriminative stimuli and generalized reinforcement (or nonspecific reinforcement). The experimental analysis of manding and tacting has resulted in a technology of training verbal behavior in humans who do not show basic verbal skills (Sundberg & Michael, 2001). Although manding and tacting may be established as independent verbal operant classes (Lamarre & Holland, 1985), the evidence from applied research suggests that the verbal contingencies are interrelated so that training in manding relations may aid in the acquisition of tacting relations, and vice versa.

ADDITIONAL VERBAL RELATIONS: INTRAVERBALS, ECHOICS, AND TEXTUALS

Intraverbal Relations

Other verbal responses also depend on discriminative stimuli. **Intraverbal behavior** is a class of verbal operants regulated by verbal discriminative stimuli. Verbal stimuli arise from verbal behavior; a verbal response by a speaker ("one, two, three . . .") may be a stimulus for a subsequent verbal operant by the same speaker ("four"). When a verbal response ("Mary") exactly replicates the verbal stimulus ("say Mary"), we may say there is correspondence between them. In this case, the verbal behavior is defined as echoic (see below). Intraverbal behavior, however, has no point-to-point correspondence between the verbal stimulus ("jack, queen . . .") and the response ("king").

In everyday language, thematically related words (or sentences) are examples of intraverbal behavior. For example, the verbal response "fish" to the spoken words "rod and reel" is an intraverbal operant; saying "water" to the written word "lake" is also intraverbal behavior. On the other hand, the person who says "water" to the spoken sound "water" is not showing intraverbal regulation; in this case, there is exact correspondence between the response and the stimulus, and the response is echoic.

Intraverbal training is part of our educational curriculum. In elementary school, students are taught to say the multiplication table, as in "5×5 equals 25" and so on. In this example, the verbal stimulus "5×5" exerts direct stimulus control over the response "25" and the relation is intraverbal. In contrast, a student who derives the answer "25" by adding five 5s, counting by 5s, or counting the cells in a 5-by-5 matrix is tacting the number or set of elements rather than emitting an intraverbal response. As you can see, the training of academic behavior in young children involves several verbal relations, including tacting and intraverbal behavior (see DeBaryshe & Whitehurst, 1986; Partington & Bailey, 1993). Children and adults with language deficits may also benefit from intraverbal training (eg., Sundberg, Endicott, & Eigenheer, 2000; Sundberg & Michael, 2001).

Echoic Relations

When there is point-to-point correspondence between the stimulus and response, verbal behavior may be classified as either echoic or textual, depending on the criterion of formal similarity. The contingencies of echoic behavior require formal similarity while the contingencies of textual behavior do not (see below). **Formal similarity** requires that the verbal stimulus and the product of the response be in the same mode (auditory, visual, etc.) and have exact physical resemblance (e.g., same sound pattern). **Echoic behavior** is defined as a class of verbal operants regulated by a verbal stimulus in which there is *correspondence and formal similarity* between the stimulus and response. Saying "this is a dog" to the spoken stimulus "this is a dog" is an example of an echoic response in human speech. Generally, *echoic behavior is generalized imitation along a vocal dimension* (see Chapter 11 and Poulson, Kymissis, Reeve, Andreatos, & Reeve, 1991).

Echoic behavior occurs at an early age in an infant's acquisition of speech. The child who repeats "dada" or "mama" to the same words uttered by a parent is showing echoic operant behavior. In this situation, any product of behavior (sound pattern of child) that closely replicates the verbal stimulus (modeled sound pattern) is reinforced.

Although reinforcement appears to occur along a dimension of acoustical correspondence, the contingencies of echoic behavior are probably based more on the matching of phonetic units. Catania (1998a) indicates that the learning of echoic behavior begins with the basic units of speech called phonemes. He explains:

> The significant dimensions of the units of speech called phonemes are more easily defined by articulations (position of the tongue, etc.) than by acoustic properties . . . The interactions of articulation and sounds are complex; for example, many English consonants (e.g., *p*, *b*, *d*) can't be produced unless accompanied by a vowel, and their acoustic properties vary as a function of context (e.g., the sounds of *l* and *k* are different in *lick* than in *kill*). Echoic behavior isn't defined by acoustic correspondence; it's defined by correspondences of the phonetic units.
>
> (p. 241)

Coordinated movements of the child's larynx, tongue, and lips result in phonemes (e.g., "ma") that replicate parts of adult speech ("ma . . . ma"). When articulations by the child correspond to those of the adult, the acoustical patterns also overlap. Adults who hear speech-relevant sounds ("ma") often provide social consequences (e.g., tickling, poking, etc.) that are paired with these acoustical patterns. On this basis, the duplication of speech sounds itself comes to function as automatic reinforcement for speech-relevant articulations by the child (Yoon & Bennett, 2000).

It is important to emphasize that echoic behavior is not simply the duplication of sounds. As a verbal operant, echoic performance is regulated by specific reinforcement contingencies based on articulation. Echoic contingencies in humans involve reinforcement by listeners of correspondence of basic speech units rather than the mere reproduction of sounds. These units begin as phonemes (i.e., smallest sound units to which listeners react), expand to words, and eventually may include full phrases and sentences. In contrast, parrots and other birds duplicate the sounds they hear (Pepperberg, 1981, 2000) but their behavior is not necessarily verbal in Skinner's (1957) sense. Parrots will reproduce sounds or noises even when these responses produce no change in the behavior of the listener. For this reason an infant's speech is echoic behavior, but a parrot's "speech" is not.

Echoic contingencies are most prevalent during language acquisition. This means that an infant's vocalizations will have more echoic components than the speech of an adult. It also implies that adult speech will become more echoic when a person is learning to speak a second language. Thus, a Spanish teacher may demonstrate word pronunciation to a student who initially makes many errors in articulation. The teacher gives repeated examples, and the student is reinforced for correct pronunciation. After some practice and correction, the student's pronunciation is close to that of the teacher's. Only when the speech units correspond is the student said to show competence in pronunciation of Spanish.

Textual Relations

Verbal behavior is textual when there is no formal similarity between the stimulus and response. **Textual behavior** is defined as a class of verbal operants regulated by verbal stimuli where there is correspondence between the stimulus and response, but no formal similarity. The most common example of textual behavior is reading out loud. The child looks at the text, See Dick see Jane, and emits the spoken words "See . . . Dick, . . . see . . . Jane." In adult reading, the behavior is also textual but the "out loud" aspect is no longer emitted—the person reads silently so that the response is now a private event. Textual behavior is also observed when a secretary *takes dictation* from his or her boss. In this case, hearing the spoken words "Dear Mr. Smith . . ." by the boss sets the occasion for writing these words by the secretary. Again, correspondence between the stimulus and response occurs but there is no formal similarity.

ANALYSIS OF COMPLEX BEHAVIOR IN THE LABORATORY

Faced with the complexity of verbal behavior, many people find it hard to believe that basic behavior principles, such as stimulus control, shaping, and schedules of reinforcement, can eventually account for this kind of human activity. It is useful therefore to step back and consider the contingencies of complex behavior. Analysis of these contingencies convinced Skinner (1957) that operant principles could eventually provide a natural-science account of human language. [Note: Chomsky (1957, 1959) argued against behavior principles and for a system of mental rules underlying the speaker's performance; Schoneberger (2000) proposes that Chomsky now rejects the mental-rules account of language and his former ties to cognitivism.]

Although there are many distinctions between the verbal behavior of humans and the complex behavior generated in pigeons, the laboratory analog identifies some of the basic contingencies that play a role in human language acquisition. In this section, we consider experimental procedures that result in pigeons showing conditional discriminations, symbolic communication, and communication of internal and private events. Many of these behaviors, if observed in humans, would be attributed to mental rules and processes rather than the contingencies of reinforcement that were known to produce them.

Let us begin with a fairly complex set of contingencies for pigeons. Consider a conditional-discrimination experiment described by Catania (1980), in which a pigeon is placed in an operant chamber with left and right keys (Figure 12.2). Stimuli can be projected on the keys, and a light is situated in one corner of the response panel, allowing general illumination of the chamber (i.e., a houselight). The stimuli consist of circles with horizontal or vertical lines, and triangles with similar angled lines (see matrix of Figure 12.2). Centered below the keys is a feeder that provides food reinforcement depending on the prevailing conditions. When the houselight is ON, pecks to the left or right keys are reinforced according to line angle— horizontal or vertical (ON = peck by line angle). If the houselight is OFF, pecks to the keys produce food on the basis of form—circle or triangle (OFF = peck by form). There are four possible arrangements of the two keys by line angle when the houselight is ON and four other arrangements by form when the houselight is OFF. For each session the houselight is illuminated or not, and the four arrangements by line angle (or form) are presented in random order.

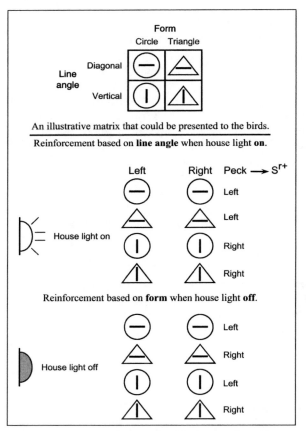

FIG. 12.2 Hypothetical experiment for conditional discrimination is shown as described by Catania (1984). A matrix of possible shapes and line angles is portrayed. When the houselight is ON, reinforcement is based on line angle; the pigeon pecks left if the line angle is horizontal and pecks right if it is vertical. When the houselight is OFF, reinforcement is based on geometric form; the bird pecks left when the shape is a circle and pecks right when it is a triangle.

Figure 12.2 portrays the contingencies based on whether the houselight is ON or OFF. During sessions when the houselight is ON, pecks to the left key are reinforced if the line angle projected on the two keys is horizontal (HORIZONTAL = peck left key) and pecking the right key is on extinction. When the line angle on the two keys is vertical, pecks to the right key produce food (VERTICAL = peck right key) and pecking the left key is on extinction. Notice that the form of the stimuli (triangles or circles) has no function when the houselight is ON or illuminated.

In contrast, when the houselight is OFF, key pecks are reinforced depending on form, and line angle no longer has a stimulus function. If circles are presented on the two keys, pecks to the left key are reinforced (CIRCLES = peck left key) and pecking the right key is on extinction. When triangles are projected on the keys, pecks to the right key produce food (TRIANGLES = peck right key) and pecking the left key is on extinction. Notice that the line angle (horizontal or vertical) has no function when the houselight is OFF.

Assuming that the bird's pecking is regulated by the appropriate stimuli, we may say that the performance demonstrates a **conditional discrimination**. Pecking the keys depends on line angle or form, conditional on the illumination of the houselight. These conditional relations among stimuli and responses are also observed in verbal behavior. A child provides the answer "five" when presented with a picture of five dimes and the question, "How many coins?" When asked "What kind of coins are these?" the child will respond "dimes." This kind of verbal performance involves contingencies similar to those that produce conditional discrimination in the laboratory.

This does not mean that the pigeon's performance should be called verbal. The laboratory procedure shows that nonverbal processes (conditional discrimination) may play a role in verbal behavior. In the pigeon experiments, the bird responded to angle and form only within the narrow context of the operant chamber. Verbal behavior in humans is not limited to specific situations or circumstances. You may also have noted that the bird's performance was maintained by food, and this is seldom the case with human verbal behavior. Additionally, no audience responded to the performance and mediated reinforcement. In each of these respects, and perhaps others, the pigeon's behavior may be distinguished from human verbal performance. The point, however, is that conditional control by stimuli (e.g., four-term contingencies) is important in an analysis of human behavior, and this is especially so for verbal behavior.

Symbolic Communication in Animals

One implication of complex stimulus control in the laboratory is that animals exposed to such contingencies often acquire behavior that in humans is said to reflect mental or cognitive processes. That is, human communication is said to be caused by our expanded brain capacity and cognitive abilities. Behavior analysts offer an alternative to the mental capacity approach, arguing that symbolic communication is caused by special contingencies of reinforcement. To test this assumption, nonhuman organisms have been trained to emit verbal responses. In this research, one subject is designated the speaker and the other the listener. The roles of speaker and listener are used here to suggest the verbal exchange between two organisms, one who asks for and uses information (listener) and the other who supplies it (speaker).

The Jack and Jill experiment

Epstein, Lanza, and Skinner (1980) first reported communication by pigeons in *Science* magazine. They wanted to show that language-like behavior could be generated in simple organisms by complex contingencies of reinforcement and, by implication, that human language could be generated by complex verbal contingencies.

The original experiment used discrimination procedures based on color; the illustrations in this textbook are in black and white and for clarity we will substitute procedures based on geometric

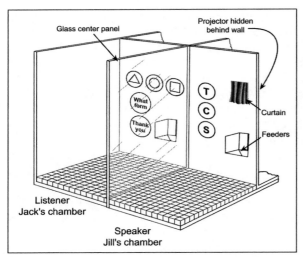

Glass center panel

Projector hidden
behind wall

What
form

Thank
you

T
C
S

Curtain

Feeders

Listener
Jack's chamber

Speaker
Jill's chamber

FIG. 12.3   Chambers and key arrangements are shown for the Jack and Jill experiment as described by Epstein, Lanza, and Skinner (1980). For clarity, we have substituted geometric forms for color stimuli. The experiment involved communication between two pigeons. The curtain in Jill's chamber hides a projected geometric form (triangle, circle, or square). The letter or symbols correspond to the geometric forms (T = triangle, C = circle, and S = square). Jack matches geometric form (triangle, circle, or square) to the symbol key (T, C, or S) pecked by Jill. See text for a description of the contingencies.

forms (e.g., triangles) rather than colors. The pigeons, called Jack and Jill, were placed in separate chambers with a clear Plexiglas partition between them (see Figure 12.3). In the original procedure, Jack was the listener and Jill was the speaker (see Epstein & Skinner, 1981, for implications of training both birds as speaker and listener). The interrelationship between the behavioral sequences of the speaker and listener defines the **interlocking contingencies** for the experiment. Following basic training for both birds to establish the respective operant chains, the interaction began when Jack pecked a key in his chamber with the words *What form?* projected on it. When this happened, one of three forms—triangle, circle, or square—was illuminated in Jill's chamber. Importantly, the form was hidden by a curtain and could not be seen by Jack (see Figure 12.3).

The speaker, Jill, thrust her head behind the curtain and looked at the geometric form projected on a disk. Following this, she pecked one of three symbol or letter keys, labeled with the letters T, C, or S (T = triangle; C = circle; S = square), that matched the form she had observed behind the curtain. When Jack looked into Jill's chamber, he saw which symbol key she had pecked; he then pecked his *Thank you* key, which in turn operated Jill's feeder for a few seconds. Following this, Jack pecked one of three form keys in his chamber (e.g., triangle, circle, or square) that corresponded to the symbol (T, C , or S) selected by Jill. If Jack matched his form key to the symbol pecked by Jill (e.g., pecked his triangle key when Jill had pecked her T symbol key), this response operated Jack's feeder for a few seconds. An incorrect response resulted in a short time out. After 5 days of this interaction, the pigeons were accurate on more than 90% of the trials.

Formally, the experiment involved training pigeons in manding and tacting. Completion of the interaction sequence between the speaker and listener is defined as a **social episode**. The role of listener (Jack) required manding *What form?* His "question" is manding that is reinforced by Jill reporting the form she had observed behind the curtain. Jill "reports" her observation by pecking one of the three symbols or letter keys. This "report" by the speaker (Jill) allows the listener (Jack) to peck the corresponding geometric form on his panel. Because pecking the correct form is part of a sequence that leads to food, hiding the geometric shape from the listener may be viewed as a conditioned establishing operation (CEO, blocked-response procedure) in this experiment.

The speaker's sequence also is initiated when the listener pecks *What form?* In the presence of this verbal stimulus, the speaker must look at the form behind the curtain and "report" on the shape she has seen. Pecking the correct symbol key is formally tacting in Skinner's (1957) classification of verbal behavior. The symbolic response qualifies as tacting; a nonverbal aspect of the environment (the hidden color) controls the response that results in nonspecific reinforcement (i.e., the food supplied when the listener pecks *Thank you*). A nonspecific reinforcer is one that does not specify the topography of a subsequent tacting response. The speaker pecks T, C, or S and is reinforced with grain. The presentation of grain at the end of the listener–speaker interaction does not control which symbol the speaker pecks on the next trial.

Communication by pigeons maintained by food reinforcement is a demonstration that complex contingencies generate complex behavior, even in relatively simple organisms like pigeons. Of course, human verbal behavior involves sound production and infinite variations and combinations of phonemes and words. But the verbal environment, composed of speakers from the verbal community, arranges intricate verbal contingencies that select the common forms and grammar of everyday speaking much as the contingencies of reinforcement did in the Jack and Jill demonstration.

Communication and generalized reinforcement

In human communication, tacting by a speaker almost never results in food reinforcement. It is therefore important to know whether animals will continue tacting when this behavior is supported by generalized conditioned reinforcement. An experiment by Lubinski and MacCorquodale (1984) with pigeons was designed to answer such a question. These researchers established a generalized reinforcer for the speaker by pairing a flashing light with the presentation of *both* food and water. On some days the pigeon was deprived of food and on other days it was deprived of water. Occasionally, the pigeon was deprived of both food and water. When deprived of food, the bird could peck a key that operated a feeder. When the bird was thirsty, it could peck a different key to produce water. Importantly, responses for food or water were only effective when a light was flashing in the chamber. The flashing light functioned as a *generalized conditioned reinforcer* because it was associated with more than one source of primary reinforcement (food and water). Using the flashing light as reinforcement, Lubinski and MacCorquodale (1984) showed that tacting in pigeons would occur even when the only consequence was reinforcement from the "flashing light."

Research on nonhuman communication plays an important role in behavior analysis (see Lubinski & Thompson, 1993, for a review). Although human communication involves far more than the manding and tacting of symbols and forms, these nonhuman experiments point to the *basic elements* that underlie symbolic communication. This research also suggests that human communication may arise from the simultaneous interplay of relatively simple principles of behavior—in this case, shaping, fading, chaining, and discrimination procedures.

FOCUS ON: Reports of private events by pigeons

One of the actions that is said to separate humans from other animals is the ability to report on internal states and feelings. Behaviorists maintain that humans do not have unique capabilities that give them self-awareness or special knowledge of themselves. Rather, behavior analysts suggest that self-description is something a person learns by interacting with others who ask questions about the person and her private events (e.g., "How do you feel?"). *It is only because of special verbal contingencies that a person acquires a repertoire of self-description* (Bem, 1965; Skinner, 1957).

As we have seen in earlier chapters, behavior analysts treat the internal and external happenings of an organism as *physical and functional* events. The only difference between the external environment and the one inside us is that internal events are *private*. This privacy means that *internal events are less accessible* to others and, as a result, it is more difficult for the verbal community to teach a person to describe internal events accurately.

When a verbal response is controlled by a nonverbal discriminative stimulus, this response is functionally defined as tacting. A person who has learned to describe the up-and-down flight of a butterfly may say "I have butterflies in my stomach" when upset or nervous. This response is analyzed as extended or *generalized tacting*—the person describes an upset stomach in the same way as a person describing the motion of a butterfly. This suggests that self-description is, in part, based on the verbal relations involved in tacting.

To set up a report on a private event (tacting), it is necessary to have a public event that is well correlated with this private happening. For example, a bump on the head and crying usually accompany painful private stimulation. A child who bumps her head and cries may occasion the response "Oh, you're hurt" by the parent. In this situation, the child is asked where it hurts and how she feels. The youngster is reinforced when she accurately reports "I hurt my head" and "it hurts a lot." Although parents use public events (bumps and crying) to train self-description, the public signs are usually well correlated with private stimulation (physical damage). Because of this correspondence, private stimulation eventually comes to regulate self-descriptive responses (e.g., "I am hurt") even in the absence of public signs like crying.

The verbal relations that are presumed to set up a self-descriptive repertoire may be arranged in a laboratory (see Lubinski & Thompson, 1993). A pigeon is a useful organism on which to test these ideas because pigeons are not usually able to describe themselves. Lubinski and Thompson (1987) therefore used pigeons that were trained to discriminate among the private stimulation produced by different drugs (S^D) and to "report" how they felt in each condition ($R_{tacting}$) for generalized conditioned reinforcement (S^r). *This is another example of communication in nonhuman organisms, but the experiment involves reporting on internal (private) drug effects rather than external events (S^Ds) like triangles, circles, or squares.* Again, the internal effects of the drugs are treated as physical events that pigeons can discriminate, just as pigeons can discriminate among shapes projected on a key. Presumably, humans also discriminate among internal stimulations and are trained by the verbal community to report on these (physical) events. The basic point is that describing one's feelings and emotions is behavior controlled by the *interlocking contingencies* among speakers and listeners (the verbal community).

In Lubinski and Thompson's (1987) experiment, two pigeons were placed in separate chambers, as shown in Figure 12.4. One bird was the "mander" or listener and the other was the "tacter" or speaker, as in other studies of communication in pigeons described in this chapter. The first step was to develop a generalized reinforcer for the tacter. That is, pecking a key for food or a key for water was reinforced only when a blue light was flashing (as in Lubinski & MacCorquodale, 1984). After

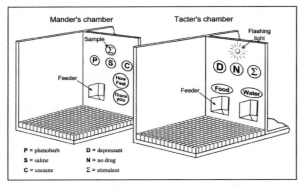

FIG. 12.4 Chambers and key arrangements for the "mander" and "tacter" pigeons are shown for the experiment on communication of internal states by pigeons, as described by Lubinski and Thompson (1987). The symbols D, N, and Σ are equivalent to depressant, no drug, and stimulant. The other symbols P, S, and C are equivalent to phenobarbital, saline, and cocaine. The flashing light is generalized conditioned reinforcement for the behavior of the tacter bird. See text for a description of the contingencies.

this training, the tacting bird was given a drug that was either a depressant, a stimulant, or a saline solution (salt water). Private stimulation consisted of the introceptive effects produced by the different kinds of drugs or chemicals.

Again after extensive training to establish the behavioral sequences, the interaction began with the mander (listener) pecking a *How do you feel?* key in its chamber. This response illuminated three keys in the tacter's (speaker's) chamber. Each key had a symbol: D for depressant, N for no drug, and Σ (sigma) for stimulant. The tacter had to peck a symbol key that corresponded to the drug it had received (D after an injection of phenobarbital; N after saline; Σ after cocaine). When this occurred, a sample disk illuminated in the mander's chamber with the symbol reported by the tacter (Σ), and at the same time a *Thank you* key was illuminated. Pecks to the *Thank you* key by the manding bird activated a flashing blue light in the tacter's chamber. The tacting bird could then receive food or water by pecking the corresponding keys.

The interaction ended with the mander pecking one of three comparison keys that matched the sample (D, N, or Σ) reported by the tacting bird. The mander's three keys had the letter P, S, or C on them: P for phenobarbital, S for saline, and C for cocaine. If the symbol N (no drug) was the sample (the tacting bird had pecked the N key), pecking the S key for saline resulted in food reinforcement for the mander. Reinforcement also occurred if the mander pecked its P key for pentobarbital when D (depressant) was the sample, or pecked the C key for cocaine when Σ (stimulant) was the sample. Notice that this experiment is similar to the experiments in which pigeons reported on hidden forms or symbols. The interesting twist on the procedure is that the tacting bird reports an internal and private drug state ("I am on a stimulant" = Σ). The mander, on the other hand, indicates her "understanding the feeling" by matching the symbol for the drug to the sample (pecking the C key for cocaine).

Although these complex behavioral sequences took a long time to train, eventually the tacter's "reports" and the mander's "comprehensions" were highly accurate—exceeding 90% reliability. At this point, Lubinski and Thompson (1987) conducted additional experiments on the communication of internal events, in order to extend the findings to human behavior. In a test for generalization, the researchers substituted the drug Dexedrine (*d*-amphetamine) for cocaine and Librium (chlordiazapoxide) for pentobarbital. Although the Dexedrine and Librium differ chemically and pharmacologically from cocaine and pentobarbital, both share pharmacological properties with these agents. *The generalization tests showed that accurate reporting of drug effects occurred even when the same bird was given a different depressant and stimulant.* This finding suggested that the tacting response (i.e., pecking the symbol key that corresponded to the drug effect) had generalized to a class of drugs with common chemical effects. In addition, the experiments showed that *accurate tacting of the drug effects could be maintained by generalized conditioned reinforcement* (as would be the case in human reports of internal states). In this case, the tacting bird was satiated on food and water, and the only result of the report was the blue flashing light. Even though the number of tacting responses declined, the pigeon was still highly reliable at reporting on the internal effects of the drugs.

The research on private events by Lubinski and Thompson (1987) is an important step in the analysis of verbal behavior and self-description. The contingencies arranged by the researchers resulted in a complex sequence of behavior between two pigeons. *When birds are exposed to verbal contingencies that are presumed to operate in human behavior, they begin to act something like humans—reporting on how they feel to one another* (Lubinski & Thompson, 1993).

Self-reference in humans is trained through the socialization practices of the community (Bem, 1965). People in different parts of the world (e.g., India) are able to contact and describe internal events that are usually unavailable to North Americans. These people receive religious and educational training that make them more "aware" of themselves. Although mystical and mentalistic explanations have been given for such abilities, contingencies of reinforcement provide a scientific account of this kind of human behavior.

SYMBOLIC BEHAVIOR AND STIMULUS EQUIVALENCE

For most Americans, the flag is a significant symbol. When we see the flag, we may think of the United States, mother, and apple pie. This suggests that symbolic behavior involves the training of **stimulus equivalence**. The presentation of one class of stimuli (e.g., flags) occasions responses made to other stimulus classes (e.g., countries). This seems to be what we mean when we say that the flag stands for, represents, or signifies our country. Equivalence relations such as these are an important aspect of human behavior. For example, in teaching a child to read, spoken words (names of animals) are trained to visual stimuli (pictures of animals) and then to written symbols (written words for animals). Eventually, the written word is then said to stand for (or mean) the actual object, in the same sense that a flag stands for a country. In this section, we will examine the behavior analysis of equivalence relations as a scientific account of symbolic activity and meaning.

Basic Equivalence Relations

When stimulus class A is shown to be interchangeable with stimulus class B (if A = B then B = A), we may say that the organism shows **symmetry** between the stimulus classes. Symmetry is only one form of equivalence relation. A more elementary form of equivalence is called **reflexivity**. In this case, an A to A relation (A = A) is established so that given the color red on a sample key, the organism responds to the comparison key with the identical color (red). A child who is given a picture of a cat and then finds a similar picture in a set of photographs is showing reflexivity (identity matching).

Reflexivity and symmetry are basic logical relations of mathematics. A child who is presented with the number 1 shows reflexivity when she points to 1 in an array of numbers {2,3,1,4,5}. The same child shows symmetry if, when given the number 2, she selects the set {X, X} rather than {X} or {X, X, X}, and when given {X, X} she selects 2 from the array {3,2,1,5,4}.

There is one other equivalence relation in mathematics. This is the relation of **transitivity**. If the written numbers one, two, and three are equivalent to the arithmetic numbers 1, 2, and 3, and these arithmetic numbers are equivalent to sets {X}, {X, X}, and {X, X, X}, it logically follows that one, two, and three are equivalent to sets {X}, {X, X}, and {X, X, X}. That is, if A = B and B = C, then A = C (transitivity).

Experimental Analysis of Equivalence Relations

Although equivalences are logically required by mathematics, it is another thing to show that the behavior of organisms is governed by such relations. In terms of behavior, three stimulus classes (A, B, and C) are called equivalent when an organism has passed tests for reflexivity, symmetry, and transitivity.

A complete experiment for stimulus equivalence consists of both identity and symbolic matching procedures. In **identity matching**, the researcher presents a sample stimulus (e.g., triangle) and two options (e.g., triangle or circle). The organism is reinforced for choosing the triangle option that corresponds to the triangle sample (i.e., matching to sample). **Symbolic matching** involves presenting one class of stimuli as the sample (e.g., geometrical forms) and another set of stimuli (e.g., different line angles) as the options. Reinforcement depends on an arbitrary relation (e.g., triangle = horizontal; flag = country). After the reinforced relations are trained, tests are made for each kind of equivalence relation. *The question is whether reflexivity, symmetry, and transitivity occur without further training.* To make this clear, identity and symbolic matching are training procedures that allow for stimulus equivalence, but the procedures do not guarantee it. We will describe such an experiment in a step-by-step manner.

Figure 12.5 presents the identity-matching procedures used to show reflexivity. The training involves identity matching for line angles or geometric forms by a pigeon. The bird is presented with three keys that may be illuminated as shown in the two displays (Display A or B). For each display, two sets alternate on the three keys. A set includes a sample key and two option keys. For the sake of clarity, in our example the option (side key) that matches the sample is always shown on the left of the displays, and the nonmatching option is on the right. *In real experiments, of course, the position of the matching stimulus varies from trial to trial, eliminating any left or right bias.* A peck on the sample key illuminates the option keys, and pecks to the matching key produce food and the next sample. Pecks to the nonmatching key are not reinforced and lead to the next trial (i.e., the next sample).

Reflexivity

Reflexivity or generalized identity matching may be shown using this identity-matching procedure. In Display A (angle match) of Figure 12.5, the sample key presents a line angle (horizontal). When the pigeon pecks the sample key, horizontal and vertical stimuli are presented on the side keys (matching and nonmatching). Pecks to the horizontal matching key are reinforced with food, while pecks to the vertical nonmatching key are not. The next trial may present Display B (angle match). Now the sample is a vertical line. If the bird pecks the vertical line matching key, it receives food, but pecks to the horizontal line nonmatching key are extinguished. Based on this training and many more matching to sample trials, the bird learns to identify line angles (identity matching).

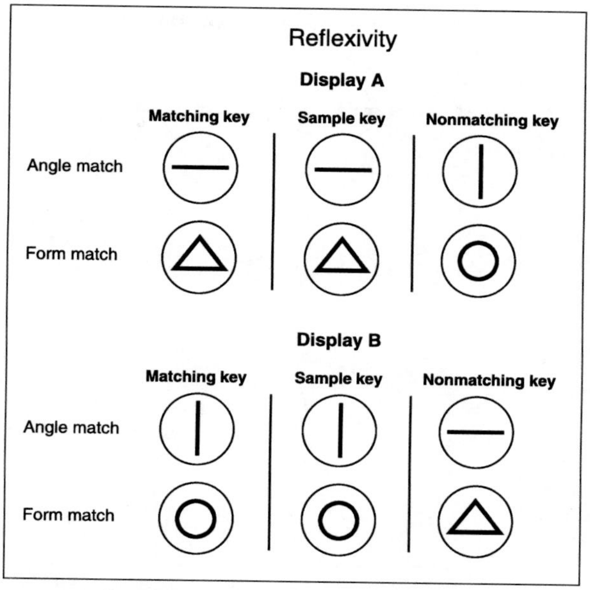

Similar procedures may be used to train identity matching based on geometric form. In Figure 12.5 Display A (form match), the form display is based on triangles and circles.

FIG. 12.5 Identity matching procedures used to establish reflexivity in pigeons, as described by Catania (1984). First, train matching to angles using the *angle match* arrangements in Displays A and B (top). Next, train matching to form using the *form match* arrangements in Displays A and B (bottom). Finally, test for reflexivity or generalized identity matching using color matching displays (not shown). See text for a description of the contingencies.

When Display A is in effect, the sample key is illuminated with a triangle. Pecks to the sample produce the two options—triangle and circle. Pecks to the key that matches the sample are reinforced, while pecks to the nonmatching geometric form are placed on extinction. A new trial may result in Display B (form match). In this case, the sample is a circle. When the bird pecks the sample, two options are presented on the side keys (circle and triangle). Pecks to the key with a circle produce food, but pecks to the triangle are extinguished. Using these procedures, the pigeon learns to identify geometric forms.

Reflexivity is shown by *a test for generalization of identity matching*. A test for reflexivity would involve testing for generalization of identity matching based on the training of matching to sample based on angle and form. For example, a bird trained to identity match to angle and form could be tested with colors (green or red) as the sample and comparison stimuli. A bird that pecks to the color that matches the sample, *without specific training* on colors, shows reflexivity or generalized identity matching. Lowenkron (1998) showed that many instances of generalized identity matching involved the training of joint stimulus control in the sense that two stimuli come to regulate a common response topography.

Symmetry

Figure 12.6 shows the procedures used to train symbolic matching and the tests for symmetry. These procedures are implemented only after a bird has shown identity matching. For example, symbolic matching occurs if the bird is trained to discriminate geometric shapes on the basis of angles (angle-to-form discrimination). Symmetry occurs if the bird can pass *a test for reversal* (form-to-angle discrimination) *without further training*.

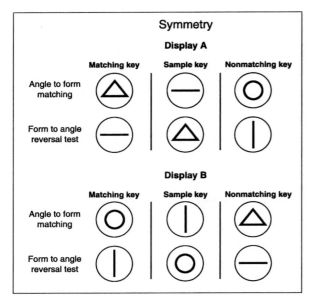

FIG. 12.6 Symbolic matching procedures used to train and test for symmetry in pigeons, as described by Catania (1984). First, train angle-to-form matching (Angle = Form) using the arrangements of Displays A and B (top). Next, test for reversal or symmetry (Form = Angle) using the form-to-angle arrangements of Displays A and B (bottom). See text for a description of the contingencies.

This procedure is shown by the angle-to-form display of Figure 12.6 (Display A). Pecks to the horizontal sample illuminate the side options—triangle or circle. In the presence of the horizontal line sample, pecks to the triangle are reinforced while pecks to the circle are not. When Display B is presented, the sample is the vertical line and pecks to the circle are reinforced while pecking the triangle is on extinction.

Once the matching of angle to geometric form is well established, a **reversal test** (form to angle) is conducted without any further reinforcement. In a reversal test of Display A, the bird is presented with a triangle as the sample and the question is whether it pecks the side key with the horizontal line. Because horizontal = triangle was trained, the bird shows symmetry if it pecks the horizontal comparison key when presented with a triangle sample (triangle = horizontal). Similarly, because vertical = circle was trained, symmetry is shown if the bird pecks the vertical side key of Display B when the circle is presented as the sample (circle = vertical). In everyday language, the bird responds as if the horizontal line stands for triangle and as if the vertical line means circle. The percentage of "correct" responses during the test (without reinforcement) is the usual measure of symbolic performance on this symmetry task.

Transitivity

Figure 12.7 illustrates the procedures that may be used to train and test a pigeon for transitivity. These procedures would be used only if a bird has passed the tests for reflexivity and symmetry. Rows 1 and 5 (Display A and Display B) of the figure present the angle-to-form (symbolic matching) procedures for symmetry that were described earlier (horizontal = triangle; vertical = circle). To test for transitivity, the pigeon is trained to produce an additional discrimination. Rows 2 and 6 of Displays A and B illustrate this training. The pigeon is reinforced for matching a geometric form to intensity of illumination on the option keys—darker or lighter key. For example, in row 2 of Display A, pecking the lighter option key is reinforced when a triangle is the sample (triangle = lighter) and pecking the darker key is not reinforced; also, row 6 of Display B shows that pecking the darker key produces food when a circle is the sample (circle = darker) while pecking the lighter option is on extinction.

Notice that the bird is trained such that horizontal = triangle and vertical = circle (rows 1 and 5) and has shown reversal on tests of symmetry. Given this performance, if triangle = lighter and circle = darker (rows 2 and 6), then the following relations could occur without explicit training on transitivity tests: horizontal = lighter, and lighter = horizontal (rows 3 and 4); also vertical = darker, and darker = vertical (rows 7 and 8). These tests would establish transitivity in the pigeon, showing that the bird responds to the set of line angles as it does to the set of geometric forms, and responds to the set of geometric forms as it does to the set of light intensities (A = B = C). This performance would be similar to a person who responds to the written word *dog* in the same way as to a picture of a dog or the spoken word "dog." The stimuli are said to be equivalent because they regulate the same operant class. Lowenkron (1998) proposed that many instances of *joint stimulus control* (equivalence between stimuli) of response forms underlie human language-related performances involving both logical (relative size and distance) and semantic (word meaning) relations.

FOCUS ON: Behavioral neuroscience and derived conceptual relations

Neuroscientists are searching for the brain mechanisms that support the behavior of language use. Major theories about concept formation difficulties often make use of stimulus equivalence operations as a basis for inferring the acquisition of new knowledge. For example, when stimulus class A is shown to be interchangeable with stimulus class B we say that the two classes show equivalence (symmetry) or that the person has formed a concept. Reinforcing behavior that is under the control of distinct sets of arbitrary conditional relations will result in the appearance of new *derived* relations.

Much is known behaviorally about the formation of equivalence relations, but the brain mechanisms and neural networks underlying this ability are not known. Recently, researchers have applied functional neuroimaging of the brain of conscious humans to reveal the neural systems involved in trained and derived conceptual relations (Schlund, Hoehn-Saric, & Cataldo, 2007). Research of this nature promises to clarify the neurobiological substrates of behavior that are usually taken to indicate conceptual and other higher cognitive processes.

Using a matching to sample task (MTS), human participants were trained to form conditional relations within stimulus classes. That is, the participants were asked to respond to sample and comparison symbols and learn the symbolic equivalences. This type of conditional responding is suspected to recruit specific frontal-parietal and frontal-subcortical brain networks central to higher cognitive functioning. A neuroimaging procedure called functional magnetic resonance imaging (fMRI) allowed the researchers to correlate blood-oxygen-level activation in areas of the brain with the behavioral discriminations for individual participants.

Responding to both conditional and derived relations activated similar regions of

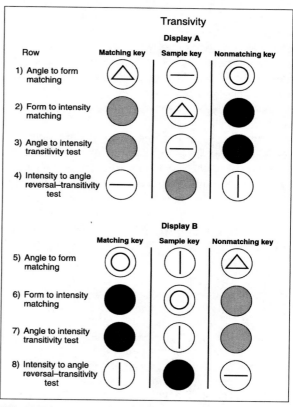

FIG. 12.7 Symbolic matching procedures used to establish and test for transitivity in pigeons, as described by Catania (1984). First, train angle-to-form matching (Angle = Form) using the arrangements in rows 1 and 5 of Displays A and B. Next, train form-to-intensity matching (Form = Intensity) using the arrangements in rows 2 and 6 of Displays A and B. Following training, conduct a transitivity test (Angle = Intensity) using the arrangements in rows 3 and 7 of Displays A and B. Finally, conduct reversal-transitivity tests (Intensity = Angle) using the arrangements in rows 4 and 8 of Displays A and B. See text for a description of the contingencies.

the brain but the magnitude was greater for trained relations in frontal areas of the brain. The researchers also observed predominantly right hemisphere activation, suggesting that the complex conditional responding in this type of task (MTS) is mediated more by nonverbal than verbal processes. The common activation of these frontal regions appears to support conditional responding to both directly trained relations and the derived relations that emerge from the reinforced relations. It is also the case that the frontal area of the brain is often where injuries occur as a result of vehicle accidents. This brain region is not critical for life and therefore victims of such injuries often survive, but are frequently cognitively impaired. Rehabilitation efforts for these victims might be improved by the combined results from neuroimaging and behavioral research. More research is required to better isolate the motor and neural functions of equivalence class formation and to specify more precisely the sensory and motivational aspects of derived conceptual behavior.

Although stimulus-equivalence training has been given to both human and nonhuman subjects, only a limited number of nonhuman studies have claimed that animals can pass tests for reflexivity, symmetry, and transitivity (McIntire, Cleary, & Thompson, 1987; Vaughn, 1988) or symmetry and transitivity (D'Amato, Salmon, Loukas, & Tomie, 1985; Richards, 1988). These studies are controversial since some researchers assert that the animals did not demonstrate generalized relations—all the relations were directly trained (e.g., Hayes, 1989a; Saunders, 1989). Also, in nonhuman research there is some question as to whether the pigeon (or ape) is picking out the key that matches the sample or is merely doing *exclusion*, or rejecting the nonmatching option (Carrigan & Sidman, 1992). These concerns are well taken because, in humans, equivalence relations are easily trained and demonstrated, even in people who are behaviorally retarded (Carr, Wilkinson, Blackman, & McIlvane, 2000).

Another issue is whether equivalent relations are stimulus classes that form on the basis of elementary principles of discrimination and generalization, or whether equivalence itself depends on even higher order operant classes. These higher order classes have been postulated because stimulus equivalence is seemingly unique to human behavior, depending on higher order language categories. Two higher order verbal classes have been proposed: naming and relational concepts or frames. It is beyond the scope of this textbook to elaborate the theories of naming (see Horne & Lowe, 1996) and relational frames (Hayes, 1991; Hayes, Barnes-Holmes, & Roche, 2001). At this point, however, it is useful to understand what is meant by higher order operant classes. Catania (1998b) states that a *higher order class* is

> ... a class that includes within it other classes that can themselves function as operant classes (as generalized imitation includes all component imitations that could be separately reinforced as a subclass) [Chapter 11 of this textbook]. A higher order class [is a generalized operant class], in the sense that contingencies arranged for some subclasses within it generalizes to all the others. ... Higher order classes may be a source of novel behavior (e.g., as in generalized imitation of behavior the imitator had not seen before). [Higher order classes] also have the property that contingencies may operate differently on the higher order class than on its component subclasses. For example, if all instances of imitation are reinforced except those within one subclass (e.g., jumping whenever the model jumps), that subclass may not become differentiated from the higher order class and so may change with the higher order class rather than with the contingencies arranged for it (i.e., the imitation of jumping may not extinguish even though it is no longer reinforced). Control by contingencies arranged for the higher order class rather than by those arranged for the subclasses defines these [higher order] classes; the subclasses may then be said to be insensitive to the contingencies arranged for them. Higher order classes of behavior are held together by the common consequences of their members.

> (p. 416)

All the features of higher order classes of behavior seem to be part of the naming and relational frame accounts of stimulus equivalence. The existence and relevance of these higher order classes is a much-disputed area of behavior analysis and learning (see, for example, the set of commentaries in the 1996 issue of the *Journal of the Experimental Analysis of Behavior, 65,* 243–353).

At the applied level, stimulus equivalence training has been helpful to those who lack reading skills. Researchers have used developmentally delayed people who could pass a reflexivity test (identity matching) but, before training, failed to show symmetry or transitivity (Sidman & Cresson, 1973; Sidman, Cresson, & Wilson-Morris, 1974; see also Lazar, 1977). These subjects were given training in symbolic matching. They were presented with one of 20 spoken names and asked to select the corresponding picture from a comparison set (A = B training). Next, the subjects were trained to select printed words from a set when given one of the 20 names (A = C training). After both training procedures, subjects displayed four untrained relations without further training—two symmetry and two transitivity relations. Subjects showed B to A and C to A reversals—given a picture, they emitted the corresponding name; and given a printed word, they said it. In addition, subjects showed two transitivity relations. When given a picture (e.g., car, boy, dog, etc.), subjects selected the corresponding printed word (B = C), and when given the printed word, they selected the corresponding picture (C = B).

During training the subjects were presented with three stimulus classes that contained 20 elements in each class (spoken words, pictures, and written words). Forty instances of symbolic matching were reinforced (spoken words = pictures, and spoken words = written words). Tests revealed that 80 new instances of correspondence were established indirectly from training (B = A; C = A; B = C; and C = B).

As you can see, the reinforcement of symbolic matching resulted in a preliminary form of reading by these individuals. The limits on this training have not been established, but it seems obvious that equivalence relations make up a large part of human education (mathematics, science, reading, etc.). Equivalence classes are not the same as discriminative stimuli because S^Ds cannot be exchanged for the responses they occasion. Clearly, equivalence relations define symbolic performance and are an important part of the experimental analysis of verbal behavior (see Sidman, 1994).

ON THE APPLIED SIDE: Three-term contingencies and natural speech

At the most basic level, behavior analysts suggest that the acquisition of verbal behavior is governed by contingencies of reinforcement. An important question is whether humans arrange verbal contingencies in their everyday interactions. Evidence of operant contingencies in casual speech is important for a comprehensive account of verbal behavior. When observational research shows natural dependencies between speakers and listeners, we can be more confident that our understanding of speaking (and writing) is not an artifact of laboratory procedures. Also, evidence of verbal contingencies without explicit control by an experimenter suggests that laboratory findings may eventually have general applicability. For both of these reasons, Moerk's (1990) analysis of contingency patterns in mother–child verbal episodes is an important contribution to the analysis of verbal behavior.

Data, Transcripts, and Findings

The data are based on a reanalysis of the verbal interactions between a child named Eve and her mother. The original observations were collected by Roger Brown (1973) as part of a larger study of mother–child interaction. Eve and her mother were observed in their home during everyday activities. When the study began Eve was 18 months old, and she was 28 months old at the end of the research. Brown collected numerous samples of verbal interaction between Eve and her mother over this 10-month period. Moerk selected all odd-numbered samples and analyzed 2 h of transcribed audio recording for each of these samples.

Transcripts were coded by Moerk and two trained research assistants. Observational categories included verbal behavior emitted by both mother and child (Eve). For example, sentence *expansion* involved the mother adding syntactic elements to her child's utterance (Eve says "see boy" and her mother says "You see the boy"), while sentence *reduction* occurred when Eve omitted elements that were originally present in her mother's speech (mother says "give the toy to mommy" and Eve says "give toy mum"). The research focuses on the arrangement of such verbal utterances in mother–child–mother interactions.

Moerk (1990) found that many different mother–child–mother verbal sequences ended with maternal reinforcement. Reinforcement was defined as feedback from the mother that confirmed that Eve's utterance was linguistically acceptable (e.g., "yes," "right," "ok," and so on). A sequence that often occurred was the mother saying a new or rare word (model) that was repeated by Eve (imitation) and followed by her acceptance by the mother (reinforcement). Another three-term pattern involved the mother repeating what she had just said, Eve emitting an approximation to this utterance, and her mother ending the sequence with words of acceptance.

The findings indicate that three-term contingencies (maternal verbal stimulus, child verbal imitation, and maternal reinforcement) characterized many of the verbal episodes of early language learning and are compatible with Skinner's functional analysis of verbal behavior (see also Moerk, 2000).

ADVANCED SECTION: A formal analysis of manding and tacting

In his book *Verbal Behavior*, Skinner (1957) discusses the formal differences in behavior regulation between manding and tacting. In this section on advanced issues, we explore the social contingencies that establish and maintain these two classes of verbal behavior. The contingencies are somewhat complex and diagrams of the interrelationship of the speaker and listener help to depict the controlling variables.

The Manding Relation

Figure 12.8 is a formal analysis of the manding relation. A *social episode* involves the social interaction of speaker and listener. The line through the middle of the diagram separates the speaker's events and actions from those of the listener. Each person completes a behavioral sequence or chain $(S^D: R \to S^r + S^D: R \to S^r . . .)$, and social interaction involves the intermingling of these chains or the *interlocking contingencies* (examine this in Figure 12.8). In the diagram of a social episode, an arrow ($\to$ horizontal or vertical) means "produces or causes"; thus, a verbal response by one person may cause an event, condition, or stimulus for the behavior of the other person (vertical arrow). That is, the verbal behavior of one person functions as a stimulus and/or consequence in the behavior chain of the other person. Also, within the behavioral sequences of each individual, the verbal operants produce effects or consequences (horizontal arrow) supplied by the behavior of the other person (check this out).

In the example of Figure 12.8, we assume that two people are seated at a counter in a cafeteria. Dinner is placed in front of the speaker, but the ketchup is out of reach and situated near the other person or listener. In this context, the presence of food on the table is an *establishing operation* (EO) for behavior that has produced ketchup in the past (see Michael, 1982a, 1993; and Chapter 2). The establishing operation also makes getting ketchup a reinforcing event in this situation.

In addition to the EO, the speaker's manding response ("pass the ketchup") in Figure 12.8 is regulated by the presence of ketchup near the listener (S_1^D for speaker). The first vertical arrow, passing from the listener's side of the interaction (operant chain) to the speaker's side, shows the causal effect of the listener. If there were no other people in the restaurant, it is likely that the speaker would get out of his or her seat and get the ketchup. The presence of a listener increases the probability that the speaker will say "pass the ketchup" rather than get it himself or herself. This means that the listener functions as part of the discriminative stimulus (S^D) in this social episode. Together, the out-of-reach ketchup and the presence of the listener (S_1^D) set the occasion for (:) a verbal response (R_1) by the speaker.

The speaker's verbal response (R_1) of "pass the ketchup" affects the listener as a

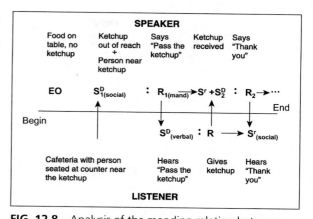

FIG. 12.8 Analysis of the manding relation between speaker and listener, based on Skinner (1957). The customer with the dinner who needs ketchup is analyzed as the speaker. EO = establishing operation; S^D = discriminative stimulus; R = operant; S^r = reinforcement. See text for a description of the verbal contingencies.

stimulus. The causal effect of the speaker's behavior on the listener is shown as a vertical downward arrow from R_1 (speaker) to the listener's side of the interaction (operant chain). The words "pass the ketchup" by the speaker are a verbal stimulus for the listener (S_1^D) that sets the occasion for (:) the listener to pass the ketchup (R_1 for listener). In this social episode, the listener's response of passing the ketchup (R_1 for listener) is reinforcement for the speaker's verbal operant (S_1^r for speaker). Because the speaker's verbal response ("pass the ketchup") produces specific reinforcement (getting ketchup) from the listener, the verbal operant is formally manding. As previously stated, *manding* is a verbal behavior that is set up by an establishing operation (out-of-reach ketchup) and maintained by specific reinforcement (getting ketchup) mediated by the listener's behavior.

In this situation, the listener's response of passing the ketchup has **multiple functions** for the speaker's behavior ($S_1^r + S_2^D$ for speaker). Passing the ketchup not only functions as reinforcement for manding, but it also functions as a discriminative stimulus for the next response by the speaker. That is, the same event (listener giving ketchup) can have several causal effects on the speaker. Based on the discriminative function of the listener's behavior (S_2^D for speaker), getting the ketchup sets the occasion for (:) the speaker saying "thank you," a verbal response (R_2 for speaker) that serves as generalized conditioned reinforcement for the listener's behavior (S_1^r for listener). The "thank you" response also serves as the ending point for this social episode, releasing the listener from obligations with respect to the speaker.

The Tacting Relation

Figure 12.9 is a formal analysis of the tacting relation. As with the manding relation, the verbal episode involves the interlocking contingencies of a speaker and listener. In this example, the speaker is a student and the listener is a teacher. The social episode begins in a classroom with the teacher showing pictures of objects to a young student.

When a picture of a red ball is displayed, this event causes (horizontal arrow) the teacher to say, "What color?" (see Figure 12.9). The teacher's question (R_1) produces a verbal stimulus to the student (vertical arrow upward). In this situation, the student's answer depends on *both* the

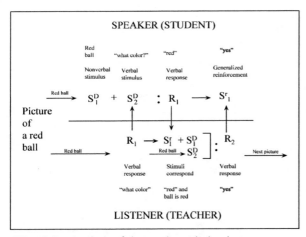

FIG. 12.9 Analysis of the tacting relation between speaker and listener, based on Skinner (1957). Both the student and teacher emit verbal behavior during the social episode, but tacting the by student (speaker) is the focus of the analysis. S^D = discriminative stimulus; R = operant; S^r = reinforcement. See text for a description of the verbal contingencies.

nonverbal stimulus of the red ball ($S^D_{1\ speaker}$) and the teacher's question ($S^D_{2\ speaker}$). Notice that the student will give a different answer if the question is, "What shape?"

The student's answer of "red" is formally tacting ($R_{1\ speaker}$) because the operant is regulated by the nonverbal stimulus (redness of ball). In this example, the student's tacting produces a verbal stimulus ($S^D_{1\ listener}$) for the teacher that may or may not *correspond* to the specified physical property of the ball ($S^D_{2\ listener}$). If the student's answer of "red" corresponds to the color of the ball, the teacher's question of "what color" is reinforced ($S^r_{1\ listener}$). Notice how speaker and listener complete individual operant chains (e.g., $S^D : R \rightarrow S^r + S^D : R \rightarrow S^r \ldots$) that are *interlocking*, in the sense that the behavior of each person causes stimulation and reinforcement for the behavior of the other.

In terms of analysis, the teacher's question "What color is the ball?" is manding. This verbal response is reinforced by correspondence between the student's tacting and the actual color of the object. When correspondence occurs, this condition sets the occasion for the teacher saying ($R_{2\ listener}$) "Yes" and turning to the next picture (noncorrespondence may lead to repeating the question, perhaps in a different way). The teacher's verbal response ("Yes") produces generalized conditioned reinforcement ($S^r_{1\ speaker}$) for the student's tacting and functions to maintain the operant class.

Finally, it is useful to compare the tacting and manding relations. As we have seen in the teacher–student example, the form or topography of tacting depends on an appropriate nonverbal stimulus. The redness of the ball regulated the student's verbal response. In contrast, manding depends on an establishing operation (EO) such as deprivation. The dinner without ketchup regulated asking for it. Generalized conditioned reinforcement (acceptance, praise, etc.) serves to maintain the operant class of tacting. In contrast, specific reinforcement related to an establishing operation (getting ketchup) maintains the operant class of manding.

CHAPTER SUMMARY

People talk to each other, and in different countries they use different languages. It seems clear that this ability is learned usually as children and according to the principles that govern other operant behavior. Evidence suggests, however, that the vocal apparatus and its neuromuscular features may have evolutionary origins allowing for extensive and complex production and control of speech sounds. Skinner defined speaking, writing, and gesturing as verbal behavior and proposed an analysis in his book of that name. This analysis begins with a description of the function of language as established by the reinforcing practices of the verbal community. Manding and tacting, are two broad classes of verbal operant behavior. Manding is a verbal form regulated by establishing operations and specific reinforcement. Tacting is a form regulated by nonverbal discriminative stimuli and maintained by generalized conditioned reinforcement. A verbal interaction between two persons may involve manding, tacting and many other verbal responses classes (e.g., intraverbals) regulated by verbal stimuli. The Jack and Jill pigeon study demonstrated some of the basic contingencies involved in communication. The study illustrated the effects of training manding and tacting repertoires in birds as an animal model for communication by humans. Pigeons have also been trained to report on their internal states or "feelings" by the interlocking contingencies among speakers and listeners. Finally, symbolic behavior and stimulus equivalence were discussed as examples of "higher order" activities involving verbal operants. The equivalence relations of reflexivity, symmetry, and transitivity were shown to extend from formal mathematics to the control of behavior. Stimulus classes exist when organisms have passed tests for these three relationships. Verbal behavior is possibly the most complex of human activities and its intricacies continue to engender much research and behavior analysis.

Key Words

Conditional discrimination
Conditioned establishing
    operation (CEO)
Echoic behavior
Formal similarity
Functional independence
Identity matching
Interlocking contingencies

Intraverbal behavior
Manding
Multiple functions
Reflexivity
Reversal test
Social episode
Stimulus equivalence
Symbolic matching

Symmetry
Tacting
Textual behavior
Transitivity
Verbal behavior
Verbal community

Applied Behavior Analysis

13

- Find out about applied behavior analysis, its methods, and data recording.
- Learn about a personalized system of instruction and precision teaching as effective behavioral applications in education.
- Discover the ABC program for the treatment of autistic behavior.
- Inquire about activity anorexia as a basis for the prevention and treatment of human anorexia.
- Focus on the problem of conditioning, overeating, and obesity.
- Explore the MammaCare program for the detection and prevention of breast cancer as an important behavioral technology.

The experimental analysis of behavior is a science that easily lends itself to application. This is because the focus of the discipline is on those environmental events that directly alter the behavior of individual organisms. Almost half a century ago (e.g., Dollard & Miller, 1950; Skinner, 1953), behavior analysts suggested that since operant and respondent principles regulate behavior in the laboratory, they likely affect human behavior in the everyday world. Thus, principles of behavior can be used to change socially significant human conduct. Based on this assumption, Skinner's second book *Walden Two* (1948) is a novelized description of a utopian society based on behavior principles. At least two communities developed utilizing many of the principles of *Walden Two*: Twin Oaks in the Eastern USA and Los Horcones near Hermosillo, Mexico (Fishman, 1991).

Principles of behavior change have been used to improve the performance of university students (Martin, Pear, & Martin, 2002; Moran & Malott, 2004; Pear & Crone-Todd, 1999), increase academic skills (Alberto & Troutman, 2006; Sulzer-Azaroff, 1986), teach developmentally delayed children self-care (Langone & Burton, 1987), reduce phobic reactions (Jones & Firman, 1999; Shabani & Fisher, 2006), get children to wear seat belts (Sowers-Hoag, Thyer, & Bailey, 1987), encourage drivers to obey stop signs (Austin, Hackett, Gravina, & Lebbon, 2006), prevent occupational injuries (Geller, 2006), prevent gun play in children (Miltenberger, Gatheridge, Satterlund, Egemo-Helm, Johnson, Jostad, et al., 2005), and help individuals stop substance abuse (Donohue, Karmely, & Strada, 2006; Higgins & Katz, 1998). Behavioral interventions have had an impact on clinical psychology, medicine, counseling, job effectiveness, sports training, and environmental protection. Applied experiments have ranged from investigating the behavior of psychotic individuals to analyzing (and altering) contingencies of entire institutions (see Kazdin, 2000). Thus, principles of behavior derived from experimental and applied research have wide-scale applicability.

CHARACTERISTICS OF APPLIED BEHAVIOR ANALYSIS

Behavioral principles, research designs, observational techniques, methods of analysis, and so on transfer readily to an applied science. When this is done to improve performance or solve social problems, the technology is called applied behavior analysis (Baer, Wolf, & Risley, 1968). Thus, **applied behavior analysis** or behavioral engineering is a field of study that focuses on the application of the principles, methods, and procedures of the science of behavior. Because applied behavior analysis is a wide field of study, it cannot be characterized by a single definition. Nonetheless, several features in combination distinguish applied behavior analysis as a unique discipline.

Concentration on Research

Behavior therapists and applied researchers are committed to a scientific analysis of human behavior. What a person does and the events that govern behavior are objectively identified. In this regard, operant and respondent conditioning are assumed to regulate most human activity regardless of how verbal behavior, generalized imitation, equivalence relationships, and physiology complicate the analysis.

Applied behavior analysis involves two major areas of research involving the application of operant and respondent principles to improve human behavior. A good deal of literature has documented the success of this enterprise (see the *Journal of Applied Behavior Analysis* from its beginning in 1968 for many examples). Thousands of experiments and applications have shown how basic conditioning principles can be used in a variety of complex settings. Problems that are unique to the applied context have been addressed, and treatment packages that are designed for the modification of behavior have been described and evaluated (see Martin & Pear, 2006).

Another set of studies have not focused directly on behavior change, but are a part of applied behavior analysis. Such investigations are involved with an analysis of everyday human behavior and have long-range implications for improving the human condition. For example, studies that investigate environmental factors that produce cooperation, competition, successful teaching, and coercive family dynamics often identify basic principles of complex human interaction (Epling & Pierce, 1986). Researchers in this area of applied behavior analysis are attempting to specify the contingencies that produce social problems (Lamal, 1997).

Behavior is the Primary Focus

Applied behavior analysts focus on the observable behavior of people. Behavior is not considered to be an expression of inner agencies or causes like personality, cognition, and attitude. Marital difficulties, children who are out of control, public littering, phobic reactions, poor performance on exams, excessive energy use, and negative self-descriptions are analyzed as problems of behavior. Interventions for these and other problems are directed at changing environmental events to improve behavior.

Of course, people think, feel, and believe a variety of things associated with what they do. Individuals experiencing difficulty in life may have unusual thoughts and feelings. A depressed person may feel worthless and think that nobody likes him or her. The same person does not spend much time visiting friends, going to social events, or engaging in the usual activities of life. A behavioral intervention for this problem would likely focus on increasing the person's activity, especially social interaction. The individual may be asked to set goals for completing various tasks, and reinforcement is arranged when they are accomplished. When people become more socially involved, physically active, and complete daily tasks, they do not describe themselves as depressed. In this and many more cases, a change in reinforcement or the density of reinforcement of daily activities produces a change in feelings and cognition.

A case study

In some cases, what a person says about his or her feelings and thoughts may be treated as verbal operant behavior that requires change (see Chapter 12). Tammi was an 8-year-old girl who was diagnosed as neurotic by a physician who saw her in his general practice. She was referred to a behavior analyst (Frank Epling) for evaluation and treatment.

It turned out that when she was 6 years old, Tammi had witnessed a gruesome farm accident in which her brother was killed. The girl frequently talked about killing herself and joining her brother in heaven. She had also cut herself with a kitchen knife on two occasions. Her parents were asked to record the circumstances that preceded and followed these episodes and the number of times they occurred.

Tammi had cut herself on two occasions since her brother's death, but had not done so during the past year. Talking about suicide had, however, increased, and she did this about three times a week. This talk usually took place during the evening meal when both parents were present. She did not talk about dying to her older siblings or to other people. Quite naturally, these episodes upset her mother and father and they routinely attempted to "calm her down and reason with her" when they occurred.

This information suggested stimulus control (parents present) and (unintentional) reinforcement by parental attention. After the mother and father were taught a few simple principles of extinction, they witheld social reinforcement when talk about suicide occurred. The parents were instructed to avoid eye contact, make no comment, and if possible turn away from Tammi when she talked about killing herself. They were also told that extinction would likely produce an initial increase in the form and frequency of the behavior. In other words, Tammi would temporarily get worse (extinction burst), but a rapid improvement could be expected to follow. At the end of 5 weeks and at a 6-month follow-up, talk of killing herself had gone to zero and cutting herself did not occur again.

The Importance of Conditioning

This discussion should make it clear that problem behavior may, in most cases, be understood in the same fashion as any other behavior. Principles of conditioning are neutral with respect to the form and frequency of behavior. Maladaptive, annoying, or dangerous responses may be inadvertently produced by environmental contingencies just as with more positive responses to life events.

Consider an institutional setting in which three staff nurses are in charge of 20 disabled children. The nurses are busy and as long as the children behave, they are left alone. This natural response to a strenuous work schedule may, for some children, result in deprivation for adult attention. When one of the children accidentally hits his or her head and is hurt, very likely a staff member rushes over and comforts the child. It is possible that head hitting will increase in frequency because it has been reinforced by contingent attention (e.g., Lovaas & Simmons, 1969). Of course, when people are injured they cannot be ignored. One way to deal with such a conundrum would be to provide lots of social reinforcement for appropriate play, academic activities, ward chores, self-hygiene, and so on. This tactic is called **differential reinforcement of other behavior**, or **DRO** (e.g., Burgio & Tice, 1985; Lowitz & Suib, 1978; Piazza, Moes, & Fisher, 1996). In the preceding example, the procedure would strengthen responses that are incompatible with self-injury and reduce deprivation for adult attention.

Although much human behavior is a function of contingencies of reinforcement, biological factors also produce behavior change. A person who has experienced a stroke, a child with fetal alcohol syndrome, an individual in the later stages of Alzheimer's, or an adult suffering from Huntington's chorea may emit responses that are a function of brain damage, toxic agents, disease, and genetics. However, even when this is the case, principles of conditioning can often be used to improve behavior (see Epling & Pierce, 1990, pp. 452–453).

Direct Treatment of Problem Behavior

Applied behavior analysts usually focus directly on the environmental events that generate and maintain behavior. Typically, target behavior and the events that precede and follow those responses are counted for several days. During this baseline, treatment is withheld so that a later change in behavior can be evaluated. This assessment also provides information about stimulus control (events that precede the behavior) and contingencies of reinforcement (events that follow behavior) that maintain responses.

Following a baseline period of assessment, a behavioral plan of action may be negotiated between the behavior therapist, the client, and concerned others (e.g., Azrin, McMahon, Donohue, Besalel, Lapinski, Kogan, et al., 1994, for a treatment program aimed at drug abuse). This plan usually includes a statement of target responses, consequences that follow different actions, and long-term goals. In many cases, a detailed **behavioral contract** is drawn up that objectively specifies what is expected of the client and the consequences that follow behavior (Hall & Hall, 1982). Figure 13.1 outlines the major principles of behavioral contracts. At a minimum, the behavior analyst should clearly identify the problem behavior; and the contract should specify in a straightforward transparent manner the reinforcement for meeting behavioral objectives, the people who provide reinforcement, and the contingencies of reinforcement.

Applied behavior analysts do not typically focus on what has been called the "therapeutic process." This is because they do not place much faith in talking about problems to relieve stress or develop insight. They prefer to arrange contingencies of reinforcement to alter behavior problems. Although this is the case, Dr. Steven Hayes at the University of Nevada in Reno is a behavior analyst who has recognized the importance of rule-governed behavior in a therapeutic setting. From his perspective, talking is a form of social influence that may be used to change the client's actions. That is, instructions and other verbal stimuli may directly alter the probability of behavior (see Hayes, 1987; Zettle & Hayes, 1982). Today, most applied behavior analysts prefer direct contingency management. Others, however, are investigating the practical importance of instructions, rules, and therapeutic advice (if it hurts when you do that then don't do that; see Hayes, 1989b)—verbal stimuli maintained by more remote contingencies of social reinforcement.

A GUIDE TO BEHAVIORAL CONTRACTING

1. Specify the target behavior.

2. Describe the behavior in a way that an observer may count or time.

3. Collect baseline data on the frequency of response or time spent responding.

4. Identify consequences that may be used to increase desired behavior (positive and negative reinforcers).

5. Find people who will monitor the behavior and provide the consequences.

6. Write the contract in clear statements of behavior and consequences (e.g., if you do "X' then you receive "y").

7. Collect data on frequency of response or time spent responding and compare with baseline level.

8. Modify the contract if the desired behavior does not increase (e.g., try different consequences).

9. Gradually, remove arbitrary consequences and replace with natural reinforcers—rewrite the contract and monitor the behavior.

10. Plan for generalization—implement the contract in a variety of settings.

FIG. 13.1   The steps in writing a behavioral contract. Based on Hall and Hall (1982).

Programming for Generality

In terms of direct treatment of problem behavior, applied behavior analysts are also concerned with the generality of behavior change (Baer, 1982; Stokes & Baer, 1977). That is, researchers attempt to ensure that their interventions produce lasting changes in behavior that occur in all relevant settings. As noted in Chapter 7, when organisms are reinforced in the presence of a particular stimulus, they typically produce a gradient of generalization that falls on both sides of the discriminative stimulus. Rather than rely on the organism to generalize automatically in an appropriate manner, the applied behavior analyst often attempts to program for generality (i.e., teach it directly).

Generality of behavior change involves three distinct processes: stimulus generalization, response generalization, and behavior maintenance (Martin & Pear, 2006). Behavior change has generality if the target response(s) occurs in a variety of situations, spreads to other related responses, and persists over time. **Stimulus generalization** occurs when the person responds similarly to different situations (e.g., a person greets one friend as she does another). **Response generalization** occurs when a target response is strengthened and other similar responses increase in frequency (e.g., a child reinforced for building a house out of Lego™ subsequently may arrange the pieces in many different ways). **Behavior maintenance** refers to how long a new behavior persists after the original contingencies are removed (e.g., an anorexic man who is taught to eat properly shows long-lasting effects of treatment if he maintains adequate weight for many years).

Donald Baer (see Chapter 11 and generalized imitation) emphasized the importance of training behavioral generality and provided the following illustration:

> Suppose that a client characterized by hypertension has been taught systematic progressive relaxation techniques on the logic that the practice of relaxation lowers blood pressure a clinically significant amount, at least during the time of relaxation, and that the technique is such that relaxation can be practiced during all sorts of everyday situations in which the client encounters the kinds of stress that would raise blood pressure if self-relaxation did not pre-empt that outcome. Suppose that the relaxation technique has been taught in the clinician's office, but is to be used by the client not only there, but in the home, at work, and recreation settings in which stress occurs. Thus, generalization of the technique across settings, as well as its maintenance after clinical treatment stops, is required.
>
> (Baer, 1982, p. 207)

To program generality of behavior change, Baer (1982) suggests a variety of procedures that affect stimulus and response generalization and behavior maintenance. Stimulus generalization of relaxation (or any other behavior) is promoted when the last few training sessions are given in situations that are as similar as possible to everyday settings. Second, when relaxation training is done in a variety of different contexts, such as different rooms with different therapists and different times of day, stimulus generalization increases. Finally, a therapist who trains relaxation in the presence of stimuli that elicit hypertension in everyday life is programming for stimulus generalization.

Response generalization is increased when the client is taught a variety of ways to obtain the same effect. For example, to relax and reduce blood pressure, the client may be taught meditation, progressive muscle relaxation, and controlled breathing. In addition, a person may be taught to produce new forms of response, as when the therapist says, "Try to find new ways of relaxing and reducing blood pressure" and reinforces novel responses.

Behavior change may be programmed to last for many years if operant responses contact sources of reinforcement outside of the therapeutic setting. Applied behavior analysts who teach their clients skills that are reinforced by members of the social community are programming for behavior maintenance. This sort of programming has been called **behavior trapping** because, once learned, the new behavior is "trapped" by natural contingencies of reinforcement (e.g., Durand,

1999; Stokes, Fowler, & Baer, 1978). The aversive consequences of hypertension are reduced when a person learns techniques of relaxation that decrease blood pressure and these practices are then trapped by automatic negative reinforcement.

In fact, relaxation training has been used to reduce hypertension over a long time with generalized effects. Usually, hypertension is treated with drugs, but there are many difficulties, including side effects of the drugs and failure by patients to follow the proposed treatment. Beiman, Graham, and Ciminero (1978) taught two men diagnosed with hypertension to relax deeply. The men were taught to practice relaxation at home and whenever they were tense, anxious, angry, or felt under pressure. Blood pressure was monitored in a variety of everyday settings and during therapy sessions. Following behavior modification, both men had blood pressure readings within the normal range. These effects were maintained at a 6-month follow-up.

Focus on the Social Environment

From a behavioral point of view, it is the physical environment and social system that requires change, not the person. James Holland at the University of Pittsburgh highlighted this issue when he said:

> Our contingencies are largely programmed in our social institutions and it is these systems of contingencies that determine our behavior. If the people of a society are unhappy, if they are poor, if they are deprived, then it is the contingencies embodied in institutions in the economic system, and in the government which must change. It takes changed contingencies to change behavior.
>
> (Holland, 1978, p. 170)

Behavior-change programs usually are more circumscribed in their focus than Holland recommends. Applied behavior analysts have seldom been in a position to change institutional contingencies. They have targeted more local contingencies involving family and community. In the case of Tammi, the social contingencies for talking about suicide were located in the family. When her parents stopped attending to such talk, she stopped saying that she wanted to kill herself. The focus of the intervention was on the family system rather than Tammi's neurosis.

Most behavior-change programs attempt to identify and alter significant variables that maintain target responses. As we have said, these variables are usually in the person's social environment. For this reason, treatment programs are often conducted in schools, hospitals, homes, prisons, and the community at large (see Glenwick & Jason, 1980; Jason, 1998; Lamal, 1997). Parents, teachers, friends, coworkers, bosses, spouses, and others typically control significant sources of reinforcement that maintain another person's behavior. These individuals are often involved and instructed in how to change contingencies of reinforcement to alter a client's behavior. This is especially relevant with interactions in a family where the "problem" is the child's behavior but the solution is changing the parent's contingency management (Latham, 1994).

RESEARCH IN APPLIED BEHAVIOR ANALYSIS

In Chapter 2, we discussed A–B–A–B reversal designs for operant research. For single-subject research, basic or applied, the A–B–A–B reversal design has the highest level of internal validity—ruling out most extraneous factors. While a reversal design is always preferred, there are practical and ethical difficulties that restrict its use in applied settings.

In natural settings, behavior is often resistant to a reversal procedure. For example, a child's shyness may be altered by using contingencies of reinforcement to increase socially acceptable playing. If the reinforcement procedure is now withdrawn, the child will probably continue playing with other children (the point of the intervention). This may occur because the shy child's behavior is maintained by the social reinforcement she now receives from playmates. In other words, the child's behavior is trapped by other sources of reinforcement. While this is a good result for the child, it is not a useful outcome in terms of inference and research design. This is because the applied analyst cannot be absolutely sure that the original improvement in behavior was caused by his or her intervention.

Another difficulty with the reversal design in applied settings is that it requires the withdrawal of a reinforcement procedure that was probably maintaining improved behavior. For example, a psychiatric patient may be restrained with leather cuffs for biting his arms. A DRO procedure is implemented and arm biting is substantially reduced, to a point at which the cuffs are no longer necessary. Although we cannot be sure that the DRO contingency caused the reduction in self-injury, it would be inadvisable to remove the contingency only to show that it was effective. Thus, the A–B–A–B reversal design is sometimes inappropriate for ethical reasons.

Multiple Baseline Designs

To solve the problems raised by the A–B–A–B reversal design, applied behavior analysts have developed other single-subject designs. **Multiple baseline designs** demonstrate experimental control and help to eliminate alternative explanations for behavior change. There are three major types of multiple baseline designs as first described by Hall, Cristler, Cranston, and Tucker (1970): **multiple baseline across stimulus conditions**, **multiple baseline across subjects**, and **multiple baseline across behaviors**.

Multiple baseline across stimulus conditions

In this design, a reinforcement procedure is applied in one situation but is withheld in other settings. When behavior only changes in the situation where it is reinforced, then the contingency is applied to the same response in another setting. Hall and associates (1970) used this design in a modification of children's tardiness in getting to class after recess or lunch.

Figure 13.2 shows the multiple baseline across stimulus conditions used by Hall and colleagues (1970). The researchers used what they called a "patriots chart" to modify lateness after lunch and after morning and afternoon recess. Children in the fifth grade who were on time for class had their names posted on the chart—an intervention that was easy and low cost to the teacher. As you can see, punctuality improved when the chart was posted. Notice that the chart was first posted after lunch time, but it was not introduced following morning or afternoon recess. The number of students who were late for class

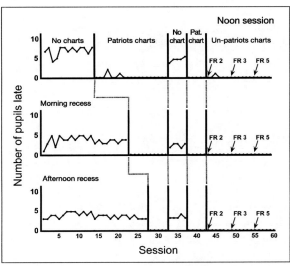

FIG. 13.2 The multiple baseline design across stimulus conditions is shown. From "Teachers and Parents as Researchers Using Multiple Baseline Designs," by R. V. Hall, C. Cristler, S. S. Cranston, and B. Tucker, 1970, *Journal of Applied Behavior Analysis*, *3*, 247–255. Copyright 1970 held by the Society for the Experimental Analysis of Behavior. Reprinted with permission.

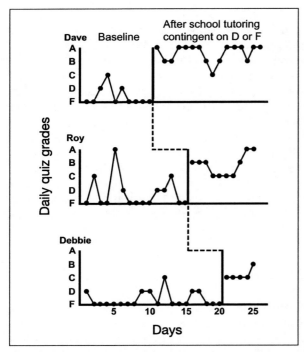

FIG. 13.3   The multiple baseline design across subjects is depicted. From "Teachers and Parents as Researchers Using Multiple Baseline Designs," by R. V. Hall, C. Cristler, S. S. Cranston, and B. Tucker, 1970, *Journal of Applied Behavior Analysis, 3*, 247–255. Copyright 1970 held by the Society for the Experimental Analysis of Behavior. Reprinted with permission.

after lunch declined from about eight to less than two. This was not the case for the recess periods; the number of students who were tardy after recess remained at four or five. Next, the researchers continued to post the patriots chart after lunch, but they added the chart following the morning recess. When this occurred, all students were on time for class following both lunch and morning recess. Finally, when the chart was also posted following the afternoon recess, all students were on time for all class periods. The multiple baseline across stimulus conditions demonstrates an effect of the intervention by staggering the introduction of the independent variable over time and settings.

Multiple baseline across subjects

A similar logic is used when an intervention is progressively introduced to different participants who exhibit similar target behavior (e.g., Alberto, Heflin, & Andrews, 2002). In this design, Hall and colleagues (1970) attempted to improve three students' scores on French quizzes. Modification involved a requirement to stay after school for tutoring if the student scored below a C on a quiz. The contingency was first introduced to Dave, then to Roy, and finally to Debbie. Figure 13.3 shows that Dave's quiz performance dramatically improved when the contingency was applied. The other students also showed improvement only after the contingency went into effect. All of the students received grades of C or better when contingency management was used to improve their performance in the French class.

Multiple baseline across behaviors

A multiple baseline design across behaviors is used when a reinforcement procedure is applied progressively to several operants. In this case, the subject, setting, and consequences remain the same, but different responses are sequentially modified. Hall and associates (1970) provided an example of this design with a 10-year-old girl when they modified her after-school reading, working on a Campfire honors project, and practicing the clarinet. The girl had to spend at least 30 min on an activity or else she had to go to bed early. She had to go to bed 1 min earlier for every minute less than 30 she spent on an activity. As you can see from Figure 13.4, practicing the clarinet was modified first, and time spent playing the clarinet increased from about 15 to 30 min. Next, both practicing the instrument and working on the Campfire project were targeted and both performances were at about 30 min. Finally, reading for book reports was modified and all three target responses occurred for 30 min. The avoidance contingency seems effective because each behavior changes when the contingency is introduced, but not before.

Multiple baseline and A–B–A–B reversal designs are the most frequently used research methods in applied behavior analysis. There are, however, many variations of these basic designs that may be used to increase internal validity or to deal with specific problems in the applied setting (e.g., Carr & Burkholder, 1998). Often the basic designs are combined in various ways to be certain that the effects are due to the independent variable. In fact, Hall and associates (1970) used a reversal phase in their experiment on tardiness and the patriots chart, but for reasons of clarity this was not shown in Figure 13.2. There are many other designs that are useful in a given situation. A **changing criterion design** involves progressive increases (or decreases) in the performance criterion for reinforcement. For example, a hyperactive child is reinforced for spending progressively more time on academic work. At first the child may be required to spend 3 min working quietly, then 5 min, then 10, and so on. The child's behavior is measured at each level of the criteria. A research example of this design is given in the section on self-control (see also Belles & Bradlyn, 1987).

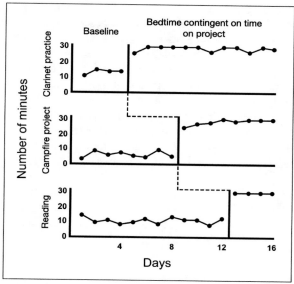

FIG. 13.4   The multiple baseline design across behaviors is depicted. From "Teachers and Parents as Researchers Using Multiple Baseline Designs," by R. V. Hall, C. Cristler, S. S. Cranston, and B. Tucker, 1970, *Journal of Applied Behavior Analysis, 3*, 247–255. Copyright 1970 held by the Society for the Experimental Analysis of Behavior. Reprinted with permission.

Issues of Measurement in Applied Behavior Analysis

It is relatively easy to define objectively an operant in the laboratory. Responses are often defined by electrical switch closures, and there is no dispute about their occurrence. When responses occur, they are recorded by computers and other electronic equipment. In the applied setting, definition and measurement of the behavior are much more difficult, especially when parents, teachers, and psychologists are used to identify problem behavior. In this regard, Kazdin (1989) has made the point that:

> Identification of the target behavior may appear to be a relatively simple task. In a given setting (e.g., the home, school, or work place), there is general agreement as to the "problems" of the clients whose behaviors need to be changed and as to the general goals of the program. Global or general statements of behavioral problems are usually inadequate for actually beginning a behavior modification program. For example, it is insufficient to select as the goal alteration of aggressiveness, learning deficits, speech, social skills, depression, psychotic symptoms, self-esteem, and similar concepts. Traits, summary labels, and personality characteristics are too general to be of much use. Moreover, definitions of the behaviors that make up such general labels may be idiosyncratic among different behavior change agents (parents, teachers, or hospital staff). The target behaviors have to be defined explicitly so that they can actually be observed, measured, and agreed upon by individuals administering the program.

> (p. 54)

Kazdin goes on to discuss three criteria of an adequate response definition (see also Johnston & Pennypacker, 1993). The first criterion is *objectivity*. This means that the response definition should refer to observable features of behavior in clearly specified situations. *Clarity* of definition is another requirement. This means that the description of the response can be read and then clearly restated by a trained research assistant or observer. Finally, the definition should be *complete* in the sense that all instances of the behavior are distinguished from all nonoccurrences. Thus, a troublesome student may be objectively defined as one who talks without permission when the teacher is talking and who is out of seat without permission during a lesson. The definition is clear in that it is easily understood and may serve as a basis for actual observation. Completeness is also shown since only these two responses are instances of the troublesome behavior class, and any other responses are not.

This definition of response assumes that there is a problem with the student's performance, not the teacher's judgment. The applied behavior analyst must be sensitive to the possibility that the teacher is too critical of the student. It is possible that many students talk without permission and leave their seats during lessons. The teacher, however, only gets upset when Anna is running about or talking during instruction. In this case, response definition may be accurate and modification successful, but the intervention is unfair. Applied behavior analysts must constantly be aware of whether they are part of the solution or part of the problem (Holland, 1978). If the problem lies with the teacher, it is his or her behavior that requires change.

Recording behavior

Once a suitable response has been defined, the next step is to record the behavior when it occurs. The simplest tactic is to record every instance of the response. Practically, this strategy may be very time-consuming and beyond the resources of most applied behavior analysts. One alternative is to count each instance of behavior only during a certain period of the day (e.g., lunch, recess, first class in the morning, and so on). This method of observation is called event recording for specified periods.

Another strategy is to select a block of time and divide the block into short, equal intervals. This is called **interval recording**. For example, a 30-min segment of a mathematics class may be divided into 10-s bits. Regardless of the number of responses, if the behavior occurs in a given 10-s segment, then the observer records it as a single event. One way this could be done is to have an observer wear a headset connected to a cassette tape recorder that plays a tape that beeps every 10 s. When the target behavior occurs, the observer records it on a piece of paper divided into segments that represent the 10-s intervals (see Figure 13.5). After each beep, the observer moves to the next interval.

Time sampling is another method of recording used in applied behavior analysis. This technique samples behavior over a long timescale, with observations made at specified times throughout the day. For example, a patient on a psychiatric ward may be observed every 30 min, as a nurse does the rounds, and instances of psychotic talk are recorded. Again, the issue is whether the target behavior is occurring at the time of the observation, not how many responses are made.

When behavior is continuous, **duration recording** is a preferred method of observation. **Continuous recording** involves responses like watching television, riding a bicycle, sitting in a chair, and so on. When behavior is continuous rather than discrete, an observer may use a stopwatch to record the duration of occurrence. When the person is sitting in a chair the watch is timing, and when the person does something else the watch is stopped.

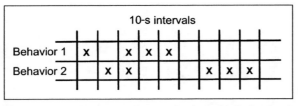

FIG. 13.5 Interval recording method used in behavioral observation and measurement.

Reliability of observations

No matter what method of recording behavior is used, reliability of observation is a critical issue. Briefly, reliability of observation involves the amount of agreement among observers who independently record the same response. For example, two observers may sit at the back of a classroom and use 10-s intervals to record the occurrence of Jessica's out-of-seat behavior. After 30 min of observation, 180 intervals of 10 s have been recorded by each researcher. One way to assess reliability is to count the number of times both observers agree that the behavior did or did not occur within an interval. This can be accomplished by video recording the participant during an observation time and then having two observers score the responses later from the tape. Reliability usually is calculated as a percentage agreement between observers, varying from zero to 100%. Generally, applied behavior analysts strive for reliability of greater than 80% agreement.

FOCUS ON: Personalized system of instruction and precision teaching

Behavior principles have been applied in a wide variety of educational settings (Sulzer-Azaroff, 1986; West & Young, 1992). University students have shown better academic performance after being taught with Fred Keller's personalized system of instruction, or PSI (Cook, 1996; Keller, 1968; Kulik, Kulik, & Cohen, 1980). In addition, learning has been accelerated for elementary school-children (and others) by precision teaching (Lindsley, 1972). Athletic performance has been improved by applying behavior principles to physical education (Martin & Hrycaiko, 1983). Autistic children have benefited from the teaching of social and living skills (Lovaas, 1987; Maurice, 1993). These are but a few of the many applications of behavior principles to education. In this section we focus on two examples, but there are many more educational applications than reported here.

A Personalized System of Instruction

The traditional lecture method used to instruct college and university students has been largely unchanged for thousands of years. A teacher stands in front of a number of students and talks about his or her area of expertise. There are variations on this theme; students are encouraged to participate in discussion, to discover new facts for themselves, to reach conclusions by being led through a series of questions, and to be active rather than passive learners. During lectures, various forms of logic are used to arrive at conclusions, classroom demonstrations are arranged, and so on. Basically, the lecture method of instruction is the same as it has always been, but presenting material is not equivalent to teaching the subject.

Fred Keller recognized that the lecture method of college teaching was inefficient and in many cases a failure. He reasoned that anyone who had acquired the skills needed to attend college was capable of successfully mastering most or all college courses. Some students might take longer than others to reach expertise in a course, but the overwhelming majority of students would be able to do so eventually. If behavior principles were to be taken seriously, there were no bad students, only bad teachers.

In a seminal article, titled "Good-bye, teacher . . .," Fred Keller outlined a college teaching method based on principles of operant conditioning (Keller, 1968). Keller called his teaching method a **personalized system of instruction**, or **PSI**. The method has also been called the "Keller Plan" (Sherman, Ruskin, & Semb, 1982). Basically, PSI courses are organized such that students move through the course at their own pace. Some students may finish the course in a few weeks, whereas others require a semester or longer.

Course material is broken down into many small units of reading and (if required) laboratory assignments. Students earn points (conditioned reinforcement) for completing unit tests and lab assignments. Mastery of the lab assignments and unit tests is required. If test scores are not close to perfect, the test (usually in a different form) is taken again. The assignments and tests build on one another so they must be completed in order. Undergraduate proctors are recruited to assist with running the course. These individuals tutor students and mark unit tests and laboratory assignments. Proctors are "chosen for [their] mastery of the course content and orientation, for [their] maturity of judgment, for [their] understanding of the special problems that confront . . . beginner[s], and for [their] willingness to assist [with the course]" (Keller, 1968, p. 81). Lectures and class demonstrations are an optional privilege; students may or may not attend them. Lectures are scheduled once the majority of students in the class have passed a sufficient number of unit tests to indicate that they are ready to appreciate the lectures; no exams are based on these lectures. The course instructor designs the course, makes up the tests, delivers the optional lectures, adjudicates disputes, and oversees the course.

Comparison studies have evaluated student performance on PSI courses against performance for those students given computer-based instruction, audio-tutorials, traditional lecture-based teaching, visual-based instruction, and other programmed instruction methods. College students instructed by PSI outperformed students taught by these other methods when given a common final exam (see Lloyd & Lloyd, 1992, for a review). Despite this positive outcome, logistical problems in organizing PSI courses, teaching to mastery level (most students get an A for the course), and allowing students more time than the allotted semester to complete the course have worked against the wide adoption of PSI in universities and colleges (Binder & Watkins, 1989).

The Method of Precision Teaching

In the early 1950s, B. F. Skinner stated, "rate of responding appears to be the only datum which varies significantly and in the expected direction under conditions which are relevant to the learning process" (Skinner, 1950). Despite this declaration, behavior analysts that moved from the laboratory to the classroom setting usually adopted "percentage correct" as a measure of academic performance, a measure that pertains only to accuracy. The temporal dimensions of behavior (e.g., rate), or fluency measures (i.e., number correct per minute), mostly were ignored except for obvious cases like typing speed.

Celeration and the charting of behavior change

Ogden Lindsley extended the method of free operant conditioning to humans, emphasizing Skinner's dictum to focus on rate of response. In what became known as **precision teaching**, Lindsley (1990b) devised a method of systematic instruction that encouraged students and teachers to target specific behaviors, count, time, and graph them, and revise instructional procedures based on the charted data (Lindsley, 1972). As part of the instructional package, Lindsley devised the *Standard Celeration Chart* for graphing the rate of a target behavior over calendar days. The word **celeration** is used to denote two kinds of behavior change: acceleration and deceleration. Acceleration occurs when the rate of target behavior (frequency/time) is increasing over days, while deceleration involves decreasing the rate over this period. Behavior graphing allows for evaluation of behavior change and revision of the instructional components based on the observed celeration (change in rate over days).

Figure 13.6 shows the Standard Celeration Chart used in educational settings (White & Haring, 1980). The chart uses a six-cycle semilogarithmic scale, with counts per minute (rate of target behavior) on the Y-axis and calendar days on the X-axis. The chart differs from a simple line graph in that tic marks on the Y-axis involve six exponential increments ranging from 0 to 1000 responses. The six-cycles or increments are: .001–.01; .01–.10; .10–1.0; 1.0–10; 10–100; 100–1000. Using this

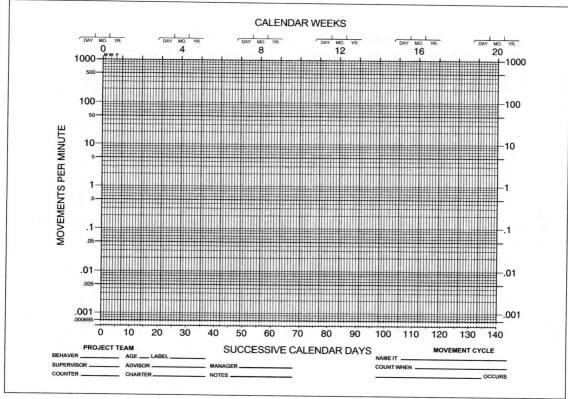

FIG. 13.6   A Standard Celeration Chart using six-cycle semilogarithmic coordinates.

scale, a student whose rate of spelling targeted words increased from 2 to 4 words (a minute) per week would appear the same as another student who increased from 20 to 40 words in the same period. That is, the students show the same relative (proportional) amount of improvement or learning when plotted on the celeration graph.

When the charted rate doubles from one week to the next, we say that it is accelerating at "times 2" or at ×2. On the other hand, a rate that is cut in half from one week to the next is said to be decelerating at "divided by 2" or at ÷2. A behavior change procedure that results in an increase from 1 to 2 (×2) would look similar to a change from 50 to 100 responses (×2). On a simple add scale, a change from 1 to 2 is +1 but also ×2 whereas a change from 80 to 100 is +20 but only ×1.25. Based on this kind of distortion, Lindsley (1990a) proposes that we discard the terms "increase" and "decrease" when describing behavior change. One of the major discoveries of precision teaching is that all behavior "multiplies" or "divides" and it is best to think in this way.

A straight line drawn from the lower left corner to the upper right corner of the Standard Celeration Chart has an angle of 33°. This angle represents a ×2 change in behavior per week and is often used as a behavioral objective for effective instruction and learning. On the other hand, a straight line from the upper left corner to the bottom right depicts a ÷2 deceleration in behavior, which is a useful target when behavior is at excessive levels. Overall, based on the celeration plotting, teachers and students work together to find instructional variables (procedures) that produce ×2 changes in academic behavior.

Basic principles of precision teaching

As an instructional system, precision teaching has four guiding principles: (1) a focus on directly observable behavior; (2) rate as the basic behavioral measure; (3) the charting of behavior on a Standard Celeration Chart; and (4) the learner knows best.

In terms of the *focus on behavior*, precision teaching involves translating learning tasks into concrete, directly observable behaviors that can be counted, timed, and recorded. Observable behavior refers to something the person is doing or the product of something that has been done. For example, during a period of oral reading, the number of words read correctly could be counted (doing), or a student could be asked to write a paragraph in so much time and the number of correctly written words could be tallied (product).

But, you say, what about private behavior, such as silent reading? In this case, the teacher must make "silent reading" public in some way. A child, Sally, who is poor at silent reading might be asked to read out loud so that counts of the number of correct words can be obtained (a measure of so-called "decoding" skills). In order to assess her comprehension skills, the teacher might provide a list of questions to Sally after she silently reads a passage from a book. Following this, the teacher would count the number of correct answers that Sally made on the quiz.

Once behavior is defined so that counts may be obtained, the rate of behavior is used as the basic measure of learning (or performance). The rate is the average number of responses during the period of assessment, or *counts per minute*. In a 4-min test of spelling, a student who spells 12 words correctly has a rate of 3 correct words per minute. The use of rate (frequency/time) focuses instruction on **fluency** or accuracy *and* high frequency. When a performance becomes fluent, the behavior is retained longer, persists during long periods on the task, is less affected by distractions, and is more likely to be available in new learning situations (i.e., to combine with other well-learned behaviors) (see Binder, 1996; West & Young, 1992).

Once the teacher has a rate measure of behavior in terms of counts per minute, the next requirement of precision teaching is to *plot the rate* on a Standard Celeration Chart. As we have seen, the celeration chart allows the teacher and student to observe improvement in the target behavior, usually against a ×2 objective for each week. The degree of acceleration (or deceleration) is a useful measure of learning in academic settings. In this regard, West and Young (1992) stated:

> When data are plotted on the standard celeration chart, learning is generally represented by a straight or nearly straight line. The value of the slope of the line which best fits the distribution of values [plotted rates over days] on a logarithmic scale is thought of as an "index of learning." The steeper the slope the faster the learning is; the flatter the slope, the slower the learning is.
>
> (p. 132)

The whole idea of precision teaching is to improve learning in a way that is objective and quantifiable. Teachers and students work out plans for improvement, implement the instructional procedures, and assess the effects of the interventions.

Instructional components of precision teaching consider four basic factors that correspond to principles of stimulus control, reinforcement, extinction, and punishment: (1) what to do before the target behavior occurs (materials, teaching assistance, etc.), (2) what to do after a correct response occurs (consequences of behavior), (3) what to do after an incorrect response occurs (ignore it or provide an aversive stimulus), and (4) what to do about how the teacher practices the task with the child. These teaching strategies are beyond the scope of this textbook but Martin and Pear (2006) provide an excellent introduction to the teaching procedures and factors influencing their effectiveness.

As a general rule, precision teaching takes the stand that "the learner knows best." This dictum arose from an incident that Lindsley (1990b) recounts about his early experience in the animal laboratory:

> When I was a graduate student, I trained a rat whose behavior did not extinguish as the charts in Skinner's (1938) book had shown. My rat at first had responded much more rapidly when his responding was no longer reinforced. The rapid responding went on for about 30 minutes, at which time the rat stopped abruptly. I took the cumulative record of the rat's unusual extinction to Dr. Skinner and asked him how this has happened. How could the rat do this when the book showed a very different gradual extinction curve? Skinner answered, "In this case, the book is wrong! *The rat knows best!* That's why we still have him in the experiment!"
>
> (p. 12)

The general rule, then, is that the *learner knows best*. That is, if a student is progressing according to the instructional plan, then the program is appropriate for that student. In contrast, if the targeted behavior for a student shows little celeration (e.g., less than ×2 or doubling), the program needs to be changed. In other words, precision teaching requires that we alter the teaching strategy rather than blame the student (e.g., "John is stupid"). That is, the student is always "right" and, in the context of low improvement, new instructional procedures are required to improve learning and performance (Carnine, 1995; see also *Behavior and Social Issues*, Special Section: What Works in Education, 1997, 7, 1–68).

Application of precision teaching

Precision teaching is a cost-effective technology (Albrecht survey cited in Lindsley, 1991) that has been successfully applied to teach learners that range from developmentally delayed to university graduate students (White, 1986). Binder and Watkins (1990) reported on a precision teaching program conducted in Great Falls, Montana in the early 1970s. Over a 4-year period, teachers at Sacajawea elementary school added 20–30 min of precision teaching to their regular curriculum. On the Iowa Test of Basic Skills, the students given precision teaching improved between 19 and 40 percentile points compared with other students in the district. More generally, improvements of two or more grade-levels per year of instruction are commonly observed in precision teaching classrooms (e.g., West, Young, & Spooner, 1990).

Similar improvements have been reported at the Morningside Academy, a school that focuses on precision teaching for developmentally delayed people. Johnson and Layng (1994) described the exceptional results at Morningside in these terms:

> Due to its successes, Morningside Academy now offers parents two money-back guarantees. The first is for [learning disabled] children who are two or more years behind in school. . . . These learners, who have rarely gained more than a half a year in any one academic year, will gain at least two grade levels per school year or their parents will receive a tuition refund in proportion to the shortfall. The second guarantee is for any other [attention deficit disordered, ADD] learners . . . who stand apart from their peers because they do not coordinate visual and motor skills effectively, as is most apparent in their handwriting. . . . Morningside Academy guarantees that these learners will increase their time-on-task endurance from 1 to 3 minutes spans to 20 minutes or more. . . . [Over seven years] . . . Morningside has never had to refund tuition for failure to meet its money-back guarantees.
>
> (pp. 174–175)

Although highly successful in promoting rapid and fluent learning, precision teaching remains only a small part of mainstream education. One possibility is that educators and psychologists in education have resisted a behavioral solution to learning, one that emphasizes the accountability of the teacher. That is, the teacher is responsible for identifying instructional procedures that result in targeted behavior changes in the student. These behavior changes are easily observed on the standardized chart, while lack of successful instruction is also apparent. Ironically, the fact that precision teaching makes learning objective and quantifiable may be the biggest reason for nonadoption by the educational community.

Another reason for the marginality of precision teaching may lie in popular negative views regarding behaviorism and behavior analysis, especially in the field of education. That is, behavioral research, theory, and philosophy are often seen to encroach on Americans' beliefs in freedom and dignity of the individual (Skinner, 1971). A behavioral technology of education appears to go against our cultural values—for example, individual responsibility suggests that students should naturally be motivated to learn. We should not have to program instruction for them! As we have seen in this section, this is a wrong-headed notion but it is upheld by our culture.

In what Skinner (1984a) called *The Shame of American Education*, he indicated that most educational problems "could be solved if students learned twice as much in the same time and with the same effort" (p. 947). This is exactly what precision teaching is all about. The problem, said Skinner, is that theories of human behavior based on humanism and developmental and cognitive psychology are most often taught in schools of education, but teaching/learning based on these theories is often ineffective. In his solution, Skinner pointed to several steps that needed to be taken to advance the educational system: (1) be clear about what is to be taught, (2) teach first things first, in an ordered sequence of progression, (3) stop making all students advance at essentially the same pace, and (4) program the subject matter—a good program of instruction guarantees a great deal of successful action.

In the end, as we have mentioned, the problem of American education rests with our culture. Skinner stated: "a culture that is not willing to accept scientific advances in the understanding of human behavior, together with the technology that emerges from these advances, will eventually be replaced by a culture that is" (Skinner, 1984a, p. 953). The survival of the American way of life depends on education of the young. The question is, are American people willing to adopt and promote a scientific approach to effective education?

APPLICATIONS OF BEHAVIOR PRINCIPLES

As noted throughout this book, behavior principles have been applied to many practical problems. In this section, we highlight a few well-known applications of operant and respondent conditioning and discuss the basic principles underlying the effectiveness of these techniques.

Training Self-Control

In applied behavior analysis, **self-control** techniques may be taught to clients, who are then better able to manage their own behavior. As we have mentioned, one common technique for self-control is called self-reinforcement. An interesting study was conducted by Belles and Bradlyn (1987), who modified the behavior of a heavy smoker by arranging self-reinforcement and self-punishment over the telephone. The client was a 65-year-old man who lived 200 miles away from the clinic. The researchers arranged a treatment program with the client and his wife. For each day that he smoked less than a specified number of cigarettes, he added $3 to a savings fund that was used to buy items that he wanted. When he exceeded the agreed-on number of cigarettes, he had to send a $25 check to the therapist, who donated the money to a charity that was unacceptable to the client. His wife verified the number of cigarettes he smoked each day by unobtrusively monitoring his behavior.

A *changing criterion design* was used to evaluate the effectiveness of the self-control procedure. In this design, the criterion for the number of cigarettes smoked each day was progressively lowered over 95 days. The effects of self-reinforcement are shown if the subject meets or falls below the criterion set by the researchers. Figure 13.7 shows the effects of the treatment. The target level for each period is shown by a horizontal line, and the client generally matched his behavior to this

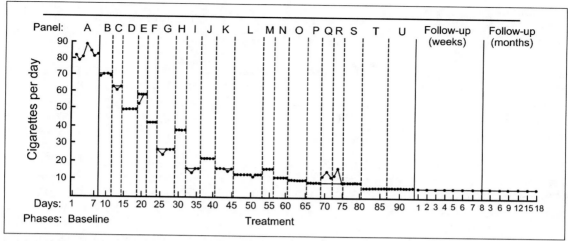

FIG. 13.7   A changing criterion design used in the modification of excessive smoking. From "The Use of the Changing Criterion Design in Achieving Controlled Smoking in a Heavy Smoker," by D. Belles and A. S. Bradlyn, 1987, *Journal of Behavior Therapy and Experimental Psychiatry, 18,* 77–82. Copyright 1987 held by Elsevier, Ltd. Published with permission.

criterion. Notice that although the criterion generally decreased, the researchers occasionally set a value higher than a previous phase and the client's behavior changed in accord with the contingencies. After 81 days on the program, the client's cigarette consumption had declined from about 85 to 5 cigarettes each day. At this point, he was satisfied with his progress and said that he wanted to remain at this level. Follow-up reports on his smoking over 18 months showed that he continued to have only five cigarettes a day.

Teaching Autistic Children

Autistic children show an early lack of social interaction with parents, other family members, and peers. For example these children often resist being held and may have a tantrum if picked up or hugged. When autistic children get older they may be mistaken as deaf because they do not talk or even establish eye contact when talked to. These children often show repeated stereotyped patterns of behavior, such as rocking back and forth, spinning a top, wiggling their fingers in front of their eyes, and so on. More than 85% of autistic children fail to speak at an age when other children are highly verbal. The long-term outcome for this disorder is grim; the overwhelming majority of such children require extended care and supervision (Ghezzi, Williams, & Carr, 1999).

Ivar Lovaas, at the time of this writing a professor of psychology at the University of California at Los Angeles, has been working on the treatment of autism since the 1960s. Lovaas and his collaborators (Lovaas, 1966, 1977, 1987; McEachin, Smith, & Lovaas, 1993) have reported on the successful behavioral treatment of autistic children. Lovaas (1977) describes **intensive behavioral intervention** (30 or more hours each week) that increases social behavior, teaches the children to speak, and eliminates self-stimulation. Most treated autistic children showed significant improvement in their daily functioning. Incredibly, when the treatment was applied to autistic children who were less than 30 months old, 50% of these children were later indistinguishable from normal school children. No other treatment of autistic children has produced such dramatic improvement (Lovaas, 1993; Maurice, 1993; Schopler & Mesibov, 1994).

FOCUS ON: Autism, mirror neurons, and applied behavior analysis

Autism is a multiply determined, multiply expressed disorder that has become alarmingly prevalent. The source of the disordered behaviors labeled as autism is not clear, but the treatment of choice is intensive behavior manipulation by skilled behavior analysts (Charlop-Christy & Kelso, 1997; Ghezzi, Williams, & Carr, 1999). Because of its unknown etiology and often extraordinary behavioral manifestations, people are desperate to try different treatments and to promote a variety of possible causes.

The definition of autism is almost exclusively based on behavior, primarily in terms of deficits such as poor eye contact, little communication skill, noncompliance, and lack of social play (Volkmar, Carter, Grossman, & Klin, 1997). The autistic child looks normal but does not show age-appropriate behavior, especially social behavior. There are several brain abnormalities and genetic defects associated with autism, but at present the evidence is limited.

The discovery of the "mirror neuron" system (see Chapter 11) and its lack of development in autistic children suggests that these youngsters may benefit from intensive behavioral training in generalized imitation (Baer, Peterson, & Sherman, 1967) and other forms of discrimination training. The mirror system allows the observer to process information about self-performed actions and, using the same system, to understand the actions, emotions, and intentions of others (Oberman & Ramachandran, 2007). The integration of behavioral neuroscience with applied behavioral interventions could greatly enhance the understanding and treatment of childhood autism (see Thompson, 2007, pp. 429–430). One possibility is that intensive early training is effective for about 50% of autistic children with intact neural systems because it organizes and activates the mirror neural system in the developing child, as Iriki (2006) suggests is the case for lower primates.

Obviously neural mechanisms are altered during early experience and the immature nervous system is especially sensitive to environmental influences during maturation and development. Thompson recently suggested that "early differential reinforcement of discriminative responding [by autistic children] to visual images of hand and arm movements may promote gene expression in the mirror neuron system" (p. 437). Intensive early behavioral intervention has the best possibility for a lasting modification of autistic behavior, and interventions aimed at priming the mirror neuron system (e.g., training to discriminate the actions and emotions modeled by others) could be even more effective.

Unfortunately, there is a subgroup of autistic children who do not benefit from 30 or more hours of weekly behavioral treatment (Thompson, 2007, p. 429). Modern neural imaging could help to demarcate autistic children who are unable to form synapses in the brain (especially the mirror neuron areas) and profit from intensive behavioral treatment. The individuals, however, could be treated by alternative behavioral procedures designed for their specific deficits.

Dr. Joe Morrow and Brenda Terzich (Figure 13.8) have established Applied Behavior Consultants or ABC, in Sacramento, California. The business is devoted to behavioral intervention for autistic children based on

FIG. 13.8   Joe Morrow and Brenda Terzich, the founders of Applied Behavioral Consultants (ABC). Reprinted with permission.

Lovaas's treatment package. Parents are taught the necessary behavioral skills for training their child. The treatment package includes specific intervention strategies for accomplishing behavioral outcomes. For example, the children are reinforced for making eye contact when the teacher talks to them. Appropriate life skills such as eating meals with utensils, dressing oneself, and personal hygiene (i.e., brushing teeth, combing hair, etc.) are reinforced with tokens and social approval. Verbal skills including, manding and tacting, are also targets for behavior change. ABC staff members monitor progress and, if necessary, advise program changes.

In 1994, Morrow and Terzich started a communication-based private school for children diagnosed as autistic. At ABC school, autistic children receive individualized behavioral training for about 5 h a day, 218 days per year. The emphasis at the school is on verbal and academic behavior as well as on social skills (Bondy, 1996; Bondy & Frost, 1994). A primary objective of the program is to move children from the ABC school to public schools, either general or special education, within 2 years. To accomplish this, ABC uses a five-step program that guides the progression of lessons from discrete trials learning to the ultimate transfer of the control of social behavior to the verbal community, including the child's peer group (Morrow, Terzich, & Williamson, 2002).

Level 1 of the program involves discrete trials procedures where the teacher presents a stimulus and the response by the child is reinforced (or corrected). The training at this level also includes training generalization of subskills to new situations, trainers, and variations within the standard teaching setting. At level 2, the teaching is focused on stimulus generalization. That is, once the child masters an appropriate response in the presence of a specific S^D (level 1), the teacher varies properties of the S^D while maintaining the appropriate response. The S^D may be "What am I doing" and hand waving by the teacher, and the child is reinforced for saying "You're waving your hand." At level 2 the teacher may say "I'm doing what?" or "Hey, what's happening here?" (varying the S^D) and reinforcement remains contingent on the response, "You're waving your hand." At level 3, the training emphasizes maintaining learned concepts and skills. The training insures that the child demonstrates generalization of skills when lessons are changed from one location or time to another. Level 3 training also involves programmed environmental distractions, similar to everyday interruptions in a classroom. The child is taught to maintain accurate responding in the face of these random interruptions.

At level 4, children are taught "splinter skills." A child may be able to use the toilet and to dress herself but she is unable to select the clothes to wear. In the classroom, a child may be able to write on a piece of paper when instructed by the teacher but be unable to get a piece of paper on her own. Formally, the training at this level is focused on completion of extended behavior chains or sequences. The final level of the program, level 5, is focused on the training and generalization of social skills (greetings, reciprocity, empathy, etc.) that will be necessary to interact with others in everyday settings (e.g., classroom, playground, and home). For example the child is taught to discriminate between greeting his or her parents and saying hello to a playmate. Training at level 5 also insures that this kind of social skill is maintained in a variety of appropriate settings.

How successful is this kind of behavioral program? Well, at the time of admission to the program, 57% of the autistic children have no speech. After 1 year, all children, both vocal and nonvocal, are *manding* (e.g., requesting, asking for, etc.) vocally, or by sign language (see Chapter 12 on manding).

What about transition from the behavioral program to regular classrooms? The first thing to note is that almost no children move from traditional, nonbehavioral treatment programs to public school classrooms (Lovaas, 1987). Over the first 4 years of ABC's school operation, 71 children had completed all five levels of behavioral training and had made the move to regular education classrooms. Of the 31 children who were 6 years or more in age (eldest group) on admission to the ABC school, none made successful transitions to public education classrooms. For the 25 children between 4 and 6 years in age at admission (middle group), only 8% made a successful transition. When the children's age at admission was 4 years or less (youngest), 40% moved into the public education system and did not return to ABC. The unpublished data indicate that intensive behavioral intervention is most successful for younger children.

The findings at the ABC school substantiate recommendations by Maurice, Green, and Luce (1996) concerning intensive behavioral treatment of autism. Their manual indicates that intensive behavioral programs work best when (1) children are less than 5 years of age—the younger the better, (2) the program includes at least 30 h of treatment per week, and (3) children continue in the program for at least 2 years. Under these conditions, even very low functioning children make behavioral gains and, as we have seen, about 40% will be able to function in the public school system. Overall, this is fantastic news for parents of autistic children.

Because of the success and subsequent demand for in-home and classroom behavioral treatment, ABC currently has hundreds of employees in California and has opened a new school in China that services about 25–30 autistic children. Since the time they started (in 1987), more than 3000 autistic children have been treated by ABC's behavioral technology. Each of these children has received about 30 h a week of one-on-one behavior therapy. ABC has been able to reach such a large number of autistic children because of their emphasis on training parents to work with these youngsters (rather than directly providing therapy themselves). Although time-consuming, early intensive behavior therapy has rescued many children from an otherwise isolated and impoverished life. Happily, this intervention is also much more cost effective than providing a lifetime of supervision or institutionalization. The state of California has recognized both of these facts and provides most, or all, of the money for the program.

THE CAUSES AND PREVENTION OF BEHAVIOR PROBLEMS

In recent years, behavior analysts have focused attention on the factors that produce behavior problems. Animal models of disordered behavior have been developed that provide insight into the causes of problem behavior (see Epling & Pierce, 1992; Keehn, 1986). Other researchers have been concerned with promoting behavior related to physical health. The area of **behavioral medicine** includes behavior-change programs that target health-related activities such as following special diets, self-examination for early symptoms of disease, exercising, taking medicine, stopping smoking, and so on (see Doleys, Meredith, & Ciminero, 1982; Friman, Finney, Glasscock, Weigel, & Christophersen, 1986). The idea is that many problems of behavior and health may be prevented before treatment is necessary.

Anorexia Nervosa and Activity Anorexia

A young woman goes on a severe diet and continues to the point of starvation. How can this person be anything but mentally disturbed? In fact, *anorexia nervosa* is currently classified as a neurotic disorder by psychiatrists and psychologists (see *Diagnostic and Statistical Manual*, 4th edition, DSM IV). Mental illness and disturbed cognitions are suggested by the many symptoms that accompany willful starvation (see Garner & Desai, 2000, for a multidimensional analysis). These symptoms include fear of being fat, obsessive food rituals, distorted body image, and disturbed self-perception.

Notably, modern psychiatry has reinforced the view that cognitive and mental events cause abnormal human behavior. This is convincing to people, because unusual thoughts often accompany bizarre behavior. Although these thoughts may occur and are associated with disturbed eating, this evidence is not sufficient to claim that they are causes. One reason for this association may be that anorexics learn to label their emotional states and behavior in accord with the expectations of therapists, family, and friends.

The numerous and varied symptoms of anorexia also arise from starvation itself (Epling & Pierce, 1992; Keys, Brozek, Henschel, Mickelsen, & Taylor, 1950). Keys and associates (1950) observed many of the symptoms of anorexia nervosa in psychologically healthy men who participated in a study of forced starvation. Symptoms similar to those found in anorexia nervosa developed as the men lost weight. On psychological tests the men became neurotic (a few scored in the psychotic range), they were obsessed with food, some became bulimic (excessive overeating), and so on. Importantly, these symptoms *followed* rather than preceded starvation—suggesting that they were not the causes of anorexia.

Physical activity and anorexia

Clinical reports of anorexia nervosa have viewed excessive physical activity as an interesting but unimportant symptom of the syndrome. For example, Feighner, Robins, Guze, Woodruff, Winokur, and Munoz (1972) have described diagnostic criteria that include periods of overactivity as one of six possible secondary symptoms. In the traditional view, activity is secondary because it is simply a way that the anorectic burns off calories. That is, physical activity reflects the patient's desire to lose weight.

Although this interpretation is widely accepted, there is evidence that it is wrong. Excessive physical activity appears central to many cases of human self-starvation (Epling & Pierce, 1992). The evidence for the importance of activity comes from a variety of sources. Controlled experiments with animals have shown that physical activity can make an animal give up eating when food is relatively abundant (Epling & Pierce, 1984, 1988). Research with humans has also suggested a link between activity and starvation (Davis, Kennedy, Ravelski, & Dionne, 1994; Davis, 1999). Beumont and colleagues asked 25 anorexics to identify their symptoms and the order of occurrence (Beumont, Booth, Abraham, Griffiths, & Turner, 1983). Of the 28 reported symptoms, only manipulating food servings and increased sport activity were present in all patients. Generally, the ordering of the symptoms indicated that changes in dieting and food intake were followed by increased physical activity. Many other studies have documented excessive physical activity in anorexic patients (see Epling, Pierce, & Stefan, 1983).

Anorexia in animals

The process of **activity anorexia** begins when rats are fed a single daily meal and are allowed to run on an activity wheel. It is important to note that the size of the meal is more than adequate for survival. Also, animals are not forced to exercise on the wheel. They can choose to remain in an attached cage or just lie in the wheel. In fact, the animals start running, and this activity increases daily because of the time-limited, one-meal a day food schedule (Epling & Pierce, 1996b).

As shown in Figure 13.9, wheel running rapidly increases to excessive levels. An adolescent rat may run up to 20 km a day at the peak. Ordinarily, these animals would run less than 1 km a day. This excessive activity is surprising because the animal is expending many more calories than it is consuming. For this reason, the activity is life-threatening.

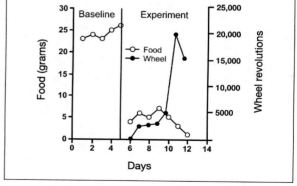

FIG. 13.9 Excessive running and reduction of food intake by an adolescent rat reported in Epling, Pierce, and Stefan (1983).

A more startling effect is that food intake remains drastically reduced as running becomes excessive. As you can see at the end of 1 week (Figure 13.9), the animal is eating very little. The rat is giving up eating in spite of increasing energy expenditure through wheel running. If this process is allowed to continue, the animal dies of starvation. The drop in running on the last day occurs because the rat is too weak to continue.

Reinforcement values of eating and running

In Chapter 7, we discussed the interrelations of eating and running (Pierce, Epling, & Boer, 1986). Recall that the research evidence indicates that rats will work more for an opportunity to run on a wheel as food deprivation increases. The animals bar pressed many more times for 60 s of wheel running as their body weights declined. Additionally, rats pressed a lever for food less when they had run on a wheel the night before a food session. This effect occurred even though the animals had several hours of rest before being placed in the operant chamber. The overall findings suggest that the reinforcing effectiveness of physical activity increased as a function of food deprivation. Also, the reinforcement value of eating food decreased when preceded by a bout of physical activity. These two reinforcement relations provide a behavioral account of the activity anorexia cycle (see Chapter 7 for the biological basis of these reinforcement relationships).

Activity-induced taste aversion

The suppression of eating during activity anorexia also involves conditioned taste aversion (CTA), although a recent experiment suggests that CTA does not fully explain the activity anorexia cycle (Sparks, Grant, & Lett, 2003). **Activity-induced taste aversion** occurs when a distinctive taste becomes a conditioned stimulus (CS) that is followed by the physiological consequences of wheel running, the unconditioned stimulus (US). Lett and Grant (1996) were the first to test the hypothesis that CTA is induced by physical activity. In their experiment, rats were exposed to flavored liquids that were paired or unpaired with wheel running. Compared with control rats that remained in their home cages, experimental rats drank less of the flavored drink when paired with wheel running—the rats showed CTA induced by wheel running. Subsequent research has replicated the basic effect and ruled out mere novelty of the wheel as the basis for the original finding (Heth, Inglis, Russell, & Pierce, 2001; Nakajima, Hayashi, & Kato, 2000).

Dr. Sarah Salvy is an assistant professor in the Department of Pediatrics at SUNY (Buffalo) and worked with David Pierce (coauthor of this textbook) on her PhD research at the University of Alberta. Her studies show that CTA induced by wheel running can be eliminated by pre-exposure to the wheel running US (Salvy, Pierce, Heth, & Russell, 2002; see Heth & Pierce, 2007, for pre-exposure to a novel food). This result is consistent with habituation effects and a respondent conditioning account of CTA induced by wheel running. Her research also indicated that CTA is related more to the contingency between a distinctive taste and wheel running than to the intensity of the physical activity. That is, the association between taste and the physiological effects of wheel running is more important than the "dose" level of physical activity. Finally, Salvy was the first researcher to find CTA induced by wheel running to food stimuli (Salvy, Pierce, Heth, & Russell, 2003). Her work on food aversion and physical activity constitutes significant "bridging experiments" between the CTA–wheel-running protocol and the animal model of activity anorexia.

FOCUS ON: Conditioned overeating and childhood obesity

Taste conditioning plays a role in the development of obesity as well as anorexia. Families that provide children with calorie-wise foods and drinks may inadvertently contribute to overeating and childhood obesity, according to new research using respondent conditioning to induced overeating

(Davidson & Swithers, 2004; Pierce, Heth, Owczarczyk, Russell, & Proctor, 2007; Swithers, Doer-flinger, & Davidson, 2006). The researchers found that food with low calories disrupted the body's capacity to regulate intake—resulting in overeating by juvenile animals. The finding may help to explain why increasing numbers of children in North America lack the ability to regulate food intake and body weight. The researchers also found that adolescent animals were not fooled by the calorie-wise foods and did not overeat at mealtimes.

Pierce and colleagues (2007) suggest that being able to match calorie intake with the body's need involves the ability to learn that the food tastes predict the amount of calories ingested. Thus, both obese-prone and lean juvenile rats are prepared to learn that particular tastes signal caloric energy. Based on this associative learning, the use of calorie-wise foods may undermine the body's natural ability to regulate food intake and weight. In this way, diet foods and drinks could lead to **conditioned overeating** and obesity in children.

Early experiences can teach juvenile rats that specific food flavors are useful in predicting the energy content of foods. Subsequently, the young animals use food tastes to determine the body's need for calories. When food flavors have been associated with low caloric energy, as with diet foods and drinks, juvenile rats eat more than their bodily need after ingesting a nutritious snack or pre-meal containing that flavor. Overall, the research shows that juvenile rats overeat when the taste of food has been associated with low energy content.

Obesity is a significant risk factor for both type 2 diabetes and cardiovascular disease and is an increasing major health problem of North America and Europe. In this regard, it is important to note that the food industry generates an extensive variety of products, some of which offer attractive tastes but have little or no caloric energy. In fact, it has become commonplace for people to eat calorie-wise foods and drinks rather than consume reduced amounts of high-energy foods. Given the ubiquity of the "diet craze," many children may learn that the taste of food often predicts low energy value. Youngsters with such a dietary history may not effectively regulate their caloric intake over the course of a day—overeating at dinner, by failing to compensate for intake of palatable high-calorie snack foods during and after school. The best strategy, say the researchers (Pierce et al., 2007), is to keep diet foods away from youngsters and give smaller portions of regular foods to avoid weight gain and obesity.

Humans and anorexia

The seemingly willful starvation of animals appears similar to cases of human anorexia. For humans, social reinforcement can increase the tendency to diet or exercise. An individual may learn these responses to escape or avoid criticism for being overweight or to gain approval for being slim and fit (see Pierce & Epling, 1997, for an analysis of the social contingencies). The type and intensity of dieting and exercise are initially regulated by the reactions of other people. However, once social reinforcement has encouraged food restriction, especially in the context of increasing exercise, the activity anorexia cycle may be initiated. When the process starts, the person is trapped by the activity/food reduction cycle.

Humans self-impose diets for a variety of reasons. All diets do not generate excessive activity. The type, severity, and pattern of diet are important factors contributing to physical activity. For example, many anorexics change their meal pattern from several meals to one per day. This change in the number of meals may be important in generating activity anorexia (Kanarek & Collier, 1978).

Mandrusiak (2002) conducted a productive experiment in our laboratory at the University of Alberta. Using a foraging model, rats had to press a procurement lever in order to produce food on a second lever (the meal lever). Michael wanted to find out whether rats would self-starve without any imposed food restriction by the experimenter. The findings indicate that rats "choose" to starve when the procurement cost of meals is high (the number of responses required to gain an opportunity to eat a meal) and an opportunity for physical activity is available. Basically, the high cost of meals drives down the number of eating bouts per day (to one meal a day); interestingly, the amount of food consumed during the meal does not compensate for the reduction in number of eating bouts (no energy balance). The rat literally places itself on a restricted food schedule.

When self-imposed food restriction is combined with the opportunity for physical activity, the activity anorexia cycle is initiated and the animals will eventually die. The foraging model is another animal analogue for human self-starvation (see also Belke, Pierce, & Duncan, 2006, for a behavioral economic model of activity anorexia). In humans, the cost of taking meals could include social contingencies based on appearance or alternative sources of reinforcement involving work, family, or school (Pierce & Epling, 1997). As the social costs increase for eating, people would self-impose food restriction and become physically active. The result would be that some people inadvertently initiate the activity anorexia cycle.

Assessment, treatment, and prevention

The activity anorexia model has important practical implications. In the book *Solving the Anorexia Puzzle: A Scientific Approach*, Epling and Pierce (1992) outline the criteria for assessment, treatment, and prevention of activity anorexia. In terms of assessment, the primary criteria involve a history of low and declining food intake, a history of excessive physical activity, and psychological symptoms that follow rather than precede weight loss. Treatment is based on traditional behavior-modification procedures but is directed at the responses that comprise the activity anorexia cycle. For example, contingencies are arranged to stop excessive dieting and exercise. In addition, patients are taught how to eat and to discriminate between moderate and excessive levels of exercise.

Prevention of activity anorexia involves changing the sociocultural conditions that promote excessive dieting and exercising. Medical doctors are in the best position to call attention to the role of diet and exercise in the onset and maintenance of eating disorders.

Self-help groups concerned with eating disorders may have members who recognize the biobehavioral processes involved in self-starvation. These groups can play an important role in preventing onset and relapse of activity anorexia. A second major function of self-help groups is education and social change. The groups may send speakers to schools, public meetings, and professional conferences. These groups may also lobby physicians, government agencies, private organizations, and public companies. Because of this active and organized involvement, self-help groups may be the most important source of prevention for activity anorexia.

ON THE APPLIED SIDE: MammaCare—detection and prevention of breast cancer

About 180,000 American women develop breast cancer each year. The disease kills an additional 46,000 women. Every woman is a potential victim and about 12% of women will develop breast cancer at some time in their lives. In addition to loss of life, victims of breast cancer often undergo surgery that may physically and emotionally disable them.

At present, doctors do not know how to prevent breast cancer, but early detection significantly improves a woman's chances of survival. Importantly, the victims of the disease are themselves almost always the first ones to detect the tumor. In most cases, however, women only detect the tumor after the cancer has reached an advanced stage. Regular and proficient self-examination by young women could substantially improve the detection of small tumors.

Surprisingly, a study by Baxter (2001) based on a summary of the literature concluded that teaching breast self-examination (BSE) to women 40–49 years old has no benefits (in terms of detection or lowering death) and is actually harmful because women are constantly going to doctors based on false readings. The conclusions of this study are controversial (Larkin, 2001), but could be accurate in terms of the BSE programs included in the review. Often BSE programs use pamphlets, posters, and films to teach the requisite skills but these teaching aids alone are not enough. There is reason to believe, however, that a strict behavioral program of BSE would fare much better—but a controlled clinical trial is unlikely in the near future (Saslow, Hannan, Osuch, Alciati, Baines, Barton et al., 2004).

The MammaCare Program

Dr. Henry S. Pennypacker (Figure 13.10) and his associates at the University of Florida have developed a behavioral program called **MammaCare** to teach women effective self-examination of their breasts (Hall, Adams, Stein, Stephenson, Goldstein, & Pennypacker, 1980; Pennypacker, Bloom, Criswell, Neelakantan, Goldstein, & Stein, 1982). He began to work on this program because:

FIG. 13.10   Henry S. Pennypacker, the founder of MammaCare. Published with permission.

> Like many before me, I took a degree in classical experimental psychology and began an academic career. I rapidly became uncomfortable with the hypocrisy inherent in my position: I was an "expert" in learning using none of my expertise in my work. My interest turned to education at all levels, partly because of the critical role it plays in the survival and evolution of the culture and partly because it looked like an easy place to make a contribution. How wrong I was! . . . [W]ith hindsight . . . I have a better understanding of the problems we face and general strategies needed to solve them. MammaCare is a step in that direction.
>
> (H. S. Pennypacker, personal communication, 22 February 1989)

The MammaCare program is based on the assumption that women often are unable to detect small tumors simply because they have not been trained to do so. The pressure receptors of the fingertips allow for subtle discrimination of surface contour (e.g., from smooth to bumpy), as is clearly demonstrated by blind people who read Braille. It follows that women may be trained to detect small lesions in the breast related to cancerous tumors. An effective program must teach women to tell the difference between small tumors and the normal lumpiness of the breast itself.

Components of MammaCare

An initial step involves *discrimination training*. The patient is trained to use her fingertips to discriminate small lesions from ordinary nodules in the breast. This training is accomplished with the used of silicone breast models that have been developed to match the physical properties of real breast tissue (Bloom, Criswell, Pennypacker, Catania, & Adams, 1982; Hall et al., 1980). A woman palpates the breast model in order to detect lumps of different hardness, located at various depths, and varying in lateral mobility. Detection of lumps functions as reinforcement that maintains searching for and reporting abnormal breast tissue.

Once the patient is able to detect small lumps (e.g., diameter of 0.4 mm) with her fingertips, she is taught additional *palpation and search skills* (Saunders, Pilgram, & Pennypacker, 1986). A vertical strips pattern of search is used because of greater success at detection when compared with concentric circles or radial spokes patterns (Saunders et al., 1986). The target of these procedures is to ensure that a woman's fingers contact a maximum volume of breast tissue during self-examination. In this phase, the woman learns palpation and search on her own breast while being carefully evaluated by a trained professional. A patient must be at least 95% proficient before leaving the training center. This level of proficiency helps to ensure that self-examination techniques become an integrated skill that may be practiced monthly as recommended.

A final component of the program ensures maintenance of self-examination by *reinforced practice*. After MammaCare training, each woman is given a take-home kit that contains a breast model that is matched to the firmness and nodularity of her own breast tissue. This breast model is used to update the patient's tactile skill just before she carries out the monthly self-examination. The practice model contains five small tumor simulations that the patient can find only if she performs the examination correctly. Based on this reinforced practice, a woman who finds nothing unusual during a breast examination can be almost certain that there was nothing there to detect.

Effectiveness of the program

Women who have learned the MammaCare method of breast self-examination are able to detect lesions as small as 0.4 mm in diameter. This compares favorably to the average tumor that women discover by accident, measuring 3.6 cm in diameter. It also compares well with conventional self-examination, in which women detect tumors in the 2.0-cm range. Evidence also shows that training in self-examination improves detection in actual breast tissue (Pennypacker et al., 1982, pp. 109–110). The effectiveness of a behavioral system of breast self-examination lies in the fact that the program directly teaches women what to feel for and how to search their breasts thoroughly. The value of the behavioral approach is that it allows for early detection of breast cancer in women who are asymptomatic and are younger than age 40 when mammograms are recommended (Saslow et al., 2004).

Extending the use of the program

The MammaCare program is now available to a greater number of women at a lower cost (for information write to The Mammacatch Corporation, 930 NW 8th Ave., Gainesville, FL 32601 or go to http://www.mammacare.com/). A woman uses the learning system to master the self-examination skills and then is asked to perform a portion of the breast examination in the presence of a trained professional who can correct any problems.

Finally, the MammaCare system is now available to physicians or other health professionals through a special 2-h clinical training course (Pennypacker, Naylor, Sander, & Goldstein, 1999; Trapp, Kottke, Viekrant, Kaur, & Sellers, 1999). Also, women who complete the 5-day program may arrange to offer the 3-day course to professionals in their own neighborhood. In this way, an effective behavioral technology for breast self-examination is transmitted to a wider circle of health-care professionals, who in turn pass these skills on to more and more women.

CHAPTER SUMMARY

This chapter has presented many examples of applied behavior analysis. Issues of observer reliability, irreversibility of treatment and multiple baseline designs, and fluency and rate as dependent measures were highlighted. We emphasize a focus on behavior and its functions, such as gaining attention for self-abusive behavior. The behavioral approach to therapy involves direct interventions on the problem behavior by manipulating the environment. Applied behavior analysts reject appeals to hypothetical mental causes and intrapsychic mechanisms in favor of changing the world in which people live.

Several systematic educational programs were described that have shown profound improvements in student achievement. For decades, precision teaching and PSI have produced superior pupil progress, but are largely ignored in mainstream education. Applications of behavior principles also have been used to educate autistic children, helping many to enter the regular educational system.

Private schools and programs such as the ABC school have flourished by producing positive behavior improvement.

The eating disorder of anorexia has been the subject of extensive behavior analysis using the animal model of activity anorexia. Much has come from this work, leading to specific recommendations for treating and preventing this dangerous human condition. We also reviewed new research on conditioned overeating and its implications for childhood obesity. Finally, we described a program for self-detection of breast cancer. This successful venture illustrates the use of behavior principles in health and medicine, indicating that applied behavior analysts are making important contributions to human welfare.

Key Words

Activity anorexia
Activity-induced taste aversion
Applied behavior analysis
Autistic children
Behavior maintenance
Behavior trapping
Behavioral contract
Behavioral medicine
Celeration
Changing criterion design
Conditioned overeating
Continuous recording

Differential reinforcement of
    other behavior (DRO)
Duration recording
Fluency
Intensive behavioral
    intervention
Interval recording
Multiple baseline across
    behaviors
Multiple baseline across
    stimulus conditions

Multiple baseline across
    subjects
Multiple baseline design
Personalized system of
    instruction (PSI)
Precision teaching
Response generalization
Self-control
Stimulus generalization
Time sampling

Three Levels of Selection: Biology, Behavior, and Culture

14

- Explore evolution, natural selection, and contingencies of survival.
- Learn about the genetic control of egg laying and the operant control of feeding in the marine snail, *Aplysia*.
- Discover how operant conditioning furthered the survival and reproductive success of organisms, including humans.
- Find out how the operant regulation of verbal behavior contributed to the transmission of cultural practices.
- Inquire about innovation and cultural evolution based on variation and selection at the behavioral and cultural levels.

Behavioral researchers have suggested that **selection by consequences** is the operating principle for biology, behavior, and culture (e.g., Pierce & Epling, 1997). It is a general form of causation that goes beyond the push–pull mechanistic Newtonian model of physics (Hull, Langman, & Glenn, 2001). In terms of biology (level 1), selection by consequences involves natural selection or the selection of genes based upon reproductive success. At the level of behavior (level 2), selection by consequences is described by the principle of reinforcement—the selection of operant behavior by the effects it produces. A third level of selection occurs in terms of culture (level 3 or cultural selection). Cultural practices (ways of doing things) are selected by macro-level consequences for the group involving greater efficiency, lower costs, and higher likelihood of survival.

In this chapter, selection by consequences is examined at the genetic, behavioral, and cultural levels (see Figure 14.1). In showing the parallels among these different levels, behavioral researchers seek to integrate the study of behavior with biology on the one hand and the social sciences on the other. The attempt is not to reduce behavior to biology, or culture to behavior. Rather, it is to show the common underpinnings of all life science in terms of the extension and elaboration of basic principles.

LEVEL 1: EVOLUTION AND NATURAL SELECTION

The evolutionary history of a species, or **phylogeny**, is the outcome of natural selection. Darwin (1859) showed how organisms change in accord with this principle (Figure 14.2). Based on a thorough analysis of life forms, Darwin concluded that reproductive success was the underlying basis of evolution. That is, individuals with more children pass on a greater number of their characteristics to the next generation.

Darwin noticed structural differences among members of sexually reproducing species. Except

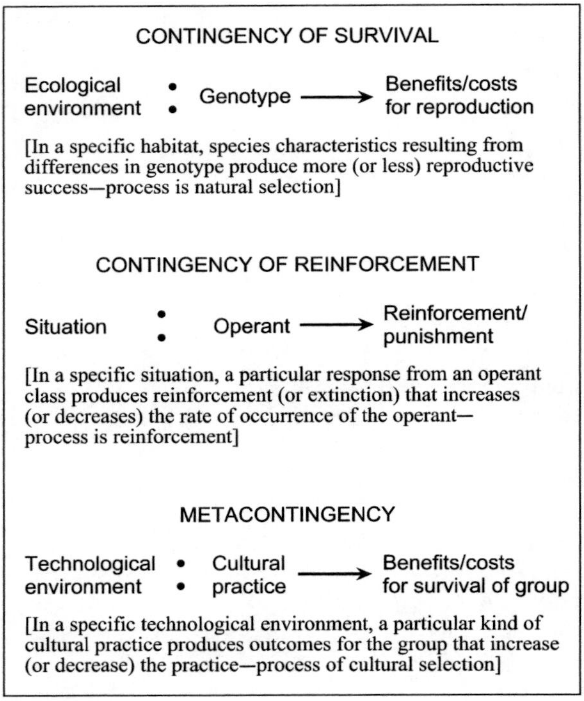

CONTINGENCY OF SURVIVAL

Ecological   •
environment   •   Genotype ⟶   Benefits/costs
                                    for reproduction

[In a specific habitat, species characteristics resulting from
differences in genotype produce more (or less) reproductive
success—process is natural selection]

CONTINGENCY OF REINFORCEMENT

                  •
Situation   •   Operant ⟶   Reinforcement/
                  •   punishment

[In a specific situation, a particular response from an operant
class produces reinforcement (or extinction) that increases
(or decreases) the rate of occurrence of the operant—
process is reinforcement]

METACONTINGENCY

Technological   •   Cultural ⟶   Benefits/costs
environment   •   practice   for survival of group

[In a specific technological environment, a particular kind of
cultural practice produces outcomes for the group that increase
(or decrease) the practice—process of cultural selection]

FIG. 14.1   Selection by consequences operates at three
levels: biology, behavior, and culture.

for identical (monozygotic) twins, individuals in the population vary in their physical features. Thus, birds like the thrush show variation in color of plumage, length of wings, and thickness of beak. Based on differences in their features, some individuals in a population are more successful than others at surviving and producing offspring. Differences in reproductive success occur when certain members of a species possess attributes that make them more likely to survive and reproduce in a given environment. Generally, individuals with features that meet the survival requirements of a habitat produce more offspring than others. As the number of descendants with those features increases, the genetic traits of these individuals are more frequently represented in the population. If there is a fecundity (surplus) of individuals produced and there exists even small variability between individuals, those with the most fit characteristics will be selected and hence multiply. This process of differential reproduction is called **natural selection**, and the change in the genetic make-up of the species is **evolution**.

Contingencies of Survival

FIG. 14.2   Charles Darwin in his later years. Darwin discovered the principle of natural selection. From the Archives of the History of American Psychology, The University of Akron. Reprinted with permission.

From a behavioral viewpoint, natural selection involves **contingencies of survival** (Skinner, 1986). The habitat or environment inadvertently sets requirements for survival of individuals. Members of a species who exhibit features and behavior appropriate to the contingencies survive and reproduce. Those with less appropriate characteristics have fewer offspring and their genetic line may become extinct. Natural selection therefore occurs as particular organisms satisfy (or fail to satisfy) the contingencies of survival.

An important implication of a contingency analysis of evolution is that the requirements for survival and reproductive success may change gradually or suddenly. For example, during the time of the dinosaurs, the collision of a large asteroid with the earth may have drastically changed the climate, fauna, and temperature of the planet in a very brief time (e.g., Alvarez, 1982; Alvarez, Alvarez, Asaro, & Michael, 1980; Alvarez, Asaro, & Michel, 1980; Alvarez, Asaro, Michel, & Alvarez, 1982). Given these changes in environmental contingencies, dinosaurs could not survive. The smaller mammals, however, that possessed features more appropriate to the new habitat lived and reproduced. Changes in the contingencies due to large-scale disasters may, therefore, occasionally favor characteristics that have advantages in a changed environment. This would occur even though these characteristics may have been a disadvantage in the past (see Gould, 1989, 2002, for a punctuated-equilibrium view of evolution; see Dawkins, 1976, 1996, 2004, for gradual genetic selection).

Phenotype, genotype, and environment

Evolutionary biologists distinguish between phenotype and genotype. An organism's **phenotype** refers to all the characteristics observed during the lifetime of an individual. For example, an individual's size, color, and shape are anatomical aspects of phenotype. Behavioral features include taste preferences, aggressiveness, shyness, and so on. Different phenotypic attributes of individuals may or may not reflect underlying genetic variation.

The **genotype** refers to the actual genetic make-up of the organism. Some observable characteristics are largely determined by genotype, while other features are strongly influenced by experience. But, as shown in Figure 14.3, most result from an interaction of genes and environment. Thus, the height of a person is attributable to both genes and nutrition. Evolution only occurs when the phenotypic differences among individuals are based on differences in genotype. If differences in height or other features did not result from genetic differences, selection for tallness (or shortness) could not occur. This is because there would be no genes for height to pass on to the next generation. People who engage in bodybuilding by lifting weights and taking steroids may substantially increase their muscle size (phenotype), but this characteristic will not be passed on to their children; it is not heritable. Natural selection can only work when there are genes that underlie physical features.

Sources of Genetic Variation

There are two major sources of heritable genetic variation: sexual recombination of existing genes and mutation. Genetic differences among individuals arise from sexual reproduction. This is because the blending of male and female genes produces an enormous number of random combinations. Although sexual recombination produces variation, the number of genetic combinations is constrained by the existing pool of genes. In other words, there are a finite number of genes in a population, and this determines the amount of variation caused by sexual reproduction.

Mutation occurs when the genetic material (e.g., genes or chromosomes) of an individual changes. These changes are accidents that affect the genetic code carried by an ovum or sperm. For example, naturally occurring background radiation may alter a gene site or a chromosome may break during the formation of sex cells or gametes. Such mutations are passed on to offspring, who display new characteristics. In most instances, mutations produce physical features that work against an organism's survival and reproductive success. However, on rare occasions mutations produce traits that improve reproductive success. The importance of mutation is that it is the source of new genetic variation. All novel genetic differences are ultimately based on mutation.

Natural selection depends on genetic variation based on sexual recombination and mutation. Genes code for proteins, which in turn regulate embryonic development and structural form. This means that differences in genes result in phenotypic differences in the structure (e.g., size and form of the brain) and physiology (e.g., release of hormones) of organisms. Selection occurs when specific genes underlying these phenotypic features contribute to fitness. Individuals with such characteristics have more offspring, ensuring that their genes occur at a higher frequency in the next generation.

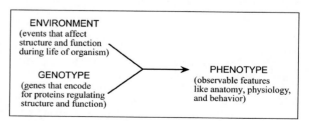

FIG. 14.3 Phenotype is a product of genotype and environment.

Genetic Regulation of Behavior

Behavioral rigidity

As we have noted, the behavior of organisms is always a phenotypic expression of genes and environment. Genes closely regulate some behavioral characteristics and in such instances the environment plays a subsidiary role. For example, in some species, defense of territory occurs as a ritualized sequence of behavior called a fixed action pattern (e.g., Tinbergen, 1951). The sequence or chain is set off by a specific stimulus, and the component responses are repeated almost identically with each presentation of the stimulus (see Chapter 3). The behavior pattern is based on a "genetic blueprint," and the environment simply initiates the sequence.

For example, the male stickleback fish will aggressively defend its territory from male intruders during mating season. The fish shows a fixed sequence of threatening actions that are elicited by the red underbelly of an intruding male. Tinbergen (1951) showed that this fixed action pattern occurred even to cigar-shaped pieces of wood that had a red patch painted on the bottom. In addition, he showed that a male intruder with its red patch hidden did not evoke the threatening sequence. Generally, the male stickleback is genetically programmed to carry out the attack sequence when given a specific stimulus at a particular moment in time.

FOCUS ON: Genetic control of a fixed action pattern

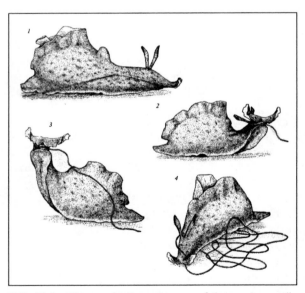

FIG. 14.4 The egg-laying sequence of the marine snail (*Aplysia*). The sequence involves (1) expelling a string of egg cases, (2) grasping the egg string by the mouth, (3) waving the head to draw the string out of the duct, and (4) affixing a triangle of string to a solid substance. This behavior was elicited by genetic procedures that activated the gene coding for egg-laying hormone (ELH) and other peptides associated with egg-laying behavior. Reproduced from Scheller and Axel (1984). Copyright 1984 held by the Estate of Bunji Tagawa. Reprinted with permission.

Richard Scheller, a geneticist at Stanford University, and Richard Axel, a professor of pathology and biochemistry at Columbia University College of Physicians and Surgeons, reported on the genetic control of a complex behavioral sequence. Scheller and Axel (1984) used the techniques of recombinant DNA to isolate a subset of gene locations that control the egg-laying sequence of the marine snail (*Aplysia*).

Techniques of recombinant DNA are beyond the scope of this book, but the important thing is that these procedures can be used to identify gene sites that encode for specific neuropeptides. In the Scheller and Axel (1984) experiment, the researchers isolated a set of gene sites that coordinated the release of several peptides. These chemicals caused neurological changes that invariably produced the egg-laying sequence (see also Hermann, de Lange, Pieneman, ter Maat, & Jansen, 1997, for genetic control of egg-laying in the pond snail, *Lymnaea stagnalis*).

Using techniques of genetic manipulation, Scheller and Axel were able to "turn on" the gene sites that controlled a complex and integrated sequence of behavior. In this sequence, the snail first contracts the muscles of the reproductive duct and expels a string of egg cases. Next, the animal grasps the egg string in its mouth and waves its head, behavior that typically functions to remove eggs from the duct. It then attaches the tangle of string to a solid surface. This behavioral sequence is shown in Figure 14.4. The fixed action pattern was activated in an unmated snail by direct manipulation of the egg-laying hormone (ELH) gene.

The DNA sequences that control egg laying may play an important role in other aspects of this animal's behavior. For example, the genetic material that encodes for head-waving behavior may be duplicated and appear in other genes that regulate feeding (Sossin, Kirk, & Scheller, 1987). In this regard, Scheller and Axel (1984) suggested:

> The same peptide may be incorporated in several different precursors encoded by different genes. Consider head waving in Aplysia. A characteristic waving of the snail's head takes place during feeding as well as during egg-laying. The same peptide or peptides could elicit the same behavioral component (head waving) in two very different contexts. To this end the head-waving peptide (or peptides) may be encoded in some other gene—one implicated in feeding behavior—as well as the ELH gene. In this way complex behaviors could be assembled by the combination of simple units of behavior, each unit mediated by one peptide or a small number of peptides.
>
> (p. 62)

When environments were stable and predictable, the replication of the same DNA sequence in a new genetic context may be one way that organisms evolved complex behavior. This solution involves using the same genetic code in different combinations. Although a high level of behavioral complexity may be achieved in this manner, the resulting behavior is tightly controlled by the underlying genetic context.

Some forms of animal communication are strongly determined by genotype. For example, the dance of the honeybee is a highly ritualized sequence of behavior that guides the travel of other bees (see Figure 14.5). After abundant foraging, a bee returns to the hive and begins to dance while other bees observe the performance in the hive in the dark. Subsequently, the bees who observe the dance fly directly to the foraging area in a so-called beeline.

The position of the sun with respect to food plays an important role in determining the initial dance. A bee may dance for several hours, and during this time the dance changes. These behavioral changes occur as the position of the sun with respect to food is altered by the rotation of the earth. That is, the bee's dancing corrects for the fact that the sun rises and falls over the course of a day.

The survival value of the dance relates to increased food supply for the hive. One problem is accounting for the occurrence of the dance before other bees responded to it—

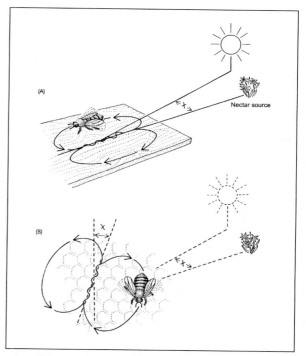

FIG. 14.5 The dance of a honeybee illustrates a phylogenetic form of communication in animals. When the bee returns from a nectar source, the dance begins with the insect waggling its abdomen. The number of waggles and direction of movement control the flight pattern of other bees that observe the performance. The orientation of the food source, relative to the current position of the sun, also is indicated by the waggle dance. From Alcock (1989). Copyright 1989 held by Sinauer Associates, Inc. Reprinted with permission.

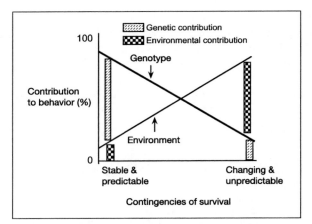

FIG. 14.6 When contingencies of survival are relatively stable and predictable, genetic regulation of behavior is predominant (e.g., fixed action patterns) and the environment plays a subsidiary role. As contingencies of survival become more uncertain, the role played by the environment and conditioning increases, while direct genetic regulation of behavior declines.

that is, before the dance had survival value. Presumably, the distance and direction that bees traveled had some effect on their behavior. Signs of fatigue and phototropic movements may have varied with distance and the position of the sun when they returned.

Bees that evolved sensitivity to what others did could respond to these aspects of behavior—relying on genes that coded for specific neurochemicals. Over time, natural selection favored variations in phototropic (and other) movements that made honeybee dancing more effective. Foraging bees would dance in conspicuous ways that allowed other bees to travel more accurately to the food source (for a similar analysis, see Skinner, 1986, p. 116).

Fixed action patterns and the communication of bees are examples of behavior that is predominantly regulated by genes and is usually called species-specific. In both instances, complex sequences of behavior are activated by specific stimuli and carried out in a highly ritualized manner. As shown in Figure 14.6, this form of behavior regulation was selected when the habitat of an animal was relatively stable and predictable.

Behavioral flexibility

When organisms were faced with unpredictable and changing environments, natural selection favored **behavioral flexibility**—adjusting one's behavior on the basis of past experience. In this case, genes played a subsidiary role, coding for general processes of learning. These processes allowed an organism to adjust to changing environmental requirements throughout its life span. Flexibility of behavior in turn contributed to the reproductive success of the organism.

Skinner (1984b) noted the reproductive advantage of behavioral flexibility:

> Reproduction under a much wider range of conditions became possible with the evolution of two processes through which individual organisms acquired behavior appropriate to novel environments. Through respondent (Pavlovian) conditioning, responses paired in advance by natural selection could come under the control of new stimuli. Through operant conditioning, new responses could be strengthened (reinforced) by events which immediately followed them.
>
> (p. 477)

In other words, respondent and operant conditioning are processes that are themselves genetically determined.

There is evidence for the selection of conditioning. Hirsch and McCauley (1977) showed that the blowfly, *Phormia regina*, could be classically conditioned and that the process of conditioning was heritable. Blowflies can be trained to extend their proboscis (or snout) whenever water is applied to their feet, if they are given sugar that is paired with foot wetting. Even though this conditioned reflex is learned, the process of establishing the reflex can be modified dramatically by artificial selection.

Flies varied in the number of elicited responses to the conditioned stimulus on trials 8–15 and were assigned a conditioning score between 0 and 8. Subjects with higher conditioning scores were selected and mated with each other, as were subjects with lower scores. A control group of flies was mated independent of their conditioning scores.

As shown in Figure 14.7, over seven generations, flies selected for conditioning showed increasingly more conditioned responses on test trials than their ancestors. When conditioning was selected against, each generation of flies showed less conditioned responses than the previous population. Flies mated regardless of conditioning scores (control) did not show a change over generations. At the end of seven generations, there was no overlap in the distribution of conditioning scores for the three groups—indicating that selection resulted in three separate populations of flies.

Hirsch and McCauley's (1977) experiment demonstrates that conditioning of a specific reflex has a range of variability. Based on this variation, selection can enhance the process of conditioning or eliminate it for distinct behavioral units. From a behavioral view, contingencies of survival continually mold the degree of behavioral flexibility of organisms—extending (or removing) the process of conditioning to a wide range of responses.

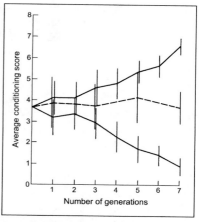

FIG. 14.7 Artificial selection for respondent conditioning in the blowfly, *Phormia regina*, reported by Hirsch and McCauley (1977). Flies mated for high-conditioning scores showed more conditioned responses over generations than flies that were randomly paired (dashed line). Other flies that were mated on the basis of low-conditioning scores (solid line downward) did progressively worse than their ancestors. Graph adapted from Hirsch and McCauley (1977) (© Elsevier, 1977).

LEVEL 2: SELECTION BY REINFORCEMENT

The evolution of operant behavior allowed variation and selection to work throughout the lifetime of an organism. Many organisms evolved genetic programs that coded for operant processes. For some species, natural selection ensured that operant processes were extended to more and more aspects of behavior. Individuals who inherited an extensive capacity for operant conditioning could adjust to complex and changing, often social, situations on the basis of behavioral consequences. Selection by reinforcement therefore became a major mode of adaptation (Glenn & Field, 1994).

Selection for Operant Processes

Glenn (1991) noted the biological advantage of operant processes and selection by behavioral consequences:

> The instability of local environments and what might be considered a limit on behavioral complexity in genetic programs appears to have given rise to a less cumbersome and more rapid sort of variation and selection. Instead of building thousands of complex behavioral relations into DNA, evolution built a few programs for behavioral processes that allowed changing environments to build behavior repertoires "as needed" during the lifetime of individuals. A relatively small change in a bit of DNA could result in profound changes in the possibility for ontogenetic adaptability if that change involved a gene for a behavioral process. All that was required as a first step was genetically uncommitted activity and susceptibility of that activity to selection by behavioral consequences.

(p. 43)

The evolution of operant conditioning, a range of uncommitted behavior, and susceptibility to certain kinds of reinforcement resulted in a second level of selection. Behavioral selection supplemented and extended selection at the biological level (i.e., natural selection).

Operant regulation in the marine snail, Aplysia

An example of how behavioral selection supplements the genetic control of behavior is seen in the marine snail, *Aplysia* (see previous FOCUS ON section). This simple organism serves as a model system for investigating the role of operant processes in the regulation of feeding (Brembs, Lorenzetti, Reyes, Baxter, & Byrne, 2002). Intact, freely behaving snails with extracellular electrodes in the buccal ganglia were observed during food ingestion. Recorded neural activity that accompanied eating was delivered contingent on spontaneous biting (no food present), and biting increased during the session, and even occurred at some level when tested 24 h later. These observations were taken as evidence of operant learning (biting reinforced by the eating-related neural activity), and also for "memory" of that behavior (reoccurrence sometime later), in the intact animal.

Subsequently, the buccal ganglia neural network was removed from trained subjects and its sensitivity to depolarizing current compared to networks taken from nontrained and yoked controls. Differential activity indicated that buccal motor patterns became ingestion-like as a result of training. Finally, one cell called B51, which is active during feeding (and could be the site of operant "memory"), was isolated and received a brief puff of dopamine contingent upon depolarization and membrane changes. There was a significant decrease in this cell's threshold compared to control cells, indicating an operant reinforcement effect at the cellular level. That is, the contingent dopamine served to differentially alter the cell's activity so that it produced ingestion-like motor patterns.

The research on operant conditioning of *Aplysia* at the cellular, neural network, and behavioral levels shows the universal nature of *selection by consequences* (see Pierce, 2001, for another example of selection at the biological, behavioral, and neural levels—activity anorexia). Clearly, the neural network and single-cell activity are modifiable by the effects of what happens when they are activated. As in any operant, the consequences at the neural and cellular levels affect the reoccurrence of the activity and thereby contribute to the regulation of feeding in *Aplysia*. Additionally, the work on *Aplysia* illustrates the continuum of behavioral regulation based on both genetic and environmental influences. That is, analysis of egg laying and feeding by *Aplysia* suggests regulation of behavior by gene-activated hormones and neurotransmitters that are combined with the operant conditioning.

Operant Selection and Extinction

The unit of selection at the behavioral level is the operant. The operant is a functional unit of behavior. At the neurocellular level operants involve increased activation, integration, and consolidation of neurons. Thus, the neuron is the physical unit on which behavioral selection works (see Chapter 4 and conditioning the neuron; also see Donahoe, 2002, and neural networks). An operant is composed of response forms that make contact with the environment, an operant class. Response forms vary from moment to moment, and some variations change the environment in ways that increase those forms (selection by consequences). A child who manipulates a rubber duck in the bathtub may inadvertently squeeze it in ways that produce a squeaking sound. If the sound functions as reinforcement, the operant of squeezing the squeaking duck increases over time. Recall that reinforcers are defined not by what they are (squeaking rubber duck) but by their effect on behavior.

If few (or no) response variations are reinforced, the operant decreases, and the process is extinct. That is, all members of an operant class cease to exist when they no longer result in reinforcement. The sound device in the toy duckling may break, and squeezing it in different ways no longer has the characteristic effect. Over time, the child will squeeze the rubber duck less and less as the operant undergoes extinction.

Extinction not only eliminates operants but also generates behavioral variation. Greater variation in the behavior increases an individual's chances of contacting the prevailing contingencies. In the bathtub, the child may push the broken rubber duck under the water, emitting a response that has never occurred before. The effect of this behavior may be to generate bubbles on the surface that, in turn, reinforce the child's behavior.

A more profound example of extinction and behavioral variation concerns people trying new ways of doing things when old ways no longer work (or do not work well). Thomas Edison's invention of the electric light bulb involved behavioral variation and selection. To generate electric light, Edison collected and tested a variety of materials to produce an effective lamp filament (Etzkowitz, 1992, p. 1005). He was known as the trial-and-error inventor, but a better description of his performance is "trial and success." Invention occurs when novel forms of response (trying different filaments) are generated by extinction and the appropriate response (using a tungsten filament) has been selected by the prevailing contingencies of reinforcement (effective and efficient light). Creativity, originality, or invention can be defined as nonrepetitive perseverance, and control by operant contingencies contributes to such behavior.

Susceptibility to Reinforcement

Contingencies of reinforcement resemble contingencies of survival (Skinner, 1986). Many animals eat and copulate simply because these responses have contributed to survival and reproduction. Male black widow spiders copulate and are then eaten by their mates. For these animals, copulating only had survival value for the species—passing on the genetic code even though the individual dies following the act. Other organisms evolved sensory systems that allowed food and sexual contact to reinforce behavior. That is, an animal whose actions resulted in sexual contact was more likely to act that way again. At this point, organisms had two redundant reasons for eating and copulating—survival of the species and reinforcement.

When food and sexual contact became reinforcing, new forms of behavior, indirectly related to eating and copulating, could be established. Animals could acquire new ways of finding, gathering, and processing foods based on reinforcement. Similarly, sexual reinforcement could establish and maintain a diversity of actions. These include looking at erotic objects, seeking out sexual partners, attracting a desirable mate, and performing a variety of sexual responses (e.g., genital contact with parts of body, position of intercourse, etc.).

Susceptibility to reinforcement may sometimes depend on the species and the particular behavior. Species-specific reinforcement is also shown by the fact that chaffinches (*Fringilla coelebs*) will peck a disk for food, but will not peck for contingent presentation of bird song. The same bird, however, will step on a perch for species-specific song, suggesting the biological preparedness of the response–reinforcer relationship (Hinde & Stevenson-Hinde, 1973; see also Chapter 5).

Primates may also be susceptible to species-specific reinforcement. The work of Harlow and Zimmerman (1959) on mother–infant attachment suggests that "contact comfort" may function as reinforcement for infants staying close to and preferring their mothers. Infants who only received food reinforcement from their mothers did not show strong attachment behavior. These findings again suggest that the response–reinforcer relationship is biologically prepared.

Organisms who are susceptible to reinforcement may acquire behavior that is not adaptive (Pierce & Epling, 1988). One paradoxical by-product of selection for operant conditioning is that people behave in ways that have distinct biological costs. Humans choose foods that are not healthful and engage in sexual behavior that is not related to procreation. In addition, conditioned reinforcement ensures that people come to value objects and events that are unrelated to survival and reproduction. Conditioned reinforcement may shape behavior that decreases reproductive success. People learn to use birth control, love adopted children, risk their lives to help others, risk their lives to kill others, and some even kill themselves.[1] The point is that susceptibility to reinforcement has been adaptive, but this sensitivity may generate behavior with no adaptive value.

Evolution, Reinforcement, and Verbal Behavior

Social signals

As noted earlier, a honeybee signals the location of food by dancing in ways that affect the travel of other bees. This form of communication involves a high degree of genetic regulation. Genes, as we have seen, code for the general behavioral processes known as respondent and operant conditioning. Once these learning capacities evolved, signaling could be acquired on the basis of an organism's interaction with the environment.

Skinner (1986) explained the acquisition of human gestures in terms of selection by consequence and susceptibility to aversive stimulation. He analyzed the contingencies as follows:

> One person can stop another by placing a hand on his chest, and if the person who is stopped finds the contact aversive, he will stop on later occasions before contact is made. The movement of the arm and hand changes from a practical response to a gesture. Once that happened, the topography can change until it would have little or no physical effect.
>
> The gesture that means "Come here" is another example. It presumably originated as practical pulling but became effective as a gesture when people who were pulled moved quickly to avoid physical contact. The topography of the gesture still varies with distance, possibly because of visibility, but also as if some practical work remained to be done: When the parties are far apart, the whole arm is moved; when they are fairly near, only the forearm; and when they are close, only a hand or a finger.
>
> (pp. 116–117)

For Skinner, gesturing is behavior that results from social contingencies of reinforcement. A social contingency involves the behavior of two (or more) people who arrange stimuli and reinforcement for each other's actions.

FIG. 14.8   How pulling a person to see a sight may have evolved into the gesture of pulling the arm toward the body (Frank Epling on left and David Pierce on the right, the original authors of this textbook).

The person who sees a surprising sight may pull a companion toward the view and be reinforced by the friend's reactions to the sight (see Figure 14.8). On later occasions, a pulling motion may occur before the companion is in reach. The friend may avoid being dragged to the sight by coming when the pulling motion is first made. The reinforcement contingencies composed of each person's behavior establish and maintain this social episode.

Although social contingencies are clearly involved in human signs and gestures, other processes may play an important role. The research on stimulus equivalence discussed in Chapter 12 is relevant to signs and gestures (Sidman & Cresson, 1973). Humans easily

---

[1] We are not making a value judgment about these activities; the point is that these behaviors do not contribute to reproductive success.

distinguish equivalent stimulus classes, but other organisms do not. Gestures and signs may stand for or be equivalent to other stimulus classes. A smile, the spoken words "good job," and the gesture for "OK" (thumb and index finger make an O) become equivalent when they have a similar effect on behavior. Equivalence relations depend on discrimination of reflexivity ($A = A$ and $B = B$), symmetry (if $A = B$ then $B = A$), and transitivity (if $A = B$ and $A = C$, then $B = C$). Complex transitivity relations seem to involve evolution of species-specific capacities for discrimination as well as general behavioral processes like operant conditioning.

Humans readily generate and respond to iconic or representational signs when there is a requirement to communicate but speaking is not possible (Kuschel, 1973; Meissner & Philpott, 1975). For example, Brown (1986) recounts a study that compared severely deaf children with a normal hearing group (Goldin-Meadow & Morford, 1985). Parents who refused to sign to them because they believed that signing would retard vocal speech raised the deaf children. Each of the 10 deaf children independently acquired a similar repertoire of iconic signs. Presumably, particular ways of signing were more effective than others in altering the behavior of the parents. The hearing children also showed iconic signing that gradually diminished as vocal speech increased. This later finding suggests that speech has some advantages over gestures and iconic signs when speakers and listeners have normal hearing.

Corballis (1999) reviewed several perspectives dealing with the probable evolution of language from manual gestures, hand to mouth. He indicated that with the emergence of the genus *Homo* and their increased brain size and adequate vocal apparatus, contingencies could have further promoted the development of speech and language. In this regard, it is useful to provide a behavior analysis of the evolution of speech sounds.

Vocal and speech sounds

Natural selection must have been important in the evolution of vocalization and speech sounds. Compared with gestures and iconic signs, sounds can affect a listener's behavior when it is too dark to see, others are out of sight, or no one is looking at the speaker. Spoken sounds are also an advantage to speakers whose hands are full—warding off prey or holding weapons to attack an enemy. Skinner (1986) noted additional benefits of speech sounds over gestures:

> There are special advantages, however, in large operant repertoires, especially the enormous variety of available speech sounds. Gestures are not as conspicuously different as speech sounds and hence are fewer in number, and the sounds one produces are more like the sounds one hears than gestures are like the gestures one sees (because they are seen from a different point of view). One learns to gesture through movement duplication, but to speak through product duplication, which is more precise.
>
> (p. 117)

Most of the organs that allowed for speech sounds probably evolved for other reasons (see Chapter 12). The diaphragm was used in breathing, the tongue and jaws were involved in eating, and the lips could take in water by sucking and sipping. The vocal cords and pharynx did not play a direct role in survival, but may have evolved in social species that could benefit from the calls and cries of others (see Blumstein & Armitage, 1997, on social alarms in marmots).

There were probably several other important steps in the evolution of human speech. One involved the extension of operant processes to a range of speech-relevant behavior. Each organ that contributed to speech was initially reflexive—the organism responding to specific stimulation. Survival must have been better served when operant processes supplemented reflexive behavior. An organism could breathe as a reflex elicited by high levels of circulating carbon dioxide, or it could hold its breath to avoid a predator. Based on natural selection, more and more speech-relevant behavior came under the control of its consequences. Compared with the great apes, humans made an evolutionary leap when the vocal apparatus was supplied with nerves (i.e., innervated) for operant regulation.

The step to operant regulation of the vocal musculature is not sufficient to account for speech. Evolution must have also resulted in the coordination of all the systems involved in the production of speech. The great apes have complete operant control of their hands but have not developed a sophisticated system of signs or gestures. Children show early iconic signing that shifts toward spoken words as more and more speech is acquired. Both iconic signing and spoken words require that the speaker and listener respond to abstract stimulus relations along several dimensions. Thus, neural coordination of speech probably built on, and added to, specialized capacities for discrimination involving the visual, auditory, and motor systems. In less technical terms, humans evolved systems for symbolic behavior and these systems were eventually integrated with those of speech (Pierce & Epling, 1988).

Speech sounds are a large pool of uncommitted behavior. This behavior is spontaneously emitted at high frequency but plays no direct role in survival (Skinner, 1984b). From a behavioral view, wide variation in spontaneous speech sounds allows for selection of vocal operants by reinforcement supplied by listeners. Thus, Osgood (1953) found that an infant's babbling included all the speech sounds that make up the different languages of the world. Vocal responses similar to the verbal community increase while dissimilar speech drops out of the repertoire (Irwin, 1948, 1952). One possibility is that a child's speech sounds are shaped toward adult forms by reinforcement of successive approximations.

Goldstein, King, and West (2003) manipulated mothers' reactions to infants' vocalizations and found that phonological aspects of babbling increase with contingent social stimulation from mothers (reinforcement) but not with noncontingent maternal behavior. Social shaping by reinforcement creates rapid shifts in infant vocalization to more advanced speech sounds. Interestingly, bird song of juvenile male cowbirds is shaped toward mature forms used in mating by subtle reactions of females called wing strokes (West & King, 1988). Thus, social shaping by reinforcement may be a general mechanism for the development of adult vocal forms of communication across diverse species.

Verbal behavior

The evolution of operant processes, the coordination of speech systems, and a large variety of uncommitted speech sounds allowed for the regulation of vocal operants by others. A person in an English-speaking community learns to speak in accord with the verbal practices of the community. That is, the way a person speaks is shaped by the reinforcement practices of others. On a specific occasion, the community provides reinforcement for certain ways of speaking and withholds reinforcement or supplies aversive stimulation for other unacceptable responses. In this manner, the individual conforms to the customary practices of the community and, in so doing, contributes to the perpetuation of the culture.

Verbal behavior (Chapter 12) allows people to coordinate their actions. When people observe rules, take advice, heed warnings, and follow instructions, their behavior is rule governed. Rule-governed behavior (Chapter 11) allows people to profit from what others say. If a fellow camper reports that a bear is near your tent, you can move the tent to a new camping site. A student looking for a good course may benefit from the advice of another student. In these examples, the listener or person who responds to the verbal report avoids an aversive event (the bear) or contacts positive reinforcement (a good course). Children are taught to follow advice and instructions. Parents and others provide simple verbal stimuli that set the occasion for reinforcement of the child's compliance. In this way, the child is taught to listen to what others say.

As we have noted, listeners benefit from the verbal reports of others. For this reason, listeners are inclined to reinforce the person who provides useful instructions. In a verbal community, people are taught to express their appreciation for the advice received from others. For example, in an English-speaking community, people say "thank you" and other variations of this response when given directions, advice, and instructions. These verbal responses by the listener reinforce the behavior of the speaker.

Verbal behavior evolved (level 2) in the sense that particular ways of speaking were more or less effective in regulating the behavior of listeners within a verbal community. Response variation ensured that many ways of speaking were tried and more and more people adopted successful combinations of speech sounds. At this point, many people were able to talk to one another on the basis of common standards for speech (grammar). These common linguistic practices by a verbal community were the underlying basis for a third level of selection: the selection and evolution of cultural practices.

LEVEL 3: THE SELECTION AND EVOLUTION OF CULTURE

The evolution of operant processes and verbal behavior allowed for the emergence of human culture. Sigrid Glenn (1988, 1989; see also Lloyd, 1985) proposed a behavior analysis of culture that builds on the works of Skinner (1953) and anthropologist Marvin Harris (1979). Although social scientists often talk about culture as the ideas and values of a group, a behavioral viewpoint suggests that a culture involves the usual ways of acting and speaking in a community. These customary forms of behavior (customs, mores, etc.) are the cultural practices of the group.

Cultural Practice

From a behavioral perspective, cultural practices involve the interlocking operant behavior of many people—the members of a culture. Each person's behavior provides stimulation and reinforcement for the actions of others. A **cultural practice** is therefore defined in terms of interlocking social contingencies—where the behavior of each person supports the behavior of other members of the community. The pattern of behavior that arises from the interlocking contingencies is the type of practice (e.g., what people do in that culture).

This view of culture suggests that what people do in a particular community is determined by the function of a practice. The ancient Romans adopted military tactics that were highly effective in most battles. For example, Roman soldiers would form a close body of men, called a phalanx, and interlock their shields as a common barrier against the enemy. Although there are many ways to conduct a battle, this military maneuver became popular because of its effectiveness. In other words, what people in a particular culture do is a function of the previous benefits and costs of that practice. With changes in technology (the products of a culture), the phalanx and the interlocking of shields became obsolete—the costs in terms of casualties and lost battles increased relative to the benefits.

Cultural practices are functionally similar to operants. Both operants and cultural practices are selected by consequences (Lamal, 1997). Thus, a cultural practice increases when people have benefited from it. The practice of making water jars involves alternative sets of interlocking operants that result in a common outcome. One person gathers clay; another person makes the pot; and a consumer trades something for the jar. The common outcome of such a practice is greater efficiency in transporting and storing water. There are many ways of storing and transporting water, including shells, hollow leaves, woven baskets, clay pots, and indoor plumbing. The cultural form that predominates (e.g., plumbing) reflects the basic processes of selection by consequences. In terms of selection, operants are selected by contingencies of reinforcement and cultural practices are selected by metacontingencies (see for example Norton, 1997, on geographic practices, rule-governed behavior, and metacontingencies).

FOCUS ON: Metacontingencies

FIG. 14.9   Sigrid Glenn. Published with permission.

Dr. Sigrid Glenn (Figure 14.9) at the University of North Texas made an important contribution to the behavior analysis of culture when she first described the metacontingencies of cultural practices. **Metacontingencies** refer to contingent relations between cultural practices and the effects of those practices for the group (Glenn, 1988). For example, competence in science is important for people who live in a technologically advanced culture. Scientific research produces a range of benefits for the general society. These include better medicine, more productive crop yields, new and better building materials, more efficient and longer-lasting appliances, and superior regulation of human behavior. Thus, a positive metacontingency exists between educational practices that increase scientific competence and long-term benefits to the group. This analysis suggests that teaching methods that promote science were selected, while alternative methods of education declined in popularity.

Metacontingency implies that there will be an increase in those forms of education that result in more and better trained students of science, but this may not occur. In complex cultures like the United States, competing (or concurrent) metacontingencies may mean that the "best" educational practice is not selected. A less than optimal form of scientific education may prevail for some time because teaching science is only part of the function of education. For example, the manifest function of education is to teach reading, writing, and arithmetic. The hidden or latent function of schooling includes keeping people out of the work force and categorizing them into high-, medium-, and low-status groups based on educational attainment. Thus, the form of education that predominates is one that has produced the most overall benefit to the community, group, or society. If the relative outcomes of an educational practice resulting in low scientific competence exceed those of a system that yields high scientific achievement, then the less adequate educational practice will predominate in the culture (see Lamal & Greenspoon, 1992, for metacontingencies and the US congress; also, Lamal, 1997).

Origin, Transmission, and Evolution of Cultural Practices

Cultural practices arise and are transmitted over generations. Galef and Allen (1995) showed how diet preferences could be established, diffused, and socially transmitted by rats. Founder colonies of four rats were taught an arbitrary food preference. Subsequently, members of the colonies were slowly replaced with naïve rats having no food preferences. The food preference was still maintained in the third generation of replacements although none of these animals had received the original training. Thus, a food practice established by arbitrary nonsocial contingencies was transmitted and maintained by implicit social contingencies of the group.

Another example comes from a story about animals in a zoo enclosure. A troop of baboons was provided with a choice between a preferred food (bananas) and less appetizing laboratory chow (Pierce, 1991). As expected, the baboons consistently chose to eat bananas. Following a baseline period, the researchers established a negative reinforcement contingency for eating the less preferred food. Whenever any animal approached the bananas, the entire colony was drenched with water from a fire hose that was used to clean the enclosure. After exposure to this contingency, the troop attacked any member that approached the bananas. Eventually, all members of the troop were exclusively eating the less preferred chow and avoiding cold showers.

The researchers then removed the reinforcement contingency—approaching and eating the bananas no longer resulted in being soaked with water. As you might expect, the group did not test the operating contingencies and continued to attack any member that went toward the preferred food. At this point, the contingencies had established a cultural taboo that was highly resistant to change. Thus, social contingencies and observational learning contributed to the maintenance of the food taboo even though the original negative reinforcement contingencies had long since been removed.

Harris (1974) has provided a functional analysis of the origin and transmission of many human cultural practices. To illustrate, in India the cow is deified and many Hindus do not eat beef. This was not always the case—when the last ice age ended, the peoples of Northern India raised and ate cattle, sheep, goats, and many agricultural products. Cattle, however, have some advantages other than just providing meat; they may be easily herded and trained to pull plows or carts.

Population density increased greatly in the Ganges River valley and by 300 BC the people of the valley had destroyed the trees surrounding the river. As a result, the risk of drought increased and farms decreased in size. Small farms have little space for animals, but draft animals were essential for working the land and transporting agricultural products. Cows provided traction, milk, and meat, but the farmer who ate his cow lost milk production and a working animal. Thus, the people of India faced a social trap involving the immediate benefit of eating beef and the long-term loss of the cows' other advantages.

A cost–benefit analysis suggests that it was better to keep a cow than eat it. To avoid this social trap, the cow was deified and eating beef became a cultural taboo. The Hindu community has maintained this practice into modern times. Other cultures have food taboos that may be analyzed in terms of the function of cultural practices. Until very recently, Catholics did not eat meat on Fridays, many Islamic and Jewish people will not eat pork, and the Chinese people despise cow's milk (Harris, 1974).

Cultural Evolution

Cultural evolution presumably begins at the level of the individual where technological effects reinforce variation in individual behavior. An inventor may discover a new way of making a wheel; a farmer finds a food crop that produces higher yields; and a teacher may find a novel way to teach reading. A culture is said to evolve when the community adopts these innovations.

Adoption of innovations depends on the metacontingencies facing the group. For example, a new food crop with higher yield is selected when the metacontingencies favor increased grain production. This could occur when a community is impoverished or when higher yielding crops support the feeding of domestic animals used for work or consumption. Higher yield crops may not be selected when food is overly abundant, when increased grain supply leads to problems of storage, or when a new crop attracts pests that spread disease.

A troop of Japanese macaques on Koshima Island is well known for its innovations and traditions (Kawamura, 1959). In one example, an infant female called Imo began to wash sweet potatoes to remove the grit. This behavior was later observed in Imo's playmates and her mother, who taught it to another offspring. Imo was also among the first to take up swimming and to throw wheat kernels on the water. Throwing wheat on the water removed the sand that the kernels were mixed with, because the sand sank and the kernels floated. Both of these practices were eventually adopted by the entire troop (see Whiten & Boesch, 2001, on chimpanzee culture).

A common observation is that cultural practices in humans often remain unchanged over many generations, even when these customs make no sense. A practice may persist for many years because the members of the group who engage in it (do not kill cows for food) fail to contact a change in the metacontingencies (cost of cows is rising relative to benefits). At the individual level, a person conforms to the taboo because the social contingencies arranged by the group (religious proclamations and sanctions) avert contact with the positive reinforcement contingency (eating beef is good).

Cultural practices also may persist when the metacontingencies are stable and the current practices are sufficient to meet the contingencies. For centuries, the only way that books were manufactured was to have scribes make written copies. As a cultural practice, copying books by hand allowed for more standardized transmission of knowledge than word of mouth. Better methods of food preparation, house construction, agriculture, waste disposal, and transportation could be described in a common manner and passed from one generation to another. Thus, written transcription satisfied the metacontingencies for passing on social knowledge, but it was not the only way to reproduce books. The advent of the printing press allowed for an alternative form of book duplication that was less costly in time and effort, more productive, and much faster. Thus, transcription by hand eventually was made obsolete by the invention of the printing press, but for a while both forms of the practice were used for social knowledge duplication. In fact, transcription by hand still is used today although it is done infrequently and for specialized purposes (e.g., translation of a work from one language to another).

A final point is that an innovation like the printing press often determines whether a culture remains static or dynamic. Individual inventions produce variation in cultural practices much as genetic mutations produce changes in species characteristics. That is, new forms of individual behavior (designing and making can-openers) are generated by aversive contingencies or extinction (satisfying a need). These novel behaviors and products (can-openers) are occasionally adopted by others and propagated as ways of meeting the metacontingencies (efficient storage and access to food with low risk of disease). Generally, variation in form and selection by consequences operate at different levels—producing both individual innovation and cultural evolution.

CHAPTER SUMMARY

This chapter provides many examples of how selection by consequences can operate at various levels of analysis. Our point has been that adaptive behaviors that provide benefits can lead to changes at the genetic, behavioral, and cultural levels. Selection is a universal process and although we, for the most part, restrict our analysis to the behavior of organisms, such a process has much greater range. The application of contingency analysis has proven useful in accounting for many diverse observations, from changes in conditioning ability in flies, to acquisition of verbal behavior in humans, to the creation and maintenance of cultural dietary taboos.

Alternative forms of explanation for these observations have not proven as helpful as assuming and applying the unifying concept of selection by consequences. A scientific approach to behavior based on selection is not only possible, but is ongoing and substantiated by thousands of research studies. The findings from these explorations have led to further questions about the regulation of behavior in more complex and widespread areas. The next step is the full integration of behavior analysis and neuroscience within a common framework based on evolution and selection.

Key Words

Behavioral flexibility	Evolution	Natural selection
Contingencies of survival	Genotype	Phenotype
Cultural evolution	Metacontingencies	Phylogeny
Cultural practice	Mutation	Selection by consequences

Glossary

A–B–A–B reversal design. This is the most basic single-subject research design and it is ideally suited to show that specific features of the environment regulate an organism's behavior. The A-phase, or baseline, is used to measure behavior before the researcher introduces an environmental change. During baseline, the experimenter takes repeated measures of the behavior under study, and this establishes a criterion against which any changes (attributed to the independent variable) may be assessed. Following the baseline phase, an environmental condition is changed (B-phase) and behavior is measured repeatedly. If the independent variable, or environmental condition, has an effect, then the behavioral measure (dependent variable) will change—increase or decrease. Next, the baseline phase is reintroduced (A) and behavior is again measured. Since the treatment is removed, behavior should return to baseline levels. Finally, the independent variable is introduced again and behavior is reassessed (B). According to the logic of the design, behavior should return to a level observed in the initial B-phase of the experiment. This second application of the independent variable helps to ensure that the behavioral effect is caused by the manipulated condition.

Absolute stimulus control. When operants are regulated by the physical properties of one stimulus (color or hue), this is called absolute stimulus control. See also **relative stimulus control**.

Activity anorexia. Following a period of food restriction, physical activity suppresses food intake and declining body weight increases activity. This negative feedback loop is called activity anorexia in rats and a similar cycle occurs in many anorexic patients.

Activity-induced taste aversion. Conditioned taste aversion (avoidance) that occurs when a novel food or liquid taste is followed by wheel running. The conditioned stimulus (CS), taste, is conditioned as an aversive stimulus when associated with the neurophysiological effects of wheel running (unconditioned stimulus, US).

Ad libitum weight. The body weight of an organism that has free access to food 24 h a day.

Adjunctive behavior. Also called interim behavior. On interval schedules of reinforcement, or time-based delivery of food, organisms often show excessive behavior within the interreinforcement interval. For example, rats may drink up to three times their usual daily water intake (polydipsia) over a 1-h session. This behavior immediately follows reinforcement and is a side effect of periodic food delivery.

Ainslie–Rachlin principle. The principle states that reinforcement value decreases as the delay between making a choice and obtaining the reinforcer increases. This principle predicts preference reversal when a delay precedes the choice between a small, immediate reward and a large, deferred reinforcer. That is, at some time prior to the choice the large, deferred reinforcer becomes more valued than the small, immediate reward.

Anticipatory contrast. The schedule of reinforcement following the target component (B) in a sequence of schedules (A→ B→ C) generates strong contrast that increases as training progresses. The strong contrast effect is called anticipatory contrast to distinguish it from the weak elicited responding by the preceding schedule.

Applied behavior analysis. This is a branch of behavior analysis that uses behavior principles to solve practical problems such as the treatment of autism or improved teaching methods. Applied behavior analysis is also referred to as behavioral engineering.

Associative strength. During respondent conditioning, the term associative strength is used to describe the relation between the conditioned stimulus (CS) and the magnitude of the conditioned response (CR). In general, associative strength increases over conditioning trials and reaches some maximum level.

Assumption of generality. The assumption of generality implies that the effects of contingencies of reinforcement extend over species, reinforcement, and behavior. For example, a fixed-interval schedule is expected to produce the scalloping pattern for a pigeon pecking a key for food and a child who is solving mathematics problems for teacher approval, all other things being equal.

Autistic children. The term refers to children who show an early lack of social interaction with parents, other family members, and peers. For example, these children often resist being held and may have a tantrum if picked up or hugged. When autistic children get older they may be mistaken as deaf because they do not talk or establish eye contact when talked to. These children often show repeated stereotyped patterns of behavior such as rocking back and forth, spinning a top, wiggling their fingers in front of their eyes, and so on.

Autoshaping. A respondent conditioning procedure that generates skeletal responses. For example, a key light is turned on a few seconds before grain is presented to a pigeon. After several pairings of key light and grain, the bird begins to peck the key. This effect was first reported as autoshaping—an automatic way to teach pigeons to key peck.

Aversive stimulus. An event or stimulus that an organism escapes or avoids.

Avoidance. See **negative reinforcement**.

Backward chaining. A procedure used to train a chained performance. The basic idea is to first train behavior that is closest to primary reinforcement; once responding is established, links in the chain are added that are farther and farther from primary reinforcement. Each link in the chain is reinforced by the discriminative stimulus (S^D), which is also a conditioned reinforcer signaling the next component in the sequence.

Backward conditioning. In the respondent procedure of backward conditioning, the unconditioned stimulus (US) comes on before the conditioned stimulus (CS). The general consensus has been that backward conditioning is unreliable, and many researchers question whether it occurs at all. There is evidence that backward conditioning can occur when the CS has biological significance (e.g., the sight of a predator).

Baseline. The term refers to the base rate of behavior against which an experimental manipulation is measured. An uncontrolled baseline is the rate of an operant before any known conditioning; a controlled baseline (e.g., the rate of response on a variable-interval 60-s schedule) may be established to assess the effects of an experimental manipulation (e.g., presentation of intermittent shocks).

Baseline sensitivity. The term means that a low dose of a drug can cause substantial changes in baseline behavior. More generally, a behavioral baseline that varies with small increases in the independent variable is said to show sensitivity.

Behavior. Everything that an organism does, including covert actions like thinking.

Behavior analysis. Behavior analysis is a comprehensive experimental approach to the study of the behavior of organisms. Primary objectives are the discovery of principles and laws that govern behavior, the extension of these principles over species, and the development of an applied technology.

Behavior analysts. These people are researchers and practitioners of behavior analysis.

Behavior maintenance. Refers to how long a new behavior persists after the original contingencies are removed (e.g., an anorexic patient who is taught to eat properly shows long-lasting effects of treatment if he maintains adequate weight for many years).

Behavior system. A species-specific set of responses elicited by a particular unconditioned stimulus (US). That is, for each species there is a behavior system related to procurement of food, another related to obtaining water, and still another for securing warmth.

Behavior trapping. Refers to the teaching of new behavior that, once established, is "trapped" by natural contingencies of reinforcement—the contingencies of everyday life.

Behavioral contract. A behavioral plan of action that is negotiated between a client, child, or spouse and concerned others is a behavioral contract. The plan usually includes a statement of target responses, consequences that follow different actions, and long-term goals. The contract objectively specifies what is expected of the person in terms of behavior and the consequences that follow.

Behavioral contrast. Contrast refers to an inverse relationship between the response rates for two components of a multiple schedule—as one goes up, the other goes down. There are two forms of contrast: positive and negative. Positive contrast occurs when rate of response in an *unchanged* component of a multiple schedule *increases* with a decline in behavior in the other component. Negative contrast is defined when rate of response in an *unchanged* component of a multiple schedule *decreases* with an increase in behavior in the other component.

Behavioral dynamics. An area of research that attempts to analyze schedule effects in terms of a few basic processes. Behavioral dynamics requires a high level of mathematical sophistication. Both linear and nonlinear calculus is used to model the behavioral impact of schedules of reinforcement. If performance on schedules can be reduced to a small number of fundamental principles, then reasonable interpretations may be made about any particular arrangement of the environment. Also, it should be possible to predict more precisely the behavior based on knowledge of the operating contingencies and the axioms that govern reinforcement schedules.

Behavioral economics. The use of economic concepts (price, substitute commodity, etc.) and principles (e.g., marginal utility) to predict, control, and analyze the behavior of organisms in choice situations.

Behavioral flexibility. When organisms were faced with unpredictable and changing environments, natural selection favored those individuals whose behavior was flexible—adjusting on the basis of past experience. In this case, genes played a subsidiary role coding for general processes of learning. These processes allowed an organism to adjust to changing environmental requirements throughout its life span. Flexibility of behavior in turn contributed to the reproductive success of the organism.

Behavioral medicine. Behavior change programs that target health-related activities such as following special diets, self-examination for early symptoms of disease, exercising, taking medicine, and so on. In many instances, the idea is that problems of behavior that affect health may be prevented before treatment is necessary.

Behavioral neuroscience. Refers to a scientific area that integrates the science of behavior (behavior analysis) with the science of the brain (neuroscience). Areas of interest include the effects of drugs on behavior (behavioral pharmacology), neural imaging and complex stimulus relations, choice and neural activity, and the brain circuitry of learning and addiction.

Behaviorism. A term that refers to the scientific philosophy of behavior analysis.

Bias. For the generalized matching equation, bias is indicated by variation in the value of k from 1. Generally, bias is produced by some unknown asymmetry between the alternatives on a concurrent schedule that affects preference over and above the relative rates of reinforcement.

Blocking. In respondent compound conditioning, a conditioned stimulus (CS) that has been associated with an unconditioned stimulus (US) blocks a subsequent CS–US association. A CS_1 is paired with a US until the conditioned response reaches maximum strength. Following this conditioning, a second stimulus or CS_2 is presented at the same time as the original CS_1, and both are paired with the US. On test trials, the original CS_1 elicits the conditioned response (CR) but the second stimulus or CS_2 does not.

Break and run. A pattern of response, seen on a cumulative record, that occasionally develops on fixed-interval schedules. There is a long postreinforcement pause (PRP) followed by a brief burst of responses that result in reinforcement.

Celeration. The word celeration is used in precision teaching to denote two kinds of behavior change: acceleration and deceleration. Acceleration occurs when the rate of target behavior (frequency/time) is increasing over days, while deceleration involves decreasing rate over this period. A graph of the rates over days allows for evaluation of behavior change and revision of the instructional components based on the observed celeration (change in rate over days).

Chain schedule of reinforcement. A chain schedule of reinforcement refers to two or more simple schedules (CRF, FI, VI, FR, or VR), each of which is presented sequentially and signaled by a discriminative stimulus (S^D). Only the final or terminal link of the chain results in primary reinforcement. See also **homogeneous** and **heterogeneous chain schedules**.

Change in associative strength. A factor that affects the increment in associative strength on any one trial is the change in associative strength, which is the difference between the present strength of the conditioned stimulus (CS) and its maximum possible value.

Changeover delay (COD). A changeover delay is a control procedure that is used to stop rapid switching between alternatives on concurrent schedules of reinforcement. The COD contingency stipulates that responses do not have an effect immediately following a change from one schedule to another. After switching to a new alternative, a brief time is required before a response is reinforced. For example, if an organism has just changed to an alternative schedule that is ready to deliver reinforcement, there is a brief delay before a response is effective. As soon as the delay has elapsed, a response is reinforced. The COD contingency operates in both directions whenever a change is made from one alternative to another.

Changeover response. On a concurrent schedule, a changeover is a response that an organism emits when it switches from one alternative to another. See also **Findley procedure**.

Changing criterion design. A research design primarily used in applied behavior analysis. The rate of target behavior is progressively changed to some new criterion (up or down). For example, the criterion for the number of cigarettes a person smokes each day could be progressively lowered over several months. The effects of the independent variable are shown if the subject meets or falls below the criterion for any set of days (e.g., the criterion is 20 cigarettes for week 3, but changes to 10 by week 6).

Choice. From a behavioral view, choice is the distribution of operant behavior among alternative sources of reinforcement (e.g., concurrent schedules of reinforcement).

Coercion. Coercion is defined as the "use of punishment and the threat of punishment to get others to act as we would like, and to our practice of rewarding people just by letting them escape from our punishments and threats" (Sidman, 2001, p. 1). That is, coercion involves the basic contingencies of punishment and negative reinforcement.

Commitment response. The commitment response is some behavior emitted at a time prior to the choice point that eliminates or reduces the probability of impulsive behavior. A student who invites a classmate over to study on Friday night (commitment response) insures that she will "hit the books" and give up partying when the choice arrives.

Compound stimuli. In respondent conditioning, two (or more) conditioned stimuli (e.g., tone and light) called a compound are presented together and acquire the capacity to evoke a single conditioned response (e.g., salivation).

Concurrent-chain schedule. Refers to two or more chain schedules that are simultaneously available. See also **chain schedule of reinforcement** and **concurrent schedules of reinforcement**.

Concurrent schedules of reinforcement. Involves two or more schedules of reinforcement (e.g., FR, VR, FI, VI) that are simultaneously available. Each alternative is associated with a separate schedule of reinforcement and the organism is free to distribute behavior to the schedules.

Conditional discrimination. A conditional discrimination is a differential response to stimuli that depends on the stimulus context (a four-term contingency of reinforcement). Consider a matching-to-sample experiment where a bird has been trained to match to triangles and squares based on the sample stimulus. To turn this experiment into a conditional-discrimination task, a house light is inserted that may be turned on or off. The bird is required to match to the sample when the house light is on and to choose the noncorresponding stimulus when the house light is off. Conditional matching to sample involves simultaneous discrimination of three elements in a display. The animal must respond to geometric form depending on the sample, to the correspondence or noncorrespondence of the comparison stimuli, and to the condition of the house light (on/off). See also **matching to sample**.

Conditioned aversive stimulus (S^{ave}). An aversive stimulus based on a history of conditioning. See **aversive stimulus**.

Conditioned establishing operation (CEO). Involves an establishing operation that depends on a history of reinforcement for completing a behavioral sequence of chain. One procedure is called the blocked-response CEO, in which a response that usually occurs is blocked because of the temporary absence of a specific condition, stimulus, or event. For example, you may leave your seminar notes at home as you rush to the university. Because you cannot complete the behavioral sequence of giving a seminar presentation, obtaining the notes would function as reinforcement for making a telephone call to get them. The notes would not have a reinforcement function during a casual lunch with an old friend because they are not necessary to this behavioral sequence. Whenever an event or stimulus is required to complete a behavior chain, withholding the event will establish it as reinforcement for operant behavior.

Conditioned overeating. Refers to a procedure of pairing a food taste (salt or sweet) with low caloric energy. When high-energy foods are consumed with tastes that have predicted low calorie content, juvenile rats overeat at their regular meals. The basic effect is that diet foods can cause overeating in children as an unintended side effect of taste conditioning.

Conditioned reflex. See **conditioned response** and **conditioned stimulus**.

Conditioned reinforcement. Refers to the presentation of a conditioned reinforcer and the subsequent increase in rate of the operant that produced it.

Conditioned reinforcer. A conditioned reinforcer is an event or stimulus that has acquired its effectiveness to increase operant rate on the basis of an organism's life or ontogenetic history.

Conditioned response (CR). An arbitrary stimulus, such as a tone, is associated with an unconditioned stimulus that elicits reflexive behavior (e.g., food elicits salivation). After several pairings, the stimulus is presented alone. If the stimulus now elicits a response (tone now elicits salivation), the response to the tone is called a conditioned response (CR).

Conditioned stimulus (CS). An arbitrary stimulus, such as a tone, is associated with an unconditioned stimulus that elicits reflexive behavior (e.g., food elicits salivation). After several pairings, the stimulus is presented alone. If the stimulus now elicits a response (tone elicits salivation), it is called a conditioned stimulus (CS).

Conditioned-stimulus function. An event or stimulus that has acquired its function to elicit a response on the basis of respondent conditioning. When a tone is followed by food in the mouth, the tone becomes a conditioned stimulus (CS) for salivation.

Conditioned suppression. In conditioned suppression, a previously conditioned stimulus (e.g., tone, light, etc.) is paired with an aversive unconditioned stimulus (US) such as an electric shock. After several pairings, the original CS becomes a conditioned aversive stimulus (CS^{ave}). Once the CS^{ave} has been conditioned, its onset suppresses ongoing operant behavior. A rat may be trained to press a lever for food. After a stable rate of response is established, the CS^{ave} is introduced. When this occurs, the animal's lever pressing is suppressed.

Conditioned withdrawal. When a conditioned stimulus (CS) that accompanies drug use is presented, people are said to have "cravings" and this respondent process is called conditioned withdrawal. The CS elicits reactions that are ordinarily countered by the unconditioned stimulus (US). However, when the US is not delivered and the conditional response (CR) reactions occur, people experience withdrawal. A heroin addict can have their withdrawal symptoms immediately terminated by a heroin injection. If you are accustomed to having a cigarette after a meal, the craving you experience can be alleviated with a smoke.

Construction of S^{D}s. In solving problems, people make up or construct their own discriminative stimuli. A person who has an important early morning appointment may set an alarm clock for 6:00 a.m. Technically, setting the alarm is precurrent behavior, or an operant that precedes some other response or performance. That is, setting the alarm is behavior that results in the alarm ringing at 6:00 a.m., setting the occasion for getting up and going to the meeting. A major function of precurrent behavior is the construction of S^Ds that regulate subsequent action. See also **precurrent behavior**.

Context for conditioning. Refers to the ontogenetic and phylogenetic histories of an organism, including its current physiological status as well as contextual events or stimuli that are present when conditioning occurs.

Context of behavior. Refers to the fact that environment–behavior relationships are always conditional—depending on other circumstances.

Contingencies of survival. The contingencies (in the sense of "if–then" requirements) that result in differential reproduction or natural selection. The habitat or ecological environment sets requirements for the survival of individuals and their genes. Members of a species who exhibit features and behavior appropriate to the contingencies survive and reproduce, and those with less appropriate characteristics have fewer offspring. Natural selection (differential reproduction) therefore occurs as particular organisms satisfy (or fail to satisfy) the contingencies of survival.

Contingency of reinforcement. A contingency of reinforcement defines the relationship between the occasion, the operant class, and the consequences that follow the behavior (e.g., S^D: $R \rightarrow S^r$). We change the contingencies by altering one of the components and observing the effect on behavior. For example, a researcher may change the rate of reinforcement for an operant in a given situation. In this case, the $R \rightarrow S^r$ component is manipulated while the S^D: R component is held constant. Contingencies of reinforcement can include more than three terms, as in conditional discrimination (e.g., four-term relations); also, the effectiveness of reinforcement contingencies depends on motivational events called establishing operations (e.g., deprivation and satiation).

Contingency-shaped behavior. Operant behavior that is directly under the control of contingencies of reinforcement, as opposed to rule-governed behavior.

Contingency-specifying stimuli. A technical term for verbal stimuli that regulate the behavior of listeners. Rules, instructions, advice, maxims, and laws are contingency-specifying stimuli in the sense that the verbal stimulus describes an actual contingency of reinforcement of everyday life. See **rule-governed behavior**.

Contingent response. In the response deprivation hypothesis, the contingent response is the activity obtained by making the instrumental response, as in the contingency if activity A occurs (instrumental response) then the opportunity to engage in activity B (contingent response) occurs.

Continuous recording. A tactic used in applied behavior analysis for assessing the rate of target behavior. Each instance of behavior is counted during certain periods of the day (e.g., lunch, recess, first class in the morning, and so on).

Continuous reinforcement (CRF). When each response produces reinforcement (e.g., each lever press produces food), the schedule is called CRF or continuous reinforcement.

Controlling stimulus (S). A controlling stimulus is any stimulus or event that changes the probability of operant behavior. There are three kinds of controlling stimuli: S^D, S^Δ, and S^{ave}. An S^D increases the probability of response, and an S^Δ makes responding less likely. An S^{ave} may increase or decrease the likelihood of operant behavior, depending on the operating contingency.

Correspondence relations. Survival or reinforcement contingencies that select for equivalence, matching, or similarity between: the behavior of a model and observer, as in imitation; what a person says and what is done (say–do correspondence); what is done and what is said (do–say correspondence); private stimulation and the verbal report (describing emotions); and an instruction or rule and what is done (rule-governed behavior).

Cultural evolution. Cultural evolution begins at the level of the individual, when its technological effects reinforce behavior: An inventor may discover a new way of making a wheel; a farmer finds a food crop that produces higher yields; and a teacher may find a novel way to teach reading. A culture is said to evolve when the community adopts these innovations and the practice (e.g., using a higher yield type of wheat) is passed on from one generation to the next.

Cultural practice. A cultural practice is defined in terms of interlocking social contingencies—where the behavior of each person supports the behavior of other members of the community. The pattern of behavior that arises from the interlocking contingencies is the type of practice (i.e., what people do in that culture).

Culture. Culture is usually defined in terms of the ideas and values of a society. However, behavior analysts define culture as all the conditions, events, and stimuli arranged by other people that regulate human action.

Cumulative record. A cumulative record is a real-time graphical representation of operant rate. Each response produces a constant upward increment on the Y-axis, and time is indexed on the X-axis. The faster the rate of response is, the steeper the slope or rise of the cumulative record. See also **cumulative recorder**.

Cumulative recorder. Refers to a laboratory instrument that is used to record the frequency of operant behavior in real time (rate of response). For example, paper is drawn across a roller at a constant speed, and each time a lever press occurs a pen steps up one increment. When reinforcement occurs, this same pen makes a downward deflection. Once the pen reaches the top of the paper, it resets to the bottom and starts to step up again. See also **cumulative record**.

Delay-reduction hypothesis. Stimuli that signal a decrease in time to positive reinforcement, or an increase in time to an aversive event, are more effective conditioned reinforcers. Generally, the value of a conditioned reinforcer is attributed to its delay reduction—how close it is to reinforcement or how far it is from punishment.

Delayed conditioning. A respondent conditioning procedure in which the conditioned stimulus (CS) is presented a few seconds before the unconditioned stimulus (US) occurs.

Delayed imitation. Refers to imitation of the modeled stimulus after a delay and in the absence of the model or modeled stimulus. Delayed imitation is considered to require more cognitive abilities than direct imitation (i.e., delayed imitation involves remembering the modeled stimulus).

Delayed matching to sample. On a matching-to-sample task, the comparison stimuli are presented some time after the sample stimulus is turned off. See also **matching to sample**.

Dependent variable. The variable that is measured in an experiment, commonly called an effect. In behavior analysis, the dependent variable is a measure of the behavior of an organism. One common dependent variable is the rate of occurrence of an operant (e.g., the rate of lever pressing for food).

Deprivation operation. Refers to the procedure of restricting access to a reinforcing event. Withholding an event or stimulus increases its effectiveness as a reinforcer.

Differential reinforcement. In *discrimination procedures*, differential reinforcement involves reinforcement in the presence of one stimulus (S^D) but not in other settings (S^Δ). The result is that the organism comes to respond when the S^D is presented and to show a low probability of response in settings that have not resulted in reinforcement (S^D). A differential response in S^D and S^Δ situations is called discrimination and an organism that shows this differential response is said to discriminate the occasion for reinforcement.

Differential reinforcement may be based on a property of operant behavior and in this case results in *response differentiation*. For example, when reinforcement is based on short inter-response times or IRTs (2–5 s) the distribution of IRTs becomes centered around short intervals. A change in the contingencies to reinforce longer IRTs (20–25 s) produces a new distribution centered around long intervals. See **response differentiation**.

Differential reinforcement of other behavior (DRO). Refers to reinforcement for any behavior other than a target operant. For example, after a period of time the applied behavior analyst delivers reinforcement for any behavior other than "getting out of seat" in a classroom. The target behavior is on extinction and any other behavior is reinforced.

Differential response. When an organism makes a response in one situation but not in another, we say that the animal discriminates between the situations or makes a differential response.

Direct replication. Repeating the procedures and measures of an experiment with several subjects of the same species (e.g., pigeons) is called direct replication. If each pigeon is exposed to a fixed-interval 30-s schedule of food reinforcement and each bird shows a scalloping pattern of pecking the key (i.e., a low rate of response following reinforcement that increases to a high rate at the moment of reinforcement), then the experimental procedures show direct replication.

Discriminated avoidance. Refers to avoidance behavior emitted to a warning stimulus. For example, a dog stops barking when its owner shouts, "Shut up!"

Discriminated extinction. A low rate of operant behavior that occurs as a function of an S^Δ. For example, the probability of putting coins in a vending machine with an "out of order" sign on it is very low.

Discrimination. When an organism makes a differential response to two or more stimuli (or events), we can say that the animal discriminates between them. This process is called discrimination.

Discrimination index (I_D). This index compares the rate of response in the S^D component to the sum of the rates in both S^D and S^Δ phases:

$$I_D = (S^D \text{ rate})/(S^D \text{ rate} + S^\Delta \text{ rate})$$

The measure is a proportion that varies between 0.00 and 1.00. Using the I_D measure, when the rates of response are the same in the S^D and S^Δ components, the value of I_D is 0.50, indicating no discrimination. When all responses occur during the S^D phase, the S^Δ rate is zero and I_D is 1. Thus, a discrimination index of 1 indicates a perfect discrimination and maximum stimulus control of behavior. Intermediate values of the index signify more or less control by the discriminative stimulus.

Discriminative function. When an organism's behavior is reinforced, those events that reliably precede responses come to have a *discriminative function*. These events are said to *set the occasion* for behavior and are called discriminative stimuli. Discriminative stimuli acquire this function because they predict (have been followed by) reinforcement.

Discriminative stimulus (S^D). An event or stimulus that precedes an operant and sets the occasion for operant behavior (antecedent stimulus).

Discriminative-stimulus account of conditioned reinforcement. The hypothesis that it is necessary for a stimulus to be an S^D in order for it to be a conditioned reinforcer. The hypothesis has been largely discounted, and the weight of the evidence supports Fantino's (1969b) delay-reduction hypothesis. See **delay-reduction hypothesis**.

Displacement behavior. Displacement behavior is observed in the natural environment and is characterized as irrelevant, incongruous, or out of context. That is, the behavior of the animal does not make sense given the situation, and the displaced responses do not appear to follow from immediately preceding behavior. Like adjunctive behavior (see definition in this glossary), displacement responses arise when consummatory activities like eating are interrupted or prevented.

Duration recording. When behavior is continuous, duration recording is a method of observation. An observer may use a stopwatch, or other timing device, to record the duration of behavior. When a person is sitting in a chair, the watch is timing; and when the person leaves the chair, the watch is stopped.

Echoic behavior. When there is point-to-point correspondence between the stimulus and response, verbal behavior may be classified as echoic. A further requirement is that the verbal stimulus and the echoic response must be in the same mode (auditory, visual, etc.) and have exact physical resemblance (e.g., same sound pattern). An echoic is a class of verbal operants regulated by a verbal stimulus in which there is correspondence and topographic similarity between the stimulus and response. Saying "this is a dog" to the spoken stimulus "this is a dog" is an example of an echoic response in human speech.

Elicited (behavior). Respondent (CR) or reflexive (UR) behavior is elicited in the sense that the behavior is made to occur by the presentation of a stimulus (CS or US).

Emitted (behavior). Operant behavior is emitted in the sense that it occurs at some probability in the presence of a discriminative stimulus, but the S^D does not force its occurrence.

Emotional response. Refers to a response such as "wing flapping" in birds that occurs with the change in contingencies from reinforcement to extinction. A common emotional response is called aggression (attacking another organism or target).

Environment. The functional environment is all of the events and stimuli that affect the behavior of an organism. The environment includes events "inside the skin" like thinking, hormonal changes, and pain stimulation.

Errorless discrimination. In errorless discrimination, the trainer does not allow the organism to make mistakes by responding to the extinction stimulus (S^Δ). Initially S^D and S^Δ are very different, but differences between the stimuli are gradually reduced as training progresses. The procedure eliminates the emotional behavior generated by extinction with other discrimination-training methods. For example, pigeons flap their wings in an aggressive manner and work for an opportunity to attack another bird during the presentation of the S^Δ on a multiple schedule. This behavior does not occur when errorless discrimination is used in training.

Escape. See **negative reinforcement**.

Established-response method. In terms of conditioned reinforcement, an operant that produces unconditioned reinforcement is accompanied by a discriminative stimulus, just prior to reinforcement. When responding is well established, extinction is implemented but half of the subjects continue to get the stimulus that accompanied unconditioned reinforcement. The other subjects undergo extinction without the discriminative stimulus. Generally, subjects with the stimulus present respond more than the subjects who do not get the stimulus associated with unconditioned reinforcement. This result is interpreted as evidence for the effects of conditioned reinforcement.

Establishing operation. Formally, an establishing operation is defined as any change in the environment that alters the effectiveness of some stimulus or event as reinforcement and simultaneously alters the momentary frequency of the behavior that has been followed by that reinforcement. Thus, an establishing operation has two major effects: it increases the momentary effectiveness of reinforcers supporting operant behavior; and it increases the momentary probability of operants that have produced such reinforcement. For example, the most common establishing operation is deprivation for primary reinforcement. This procedure has two effects. First, food becomes an effective reinforcer for any operant that produces it. Second, behavior that has previously resulted in getting food becomes more likely.

Evolution. In terms of biology, the change in the genetic make-up of the species as observed in the expressed characteristics of its members.

Experimental analysis of behavior. The method of investigation most commonly used in behavior analysis. The method involves breaking down complex environment–behavior relations into component principles of behavior. The analysis is verified by arranging experimental procedures that reveal the underlying basic principles and controlling variables. This involves intensive experimentation with a single organism over an extended period, rather than statistical assessment of groups exposed to experimental treatments.

Extinction. The procedure of extinction involves the breaking of the contingency between an operant and its consequence. For example, bar pressing followed by food reinforcement no longer produces food. As a behavioral process, extinction refers to a decline in the frequency of the operant when an extinction procedure is in effect. In both instances, the term extinction is used correctly.

Extinction burst. A rapid burst of responses when an extinction procedure is first implemented.

Extraneous sources of reinforcement. Involves all nonprogrammed sources of reinforcement that regulate alternative behavior—reducing the control of behavior on a specified schedule of reinforcement. Extraneous sources of reinforcement include any unknown contingencies that support the behavior of the organism. For example, a rat that is pressing a lever for food on a particular schedule of reinforcement could receive extraneous reinforcement for scratching, sniffing, and numerous other behaviors. The rate of response for food will be a function of the programmed schedule as well as the extraneous schedules controlling other behavior. In humans, a student's mathematical performance will be a function of the schedule of correct solutions as well as extraneous reinforcement for other behavior from classmates or teachers, internal neurochemical processes, and changes to the physical/chemical environment (e.g., smell of food drifting from the cafeteria). See also **quantitative law of effect**.

Facultative behavior. Collateral behavior generated by properties of a schedule of reinforcement is called facultative behavior. See also **adjunctive behavior**.

Fading. The procedure involves transferring stimulus control from one value of a stimulus to another. This is done by gradually changing a controlling stimulus from an initial value to some designated criterion.

Findley procedure. An experimental method used to present concurrent schedules in the operant laboratory. Separate schedules are programmed on a single key, and the organism may switch schedules (and associated S^Ds) by making a response on a changeover key.

First-order conditioning. In first-order respondent conditioning, an apparently neutral stimulus is paired with an unconditioned stimulus (US). When this occurs, the control of the response to the US is transferred to the neutral stimulus, which is now called a conditioned stimulus (CS).

Fixed action pattern (FAP). A sequence or chain of behavior set off by a specific stimulus. The component responses are repeated almost identically with each presentation of the stimulus. Fixed action patterns are based on a "genetic blueprint," and the environment simply initiates the sequence. For example, the male stickleback fish will aggressively defend its territory from male intruders during mating season. The fish shows a fixed sequence of threatening actions that are elicited by the red underbelly of an intruding male.

Fixed interval (FI). The fixed interval is a schedule of reinforcement in which an operant is reinforced after a fixed amount of time has passed. For example, on a fixed-interval 90-s schedule (FI 90), one bar press after 90 s results in reinforcement. Following reinforcement, another 90-s period goes into effect; and after this time has passed, another response will produce reinforcement.

Fixed ratio (FR). The fixed ratio is a response-based schedule of reinforcement that delivers reinforcement after a fixed number of responses are made. For example, on a fixed ratio of 10 (FR 10), the organism must make 10 responses per reinforcement.

Fluency. In precision teaching, the use of rate (frequency/time) focuses instruction on *fluency* or accuracy *and* high frequency. When a performance becomes fluent, the behavior is retained longer, persists during long periods on the task, is less affected by distractions, and is more likely to be available in new learning situations (i.e., to combine with other well-learned behaviors).

Formal similarity. A term used in verbal behavior to define echoic behavior. Formal similarity requires that the verbal stimulus and the product of the response be in the same mode (auditory, visual, etc.) and have exact physical resemblance (e.g., same sound pattern).

Free operant method. In the free operant method, an organism may repeatedly respond over an extensive period of time. The organism is "free" to emit many responses or none at all. More accurately, responses can be made without interference from the experimenter (as in a trials procedure).

Function-altering event. Verbal stimuli such as rules and instructions can alter the function of other stimuli and, thereby, the strength of relations among stimuli and behavior. For example, an instruction about what to do in an airline emergency can establish stimulus control by a "dangling yellow mask" over the behavior of "placing the mask over your face and breathing normally."

Functional analysis. An analysis of behavior in terms of its products or consequences. Functionally, there are two basic types of behavior: operant and respondent. The term respondent defines behavior that increases or decreases because of the presentation of a stimulus (or event) that precedes the response. Such behavior is said to be elicited, in the sense that it reliably occurs when the stimulus is presented. There is a large class of behavior that does not depend on an eliciting stimulus. This behavior is called emitted and spontaneously occurs at some frequency. When emitted behavior is strengthened or weakened by the events that follow the response, it is called operant behavior. Thus, operants are emitted responses that increase or decrease depending on the consequences they produce.

Functional independence. A term used in verbal behavior to describe the independence of the operant classes of manding and tacting. Formally, each operant class is controlled by separate contingencies of reinforcement; training in manding relations would not necessarily affect the training in tacting relations, or vice versa.

Generality. An experimental result has generality when it is observed in different environments, organisms, and so on. For example, the principle of reinforcement generalizes over species, settings, responses, and reinforcers. In a pigeon, the peck-for-food relationship depends on the establishing operation of deprivation for food in the immediate past. For humans, who have an extensive capacity for operant conditioning, going to a soda machine to get a cold drink on a hot afternoon is an effective contingency. In both examples, establishing operations and reinforcement are the operating principles.

Generalization. The spread of stimulus control from one stimulus to another, as in stimulus generalization. The control by a 60-Hz tone over key pecking for food may generalize to an 80-Hz tone. In another usage, generalization may refer to the spread of behavior from one response form to another when the stimulus remains constant. A rat may acquire lever pressing to a tone with its right paw but also presses with its left paw or even its nose. The rat's lever pressing in the presence of the tone is said to show response generalization.

Generalization gradient (operant). Generalization occurs when an organism responds to values of the S^D (or fewer responses to the S^Δ) that were not trained during acquisition. A generalization gradient is the function (graph) that relates values of the S^D (intensity of light) to a measure of response strength (operant rate).

Generalization gradient (respondent). Generalization occurs when an organism shows a conditioned response (CR) to values of the conditioned stimulus (CS) that were not trained during acquisition. A generalization gradient is the function (graph) that relates values of the CS (loudness of tone) to a measure of response strength (amount of CR).

Generalized conditioned reinforcer. A conditioned reinforcer that is backed up by many other sources of reinforcement is a generalized conditioned reinforcer. Money is a good example. Cash may be exchanged for a large variety of goods and services. Human behavior is regulated by generalized reinforcement, involving social attention, approval, and affection.

Generalized imitation. A reinforcement procedure used to teach the generalized response and stimulus classes "do as I do." The procedure involves reinforcement of correspondence between modeled performance and imitative operants. After training a number of exemplars, a novel modeled stimulus is presented without reinforcement and a new imitative response occurs that matches the modeled performance. Generalized imitation involves both stimulus generalization of the class of modeled stimuli and response generalization of the class of imitative responses.

Generalized matching law. Proportion equations like $B_a/(B_a + B_b) = R_a/(R_a + R_b)$ describe concurrent performance when alternatives differ only in rate of reinforcement. However, in complex environments, other factors also contribute to choice and preference. These factors arise from the biology and environmental history of the organism. For example, sources of error may include different amounts of effort for the responses, qualitative differences in reinforcement such as food versus water, a history of punishment, a tendency to respond to the right alternative rather than the left, and sensory capacities.

To include these and other conditions within the matching law, it is useful to express the law in terms of ratios rather than proportions (i.e., $B_a/B_b = R_a/R_b$). When relative rate of response matches relative rate of reinforcement, the ratio equation is simply a restatement of the proportional form of the matching law. A generalized form of the ratio equation may, however, be used to handle the situation in which unknown factors influence the distribution of behavior. These factors produce systematic departures from ideal matching but may be represented as two constants (parameters) in the generalized matching equation:

$$B_a/B_b = k(R_a/R_b)^a$$

In this form, the matching equation is known as the generalized matching law. The coefficient k and the exponent a are values that represent two sources of error for a given experiment. When these parameters are equal to 1, the equation is the simple ratio form of the matching law. See also **matching law**.

Generalized social reinforcement. A generalized conditioned reinforcer that is also a social reinforcer increases or maintains operant behavior. Praise is a social reinforcer backed up by many sources of reinforcement. See also **generalized conditioned reinforcer**.

Genotype. Genotype refers to the genetic make-up of the organism. Some observable characteristics are largely determined by genotype, other features are strongly influenced by experience, but most result from an interaction of genes and environment. Thus, the height of a person is attributable to both genes and nutrition.

Habituation. Habituation occurs when an unconditioned stimulus (US) repeatedly elicits an unconditioned response (UR). The frequent presentation of the US produces a gradual decline in the magnitude of the UR. When the UR is repeatedly elicited it may eventually fail to occur at all.

Heterogeneous chain schedule. A heterogeneous chain requires different responses for each link of the chain schedule. Dog trainers make use of heterogeneous chains when they teach complex behavioral sequences to their animals. In going for a walk, a seeing-eye dog stops at intersections, moves forward when the traffic is clear, pauses at a curb, avoids potholes, and finds the way home. Each of these different responses is occasioned by specific stimuli and results in conditioned reinforcement. See also **chain schedule of reinforcement**.

History of reinforcement. Refers to the reinforcement contingencies that an organism has been exposed to during its lifetime, including the changes in behavior due to such exposure.

Homeostasis. Walter Cannon coined the word in 1932 as the tendency of a system to remain stable and to resist change. In terms of a biological system, homeostasis refers to the regulation of the system by negative feedback loops. For example, the body maintains a temperature within a very fine tolerance. If the environment warms up or cools down, physiological mechanisms (sweating or shivering) involving the sympathetic and parasympathetic nervous systems are activated to reduce the drift from normal body temperature. Homeostasis involves self-regulation to maintain an internal environment in a stable or constant condition by means of multiple dynamic equilibrium adjustments.

Homogeneous chain schedule. Operant chains are classified as homogeneous when the topography or form of response is similar in each link of the schedule. For example, a bird pecks the same key in each component of the chain. Each link in the schedule produces a discriminative stimulus for the next link, and the S^D is also a conditioned reinforcer for the behavior that produces it. See also **chain schedule of reinforcement**.

Hypothetical construct. Unobservable events or processes that are postulated to occur and that are said to explain behavior are called hypothetical constructs. For example, Freud's mental device "ego" is a hypothetical construct that is used to explain self-gratifying behavior. In cognitive psychology, "cognitive representation" or "mental imagery" are hypothetical terms that are said to explain the behavior of knowing and observing the world. From a behavioral perspective, the difficulty is that the mental constructs are easily invented, are inferred from the behavior they are said to explain, and are inherently unobservable with direct observation. That is, there is no objective way of getting information about such events except by observing the behavior of people or other organisms.

Identity matching. In identity matching or discrimination, the researcher presents a sample stimulus (e.g., vertical line) and two side-key options (e.g., vertical line and horizontal line). The organism is reinforced for selecting the comparison stimulus that corresponds to the sample (e.g., pecking the side key with a vertical line when the sample is a vertical line). See also **matching to sample**.

Imitation. True imitation requires that the learner emits a novel response that could only occur by observing a model emit a similar response.

Immediate causation. An event (X) immediately preceding some occurrence (Y) is said to cause it if the event produces or results in the occurrence. The motion of the cue ball hitting the colored billiard ball (X) causes the colored ball to move in a particular trajectory (Y). A tap on the patellar tendon (X) causes the knee jerk (Y), as in a simple reflex. In a neuroscience example, the release of NPY (the feeding peptide) causes the rat to eat.

Impulsive behavior. When a person (or other animal) selects the smaller, immediate payoff over the larger, delayed benefits, we may say that the person shows impulsive behavior.

In vitro reinforcement. A method used to investigate reinforcement in the neuron: increasing calcium bursts or firings by injection of dopamine agonists or other agents.

Independent variable. The variable that is manipulated, changed, or controlled in an experiment, commonly called a cause. In behavior analysis, it is a change in the contingencies of reinforcement, the arrangement of events that precede and follow the behavior of an organism (e.g., changing the rate of reinforcement).

Instinctive drift. Species-characteristic behavior that becomes more and more invasive during operant training is called instinctive drift.

Instrumental response. In the response deprivation hypothesis, the instrumental response is the behavior that produces the opportunity to engage in some activity.

Intensive behavioral intervention. A term used in the treatment of autisic behavior where the child is given targeted or planned interventions for behavioral excesses and deficits of 30 or more hours each week. This kind of programmed behavioral intervention is most effective with youngsters under 4 years of age.

Interim behavior. See **adjunctive behavior**.

Interlocking contingencies. In social episodes involving manding and tacting, each person (speaker and listener) completes a behavioral sequence or chain ($S^D: R \rightarrow S^r + S^D: R \rightarrow S^r \ldots$), and the verbal relations involve the intermingling of these chains or the interlocking contingencies. In an interlocking contingency the behavior of one person causes stimulation and reinforcement for the behavior of the other, and vice versa.

Intermittent reinforcement schedule. A schedule programmed so that some rather than all operants are reinforced. In other words, an intermittent schedule is any schedule of reinforcement other than continuous reinforcement (CRF).

Interreinforcement interval (IRI). The interreinforcement interval (IRI) is the time between any two reinforcers. Research shows that the postreinforcement pause (PRP) is a function of the IRI. As the time between reinforcements becomes longer, the PRP increases. On fixed-interval (FI) schedules the PRP is approximately half of the IRI. For example, on an FI 300-s schedule (in which the time between reinforcements is 300 s) the average PRP will be 150 s. On fixed-ratio (FR) schedules, the evidence indicates similar control by the IRI: as the ratio requirement increases, the PRP becomes longer. See **postreinforcement pause (PRP)**.

Interresponse time (IRT). The time between any two responses is called the interresponse time. The interresponse time may be treated as a conditionable property of operant behavior; for example, the IRTs on a variable-interval (VI) schedule of reinforcement are much longer than on a variable-ratio (VR) schedule. Variable-interval schedules are said to differentially reinforce long IRTs, while VR schedules differentially reinforce short interresponse times.

Interval recording. A measurement strategy used in applied behavior analysis to assess the rate of target behavior. A block of time is selected and divided into short equal intervals, and if the target behavior occurs it is recorded once in an appropriate time bin. For example, a 30-min segment of a mathematics class may be divided into 10-s bins. Regardless of the number of responses, if the behavior occurs in a given 10-s segment, then the observer records it as a single event.

Interval schedules. These are schedules of reinforcement based on the passage of time and one response after that time has elapsed.

Intraverbal behavior. Intraverbal behavior involves a class of verbal operants regulated by verbal discriminative stimuli. In everyday language, thematically related words (or sentences) are examples of intraverbal relations. For example, the verbal response "fish" to the spoken words "rod and reel" is an intraverbal response; saying "water" to the written word LAKE is also intraverbal behavior. Thus, intraverbal relations arise from verbal behavior itself. A previous verbal response by a speaker is a stimulus for a subsequent verbal operant.

Joint control. Refers to the notion that two verbal stimuli exert stimulus control over a common verbal topography. In finding the correct sequence of numbers in an array, repeating the required number and identifying that number in the array both jointly control the terminal verbal response "[number] I found it."

Latency. The time from the onset of one event to the onset of another. For example, the time it takes a rat to reach a goal box after it has been released in a maze.

Law of effect. As originally stated by Thorndike, the law refers to stamping in (or out) some response. A cat opened a puzzle-box door more rapidly over repeated trials. Currently the law is stated as the principle of reinforcement: Operants may be followed by consequences that increase (or decrease) the probability or rate of response.

Law of intensity–magnitude. As the intensity of an unconditioned stimulus increases, so does the magnitude or size of the unconditioned response.

Law of latency. As the intensity of the unconditioned stimulus increases, the latency (time to onset) of the unconditioned response decreases.

Law of the threshold. At very weak intensities a stimulus will not elicit a response, but as the intensity of the eliciting stimulus increases there is a point at which the response is elicited. That is, there is a point below which no response is elicited and above which a response always occurs.

Learned helplessness. Learned helplessness involves exposing an animal to inescapable and severe aversive stimulation (shocks). Eventually the animal gives up and stops attempting to avoid or escape the situation. Next, an escape response that under ordinary circumstances would be acquired easily is made available, but the animal does not make the response. The organism seems to give up and become helpless when presented with inescapable aversive stimulation.

Learning. The acquisition, maintenance, and change of an organism's behavior as a result of lifetime events (the ontogeny of behavior). In everyday language, learning often is used to refer to transitional changes in behavior (e.g., from not knowing to knowing one's ABC) but conditions that maintain behavior in a steady state are also part of what we mean by learning (e.g., continuing to recite the alphabet).

Limited hold. A limited hold is a contingency where the reinforcer is available for a set time after an interval schedule has timed out. Adding a limited hold to a variable-interval schedule increases the rate of responding by reinforcing short interresponse times.

Log-linear matching equation. To write the matching law as a straight line, we may write the log-linear equation:

$$\log(B_a/B_b) = \log k + [a \times \log(R_a/R_b)]$$

Notice that in this form, $\log(B_a/B_b)$ is the Y variable and $\log(R_a/R_b)$ is the X variable. The constants a and $\log k$ are the slope and intercept, respectively. See **generalized matching law**.

Magazine training. Refers to following the click of the feeder (stimulus) with the presentation of food (reinforcement). For example, a rat is placed in an operant chamber and a microcomputer periodically turns on the feeder. When the feeder is turned on, it makes a click and a food pellet falls into a cup. Because the click and the appearance of food are associated in time you would, after training, observe a typical rat staying close to the food magazine, quickly moving toward it when the feeder is operated. See **conditioned reinforcer**.

MammaCare. A behavioral program used to teach women effective self-examination of their breasts.

Manding. The word manding comes from the common English word *commanding*, but commanding is only part of this operant class. Manding is a class of verbal operants whose form is regulated by specific establishing operations (e.g., deprivation, aversive stimulation, etc.) and specific reinforcement. When you say "give me the book," "don't do that," "stop," and so on, your words are regulated by motivational conditions or establishing operations (e.g., deprivation for the book, or by another person doing something unpleasant). The establishing operation (no ketchup) regulates the topography of manding ("give ketchup") and insures that a particular event functions as specific reinforcement (getting ketchup).

Matching. The term is used to describe the relationship between the distribution of behavior and the distribution of reinforcement in choice situations. When the distribution of behavior (percentage or ratio) equals the distribution of reinforcement (percentage or ratio) we say that the organism shows matching.

Matching law. When two or more concurrent-interval schedules are available, the relative rate of response matches (or equals) the relative rate of reinforcement. More generally, the matching law states that the distribution of behavior between (or among) alternative sources of reinforcement is equal to the distribution of reinforcement for these alternatives. See **relative rate of response** and **relative rate of reinforcement**.

Matching to sample. A procedure used to investigate recognition of stimuli is called matching to sample. For example, a pigeon may be presented with three keys. A triangle or sample stimulus is projected onto the center key. To ensure that the bird attends to the sample, the pigeon is required to peck the sample key. When this happens, two side keys are illuminated with a triangle on one and a square on the other, called the comparison stimuli. If the bird pecks the comparison stimulus that corresponds to the sample, this behavior is reinforced and leads to the presentation of a new sample. Pecks to the noncorresponding stimulus result in extinction and the next trial. See **identity matching**.

Maximization. In this economic view of behavior, humans and other animals are like organic computers that compare their behavioral distributions with overall outcomes and eventually stabilize on a response distribution that maximizes overall rate of reinforcement. See **melioration** as an alternative view.

Maximum associative strength. In the Rescorla–Wagner model, a conditioned stimulus (CS) can acquire only so much control over a conditioned response (CR). This is the maximum associative strength for the CS. Thus, a tone (CS) that is paired with 1 g of food will have maximum associative strength when conditioned salivation (the conditioned response, CR) to the tone is about the same amount as the unconditioned salivation (unconditioned stimulus, UR) elicited by the food (US). That is, a US elicits a given magnitude of the UR. This magnitude sets the upper limit for the CR. The CS cannot elicit a greater response than the one produced by the US.

Mechner notation. A notation system that describes the independent variables that produce operant behavior. That is, Mechner notation is a set of symbols for programming schedules of reinforcement arranged in the laboratory.

Melioration. An explanation of how organisms come to produce matching on concurrent schedules of reinforcement. In contrast to overall maximizing of reinforcement, Herrnstein (1982) proposed a process of melioration (doing the best at the moment). Organisms, he argued, are sensitive to fluctuations in the momentary rates of reinforcement rather than to long-term changes in overall rates of reinforcement.

Metacontingencies. The contingent relations among cultural practices and the effects of those practices for the group. For example, competence in science is important for people who live in a technologically advanced culture. Scientific research produces a range of benefits for the general society. These include better medicine, more productive crop yields, new and better building materials, more efficient and longer-lasting appliances, and superior regulation of human behavior. Thus, a positive metacontingency exists between educational practices that increase scientific competence and long-term benefits to the group.

Mixed schedule of reinforcement. A mixed schedule is two or more basic schedules (CRF, FR, FI, VI, VR) presented sequentially in which each link ends with primary reinforcement (or in some cases extinction) and the component schedules are not signaled by discriminative stimuli. In other words, a mixed schedule is the same as an unsignaled multiple schedule. See **multiple schedule**.

Molar perspective (or account). Molar perspectives of behavior on schedules of reinforcement or punishment are concerned with large-scale factors that regulate responding over a long period of time. For example, the average time between reinforcers for an entire session and the overall reduction in shock frequency are molar-level variables.

Molecular perspective (or account). Molecular perspectives of behavior on schedules of reinforcement or punishment focus on small moment-to-moment relationships between behavior and its consequences. For example, the time between any two responses (the interresponse time) and the response–shock interval (R–S) are molecular-level variables.

Multiple baseline across behaviors. A multiple baseline research design across behaviors is used when a reinforcement procedure is applied progressively to several operants. In this case, the subject, setting, and consequences remain the same, but different responses are modified sequentially.

Multiple baseline across stimulus conditions. In this research design, a reinforcement procedure is applied in one situation but is withheld in other settings. When behavior changes in the situation where it is reinforced, the contingency is applied to the same response in another setting.

Multiple baseline across subjects. A research design in which an intervention is introduced progressively for different subjects who exhibit similar target behavior. The same behavior (e.g., stealing) is first modified for subject 1, and baselines are collected for subjects 2 and 3. Next, the behavior of subject 2 is changed while the rate of target behavior for subjects 1 and 3 continues to be assessed. Finally, the treatment procedure is applied to subject 3.

Multiple baseline design. A class of research designs used primarily in applied behavior analysis. See **multiple baseline across behaviors**, **multiple baseline across stimulus conditions**, and **multiple baseline across subjects**.

Multiple functions (of stimuli). A given event or stimulus such as a student saying "the ball is red" can have several functions in the control of behavior (e.g., $S^r + S^D$). For example, the response can function as reinforcement for the teacher's question "what color is the ball?" and at the same time function as a discriminative stimulus for the teacher saying "Yes."

Multiple schedule. A multiple schedule is two or more basic schedules (CRF, FR, FI, VI, VR) presented sequentially, each link ending with primary reinforcement (or in some cases extinction); the component schedules are signaled by discriminative stimuli. In other words, a multiple schedule is the same as a chain schedule, but each link produces primary reinforcement. See **chain schedule of reinforcement**.

Mutation. Mutation occurs when the genetic material (e.g., genes or chromosomes) of an individual changes. These changes are accidents that affect the genetic code carried by an ovum or sperm. For example, naturally occurring background radiation may alter a gene site or a chromosome may break during the formation of sex cells or gametes. Such mutations are passed on to offspring, who display new characteristics.

Natural selection. The differential reproduction of the members of a species and their genetic endowment. Based on a thorough analysis of life forms, Darwin concluded that reproductive success was the underlying basis of evolution. That is, individuals with more offspring pass on a greater number of their characteristics (genes) to the next generation.

Negative automaintenance. Birds are autoshaped to peck a key, but in negative automaintenance food is not presented if the bird pecks the key. This is also called an omission procedure because food reinforcement is omitted if key pecking occurs.

Negative contrast. See **behavioral contrast**.

Negative punishment. Negative punishment is a contingency that involves the removal of an event or stimulus following behavior that has the effect of decreasing the rate of response. The negative punishment procedure requires that behavior (watching television) is maintained by positive reinforcement (entertaining programs) and the reinforcer is removed (TV turned off) if a specified response occurs (yelling and screaming). The probability of response is reduced by the procedure.

Negative reinforcement. Negative reinforcement is a contingency where an ongoing stimulus or event is removed (or prevented) by some response (operant) and the rate of response increases. If it is raining, opening and standing under an umbrella removes the rain and maintains the use of the umbrella on rainy days. When operant behavior increases by removing an ongoing event or stimulus the contingency is called *escape*. The contingency is called *avoidance* when the operant increases by preventing the onset of the event or stimulus. Both escape and avoidance involve negative reinforcement.

Negative reinforcer. A negative reinforcer is any event or stimulus that increases the probability (rate of occurrence) of an operant when it is removed or prevented. See also **negative reinforcement**.

New-response method (for conditioned reinforcement). First, a nonreinforcing stimulus is associated with a reinforcing event (sound of feeder is followed by food), and after this procedure the stimulus (sound of feeder) is shown to increase the frequency of some operant behavior.

Nondiscriminated avoidance. A procedure used to train avoidance responding in which no warning stimulus is presented is called nondiscriminated or Sidman avoidance. See also **negative reinforcement**.

Observational learning. From a social cognitive viewpoint, the observer pays attention to the modeled sequence, noting the arrangement of each action. The general information in the sequence must be coded and rehearsed. Once this abstract information is retained in memory, imitation is a matter of reproducing the component responses in the correct sequences. From a behavioral perspective, observational learning involves the integration of generalized imitation, rule-governed behavior, and verbal behavior. Each of these components is addressed separately in behavior analysis.

Observing response. The observing response is a topographically different operant that functions to produce an S^D or S^Δ depending on whether reinforcement or extinction is in effect. In other words, an observing response changes a mixed schedule of reinforcement to a multiple schedule. See **mixed schedule of reinforcement** and **multiple schedule**.

Omission procedure. See **negative automaintenance**.

Ontogenetic. Each organism has a unique life history (ontogeny) that contributes to its behavior. Ontogenetic changes in behavior are caused by events that occur over the lifetime of an individual. Ontogenetic history builds on species history (phylogeny) to determine when, where, and what kind of behavior will occur at a given moment. See also **phylogenetic**.

Ontogenetic selection. The selection of operant behavior during the lifetime of an organism is ontogenetic selection. The process involves operant variability during periods of extinction and selection by contingencies of reinforcement. An organism that alters its behavior (adaptation) on the basis of changing life experiences is showing ontogenetic selection. In this ontogenetic form of adaptation, the topography and frequency of behavior increase when reinforcement is withheld (increase in operant variability). These behavioral changes during extinction allow for the selection of behavior by new contingencies of reinforcement. Thus, a wild rat that has been exploiting a compost heap may find that the homeowner has covered it. In this case, the rat emits various operants that may eventually uncover the food. The animal may dig under the cover, gnaw a hole in the sheathing, or search for some other means of entry. A similar effect occurs when food in the compost heap is depleted and the animal emits behavior that results in getting to a new food patch. In the laboratory, this behavior is measured as an increase in the topography and frequency of bar pressing as the schedules of reinforcement change.

Operant. An operant is behavior that operates on the environment to produce a change, effect, or consequence. These environmental changes select the operant appropriate to a given setting or circumstance. That is, particular responses increase or decrease in a situation as a function of the consequences they produced in the past. Operant behavior is said to be emitted (rather than elicited) in the sense that the behavior may occur at some frequency before any known conditioning.

Operant aggression. Aggressive behavior that is reinforced (increased) by the removal of an aversive event arranged by another member of the species. See also **negative reinforcement**.

Operant chamber. A laboratory enclosure or box used to investigate operant conditioning. An operant chamber for a rat is a small, enclosed box that typically contains a lever with a light above it and a food magazine or cup connected to an external feeder. The feeder delivers a small food pellet when electronically activated.

Operant class. A class or set of responses that vary in topography but produce a common environmental consequence or effect. The response class of turning on the light has many variations in form (turn on light with left index finger, or right one, or side of the hand, or saying to someone "please turn on the light").

Operant conditioning. An increase or decrease in operant response as a function of the consequences that have followed the response.

Operant imitation. Operant imitation is imitative behavior controlled by its consequences. See **imitation**.

Operant level. The rate of an operant before any known conditioning. For example, the rate of key pecking before a peck–food contingency has been established.

Operant rate. See **rate of response**.

Operant variability. Operant behavior becomes increasingly more variable as extinction proceeds. From an evolutionary view, it makes sense to try different ways of acting when something no longer works. That is, behavioral variation increases the chances that the organisms will reinstate reinforcement or contact other sources of reinforcement, increasing the likelihood of survival and reproduction of the organism.

Overmatching. In the generalized matching equation, a value of a greater than 1 indicates that changes in the response ratio (B_a/B_b) are larger than changes in the ratio of reinforcement (R_a/R_b). This outcome occurs because relative behavior increases faster than predicted from the relative rate of reinforcement. See also **generalized matching law**.

Overshadowing. This effect occurs when a compound stimulus is used as the conditioned stimulus (CS) in a respondent conditioning experiment. For example, a light + tone (CS) may be presented at the same time and be associated with an unconditioned stimulus (US) such as food. The most *salient* property of the compound stimulus comes to regulate exclusively the conditioned response. Thus, if the tone is more salient than the light, only the tone will elicit salivation.

Partial reinforcement effect (PRE). Partial or intermittent reinforcement generates greater resistance to extinction than continuous reinforcement (CRF). The higher the rate of reinforcement, the greater the resistance to change; however, the change from CRF to extinction is discriminated more rapidly than between partial reinforcement and extinction.

Peak shift. A shift that occurs in the peak of a generalization gradient away from an extinction (S^Δ) stimulus is called a peak shift. See **generalization gradient (operant)** and **generalization gradient (respondent)**.

Personalized system of instruction (PSI). A college teaching method based on principles of operant conditioning and designed by Fred Keller (Keller, 1968). Keller called his teaching method a personalized system of instruction or PSI. Basically, PSI courses are organized so that students move through the course at their own pace and they are reinforced for completing small course units.

Phenotype. An organism's phenotype refers to anatomical and behavioral characteristics observed during the lifetime of the individual. For example, an individual's size, color, and shape are anatomical aspects of phenotype. Behavioral features include taste preferences, aggressiveness, and shyness. Different phenotypic attributes of individuals may or may not reflect underlying genetic variation.

Phylogenetic. Behavior relations that are based on the genetic endowment of an organism are called phylogenetic and are present on the basis of species history. Behavior that aids survival or procreation is often (but not always) unlearned. This is because past generations of organisms that engaged in such behavior survived and reproduced. These animals passed on (to the next generation) the characteristics (via genes) that allowed similar behavior. Thus, species history provides the organism with a basic repertoire of responses that are evoked by environmental conditions. See also **ontogenetic**.

Phylogeny. Phylogeny is the species history of an organism.

Placebo effect. Concerns the effect of an inert substance such as a sugar pill on the "physiological well-being" of a patient. That is, patients treated with sugar pills show improvements relative to a no-treatment control group.

Polydipsia. Polydipsia or excessive drinking is adjunctive behavior induced by the time-based delivery of food. For example, a rat that is working for food on an intermittent schedule may drink as much as half its body weight during a single session. This drinking occurs even though the animal is not water deprived. See also **adjunctive behavior**.

Positive contrast. See **behavioral contrast**.

Positive punishment. A procedure that involves the presentation of an event or stimulus following behavior that has the effect of decreasing the rate of response. A child is given a spanking for running into the street and the probability of the behavior is decreased.

Positive reinforcement. Positive reinforcement is a contingency that involves the presentation of an event or stimulus following an operant that increases the rate of response.

Positive reinforcer. A positive reinforcer is any stimulus or event that increases the probability (rate of response) of an operant when presented.

Postreinforcement pause (PRP). The pause in responding that occurs after reinforcement on some intermittent schedules (e.g., FR, FI).

Power law for matching. See **generalized matching law**.

Precision teaching. In what became known as *precision teaching*, Ogden Lindsley devised a method of systematic instruction that encouraged students and teachers to target specific behaviors, count, time, and graph them, and revise instructional procedures based on the charted data. The use of the Standard Celeration Chart for graphing change in response rate over days is a prominent feature of this teaching method.

Precurrent behavior. Operant behavior that precedes a current response. Precurrent behavior often functions to establish stimulus control over subsequent operant behavior, as when a person sets the alarm for 6:00 a.m. (precurrent behavior) to insure stimulus control by the clock over waking up and going to an appointment or job (current behavior). In this example, both the precurrent and current behavior are maintained by the reinforcement contingency (e.g., avoiding the consequences of being late). When precurrent behavior is private, as in thinking about chess moves, the behavior provides S^D control over the actual movement of the chess pieces. Thinking about chess moves and actual moves are maintained by the contingency of reinforcement, involving getting a momentary advantage and ultimately winning the game. See **construction of S^Ds**.

Preference. When several schedules of reinforcement are available concurrently, one alternative may be chosen more frequently than others. When this occurs, we say that the organism shows a preference for that alternative.

Preference reversal. The change in value of a reinforcer as a function of time to the choice point (as in self-control). For example, people make a commitment to save their money (monthly deduction at the bank) rather than spend it because the value of saving is greater than spending when far from the choice point (getting paid). At the choice point, spending is always higher in value than saving the money. See **Ainslie–Rachlin principle**.

Premack principle. A higher frequency behavior will function as reinforcement for a lower frequency behavior.

Preparedness. Some relations between stimuli, and between stimuli and responses, are more likely because of phylogenetic history. This phenomenon has been called preparedness. For example, a bird that relies on sight for food selection would be expected to associate the appearance of a particular food item with illness, but rats that select food on the basis of taste quickly make a flavor–illness association.

Preratio pause. The number of responses (ratio size) required and the magnitude of the reinforcer have both been shown to influence the postreinforcement pause (PRP). Calling this pause a "post" reinforcement event accurately locates the pause but the ratio size is what actually controls it. Hence, many researchers refer to the PRP as a preratio pause. See **postreinforcement pause (PRP)**.

Primary aversive stimulus. An aversive stimulus that has acquired its properties as a function of species history. See **aversive stimulus**.

Primary laws of the reflex. The primary laws of the reflex include (1) the law of the threshold, (2) the law of intensity–magnitude, and (3) the law of latency. These laws govern the unconditioned stimulus (US) → unconditioned response (UR) relationship.

Private behavior. Behavior that is only accessible to the person who emits it (e.g., thinking).

Probability of response. The probability that an operant will occur on a given occasion (measured as rate of response).

Progressive ratio schedule. A schedule where the number of responses (ratio) increases (or decreases) after reinforcement. For example, a pigeon on an increasing progressive ratio may be required to make 2 responses for access to food, then 4, 8, 16, 32, and higher ratios. In a foraging model, the increasing progressive ratio schedule simulates a depleting patch of food.

Punisher. A stimulus that decreases the frequency of an operant that produces it.

Punishment. As a procedure, punishment involves following an operant with a punisher. Usually, the operant is maintained by positive reinforcement so that punishment is superimposed on a baseline of positive reinforcement. Punishment also refers to a decrease in operant behavior when followed by a punisher or when reinforcement is withdrawn contingent on responding. See **positive** and **negative punishment**.

Quantitative law of effect. The law states that the absolute rate of response on a schedule of reinforcement is a hyperbolic function of rate of reinforcement on the schedule relative to the total rate of reinforcement (both scheduled and extraneous reinforcement). That is, as the rate of reinforcement on the schedule increases, the rate of response also rises, but eventually further increases in rate of reinforcement produce less and less of an increase in rate of response (hyperbolic). Also, the rise in rate of response with increasing rate of reinforcement is modified by extraneous sources of reinforcement. Extraneous reinforcement reduces the rate of response on the reinforcement schedule. One implication is that control of behavior by a schedule of reinforcement is weakened by sources of extraneous reinforcement.

A proportional matching equation is one mathematical expression of quantitative law of effect. The equation relates absolute response and reinforcement rates, using alternative sources of reinforcement as the context. The equation may be derived from a restatement of the proportional matching law and is written as $B_a/(B_a + B_e) = R_a/(R_a + R_e)$. In this equation, B_e refers to all behavior directed to extraneous sources of reinforcement, and R_e represents these sources.

The term B_a represents rate of response on the programmed schedule, and R_a is the rate of scheduled reinforcement.

Rate of response. Rate of response (or operant rate) is the number of responses that occur in a given interval. For example, a bird may peck a key for food 2 times per second; a student may do math problems at the rate of 10 per hour.

Ratio schedule. Response-based schedules of reinforcement that are set to deliver reinforcement following a prescribed number of responses. The ratio specifies the number of responses for each reinforcer.

Ratio strain. A disruption of responding that occurs when a ratio schedule is increased rapidly. For example, faced with a change in the schedule from continuous reinforcement to the large fixed-ratio value, an animal will probably show ratio strain in the sense that it pauses longer and longer after reinforcement. This occurs because the time between successive reinforcements contributes to the postreinforcement pause (PRP). The pause gets longer as the interreinforcement interval (IRI) increases. Because the PRP makes up part of the interval between reinforcements and is controlled by it, the animal eventually stops responding. Thus, there is a negative feedback loop between increasing PRP length and the time between reinforcements (IRI). See **postreinforcement pause (PRP)** and **interreinforcement interval (IRI)**.

Reaction chain. Reaction chains are phylogenetic sequences of behavior. An environmental stimulus sets off behavior that produces stimuli that set off the next set of responses in the sequence; these behaviors produce the next set of stimuli, and so on. Presenting stimuli that prompt responses ordinarily occurring in the middle part of the sequence will start the chain at that point rather than at the beginning. Reaction chains are like consecutive sets of reflexes where the stimulus that elicits the next response in the sequence is produced by the previous reflex.

Reflex. When an unconditioned stimulus elicits an unconditioned response (US → UR), the relationship is called a reflex.

Reflexive aggression. Aggression elicited by the presentation of an aversive stimulus or event. Reflexive aggression is elicited by an aversive unconditioned stimulus like a shock in the presence of another member of the species, and in humans may involve aversive conditioned stimuli such as the verbal stimulus "You idiot" (respondent aggression). Reflexive aggression is also called pain-elicited aggression.

Reflexivity. Involves responding to a one-to-one relationship (A = A) between stimulus classes. For example, a pigeon is presented with the color red on a sample key and the bird responds to a comparison key with the identical color (red). A child who is given a picture of a cat and then finds a similar picture in a set of photographs is showing reflexivity. See also **identity matching**.

Reinforcement function. Any event (or stimulus) that follows a response and increases its frequency is said to have a reinforcement function. If an infant's babbling increases due to touching by the mother, we can say that maternal touching has a reinforcement function.

Relative rate of reinforcement. When two or more sources of reinforcement are available (as on a concurrent schedule), the relative rate of reinforcement refers to the rate of reinforcement delivered on one alternative divided by the sum of the rates of reinforcement from all sources of reinforcement. Relative rate of reinforcement is a measure of the distribution of reinforcement between or among alternatives.

Relative rate of response. When two or more sources of reinforcement are available (as on a concurrent schedule), relative rate of response refers to the rate of response on one alternative divided by the sum of the response rates on all alternatives. Relative rate of response is a measure of the distribution of behavior between or among alternative sources of reinforcement.

Relative stimulus control. Relative stimulus control involves the organism responding to differences between two or more stimuli. For example, a pigeon may be trained to peck in the presence of the larger of two triangles rather than to the absolute size of a triangle. See also **absolute stimulus control**.

Relativity of punishment. The Premack principle states that a lower frequency operant will punish a higher frequency behavior. For example, when wheel running is a lower frequency operant, drinking is punished when followed by wheel running. In contrast, drinking is reinforced by wheel running when running in a wheel is a higher frequency operant. According to the Premack principle, we cannot make an absolute statement about whether wheel running is a punisher or a reinforcer for drinking.

Remembering. The verb remembering (or forgetting) is used to refer to the effect of some event on behavior after the passage of time (as opposed to the noun "memory," which seems to refer to a mental representation stored in the brain).

Remote causation. The current status of some system is brought about or caused by the long-term interactions between the system and the universe (niche or environment) of which it is a part. In biology, the current genome of a species is caused by natural selection (a causal process) whereby the genes, underlying the expressed characteristics of these organisms, have been selected by differential reproduction over extended periods. We can say that the history of natural selection causes or results in the current genome. In behavior, the current probability of pecking a key for food is caused by the repeated interaction between the bird's key pecking and the presentation of food. We can say that the current probability of response is caused by or brought about by the history of reinforcement (the causal process). In both natural selection and reinforcement, an adequate causal explanation must precisely specify the particular history of interaction that has resulted in the current status (genetic or behavioral) of the organism.

Repertoire. All the behavior an organism is capable of emitting on the basis of species and environmental history.

Replication. Replication of results is used to enhance both internal and external validity of an experiment. If results replicate over time and place, it is likely that the original findings were due to the experimental variable and not to extraneous conditions (internal validity). Replication also establishes that the findings have generality in the sense that the effects are not limited to specific procedures, behaviors, or species (external validity). See also **direct** and **systematic replication**.

Rescorla–Wagner model. The basic idea of the Rescorla–Wagner model of respondent conditioning is that a conditioned stimulus acquires a limited amount of associative strength on any one trial. The term associative strength describes the relation between the conditioned stimulus (CS) and the magnitude of the conditioned response (CR). In general, associative strength increases over conditioning trials and reaches some maximum level. A given CS can acquire only so much control over a CR. This is the maximum associative strength for the CS. Thus, a tone (CS) paired with 1 g of food will have maximum associative strength when conditioned salivation (CR) has the same strength as unconditioned salivation (unconditioned response, UR) elicited by the gram of food (unconditioned stimulus, US). The magnitude of the UR to the US sets the upper limit for the CR. The CS cannot elicit a greater CR than the one produced by the US.

Resistance to extinction. The perseverance of operant behavior when it is placed on extinction. Resistance to extinction is substantially increased when an intermittent schedule of reinforcement has been used to maintain behavior. See **partial reinforcement effect (PRE)**.

Respondent. A respondent is behavior that increases or decreases by the presentation of a conditioned stimulus (CS) that *precedes* the conditioned response (CR). We say that the presentation of the CS regulates or controls the CR. Respondent behavior is elicited, in the sense that it reliably occurs when the CS is presented. The notation system used with elicited behavior is CS $\rightarrow$ CR. The CS causes (arrow) the CR.

Respondent acquisition. The procedure of pairing the conditioned stimulus (CS) with the unconditioned stimulus (US) over trials when respondent level for the CS is near zero. Also, refers to the increase in magnitude of the conditioned response (CR) when respondent level for the CS is near zero.

Respondent conditioning. Respondent conditioning occurs when an organism responds to a new event based on a history of pairing with a biologically important stimulus. The Russian physiologist Ivan Pavlov discovered this form of conditioning at the turn of the century. He showed that dogs salivated when food was placed in their mouths. This relation between the food stimulus and salivation is called a reflex and occurs because of the animal's biological history. When Pavlov rang a bell just before feeding the dog, it began to salivate at the sound of the bell. In this way, new features (sound of bell) controlled the dog's respondent behavior (salivation). Thus, presenting stimuli together in time (typically conditioned and then unconditioned stimuli) is the procedure for respondent conditioning. If a conditioned stimulus comes to regulate the occurrence of a conditioned response, then respondent conditioning has occurred.

Respondent discrimination. Respondent discrimination occurs when an organism shows a conditioned response to one stimulus but not to other similar events. A discrimination procedure involves positive and negative conditioning trials. For example, a positive trial occurs when a CS^+ such as a 60-dB tone is followed by an unconditioned stimulus like food. On negative trials, a 40-dB tone is presented (CS^-) but not followed by food. Once a differential response occurs (salivation to 60 dB but not to 40 dB), we may say that the organism discriminates between the tones.

Respondent extinction. The procedure of respondent extinction involves the presentation of the conditioned stimulus without the unconditioned stimulus after acquisition has occurred. As a behavioral process, extinction refers to a decline in the strength of the conditioned response when an extinction procedure is in effect. In both instances, the term extinction is used correctly.

Respondent generalization. Respondent generalization occurs when an organism shows a conditioned response (CR) to values of the conditioned stimulus that have not been trained. For example, if a tone of 375 Hz is followed by food, a dog will salivate at maximum level when this tone is presented. The animal, however, may salivate to other values of the tone. As the tone differs more and more from 375 Hz, the CR decreases in magnitude.

Respondent level. The baseline level (magnitude) of the conditioned response (CR) to the conditioned stimulus (CS) before any known conditioning has taken place is the respondent level. For example, the amount of salivation (CR) to a tone (CS) before the tone has been paired with food in the mouth is usually zero (no salivation).

Response class. A response class refers to all the forms of the performance that have a similar function (e.g., putting on a coat to keep warm). In some cases, the responses in a class have close physical resemblance, but this is not always the case. For example, saying "Please open the door" and physically opening the door are members of the same response class if both result in an open door.

Response deprivation. Response deprivation is the principle that organisms work to gain access to activities that are restricted or withheld (deprivation), presumably to reinstate equilibrium or free-choice levels of behavior. This principle is more general than the Premack principle, predicting when any activity (high or low in rate) will function as reinforcement.

Response differentiation. When reinforcement is contingent on some difference in response properties, that form of response will increase. For example, the force or magnitude of response can be differentiated; if the contingencies of reinforcement require a forceful or vigorous response in a particular situation then that form of response will predominate. In another example, when reinforcement is based on short interresponse times or IRTs (2–5 s) the distribution of IRTs becomes centered on short intervals. Changing the contingencies to reinforce longer IRTs (20–25 s) produces a new distribution centered on long intervals. See **differential reinforcement**.

Response generalization. Response generalization occurs when a target response is strengthened and other similar responses increase in frequency (e.g., a child reinforced for building a house out of Lego™ subsequently may arrange the pieces in many different ways).

Response hierarchy. The differences in relative frequency or probability of different responses in a free-choice or baseline setting is called a response hierarchy. For a rat the probability of eating, drinking, and wheel running might form a hierarchy, with eating occurring most often and wheel running least.

Response–shock interval (R–S). On an avoidance schedule, the response–shock interval is the time from a response that postpones shock to the onset of the aversive stimulus, assuming that another response does not occur. See also **shock–shock interval (S–S)**.

Resurgence. After a period of reinforcement, the increase in behavioral variability or topography during extinction is called resurgence.

Retention interval. The time between the offset of the sample stimulus and the onset of the comparison stimuli is the retention interval.

Reversal test. Once the matching of angle to geometric form is well established, a reversal test (form to angle) is conducted without any further reinforcement. In a reversal test, the bird is presented with a triangle as the sample and the question is whether it pecks the side key with the horizontal line. Because horizontal = triangle was trained, the bird shows symmetry if it pecks the horizontal comparison key when presented with a triangle sample (triangle = horizontal). Similarly, because vertical = circle was trained, symmetry is shown if the bird pecks the vertical side key when the circle is presented as the sample (circle = vertical). In everyday language, the bird responds as if the horizontal line stands for triangle and as if the vertical line means circle. The percentage of "correct" responses during the test (without reinforcement) is the usual measure of symbolic performance on this reversal test.

Rule-governed behavior. Refers to the effects of contingency-specifying stimuli on the listener's behavior. When instructions, rules, advice, maxims, and laws regulate operant behavior, the behavior is said to be rule-governed. Control by instructions can make operant behavior insensitive to the operating contingencies of reinforcement.

Run of responses. A fast burst of responding is called a run of responses. For example, after the postreinforcement pause on a fixed-ratio schedule, an organism will rapidly emit the responses required by the ratio.

Salience. The symbol S in the Rescorla–Wagner equation is a constant that varies between 0 and 1, and may be interpreted as the salience (e.g., dim light versus bright light) of the conditioned stimulus (CS) based on the sensory capacities of the organism. The constant S (salience) is estimated after conditioning and determines how quickly the associative strength of the CS rises to a maximum. That is, a larger salience coefficient makes the associative strength of the CS rise more quickly to its maximum.

Satiation. Repeated presentations of a reinforcer weaken its effectiveness, and for this reason the rate of response declines. Satiation refers to this effect, and the repeated presentation of a reinforcer is called a satiation operation.

Scalloping. The characteristic pattern of response seen on a cumulative record produced by a fixed-interval schedule is called scalloping. There is a pause after reinforcement, then a few probe responses, and finally an increasingly accelerated rate of response to the moment of reinforcement.

Schedule of reinforcement. In relation to responses, a schedule of reinforcement is the arrangement of the environment in terms of discriminative stimuli and behavioral consequences. Mechner notation describes these behavioral contingencies. See **Mechner notation**.

Schedule-induced behavior. See **adjunctive behavior**.

Science of behavior. See **behavior analysis**.

S-delta (S^Δ). When an operant does not produce reinforcement, the stimulus that precedes the operant is called an S-delta (S^Δ). In the presence of an S-delta, the probability of emitting an operant declines.

Second-order conditioning. Second-order conditioning involves pairing two conditioned stimuli ($CS_1 + CS_2$), rather than a conditioned and unconditioned stimulus (CS + US). Pavlov (1927/1960) conducted the early experiments on second-order conditioning. The tick of a metronome was paired with food. The sound of the metronome came to elicit salivation. Once the ticking sound reliably elicited salivation, Pavlov paired it with the sight of a black square ($CS_1 + CS_2$). Following several pairings of the metronome beat with the black square, the sight of the black square elicited salivation.

Selection by consequences. From a behavioral viewpoint, the principle of causation for biology, behavior, and culture is selection by consequences. With regard to biology, mutation and sexual reproduction ensure a range of variation in genes that code for the features of organisms. Some physical attributes of the organisms, coded by genes, meet the requirements of the environment. Organisms with these adaptive features survive and reproduce, passing their genes to the next generation (phylogenetic). Organisms without these characteristics do not reproduce as well and their genes are less represented in the subsequent generations. Natural selection is a form of selection by consequences that occurs at the biological level.

Selection by consequences has been extended to the level of behavior as the principle of reinforcement. Operant behavior is an expressed characteristic of many organisms, including humans. Organisms with an extensive range of operant behavior adjust to new environmental situations on the basis of the consequences that follow behavior. This kind of selection occurs over the lifetime of the individual (ontogenetic) and behavior change is a form of evolution. Brain neurons are probably the units selected at the behavioral level; the interplay of neurons allows for behavior to be passed on from one moment to the next (transmitted). The process of the selection and change of operant behavior is analogous to evolution and natural selection at the genetic level. Reinforcement is therefore an ontogenetic process that extends selection by consequences to the level of behavior.

A third level of evolution and selection occurs at the cultural level (cultural selection). The unit of selection at this level is the cultural practice or meme (Dawkins, 1976). A cultural practice involves the interlocking behavior of many people. As with operant behavior itself, cultural practices vary in form and frequency. Different ways of doing things are more or less successful in terms of efficiency, productivity, and survival of group members. Generally, group level outcomes or effects (metacontingencies) increase or decrease the rate of adoption and transmission of practices in the population. The fit between current practices and new ways of doing things (e.g., technology) plays a role in adoption and transmission of innovations by the group. Although an innovative technology or method may be more efficient, it may also be more costly to change from traditional to new ways of doing things.

Self-control. From a behavioral perspective, self-control occurs when a person emits a response that affects the probability of subsequent behavior—giving up immediate gains for greater long-term benefits or accepting immediate costs for later rewards. When people (and other organisms) manage their behavior in such a way that they choose the more beneficial long-range consequences, they are said to show self-control.

Sensory preconditioning. In respondent compound conditioning, two stimuli such as light and tone are repeatedly presented together (light + tone) without the occurrence of an unconditioned stimulus (preconditioning). Later, one of these stimuli (CS_1) is paired with an unconditioned stimulus (US) and the other stimulus (CS_2) is tested for conditioning. Even though the second stimulus (CS_2) has never been directly associated with the US, it comes to elicit the conditioned response (CR).

Shaping. The method of successive approximation or shaping may be used to establish a response. This method involves the reinforcement of closer and closer approximations to the final performance. For example, a rat may be reinforced for standing in the vicinity of a lever. Once the animal is reliably facing the lever, a movement of the head toward the bar is reinforced. Next, closer and closer approximations to pressing the lever are reinforced. Each step of the procedure involves reinforcement of closer approximations and nonreinforcement of more distant responses. Many novel forms of behavior may be shaped by the method of successive approximation.

Shock–shock interval (S–S). The shock–shock interval is the scheduled time between shocks using an avoidance procedure and it is the time from one shock to the next if the avoidance response does not occur. See also the **response–shock interval (R–S)**.

Sidman avoidance. See **nondiscriminated avoidance**.

Sign tracking. Sign tracking refers to approaching a sign (or stimulus) that signals a biologically relevant event. For example, dogs are required to sit on a mat and a stimulus that signals food is presented to the animal. When the food signal is presented, the dogs approach the stimulus and make food-soliciting responses to it.

Simultaneous conditioning. A respondent conditioning procedure in which the conditioned stimulus (CS) and unconditioned stimulus (US) are presented at the same moment. Compared with delayed conditioning, simultaneous conditioning produces a weaker conditioned response (CR).

Simultaneous discrimination. In simultaneous discrimination, the S^D and S^Δ are presented at the same time and the organism is reinforced for responding to the relative properties of one or the other. For example, a pigeon may be presented with two keys, both illuminated with white lights, but one light is brighter than the other. The bird is reinforced for pecking the dimmer of the two keys. Pecks to the other key are placed on extinction. After training, the pigeon will peck the darker of any two keys. See also **relative stimulus control**.

Single-subject research. Experimental research that is concerned with discovering principles and conditions that govern the behavior of single or individual organisms. Each individual's behavior is studied to assess the impact of a given experimental variable. In behavioral research, a change in the contingencies of reinforcement is assessed for each bird, rat, or human (e.g., changing the schedule of reinforcement, the operant, or the discriminative stimuli).

Social disruption. A negative side effect of punishment in which the person who delivers punishment and the context become conditioned aversive stimuli. Individuals will attempt to escape from or avoid the punishing person or setting.

Social episode. A social episode involves the interlocking contingencies between speaker and listener, as when a customer asks the waiter for a napkin and gets it (manding). The episode begins with the customer spilling her coffee (establishing the napkin as reinforcement) and ends when the waiter provides the napkin (reinforcement) and the customer says "Thank you."

Spontaneous imitation. Innate imitation based on evolution and natural selection (a characteristic of the species) rather than experiences during the lifetime of the individual. See **imitation** and **generalized imitation**.

Spontaneous recovery (operant). After a period of extinction, an organism's rate of response may be close to operant level. After some time, the organism is again placed in the setting and extinction is continued. Responding initially recovers, but over repeated sessions of extinction the amount of recovery decreases. Repeated sessions of extinction eliminate stimulus control by extraneous features of the situation and eventually "being placed in the setting" no longer occasions the operant.

Spontaneous recovery (respondent). An increase in the magnitude of the conditioned response (CR) after respondent extinction has occurred and time has passed. A behavioral analysis of spontaneous recovery suggests that the relation between conditioned stimulus (CS) and CR is weakened by extinction, but the context or features of the situation elicit some level of the CR. During respondent conditioning, many stimuli not specified by the researcher as the CS, but present in the experimental situation, come to regulate behavior.

S–S account of conditioned reinforcement. Refers to the hypothesis that it is necessary for a stimulus to be paired with primary reinforcement to become a conditioned reinforcer. The hypothesis has been largely discounted, and the weight of the evidence supports Fantino's (1969b) delay-reduction hypothesis. See **delay-reduction hypothesis**.

Steady-state performance. Schedule-controlled behavior that is stable and does not change over time is called steady-state performance. For example, after an extensive history on VI 30 s, a rat may press a lever at approximately the same rate day after day.

Stimulus class. Stimuli that vary across physical dimensions but have a common effect on behavior belong to the same stimulus class.

Stimulus control. A change in operant behavior that occurs when either an S^D or S^Δ is presented is called stimulus control. When an S^D is presented, the probability of response increases; and when an S^Δ is given, operant behavior has a low probability of occurrence.

Stimulus equivalence. Involves the presentation of one class of stimuli (e.g., flags) that occasions responses to other stimulus classes (e.g., countries). This seems to be what we mean when we say that the flag stands for, represents, or signifies our country. Equivalence relations such as these are an important aspect of human behavior. For example, in teaching a child to read, spoken words (names of animals) are trained to visual stimuli (pictures of animals) and then to written symbols (written words for animals). Eventually, the written word is said to stand for the actual object, in the same sense that a flag stands for a country.

Stimulus function. When the occurrence of an event changes the behavior of an organism, we may say that the event has a stimulus function. Both respondent and operant conditioning are ways to create stimulus functions. During respondent conditioning, an arbitrary event like a tone comes to elicit a particular response, like salivation. Once the tone is effective, it is said to have a conditioned-stimulus function for salivation. In the absence of a conditioning history, the tone may have no specified function and does not affect the specified behavior.

Stimulus generalization. Stimulus generalization occurs when an operant reinforced in the presence of a specific discriminative stimulus also is emitted in the presence of other stimuli. The process is called stimulus generalization because the operant is emitted to new stimuli that presumably share common properties with the discriminative stimulus.

Stimulus substitution. When a conditioned stimulus (e.g., light) is paired with an unconditioned stimulus (e.g., food), the conditioned stimulus is said to substitute for the unconditioned stimulus. That is, food elicits salivation, and by conditioning, the light elicits similar behavior.

Structural approach. In the structural approach, behavior is classified in terms of its form or topography. For example, many developmental psychologists are interested in the intellectual growth of children. These researchers often investigate what a person does at a given stage of development. The structure of behavior is emphasized because it is said to reveal the underlying stage of intellectual development. See also **functional analysis of behavior**.

Successive approximation. See **shaping**.

Successive discrimination. A procedure used to train differential responding. The researcher arranges the presentation of S^D and S^Δ so that one follows the other. For example, a multiple schedule is programmed so that a red light signals variable-interval food reinforcement; this is followed by a green light that indicates extinction is in effect.

Superstitious behavior. Behavior that is accidentally reinforced is called superstitious. For example, a parent may inadvertently strengthen aggressive behavior when a child is given his or her allowance just after fighting with a playmate. Switching from one alternative to another may be accidentally reinforced on a concurrent schedule if the alternative schedule has a reinforcement setup. In this case, the organism is accidentally reinforced for a change from one schedule to another.

Symbolic matching. In a matching-to-sample task, symbolic matching involves the presentation of one class of stimuli as the sample (geometrical forms) and another set of stimuli (different line angles) as the comparisons. Reinforcement depends on an arbitrary relation (triangle = vertical).

Symmetry. When stimulus class A is shown to be interchangeable with stimulus class B (if A = B then B = A), we may say that the organism shows symmetry between the stimulus classes. After training a form-to-angle discrimination (triangle = vertical), a reversal test is conducted without reinforcement using line angles as the sample and geometric shapes as the comparisons (vertical = triangle). An organism that passes the reversal test is said to demonstrate symmetry of angles and forms. See also **reversal test**.

Systematic replication. Refers to increasing the generality of an experimental finding by conducting other experiments in which the procedures are different but are logically related to the original research. An experiment is conducted with rats to find out what happens when food pellets are presented contingent on lever pressing. The observation is that lever pressing increases when followed by food pellets. In a systematic replication, elephants step on a treadle to produce peanuts. The observation is that treadle pressing increases. Both experiments are said to show the effects of positive reinforcement contingencies on operant behavior. See also **direct replication**.

Tacting. A class of verbal operants whose form is regulated by specific nonverbal discriminative stimuli. For example, a child may see a cat and say, "kitty." The word tacting comes from the more familiar term contact. Tacting is verbal behavior that makes contact with the environment. In common parlance we say that people make reference to the world (language of reference), but in behavior analysis the world (stimuli) controls the verbal response class of tacting.

Tandem schedule. A tandem schedule is two or more basic schedules (CRF, FR, FI, VI, VR) presented sequentially in which only the final link ends with primary reinforcement (or in some cases extinction) and the component schedules are not signaled by discriminative stimuli. In other words, a tandem schedule is the same as an unsignaled chain schedule.

Taste aversion learning. When a distinctive taste (e.g., flavored liquid) is paired with nausea or sickness induced by a drug, X-ray, or even physical activity, the organism shows suppression of intake of the paired flavor.

Terminal behavior. On a schedule of reinforcement, as the time for reinforcement gets close, animals engage in activities related to the presentation of the reinforcer. For example, a rat will orient toward the food cup.

Textual behavior. A class of verbal operants regulated by verbal stimuli where there is correspondence between the stimulus and response but no topographical similarity. The most common example of textual behavior is reading out loud. The child looks at the text *See Dick, see Jane* and emits the spoken words "See Dick, see Jane." The stimulus and response correspond, but the stimulus is visual and the response is vocal.

Time sampling. A method of recording used mostly in applied behavior analysis. Behavior is sampled over a long timescale. The idea is to make observations at specified times throughout the day. For example, a patient on a psychiatric ward may be observed every 30 min, as a nurse does the rounds, and instances of psychotic talk are recorded.

Token economy. A reinforcement system based on token reinforcement; the contingencies specify when, and under what conditions, particular forms of behavior are reinforced. The system is an economy in the sense that tokens may be exchanged for goods and services, much like money is in our economy. This exchange of tokens for a variety of back-up reinforcers ensures that the tokens are conditioned reinforcers. Token economies have been used to improve the behavior of psychiatric patients, juvenile delinquents, pupils in remedial classrooms, medical patients, alcoholics, drug addicts, prisoners, nursing home residents, and retarded persons.

Tolerance. When more of a drug (unconditioned stimulus) is needed to obtain the same drug effects (unconditioned response), we talk about drug tolerance. In respondent conditioning, the counteractive effects to conditioned stimuli are major components of drug tolerance.

Topography. Refers to the physical form or characteristics of the response—for example, the way that a rat presses a lever with the left paw, the hind right foot, and so on. The topography of response is related to the contingencies of reinforcement in the sense that the form of response can be broadened or restricted by the contingencies. The contingency of reinforcement may require only responses with the left paw rather than any response that activates the microswitch—under theses conditions left paw responses will predominate. Generally, topography or form is a function of the contingencies of reinforcement.

Trace conditioning. A respondent conditioning procedure in which the conditioned stimulus (CS) is presented for a brief period and after some time passes the unconditioned stimulus (US) occurs. Generally, as the time between the CS presentation and the occurrence of the US increases, the conditioned response becomes weaker. When compared to delayed conditioning, trace conditioning is not as effective.

Transition-state performance. The instability of behavior generated by a change in contingencies of reinforcement. For example, when continuous reinforcement is changed to fixed ratio (FR) 10, the pattern of response is unstable during the transition. After prolonged exposure to the FR contingency the performance eventually stabilizes into a regular or characteristic pattern. See also **steady-state performance**.

Transitivity. An organism shows transitivity when it responds to stimulus class A as it does to stimulus class C, or A = C after training that A = B and B = C. For example, if the written words *one, two, and three* are equivalent to the arithmetic numbers 1, 2, and 3, and the words and these arithmetic numbers are equivalent to sets {X}, {X, X}, and {X, X, X}, then it logically follows that the words *one, two, and three* are equivalent to sets {X}, {X, X}, and {X, X, X}—the relationship is transitive. An organism is said to show transitivity when it passes tests for transitivity after training for symbolic matching of stimulus class A (angles) to stimulus class B (geometric forms), and B (geometric forms) to C (intensity of illumination).

Trend (in baseline). A trend is a systematic decline or rise in the baseline values of the dependent variable. A drift in baseline measures can be problematic when the treatment is expected to produce a change in the same direction as the trend.

Trial-and-error learning. A term coined by Thorndike (1898, 1911) that he used to describe results from his puzzle box and maze learning experiments. Animals were said to make fewer and fewer errors over repeated trials, learning by trial and error.

Two-key procedure. On a concurrent schedule of reinforcement, the alternative schedules are presented on separate response keys.

Unconditioned reinforcer. A reinforcing stimulus that has acquired its properties as a function of species history. Although many reinforcers such as food and sex are general over species, other reinforcers such as the song of a bird or the scent of a mate are particular to a species. Behavior analysis, evolutionary biology, and neuroscience are necessary to describe, predict, and control the behavior regulated by unconditioned reinforcement.

Unconditioned response (UR). All organisms are born with a set of reflexes (US → UR). These relationships are invariant and biologically based. The behavior elicited by the unconditioned stimulus (US) is called the unconditioned response (UR).

Unconditioned stimulus (US). All organisms are born with a set of reflexes (US → UR). These relationships are invariant and biologically based. The eliciting event for the reflex is called the unconditioned stimulus (US).

Undermatching. In the generalized matching equation, the exponent *a* takes on a value of less than 1. This result is described as undermatching and occurs when changes in the response ratio are less than changes in the reinforcement ratio. The effect is interpreted as low sensitivity to the programmed schedules of reinforcement. See also **generalized matching law**.

Variable interval (VI). A schedule of reinforcement in which one response is reinforced after a variable amount of time has passed. For example, on a VI 30-s schedule, the time to each reinforcement changes but the average time is 30 s.

Variable ratio (VR). A response-based schedule of reinforcement in which the number of responses required for reinforcement changes after each reinforcer. The average number of responses is used to index the schedule. For example, a rat may press a lever for reinforcement 50 times, and then 150, 70, 30, and 200. Adding these response requirements for a total of 500 and then dividing by the number of separate response runs (5) yields the schedule value, VR 100.

Verbal behavior. Verbal behavior refers to the vocal, written, and gestural performances of a speaker, writer, or communicator. This behavior operates on the listener, reader, or observer, who arranges for reinforcement of the verbal performance. Verbal behavior only has indirect effects on the environment. This contrasts with nonverbal behavior, which usually results in direct and automatic consequences. When you walk toward an object, you come closer to it. Verbal behavior, on the other hand, works through its effects on other people. To change the position of a lamp, the speaker states "Lift the lamp at the back of the room" to a listener who is inclined to respond. Although verbal behavior is usually equated with speaking, vocal responses are only one of its forms. For example, a person may emit gestures and body movements that indirectly operate on the environment through their effects on others. A frown sets the occasion for others to remove some aversive event, while a smile may signal the observer to behave in ways that produce positive reinforcement.

Verbal community. The contingencies that regulate verbal behavior arise from the practices of people in the verbal community. The verbal community refers to the customary ways that people reinforce the behavior of the speaker. These customary ways or practices have evolved as part of cultural evolution. The study of the semantics and syntax of words and sentences (linguistics) describes the universal and specific contingencies arranged by the verbal community. In the behavioral view, language does not reside in the mind but in the social environment of the speaker.

References

Abramson, L. Y., Seligman, M. E. P., & Teasdale, J. D. (1978). Learned helplessness in humans: Critique and reformulation. *Journal of Abnormal Psychology, 87*, 49–74.

Ader, R., & Cohen, N. (1981). Conditioned immunopharmacologic responses. In R. Ader (Ed.), *Psycho-neuroimmunology* (pp. 281–319). New York: Academic Press.

Ader, R., & Cohen, N. (1985). CNS–immune system interactions: Conditioning phenomena. *Behavior and Brain Sciences, 8*, 379–394.

Ader, R., & Cohen, N. (1993). Psychoneuroimmunology: Conditioning and stress. *Annual Review of Psychology, 44*, 53–85.

Ainslie, G. (2005) Précis of breakdown of will. *Behavioral and Brain Sciences, 28*, 635–673.

Ainslie, G. W. (1974). Impulse control in pigeons. *Journal of the Experimental Analysis of Behavior, 21*, 485–489.

Ainslie, G. W. (1975). Specious reward: A behavioral theory of impulsiveness and impulse control. *Psychological Bulletin, 82*, 463–496.

Alberto, P. A., & Troutman, A. C. (2006). *Applied behavior analysis for teachers* (7th ed.). Upper Saddle River, NJ: Merrill/Prentice Hall.

Alberto, P. A., Heflin, L. J., & Andrews, D. (2002). Use of the timeout ribbon procedure during community-based instruction. *Behavior Modification, 26*, 297–311.

Alcock, J. (1969). Observational learning in three species of birds. *Ibis, 11*, 308–321.

Alferink, L. A., Crossman, E. K., & Cheney, C. D. (1973). Control of responding by a conditioned reinforcer in the presence of free food. *Animal Learning and Behavior, 1*, 38–40.

Allen, C. M. (1981). On the exponent in the "generalized" matching equation. *Journal of the Experimental Analysis of Behavior, 35*, 125–127.

Alvarez, L. W. (1982). Experimental evidence that an asteroid impact led to the extinction of many species 65 million years ago. *Proceedings of the National Academy of Sciences, 80*, 627–642.

Alvarez, L. W., Alvarez, W., Asaro, F., & Michel, H. V. (1980). Extraterrestrial cause for the Cretaceous–Tertiary extinction. *Science, 208*, 1095–1108.

Alvarez, L. W., Asaro, F., & Michel, H. V. (1980). Extraterrestrial cause for the Cretaceous–Tertiary extinction—Experimental results and theoretical interpretation. *Science, 206*, 1095–1108.

Alvarez, W., Asaro, F., Michel, H. V., & Alvarez, L. W. (1982). Iridium anomaly approximately synchronous with terminal Eocene extinction. *Science, 216*, 886–888.

Alvord, J. R., & Cheney, C. D. (1994). *The home token economy*. Cambridge, MA: Cambridge Center for Behavioral Studies.

Anderson, C. D., Ferland, R. J. and Williams, M. D. (1992). Negative contrast associated with reinforcing stimulation of the brain. *Society for Neuroscience Abstracts, 18*, 874.

Anderson, N. D., & Craik, F. I. (2006). The mnemonic mechanisms of errorless learning. *Neuropsychologica, 44*, 2806–2813.

Andre, J., Albanos, K., & Reilly, S. (2007). *c*-Fos expression in the rat brain following lithium chloride-induced illness. *Brain Research, 1135*, 122–128.

Anger, D. (1956). The dependence of interresponse times upon the relative reinforcement of different interresponse times. *Journal of Experimental Psychology, 52*, 145–161.

Anisfeld, M. (1996). Only tongue protusion modeling is matched by neonates. *Developmental Review, 16*, 149–161.

Anrep, G. V. (1920). Pitch discrimination in a dog. *Journal of Physiology, 53*, 367–385.

Antonitis, J. J. (1951). Response variability in the white rat during conditioning, extinction, and reconditioning. *Journal of Experimental Psychology, 42*, 273–281.

Appel, J. B. (1961). Punishment in the squirrel monkey *Saimiri sciurea*. *Science, 133*, 36.

Appel, J. B., & Peterson, N. J. (1965). Punishment: Effects of shock intensity on response suppression. *Psychological Reports, 16*, 721–730.

Arbuckle, J. L., & Lattal, K. A. (1988). Changes in functional response units with briefly delayed reinforcement. *Journal of the Experimental Analysis of Behavior, 49*, 249–263.

Arcediano, F., & Miller, R. R. (2002). Some constraints for models of timing: A temporal coding hypothesis perspective. *Learning and Motivation, 33*, 105–123.

Armstrong, E. A. (1950). The nature and function of displacement activities. *Symposia of the Society for Experimental Biology, 4*, 361–384.

Arwas, S., Rolnick, A., & Lubow, R. E. (1989) Conditioned taste aversion in humans using motion-induced sickness as the US. *Behavior Research and Therapy, 27*, 295–301.

Ator, N. A. (1991). Subjects and instrumentation. In I. H. Iverson & K. A. Lattal (Eds.), *Experimental analysis of behavior: Part 1* (pp. 1–62). New York: Elsevier.

Austin, J., Hackett, S., Gravina, N., & Lebbon, A. (2006). The effects of prompting and feedback on drivers' stopping at stop signs. *Journal of Applied Behavior Analysis, 39*, 117–121.

Autor, S. M. (1960). *The strength of conditioned reinforcers as a function of frequency and probability of reinforcement.* Unpublished doctoral dissertation, Harvard University, Cambridge, MA.

Ayllon, T., & Azrin, N. H. (1968). *The token economy: A motivational system for therapy and rehabilitation.* New York: Appleton-Century-Crofts.

Azar, B. (2002). Pigeons as baggage screeners, rats as rescuers. *Monitor on Psychology, 33*, 42–44.

Azrin, N. H. (1956). Effects of two intermittent schedules of immediate and nonimmediate punishment. *Journal of Psychology, 42*, 3–21.

Azrin, N. H. (1958). Some effects of noise on human behavior. *Journal of the Experimental Analysis of Behavior, 1*, 183–200.

Azrin, N. H. (1959). Punishment and recovery during fixed ratio performance. *Journal of the Experimental Analysis of Behavior, 2*, 303–305.

Azrin, N. H. (1960). Effects of punishment intensity during variable-interval reinforcement. *Journal of the Experimental Analysis of Behavior, 3*, 123–142.

Azrin, N. H., Hake, D. F., & Hutchinson, R. R. (1965). Elicitation of aggression by a physical blow. *Journal of the Experimental Analysis of Behavior, 8*, 55–57.

Azrin, N. H., & Holz, W. C. (1961). Punishment during fixed interval reinforcement. *Journal of the Experimental Analysis of Behavior, 4*, 343–347.

Azrin, N. H., & Holz, W. C. (1966). Punishment. In W. K. Honig (Ed.), *Operant behavior: Areas of research and application* (pp. 380–447). New York: Appleton-Century-Crofts.

Azrin, N. H., Holz, W. C., & Hake, D. (1963). Fixed-ratio punishment. *Journal of the Experimental Analysis of Behavior, 6*, 141–148.

Azrin, N. H., Hutchinson, R. R., & Hake, D. F. (1963). Pain-induced fighting in the squirrel monkey. *Journal of the Experimental Analysis of Behavior, 6*, 620.

Azrin, N. H., Hutchinson, R. R., & Hake, D. F. (1966). Extinction-induced aggression. *Journal of the Experimental Analysis of Behavior, 9*, 191–204.

Azrin, N. H., Hutchinson, R. R., & Sallery, R. D. (1964). Pain aggression toward inanimate objects. *Journal of the Experimental Analysis of Behavior, 7*, 223–228.

Azrin, N. H., McMahon, P. T., Donohue, B., Besalel, V., Lapinski, K. J., Kogan, E., et al. (1994). Behavioral therapy for drug abuse: a controlled treatment outcome study. *Behavior Research and Therapy, 32*, 857–866.

Baars, B.J. (1986). *The cognitive revolution in psychology.* New York: Guilford Press.

Badia, P., Harsh, J., Coker, C. C., & Abbott, B. (1976). Choice and the dependability of stimuli that predict shock and safety. *Journal of the Experimental Analysis of Behavior, 26*, 95–111.

Baer, D. M. (1981). A flight of behavior analysis. *The Behavior Analyst, 4*, 85–91.

Baer, D. M. (1982). The role of current pragmatics in the future analysis of generalization technology. In R. B. Stuart (Ed.), *Adherence, compliance and generalization in behavioral medicine* (pp. 192–212). New York: Brunner/Mazel.

Baer, D. M., & Detrich, R. (1990). Tacting and manding in correspondence training: Effects of child selection of verbalization. *Journal of Experimental Analysis of Behavior, 54*, 23–30.

Baer, D. M., & Guess, D. (1971). Receptive training of adjectival inflections in mental retardates. *Journal of Applied Behavior Analysis, 4*, 129–139.

Baer, D. M., Peterson, R. F., & Sherman, J. A. (1967). The development of imitation by reinforcing behavioral similarity to a model. *Journal of the Experimental Analysis of Behavior, 10*, 405–416.

Baer, D. M., & Sherman, J. A. (1964). Reinforcement control of generalized imitation in young children. *Journal of Experimental Child Psychology, 1*, 37–49.

Baer, D. M., Wolf, M. M., & Risley, T. R. (1968). Some current dimensions of applied behavior analysis. *Journal of Applied Behavior Analysis, 1*, 91–97.

Baker, A. G. (1976). Learned irrelevance and learned helplessness: Rats learn that stimuli, reinforcers, and responses are uncorrelated. *Journal of Experimental Psychology: Animal Behavior Processes, 2*, 130–141.

Baker, T. B., & Tiffany, S. T. (1985). Morphine tolerance as habituation. *Psychological Review, 92*, 78–108.

Baldwin, J. M. (1906). *Mental development, methods, and processes.* New York: Macmillan.

Ball, J. (1938). A case of apparent imitation in a monkey. *Journal of Genetic Psychology, 52*, 439–442.

Bandura, A. (1965). Influence of models' reinforcement contingencies on the acquisition of imitative responses. *Journal of Personality and Social Psychology, 1*, 589–595.

Bandura, A. (1969). *Principles of behavior modification.* New York: Holt, Rinehart & Winston.

Bandura, A. (1971). Vicarious an self-reinforcement processes. In R. Glaser (Ed.), *The nature of reinforcement* (pp. 228–278). New York: Academic Press.

Bandura, A. (1974). Behavior theory and the models of man. *American Psychologist, 29*, 859–869.

Bandura, A. (1977). *Social learning theory.* Englewood Cliffs, NJ: Prentice-Hall.

Bandura, A. (1986). *Social foundations of thought and action: A social cognitive theory.* Englewood Cliffs, NJ: Prentice-Hall.

Bandura, A. (1997). *Self-efficacy: The exercise of control.* New York: Freeman.

Bandura, A., Ross, D., & Ross, S. A. (1963). Imitation of film-mediated aggressive models. *Journal of Abnormal and Social Psychology, 66*, 3–11.

Bard, K. (2007). Neonatal imitation in chimpanzees (*Pan troglodytes*) tested with two paradigms. *Animal Cognition, 10*, 233–242.

Barker, L. M., Best, M. R., & Domjan, M. (1977). *Learning mechanisms in food selection.* Waco, TX: Baylor University Press.

Barnet, R. C., & Miller, R. R. (1996). Second-order excitation mediated by a backward conditioned inhibitor. *Journal of Experimental Psychology: Animal Behavior Processes, 2*, 279–296.

Baron, A. (1991). Avoidance and punishment. In I. H. Iverson & K. A. Lattal (Eds.), *Experimental analysis of behavior: Part 1* (pp. 171–217). New York: Elsevier Science.

Baron, A., & Galizio, M. (1983). Instructional control of human operant behavior. *The Psychological Record, 33*, 495–520.

Baron, A., & Galizio, M. (2005). Positive and negative reinforcement: Should the distinction be preserved? *The Behavior Analyst, 28*, 85–95.

Baron, A., & Galizio, M. (2006). The distinction between positive and negative reinforcement: Use with care. *The Behavior Analyst, 29*, 141–151.

Baron, R. A., & Richardson, D. R. (1993). *Human aggression.* New York: Plenum Press.

Baron, R. A., Russell, G. W., & Arms, R. L. (1985). Negative ions and behavior: Impact on mood, memory, and aggression among Type A and Type B persons. *Journal of Personality and Social Psychology, 48*, 746–754.

Barr, R., & Hayne, H. (1996). The effect of event structure on imitation in infancy: Practice makes perfect? *Infant Behavior and Development, 19*, 253–257.

Baum, M. (1965). An automated apparatus for the avoidance training of rats. *Psychological Reports, 16*, 1205–1211.

Baum, M. (1969). Paradoxical effect of alcohol on the resistance to extinction of an avoidance response in rats. *Journal of Comparative and Physiological Psychology, 69*, 238–240.

Baum, W. M. (1974a). Choice in free-ranging wild pigeons. *Science, 185*, 78–79.

Baum, W. M. (1974b). On two types of deviation from the matching law: Bias and undermatching. *Journal of the Experimental Analysis of Behavior, 22*, 231–242.

Baum, W. M. (1979). Matching, undermatching, and overmatching in studies of choice. *Journal of the Experimental Analysis of Behavior, 32*, 269–281.

Baum, W. M. (1983). Studying foraging in the psychological laboratory. In R. L. Mellgren (Ed.), *Animal cognition and behavior* (pp. 253–278). New York: North-Holland.

Baum, W. M. (1992). In search of the feedback function for variable-interval schedules. *Journal of the Experimental Analysis of Behavior, 57*, 365–375.

Baum, W. M. (1993). Performance on ratio and interval schedules of reinforcement: Data and theory. *Journal of the Experimental Analysis of Behavior, 59*, 245–264.

Baum, W. M. (1995). Rules, culture, and fitness. *The Behavior Analyst, 18*, 1–21.

Baum, W. M. (2001). Molar versus molecular as a paradigm clash. *Journal of the Experimental Analysis of Behavior, 75*, 338–341.

Baum, W. M. (2002). From molecular to molar: A paradigm shift in behavior analysis. *Journal of the Experimental Analysis of Behavior, 78*, 95–116.

Baum, W. M. (2005). *Understanding behaviorism: Behavior, culture and evolution.* Malden, MA: Blackwell.

Baum, W. M., & Rachlin, H. C. (1969). Choice as time allocation. *Journal of the Experimental Analysis of Behavior, 12*, 861–874.

Baxley, N. (Producer). (1982). *Cognition, creativity and behavior: The Columban simulations* [Film]. Champaign, IL: Research Press.

Baxter, N. (Canadian Task Force on Preventive Health Care) (2001). Preventive health care, 2001 update: Should women be routinely taught breast self-examination to screen for breast cancer? *Canadian Medical Association Journal, 164*, 1837–1846.

Beiman, I., Graham, L. E., & Ciminero, A. R. (1978). Self-control progressive relaxation training as an alternative nonpharmacological treatment for essential hypertension: Therapeutic effects in the natural environment. *Behavior Research and Therapy, 16*, 371–375.

Belke, T. W., Pierce, W. D., & Duncan, I. D. (2006). Reinforcement value and substitutability of sucrose and wheel running: Implications for activity anorexia. *Journal of the Experimental Analysis of Behavior, 86*, 97–109.

Belke, T. W., Pierce, W. D., & Powell, R. A. (1989). Determinants of choice for pigeons and humans on concurrent-chains schedules of reinforcement. *Journal of the Experimental Analysis of Behavior, 52*, 97–109.

Belles, D., & Bradlyn, A. S. (1987). The use of the changing criterion design in achieving controlled smoking in a heavy smoker: A controlled case study. *Journal of Behavior Therapy and Experimental Psychiatry, 18*, 77–82.

Bem, D. J. (1965). An experimental analysis of self-persuasion. *Journal of Experimental Social Psychology, 1*, 199–218.

Bem, D. J. (1972). Self-perception theory. In L. Berkowitz (Ed.), *Advances in experimental social psychology* (Vol. 6, pp. 1–62). New York: Academic Press.

Benbasset, D., & Abramson, C. I. (2002). Errorless discrimination learning in simulated landing flares. *Human Factors and Aerospace Safety, 2*, 319–338.

Beninger, R. J., & Kendall, S. B. (1975). Behavioral contrast in rats with different reinforcers and different response topographies. *Journal of the Experimental Analysis of Behavior, 24*, 267–280.

Bering, J. M., Bjorklund, D. F., & Ragan, P. (2000). Deferred imitation of object-related actions in human-reared juvenile chimpanzees and orangutans. *Developmental Psychobiology, 36*, 218–232.

Berkowitz, L., & Donnerstein, E. (1982). External validity is more than skin deep: Some answers to criticism of laboratory experiments. *American Psychologist, 37*, 245–257.

Bernard, C. (1927). *An introduction to the study of experimental medicine.* New York: Macmillan. (Original work published 1865.)

Bertaina-Anglade, V., La Rochelle, C. D., & Scheller, D. K. (2006). Antidepressant properties of rotigotine in experimental models of depression. *European Journal of Pharmacology, 548*, 106–114.

Berton, O., McClung, C., DiLeone, R. J., Krishnan, V., & Renthal, W. (2006). Essential role of BDNF in the mesolimbic dopamine pathway in social defeat stress. *Science, 311*, 864–868.

Besson, A., Privat, A. M., Eschalier, A., & Fialip, J. (1999). Dopaminergic and opiodergic mediations of tricyclic antidepressants in the learned helplessness paradigm. *Pharmacology, Biochemistry, and Behavior, 64*, 541–548.

Beumont, A. L., Booth, S. F., Abraham, D. A., Griffiths, D. A., & Turner, T. R. (1983). Temporal sequence of symptoms in patients with anorexia nervosa: A preliminary report. In P. L. Darby, P. E. Garfinkel, D. M. Garner, & D. V. Coscina (Eds.), *Anorexia nervosa: Recent developments in research* (pp. 129–136). New York: Alan R. Liss.

Bickel, W. K., & Vuchinich, R. E. (2000). *Reframing health behavior change with behavioral economics.* Mahwah, NJ: Lawrence Erlbaum Associates.

Biederman, G. B., & Vanayan, M. (1988). Observational learning in pigeons: The function of quality of observed performance in simultaneous discrimination. *Learning and Motivation, 19*, 31–43.

Bijou, S., & Baer, D. M. (1978). *Behavior analysis of child development.* Englewood Cliffs, NJ: Prentice-Hall.

Binder, C. (1996). Behavioral fluency: Evolution of a new paradigm. *The Behavior Analyst, 19*, 163–197.

Binder, C., & Watkins, C. L. (1989). Promoting effective instructional methods: Solutions to America's educational crisis. *Future Choices, 1*, 33–39.

Binder, C., & Watkins, C. L. (1990). Precision teaching and direct instruction: Measurably superior instructional technology in schools. *Performance Improvement Quarterly, 3*, 74–96.

Bjork, D. W. (1993). *B. F. Skinner: A life*. New York: Basic Books.

Bjorklund, D. F. (1987). A note on neonatal imitation. *Developmental Review, 7*, 86–92.

Blanchard, R. J. (1975). The effect of S⁻ on observing behavior. *Learning and Motivation, 6*, 1–10.

Bloom, H. S., Criswell, E. L., Penneypacker, H. S., Catania, A. C., & Adams, C. K. (1982). Major stimulus dimensions determining detection of simulated breast lesions. *Perception and Psychophysics, 32*, 251–260.

Blough, D. S. (1957). Spectral sensitivity in the pigeon. *Journal of the Optical Society of America, 47*, 827–833.

Blough, D. S. (1959). Delayed matching in the pigeon. *Journal of the Experimental Analysis of Behavior, 2*, 151–160.

Blough, D. S. (1966). The reinforcement of least-frequent interresponse times. *Journal of the Experimental Analysis of Behavior, 9*, 581–591.

Blough, D. S. (1982). Pigeon perception of letters of the alphabet. *Science, 218*, 397–398.

Blumstein, D. T., & Armitage, K. B. (1997). Alarm calling in yellow-bellied marmots: 1. The meaning of situationally variable alarm calls. *Animal Behaviour, 53*, 143–171.

Bolles, R. C. (1970). Species-specific defense reactions and avoidance learning. *Psychological Review, 77*, 32–48.

Bolles, R. C. (1979). *Learning theory*. New York: Holt, Rinehart & Winston.

Bondy, A. (1996). *The pyramid approach to education: An integrative approach to teaching children and adults with autism*. Cherry Hill, NJ: Pyramid Education Consultants, Inc.

Bondy, A., & Frost, L. (1994). The picture exchange communication system. *Focus on Autistic Behavior, 9*, 1–19.

Borden, R. J., Bowen, R., & Taylor, S. P. (1971). Shock setting behavior as a function of physical attack and extrinsic reward. *Perceptual and Motor Skills, 33*, 563–568.

Boren, J. J. (1961). Resistance to extinction as a function of the fixed ratio. *Journal of Experimental Psychology, 4*, 304–308.

Borrero, J. C., & Vollmer, T. R. (2002). An application of the matching law to severe problem behavior. *Journal of Applied Behavior Analysis, 35*, 13–27.

Bower, G. H., & Hilgard, E. R. (1981). *Theories of learning*. Englewood Cliffs, NJ: Prentice-Hall.

Bradshaw, C. M., Ruddle, H. V., & Szabadi, E. (1981). Studies of concurrent performance in humans. In C. M. Bradshaw, E. Szabadi, & C. F. Lowe (Eds.), *Quantification of steady-state operant behaviour* (pp. 79–90). Amsterdam: Elsevier/North-Holland.

Bradshaw, C. M., & Szabadi, E. (1988). Quantitative analysis of human operant behavior. In G. Davey & C. Cullen (Eds.), *Human operant conditioning and behavior modification* (pp. 225–259). New York: John Wiley.

Brandon, P. K. (2005). Commentary on *Behavior analysis and learning* (3rd ed., p. 11). Available at http://krypton.mnsu.edu/%7Epkbrando/CommentaryP_C.htm.

Brandon, P. K., & Houlihan, D. (1997). Applying behavior theory to practice: An examination of the behavioral momentum metaphor. *Behavioral Interventions, 2*, 113–131.

Bratcher, N. A., Farmer-Dougan, V., Dougan, J. D., Heidenreich, B. A., & Garris, P. A. (2005). The role of dopamine in reinforcement: Changes in reinforcement sensitivity induced by D1-type, D2-type, and non-selective dopamine receptor agonists. *Journal of the Experimental Analysis of Behavior, 84*, 371–399.

Breland, K., & Breland, M. (1961). The misbehavior of organisms. *American Psychologist, 16*, 681–684.

Brembs, B., Lorenzetti, F. D., Reyes, F. D., Baxter, D. A., & Byrne, J. H. (2002). Operant reward learning in *Aplysia*: Neuronal correlates and mechanisms. *Science, 296*, 1706–1708.

Breuggeman, J. A. (1973). Parental care in a group of free-ranging rhesus monkeys. *Folia Primatologica, 20*, 178–210.

Breyer, N. L., & Allen, G. L. (1975). Effects of implementing a token economy on teacher attending behavior. *Journal of Applied Behavior Analysis, 8*, 373–380.

Brody, H. (2000). *The placebo response*. New York: Harper Collins.

Brogden, W. J. (1939). Sensory pre-conditioning. *Journal of Experimental Psychology, 25*, 323–332.

Brooks, D. C., & Bouton, M. E. (1993). A retrieval cue for extinction attenuates spontaneous recovery. *Journal of Experimental Psychology: Animal Behavior Processes, 19*, 77–89.

Brosnan, S. F. (2005). Responses to a simple barter task in chimpanzees, *Pan troglodytes*. *Primates, 46*, 173–182.

Brown, P. L., & Jenkins, H. M. (1968). Auto-shaping of the pigeon's key-peck. *Journal of the Experimental Analysis of Behavior, 11*, 1–8.

Brown, R. (1973). *A first language: The early stages.* Cambridge, MA: Harvard University Press.

Brown, R. (1986). *Social psychology: The second edition.* New York: Free Press.

Brownstein, A. J., & Pliskoff, S. S. (1968). Some effects of relative reinforcement rate and changeover delay in response-independent concurrent schedules of reinforcement. *Journal of the Experimental Analysis of Behavior, 11*, 683–688.

Buccino, G., Vogt, S., Ritzl, A., Fink, G. R., Zilles, K., Freund, H. J., et al. (2004). Neural circuits underlying learning of hand actions: An event-related fMRI study. *Neuron, 42*, 323–334.

Buckleitner, W. (2006). Relationship between software design and children's engagement. *Early Education and Development, 17*, 489–505.

Buckley, K. B. (1989). *Mechanical man: John Broadus Watson and the beginnings of behaviorism.* New York: Guilford Press.

Burgess, R. L., & Bushell, D., Jr. (1969). *Behavioral sociology: The experimental analysis of social processes.* New York: Columbia University Press.

Burgio, L. D., & Tice, L. (1985). The reduction of seizure-like behaviors through contingency management. *Journal of Behavior Therapy and Experimental Psychiatry, 16*, 71–75.

Bushell, D., Jr., & Burgess, R. L. (1969). Characteristics of the experimental analysis. In R. L. Burgess & D. Bushell, Jr. (Eds.), *Behavioral sociology: The experimental analysis of social processes* (pp. 145–174). New York: Columbia University Press.

Buske-Kirschbaum, A., Kirschbaum, C., Stierle, H., Jabij, L., & Hellhammer, D. (1994). Conditioned manipulation of natural killer (NK) cells in humans using a discriminative learning protocol. *Biological Psychology, 38*, 143–155.

Buskist, W. F., & Miller, H. L. (1986). Interaction between rules and contingencies in the control of fixed-interval performance. *The Psychological Record, 36*, 109–116.

Byrne, D. (1971). *The attraction paradigm.* New York: Academic Press.

Cameron, J., Banko, K., & Pierce, W. D. (2001). Pervasive negative effects of rewards on intrinsic motivation: The myth continues. *The Behavior Analyst, 24*, 1–44.

Cameron, J., & Pierce, W. D. (1994). Reinforcement, reward and intrinsic motivation: A meta-analysis. *Review of Educational Research, 64*, 363–423.

Cameron, J., & Pierce, W. D. (2002). *Rewards and intrinsic motivation: Resolving the controversy.* Westport, CT: Bergin & Garvey.

Carnine, D. (1995). Rational schools: The role of science in helping education become a profession. *Behavior and Social Issues, 5*, 5–19.

Carr, D., Wilkinson, K. M., Blackman, D., & McIlvane, W. J. (2000). Equivalence classes in individuals with minimal verbal repertoires. *Journal of the Experimental Analysis of Behavior, 74*, 101–114.

Carr, E. G., & McDowell, J. J. (1980). Social control of self-injurious behavior of organic etiology. *Behavior Therapy, 11*, 402–409.

Carr, J. E., & Burkholder, E. O. (1998). Creating single-subject design graphs with Microsoft Excel™. *Journal of Applied Behavior Analysis, 31*, 245–251.

Carrigan, P. F., Jr., & Sidman, M. (1992). Conditional discrimination and equivalence relations: A theoretical analysis of control by negative stimuli. *Journal of the Experimental Analysis of Behavior, 58*, 183–204.

Carroll, M. E. (1993). The economic context of drug and non-drug reinforcers affects acquistion and maintenance of drug-reinforced behavior and withdrawal effects. *Drug and Alcohol Dependence, 33*, 201–210.

Carroll, M. E., Lac, S. T., & Nygaard, S. L. (1989). A concurrently available nondrug reinforcer prevents the acquisition of decreases in the maintenance of cocaine-reinforced behavior. *Psychopharmacology, 97*, 23–29.

Carroll, R. J., & Hesse, B. E. (1987). The effects of alternating mand and tact training on the acquisition of tacts. *The Analysis of Verbal Behavior, 5*, 55–65.

Carton, J. S., & Schweitzer, J. B. (1996). Use of a token economy to increase compliance during hemodialysis. *Journal of Applied Behavior Analysis, 29*, 111–113.

Case, D. A., Ploog, B. O., & Fantino, E. (1990). Observing behavior in a computer game. *Journal of the Experimental Analysis of Behavior, 54*, 185–199.

Catania, A. C. (1966). Concurrent operants. In W. K. Honig (Ed.), *Operant behavior: Areas of research and application* (pp. 213–270). Englewood Cliffs, NJ: Prentice-Hall.

Catania, A. C. (1973). The concept of the operant in the analysis of behavior. *Behaviorism, 1*, 103–116.

Catania, A. C. (1980). Autoclitic processes and the structure of behavior. *Behaviorism, 8*, 175–186.

Catania, A. C. (1998a). *Learning*. Englewood Cliffs, NJ: Prentice-Hall.

Catania, A. C. (1998b). The taxonomy of verbal behavior. In K. A. Lattal & M. Perone (Eds.), *Handbook of research methods in human operant behavior: Applied clinical psychology* (pp. 405–433). New York: Plenum Press.

Catania, A. C., & Harnard, S. (1988). *The selection of behavior*. New York: Cambridge University Press.

Catania, A. C., Matthews, B. A., & Shimoff, E. H. (1990). Properties of rule-governed behaviour and their implications. In D. E. Blackman, & Lejeune, H. (Eds.), *Behaviour analysis in theory and practice: Contributions and controversies* (pp. 215–230). Hillsdale, NJ: Lawrence Erlbaum Associates.

Catania, A. C., & Reynolds, G. S. A. (1968). A quantitative analysis of the responding maintained by interval schedules of reinforcement. *Journal of the Experimental Analysis of Behavior, 11*, 327–383.

Cerutti, D. (1989) Discrimination theory of rule-governed behavior. *Journal of the Experimental Analysis of Behavior, 51*, 251–259.

Chance, P. (1999). Thorndike's puzzle boxes and the origins of the experimental analysis of behavior. *Journal of the Experimental Analysis of Behavior, 72*, 433–440.

Charlop-Christy, M. H. & Kelso, S. E. (1997). How to treat the child with autism: A guide to treatment at the Claremont Autism Center. Claremont, CA: Marjorie H. Charlop-Christy.

Charnov, E. L. (1976). Optimal foraging: The marginal value theorem. *Theoretical Population Biology, 9*, 129–136.

Chen, X., Striano, T., & Rakoczy, H. (2004). Auditory–oral matching behavior in newborns. *Developmental Science, 7*, 42–47.

Cheney, C. D., Bonem, E., & Bonem, M. (1985). Changeover cost and switching between concurrent adjusting schedules. *Behavioural Processes, 10*, 145–155.

Cheney, C. D. , DeWulf, M. J., and Bonem, E. J. (1993). Prey vulnerability effects in an operant simulation of foraging. *Behaviorology, 1*, 23–30.

Cheney, C. D., & Eldred, N. L., (1980). Lithium-chloride-induced aversions in the opossum (*Didelphis virginiana*). *Physiological Psychology, 8*, 383–385.

Cheney, C. D., & Epling, W. F. (1968). *Running wheel activity and self-starvation in the white rat*. Unpublished manuscript, Department of Psychology, Eastern Washington State University.

Cheney, C. D., & Tam, V. (1972). Interocular transfer of a line tilt discrimination without mirror-image reversal using fading in pigeons. *The Journal of Biological Psychology, 14*, 17–20.

Cheney, C. D., van der Wall, S. B., & Poehlmann, R. J. (1987). Effects of strychnine on the behavior of Great Horned Owls and Red-Tailed Hawks. *Journal of Raptor Research, 21*, 103–110.

Cheng, J., & Feenstra, M. G. P. (2006). Individual differences in dopamine efflux in nucleus accumbens shell and core during instrumental learning. *Learning and Memory, 13*, 168–177.

Cheng, K., & Spetch, M. L. (2002). Spatial generalization and peak shift in humans. *Learning and Motivation, 33*, 358–389.

Chillag, D., & Mendelson, J. (1971). Schedule-induced airlicking as a function of body-weight in rats. *Physiology and Behavior, 6*, 603–605.

Chomsky, N. (1957). *Syntactic structures*. The Hague: Mouton.

Chomsky, N. (1959). Review of B. F. Skinner's verbal behavior. *Language, 35*, 26–58.

Cohen, D., Nisbett, R. E., Bowdle, B. F., & Schwarz, N. (1996). Insult, aggression, and the southern culture of honor: An "experimental ethnography." *Journal of Personality and Social Psychology, 70*, 945–960.

Cohen, P. S. (1968). Punishment: The interactive effects of delay and intensity of shock. *Journal of the Experimental Analysis of Behavior, 11*, 789–799.

Cohn, S. L. (1998). Behavioral momentum: The effects of the temporal separation of rates of reinforcement. *Journal of the Experimental Analysis of Behavior, 69*, 29–47.

Cole, R. P., & Miller, R. R. (1999). Conditioned excitation and conditioned inhibition acquired through backward conditioning. *Learning and Motivation, 30*, 129–156.

Conger, R., & Killeen, P. (1974). Use of concurrent operants in small group research. *Pacific Sociological Review, 17*, 399–416.

Cook, D. (1996). Reminiscences: Fred S. Keller: An appreciation. *Behavior and Social Issues, 6*, 61–71.

Corballis, M. C. (1999). The gestural origins of language. *American Scientist, 87*, 138–145.

Coren, S., Ward, L. M., & Enns, J. T. (2004). *Sensation and perception*. Hoboken, NJ: John Wiley.

Courage, M. L., & Howe, M. L. (2002) From infant to child: The dynamics of cognitive change in the second year of life. *Psychological Bulletin, 129*, 250–277.

Cowles, J. T. (1937). Food-tokens as incentive for learning by chimpanzees. *Comparative Psychology Monographs, 14*, 1–96.

Crossman, E. K., Trapp, N. L., Bonem, E. J., & Bonem, M. K. (1985). Temporal patterns of responding in small fixed-ratio schedules. *Journal of the Experimental Analysis of Behavior, 43*, 115–130.

Cullen, C. (1998). The trouble with rules. *The Psychologist, 11*, 471–475.

Cumming, W. W. (1966). A bird's eye glimpse of men and machines. In R. Ulrich, T. Stachnik, & J. Mabry (Eds.), *Control of human behavior* (pp. 246–256). Glenview, IL: Scott Foresman & Co.

Cumming, W. W., & Schoenfeld, W. (1960). Behavior stability under extended exposure to a time-correlated reinforcement contingency. *Journal of the Experimental Analysis of Behavior, 3*, 71–82.

Custance, D. M., Whiten, A., Sambrook, T., & Galdikas, B. (2001). Testing for social learning in the "artificial fruit" processing of wildborn orangutans (*Pongo pygmaeus*), Tanjung Puting, Indonesia. *Animal Cognition, 4*, 305–313.

D'Amato, M. R., Salmon, D. P., Loukas, E., & Tomie, A. (1985). Symmetry and transitivity of conditional relations in monkeys (*Cebus apella*) and pigeons (*Columba livia*). *Journal of the Experimental Analysis of Behavior, 44*, 35–47.

Dapcich-Miura, E., & Hovell, M. F. (1979). Contingency management of adherence to a complex medical regimen in elderly heart patients. *Behavior Therapy, 10*, 193–201.

Darley, J. M., Glucksberg, S., & Kinchla, R. A. (1991). *Psychology*. Englewood Cliffs, NJ: Prentice-Hall.

Darwin, C. (1859). *On the origin of species by means of natural selection*. London: John Murray.

Davidson, T. L., & Swithers, S. E. (2004). A Pavlovian approach to the problem of overeating. *International Journal of Obesity, 28*, 933–935.

Davis, C. (1999). Excessive exercise and anorexia nervosa: Addictive and compulsive behaviors. *Psychiatric Annals, 29*, 221–224.

Davis, C., Kennedy, S. H., Ravelski, E., & Dionne, M. (1994). The role of physical activity in the development and maintenance of eating disorders. *Psychological Medicine, 24*, 957–967.

Davis, J. M. (1973). Imitation: A review and critique. In P. P. G. Bateson & P. H. Klopfer (Eds.), *Perspectives in ethology* (Vol. 1, pp. 43–72). New York: Plenum Press.

Davison, M. C. (1969). Preference for mixed-interval versus fixed-interval schedules. *Journal of the Experimental Analysis of Behavior, 12*, 247–252.

Davison, M. C. (1972). Preference for mixed-interval versus fixed-interval schedules: Number of component intervals. *Journal of the Experimental Analysis of Behavior, 17*, 169–176.

Davison, M. C. (1981). Choice between concurrent variable-interval and fixed-ratio schedules: A failure of the generalized matching law. In C. M. Bradshaw, E. Szabadi, & C. F. Lowe (Eds.), *Quantification of steady-state operant behaviour* (pp. 91–100). Amsterdam: Elsevier/North-Holland.

Davison, M. C., & Ferguson, A. (1978). The effect of different component response requirements in multiple and concurrent schedules. *Journal of the Experimental Analysis of Behavior, 29*, 283–295.

Davison, M. C., & Hunter, I. W. (1976). Performance on variable-interval schedules arranged singly and concurrently. *Journal of the Experimental Analysis of Behavior, 25*, 335–345.

Davison, M. C., & Jenkins, P. E. (1985). Stimulus discrininability, contingency discriminability, and schedule performance. *Animal Learning and Behavior, 13*, 147–162.

Davison, M. C., & McCarthy, D. (1988). *The matching law: A research review*. Hillsdale, NJ: Lawrence Erlbaum Associates.

Dawkins, R. (1976). *The selfish gene*. London: Oxford University Press.

Dawkins, R. (1996). *Climbing Mount Improbable*. New York: W. W. Norton.

Dawkins, R. (2004). *The ancestor's tale: A pilgrimage to the dawn of evolution*. Boston, MA: Houghton Mifflin.

Dawson, B. V., & Foss, B. M. (1965). Observational learning in budgerigars. *Animal Behaviour, 13*, 470–474.

Deacon, J. R., & Konarski, E. A., Jr. (1987). Correspondence training: An example of rule-governed behavior? *Journal of Applied Behavior Analysis, 20*, 391–400.

DeBaryshe, B. D., & Whitehurst, G. J. (1986). Intraverbal acquisition of semantic concepts by preschoolers. *Journal of Experimental Child Psychology, 42*, 169–186.

Deci, E. L., Koestner, R., & Ryan, R. M. (1999). A meta-analytic review of experiments examining the effects of extrinsic rewards on intrinsic motivation. *Psychological Bulletin, 125*, 627–668.

DeFran, R. H. (1972). *Reinforcing effects of stimuli paired with schedules of aversive control.* Unpublished doctoral dissertation, Bowling Green State University, Bowling Green, OH.

De Houwer, J., Thomas, S., & Baeyens, F. (2001). Association learning of likes and dislikes: A review of 25 years of research on human evaluative conditioning. *Psychological Bulletin, 127,* 853–869.

Deitz, S. M. (1978). Current status of applied behavior analysis: Science versus technology. *American Psychologist, 33,* 805–814.

Derenne, A., & Baron, A. (2002). Preratio pausing: Effects of an alternative reinforcer on fixed- and variable-ratio responding. *Journal of the Experimental Analysis of Behavior, 77,* 273–282.

Derenne, A., Richardson, J. V., & Baron, A. (2006). Long-term effects of suppressing the preratio pause. *Behavioral Processes, 72,* 32–37.

Dessalles, J. L. (2007). *Why we talk: The evolutionary origins of language.* New York: Oxford University Press.

De Villiers, P. (1977). Choice in concurrent schedules and a quantitative formulation of the law of effect. In W. K. Honig & J. E. R. Staddon (Eds.), *Handbook of operant behavior* (pp. 233–287). Englewood Cliffs, NJ: Prentice-Hall.

Dews, P. B. (1963). Behavioral effects of drugs. In S. M. Farber & R. H. L. Wilson (Eds.), *Conflict and creativity* (pp. 138–153). New York: McGraw-Hill.

Dews, P. B. (1969). Studies on responding under fixed-interval schedules of reinforcement: The effects on the pattern of responding of changes in requirements at reinforcement. *Journal of the Experimental Analysis of Behavior, 12,* 191–199.

DiCara, L. V. (1970). Learning in the autonomic nervous system. *Scientific American, 222,* 30–39.

Dickinson, A., Hall, G., & Mackintosh, N. J. (1976). Surprise and the attenuation of blocking. *Journal of Experimental Psychology: Animal Behavior Processes, 2,* 313–322.

Dinsmoor, J. A. (1951). The effect of periodic reinforcement of bar-pressing in the presence of a discriminative stimulus. *Journal of Comparative and Physiological Psychology, 44,* 354–361.

Dinsmoor, J. A. (1952). A discrimination based on punishment. *Quarterly Journal of Experimental Psychology, 4,* 27–45.

Dinsmoor, J. A. (1977). Escape, avoidance, punishment: Where do we stand? *Journal of the Experimental Analysis of Behavior, 28,* 83–95.

Dinsmoor, J. A. (2001a). Stimuli inevitably generated by behavior that avoids electric shock are inherently reinforcing. *Journal of the Experimental Analysis of Behavior, 75,* 311–333.

Dinsmoor, J. A. (2001b). Still no evidence for temporally extended shock-frequency reduction as a reinforcer. *Journal of the Experimental Analysis of Behavior, 75,* 367–378.

Dinsmoor, J. A., Brown, M. P., & Lawrence, C. E. (1972). A test of the negative discriminative stimulus as a reinforcer of observing. *Journal of the Experimental Analysis of Behavior, 18,* 79–85.

Dinsmoor, J. A., Flint, G. A., Smith, R. F., & Viemeister, N. F. (1969). Differential reinforcing effects of stimuli associated with the presence or absence of a schedule of punishment. In D. P. Hendry (Ed.), *Conditioned reinforcement* (pp. 357–384). Homewood, IL: Dorsey Press.

Doleys, D. M., Meredith, R. L., & Ciminero, A. R. (1982). *Behavioral medicine: Assessment and treatment strategies.* New York: Plenum Press.

Dollard, J., & Miller, N. E. (1950). *Personality and psychotherapy.* New York: McGraw-Hill.

Donahoe, J. W. (2002). Behavior analysis and neuroscience. *Behavioural Processes, 57,* 241–259.

Donahoe, J. W., & Palmer, J. W. (1994). *Learning and complex behavior.* Boston, MA: Allyn & Bacon.

Donegan, N. H., & Wagner, A. R. (1987). Conditioned diminution and facilitation of the UR: A sometimes opponent-process interpretation. In I. Gomezano, W. F. Prokasy, & R. F. Thompson (Eds.), *Classical conditioning* (pp. 339–369). Hillsdale, NJ: Lawrence Erlbaum Associates.

Donohue, B. C., Karmely, J., & Strada, M. J. (2006). Alcohol and drug abuse. In M. Hersen (Ed.), *Clinician's handbook of child behavioral assessment* (pp. 337–375). San Diego, CA: Elsevier Academic Press.

Donovan, W. J. (1978). Structure and function of the pigeon visual system. *Physiological Psychology, 6,* 403–437.

Dorrance, B. R. (2001). Imitative learning of conditional discriminations in pigeons. *Dissertation Abstracts International: Section B: The Sciences & Engineering, 61*(11-B), No. 6169.

Dorrance, B. R., & Zentall, T. R. (2001). Imitative learning in Japanese quail depends on the motivational state of the observer at the time of observation. *Journal of Comparative Psychology, 115,* 62–67.

Dove, L. D. (1976). Relation between level of food deprivation and rate of schedule-induced attack. *Journal of the Experimental Analysis of Behavior, 25,* 63–68.

Dube, W. V., & McIlvane, W. J. (2001). Behavioral momentum in computer-presented discriminations in individuals with severe mental retardation. *Journal of the Experimental Analysis of Behavior*, *75*, 15–23.

Ducharme, J. M., & Worling, D. E. (1994). Behavioral momentum and stimulus fading in the acquisition and maintenance of child compliance in the home. *Journal of Applied Behavior Analysis*, *27*, 639–647.

Dulany, D. E. (1968). Awareness, rules, and propositonal control: A confrontation with S–R behavior theory. In T. Dixon & D. Horton (Eds.), *Verbal behavior and behavior theory* (pp. 340–387). New York: Prentice-Hall.

Durand, V. M. (1999). Functional communication training using assistive devices: Recruiting natural communities of reinforcement. *Journal of Applied Behavior Analysis*, *32*, 247–267.

Dworkin, B., & Miller, N. (1986). Failure to replicate visceral learning in the acute curarized rat preparation. *Behavioral Neuroscience*, *100*, 299–314.

Eckerman, D. A., & Lanson, R. N. (1969). Variability of response location for pigeons responding under continuous reinforcement, intermittent reinforcement, and extinction. *Journal of the Experimental Analysis of Behavior*, *12*, 73–80.

Egger, M. D., & Miller, N. E. (1962). Secondary reinforcement in rats as a function of information value and reliability of the stimulus. *Journal of Experimental Psychology*, *64*, 97–104.

Egger, M. D., & Miller, N. E. (1963). When is reward reinforcing?: An experimental study of the information hypothesis. *Journal of Comparative and Physiological Psychology*, *56*, 132–137.

Eibl-Eibesfeldt, I. (1975) *Ethology: The biology of behavior*. New York: Holt, Rinehart & Winston.

Eisenberger, R., & Armeli, S. (1997). Can salient reward increase creative performance without reducing intrinsic creative interest? *Journal of Personality and Social Psychology*, *72*, 652–663.

Eisenberger, R., & Cameron, J. (1996). The detrimental effects of reward: Myth or reality? *American Psychologist*, *51*, 1153–1166.

Ekman, P., & Friesen, W. V. (1975). *Unmasking the face*. Englewood Cliffs, NJ: Prentice-Hall.

Ellison, G. D. (1964). Differential salivary conditioning to traces. *Journal of Comparative and Physiological Psychology*, *57*, 373–380.

Elsmore, T. F., & McBride, S. A. (1994). An eight-alternative concurrent schedule: Foraging in a radial maze. *Journal of the Experimental Analysis of Behavior*, *61*, 331–348.

Engle, B. T. (1993). Autonomic behavior. *Experimental Gerontology*, *28*, 499–502.

Epling, W. F., & Cameron, J. (1994). Gibbons on conditioned seeing. From Gibbons, E. (1970), Stalking the wild asparagus: Field guide edition (pp. 28–32). Quotation contributed to the *Journal of the Experimental Analysis of Behavior*, *61*, 280.

Epling, W. F., & Pierce, W. D. (1983). Applied behavior analysis: New directions from the laboratory. *The Behavior Analyst*, *6*, 27–37.

Epling, W. F., & Pierce, W. D. (1984). Activity-based anorexia in rats as a function of opportunity to run on an activity wheel. *Nutrition and Behavior*, *2*, 37–49.

Epling, W. F., & Pierce, W. D. (1986). The basic importance of applied behavior analysis. *The Behavior Analyst*, *9*, 89–99.

Epling, W. F., & Pierce, W. D. (1988). Activity-based anorexia: A biobehavioral perspective. *International Journal of Eating Disorders*, *7*, 475–485.

Epling, W. F., & Pierce, W. D. (1990). Laboratory to application: An experimental analysis of severe problem behaviors. In A. C. Repp & N. N. Singh (Eds.), *Perspectives on the use of nonaversive and aversive interventions for persons with developmental disabilities* (pp. 451–464). Sycamore, IL: Sycamore Publishing Co.

Epling, W. F., & Pierce, W. D. (1992). *Solving the anorexia puzzle: A scientific approach*. Toronto: Hogrefe & Huber.

Epling, W. F., & Pierce, W. D. (1996a). *Activity anorexia: Theory, research, and treatment*. Mahwah, NJ: Lawrence Erlbaum Associates.

Epling, W. F., & Pierce, W. D. (1996b). An overview of activity anorexia. In W. F. Epling & W. D. Pierce (Eds.), *Activity anorexia: Theory, research, and treatment* (pp. 1–4). Mahwah, NJ: Lawrence Erlbaum Associates.

Epling, W. F., Pierce, W. D., & Stefan, L. (1983). A theory of activity-based anorexia. *International Journal of Eating Disorders*, *3*, 27–46.

Epstein, R. (1983). Resurgence of previously reinforced behavior during extinction. *Behavior Analysis Letters*, *3*, 391–397.

Epstein, R. (1984). Spontaneous and deferred imitation in the pigeon. *Behavioral Processes*, *9*, 347–354.

Epstein, R. (1985). Extinction-induced resurgence: Preliminary investigation and possible application. *Psychological Record*, *35*, 143–153.

Epstein, R., Lanza, R. P., & Skinner, B. F. (1980). Symbolic communication between two pigeons (*Columba livia domestica*). *Science, 207*, 543–545.

Epstein, R., & Skinner, B. F. (1981). The spontaneous use of memoranda by pigeons. *Behavior Analysis Letters, 1*, 241–246.

Erlich, P. R. (2000). *Human natures: Genes, cultures, and the human prospect*. New York: Penguin.

Ernst, A. J., Engberg, L., & Thomas, D. R. (1971). On the form of stimulus generalization curves for visual intensity. *Journal of the Experimental Analysis of Behavior, 16*, 177–180.

Estes, W. K. (1944). An experimental study of punishment. *Psychological Monographs, 57* (Serial No. 3).

Estes, W. K., & Skinner, B. F. (1941). Some quantitative properties of anxiety. *Journal of Experimental Psychology, 29*, 390–400.

Ettinger, R. H., & McSweeney, F. K. (1981). Behavioral contrast and responding during multiple food–food, food–water, and water-water schedules. *Animal Learning and Behavior, 9*, 216–222.

Etzkowitz, H. (1992). Inventions. In E. F. Borgatta & M. L. Borgatta (Eds.), *Encyclopedia of sociology* (Vol. 2, pp. 1004–1005). New York: Macmillan.

Evans, R. I. (1989). *Albert Bandura, the man and his ideas—A dialogue*. New York: Praeger.

Falck-Ytter, T., Gredeback, G., & von Hofsten, C. (2006). Infants predict other people's action goals. *Nature Neuroscience, 9*, 878–879.

Falk, J. L. (1961). Production of polydipsia in normal rats by an intermittent food schedule. *Science, 133*, 195–196.

Falk, J. L. (1964). Studies on schedule-induced polydipsia. In M. J. Wayner (Ed.), *Thirst: First international symposium on thirst in the regulation of body water* (pp. 95–116). New York: Pergamon Press.

Falk, J. L. (1969). Schedule-induced polydipsia as a function of fixed interval length. *Journal of the Experimental Analysis of Behavior, 9*, 37–39.

Falk, J. L. (1971). The nature and determinants of adjunctive behavior. *Physiology and Behavior, 6*, 577–588.

Falk, J. L. (1977). The origin and functions of adjunctive behavior. *Animal Learning and Behavior, 5*, 325–335.

Falk, J. L., D'Mello, K., & Lau, C. E. (2001). Two procedures establishing preference for oral cocaine and lidocane solutions which do not use an associative history with a reinforcer. *Behavioral Pharmacology, 12*, 117–123.

Falk, J. L., & Lau, C. E. (1997). Establishing preference for oral cocaine without an associative history with a reinforcer. *Drug and Alcohol Dependence, 46*, 159–166.

Fantino, E. (1965). Some data on the discriminative stimulus hypothesis of secondary reinforcement. *Psychological Record, 15*, 409–414.

Fantino, E. (1967). Preference for mixed- versus fixed-ratio schedules. *Journal of the Experimental Analysis of Behavior, 10*, 35–43.

Fantino, E. (1969a). Choice and rate of reinforcement. *Journal of the Experimental Analysis of Behavior, 12*, 723–730.

Fantino, E. (1969b). Conditioned reinforcement, choice, and the psychological distance to reward. In D. P. Hendry (Ed.), *Conditioned reinforcement* (pp. 163–191). Homewood, IL: Dorsey Press.

Fantino, E. (1977). Conditioned reinforcement: Choice and information. In W. K. Honig & J. E. R. Staddon (Eds.), *Handbook of operant behavior* (pp. 313–339). Englewood Cliffs, NJ: Prentice-Hall.

Fantino, E., & Logan, C. A. (1979). *The experimental analysis of behavior: A biological perspective*. San Francisco, CA: W. H. Freeman.

Feighner, J. P., Robins, E., Guze, S. B., Woodruff, R. A., Winokur, G., & Munoz, R. (1972). Diagnostic criteria for use in psychiatric research. *Archives of General Psychiatry, 26*, 57–63.

Feldman, M. A. (1990). Balancing freedom from harm and right to treatment for persons with developmental disabilities. In A. C. Repp & N. N. Singh (Eds.), *Perspectives on the use of nonaversive and aversive interventions for persons with developmental disabilities* (pp. 261–271). Sycamore, IL: Sycamore Publishing Co.

Ferrari, P. F., Rozzi, S., &. Fogassi, L. (2005). Mirror neurons responding to observation of actions made with tools in monkey ventral premotor cortex. *Journal of Cognitive Neuroscience, 17*, 212–226.

Ferrari, P. F., Visalberghi, E., Pauker, A., Fogassi, L., Ruggiero, A., & Suomi, S. J. (2006). Neonatal imitation in rhesus macaques. *PLoS Biology, 4*, 1501–1508.

Ferster, C. B. (1979). Psychotherapy from the standpoint of a behaviorist. In J. D. Keehn (Ed.), Psychopathology in animals: Research and clinical implications (pp. 279–303). San Diego, CA: Academic Press.

Ferster, C. B. (2000). Schedules of reinforcement with Skinner. *Journal of the Experimental Analysis of Behavior, 77*, 303–311.

Ferster, C. B., Culbertson, S., & Boren, M. C. P. (1975). *Behavior principles*. Englewood Cliffs, NJ: Prentice-Hall.

Ferster, C. B., & Skinner, B. F. (1957). *Schedules of reinforcement*. New York: Appleton-Century-Crofts.

Festinger, L. (1957). *A theory of cognitive dissonance*. Stanford, CA: Stanford University Press.

Field, T. M., Woodson, R., Greenberg, R., & Cohen, D. (1982). Discrimination and imitation of facial expressions by neonates. *Science, 218*, 179–181.

Filby, Y., & Appel, J. B. (1966). Variable-interval punishment during variable-interval reinforcement. *Journal of the Experimental Analysis of Behavior, 9*, 521–527.

Findley, J. D. (1958). Preference and switching under concurrent scheduling. *Journal of the Experimental Analysis of Behavior, 1*, 123–144.

Fiorillo, C. D., Tobler, P. N., & Schultz, W. (2003). Discrete coding of reward probability and uncertainty by dopamine neurons. *Science, 299*, 1898–1902.

Fisher, J., & Hinde, C. A. (1949). The opening of milk bottles by birds. *British Birds, 42*, 347–357.

Fisher, W. W., & Mazur, J. E. (1997). Basic and applied research on choice responding. *Journal of Applied Behavior Analysis, 30*, 387–410.

Fishman, S. (1991). The town B. F. Skinner boxed. *Health, 5*, 50–60.

Fixsen, D. L., Phillips, E. L., Phillips, E. A., & Wolf, M. M. (1976). The teaching family-model of group home treatment. In W. E. Craighead, A. E. Kazdin, & M. J. Mahoney (Eds.), *Behavior modification: Principles, issues, and applications* (pp. 310–320). Boston, MA: Houghton Mifflin.

Flory, R. K. (1969). Attack behavior as a function of minimum inter-food interval. *Journal of the Experimental Analysis of Behavior, 12*, 825–828.

Friman, P. C., Finney, J. W., Glasscock, S. T., Weigel, J. W., & Christophersen, E. R. (1986). Testicular self-examination: Validation of a training strategy for early cancer detection. *Journal of Applied Behavior Analysis, 19*, 87–92.

Galbicka, G. (1992). The dynamics of behavior. *Journal of the Experimental Analysis of Behavior, 57*, 243–248.

Galef, B. G. (1988). Imitation in animals: History, definition, and interpretation of data from the psychological laboratory. In T. R. Zentall & B. G. Galef, Jr. (Eds.), *Social learning: Psychological and biological perspectives* (pp. 3–28). Hillsdale, NJ: Lawrence Erlbaum Associates.

Galef, B. G. (1990). Necessary and sufficient conditions for communication of diet preferences by Norway rats. *Animal Learning and Behavior, 18*, 347–351.

Galef, B. G., & Allen, C. (1995). A new model system for studying behavioural traditions in animals. *Animal Behaviour, 50*, 705–717.

Galizio, M. (1979). Contingency-shaped and rule-governed behavior: Instructional control of human loss avoidance. *Journal of the Experimental Analysis of Behavior, 31*, 53–70.

Gallese, V., Fadiga, L., Fogassi, L., & Rizzolatti, G. (1996). Action recognition in the premotor cortex. *Brain, 119*, 593–609.

Garcia, J., & Koelling, R. A. (1966). Relation of cue to consequence in avoidance learning. *Psychonomic Science, 4*, 123–124.

Gardner, E. T., & Lewis, P. (1976). Negative reinforcement with shock-frequency increase. *Journal of the Experimental Analysis of Behavior, 25*, 3–14.

Garner, D. M., & Desai, J. J. (2000). Eating disorders. In M. Hersen & A. S. Bellack (Eds.), *Psychopathology in adulthood* (2nd ed., pp. 419–441). Needham Heights, MA: Allyn & Bacon.

Geen, R. G. (1968). Effects of frustration, attack, and prior training in aggressiveness upon aggressive behavior. *Journal of Personality and Social Psychology, 9*, 316–321.

Geller, E. S. (2006). Occupational injury prevention and applied behavior analysis. In A. C. Gielen, D. A. Sleet, & R. J. DiClemente (Eds.), *Injury and violence prevention: Behavioral science theories, methods, and applications* (pp. 297–322). San Francisco, CA: Jossey-Bass.

Geller, I., Kulak, J. T., Jr., & Seifter, J. (1962). The effects of chlordiazepoxide and chlorpromazine on punished discrimination. *Psychopharmacologia, 3*, 374–385.

Geller, I., & Seifter, J. (1960). The effects of meprobamate, barbiturates, *d*-amphetamine and promazine on experimentally induced conflict in the rat. *Psychopharmacologia, 1*, 482–492.

Gerard, H. B. (1994). A retrospective review of Festinger's *A theory of cognitive dissonance*: *Psychological critiques, 39*, 1013–1017.

Gershoff, E. T. (2002). Corporal punishment by parents and associated child behaviors and experiences: A meta-analytic and theoretical review. *Psychological Bulletin, 128*, 539–579.

Gewirtz, J. L. (1971). The roles of overt responding and extrinsic reinforcement in "self-" and "vicarious-reinforcement" phenomena and in "observational learning" and imitation. In R. Glaser (Ed.), *The nature of reinforcement* (pp. 279–309). New York: Academic Press.

Ghezzi, P., Williams, W. L., & Carr, J. (1999). *Autism: Behavior Analytic Perspectives*. Reno, NV: Context Press.

Gibbon, J., & Church, R. M. (1992). Comparison of variance and covariance patterns in parallel and serial theories of timing. *Journal of the Experimental Analysis of Behavior, 57*, 393–406.

Glazer, H. I., & Weiss, J. M. (1976a). Long-term interference effect: An alternative to "learned helplessness." *Journal of Experimental Psychology: Animal Behavior Processes, 2*, 202–213.

Glazer, H. I., & Weiss, J. M. (1976b). Long-term and transitory interference effects. *Journal of Experimental Psychology: Animal Behavior Processes, 2*, 191–201.

Gleeson, S. (1991). Response acquisition. In I. H. Iverson & K. A. Lattal (Eds.), *Experimental analysis of behavior: Part 1* (pp. 63–86). New York: Elsevier.

Glenn, S. S. (1988). Contingencies and metacontingencies: Toward a synthesis of behavior analysis and cultural materialism. *The Behavior Analyst, 11*, 161–179.

Glenn, S. S. (1989). Verbal behavior and cultural practices. *Behavior Analysis and Social Action, 7*, 10–14.

Glenn, S. S. (1991). Contingencies and metacontingencies: Relations among behavioral, cultural, and biological evolution. In P. A. Lamal (Ed.), *Behavioral analysis of societies and cultural practices* (pp. 39–73). New York: Hemisphere.

Glenn, S. S., & Field, D. P. (1994). Functions of the environment in behavioral evolution. *The Behavior Analyst, 17*, 241–259.

Glenwick, D., & Jason, L. (1980). *Behavioral community psychology: Progress and prospects*. New York: Praeger.

Goetz, E. M., & Baer, D. M. (1973). Social control of form diversity and the emergence of new forms in children's blockbuilding. *Journal of Applied Behavior Analysis, 6*, 209–217.

Goldin-Meadow, S., & Morford, M. (1985). Gesture in early child language: Studies of deaf and hearing children. *Merrill-Palmer Quarterly, 31*, 145–176.

Goldsmith, T. H. (2006). What birds see. *Scientific American, 295*, 68–75.

Goldsmith, T. H., & Butler, B. K. (2005). Color vision of the budgerigar (*Melopsittacus undulates*): Hue matches, tetrachromacy, and intensity discrimination. *Journal of Comparative Physiology A: Neuroethology, Sensory, Neural, and Behavioral Physiology, 191*, 933–951.

Goldstein, M. H., King, A. P., & West, M. J. (2003). Social interaction shapes babbling: Testing parallels between birdsong and speech. *Proceedings of the National Academy of Sciences, 100*, 8030–8035.

Gollub, L. R. (1958). *The chaining of fixed-interval schedules*. Unpublished doctoral dissertation, Harvard University, Cambridge, MA.

Gollub, L. R. (1977). Conditioned reinforcement: Schedule effects. In W. K. Honig & J. E. R. Staddon (Eds.), *Handbook of operant behavior* (pp. 288–312). Englewood Cliffs, NJ: Prentice-Hall.

Gollub, L. R. (1991) The use of computers in the control and recording of behavior. In I. H. Iverson & K. A. Lattal (Eds.), *Experimental analysis of behavior: Part 2* (pp. 155–192). New York: Elsevier.

Gott, C. T., & Weiss, B. (1972). The development of fixed-ratio performance under the influence of ribonucleic acid. *Journal of the Experimental Analysis of Behavior, 18*, 481–497.

Gould, S. J. (1989). *Wonderful life*. New York: W. W. Norton.

Gould, S. J. (2002). *The structure of evolutionary theory*. Cambridge, MA: Harvard University Press.

Grant, D. S. (1975). Proactive interference in pigeon short-term memory. *Journal of Experimental Psychology: Animal Behavior Processes, 1*, 207–220.

Grant, D. S. (1981). Short-term memory in the pigeon. In N. E. Spear & R. R. Miller (Eds.), *Information processing in animals: Memory mechanisms* (pp. 227–256). Hillsdale, NJ: Lawrence Erlbaum Associates.

Green, D. M., & Swets, J. A. (1966). *Signal detection theory and psychophysics*. New York: John Wiley.

Green, L., & Freed, D. E. (1993). The substitutability of reinforcers. *Journal of the Experimental Analysis of Behavior, 60*, 141–158.

Green, L., Fisher, E. B., Perlow, S., & Sherman, L. (1981). Preference reversal and self control: Choice as a function of reward amount and delay. *Behavior Analysis Letters, 1*, 43–51.

Green, L., Fry, A. F., & Myerson, J. (1994). Discounting of delayed rewards: A life-span comparison. *Psychological Science, 5*, 33–36.

Greene, W. A., & Sutor, L. T. (1971). Stimulus control of skin resistance responses on an escape–avoidance schedule. *Journal of the Experimental Analysis of Behavior, 16*, 269–274.

Guess, D. (1969). A functional analysis of receptive language and productive speech: Acquisition of the plural morpheme. *Journal of Applied Behavior Analysis, 2*, 55–64.

Guess, D., & Baer, D. M. (1973). An analysis of individual differences in generalization between receptive and productive language in retarded children. *Journal of Applied Behavior Analysis, 6*, 311–329.

Guess, D., Helmstetter, E., Turnbull, H. R., & Knowlton, S. (1986). *Use of aversive procedures with persons who are disabled: An historical review and critical analysis* (Monograph No. 2). Seattle, WA: The Association for Persons with Severe Handicaps.

Guess, D., Sailor, W., Rutherford, G., & Baer, D. M. (1968). An experimental analysis of linguistic development: The productive use of the plural morpheme. *Journal of Applied Behavior Analysis, 1*, 297–306.

Gully, K. J., & Dengerink, H. A. (1983). The dyadic interaction of persons with violent and nonviolent histories. *Aggressive Behavior, 7*, 13–20.

Gustafson, R. (1989). Frustration and successful vs. unsuccessful aggression: A test of Berkowitz' completion hypothesis. *Aggressive Behavior, 15*, 5–12.

Guttman, A. (1977). Positive contrast, negative induction, and inhibitory stimulus control in the rat. *Journal of the Experimental Analysis of Behavior, 27*, 219–233.

Guttman, N., & Kalish, H. I. (1956). Discriminability and stimulus generalization. *Journal of Experimental Psychology, 51*, 79–88.

Hackenberg, T. D., & Hineline, P. H. (1987). Remote effects of aversive contingencies: Disruption of appetitive behavior by adjacent avoidance sessions. *Journal of the Experimental Analysis of Behavior, 48*, 161–173.

Hackenberg, T. D., & Joker, V. R. (1994). Instructional versus schedule control of humans' choices in situations of diminishing returns. *Journal of the Experimental Analysis of Behavior, 62*, 367–383.

Hake, D. F., Donaldson, T., & Hyten, C. (1983). Analysis of discriminative control by social behavioral stimuli. *Journal of the Experimental Analysis of Behavior, 39*, 7–23.

Hall, D. C., Adams, C. K., Stein, G. H., Stephenson, H. S., Goldstein, M. K., & Pennypacker, H. S. (1980). Improved detection of human breast lesions following experimental training. *Cancer, 46*, 408–414.

Hall, G., & Sundberg, M. L. (1987). Teaching mands by manipulating conditioned establishing operations. *The Analysis of Verbal Behavior, 5*, 41–53.

Hall, R. V., Cristler, C., Cranston, S. S., & Tucker, B. (1970). Teachers and parents as researchers using multiple baseline designs. *Journal of Applied Behavior Analysis, 3*, 247–255.

Hall, R. V., & Hall, M. C. (1982). *How to negotiate a behavioral contract.* Lawrence, KS: H. & H. Enterprises.

Hanna, E., & Meltzoff, A. N. (1993). Peer imitation by toddlers in laboratory, home and day care contexts: Implications for social learning and memory. *Developmental Psychology, 29*, 701–710.

Hanson, H. M. (1959). Effects of discrimination training on stimulus generalization. *Journal of Experimental Psychology, 58*, 321–334.

Harlow, H. F., & Zimmerman, R. R. (1959). Affectional responses in the infant monkey. *Science, 130*, 421–432.

Harper, D. N., & McLean, A. P. (1992). Resistance to change and the law of effect. *Journal of the Experimental Analysis of Behavior, 57*, 317–337.

Harris, M. (1974). *Cows, pigs, wars, and witches.* New York: Vintage Books.

Harris, M. (1979). *Cultural materialism.* New York: Random House.

Harrison, J. M. (1991). Stimulus control. In I. H. Iversion & K. A. Lattal (Eds.), *Experimental Analysis of Behavior: Part 1* (pp. 251–300). Amsterdam: Elsevier.

Hausmann, F., Arnold, K. E., Marshall, N. J., & Owens, I. P. F. (2003). Ultraviolet signals in birds are special. *Proceedings of the Royal Society B, 270, (1510)*, 61–67.

Hayes, S. C. (1987). A contextual approach to therapeutic change. In N. Jacobson (Ed.), *Psychotherapists in clinical practice: Cognitive and behavioral perspectives* (pp. 329–383). New York: Guilford Press.

Hayes, S. C. (1989a). Nonhumans have not yet shown stimulus equivalence. *Journal of the Experimental Analysis of Behavior, 51*, 385–392.

Hayes, S. C. (1989b). *Rule-governed behavior: Cognition, contingencies, and instructional control.* New York: Plenum Press.

Hayes, S. C. (1991). A relational control theory of stimulus equivalence. In L. J. Hayes & P. N. Chase (Eds.), *Dialogues on verbal behavior* (pp. 19–40). Reno, NV: Context Press.

Hayes, S. C., Barnes-Holmes, D., & Roche, B. (2001). *Relational frame theory: A post-Skinnerian account of human language and cognition.* New York: Plenum Press.

Hayes, S. C., Brownstein, A. J., Haas, J. R., & Greenway, D. E. (1986). Instructions, multiple schedules, and extinction: Distinguishing rule-governed from schedule-controlled behavior. *Journal of the Experimental Analysis of Behavior, 46,* 137–147.

Hayes, S. C., & Ju, W. (1997). The applied implications of rule-governed behavior. In W. T. O'Donohue (Ed.), *Learning and behavior therapy* (pp. 374–391). Needham Heights, MA: Allyn & Bacon.

Hayes, S. C., Rincover, A., & Solnick, J. V. (1980). The technical drift of applied behavior analysis. *Journal of Applied Behavior Analysis, 13,* 275–285.

Hayes, L. A., & Watson, J. S. (1981). Neonatal imitation: Fact or artifact. *Developmental Psychology, 17,* 655–660.

Hearst, E. (1961). Resistance-to-extinction functions in the single organism. *Journal of the Experimental Analysis of Behavior, 4,* 133–144.

Hearst, E., & Jenkins, H. M. (1974). *Sign tracking: The stimulus–reinforcer relation and directed action.* Austin, TX: The Psychonomic Society.

Heath, R. G. (1963). Electrical self-stimulation of the brain in man. *American Journal of Psychiatry, 120,* 571–577.

Heinemann, E. G., & Chase, S. (1970). On the form of stimulus generalization curves for auditory intensity. *Journal of Experimental Psychology, 84,* 483–486.

Hemmes, N. S. (1973). Behavioral contrast in pigeons depends upon the operant. *Journal of Comparative and Physiological Psychology, 85,* 171–178.

Hendry, D. P. (1969). *Conditioned reinforcement.* Homewood, IL: Dorsey Press.

Herbert, J. J., & Harsh, C. M. (1944). Observational learning by cats. *Journal of Comparative Psychology, 37,* 81–95.

Herman, R. L., & Azrin, N. H. (1964). Punishment by noise in an alternative response situation. *Journal of the Experimental Analysis of Behavior, 7,* 185–188.

Hermann, P. M., de Lange, R. P. J., Pieneman, A. W., ter Maat, A., & Jansen, R. F. (1997). Role of neuropeptides encoded on CDCH-1 gene in the organization of egg-laying behavior in the pond snail, *Lymnaea stagnalis. Journal of Neurophysiology, 78,* 2859–2869.

Herrnstein, R. J. (1961a). Stereotypy and intermittent reinforcement. *Science, 133,* 2067–2069.

Herrnstein, R. J. (1961b). Relative and absolute strength of responses as a function of frequency of reinforcement. *Journal of the Experimental Analysis of Behavior, 4,* 267–272.

Herrnstein, R. J. (1964a). Aperiodicity as a factor in choice. *Journal of the Experimental Analysis of Behavior, 7,* 179–182.

Herrnstein, R. J. (1964b). Secondary reinforcement and the rate of primary reinforcement. *Journal of the Experimental Analysis of Behavior, 7,* 27–36.

Herrnstein, R. J. (1970). On the law of effect. *Journal of the Experimental Analysis of Behavior, 13,* 243–266.

Herrnstein, R. J. (1974). Formal properties of the matching law. *Journal of the Experimental Analysis of Behavior, 21,* 159–164.

Herrnstein, R. J. (1979). Acquisition, generalization, and reversal of a natural concept. *Journal of Experimental Psychology: Animal Behavior Processes, 5,* 116–129.

Herrnstein, R. J. (1982). Melioration as behavioral dynamicism. In M. L. Commons, R. J. Herrnstein, & H. Rachlin (Eds.), *Quantitative analyses of behavior: Vol 2. Matching and maximizing accounts of behavior* (pp. 433–458). Cambridge, MA: Ballinger.

Herrnstein, R. J. (1990). Rational choice theory: Necessary but not sufficient. *American Psychologist, 45,* 336–346.

Herrnstein, R. J. (1997). Melioration as behavioral dynamics. In H. Rachlin & D. I. Laibson (Eds.), *The matching law: Papers in psychology and economics by Richard J. Herrnstein* (pp. 74–99). Cambridge, MA: Harvard University Press.

Herrnstein, R. J., & de Villiers, P. A. (1980). Fish as a natural category for people and pigeons. In G. H. Bower (Ed.), *The psychology of learning and motivation* (Vol. 14, pp. 60–95). New York: Academic Press.

Herrnstein, R. J., & Hineline, P. N. (1966). Negative reinforcement as shock frequency reduction. *Journal of the Experimental Analysis of Behavior, 9,* 421–430.

Herrnstein, R. J., & Loveland, D. H. (1964). Complex visual concept in the pigeon. *Science, 146,* 549–551.

Herrnstein, R. J., & Loveland, D. H. (1975). Maximizing and matching on concurrent ratio schedules. *Journal of the Experimental Analysis of Behavior, 24,* 107–116.

Herrnstein, R. J., & Prelec, D. (1997). Melioration: A theory of distributed choice. . In H. Rachlin & D. I.

Laibson (Eds.), *The matching law: Papers in psychology and economics by Richard J. Herrnstein* (pp. 274–292). Cambridge, MA: Harvard University Press.

Herrnstein, R. J., Loveland, D. H., & Cable, C. (1976). Natural concepts in pigeons. *Journal of Experimental Psychology: Animal Behavior Processes, 2*, 285–302.

Heth, C. D. (1976). Simultaneous and backward fear conditioning as a function of number of CS–UCS pairings. *Journal of Experimental Psychology: Animal Behavior Processes, 2*, 117–129.

Heth, C. D., Inglis, P., Russell, J. C., & Pierce, W. D. (2001). Conditioned taste aversion induced by wheel running is not due to novelty of the wheel. *Physiology and Behavior, 74*, 53–56.

Heth, C. D., & Pierce, W. D. (2007). The role of pre-exposure to novel food tastes in activity-based conditioned taste avoidance. *Learning and Motivation, 38*, 35–43.

Higgins, S. T., & Katz, J. L. (1998). *Cocaine abuse: Behavior, pharmacology, and clinical applications.* San Diego, CA: Academic Press.

Higgins, S. T., Bickel, W. K., & Hughes, J. R. (1994). Influence of an alternative reinforcer on human cocaine self-administration. *Life Sciences, 55*, 179–187.

Hilgard, E. R., & Marquis, D. G. (1961). *Conditioning and learning.* New York: Appleton. (Original work published 1940.)

Hinde, R. A., & Stevenson-Hinde, J. (1973). *Constraints on learning: Limitations and predispositions.* New York: Academic Press.

Hineline, P. N. (1970). Negative reinforcement without shock reduction. *Journal of the Experimental Analysis of Behavior, 14*, 259–268.

Hineline, P. N. (1977). Negative reinforcement and avoidance. In W. K. Honig & J. E. R. Staddon (Eds.), *Handbook of operant behavior* (pp. 364–414). Englewood Cliffs, NJ: Prentice-Hall.

Hineline, P. N. (1984). Aversive control: A separate domain? *Journal of the Experimental Analysis of Behavior, 42*, 495–509.

Hineline, P. N. (2001). Beyond the molar–molecular distinction: We need multiscaled analyses. *Journal of the Experimental Analysis of Behavior, 75*, 342–347.

Hinson, R. E., Poulos, C. X., & Cappell, H. (1982). Effects of pentobarbital and cocaine in rats expecting pentobarbital. *Pharmacology, Biochemistry and Behavior, 16*, 661–666.

Hiroto, D. S., & Seligman, M. E. P. (1975). Generality of learned helplessness in man. *Journal of Personality and Social Psychology, 31*, 311–327.

Hirsch, J., & McCauley, L. (1977). Successful replication of, and selective breeding for, classical conditioning in the blowfly (*Phorma regina*). *Animal Behaviour, 25*, 784–785.

Hockett, C. F. (1958). *A course in modern linguistics.* New York: Macmillan.

Hockett, C. F. (1968). *The state of the art.* The Hague: Mouton.

Holland, J. G. (1978). Behaviorism: Part of the problem or part of the solution? *Journal of Applied Behavior Analysis, 11*, 163–174.

Hollerman, J. R., & Schultz, W. (1998). Dopamine neurons report an error in temporal prediction of reward during learning. *Nature Neuroscience , 1*, 304–309.

Horne, P. J., & Erjavec, M. (2007). Do infants show generalized imitation of gestures? *Journal of the Experimental Analysis of Behavior, 87*, 63–88.

Horne, P. J., & Lowe, C. F. (1993). Determinants of human performance on concurrent schedules. *Journal of the Experimental Analysis of Behavior, 59*, 29–60.

Horne, P. J., & Lowe, C. F. (1996) On the origins of naming and other symbolic behavior. *Journal of the Experimental Analysis of Behavior, 65*, 185–242.

Hothersall, D. (1990) *History of psychology.* New York: McGraw-Hill.

Houston, A. (1986). The matching law applies to wagtails' foraging in the wild. *Journal of the Experimental Analysis of Behavior, 45*, 15–18.

Hoyert, M. S. (1992). Order and chaos in fixed-interval schedules of reinforcement. *Journal of the Experimental Analysis of Behavior, 57*, 339–363.

Hull, D. L., Langman, R. E., & Glenn, S. S. (2001). A general account of selection: Biology, immunology, and behavior. *Behavioral and Brain Sciences, 24*, 511–573.

Hung, D. (1980). Training and generalization of "yes" and "no" as mands in two autistic children. *Journal of Autism and Developmental Disorders, 10*, 130–152.

Hunt, H. F., & Brady, J. V. (1955). Some effects of punishment and intercurrent anxiety on a simple operant. *Journal of Comparative and Physiological Psychology, 48*, 305–310.

Hursh, S. R. (1991). Behavioral economics of drug self-administration and drug abuse policy. *Journal of the Experimental Analysis of Behavior, 56*, 377–393.

Hursh, S. R., Navarick, D. J., & Fantino, E. (1974). "Automaintenance": The role of reinforcement. *Journal of the Experimental Analysis of Behavior, 21*, 112–124.

Hutchinson, G. E. (1981). Random adaptation and imitation in human evolution. *American Scientist, 69*, 161–165.

Hutchinson, R. R. (1977). By-products of aversive control. In W. K. Honig & J. E. R. Staddon (Eds.), *Handbook of operant behavior* (pp. 415–431). Englewood Cliffs, NJ: Prentice-Hall.

Hutchinson, R. R., Azrin, N. H., & Hunt, G. M. (1968). Attack produced by intermittent reinforcement of a concurrent operant response. *Journal of the Experimental Analysis of Behavior, 11*, 489–495.

Iacobini, M., Woods, R. P., Brass, M., Bekkering, H., Mazziota, J. C., & Rizzolatti. G. (1999). Cortical mechanisms of human imitation. *Science, 286*, 2526–2528.

Inman, D., & Cheney, C. (1974). Functional variables in fixed ratio pausing with rabbits. *The Psychological Record, 24*, 193–202.

Iriki, A. (2006). The neural origins and implications of imitation, mirror neurons and tool use. *Current Opinion in Neurobiology, 16*, 660–667.

Irwin, O. C. (1948). Infant speech: Development of vowel sounds. *Journal of Speech and Hearing, 13*, 31–34.

Irwin, O. C. (1952). Speech development in the young child: 2. Some factors related to the speech development of the infant and the young child. *Journal of Speech and Hearing, 17*, 209–279.

Ishaq, F. S. (1991). *Human behavior in today's world*. New York: Praeger.

Jackson, K., & Hackenberg, T. D. (1996). Token reinforcement, choice, and self-control in pigeons. *Journal of the Experimental Analysis of Behavior, 66*, 29–49.

Jackson, R. L., Alexander, J. H., & Maier, S. F. (1980). Learned helplessness, inactivity, and associative deficits: Effects of inescapable shock on response choice escape learning. *Journal of Experimental Psychology: Animal Behavior Processes, 6*, 1–20.

Jacobson, S. W. (1979). Matching behavior in the young infant. *Child Development, 50*, 425–430.

James, W. (1890). *Principles of psychology*. New York: Holt, Rinehart & Winston.

Jason, L. A. (1998). Tobacco, drug, and HIV preventive media interventions. *American Journal of Community Psychology, 26*, 151–187.

Jenkins, H. M., Barrera, F. J., Ireland, C., & Woodside, B. (1978). Signal-centered action patterns of dogs in appetitive classical conditioning. *Learning and Motivation, 9*, 272–296.

Jenkins, H. M., & Boakes, R. A. (1973). Observing stimulus sources that signal food or no food. *Journal of the Experimental Analysis of Behavior, 20*, 197–207.

Jenkins, W. O., & Stanley, J. C. (1950). Partial reinforcement: A review and critique. *Psychological Bulletin, 47*, 193–234.

Johnston, J. M., & Pennypacker, H. S. (1993). *Strategies and tactics of human behavioral research*. Hillsdale, NJ: Lawrence Erlbaum Associates.

Johnson, K. R., & Layng, T. V. J. (1994). The Morningside Model of generative instruction. In R. Gardner III, D. M. Sainato, J. O. Cooper, T. E. Heron, W. L. Heward, J. Eshleman, et al. (Eds.), *Behavior analysis in education: Focus on measurably superior instruction* (pp. 173–197). Monterey, CA: Brooks/Cole.

Jolly, A. (1985). *The evolution of primate behavior*. New York: Macmillan.

Jonas, G. (1973). *Visceral learning: Toward a science of self-control*. New York: Viking Press.

Jones, K. M., & Firman, P. C. (1999). A case study of behavioral assessment and treatment of insect phobia. *Journal of Applied Behavior Analysis, 32*, 95–98.

Jones, S. S. (1996) Imitation or exploration? Young infants' matching of adults' oral gestures. *Child Development, 67*, 1952–1969.

Jones, S. S. (2006). Exploration or imitation? The effect of music on 4-week old infant's tongue protrusions. *Infant Behavior and Development, 29*, 126–130.

Juujaevari, P., Kooistra, L., Kaartinen, J., & Pulkkinen, L. (2001) An aggression machine. V: Determinants in reactive aggression revisited. *Aggressive Behavior, 27*, 430–445.

Kaiser, D. H., Zentall, T. R., & Galef, B. G., Jr. (1997). Can imitation in pigeons be explained by local enhancement together with trial-and-error learning? *Psychological Science, 8*, 459–460.

Kamin, L. J. (1969). Predictability, surprise, attention, and conditioning. In B. A. Campbell & R. M. Church (Eds.), *Punishment and aversive behavior* (pp. 279–296). New York: Appleton-Century-Crofts.

Kanarek, R. B., & Collier, G. (1978). Patterns of eating as a function of the cost of the meal. *Physiology and Behavior, 23,* 141–145.

Kattal, K. A., & Doepke, K. J. (2001). Correspondence as conditional stimulus control: Insights from experiments with pigeons. *Journal of Applied Behavior Analysis, 34,* 127–144.

Katz, N. H. (1976). A test of the reinforcing properties of stimuli correlated with nonreinforcement. *Journal of the Experimental Analysis of Behavior, 26,* 45–56.

Kaufman, A., Baron, A., & Kopp, R. E. (1966). Some effects of instructions on human operant behavior. *Psychonomic Monograph Supplements, 11,* 243–250.

Kawai, M. (1965). Newly acquired pre-cultural behavior of the natural troop of Japanese monkeys on Koshima Islet. *Primates, 6,* 1–30.

Kawamura, S. (1959). The process of sub-culture propagation among Japanese macaques. *Primates, 2,* 43–60.

Kazdin, A. E. (1977). *The token economy: A review and evaluation.* New York: Plenum Press.

Kazdin, A. E. (1982). *Single-case research designs: Methods for clinical and applied settings.* New York: Oxford University Press.

Kazdin, A. E. (1983). Failure of persons to respond to the token economy. In E. B. Foa & P. M. G. Emmelkamp (Eds.), *Failures in behavior therapy* (pp. 335–354). New York: John Wiley.

Kazdin, A. E. (1989). *Behavior modification in applied settings.* Belmont, CA: Brooks/Cole.

Kazdin, A. E. (1998). *Methodological issues & strategies in clinical research* (2nd ed.). Washington, DC: American Psychological Association.

Kazdin, A. E., & Klock, J. (1973). The effect of nonverbal teacher approval on student attentive behavior. *Journal of Applied Behavior Analysis, 6,* 643–654.

Keehn, J. D. (1986). *Animal models for psychiatry.* London: Routledge & Kegan Paul.

Keehn, J. D., & Jozsvai, E. (1989). Induced and noninduced patterns of drinking by food-deprived rats. *Bulletin of the Psychonomic Society, 27,* 157–159.

Keith-Lucas, T., & Guttman, N. (1975). Robust single-trial delayed backward conditioning. *Journal of Comparative and Physiological Psychology, 88,* 468–476.

Kelleher, R. T. (1956) Intermittent conditioned reinforcement in chimpanzees. *Science, 124,* 279–280.

Kelleher, R. T. (1958). Fixed-ratio schedules of conditioned reinforcement with chimpanzees. *Journal of the Experimental Analysis of Behavior, 1,* 281–289.

Kelleher, R. T., Fry, W., & Cook, L. (1959). Inter-response time distribution as a function of differential reinforcement of temporally spaced responses. *Journal of the Experimental Analysis of Behavior, 2,* 91–106.

Kelleher, R. T., & Gollub, L. R. (1962). A review of positive conditioned reinforcement. *Journal of the Experimental Analysis of Behavior, 5,* 543–597.

Keller, F. S. (1968). "Good-bye, teacher . . ." *Journal of Applied Behavior Analysis, 1,* 79–89.

Keller, F. S. (1977). *Summers and sabbaticals.* Champaign, IL: Research Press.

Keller, F. S. (1981). Charles Bohris Ferster (1922–1981) an appreciation. *Journal of the Experimental Analysis of Behavior, 36,* 299–301.

Keys, A., Brozek, J., Henschel, A., Mickelsen, O., & Taylor, H. L. (1950). *The biology of human starvation.* Minneapolis: University of Minnesota Press.

Khalili, J., & Cheney, C. D. (1969). Development and maintenance of FR escape with titrated reinforcement. *Psychonomic Science, 15,* 10–11.

Khalili, J., Daley, M. F., & Cheney, C. D. (1969). A titration procedure for generating escape behavior.*Behavior Research Methods and Instrumentation, 6,* 293–294.

Killeen, P. R. (1974). Psychophysical distance functions for hooded rats. *The Psychological Record, 24,* 229–235.

Killeen, P. R. (1975). On the temporal control of behavior. *Psychological Review, 82,* 89–115.

Killeen, P. R. (1985). Incentive theory. IV: Magnitude of reward. *Journal of the Experimental Analysis of Behavior, 43,* 407–417.

Killeen, P. R. (1992). Mechanics of the animate. *Journal of the Experimental Analysis of Behavior, 57,* 429–463.

Killeen, P. R., Wald, B., & Cheney, C. (1980). Observing behavior and information. *The Psychological Record, 30,* 181–190.

Kimmel, E., & Kimmel, H. D. (1963). Replication of operant conditioning of the GSR. *Journal of Experimental Psychology, 65,* 212–213.

Kimmel, H. D. (1974). Instrumental conditioning of autonomically mediated responses in human beings. *American Psychologist, 29,* 325–335.

Kintsch, W. (1965). Frequency distribution of interresponse times during VI and VR reinforcement. *Journal of the Experimental Analysis of Behavior, 8,* 347–352.

Kirby, F. D., & Shields, F. (1972). Modification of arithmetic response rate and attending behavior in a seventh-grade student. *Journal of Applied Behavior Analysis, 5,* 79–84.

Kohler, W. (1927). *The mentality of apes* (2nd rev. ed., E. Winter, Trans.). London: Routledge & Kegan Paul.

Komar, I. (1983). *Living a dream: A documentary study of the Twin Oaks community.* Norwood, PA: Norwood Editions.

Kram, M. L., Kramer, G. L., Ronan, P. J., & Petty, F. (2002). Dopamine receptors and learned helplessness in the rat: An autoradiographic study. *Progress in Neuropsychopharmacology and Biological Psychiatry, 26,* 639–645.

Krebs, J. R., & Davies, N. B. (1978). *Behavioural ecology: An evolutionary approach.* Oxford: Blackwell Scientific Publications.

Kuhl, P. K., & Meltzoff, A. N. (1996). Infant vocalizations in response to speech: Vocal imitation and developmental change. *Journal of the Acoustical Society of America, 100,* 2425–2438.

Kulik, C. C., Kulik, J. A., & Cohen, P. A. (1980). Instructional technology and college teaching. *Teaching of Psychology, 7,* 199–205.

Kunkel, J. H. (1997). The analysis of rule-governed behavior in social psychology. *The Psychological Record, 47,* 698–716.

Kuschel, R. (1973). The silent inventor: The creation of a sign language by the only deaf mute on a Polynesian island. *Sign Language Studies, 3,* 1–28.

Kushner, M. (1970). Faradic aversive control in clinical practice. In C. Neuringer and J. Michael (Eds.), *Behavior modification in clinical psychology* (pp. 26–51). New York: Appleton-Century-Crofts.

Laitman, J. T., & Reidenberg, J. S. (1993). Specializations of the human upper respiratory and upper digestive systems as seen through comparative and developmental anatomy. *Dysphagia, 8,* 318–325.

Lamal, P. A. (1997). *Cultural contingencies: Behavior analytic perspectives on cultural practices.* Westport, CT: Praeger.

Lamal, P. A., & Greenspoon, J. (1992). Congressional metacontingencies. *Behavior and Social Issues, 2,* 71–81.

Lamarre, J., & Holland, J. G. (1985). The functional independence of mands and tacts. *Journal of the Experimental Analysis of Behavior, 43,* 5–19.

Lane, H. (1961). Operant control of vocalizing in the chicken. *Journal of the Experimental Analysis of Behavior, 4,* 171–177.

Langone, J., & Burton, T. A. (1987). Teaching adaptive behavior skills to moderately and severely handicapped individuals: Best practices for facilitating independent living. *Journal of Special Education, 21,* 149–165.

Larkin, M. (2001). Breast self examination does more harm than good, says task force. *Lancet, 357,* 2109.

Latham, G. (1994). *The power of positive parenting.* North Logan, UT: P&T.

Lattal, K. A. (1984). Signal functions in delayed reinforcement. *Journal of the Experimental Analysis of Behavior, 42,* 239–253.

Lattal, K. A., & Doepke, K. J. (2001). Correspondence as conditional stimulus control: Insights from experiments with pigeons. *Journal of Applied Behavior Analysis, 34,* 127–144.

Lattal, K. A., Reilly, M. P., & Kohn, J. P. (1998). Response persistence under ratio and interval reinforcement schedules. *Journal of the Experimental Analysis of Behavior, 70,* 165–183.

Lattal, K. A., & Ziegler, D. R. (1982). Briefly delayed reinforcement: An interresponse time analysis. *Journal of the Experimental Analysis of Behavior, 37,* 407–416.

LaVigna, G. W., & Donnellan, A. W. (1986). *Alternatives to punishment: Solving behavior problems with non-aversive strategies.* New York: Irvington.

Lazar, R. (1977). Extending sequence-class membership with matching to sample. *Journal of the Experimental Analysis of Behavior, 27,* 381–392.

Leaf, R. C. (1965). Acquisition of Sidman avoidance responding as a function of S–S interval. *Journal of Comparative and Physiological Psychology, 59,* 298–300.

Lee, V. L. (1981a). Prepositional phrases spoken and heard. *Journal of the Experimental Analysis of Behavior, 35,* 227–242.

Lee, V. L. (1981b). Terminological and conceptual revision in the experimental analysis of language development: Why? *Behaviorism, 9,* 25–53.

Lerman, D. C., Iwata, B. A., Zarcone, J. R., & Ringdahl, J. (1994). Assessment of stereotypic and self-injurious behavior as adjunctive responses. *Journal of Applied Behavior Analysis, 27,* 715–728.

Lett, B. T., & Grant, V. L. (1996). Wheel running induces conditioned taste aversion in rats trained while hungry and thirsty. *Physiology and Behavior, 59*, 699–702.

Lewis, P., Gardner, E. T., & Hutton, L. (1976). Integrated delays to shock as negative reinforcement. *Journal of the Experimental Analysis of Behavior, 26*, 379–386.

Lieberman, D. A., Cathro, J. S., Nichol, K., & Watson, E. (1997). The role of S– in human observing behavior: Bad news is sometimes better than no news. *Learning and Motivation, 28*, 20–42.

Lieberman, P., Laitman, J. T., Reidenberg, J. S., & Gannon, P. J. (1991). The anatomy, physiology, acoustic and perception of speech: Essential elements in analysis of the evolution of human speech. *Journal of Human Evolution, 23*, 447–467.

Lindsley, O. R. (1972). From Skinner to precision teaching: The child knows best. In J. B. Jordan & L. S. Robbins (Eds.), *Let's try something else kind of thing: Behavioral principles of the exceptional child* (pp. 1–11). Arlington, VA: The Council for Exceptional Children.

Lindsley, O. R. (1990a). Our aims, discoveries, failures, and problem. *Journal of Precision Teaching, 7*, 7–17.

Lindsley, O. R. (1990b). Precision teaching: By teachers for children. *Teaching Exceptional Children, 22*, 10–15.

Lindsley, O. R. (1991). Precision teaching's unique legacy from B. F. Skinner. *Journal of Behavioral Education, 1*, 253–266.

Linscheid, T. R., & Meinhold, P. (1990). The controversy over aversives: Basic operant research and the side effects of punishment. In A. C. Repp & N. N. Singh (Eds.), *Perspectives on the use of nonaversive and aversive interventions for persons with developmental disabilities* (pp. 434–450). Sycamore, IL: Sycamore Publishing Co.

Lippman, L. G., & Meyer, M. E. (1967). Fixed-interval performance as related to instructions and to the subject's vocalizations of the contingency. *Psychonomic Science, 8*, 135–136.

Lloyd, K. E. (1985). Behavioral anthropology: A review of Marvin Harris' *Cultural materialism. Journal of the Experimental Analysis of Behavior, 43*, 279–287.

Lloyd, K. E., & Lloyd, M. E. (1992). Behavior analysis and technology in higher education. In R. P. West & L. A. Hamerlynck (Eds.) *Designs for excellence in education: The legacy of B. F. Skinner* (pp. 147–160). Longmont, CO: Sopris West, Inc.

Logue, A. W. (1979). Taste aversion and the generality of the laws of learning. *Psychological Bulletin, 86*, 276–296.

Logue, A. W. (1985). Conditioned food aversion learning in humans. In N. S. Braveman & P. Bronstein (Eds.), *Experimental assessments and clinical applications of conditioned food aversions* (pp. 316–329). New York: New York Academy of Sciences.

Logue, A. W. (1988a). A comparison of taste aversion learning in humans and other vertebrates: Evolutionary pressures in common. In R. C. Bolles & M. D. Beecher (Eds.), *Evolution and learning* (pp. 97–116). Hillsdale, NJ: Lawrence Erlbaum Associates.

Logue, A. W. (1988b). Research on self-control: An integrating framework. *Behavioral and Brain Sciences, 11*, 665–709.

Logue, A. W. (1998). Laboratory research on self-control: Applications to administration. *Review of General Psychology, 2*, 221–238.

Logue, A. W., Pena-Correal, T. E., Rodriguez, M. L., & Kabela, E. (1986). Self-control in adult humans: Variation in positive reinforcer amount and delay. *Journal of the Experimental Analysis of Behavior, 46*, 159–173.

Lohrman-O'Rourke, S., & Zirkel, P. A. (1998). The case law on aversive interventions for students with disabilities. *Exceptional Children, 65*, 101–123.

Lovaas, O. I. (1961). Interaction between verbal and nonverbal behavior. *Child Development, 32*, 329–336.

Lovaas, O. I. (1966). A program for the establishment of speech in psychotic children. In J. K. Wing (Ed.), *Early childhood autism* (pp. 115–144). Elmsford, NY: Pergamon Press.

Lovaas, O. I. (1977). *The autistic child: Language development through behavior modification.* New York: Irvington.

Lovaas, O. I. (1987). Behavioral treatment and normal educational and intellectual functioning in young autistic children. *Journal of Consulting and Clinical Psychology, 55*, 3–9.

Lovaas, O. I. (1993). The development of a treatment-research project for developmentally disabled and autistic children. *Journal of Applied Behavior Analysis, 26*, 617–630.

Lovaas, O. I., & Simmons, J. Q. (1969). Manipulation of self-destruction in three retarded children. *Journal of Applied Behavior Analysis, 2*, 143–157.

Lowe, F. C. (1979). Determinants of human operant behavior. In M. D. Zeiler & P. Harzem (Eds.), *Reinforcement and the organization of behaviour* (pp. 159–192). New York: John Wiley.

Lowe, F. C., Beasty, A., & Bentall, R. P. (1983). The role of verbal behavior in human learning: Infant performance on fixed-interval schedules. *Journal of the Experimental Analysis of Behavior, 39,* 157–164.

Lowenkron, B. (1998). Some logical functions of joint control. *Journal of the Experimental Analysis of Behavior, 69,* 327–354.

Lowenkron, B. (1999). Joint control of rule following: An analysis of purpose. *Annual Meeting of the Association for Behavior Analysis,* May, Chicago.

Lowitz, G. H., & Suib, M. R. (1978). Generalized control of persistent thumbsucking by differential reinforcement of other behaviors. *Journal of Behavior Therapy and Experimental Psychiatry, 9,* 343–346.

Lubinski, D., & MacCorquodale, K. (1984). "Symbolic communication" between two pigeons (*Columba livia*) without unconditioned reinforcement. *Journal of Comparative Psychology, 98,* 372–380.

Lubinski, D., & Thompson, T. (1987). An animal model of the interpersonal communication of introceptive (private) states. *Journal of the Experimental Analysis of Behavior, 48,* 1–15.

Lubinski, D., & Thompson, T. (1993). Species and individual differences in communication based on private states. *Behavioral and Brain Science, 16,* 627–680.

Lubow, R. E. (1974). High-order concept formation in the pigeon. *Journal of the Experimental Analysis of Behavior, 21,* 475–483.

Lucas, G. A., Deich, J. D., & Wasserman, E. A. (1981). Trace autoshaping: Acquisition, maintenance, and path dependence at long trace intervals. *Journal of the Experimental Analysis of Behavior, 36,* 61–74.

Lucas, K. E., Marr, M. J., & Maple, T. L. (1998). Teaching operant conditioning at the zoo. *Teaching of Psychology, 25,* 112–116.

Luciano, M. C. (1986). Acquisition, maintenance, and generalization of productive intraverbal behavior through transfer of stimulus control procedures. *Applied Research in Mental Retardation, 7,* 1–20.

Luciano, M. C. (2000). Applications of research on rule-governed behavior. In J. C. Leslie & D. Blackman (Eds.), *Experimental and applied analysis of human behavior* (pp. 181–204). Reno, NV: Context Press.

Luciano, M. C., Herruzo, J., & Barnes-Holmes, D. (2001). Generalization of say–do correspondence. *Psychological Record, 51,* 111–130.

Luiselli, J. K., Ricciardi, J. N., & Gilligan, K. (2005). Liquid fading to establish milk consumption by a child with autism. *Behavioral Interventions, 20,* 155–163.

MacCorquodale, K. (1970). On Chomsky's review of Skinner's *Verbal behavior. Journal of the Experimental Analysis of Behavior, 13,* 83–99.

Mace, F. C. (1996). In pursuit of general behavioral relations. *Journal of Applied Behavior Analysis, 29,* 557–563.

Mace, F. C., Neef, N. A., Shade, D., & Mauro, B. C. (1994). Limited matching on concurrent schedule reinforcement of academic behavior. *Journal of Applied Behavior Analysis, 27,* 585–596.

Machado, A. (1989). Operant conditioning of behavioral variability using a percentile reinforcement schedule. *Journal of the Experimental Analysis of Behavior, 52,* 155–166.

Machado, A. (1992). Behavioral variability and frequency dependent selection. *Journal of the Experimental Analysis of Behavior, 58,* 241–263.

Machado, A. (1997). Increasing the variability of response sequences in pigeons by adjusting the frequency of switching between two keys. *Journal of the Experimental Analysis of Behavior, 68,* 1–25

Macphail, E. M. (1968). Avoidance responding in pigeons. *Journal of the Experimental Analysis of Behavior, 11,* 629–632.

Madden, G. J., Peden, B. F., & Yamaguchi, T. (2002). Human group choice: Discrete-trial and free-operant tests of the ideal free distribution. *Journal of the Experimental Analysis of Behavior, 78,* 1–15.

Maier, S. F. (1970). Failure to escape traumatic electric shock: Incompatible skeletal-motor responses or learned helplessness. *Learning and Motivation, 1,* 157–169.

Maier, S. F., Albin, R. W., & Testa, T. J. (1973). Failure to learn to escape in rats previously exposed to inescapable shock depends on nature of the escape response. *Journal of Comparative and Physiological Psychology, 85,* 581–592.

Maier, S. F., & Seligman, M. E. P. (1976). Learned helplessness: Theory and evidence. *Journal of Experimental Psychology: General, 105,* 3–46.

Maier, S. F., Seligman, M. E. P., & Solomon, R. L. (1969). Pavlovian fear conditioning and learned helplessness. In B. A. Campbell & R. M. Church (Eds.), *Punishment and aversive behavior* (pp. 299–342). New York: Appleton-Century-Crofts.

Maki, W. S., & Hegvik, D. K. (1980). Directed forgetting in pigeons. *Animal Learning and Behavior, 8*, 567–574.

Malott, R. W. (1988). Rule-governed behavior and behavioral anthropology. *The Behavior Analyst, 11*, 181–203.

Mandrusiak, M. (2002). *Activity anorexia induced by increased procurement cost of meals and opportunity for physical activity*. Honors thesis submitted to the Faculty of Science, Department of Psychology, University of Alberta.

Markowitz, H., Schmidt, M., Nadal, L., & Squier, L. (1975). Do elephants ever forget? *Journal of Applied Behavior Analysis, 8*, 333–335.

Marr, J. M. (1992). Behavior dynamics: One perspective. *Journal of the Experimental Analysis of Behavior, 57*, 249–266.

Marsh, G., & Johnson, R. (1968). Discrimination reversal learning without "errors." *Psychonomic Science, 10*, 261–262.

Martens, B. K., Lochner, D. G., & Kelly, S. Q. (1992). The effects of variable-interval reinforcement on academic engagement: A demonstration of matching theory. *Journal of Applied Behavior Analysis, 25*, 143–151.

Martin, D. G. (1991). *Psychology: Principles and applications*. Scarborough, Ontario: Prentice-Hall.

Martin, G., & Hrycaiko, D. (1983). *Behavior modification and coaching: Principles, procedures and research*. Springfield, IL: Charles C. Thomas

Martin, G., & Pear, J. (2006). *Behavior modification: What is it and how to do it*. Upper Saddle River, NJ: Prentice-Hall.

Martin, T. L., Pear, J. J., & Martin, G. L. (2002). Feedback and its effectiveness in a computer-aided personalized system of instruction course. *Journal of Applied Behavior Analysis, 35*, 427–430.

Masserman, J. H. (1946). *Principles of dynamic psychiatry*. Philadelphia, PA: Saunders.

Matson, J. L., & Taras, M. E. (1989). A 20 year review of punishment and alternative methods to treat problem behaviors in developmentally disabled persons. *Research in Developmental Disabilities, 10*, 85–104.

Matthews, B. A., Shimoff, E., & Catania, A. C. (1987). Saying and doing: A contingency-space analysis. *Journal of Applied Behavior Analysis, 20*, 69–74.

Matthews, L. R., & Temple, W. (1979). Concurrent schedule assessment of food preference in cows. *Journal of the Experimental Analysis of Behavior, 32*, 245–254.

Maurice, C. (1993). *Let me hear your voice*. New York: Knopf.

Maurice, C., Green, G., & Luce, S. C. (1996). *Behavioral intervention for young children with autism—A manual for parents and professionals*. Sarasota, FL: Pro-Ed.

May, J. G., & Dorr, D. (1968). Imitative pecking in chicks as a function of early social experience. *Psychonomic Science, 11*, 109–129.

Mazur, J. E. (1983). Steady-state performance on fixed-, mixed-, and random-ratio schedules. *Journal of the Experimental Analysis of Behavior, 39*, 293–307.

Mazur, J. E. (1990). *Learning and behavior*. Englewood Cliffs, NJ: Prentice-Hall.

McDonald, J. S. (1988). Concurrent variable-ratio schedules: Implications for the generalized matching law. *Journal of the Experimental Analysis of Behavior, 50*, 55–64.

McDougall, W. (1908). *An introduction to social psychology*. London: Methuen.

McDowell, J. J. (1981). On the validity and utility of Herrnstein's hyperbola in applied behavior analysis. In C. M. Bradshaw, E. Szabadi, & C. F. Lowe (Eds.), *Quantification of steady-state operant behaviour* (pp. 311–324). Amsterdam: Elsevier/North-Holland.

McDowell, J. J. (1982). The importance of Herrnstein's mathematical statement of the law of effect for behavior therapy. *American Psychologist, 37*, 771–779.

McDowell, J. J. (1988). Matching theory in natural human environments. *The Behavior Analyst, 11*, 95–109.

McDowell, J. J., Bass, R., & Kessel, R. (1992). Applying linear systems analysis to dynamic behavior. *Journal of the Experimental Analysis of Behavior, 57*, 377–391.

McEachin, J. J., Smith, T., & Lovaas, I. O. (1993). Long-term outcome for children with autism who received early intensive behavioral treatment. *American Journal on Mental Retardation, 97*, 359–372.

McGinnis, J. C., Firman, P. C., & Carlyon, W. D. (1999). The effect of token rewards on "intrinsic" motivation for doing math. *Journal of Applied Behavior Analysis, 32*, 375–379.

McIntire, K. D., Cleary, J., & Thompson, T. (1987). Conditional relations by monkeys: Reflexivity, symmetry, and transitivity. *Journal of the Experimental Analysis of Behavior, 47*, 279–285.

McLean, A., & Blampied, N. (1995). Resistance to reinforcement change in multiple and concurrent schedules assessed in transition and at steady state. *Journal of the Experimental Analysis of Behavior, 63*, 1–17.

McSweeney, F. K., Ettinger, R. A., & Norman, W. D. (1981). Three versions of the additive theories of behavioral contrast. *Journal of the Experimental Analysis of Behavior, 36,* 285–297.

McSweeney, F. K., Melville, C. L., & Higa, J. (1988). Positive behavioral contrast across food and alcohol reinforcers. *Journal of the Experimental Analysis of Behavior, 50,* 469–481.

McSweeney, F. K., Murphy, E. S., & Kowal, B. P. (2003). Dishabituation with component transitions may contribute to the interactions observed during multiple schedules. *Behavioral Processes, 64,* 77–89.

McSweeney, F. K., & Weatherly, J. N. (1998). Habituation to the reinforcer may contribute to multiple-schedule behavioral contrast. *Journal of the Experimental Analysis of Behavior, 69,* 199–221.

Mechner, F. (1959). A notation system for the description of behavioral procedures. *Journal of the Experimental Analysis of Behavior, 2,* 133–150.

Meissner, M., & Philpott, S. B. (1975). The sign language of sawmill workers in British Columbia. *Sign Language Studies, 9,* 291–308.

Mellitz, M., Hineline, P. N., Whitehouse, W. G., & Laurence, M. T. (1983). Duration reduction of avoidance sessions as negative reinforcement. *Journal of the Experimental Analysis of Behavior, 40,* 57–67.

Meltzoff, A. N. (1988a). Imitation of televised models by infants. *Child Development, 59,* 1221–1229.

Meltzoff, A. N. (1988b). Infant imitation after a 1-week delay: Long-term memory for novel acts and multiple stimuli. *Developmental Psychology, 24,* 470–476.

Meltzoff, A. N. (1988c). Infant imitation and memory: Nine-month-olds in immediate and deferred tests. *Child Development, 59,* 217–225.

Meltzoff, A. N. (1999). Born to learn: What infants learn from watching us. In N. Fox & J. G. Worhol (Eds.), *The role of early experience in infant development* (pp. 1–10). Skillman, NJ: Pediatric Institute Publications.

Meltzoff, A. N., & Moore, M. K. (1977). Imitation of facial and manual gestures by human neonates. *Science, 198,* 75–78.

Meltzoff, A. N., & Moore, M. K. (1983). Newborn infants imitate adult facial gestures. *Child Development, 54,* 702–709.

Meltzoff, A. N., & Moore, M. K. (1999). Resolving the debate about early imitation. In A. Slater & D. Muir (Eds.), *Reader in developmental psychology* (pp. 151–155). Oxford: Blackwell Science.

Mendelson, J., & Chillag, D. (1970). Schedule-induced air licking in rats. *Physiology and Behavior, 5,* 535–537.

Meyer, D. R., Cho, C., & Wesemann, A. F. (1960). On problems of conditioning discriminated lever-press avoidance responses. *Psychological Review, 67,* 224–228.

Meyer, L. H., & Evans, I. M. (1989). *Non-aversive intervention for behavior problems: A manual for home and community.* Baltimore, MD: Paul H. Brookes.

Michael, J. L. (1975). Positive and negative reinforcement, a distinction that is no longer necessary: Or a better way to talk about bad things. *Behaviorism, 3,* 33–44.

Michael, J. L. (1980). Flight from behavior analysis. *The Behavior Analyst, 3,* 1–24.

Michael, J. L. (1982a). Distinguishing between discriminative and motivational functions of stimuli. *Journal of the Experimental Analysis of Behavior, 37,* 149–155.

Michael, J. L. (1982b). Skinner's elementary verbal relations: Some new categories. *The Analysis of Verbal Behavior, 1,* 1–3.

Michael, J. L. (1984). Behavior analysis: A radical perspective. In B. L. Hammonds & C. J. Scheirer (Eds.), *Master lecture series: Psychology of learning* (Vol. 4, pp. 99–121). Washington, DC: American Psychological Association.

Michael, J. L. (1988). Establishing operations and the mand. *The Analysis of Verbal Behavior, 6,* 3–9.

Michael, J. L. (1993). Establishing operations. *The Behavior Analyst, 16,* 191–206.

Michael, J. L. (2000). Implications and refinements of the establishing operation concept. *Journal of Applied Behavior Analysis, 33,* 401–410.

Michael, J. L., Whitley, P., & Hesse, B. E. (1983). The pigeon parlance project. *The Analysis of Verbal Behavior, 1,* 6–9.

Milgram, S. (1974). *Obedience to authority.* New York: Harper & Row.

Millard, W. J. (1979). Stimulus properties of conspecific behavior. *Journal of the Experimental Analysis of Behavior, 32,* 283–296.

Millenson, J. R. (1967). *Principles of behavioral analysis.* New York: Macmillan.

Miller, H. L., & Loveland, D. H. (1974). Matching when the number of response alternatives is large. *Animal Learning and Behavior, 26,* 106–110.

Miller, N. E. (1951). Learnable drives and rewards. In S. S. Stevens (Ed.), *Handbook of experimental psychology* (pp. 435–472). New York: John Wiley.

Miller, N. E. (1960). Learning resistance to pain and fear effects overlearning, exposure, and rewarded exposure in context. *Journal of Experimental Psychology, 60*, 137–145.

Miller, N. E. (1969). Learning of visceral and glandular responses. *Science, 163*, 434–445.

Miller, N. E., & Banuazizi, A. (1968). Instrumental learning by curarized rats of a specific visceral response, intestinal or cardiac. *Journal of Comparative and Physiological Psychology, 65*, 1–7.

Miller, N. E., & Carmona, A. (1967). Modification of a visceral response, salivation in thirsty dogs, by instrumental training with water reward. *Journal of Comparative and Physiological Psychology, 63*, 1–6.

Miller, N. E., & DiCara, L. (1967). Instrumental learning of heart rate changes in curarized rats: Shaping and specificity to discriminative stimulus. *Journal of Comparative and Physiological Psychology, 63*, 12–19.

Miller, N. E., & Dollard, J. (1941). *Social learning and imitation*. New Haven, CT: Yale University Press.

Miller, N. E., & Dworkin, B. R. (1974). Visceral learning: Recent difficulties with curarized rats and significant problems for human research. In P. A. Obrist, A. H. Black, J. Brener, & L. V. DiCara (Eds.), *Cardiovascular psychophysiology: Current issues in response mechanisms, biofeedback and methodology* (pp. 295–331). Chicago, IL: Aldine.

Miltenberger, R. G., Gatheridge, B. J., Satterlund, M., Egemo-Helm, K. R., Johnson, B. M., Jostad, C., et al. (2005) Teaching safety skills to children to prevent gun play: An evaluation of in situ training. *Journal of Applied Behavior Analysis, 38*, 395–398.

Misanin, J. R., Goodhart, M. G., Anderson, M. J., & Hinderliter, C. F. (2002). The interaction of age and unconditioned stimulus intensity on long-trace conditioned flavor aversion in rats. *Developmental Psychobiology, 40*, 131–137.

Mitchell, C. J., Heyes, C. M., Gardner, M. R., & Dawson, G. R. (1999). Limitations of a bidirectional control procedure for the investigation of imitation in rats: Odor cues on the manipulandum *Quarterly Journal of Experimental Psychology. B, Comparative & Physiological Psychology, 52B*, 193–202.

Mitchell, D., Kirschbaum, E. H., & Perry, R. L. (1975). Effects of neophobia and habituation on the poison-induced avoidance of extroceptive stimuli in the rat. *Journal of Experimental Psychology: Animal Behavior Processes, 104*, 47–55.

Modaresi, H. A. (1990). The avoidance barpress problem: Effects of enhanced reinforcement and an SSDR-congruent lever. *Learning and Motivation, 21*, 199–220.

Moerk, E. L. (1990). Three-term contingency patterns in mother–child verbal interactions during first-language acquisition. *Journal of the Experimental Analysis of Behavior, 54*, 293–305.

Moerk, E. L. (2000). *The guided acquisition of first language skills*. Stamford, CT: Ablex Publishing.

Moore, B. R. (1992). Avian movement imitation and a new form of mimicry: Tracing the evolution of a complex form of learning. *Behaviour, 122*, 231–263.

Moore, J. (2003). Some further thoughts on the pragmatic and behavioral conception of private events. *Behavior and Philosophy, 31*, 151–157.

Moran, D. J., & Malott, R. W. (2004). *Evidence-based educational methods*. San Diego, CA: Elsevier Academic Press.

Morgan, C. L. (1894). *An introduction to comparative psychology*. London: W. Scott.

Morgan, L., & Neuringer, A. (1990). Behavioral variability as a function of response topography and reinforcement contingency. *Animal Learning and Behavior, 18*, 257–263.

Morris, E. K. (1988). Contexualism: The world view of behavior analysis. *Journal of Experimental Child Psychology, 46*, 289–323.

Morris, E. K. (1992). The aim, progress, and evolution of behavior analysis. *The Behavior Analyst, 15*, 3–29.

Morrow, J. E., Terzich, B. J., & Williamson, P. N. (2002). Behavior analytic treatment of autism in a private school. Invited address, *The Ohio State University's Third Focus on Behavior Analysis in Education Conference*, September, 2002.

Morse, W. H. (1966). Intermittent reinforcement. In W. K. Honig (Ed.), *Operant behavior: Areas of research and application* (pp. 52–108). New York: Appleton-Century-Crofts.

Moseley, J. B., O'Malley, K., Petersen, N. J., Menke, T. J., Brody, B. A., Kuykendall, D. H., et al. (2002). A controlled trial of arthroscopic surgery for osteoarthritis of the knee. *New England Journal of Medicine, 347*, 81–88.

Mueller, K. L., & Dinsmoor, J. A. (1986). The effect of negative stimulus presentations on observing-response rates. *Journal of the Experimental Analysis of Behavior, 46*, 281–291.

Muller, P. G., Crow, R. E., & Cheney, C. D. (1979). Schedule-induced locomotor activity in humans. *Journal of the Experimental Analysis of Behavior*, *31*, 83–90.

Myers, D. L., & Myers, L. E. (1977). Undermatching: A reappraisal of performance on concurrent variable-interval schedules of reinforcement. *Journal of the Experimental Analysis of Behavior*, *25*, 203–214.

Myers, J. L. (1958). Secondary reinforcements: A review of recent experimentation. *Psychological Bulletin*, *55*, 284–301.

Myers, R. D., & Mesker, D. C. (1960). Operant conditioning in a horse under several schedules of reinforcement. *Journal of the Experimental Analysis of Behavior*, *3*, 161–164.

Myerson, J., & Hale, S. (1984). Practical implications of the matching law. *Journal of Applied Behavior Analysis*, *17*, 367–380.

Nader, M. A., & Woolverton, W. L. (1992). Effects of increasing response requirement on choice between cocaine and food in rhesus monkeys. *Psychopharmacology*, *108*, 295–300.

Nagy, E., Compagne, H., Orvos, H., Pal, A., Molnar, P., Janszky, I., et al. (2005). Index finger movement imitation by human neonates: Motivation, learning and left-hand preference. *Pediatric Research*, *58*, 749–753.

Nakajima, S., Hayashi, H., & Kato, T. (2000). Taste aversion induced by confinement in a running wheel. *Behavioral Processes*, *49*, 35–42.

Naqvi, N., Rudrauf, D., Damasio, H., & Bechara, A. (2007). Damage to the insula disrupts addiction to cigarette smoking. *Science*, *315*, 531–534.

Neal, D. T., Wood, W., & Quinn, J. M. (2006). Habits—A repeat performance. *Current Directions in Psychological Science*, *15*, 198–202.

Neuringer, A. J. (1986). Can people behave "randomly?": The role of feedback. *Journal of Experimental Psychology: General*, *115*, 62–75.

Neuringer, A. J. (2002). Operant variability: Evidence, function, and theory. *Psychonomic Bulletin and Review*, *9*, 672–705.

Neuringer, A. J. (2004). Reinforced variability in animals and people. *American Psychologist*, *59*, 891–906.

Nevin, J. A., (1974). Response strength in multiple schedules. *Journal of the Experimental Analysis of Behavior*, *21*, 389–408.

Nevin, J. A. (1988a). Behavioral momentum and the partial reinforcement effect. *Psychological Bulletin*, *103*, 44–56.

Nevin, J. A. (1988b). The momentum of warmaking. *Behavior Analysis and Social Action*, *2*, 46–50.

Nevin, J. A. (1992). An integrative model for the study of behavioral momentum. *Journal of the Experimental Analysis of Behavior*, *57*, 301–316.

Nevin, J. A., & Grace, R. C. (2000). Behavior momentum and the law of effect. *Behavioral and Brain Sciences*, *23*, 73–130.

Nonacs, P. (2001). State-dependent behavior and the marginal value theorem. *Behavioral Ecology*, *12*, 71–83.

Norman, W. D., & McSweeney, F. K. (1978). Matching, contrast, and equalizing in the concurrent lever-press responding of rats. *Journal of the Experimental Analysis of Behavior*, *29*, 453–462.

Norton, W. (1997). Human geography and behavior analysis: An application of behavior analysis to the explanation of the evolution of human landscapes. *Psychological Record*, *47*, 439–460.

Norton, W. (2001). Following rules in the intermontaine West: 19th-century Mormon settlement. *The Behavior Analyst*, *24*, 57–73.

Notterman, J. M. (1959). Force emission during bar pressing. *Journal of Experimental Psychology*, *58*, 341–347.

Nurnberger, J. I., Ferster, C. B., & Brady, J. P. (1963). *An introduction to the science of human behavior.* New York: Appleton-Century-Crofts.

Oah, S., & Dickinson, A. M. (1989). A review of empirical studies of verbal behavior. *The Analysis of Verbal Behavior*, *7*, 53–68.

Oberman, L. M., Hubbard, E. M., McCleery, J. P., Altschuler, E. L., Ramachandran, V. S., & Pineda, J. A. (2005). EEG evidence for mirror neuron dysfunction in autism spectrum disorders. *Cognitive Brain Research*, *24*, 190–198.

Oberman, L. M., & Ramachandran, V. S. (2007). The stimulating social mind: The role of the mirror neuron system and simulation in the social and communicative deficits of autism spectrum disorders. *Psychological Bulletin*, *133*, 310–327.

O'Brien, R. M., & Simek, T. C. (1983). A comparison of behavioral and traditional methods for teaching golf. In G. L. Martin & D. Harycaiko (Eds.), *Behavior modification and coaching: Principles, procedures and research* (pp. 175–183). Springfield, IL: Charles C. Thomas.

Odum, A. L., Ward, R. D., Barnes, C. A., & Burke, K. A. (2006). The effects of delayed reinforcement on variability and repetition of response sequences. *Journal of the Experimental Analysis of Behavior, 86, 159–179.*

O'Kelly, L. E., & Steckle, L. C. (1939). A note on long enduring emotional responses in rats. *Journal of Psychology, 8,* 125–131.

Olds, J., & Milner, P. (1954). Positive reinforcement produced by electrical stimulation of the septal area and other regions of the rat brain. *Journal of Comparative and Physiological Psychology, 47,* 419–428.

O'Leary, M. R., & Dengerink, H. A. (1973). Aggression as a function of the intensity and pattern of attack. *Journal of Experimental Research in Personality, 7,* 61–70.

Orlando, R., & Bijou, S. W. (1960). Single and multiple schedules of reinforcement in developmentally retarded children. *Journal of the Experimental Analysis of Behavior, 3,* 339–348.

Orne, M. T., & Evans, F. J. (1965). Social control in the psychology experiment: Antisocial behavior and hypnosis. *Journal of Personality and Social Psychology, 1,* 189–200.

Osborne, J. G. (2002). Response-contingent water misting. *Encyclopedia of Psychotherapy, 2,* 553–560.

Osgood, C. E. (1953). *Method and theory in experimental psychology.* New York: Oxford University Press.

Overmier, J. B., & Seligman, M. E. P. (1967). Effects of inescapable shock upon subsequent escape and avoidance responding. *Journal of Comparative and Physiological Psychology, 63,* 28–33.

Page, S., & Neuringer, A. J. (1985). Variability as an operant. *Journal of Experimental Psychology: Animal Behavior Processes, 11,* 429–452.

Palmer, D. C. (1991). A behavioral interpretation of memory. In L. J. Hayes & P. N. Chase (Eds.), *Dialogues on verbal behavior* (pp. 261–279). Reno, NV: Context Press.

Palya, W. L. (1992). Dynamics in the fine structure of schedule-controlled behavior. *Journal of the Experimental Analysis of Behavior, 57,* 267–287.

Paniagua, F. A. (1989) Lying by children: Why children say one thing, do another? *Psychological Reports, 64,* 971–984.

Paniagua, F. A., & Baer, D. M. (1982). The analysis of correspondence as a chain reinforceable at any point. *Child Development, 53,* 786–798.

Papachristos, E. B., & Gallistel, C. R. (2006). Autoshaped head poking in the mouse: A quantitative analysis of the learning curve. *Journal of the Experimental Analysis of Behavior, 85,* 293–308.

Papini, M. R., & Bitterman, M. E. (1990). The role of contingency in classical conditioning. *Psychological Review, 97,* 396–403.

Park, R. D. (2002). Punishment revisited—science, values, and the right question: Comment on Gershoff (2002). *Psychological Bulletin, 128,* 596–601.

Parker, L. A. (2003). Taste avoidance and taste aversion: Evidence for two different processes. *Learning and Behavior, 31,* 165–172.

Parkinson, J. A., Crofts, H. S., McGuigan, M., Tomic, D. L., Everitt, B. J., & Roberts. A. C. (2001). The role of the primate amygdale in conditioned reinforcement. *Journal of Neuroscience, 21,* 7770–7780.

Parrott, L. J. (1987). Rule-governed behavior: An implicit analysis of reference. In S. Modgil & C. Modgil (Eds.), *B. F. Skinner: Consensus and controversy* (pp. 265–276). New York: Falmer Press.

Partington, J. W., & Bailey, J. S. (1993). Teaching intraverbal behavior to preschool children. *Analysis of Verbal Behavior, 11,* 9–18.

Partington, J. W., Sundberg, M. L., Newhouse, L., & Spengler, S. M. (1994). Overcoming an autistic child's failure to acquire a tact repertoire. *Journal of Applied Behavior Analysis, 27,* 733–734.

Patterson, G. R. (1976) The aggressive child: Victim and architect of a coercive system. In E. J. Mash, L. A. Hamerlynck, & L. H. Hendy (Eds.), *Behavior modification and families* (pp. 269–316). New York: Brunner/ Mazel.

Patterson, G. R. (1982). *Coercive family processes.* Eugene, OR: Castalia.

Patterson, G. R. (2002). Etiology and treatment of child and adolescent antisocial behavior. *The Behavior Analyst Today, 3,* 133–144.

Paul, G. L. (2006). Myth and reality in Wakefield's assertions regarding Paul and Lentz (1977). *Behavior and Social Issues, 15,* 244–252.

Pauley, P. J. (1987). *Controlling life: Jacques Loeb & the engineering ideal in biology*. New York: Oxford University Press.

Pavlov, I. P. (1960). *Conditioned reflexes. An investigation of the physiological activity of the cerebral cortex* (G. V. Anrep, Trans.). New York: Dover. (Original work published 1927.)

Pear, J. J. (1985). Spatiotemporal patterns of behavior produced by variable-interval schedules of reinforcement. *Journal of the Experimental Analysis of Behavior, 44*, 217–231.

Pear, J. J. (2001). *The science of learning*. Philadelphia, PA: Psychology Press.

Pear, J. J., & Crone-Todd, D. E. (1999). Personalized system of instruction in cyberspace. *Journal of Applied Behavior Analysis, 32*, 205–209.

Pear, J. J., & Wilkie, D. M. (1971). Contrast and induction in rats on multiple schedules. *Journal of the Experimental Analysis of Behavior, 15*, 289–296.

Pedersen, W. C., Gonzales, C., & Miller, N. (2000). The moderating effect of trivial triggering provocation on displaced aggression. *Journal of Personality & Social Psychology, 78*, 913–927.

Pennypacker, H. S., Bloom, H. S., Criswell, E. L., Neelakantan, P., Goldstein, M. K., & Stein, G. H. (1982). Toward an effective technology of instruction in breast self-examination. *International Journal of Mental Health, 11*, 98–116.

Pennypacker, H. S., Naylor, L., Sander, A. A., & Goldstein, M. K. (1999). Why can't we do better breast examinations? *Nurse Practitioner Forum, 10*, 122–128.

Pepperberg, I. M. (1981). Functional vocalizations by an African gray parrot (*Psittacus erithacus*). *Zeitschrift fur Tierpsychologie, 58*, 193–198.

Pepperberg, I. M. (2000). *The Alex studies: Cognitive and communicative abilities of grey parrots*. Cambridge, MA: Harvard University Press.

Perin, C. T. (1942). Behavior potentiality as a joint function of the amount of training and the degree of hunger at the time of extinction. *Journal of Experimental Psychology, 30*, 93–113.

Perone, M. (1991). Experimental design in the analysis of free-operant behavior. In I. H. Iverson & K. A. Lattal (Eds.), *Experimental analysis of behavior: Part 1* (pp. 135–172). New York: Elsevier.

Perone, M., Galizio, M., & Baron, A. (1988). The relevance of animal-based principles in the laboratory study of human operant conditioning. In G. Davy & C. Cullen (Eds.), *Human operant conditioning and behavior modification* (pp. 59–85). New York: John Wiley.

Peterson, C., & Seligman, M. E. P. (1984). Causal explanations as a risk factor for depression: Theory and evidence. *Psychological Review, 91*, 347–374.

Peterson, G. B. (2004). A day of great illumination: B.F. Skinner's *discovery* of shaping. *Journal of the Experimental Analysis of Behavior, 82*, 317.

Peterson, G. B., Ackil, J. E., Frommer, G. P., & Hearst, E. S. (1972). Conditioned approach and contact behavior toward signals for food or brain-stimulation reinforcement. *Science, 177*, 1009–1011.

Pfautz, P. L., Donegan, N. H., & Wagner, A. R. (1978). Sensory preconditioning versus protection from habituation. *Journal of Experimental Psychology: Animal Behavior Processes, 4*, 286–292.

Piazza, C. C., Moes, D. R., & Fisher, W. W. (1996). Differential reinforcement of alternative behavior and demand fading in the treatment of escape-maintained destructive behavior. *Journal of Applied Behavior Analysis, 29*, 569–572.

Pierce, W. D. (1991). Culture and society: The role of behavioral analysis. In P. A. Lamal (Ed.), *Behavioral analysis of societies and cultural practices* (pp. 13–37). New York: Hemisphere.

Pierce, W. D. (2001). Activity anorexia: Biological, behavioral, and neural levels of selection. *Behavioral and Brain Sciences, 24*, 551–552.

Pierce, W. D., & Cameron, J. (2002). A summary of the effects of reward contingencies on interest and performance. *The Behavior Analyst Today, 3*, 221–228.

Pierce, W. D., & Epling, W. F. (1980). What happened to analysis in applied behavior analysis? *The Behavior Analyst, 3*, 1–9.

Pierce, W. D., & Epling, W. F. (1983). Choice, matching, and human behavior: A review of the literature. *The Behavior Analyst, 6*, 57–76.

Pierce, W. D., & Epling, W. F. (1988). *Biobehaviorism: Genes, learning and behavior* (Working paper No. 88–5). Edmonton: Center for Systems Research, University of Alberta.

Pierce, W. D., & Epling, W. F. (1991). Activity anorexia: An animal model and theory of human self-starvation. In A. Boulton, G. Baker, & M. Martin-Iverson (Eds.), *Neuromethods: Animal models in psychiatry, 1* (Vol. 18, pp. 267–311). Clifton, NJ: Humana Press.

Pierce, W. D., & Epling, W. F. (1997). Activity anorexia: The interplay of culture, behavior, and biology. In P. A. Lamal (Ed.), *Cultural contingencies: Behavior analytic perspectives on cultural practices* (pp. 53–85). Westport, CT: Praeger.

Pierce, W. D., Epling, W. F., & Boer, D. P. (1986). Deprivation and satiation: The interrelations between food and wheel running. *Journal of the Experimental Analysis of Behavior, 46,* 199–210.

Pierce, W. D., Epling, W. F., & Greer, S. M. (1981). Human communication and the matching law. In C. M. Bradshaw, E. Szabadi, & C. F. Lowe (Eds.), *Quantification of steady-state operant behaviour* (pp. 345–352). Amsterdam: Elsevier/North-Holland.

Pierce, W. D., Heth, C. D., Owczarczyk, J., Russell, J. C., & Proctor, S. D. (2007). Overeating by young obese-prone and lean rats caused by tastes associated with low energy foods. *Obesity, 15,* 1069–1079.

Pierrel, R., Sherman, G. J., Blue, S., & Hegge, F. W. (1970). Auditory discrimination: A three-variable analysis of intensity effects. *Journal of the Experimental Analysis of Behavior, 13,* 17–35.

Pitts, R. C., & Malagodi, E. F. (1996). Effects of reinforcement amount on attack induced under a fixed interval schedule in pigeons. *Journal of the Experimental Analysis of Behavior, 65,* 93–110.

Platt, J. R. (1979). Interresponse-time shaping by variable-interval-like interresponse-time reinforcement contingencies. *Journal of the Experimental Analysis of Behavior, 31,* 3–14.

Plaud, J. J. (1992). The prediction and control of behavior revisited: A review of the matching law. *Journal of Behavior Therapy and Experimental Psychiatry, 23,* 25–31.

Plaud, J. J., & Newberry, D. E. (1996). Rule-governed behavior and pedophilia. *Sexual Abuse: Journal of Research and Treatment, 8,* 143–159.

Pliskoff, S. S., & Brown, T. G. (1976). Matching with a trio of concurrent variable-interval schedules of reinforcement. *Journal of the Experimental Analysis of Behavior, 25,* 69–74.

Poling, A. (1978). Performance of rats under concurrent variable-interval schedules of negative reinforcement. *Journal of the Experimental Analysis of Behavior, 30,* 31–36.

Poling, A., Nickel, M., & Alling, K. (1990). Free birds aren't fat: Weight gain in captured wild pigeons maintained under laboratory conditions. *Journal of the Experimental Analysis of Behavior, 53,* 423–424.

Poppen, R. (1982). The fixed-interval scallop in human affairs. *The Behavior Analyst, 5,* 127–136.

Porter, J. P. (1910). Intelligence and imitation in birds: A criterion of imitation. *American Journal of Psychology, 21,* 1–71.

Poulos, C. X., Wilkinson, D. A., & Cappell, H. (1981). Homeostatic regulation and Pavlovian conditioning intolerance to amphetamine-induced anorexia. *Journal of Comparative and Physiological Psychology, 95,* 735–746.

Poulson, C. L., Kymissis, E., Reeve, K. F., Andreatos, M., & Reeve, L. (1991). Generalized vocal imitation in infants. *Journal of Experimental Child Psychology, 51,* 267–279.

Powell, R. W. (1968). The effect of small sequential changes in fixed-ratio size upon the post-reinforcement pause. *Journal of the Experimental Analysis of Behavior, 11,* 589–593.

Powers, R., Cheney, C. D., & Agostino, N. R. (1970). Errorless training of a visual discrimination in preschool children. *The Psychological Record, 20,* 45–50.

Prelec, D. (1984). The assumptions underlying the generalized matching law. *Journal of the Experimental Analysis of Behavior, 41,* 101–107.

Premack, D. (1959). Toward empirical behavioral laws: 1. Positive reinforcement. *Psychological Review, 66,* 219–233.

Premack, D. (1962). Reversability of the reinforcement relation. *Science, 136,* 235–237.

Premack, D. (1971). Catching up with common sense or two sides of a generalization: Reinforcement and punishment. In R. Glaser (Ed.), *The nature of reinforcement* (pp. 121–150). New York: Academic Press.

Prewitt, E. P. (1967). Number of preconditioning trials in sensory preconditioning using CER training. *Journal of Comparative and Physiological Psychology, 64,* 360–362.

Provenza, F. D., Lynch, J. J., & Nolan, J. V. (1994). Food aversion conditioned in anesthetized sheep. *Physiology and Behavior, 55,* 429–432.

Provine, R. R. (1989). Contagious yawning and infant imitation. *Bulletin of the Psychonomic Society, 27,* 125–126.

Pryor, K. W. (1999). *Don't shoot the dog.* New York: Bantum.

Pryor, K. W., Haag, R., & O'Reilly, J. (1969). The creative porpoise: Training for novel behavior. *Journal of the Experimental Analysis of Behavior, 12,* 653–651.

Rachlin, H. (1969). Autoshaping of key pecking in pigeons with negative reinforcement. *Journal of the Experimental Analysis of Behavior, 12*, 521–531.

Rachlin, H. (1970). *Introduction to modern behaviorism.* San Francisco, CA: W. H. Freeman.

Rachlin, H. (1974). Self-control. *Behaviorism, 2*, 94–107.

Rachlin, H. (1976). *Behavior and learning.* San Francisco, CA: W. H. Freeman.

Rachlin, H. (1992). Diminishing marginal value as delay discounting. *Journal of the Experimental Analysis of Behavior, 57*, 407–415.

Rachlin, H. (2000). *The science of self-control.* Cambridge, MA: Harvard University Press.

Rachlin, H., & Green, L. (1972). Commitment, choice and self-control. *Journal of the Experimental Analysis of Behavior, 17*, 15–22.

Rachlin, H., Green, L., Kagel, J. H., & Battalio, R. C. (1976). Economic demand theory and psychological studies of choice. In G. H. Bower (Ed.), *The psychology of learning and motivation* (Vol. 10, pp. 129–154). New York: Academic Press.

Rachlin, H., & Laibson, D. I. (1997). *The matching law: Papers in psychology and ecomomics by Richard J. Herrnstein.* Cambridge, MA: Harvard University Press.

Ray, E. D., Gardner, M. R., & Heyes, C. M. (2000). Seeing how it's done: Matching conditions for observer rats (*Rattus norvegicus*) in bidirectional control. *Animal Cognition, 3*, 147–157.

Razran, G. (1949). Stimulus generalization of conditioned responses. *Psychological Bulletin, 46*, 337–365.

Repacholi, B. M., & Meltzoff, A. N. (2007). Emotional eavesdropping: Infants selectively respond to indirect emotional signals. *Child Development, 78*, 503–521.

Rescorla, R. A. (1966). Predictability and number of pairings in Pavlovian fear conditioning. *Psychonomic Science, 4*, 383–384.

Rescorla, R. A., & Wagner, A. R. (1972). A theory of Pavlovian conditioning: Variations in the effectiveness of reinforcement and nonreinforcement. In A. H. Black & W. F. Prokasy (Eds.), *Classical conditioning II: Current research and theory* (pp. 64–69). New York: Appleton-Century-Crofts.

Revusky, S. H., & Bedarf, E. W. (1967). Association of illness with prior ingestion of novel foods. *Science, 155*, 219–220.

Revusky, S. H., & Garcia, J. (1970). Learned associations over long delays. In G. H. Bower (Ed.), *The psychology of learning and motivation: Advances in research and theory* (Vol. 4, pp. 1–84). New York: Academic Press.

Reynolds, G. S. (1961a). An analysis of interactions in a multiple schedule. *Journal of the Experimental Analysis of Behavior, 4*, 107–117.

Reynolds, G. S. (1961b). Behavioral contrast. *Journal of the Experimental Analysis of Behavior, 4*, 57–71.

Reynolds, G. S. (1963). Some limitations on behavioral contrast and induction during successive discrimination. *Journal of the Experimental Analysis of Behavior, 6*, 131–139.

Reynolds, G. S. (1966a). *A primer of operant conditioning.* Glenview, IL: Scott, Foresman.

Reynolds, G. S. (1966b). Discrimination and emission of temporal intervals by pigeons. *Journal of the Experimental Analysis of Behavior, 9*, 65–68.

Rheingold, H. L., Gewirtz, J. L., & Ross, H. W. (1959). Social conditioning of vocalizations in the infant. *Journal of Comparative and Physiological Psychology, 52*, 68–73.

Ribes, E. M., & Martinez, C. (1998). Second-order discrimination in humans: The roles of explicit instructions and constructed verbal responding. *Behavioural Processes, 42*, 1–18.

Ribes, E. M., & Rodriguez, M. E. (2001). Correspondence between instructions, performance, and self-descriptions in a conditional discrimination task: The effects of feedback and type of matching response. *Psychological Record, 51*, 309–333.

Richards, R. W. (1988) The question of bidirectional associations in pigeons' learning of conditional discrimination tasks. *Bulletin of the Psychonomic Society, 26*, 577–579.

Risley, T. R., & Hart, B. (1968). Developing correspondence between the nonverbal and verbal behavior of preschool children. *Journal of Applied Behavior Analysis, 1*, 267–281.

Rizley, R. C., & Rescorla, R. A. (1972). Associations in second-order conditioning and sensory preconditioning. *Journal of Comparative and Physiological Psychology, 81*, 1–11.

Rizzolatti, G., & Craighero, L. (2004). The mirror-neuron system. *Annual Review of Neuroscience, 27*, 169–192.

Rogers-Warren, A., & Warren, S. (1980). Mands for verbalization: Facilitating the display of newly trained language in children. *Behavior Modification, 4*, 361–382.

Roll, J. M., Higgins, S. T., & Badger, G. J. (1996). An experimental comparison of three different schedules of reinforcement of drug abstinence using cigarette smoking as an exemplar. *Journal of Applied Behavior Analysis, 29*, 495–505.

Rosenberg, E. L., & Ekman, P. (1995). Conceptual and methodological issues in the judgment of facial expressions of emotion. *Motivation and Emotion, 19*, 111–138.

Roth, W. J. (2002). Teaching dolphins to select pictures in response to recorded dolphin whistles with few errors. *Dissertation Abstracts International: Section B: The Sciences & Engineering, 62* (10-B), No. 95008.

Routtenberg, A., & Kuznesof, A. W. (1967). Self-starvation of rats living in activity wheels on a restricted feeding schedule. *Journal of Comparative and Physiological Psychology, 64*, 414–421.

Rozin, P., & Kalat, J. (1971). Adaptive specializations in learning and memory. *Psychological Review, 78*, 459–486.

Ruggles, T. R., & LeBlanc, J. M. (1982). Behavior analysis procedures in classroom teaching. In A. S. Bellack, M. Hersen, & A. E. Kazdin (Eds.), *International handbook of behavior modification and therapy* (pp. 959–996). New York: Plenum Press.

Salamone, J. D., Mingote, C. S., & Weber, S. M. (2003). Nucleus accumbens dopamine and the regulation of effort in food-seeking behavior: Implications for studies of natural motivation, psychiatry, and drug abuse. *Journal of Pharmacology and Experimental Therapeutics, 305*, 1–8.

Salvy, S. J., Heth, C. D., Pierce, W. D., & Russell, J. C. (2004). Conditioned taste aversion induced by wheel running: Further evidence on wheel running duration. *Behavioural Processes, 66*, 101–106.

Salvy S., Mulick, J. A., Butter, E., Bartlett, R. K., & Linscheid, T. R. (2004) Contingent electric shock (SIBIS) and a conditioned punisher eliminate severe head banging in a preschool child. *Behavioral Interventions, 19*, 59–72.

Salvy, S., Pierce, W. D., Heth, C. D., & Russell, J. C. (2002). Pre-exposure to wheel running disrupts taste aversion conditioning. *Physiology and Behavior, 76*, 51–56.

Salvy, S. J., Pierce, W. D., Heth, C. D., & Russell, J. C. (2003). Wheel running produces conditioned food aversion. *Physiology and Behavior, 80*, 89–94.

Sanders, G. A. (1974). Introduction. In D. Cohen (Ed.), *Explaining linguistic phenomena* (pp. 1–20). Washington, DC: Hemisphere.

Sargisson, R. J., & White, K. G. (2001). Generalization of delayed matching-to-sample performance following training at different delays. *Journal of the Experimental Analysis of Behavior, 75*, 1–14.

Saslow, D., Hannan, J., Osuch, J., Alciati, M. H., Baines, C., Barton, M., et al. (2004). Clinical breast examination: Practical recommendations for optimizing performance and reporting. *CA: A Cancer Journal for Clinicians, 54*, 327–344.

Saunders, K. J. (1989). Naming in conditional discrimination and stimulus equivalence. *Journal of the Experimental Analysis of Behavior, 51*, 379–384.

Saunders, K. J., Pilgram, C. A., & Pennypacker, H. S. (1986). Increased proficiency of search in breast self-examination. *Cancer, 58*, 2531–2537.

Savage-Rumbaugh, S. E. (1984). Verbal behavior at a procedural level in the chimpanzee. *Journal of the Experimental Analysis of Behavior, 41*, 223–250.

Savage-Rumbaugh, S. E. (1986). *Ape language: From conditioned response to symbol.* New York: Columbia University Press.

Savage-Rumbaugh, S. E., & Lewin, R. (1994). *Kanzi: The ape at the brink of the human mind.* New York: Wiley.

Savage-Rumbaugh, S. E., Murphy, J., Sevcik, R. A., Brakke, K. E., Williams, S. L., & Rumbaugh, D. M. (1993). Language comprehension in ape and child. *Monographs of the Society for Research in Child Development, 58*, (3–4), No. 233.

Savage-Rumbaugh, S. E., Shanker, S. G., & Taylor, T. J. (1998). *Apes, language, and the human mind.* New York: Oxford University Press.

Schaefer, H. H., & Martin, P. L. (1966). Behavior therapy for "apathy" of hospitalized patients. *Psychological Reports, 19*, 1147–1158.

Scheller, R. H., & Axel, R. (1984). How genes control innate behavior. *Scientific American, 250*, 54–62.

Schlinger, H., & Blakely, E. (1987). Function-altering effects of contingency-specifying stimuli. *The Behavior Analyst, 10*, 41–45.

Schlund, M. W., Hoehn-Saric, R., & Cataldo, M. F. (2007). New knowledge derived from learned knowledge: Functional-anatomic correlates of stimulus equivalence. *Journal of the Experimental Analysis of Behavior, 87*, 287–307.

Schmitt, D. R. (2001). Delayed rule following. *The Behavior Analyst, 24*, 181–189.

Schneiderman, N. (1966). Interstimulus interval function of the nicitating membrane response of the rabbit under delay versus trace conditioning. *Journal of Comparative and Physiological Psychology, 62*, 397–402.

Schoenfeld, W. N., Antonitis, J. J., & Bersh, P. J. (1950). A preliminary study of training conditions necessary for conditioned reinforcement. *Journal of Experimental Psychology, 40*, 40–45.

Schoneberger, T. (2000). A departure from cognitivism: Implications of Chomsky's second revolution in linguistics. *Analysis of Verbal Behavior, 17*, 57–73.

Schopler, E., & Mesibov, G. B. (1994). *Behavioral issues in autism.* New York: Plenum Press.

Schrier, A. M., & Brady, P. M. (1987). Categorization of natural stimuli by monkeys (*Macaca mulatta*): Effects of stimulus set size and modification of exemplars. *Journal of Experimental Psychology: Animal Behavior Processes, 13*, 136–143.

Schwartz, B. (1980). Development of complex stereotyped behavior in pigeons. *Journal of the Experimental Analysis of Behavior, 33*, 153–166.

Schwartz, B. (1982a). Failure to produce response variability with reinforcement. *Journal of the Experimental Analysis of Behavior, 37*, 171–181.

Schwartz, B. (1982b). Reinforcement-induced stereotypy: How not to teach people to discover rules. *Journal of Experimental Psychology: General, 111*, 23–59.

Schwartz, B., & Gamzu, E. (1977). Pavlovian control of operant behavior: An analysis of autoshaping and its implication for operant conditioning. In W. K. Honig & J. E. R. Staddon (Eds.), *Handbook of operant behavior* (pp. 53–97). Englewood Cliffs, NJ: Prentice-Hall.

Schwartz, B., & Lacey, H. (1982). *Behaviorism, science, and human nature* (pp. 160–191). New York: W. W. Norton & Co.

Schwartz, B., & Williams, D. R. (1972a). The role of response reinforcer contingency in negative auto-maintenance. *Journal of the Experimental Analysis of Behavior, 18*, 351–357.

Schwartz, B., & Williams, D. R. (1972b). Two different kinds of key peck in the pigeon: Some properties of responses maintained by negative and positive response-reinforcer contingencies. *Journal of the Experimental Analysis of Behavior, 18*, 201–216.

Scott, J. F. (1971). *Internalization of norms: A sociological theory of moral commitment.* Englewood Cliffs, NJ: Prentice-Hall.

Segal, E. F. (1962). Effects of *dl*-amphetamine under concurrent VI DRL reinforcement. *Journal of the Experimental Analysis of Behavior, 5*, 105–112.

Seligman, M. E. P. (1970). On the generality of the laws of learning. *Psychological Review, 77*, 406–418.

Seligman, M. E. P. (1975). *Helplessness: On depression, development, and death.* San Francisco, CA: Freeman.

Seligman, M. E. P., & Maier, S. F. (1967). Failure to escape traumatic shock. *Journal of Experimental Psychology, 74*, 1–9.

Sepinwall, J., & Cook, L. (1978). Behavioral pharmacology of antianxiety drugs. In L. L. Iversen, S. D. Iverson, & S. H. Snyder (Eds.), *Handbook of psychopharmacology* (Vol. 13, pp. 345–393). New York: Plenum Press.

Shabani, D. B., & Fisher, W. W. (2006) Stimulus fading and differential reinforcement for the treatment of needle phobia in a youth with autism. *Journal of Applied Behavior Analysis, 39*, 449–452.

Shapiro, M. M. (1960). Respondent salivary conditioning during operant lever pressing in dogs. *Science, 132*, 619–620.

Shaver, K.G. (1985). *The attribution of blame.* New York: Springer-Verlag.

Shearn, D. W. (1962). Operant conditioning of heart rate. *Science, 137*, 530–531.

Sherman, J. A. (1965). Use of reinforcement and imitation to reinstate verbal behavior in mute psychotics. *Journal of Abnormal Psychology, 70*, 155–164.

Sherman, J. G., Ruskin, G., & Semb, G. B. (1982). *The personalized system of instruction: 48 seminal papers.* Lawrence, KS: TRI Publications.

Sherrington, C. (1906) *The integrative action of the nervous system* (2nd ed. 1947). New Haven, CT: Yale University Press.

Shimp, C. P. (1969). The concurrent reinforcement of two interresponse times: The relative frequency of an interresponse time equals its relative harmonic length. *Journal of the Experimental Analysis of Behavior, 12*, 403–411.

Shimp, C. P. (1992). Computational behavior dynamics: An alternative description of Nevin (1969). *Journal of the Experimental Analysis of Behavior, 57*, 289–299.

Shizgal, P., & Arvanitogiannis, A. (2003). Gambling on dopamine. *Science, 299*, 1856–1858.

Shull, R. L. (1979). The postreinforcement pause: Some implications for the correlational law of effect. In M.

D. Zeiler & P. Harzem (Eds.), *Reinforcement and the organization of behaviour* (pp. 193–221). New York: John Wiley.

Shull, R. L., Gaynor, S. T., & Grimer, J. A. (2002). Response rate measured as engagement bouts: Resistance to extinction. *Journal of the Experimental Analysis of Behavior, 77*, 211–231.

Shull, R. L., & Pliskoff, S. S. (1967). Changeover delay and concurrent schedules: Some effects on relative performance measures. *Journal of the Experimental Analysis of Behavior, 10*, 517–527.

Sidman, M. (1953). Two temporal parameters in the maintenance of avoidance behavior of the white rat. *Journal of Comparative and Physiological Psychology, 46*, 253–261.

Sidman, M. (1960). *Tactics of scientific research.* New York: Basic Books.

Sidman, M. (1962). Reduction of shock frequency as reinforcement for avoidance behavior. *Journal of the Experimental Analysis of Behavior, 5*, 247–257.

Sidman, M. (1994). *Equivalence relations and behavior: A research story.* Boston, MA: Authors Cooperative, Inc.

Sidman, M. (1999). *B. F. Skinner: A fresh appraisal.* Film available from Cambridge Center for Behavioral Studies (www.behavior.org).

Sidman, M. (2001). *Coercion and its fallout.* Boston, MA: Authors Cooperative, Inc.

Sidman, M., Brady, J. V., Boren, J. J., Conrad, D. G., & Schulman, A. (1955). Reward schedules and behavior maintained by intracranial self-stimulation. *Science, 122*, 925.

Sidman, M., & Cresson, O., Jr. (1973). Reading and crossmodal transfer of stimulus equivalences in severe retardation. *American Journal of Mental Deficiency, 77*, 515–523.

Sidman, M., Cresson, O., Jr., & Wilson-Morris, M. (1974). Acquisition of matching to sample via mediated transfer. *Journal of the Experimental Analysis of Behavior, 22*, 261–273.

Siegel, S. (1972). Conditioning of insulin-induced glycemia. *Journal of Comparative and Physiological Psychology, 78*, 233–241.

Siegel, S. (1975). Conditioning insulin effects. *Journal of Comparative and Physiological Psychology, 89*, 189–199.

Siegel, S. (2001). Pavlovian conditiioning and drug overdose: When tolerance fails. *Addiction Research and Theory, 9*, 503–513.

Siegel, S., & Domjan, M. (1971). Backward conditioning as an inhibitory procedure. *Learning and Motivation, 2*, 1–11.

Siegel, S., Hinson, R. E., Krank, M. D., & McCully, J. (1982). Heroin "overdose" death: The contribution of drug-associated environmental cues. *Science, 216*, 436–437.

Sigafoos, J., Doss, S., & Reichle, J. (1989). Developing mand and tact repertoires in persons with severe developmental-disabilities using graphic symbols. *Research in Developmental Disabilities, 10*, 183–200.

Sigafoos, J., Reichle, J., Doss, S., Hall, K., & Pettitt, L. (1990). Spontaneous transfer of stimulus control from tact to mand contingencies. *Research in Developmental Disabilities, 11*, 165–176.

Simic, J., & Bucher, B. (1980). Development of spontaneous manding in nonverbal children. *Journal of Applied Behavior Analysis, 13*, 523–528.

Simon, S. J., Ayllon, T., & Milan, M. A. (1982). Behavioral compensation: Contrastlike effects in the classroom. *Behavior Modification, 6*, 407–420.

Sitharthan, G., Hough, M. J., Sitharthan, T., & Kavanagh, D. J. (2001). The Alcohol Helplessness Scale and its prediction of depression among problem drinkers. *Journal of Clinical Psychology, 57*, 1445–1457.

Skinner, B. F. (1935). Two types of conditioned reflex and a pseudo type. *Journal of General Psychology, 12*, 66–77.

Skinner, B. F. (1937). Two types of conditioned reflex: A reply to Konorski and Miller. *Journal of General Psychology, 16*, 272–279.

Skinner, B. F. (1938). *The behavior of organisms.* New York: Appleton-Century-Crofts.

Skinner, B. F. (1945). Baby in a box. *Ladies Home Journal, October*, 30–31, 135–136, 138.

Skinner, B. F. (1948). *Walden two.* New York: Macmillan.

Skinner, B. F. (1950). Are theories of learning necessary? *Psychological Review, 57*, 193–216.

Skinner, B. F. (1953). *Science and human behavior.* New York: Free Press.

Skinner, B. F. (1957). *Verbal behavior.* New York: Appleton-Century-Crofts.

Skinner, B. F. (1960). Pigeons in a pelican. *American Psychologist, 15*, 28–37.

Skinner, B. F. (1968). *The technology of teaching.* New York: Appleton-Century-Crofts.

Skinner, B. F. (1969). *Contingencies of reinforcement: A theoretical analysis.* New York: Appleton-Century-Crofts.

Skinner, B. F. (1971). *Beyond freedom and dignity.* New York: Alfred A. Knopf.

Skinner, B. F. (1974). *About behaviorism.* New York: Alfred A. Knopf.

Skinner, B. F. (1976). *Particulars of my life.* New York: McGraw-Hill.

Skinner, B. F. (1978). *Reflections on behaviorism and society.* Englewood Cliffs, NJ: Prentice-Hall.

Skinner, B. F. (1979). *The shaping of a behaviorist.* New York: Alfred A. Knopf.

Skinner, B. F. (1983). *A matter of consequences.* New York: Alfred A. Knopf.

Skinner, B. F. (1984a). The shame of American education. *American Psychologist, 39,* 947–954.

Skinner, B. F. (1984b). The evolution of behavior. *Journal of the Experimental Analysis of Behavior, 41,* 217–222.

Skinner, B. F. (1986). The evolution of verbal behavior. *Journal of the Experimental Analysis of Behavior, 45,* 115–122.

Skinner, B. F. (1988). An operant analysis of problem solving. In A. C. Catania & S. Harnad (Eds.), *The selection of behavior—The operant behaviorism of B. F. Skinner: Comments and consequences* (pp. 218–277). New York: Cambridge University Press.

Skinner, B. F. & Vaughan, M. E. (1983). *Enjoy old age: A program of self-management.* New York: W. W. Norton.

Smith, M. C., & Gormezano, I. (1965). *Conditioning of the nictitating membrane response of the rabbit as a function of backward, simultaneous, and forward CS–UCS intervals.* Paper presented at the meeting of the Psychonomic Society, Chicago, IL.

Sobsey, D. (1990). Modifying the behavior of behavior modifiers: Arguments for countercontrol against aversive procedures. In A. C. Repp & N. N. Singh (Eds.), *Perspectives on the use of nonaversive and aversive interventions for persons with developmental disabilities* (pp. 421–433). Sycamore, IL: Sycamore Publishing Co.

Solomon, P. R., Blanchard, S., Levine, E., Velazquez, E., & Groccia-Ellison, M. (1991). Attenuation of age-related deficits in humans by extension of the interstumulus interval. *Psychology of Aging, 6,* 36–42.

Solomon, R. L. (1969). Punishment. In D. Rosenhan & P. London (Eds.), *Theory and research in abnormal psychology* (pp. 75–119). New York: Holt, Rinehart & Winston.

Solomon, R. L., & Brush, E. S. (1956). Experimentally derived conceptions of anxiety and aversion. In M. R. Jones (Ed.), *Nebraska symposium on motivation* (pp. 212–305). Lincoln: University of Nebraska Press.

Solzhenitsyn, A. (1973). *The first circle.* London: Collins Fontana Books.

Sossin, W. S., Kirk, M. D., & Scheller, R. H. (1987). Peptidergic modulation of neuronal circuitry controlling feeding in Aplysia. *Journal of Neuroscience, 7,* 671–681.

Sousa, C., & Matsuzawa, T. (2001). The use of tokens as rewards and tools by chimpanzees (*Pan troglodytes*). *Animal Cognition, 4,* 213–221.

Sowers-Hoag, K. M., Thyer, B. A., & Bailey, J. S. (1987). Promoting automobile safety belt use by young children. *Journal of Applied Behavior Analysis, 20,* 133–138.

Sparks, S., Grant, V. L., & Lett, B. T. (2003). Role of conditioned taste aversion in the development of activity anorexia. *Appetite, 41,* 161–165.

Spetch, M. L., & Friedman, A. (2006). Pigeons see correspondence between objects and their pictures. *Psychological Science, 17,* 966–972.

Spetch, M. L., Cheng, K., & Clifford, C. W. G. (2004). Peak shift but not range effects in recognition of faces. *Learning and Motivation, 35,* 221–241.

Squires, N., & Fantino, E. (1971). A model for choice in simple concurrent and concurrent-chains schedules. *Journal of the Experimental Analysis of Behavior, 15,* 27–38.

Staats, A. W. (1975). *Social behaviorism.* Chicago, IL: Dorsey Press.

Staddon, J. E. R. (1977). Schedule-induced behavior. In W. K. Honig & J. E. R. Staddon (Eds.), *Handbook of operant behavior* (pp. 125–152). Englewood Cliffs, NJ: Prentice-Hall.

Staddon, J. E. R., & Simmelhag, V. L. (1971). The "superstition" experiment: A re-examination of its implications for the principles of adaptive behavior. *Psychological Review, 78,* 3–43.

Stafford, D., & Branch, M. (1998). Effects of step size and break-point criterion on progressive-ratio performance. *Journal of the Experimental Analysis of Behavior, 70,* 123–138.

Stein, L., & Belluzzi, J. D. (1988). Operant conditioning of individual neurons. In M. L. Commons, R. M.

Church, J. R. Stellar, & A. R. Wagner (Eds.), *Quantitative analyses of behavior: Vol. 7. Biological determinants of reinforcement and memory* (pp. 249–264). Hillsdale, NJ: Lawrence Erlbaum Associates.

Stein, L., Xue, B. G., & Belluzzi, J. D. (1994). In vitro reinforcement of hippocampal bursting: A search for Skinner's atoms of behavior. *Journal of the Experimental Analysis of Behavior, 61*, 155–168.

Stevenson-Hinde, J. (1983). Constraints on reinforcement. In R. A. Hinde & J. Stevenson-Hinde (Eds.), *Constraints on learning: Limitations and predispositions* (pp. 285–296). New York: Academic Press.

Stiers, M., & Silberberg, A. (1974). Lever-contact responses in rats: Automaintenance with and without a negative response-reinforcer dependency. *Journal of the Experimental Analysis of Behavior, 22*, 497–506.

Stokes, P. D., Mechner, F., & Balsam, P. D. (1999). Effects of different acquisition procedures on response variability. *Animal Learning and Behavior, 27*, 28–41.

Stokes, T. F., & Baer, D. M. (1977). An implicit technology of generalization. *Journal of Applied Behavior Analysis, 10*, 349–367.

Stokes, T. F., Fowler, S. A., & Baer, D. M. (1978). Training preschool children to recruit natural communities of reinforcement. *Journal of Applied Behavior Analysis, 11*, 285–303.

Stonebraker, T. B., & Rilling, M. (1981). Control of delayed matching-to-sample using directed forgetting techniques. *Animal Learning and Behavior, 9*, 196–201.

Stonebraker, T. B., Rilling, M., & Kendrick, D. F. (1981). Time dependent effects of double cuing in directed forgetting. *Animal Learning and Behavior, 9*, 385–394.

Storms, L. H., Boroczi, G., & Broen, W. E., Jr. (1962). Punishment inhibits an instrumental response in hooded rats. *Science, 135*, 1133–1134.

Stroop, J. R. (1935). Studies of interference in serial verbal reactions. *Journal of Experimental Psychology, 18*, 643–662.

Sulzer-Azaroff, B. (1986). Behavior analysis and education: Crowning achievements and crying needs. *Division 25 Recorder, 21*, 55–65.

Sunahara, D., & Pierce, W. D. (1982). The matching law and bias in a social exchange involving choice between alternatives. *Canadian Journal of Sociology, 7*, 145–165.

Sundberg, M. L. (1985). Teaching verbal behavior to pigeons. *The Analysis of Verbal Behavior, 3*, 11–17.

Sundberg, M. L. (1996). Toward granting linguistic competence to apes: A review of Savage-Rumbaugh et al.'s *Language comprehension in ape and child. Journal of the Experimental Analysis of Behavior, 65*, 477–492.

Sundberg, M. L., Endicott, K., & Eigenheer, P. (2000). Using intraverbal prompts to establish tacts for children with autism. *Analysis of Verbal Behavior, 17*, 89–104.

Sundberg, M. L., & Michael, J. (2001). The benefits of Skinner's analysis of verbal behavior for children with autism. *Behavior Modification, 25*, 698–724.

Svartdal, F. (1992). Operant modulation of low-level attributes of rule-governed behavior by nonverbal contingencies. *Learning and Motivation, 22*, 406–420.

Swithers, S. E., Doerflinger, A., & Davidson, T. L. (2006). Consistent relationships between sensory properties of savory snack foods and calories influence food intake in rats. *International Journal of Obesity, 30*, 1685–1692.

Tait, R. W., & Saladin, M. E. (1986). Concurrent development of excitatory and inhibitory associations during backward conditioning. *Animal Learning and Behavior, 14*, 133–137.

Takamori, K., Yoshida, S., & Okuyama, S. (2001). Repeated treatment with imipramine, fluvoxamine, and tranylcypromine decreases the number of escape failures by activating dopaminergic systems in a rat learned helplessness test. *Life Sciences, 69*, 1919–1926.

Taylor, C. K., & Saayman, G. S. (1973). Imitative behavior by Indian Ocean bottlenose dolphins (*Tursiops aduncus*) in captivity. *Behaviour, 44*, 286–298.

Taylor, I., & O'Reilly, M. F. (1997). Toward a functional analysis of private verbal self-regulation. *Journal of Applied Behavior Analysis, 30*, 43–58.

Taylor, S. P., & Pisano, R. (1971). Physical aggression as a function of frustration and physical attack. *Journal of Social Psychology, 84*, 261–267.

Terrace, H. S. (1963). Discrimination learning with and without "errors." *Journal of the Experimental Analysis of Behavior, 6*, 1–27.

Terrace, H. S. (1972). By-products of discrimination learning. In G. H. Bower (Ed.), *The psychology of learning and motivation* (Vol. 5, pp. 195–265). New York: Academic Press.

Thomas, D. R., & Setzer, J. (1972). Stimulus generalization gradients for auditory intensity in rats and guinea pigs. *Psychonomic Science, 28*, 22–24.

Thompson, R. F., & Glanzman, D. L. (1976). Neural and behavioral mechanisms of habituation and sensitization. In T. J. Tighe & R. N. Leaton (eds.), *Habituation* (pp. 49–93). Hillsdale, NJ: Lawrence Erlbaum Associates.

Thompson, R. F. & Spencer, W. A. (1966). Habituation: A model phenomenon for the study of neuronal substrates of behavior. *Psychological Review, 73*, 16–43.

Thompson, T. (2007). Relations among functional systems in behavior analysis. *Journal of the Experimental Analysis of Behavior, 87*, 423–440.

Thorndike, E. L. (1898). Animal intelligence. *Psychological Review Monograph Supplements* (Serial No. 8).

Thorndike, E. L. (1911). *Animal intelligence.* New York: Macmillan.

Thorpe, W. H. (1963). *Learning and instinct in animals.* Cambridge, MA: Harvard University Press.

Tighe, T. J., & Leaton, R. N. (1976). *Habituation.* Hillsdale, NJ: Lawrence Erlbaum Associates.

Timberlake, W. (1983). Rats responses to a moving object related to food or water: A behavior-systems analysis. *Animal Learning and Behavior, 11*, 309–320.

Timberlake, W. (1993). Behavior systems and reinforcement: An integrative approach. *Journal of the Experimental Analysis of Behavior, 60*, 105–128.

Timberlake, W., & Allison, J. (1974). Response deprivation: An empirical approach to instrumental performance. *Psychological Review, 81*, 146–164.

Timberlake, W., & Grant, D. L. (1975). Auto-shaping in rats to the presentation of another rat predicting food. *Science, 190*, 690–692.

Tinbergen, N. (1951). *The study of instinct.* Oxford: Oxford University Press.

Tinbergen, N., & Kuenen, D. J. (1957). Feeding behavior in young thrushes. In C. H. Schiller (Ed.), *Instinctive behavior: Development of a modern concept* (pp. 209–236). Methuen: London.

Tobler, P. N., Fiorillo, C. D., & and Schultz, W. (2005). Adaptive coding of reward value by dopamine neurons. *Science, 307*, 1642–1645.

Todd, J. T., & Morris, E. K. (1992). Case histories in the great power of steady misrepresentation. *American Psychologist, 47*, 1441–1453.

Todd, J. T., & Morris, E. K. (1986). The early research of John B. Watson: Before the behavioral revolution. *The Behavior Analyst, 9*, 71–88.

Tomasello, M., Savage-Rumbaugh, S., & Kruger, A. C. (1993). Imitative learning of actions on objects by, children, chimpanzees, and enculturated chimpanzees. *Child Development, 64*, 1688–1705.

Tourinho, E. Z. (2006). Private stimuli, covert responses and private events: Conceptual remarks. *The Behavior Analyst, 29*, 13–31.

Towe, A. L. (1954). A study of figural equivalence in the pigeon. *Journal of Comparative and Physiological Psychology, 47*, 283–287.

Trapp, M. A., Kottke, T. E., Viekrant, R. A., Kaur, J. S., & Sellers, T. A. (1999). The ability of trained nurses to detect lumps in a test set of silicone breast models. *Cancer, 86*, 1750–1756.

Tulving, E. (1983). *Elements of episodic memory.* New York: Oxford University Press.

Turney, T. H. (1982). The association of visual concepts and imitative vocalization in the mynah (*Gracula religiosa*). *Bulletin of the Psychonomic Society, 19*, 59–62.

Twinge, J. M., Baumeister, R. F., Tice, D. M., & Stucke, T. S. (2001). If you can't join them, beat them: Effects of social exclusion on aggressive behavior. *Journal of Personality and Social Psychology, 81*, 1058–1069.

Ullstadius, E. (2000). Variability in judgment of neonatal imitation. *Journal of Reproductive and Infant Psychology, 18*, 239–247.

Ulrich, R. E., & Azrin, N. H. (1962). Reflexive fighting in response to aversive stimulation. *Journal of the Experimental Analysis of Behavior, 5*, 511–520.

Ulrich, R. E., Wolff, P. C., & Azrin, N. H. (1964). Shock as an elictor of intra- and inter-species fighting behavior. *Animal Behaviour, 12*, 14–15.

Van Hess, A., van Haaren, F., & van de Poll, N. E. (1989). Operant conditioning of response variability in male and female Wistar rats. *Physiology and Behavior, 45*, 551–555.

Van Houten, R., Axelrod, S., Bailey, J. S., Favell, J. E., Foxx, R. M., Iwata, B. A., et al. (1988). The right to effective treatment. *Journal of Applied Behavior Analysis, 21*, 381–384.

Vargas, E. A. (1998). Verbal behavior: Implications of its mediational and relational characteristics. *Analysis of Verbal Behavior, 15*, 149–151.

Vargas, J. S. (1990). B. F. Skinner fact and fiction. *The International Behaviorology Association Newsletter, 2*, 8–11.

Vaughn, W., Jr. (1988). Formation of equivalence sets in pigeons. *Journal of Experimental Psychology: Animal Behavior Processes, 14*, 36–42.

Ventura, R., Morrone, C., & Puglisi-Allegra, S. (2007). Prefrontal/accumbal catecholamine system determines motivational salience attribution to both reward- and aversion-related stimuli. *Proceedings of the National Academy of Science, 104*, 5181–5186.

Verhave, T. (1966). The pigeon as a quality control inspector. *American Psychologist, 21*, 109–115.

Villareal, J. (1967). Shedule-induced pica. *Physiology and Behavior, 6*, 577–588.

Volkmar, F., Carter, A., Grossman, J., & Klin, A. (1997). Social development in autism. In D. J. Cohen, & F. R. Volkmar (Eds.), *Handbook of autism and pervasive developmental disorders* (2nd ed., pp. 171–194). New York: John Wiley.

Vollmer, T. R., & Hackenberg, T. D. (2001). Reinforcement contingencies and social reinforcement: Some reciprocal relations between basic and applied research. *Journal of Applied Behavior Analysis, 34*, 241–253.

Vorndran, C. M., & Lerman, D. C. (2006). Establishing and maintaining treatment effects with less intrusive consequences via a pairing procedure. *Journal of Applied Behavior Analysis, 39*, 35–48.

Vuchinich, R. E. (1999). Behavioral economics as a framework for organizing the expanded range of substance abuse interventions. In J. A. Tucker, D. M. Donovan, & G. A. Marlatt (Eds.), *Changing addictive behavior: Bridging clinical and public health strategies* (pp. 191–218). New York: Guilford Press.

Wagner, A. R., & Rescorla, R. A. (1972). Inhibition in Pavlovian conditioning: Applications of a theory. In R. A. Boakes & M. S. Halliday (Eds.), *Inhibition and learning* (pp. 301–359). London: Academic Press.

Wakefield, J. C. (2006). Is behaviorism becoming a pseudo-science?: Power versus scientific rationality in the eclipse of token economies by biological psychiatry in the treatment of schizophrenia. *Behavior and Social Issues, 15*, 202–221.

Walker, S. (1987). *Animal learning*. New York: Routledge & Kegan Paul.

Waller, M. B. (1961). Effects of chronically administered chlorpromazine on multiple-schedule performance. *Journal of the Experimental Analysis of Behavior, 4*, 351–359.

Wanchisen, B. A., Tatham, T. A., & Mooney, S. E. (1989). Variable-ratio conditioning history produces high- and low-rate fixed-interval performance in rats. *Journal of the Experimental Analysis of Behavior, 52*, 167–179.

Warden, C. J., Fjeld, H. A., & Koch, A. M. (1940). Imitative behavior in the rhesus monkeys. *Pedagogical Seminary and Journal of Genetic Psychology, 56*, 311–322.

Warden, C. J., & Jackson, T. A. (1935). Imitative behavior in the rhesus monkeys. *Pedagogical Seminary and Journal of Genetic Psychology, 46*, 103–125.

Wasserman, E. A. (1973). Pavlovian conditioning with heat reinforcement produces stimulus-directed pecking in chicks. *Science, 181*, 875–877.

Watson, J. B. (1903). *Animal education: An experimental study on the psychical development of the white rat, correlated with the growth of its nervous system*. Chicago, IL: University of Chicago Press.

Watson, J. B. (1913). Psychology as the behaviorist views it. *Psychological Review, 20*, 158–177.

Watson, J. B. (1936). John Broadus Watson. In C. Murchison (Ed.), *A history of psychology in autobiography* (Vol. 3, pp. 271–281). Worcester, MA: Clark University Press.

Watson, J. B., & Rayner, R. (1920). Conditioned emotional reactions. *Journal of Experimental Child Psychology, 3*, 1–14.

Wawrzyncyck, S. (1937) Badania and parecia *Spirostomum ambiguum major. Acta Biologica Experimentalis (Warsaw), 11*, 57–77.

Wearden, J. H. (1983). Undermatching and overmatching as deviations from the matching law. *Journal of the Experimental Analysis of Behavior, 40*, 333–340.

Wearden, J. H., & Burgess, I. S. (1982). Matching since Baum (1979). *Journal of the Experimental Analysis of Behavior, 38*, 339–348.

Webbe, F. M., DeWeese, J., & Malagodi, E. F. (1978). Induced attack during multiple fixed-ratio, variable-ratio schedules of reinforcement. *Journal of the Experimental Analysis of Behavior, 20*, 219–224.

Weiner, H. (1969). Controlling human fixed-interval performance. *Journal of the Experimental Analysis of Behavior, 12*, 349–373.

Weiss, B., & Gott, C. T. (1972). A microanalysis of drug effects on fixed-ratio performance in pigeons. *Journal of Pharmacology and Experimental Therapeutics, 180*, 189–202.

Weissman, N. W., & Crossman, E. K. (1966). A comparison of two types of extinction following fixed-ratio training. *Journal of the Experimental Analysis of Behavior, 9*, 41–46.

West, M. J., & King, A. P. (1988). Female visual displays affect the development of male song in the cowbird. *Nature, 334*, 244–246.

West, R. P., & Young, K. R. (1992). Precision teaching. In R. P. West & L. A. Hamerlynck (Eds.), *Designs for excellence in education: The legacy of B. F. Skinner* (pp. 113–146). Longmont, CO: Sopris West, Inc.

West, R. P., Young, R., & Spooner, F. (1990). Precision teaching: An introduction. *Teaching Exceptional Children, 22*, 4–9.

Westbrook, R. F. (1973). Failure to obtain positive contrast when pigeons press a bar. *Journal of the Experimental Analysis of Behavior, 20*, 499–510.

Wheeler, H. (1973). *Beyond the punitive society.* San Francisco, CA: W. H. Freeman.

White, A. J., & Davison, M. C. (1973). Performance in concurrent fixed-interval schedules. *Journal of the Experimental Analysis of Behavior, 19*, 147–153.

White, C. T., & Schlosberg, H. (1952). Degree of conditioning of the GSR as a function of the period of delay. *Journal of Experimental Psychology, 43*, 357–362.

White, K. G. (2002). Psychophysics of remembering: The discrimination hypothesis. *Current Directions in Psychological Science, 11*, 141–145.

White, K. G., Parkinson, A. E., Brown, G. S., & Wixted, J. T. (2004). Local proactive interference in delayed matching to sample: the role of reinforcement. *Journal of Experimental Psychology: Animal Behavior Processes, 32*, 83–95.

White, K. G., & Wixted, J. T. (1999). Psychophysics of remembering. *Journal of the Experimental Analysis of Behavior, 71*, 91–113.

White, O. R. (1986). Precision teaching—Precision learning. *Exceptional Children, 52*, 522–534.

White, O. R., & Haring, N. G. (1980). *Exceptional teaching* (2nd ed.). Columbus, OH: Merrill.

Whiten, A., & Boesch, C. (2001). The cultures of chimpanzees. *Scientific American, 284*, 60–68.

Wike, E. L. (1966). *Secondary reinforcement: Selected experiments.* New York: Harper & Row.

Wilcoxon, H. C., Dragoin, W. B., & Kral, P. A. (1971). Illness-induced aversions in rat and quail: Relative salience of visual and gustatory cues. *Science, 171*, 826–828.

Wilkes, G. (1994). *A behavior sampler.* North Bend, WA: Sunshine Books.

Williams, A. R. (1997). Under the volcano: Montserrat. *National Geographic, 192*, 59–75.

Williams, B. A. (1974). The role of local interactions in behavioral contrast. *Bulletin of the Psychonomic Society, 4*, 543–545.

Williams, B. A. (1976). Behavioral contrast as a function of the temporal location of reinforcement. *Journal of the Experimental Analysis of Behavior, 26*, 57–64.

Williams, B. A. (1979). Contrast, component duration, and the following schedule of reinforcement. *Journal of Experimental Psychology: Animal Behavior Processes, 5*, 379–396.

Williams, B. A. (1981). The following schedule of reinforcement as a fundamental determinant of steady state contrast in multiple schedules. *Journal of the Experimental Analysis of Behavior, 12*, 293–310.

Williams, B. A. (1990). Pavlovian contingencies and anticipatory contrast. *Animal Learning and Behavior, 18*, 44–50.

Williams, B. A. (1992). Competition between stimulus-reinforcer contingencies and anticipatory contrast. *Journal of the Experimental Analysis of Behavior, 58*, 287–302.

Williams, B. A. (2002). Behavioral contrast redux. *Animal Learning and Behavior, 30*, 1–20.

Williams, C. D. (1959). The elimination of tantrum behavior by extinction procedures. *Journal of Abnormal and Social Psychology, 59*, 269.

Williams, D. R., & Williams, H. (1969). Automaintenance in the pigeon: Sustained pecking despite contingent non-reinforcement. *Journal of the Experimental Analysis of Behavior, 12*, 511–520.

Williams, J. L., & Lierle, D. M. (1986). Effects of stress controllability, immunization, and therapy on the subsequent defeat of colony intruders. *Animal Learning and Behavior, 14*, 305–314.

Wilson, L., & Rogers, R. W. (1975). The fire this time: Effects of race of target, insult, and potential retaliation on black aggression. *Journal of Personality and Social Psychology, 32*, 857–864.

Witoslawski, J. J., Anderson, R. B., & Hanson, H. M. (1963). Behavioral studies with a black vulture, *Coragyps atratus. Journal of the Experimental Analysis of Behavior, 6*, 605–606.

Wixted, J. T., & Gaitan, S. C. (2002). Cognitive theories as reinforcement history surrogates: The case of likelihood ratio models of human recognition memory. *Learning and Behavior, 30*, 289–305.

Wolfe, B. M., & Baron, R. A. (1971). Laboratory aggression related to aggression in naturalistic social situations: Effects of an aggressive model on the behavior of college students and prisoner observers. *Psychonomic Science, 24*, 193–194.

Wolfe, J. B. (1936). Effectiveness of token rewards for chimpanzees. *Comparative Psychology Monographs, 12*, 1–72.

Wyckoff, L. B., Jr. (1952). The role of observing responses in discrimination learning. Part 1. *Psychological Review, 59*, 431–442.

Wyckoff, L. B., Jr. (1969). The role of observing responses in discrimination learning. In D. P. Hendry (Ed.), *Conditioned reinforcement* (pp. 237–260). Homewood, IL: Dorsey Press.

Xue, B. G., Belluzzi, J. D., & Stein, L. (1993). In vitro reinforcement of hippocampal bursting activity by the cannabinoid receptor agonist (-)-CP-55,940. *Brain Research, 626*, 272–277.

Yamamoto, J., & Mochizuki, A, (1988). Acquisition and functional analysis of manding with autistic students. *Journal of Applied Behavior Analysis, 21*, 57–64.

Yamamoto, T. (2007). Brain regions responsible for the expression of conditioned taste aversion in rats. *Chemical Senses, 32*, 105–109.

Yi, J. I., Christian, L., Vittimberga, G., & Lowenkron, B. (2006). Generalized negatively reinforced manding in children with autism. *Analysis of Verbal Behavior, 22*, 21–33.

Yoon, S., & Bennett, G. M. (2000). Effects of a stimulus–stimulus pairing procedure on conditioning vocal sounds as reinforcers. *Analysis of Verbal Behavior, 17*, 75–88.

Zajonc, R. B. (1965). Social facilitation. *Science, 149*, 269–274.

Zeiler, M. D. (1977). Schedules of reinforcement: The controlling variables. In W. K. Honig & J. E. R. Staddon (Eds.), *Handbook of operant behavior* (pp. 201–232). Englewood Cliffs, NJ: Prentice-Hall.

Zeiler, M. D. (1992). On immediate function. *Journal of the Experimental Analysis of Behavior, 57*, 417–427.

Zentall, T. R. (2006). Imitation: Definitions, evidence and mechanisms. *Animal Cognition, 9*, 335–353.

Zentall, T. R., Sutton, J. E., & Sherburne, L. M. (1996). True imitative learning in pigeons. *Psychological Science, 7*, 343–346.

Zettle, R. D., & Hayes, S. C. (1982). Rule-governed behavior: A potential theoretical framework for cognitive-behavior therapy. In P. C. Kendall (Ed.), *Advances in cognitive behavioral research and therapy* (Vol. 1, pp. 73–118). New York: Academic Press.

Zillmann, D. (1988). Cognition–excitation interdependencies in aggressive behavior. *Aggressive Behavior, 14*, 51–64.

Zimmerman, J., & Ferster, C. B. (1963). Intermittent punishment of S^{Δ} responding in matching-to-sample. *Journal of the Experimental Analysis of Behavior, 6*, 349–356.

Zink, C. F., Pagnoni, G., Martin-Skursky, M. E., Chappelow, J. C., & Berns, G. S. (2004). Human striatal responses to monetary reward depend on saliency. *Neuron, 42*, 509–517.

Author Index

Biographical information about authors is listed in the Subject Index.

Abbott, B., 229
Abraham, D. A., 315
Abraham, L. Y., 139
Abramson, C. I., 183
Ackil, J. E., 154
Adams, C. K., 319
Ader, R., 56
Agostino, N. R., 184
Ainslie, G., 207, 208
Albanos, K., 160
Alberto, P. A., 295, 302
Albin, R. W., 137
Alciati, M. H., 319, 320
Alcock, J., 243, 327
Alexander, J. H., 138
Alferink, L. A., 222
Allen, C, M., 213, 336
Allen, G. L., 236
Alling, K., 76
Allison, J., 72
Altschuler, E. L., 250
Alvarez, L. W., 324
Alvarez, W., 324
Alvord, J. R., 236
Anderson, C. D., 178
Anderson, M. J., 52
Anderson, N. D., 184
Anderson, R. B., 97
Andre, J., 160
Andreatos, M., 276
Andrews, D., 302
Angell, J., 13
Anisfeld, M., 248
Anrep, G. V., 47, 48
Antonitis, J. J., 83, 102, 227
Appel, J. B., 125, 126
Arbuckle, J. L., 115
Arcediano, F., 53
Armitage, K. B., 333
Arms, R. L., 142
Armstrong, E. A., 164
Arnold, K. E., 173
Arvanitogiannis, A., 5
Arwas, S., 161
Asaro, F., 324
Ator, N. A., 75
Austin, J., 295
Autor, S. M., 225
Axel, R., 326, 327
Axelrod, S., 127

Ayllon, T., 178, 236
Azar, B., 191
Azrin, H. N., 84, 99, 121, 124, 125, 126, 127, 128, 129, 140, 141, 144, 163, 236, 298

Baars, B. J., 18
Badger, G. J., 112, 113
Badia, P., 229
Baer, D. M., 10, 17, 31, 82, 241, 242, 251, 252, 253, 254, 267, 275, 296, 299, 300, 312
Baeyens, F., 53
Bailey, J. S., 127, 276, 295
Baines, C., 319, 320
Baker, A. G., 137
Baker, T. B., 54
Baldwin, J. M., 243
Ball, J., 243
Balsam, P. D., 82
Bandura, A., 251, 254/**254**, 255, 256, 257, 261
Banko, K., 69, 70
Banuazizi, A., 156, 157
Bard, K., 248
Barker, L. M., 161
Barnes, C. A., 82
Barnes-Holmes, D., 241, 288
Barnet, R. C., 52
Baron, A., 104, 107, 108, 118, 129, 134, 261
Baron, R. A., 142
Barr, R., 248
Barrera, F. J., 152
Bartlett, R. K., 127
Barton, M., 319, 320
Bass, R., 118
Battalio, R. C., 205
Baum, M., 132, 202
Baum, W. M., xi, 6, 116, 118, 134, 145, 201, 205, 212, 213, 214, 219, 261
Baumeister, R. F., 143
Baxley, N. (Film Producer), 99
Baxter, D. A., 330
Baxter, N., 318
Beasty, A., 107
Bechera, A., 160
Bedarf, E. W., 161
Beiman, I., 300
Bekkering, H., 250
Belke, T. W., 166, 167, 206, 235, 318
Belles, D., 302, 310, 311
Belluzzi, J. D., 74
Bem, D. J., 242, 272, 281

Benbasset, D., 183
Beninger, R. J., 178
Bennett, G. M., 277
Bentall, R. P., 107
Bering, J. M., 243, 250
Berkowitz, L., 142
Bernard, C., 28
Berns, G. S., 62
Bersh, P. J., 227
Bertaina-Anglade, V., 139
Berton, O., 139, 140
Besalel, V., 298
Besson, A., 139
Best, M. R., 161
Beumont, A. L., 315
Bickel, W. K., 112, 206
Biederman, G. B., 244
Bijou, S. W., 97
Binder, C., 306, 308, 309
Bitterman, M. E., 52
Bjork, D. W., 16
Bjorklund, D. F., 243, 248, 250
Blackman, D., 288
Blakely, E., 263
Blampied, N., 110
Blanchard, R. J., 230
Blanchard, S., 51
Bloom, H. S., 319, 320
Blough, D. S., 82, 173, 186, 189
Blue, S., 174, 175
Blumstein, D. T., 333
Boakes, R. A., 230
Boer, D. P., 165, 166, 316
Boesch, C., 337
Bolles, R. C., 58, 59, 61, 131
Bondy, A., 313
Bonem, E. J., 98, 104, 178
Bonem, M. K., 98, 104
Booth, S. F., 315
Borden, R. J., 143
Borem, M. C. P., 103, 111, 190
Boren, J. J., 124
Boroczi, G., 125
Borrero, J. C., 203
Bouton, M. E., 49
Bowdle, B. F., 143
Bowen, R., 143
Braake, K. E., 274
Bradlyn, A. S., 302, 310, 311
Bradshaw, C. M., 201
Brady, J. P., 95
Brady, J. V., 124, 125
Brady, P. M., 189
Branch, M., 110
Brandon, P. K, 110, 145
Brass, M., 250
Bratcher, N. A., 5, 218, 219
Breland, K., 151, 169
Breland, M., 151, 169
Brembs, B., 330
Breuggeman, J. A., 243

Breyer, N. L., 236
Brody, B. A., 56
Brody, H., 56
Broen, W. E., Jr., 125
Brogden, W. J., 58
Bronsnan, S. F., 235
Brooks, D. C., 49
Brown, G. S., 188
Brown, M. P., 230
Brown, P. L., 153, 154
Brown, R., 168, 229, 289, 333
Brown, T. G., 203
Brownstein, A. J., 202, 262
Brozec, J., 315
Brush, E. S., 132
Buccino, G., 250
Bucher, B., 273
Buckleitner, W., 233
Buckley, K. B., 14
Burgess, I. S., 213
Burgess, R. L., 28, 29, 30
Burgio, L. D., 297
Burke, K. A., 82
Burkholder, E. O., 302
Burton, T. A., 295
Bushell, D., Jr., 28, 29, 30
Buske-Kirschbaum, A., 56
Buskist, W. F., 262
Butler, B. K., 173
Butter, E., 127
Byrne, D., 4
Byrne, J. H., 330

Cable, C., 189
Cameron, J., 38, 69, 70, 146
Cappell, H., 54
Carmona, A., 155, 156
Carnine, D., 309
Carr, D., 288, 303, 311, 312
Carr, J. E., 210, 211
Carrigan, P. F., Jr., 288
Carroll, M. E., 205
Carroll, R. J., 273, 275
Carter, A., 312
Carton, J. S., 236
Carylon, W. D., 70
Case, D. A., 230
Cataldo, M. F., 287
Catania, A. C., 10, 66, 130, 194, 196, 209, 241, 259, 267, 277, 278, 286, 288, 319
Cathro, J. S., 230
Cattell, J. M., 15
Cerutti, D., 264
Chance, P., 15
Chappelow, J. C., 62
Charlop-Christy, M. H., 312
Charnov, E. L., 204
Chase, S., 50
Chen, X., 247, 248
Cheney, C. D., xii, xiii–xv, 98, 104, 106, 130, 131, 160, 161, 163, 164, 178, 184, 222, 229, 236

Cheng, J., 228
Cheng, K., 181
Chillag, D., 163
Cho, C., 132
Chomsky, N., 268, 278
Christian, L., 274
Christopherson, E. R., 314
Church, R. M., 118
Ciminero, A. R., 300, 314
Cleary, J., 288
Clifford, C. W. G., 181
Cohen, D., 143, 247, 248
Cohen, N., 56
Cohen, P. A., 305
Cohen, P. S, 125
Cohn, S. L., 110
Coker, C. C., 229
Cole, R. P., 53
Collier, G., 317
Compagne, H., 247, 248
Conger, R., 201
Conrad, D. G., 124
Cook, D., 305
Cook, L., 32, 115
Corballis, M. C., 333
Coren, S., 249
Courage, M. L., 243, 249
Cowles, J. T., 234
Craighero, L., 249
Craik, F. I., 184
Cranston, S. S., 301, 302, 303
Cresson, O., Jr., 289, 332
Cristler, C., 301, 302, 303
Criswell, E. L., 319, 320
Crofts, H. S., 227
Crone-Todd, D. E., 295
Crossman, E. K., 104, 222
Crowe, R. E., 106, 163
Culbertson, S., 103, 111, 190
Cullen, C., 263
Cumming, W. W., 110, 191
Custance, D. M., 243

Daley, M. F., 130
Damasio, H., 160
D'Amato, M. R., 288
Dapcich-Miura, E., 236
Darley, J. M., 36, 37
Darwin, C., 4, 7, 8, 323, 324/**324**
Davidson, T. L., 317
Davies, N. B., 204
Davis, C., 315
Davis, J. M., 243
Davison, M. C., 200, 203, 213, 217, 226
Dawkins, R., 4, 173, 325
Dawson, B. V., 243
Dawson, G. R., 246
Deacon, J. R., 242
DeBaryshe, B. D., 276
Deci, E. L., 69
DeFran, R. H., 230

De Houwer, J., 53
Deich, J. D., 52
Deitz, S. M., 17
de Lange, R. P. J., 326
Dengerink, H. A., 142, 143
Derenne, A., 104, 118
Desai, J. J., 314
Dessalles, J. L., 268
Detrich, R., 242
de Villiers, P., 177, 189, 196, 200, 201, 209
Deweese, J., 105
Dewey, J., 13
Dews, P. B., 106, 115
DeWulf, M. J., 178
DiCara, L. V., 156, 157
Dickinson, A. M., 271
DiLione, R. J., 139, 140
Dinsmoor, J. A., 17, 127, 134, 174, 229, 230
Dionne, M., 315
D'Mello, K., 163
Doepke, K. J., 241
Doerflinger, A., 317
Doleys, D. M., 314
Dollard, J., 251, 295
Domjan, M., 53, 161
Donahoe, J. W., 87, 330
Donaldson, H., 13
Donaldson, T., 251
Donegan, N. H., 58
Donnellan, A. W., 127
Donnerstein, E., 142
Donohue, B. C., 295, 298
Donovan, W. J., 173
Dorr, D., 246
Dorrance, B. R., 246
Doss, S., 275
Dougan, J. D., 5, 218, 219
Dove, L. D., 163
Dragoin, W. B., 158, 159
Dube, W. V., 110
Ducharme, J. M., 17
Dulany, D. E., 262
Duncan, I. D., 166, 167, 206, 318
Durand, V. M., 299
Dworkin, B., 157

Eckerman, D. A., 102
Egemo-Helm, K. R., 295
Egger, M. D., 228
Eibl-Eibesfeldt, I., 42
Eigenheer, P., 276
Eisenberger, R., 70
Ekman, P., 270
Eldred, N. L., 161
Ellison, G. D., 52
Elsmore, T. F., 202
Endicott, K., 276
Engberg, L., 50
Engle, B. T., 157
Enns, J. T., 249

Epling, W. F., xiii, 17, 38, 127, 161, 164, 165, 166, 201, 203, 206, 296, 297, 298, 314, 315, 316, 317, 318, 323, 331, 332, 334
Epstein, R., 17, 102, 244, 245, 246, 279, 280
Erjavac, M., 250
Erlich, P. R., 268
Ernst, A.J., 50
Eschelier, A., 139
Estes, W. K., 17, 57, 125
Ettinger, R. H., 177, 178
Etzkowitz, H., 331
Evans, F. J., 260
Evans, I. M., 127
Evans, R. I., 257
Everitt, B. J., 227

Fadiga, L., 249
Falck-Ytter, T., 249
Falk, J. L., 162, 163, 164
Fantino, E., 169, 226, 230, 232, 238, 239
Farmer-Dougan, V., 5, 218, 219
Favell, J. E., 127
Feenstra, M. G. P., 228
Feighner, J. P., 315
Feldman, M. A., 126
Ferguson, A., 200
Ferland, R. J., 178
Ferrari, P. F., 244, 250
Ferster, C. B., xiv, 11, 74, 79, 93, 94–5, 97, 103, 104, 106, 111, 115, 126, 145, 190, 194, 222
Festinger, L., 241
Fialip, J., 139
Field, D. P., 329
Field, T. M., 247, 248
Filby, Y., 126
Findley, J. D., 110, 197
Fink, G. R., 250
Finney, J. W., 314
Fiorillo, C. D., 5, 6
Firman, P. C., 70, 295
Fisher, E. B., 208
Fisher, J., 243
Fisher, W. W., 211, 295, 297
Fishman, S., 295
Fixsen, D. L., 236
Fjeld, H. A., 244
Flint, G. A., 230
Flory, R. K., 163
Fogassi, L., 244, 249, 250
Foss, B. M., 243
Fowler, S. A., 300
Foxx, R. M., 127
Freed, D. E., 206
Freud, S., 14
Freund, H. J., 250
Friedman, A., 189
Friesen, W. V., 270
Friman, P. C., 314
Frommer, G. P., 154
Frost, L., 313
Fry, A. F., 207

Fry, W., 115

Gaitan, S. C., 187
Galbicka, G., 118
Galdikas, B., 243
Galef, B. G., 244, 246, 336
Galizio, M., 107, 108, 129, 262, 263
Gallese, V., 249
Gallistel, C. R., 169
Gamzu, E., 177
Gannon, P. J., 268, 269
Garcia, J., 159, 161, 170
Gardner, E. T., 134
Gardner, M. R., 246
Garner, D. M., 314
Garris, P. A., 5, 218, 219
Gatheridge, B. J., 295
Gaynor, S. T., 109
Geen, R. G., 143
Geller, E. S., 295
Geller, I., 33
Gerard, H. B., 241
Gerbrands, R., 94
Gershoff, E. T., 122
Gewirtz, J. L., 253
Ghezzi, P., 311, 312
Gibbon, J., 118
Gibbons, E., 38
Gilligan, K., 185
Glanzman, D. L., 45
Glasscock, S. T., 314
Glazer, H. I., 137
Gleeson, S., 77
Glenn, S. S., 8, 323, 329, 335, 336
Glenwick, D., 9, 237, 300
Glucksberg, S., 36, 37
Goetz, E. M., 31, 82
Goldin-Meadow, S., 333
Goldsmith, T. H., 173
Goldstein, M. H., 319, 320, 334
Gollub, L. R., 79, 222, 226, 227
Gonzales, C., 143
Goodheart, M. G., 52
Gormezano, I., 52
Gott, C. T., 115, 116
Gould, S. J., 325
Grace, R. C., 109
Graham, L. E., 300
Grant, D. L., 154, 155
Grant, D. S., 161, 162, 186, 316
Grant, V. L., 316
Gravina, N., 295
Gredeback, G., 249
Green, D. M., 39
Green, G., 314
Green, L., 205, 206, 207, 208
Greenberg, R., 247, 248
Greene, W. A., 157
Greenspoon, J., 336
Greenway, D. E., 262
Greer, S. M., 201

Griffiths, D. A., 315
Grimer, J. A., 109
Groccia-Ellison, M., 51
Grossman, J., 312
Guess, D., 126, 267, 275
Gully, K. J., 142
Gustafson, R., 142
Guttman, A., 52
Guttman, N., 174, 177, 180, 181
Guze, S. B., 315

Haag, R., 82
Haas, J. R., 262
Hackenberg, T. D., 135, 233, 235, 261
Hackett, S., 295
Hake, D. F., 84, 124, 126, 127, 128, 140, 251
Hale, S., 203, 204
Hall, D. C., 319
Hall, G., 273
Hall, K., 275
Hall, M. C., 298
Hall, R. V., 298, 301, 302, 303
Hanna, E., 249
Hannan, J., 319, 320
Hanson, H. M., 97, 181
Harlow, H. F., 331
Harnard, S., 10
Harper, D. N., 101, 110, 118
Harring, N. G., 306
Harris, M., 335, 336
Harrison, J. M., 174
Harsh, C. M., 244
Harsh, J., 229
Hart, B., 241
Hausmann, F., 173
Hayashi, H., 316
Hayes, L. A., 248
Hayes, S. C., xi, 17, 259, 260, 262, 288, 298
Hayne, H., 248
Hearst, E. S., 85, 101, 154
Heath, R. G., 124
Heflin, L. J., 302
Hegge, F. W., 174, 175
Hegvik, D. K., 186
Heidenreich, B. A., 5, 218, 219
Heinemann, E. G., 50
Helhammer, D., 56
Helmstetter, E., 126
Hemmes, N. S., 178
Hendry, D. P., 227
Henschel, A., 315
Herbert, J. J., 244
Herman, R. L., 129
Hermann, P. M., 326
Herrnstein, R. J., xi, 102, 134, 188, 189, 195, 198, 199, 200, 201, 203, 204, 208, 209, 210, 211, 219, 226
Herruzo, J., 241
Hesse, B. E., 273, 274, 275
Heth, C. D., 52, 162, 316, 317
Heyes, C. M., 246
Higa, J., 178

Higgins, S. T., 112, 113, 295
Hilgard, E. R., 13
Hinde, C. A., 243
Hinde, R. A., 331
Hinderliter, C. F., 52
Hineline, P. N., 129, 130, 134, 135
Hinson, R. E., 54, 55
Hiroto, D. S., 138
Hirsch, J., 328, 329
Hockett, C. F., 267
Hoehn-Saric, R., 287
Holland, J. G., 275, 300, 304
Hollerman, J. R., 5
Holz, W. C., 99, 121, 124, 126, 127, 128, 129, 141, 144
Horne, P. J., 250, 252, 288
Hothersall, D., 44
Hough, M. J., 139
Houlihan, D., 110
Houston, A., 200
Hovell, M. F., 236
Howe, M. L., 243, 249
Hoyert, M. S., 118
Hrycaiko, D., 305
Hubbard, E. M., 250
Hughes, J. R., 112
Hull, D. L., 323
Hung, D., 273
Hunt, H. F., 125, 163
Hunter, I. W., 203
Hursh, S. R., 169, 205
Hutchinson, G. E., 243
Hutchinson, R. R., 84, 140, 141, 163
Hutton, L., 134
Hyten, C., 251

Iacobini, M., 250
Inglis, P., 162, 316
Inman, D., 104
Ireland, C., 152
Iriki, A., 249, 312
Irwin, O. C., 334
Ishaq, F. S., 3
Iwata, B. A., 127, 163

Jabaij, L., 56
Jackson, K., 235
Jackson, R. L., 138
Jackson, T. A., 244
Jacobson, S. W., 247, 248
James, W., 15, 243
Jansen, R. F., 326
Janszky, I., 247, 248
Jason, L. A., 9, 237, 300
Jenkins, H. M., 152, 153, 154, 168, 230
Jenkins, P. E., 213
Jenkins, W. O., 101
Johnson, B. M., 295
Johnson, K. R., 309
Johnson, R., 183
Johnston, J. M., 28, 303
Joker, V. R., 261

Jonas, G., 157
Jones, K. M., 295
Jones, S. S., 248
Jostad, C., 295
Jozsvai, E., 163
Ju, W., 262
Juujaevari, P., 143

Kaartinen, L., 143
Kabela, E., 207
Kagel, J. H., 205
Kaiser, D. H., 246
Kalat, J., 161
Kalish, H. I., 174, 180, 181
Kamin, L. J., 57, 58
Kanarek, R. B., 317
Karmely, J., 295
Kato, T., 316
Katz, J. L., 230
Katz, N. H., 295
Kaufman, A., 261
Kaur, J. S., 320
Kavanagh, D. J., 139
Kawai, M., 243
Kawamura, S., 337
Kazdin, A. E., 233, 236, 237, 295, 303
Keehn, J. D., 163, 314
Keith-Lucas, T., 52
Kelleher, R. T., 115, 222, 235
Keller, F. S., xii, 16, **17**, 305, 306
Kelly, S. Q., 211
Kelso, S. E., 312
Kendall, S. B., 178
Kendrick, D. F., 186
Kennedy, S. H., 315
Kessel, R., 118
Keys, A., 315
Khalili, J., 130, 131
Killeen, P. R., 118, 201, 229
Kimmel, E., 155
Kimmel, H. D., 155, 156
Kinchla, R. A., 36, 37
King, A. P., 334
Kintsch, W., 105
Kirby, F. D., 233
Kirk, M. D., 327
Kirschbaum, C., 56, 161
Kirschbaum, E. H., 161
Klin, A., 312
Klock, J., 233
Knowlton, S., 126
Koch, A. M., 244
Koelling, R. A., 159, 170
Koestner, R., 69
Kogan, E., 298
Kohler, W., 176
Kohn, J. P., 110
Komar, I., 9
Konarski, E. A., Jr., 242
Kooistra, L., 143
Kopp, R. E., 261

Kottke, T. E., 320
Kowal, B. P., 177
Kral, P. A., 158, 159
Kram, M. L., 139
Kramer, G. L., 139
Krank, M. D., 55
Krebs, J. R., 204
Krishnan, V., 139, 140
Kruger, A. C., 250
Kuenen, D. J., 41
Kuhl, P. K., 247
Kulak, J. T., Jr., 33
Kulik, C. C., 305
Kulik, J. A., 305
Kunkel, J. H., 242
Kurschel, R., 333
Kushner, M., 127
Kuykendall, D. H., 56
Kuznesof, A. W., 162, 164, 206
Kymissis, E., 276

Lac, S. T., 205
Laibson, D. I., 208
Laitman, J. T., 268, 269
Lamal, P. A., 8, 296, 300, 335, 336
Lamarre, J., 275
Lane, H., 97
Langman, R. E., 323
Langone, J., 295
Lanson, R. N., 102
Lanza, R. P., 279, 280
Lapinski, K. J., 298
Larkin, M., 318
La Rochelle, C. D., 139
Latham, G., 300
Lattal, K. A., 110, 115, 241
Lau, C. E., 163
Laurence, M. T., 134
LaVigna, G. W., 127
Lawrence, C. E., 229, 230
Layng, T. V. J., 309
Lazar, R., 289
Leaf, R. C., 133
Leaton, R. N., 45
Lebbon, A., 295
LeBlanc, J. M., 233
Lee, V. L., 267, 275
Lerman, D. C., 127, 163
Lett, B. T., 161, 162, 316
Levine, E., 51
Lewin, R., 273
Lewis, P., 134
Lieberman, D. A., 230
Lieberman, P., 268, 269
Lierle, D. M., 139
Lindsley, O. R., 305, 306, 308, 309
Linscheid, T. R., 127
Lippman, L. G., 261
Lloyd, K. E., **17**, 306, 335
Lloyd, M. E., 306
Lochner, D. G., 211

Loeb, J., 13
Logan, C. A., 230
Logue, A. W., 161, 207
Lohrman-O'Rourke, S., 127
Lorenzetti, F. D., 330
Loukas, E., 288
Lovaas, O. I., 128, 129, 241, 297, 305, 311, 313
Loveland, D. H., 188, 189, 195, 203
Lowe, F. C., 106–7, 262, 288
Lowenkron, B., 264, 274, 285, 287
Lowitz, G. H., 297
Lubinski, D., 242, 281, 282, 283
Lubow, R. E., 161, 189
Lucas, G. A., 52, 222
Lucas, K. E., 222
Luce, S. C., 314
Luciano, M. C., 184, 241, 263
Luiselli, J. K., 185
Lynch, J. J., 160

MacCorquodale, K., 271, 281, 282
Mace, F. C., 17, 201
Machado, A., 82
Macphail, E. M., 132
Madden, G. J., 201
Magnus, R., 16
Maier, S. F., 137, 138, 139
Maki, W. S., 186
Malagodi, E. F., 105, 163
Malott, R. W., 263, 295
Mandrusiak, M., 317
Maple, T. L., 222
Markowitz, H., 88
Marquis, D. G., 13
Marr, J. M., 222
Marr, M. J., 118
Marsh, G., 183
Marshall, N. J., 173
Martens, B. K., 211
Martin, D. G., 36
Martin, G., 53, 295, 296, 299, 305, 308
Martin, P. L., 236, 237
Martin, T. L., 295
Martin-Skursky, M. E., 62
Martinez, C., 262
Masserman, J. H., 125, 128
Matson, J. L., 127
Matsuzawa, T., 235
Matthews, B. A., 241, 259
Matthews, L. R., 200
Maurice, C., 305, 311, 314
Mauro, B. C., 201
May, J. G., 134, 246
Mazziota, J. C., 250
Mazur, J. E., 105, 211
McBride, S. A., 203
McCarthy, D., 213
McCauley, L., 328, 329
McCleery, J. P., 250
McClung, C., 139, 140
McCully, J., 55

McDonald, J. S., 195
McDougall, W., 243
McDowell, J. J., 118, 203, 210, 211
McEachin, J. J., 311
McGinnis, J. C., 70
McGuigan, M., 227
McIlvane, W. J., 110, 288
McIntire, K. D., 288
McLean, A. P., 101, 110, 118
McMahon, P. T., 298
McSweeney, F. K., 177, 178, 201
Mechner, F., 82, 99
Meinhold, P., 127
Meissner, M., 333
Mellitz, M., 134
Meltzoff, A. N., 246, 247, 248, 249, 250, 254
Melville, C. L., 178
Mendelson, J., 163
Menke, T. J., 56
Meredith, R. L., 314
Mesibov, G.B., 311
Mesker, D. C., 97
Meyer, D. R., 132
Meyer, L. H., 127
Meyer, M. E., 261
Michael, J. L., xi, 17, 27, 129, 226, 263, 271, 273, 274, 275, 276, 290, 324
Michel, H. V., 324
Mickelsen, O., 315
Milan, M. A., 178
Milgram, S., 260
Millard, W. J., 243
Millenson, J. R., 1, 48
Miller, H. L., 203, 262
Miller, N. E., 124, 143, 157, 155, 156, 222, 228, 251, 295
Miller, R. R., 52, 53
Milner, P., 227
Miltenberger, R. G., 295
Mingote, C. S., 228
Misanin, J. R., 52
Mitchell, C. J., 246
Mitchell, D., 161
Mochizuki, A., 273
Modaresi, H. A., 132
Moerk, E. L., 289, 290
Moes, D. R., 297
Molnar, P., 247, 248
Mooney, S. E., 108
Moore, B. R., 244,
Moore, J., 20
Moore, M. K., 246, 247, 248, 249, 254
Moran, D. J., 295
Morford, M., 333
Morgan, C. L., 243
Morgan, L., 82,
Morris, E., 158
Morris, E. K., 7
Morrone, C., 228
Morrow, J. E., 312, 313
Morse, W. H., 93, 97, 106, 115, 116
Moseley, J. B., 56

Mueller, K. L., 230
Mulick, J. A., 127
Muller, P. G., 106, 163
Munoz, R., 315
Murphy, E. S., 177
Murphy, J., 274
Myers, D. L., 213
Myers, J. L., 222
Myers, L. E., 213
Myers, R. D., 97
Myerson, J., 203, 204, 207

Nadal, L., 88
Nader, M. A., 205
Nagi, E., 247, 248
Nakajima, S., 316
Naqvi, N., 160
Navarick, D. J., 169
Naylor, L., 320
Neal, D. T., 97
Neef, N. A., 201
Neelakantan, P., 319, 320
Neuringer, A. J., 82
Nevin, J. A., xi, 85, 109, 118
Newberry, D. E., 262
Newhouse, L., 275
Nichol, K., 230
Nickel, M., 76
Nisbett, R. E., 143
Nolan, J. V., 160
Nonacs, P., 204
Norman, W. D., 177, 201
Norton, W., 259, 335
Notterman, J. M., 84
Nurnberger, J. I., 95
Nygaard, S. L., 205

Oah, S., 271
Oberman, L. M., 250, 312
Odum, A. L., 82
O'Brien, R. M., 225
O'Kelly, L. E., 140
Okuyama, S., 139
O'Leary, M. R., 143
Olds, J., 227
O'Malley, K., 56
O'Reilly, J., 82
O'Reilly, M. F., 258
Orlando, R., 97
Orne, M. T., 260
Orvos, H., 247, 248
Osborne, J. G., 126
Osgood, C. E., 334
Osuch, J., 319, 320
Overmier, J. B., 138
Owczarczyk, J., 317
Owens, I. P. F., 173

Page, S., 82
Pagnoni, G., 62
Pal, A., 247, 248

Palmer, D. C., 87
Palya, W. L., 118
Paniagua, F. A., 241, 242
Papachristos, E. B., 169
Papini, M. R., 52
Parker, L. A., 161
Parkinson, A. E., 188
Parkinson, J. A, 227
Parrott, L. J., 271
Partington, J. W., 275, 276
Patterson, G. R., 142, 233
Pauker, A., 244
Paul, G. L., 237
Pauley, P. J., 13
Pavlov, I. P., 3, 7, 11, 12–13, 16, 44, 46, 47, 48, 49, 50, 57, 66, 160
Pear, J. J., 53, 62, 83, 178, 181, 246, 295, 296, 299, 308
Peden, B. F., 201
Pedersen, W. C., 143
Pena-Correal, T. E., 207
Pennypacker, H. S., 28, 303, 310, 319, 320
Pepperberg, I. M., 189, 277
Perin, C. T., 85
Perlow, S., 208
Perone, M., 75, 108
Perry, R. L., 161
Petersen, N. J., 56
Peterson, C., 139
Peterson, G. B., 154
Peterson, N. J., 125, 222
Peterson, R. F., 251, 312
Pettitt, L., 275
Petty, F., 139
Pfautz, P. L., 58
Phillips, E. A., 236
Phillips, E. L., 236
Philpott, S. B., 333
Piazza, C. C., 297
Pieneman, A. W., 326
Pierce, W. D., xii, xiii–xv, 6, 17, 69, 70, 127, 146, 161, 162, 164, 165, 166, 167, 198, 201, 203, 206, 235, 296, 298, 314, 314, 315, 316, 317, 318, 323, 330, 331, 332, 334, 336
Pierrel, R., 174, 175
Pilgram, C. A., 319
Pineda, J. A., 250
Pisano, R., 143
Pitts, R. C., 163
Platt, J. R., 115
Plaud, J. J., 203, 262
Pliskoff, S. S., 197, 202, 203
Ploog, B. O., 230
Poehlmann, R. J., 160
Poling, A., 76, 200
Poppen, R., 263
Porter, J. P., 243
Poulos, C. X., 54
Poulson, C. L., 276
Powell, R. A., 235
Powell, R. W., 117
Powers, R., 184
Prelec, D., 204

Premack, D., 71, 123, 124, 213
Prewitt, E. P., 58
Privat, A. M., 139
Proctor, S. D., 317
Provenza, F. D., 160
Provine, R. R., 248
Pryor, K. W, 78, 82, 222
Puglisi-Allegra, S., 228
Pulkkinen, L., 143

Quinn, J. M., 98

Rachlin, H. C, 118, 154, 202, 205, 207, 208
Ragan, P., 243, 250
Rakoczy, H., 247, 248
Ramachandran, V. S., 250, 312
Ravelski, E., 315
Ray, E. D., 246
Rayner, R., 14, 44
Razran, G., 50
Reeve, K. F., 276
Reeve, L., 276
Reichle, J., 275
Reidenberg, J. S., 268, 269
Reilly, M. P., 110
Reilly, S., 160
Renthal, W., 139, 140
Repacholi, B. M., 250
Rescorla, R. A., 52, 53, 59, 61, 62, 226
Revusky, S. H., 161
Reyes, F. D., 330
Reynolds, G. S., 95, 115, 177, 209
Ribes, E. M., 262
Ricciardi, J. N., 185
Richards, R. W., 288
Richardson, D. R., 142
Richardson, J. V., 104
Rilling, M., 186
Rincover, A., 17
Ringdahl, J., 163
Risley, T. R., 10, 241, 253, 254, 296
Ritzl, A., 250
Rizley, R. C., 53
Rizzolatti, G., 249, 250
Roberts, A. C., 227
Robins, E., 315
Roche, B., 288
Rodriguez, M. L., 207, 262
Rogers, R. W., 143
Rogers-Warren, A., 273
Roll, J. M., 112, 113
Rolnick, A., 161
Ronan, P. J., 139
Rosenberg, E. L., 270
Ross, D., 255
Ross, S. A., 255
Roth, W. J., 183
Routtenberg, A., 162, 164, 206
Rozin, P., 161
Rozzi, S., 250
Ruddle, H. V., 201

Rudrauf, D., 160
Ruggiero, A., 244
Ruggles, T. R., 233
Rumbaugh, D. M., 274
Ruskin, G., 305
Russell, G. W., 142
Russell, J. C., 162, 316, 317
Rutherford, G., 275
Ryan, R. M., 69

Saayman, G. S., 244
Sailor, W., 275
Saladin, M. E., 53
Salamone, J. D., 228
Sallery, R. D., 140
Salmon, D. P., 288
Salvy, S. J., 127, 162, 316
Sambrook, T., 243
Sander, A. A., 320
Sanders, G. A., 268
Sargisson, R. J., 187
Saslow, D., 319, 320
Satterlund, M., 295
Saunders, K. J., 288, 319
Savage-Rumbaugh, S. E., 250, 273, 274
Schaefer, H. H., 236, 237
Scheller, D. K., 139
Scheller, R. H, 326, 327
Schlinger, H., 263
Schlosberg, H., 52
Schlund, M. W., 287
Schmidt, M., 88
Schmitt, D. R., 263
Schneiderman, N., 52
Schoenfeld, W. N., xii, 16, 17, 110, 227
Schoneberger, T., 278
Schopler, E., 311
Schrier, A. M., 189
Schulman, A., 124
Schultz, W., 5, 6
Schwartz, B., 81, 82, 168, 169, 177
Schwarz, N., 143
Schweitzer, J. B., 236
Scott, J. F., 137
Segal, E. F., 109
Seifter, J., 33
Seligman, M. E. P., 137, 138, 139, 160
Sellers, T. A., 320
Semb, G. B., 305
Sepinwall, J., 32
Setzer, J., 50
Sevcik, R. A., 274
Shabani, D. B., 295
Shade, D., 201
Shanker, S. G., 274
Shapiro, M. M., 149
Shaver, K. G., 177
Shearn, D. W., 155, 156
Sherburne, L. M., 246
Sherman, G. J., 174, 175
Sherman, J. A., 184, 251, 252, 305, 312

Sherman, L., 208
Sherrington, C., 43, 44
Shields, F., 233
Shimoff, E. H., 241, 259
Shimp, C. P., 115, 118
Shizgal, P., 5
Shull, R. L., 109, 118, 197
Sidman, M., 11, 28, 32, 97, 109, 110, 122, 124, 127, 133, 134, 138, 144, 145, 146, 288, 289, 332
Siegel, S., 53, 54, 55
Sigafoos, J., 275
Silberberg, A., 154
Simek, T. C., 225
Simic, J., 273
Simmelhag, V. L., 117, 162
Simmons, J. Q., 128, 129, 297
Simmons, J., 191
Simon, S. J., 178
Sitharthan, G., 139
Sitharthan, T., 139
Skinner, B. F., xi, xii, 1, 4, 7, 8, 9–11, 16, 17, 18, 20, 38, 57, 67, 73, 74, 75, 79, 82, 86, 87, 88, 89, 93, 94, 95, 97, 103, 104, 106, 112, 114, 115, 118, 125, 135, 136, 137, 142, 143, 145, 149, 151, 158, 191, 194, 221, 222, 232, 233, 238, 242, 250, 257, 259, 261, 268, 270, 271, 273, 275, 277, 278, 279, 280, 281, 290, 291, 292, 295, 306, 309, 310, 323, 328, 331, 332, 333, 334, 335
Smith, M. C., 52
Smith, R. F., 230
Smith, T., 311
Sobsey, D., 126
Socrates, 1
Solnick, J. V., 17
Solomon, P. R., 51,
Solomon, R. L., 127, 132, 138
Solzhenitsyn, A., 36
Sossin, W. S., 327
Sousa, C., 235
Sowers-Hoag, K. M., 295
Sparks, S., 162, 316
Spencer, W. A., 45
Spengler, S. M., 275
Spetch, M. L., 181, 189
Spooner, F., 309
Squier, L., 88
Squires, N., 230
Staats, A. W., 53
Staddon, J. E. R., 117, 162, 163
Stafford, D., 110
Stanley, J. C., 101
Steckle, L. C., 140
Stefan, L., 161, 165, 206, 315
Stein, G. H., 319, 320
Stein, L., 74
Stephenson, H. S., 319
Stevenson-Hinde, J., 331
Stierle, H., 56
Stiers, M., 154
Stokes, P. D., 82
Stokes, T. F., 300
Stonebraker, T. B., 186

Storms, L. H., 125, 128
Strada, M. J., 295
Striano, T., 247, 248
Stroop, J. R., 36
Stucke, T. S., 143
Suib, M. R., 297
Sulzer-Azaroff, B., 295, 305
Sunahara, D., 198
Sundberg, M. L., 273, 274, 275, 276
Suomi, S. J., 244
Sutor, L. T., 157
Sutton, J. E., 246
Swets, J. A., 39
Swithers, S. E., 317
Szabadi, E., 201

Tait, R. W., 53
Tam, V., 184
Taras, M. E., 127
Takamori, K., 139
Tatham, T. A., 108
Tayler, C. K., 244
Taylor, H. L., 315
Taylor, I., 258
Taylor, S.P., 143
Taylor, T. J., 274
Teasedale, J. D., 139
Temple, W., 200
ter Maat, A., 326
Terrace, H. S., 183, 184
Terzich, B. J., 312, 313
Testa, T. J., 138
Thomas, D. R., 50
Thomas, S., 53
Thompson, R. F., 45
Thompson, T., 242, 281, 282, 283, 288, 312
Thorndike, E. L., 14–15, 16, 72, 73, 75, 244
Thorndike, R. L., 15, 16
Thorpe, W. H., 242, 243
Thyer, B. A., 295
Tice, D. M., 143
Tice, L., 297
Tiffany, S. T., 54
Tighe, T., J., 45
Timberlake, W., 72/**72**, 154, 155
Tinbergen, N., 41, 42, 326
Tobler, P. N., 5, 6
Tomasello, M., 250
Tomic, D. L., 227
Tomie, A., 288
Tourinho, E. Z., 20
Towe, A. L., 189
Trapp, M. A., 320
Trapp, N. L., 104
Troutman, A. C., 295
Tucker, B., 301, 302, 303
Tulving, E., 186
Turnbull, H. R., 126
Turner, T. R., 315
Turney, T. H., 189
Twinge, J. M., 143

Ullstadius, E., 248
Ulrich, R. E., 140, 141

Vanayan, M., 244
van de Poll, N. E., 82
van der Wall, S. B., 160
van Haaren, F., 82
van Hess, A., 82
Van Houten, R., 127
Vargas, E. A., 7, 8, 10
Vargas, J. S., 269, 271
Vaughan, M. E., 11
Vaughn, W., Jr., 112, 288
Velazquez, E., 51
Ventura, R., 228
Verhave, T., 190, 191
Viekrant, R. A., 320
Viemeister, N. F., 230
Villareal, J., 163
Visal-berghi, E., 244
Vittimberga, G., 274
Vogt, S., 250
Volkmar, F., 312
Vollmer, T. R., 203, 233
von Hofsten, C., 249
Vorndran, C. M., 127
Vuchinich, R. E., 205, 206

Wagner, A. R., 58, 59, 61, 62,
    226
Wakefield, J. C., 237
Wald, B., 229
Walker, S., 41
Wanchisen, B. A., 108
Ward, L. M., 249
Ward, R. D., 82
Warden, C. J., 244
Warren, S., 273
Wasserman, E. A., 52, 154, 155
Watkins, C. L., 306, 309
Watson, E., 230
Watson, J. B., 7, 13–14, 16, 44
Watson, J. S., 248
Wawrzyncyck, S., 44
Wearden, J. H., 213
Weatherly, J. N., 177
Webbe, F. M., 105
Weber, S. M., 228
Weigel, J. W., 314
Weiner, H., 107
Weiss, B., 116
Weiss, J. M., 137
Weissman, N. W., 104
Wesemann, A. F., 132
West, M. J., 334
West, R. P., 305, 308, 309
Westbrook, R. F., 178
Wheeler, H., 10
White, A. J., 309
White, C. T., 52
White, K. G., 87, 186, 187, 188, 217

White, O. R., 306
Whitehead, A. N., 1
Whitehurst, G. L., 276
Whitehouse, W. G., 134
Whiten, A., 243, 337
Whitley, P., 274
Wike, E. L., 222
Wilcoxon, H. C., 158, 159
Wilkes, G., 222
Wilkie, D. M., 178
Wilkinson, D. A., 54
Wilkinson, K. M., 288
Williams, A. R., 45
Williams, B. A., 178/**178**, 179
Williams, C. D., 89, 168, 169
Williams, D. R., 168, 169
Williams, H., 168
Williams, J. L., 139
Williams, M. D., 311, 312
Williams, S. L., 274
Williamson, P. N., 313
Wilson, L., 143
Wilson-Morris, M., 289
Winokur, G., 315
Witolawski, J. J., 97
Wixted, J. T., 87, 187, 188
Wolf, M. M., 10, 236, 253, 254, 296
Wolfe, B. M., 234
Wolfe, J. B., 142
Wolff, P. C., 140
Wood, W., 98
Woodruff, R. A., 315
Woods, R. P., 250
Woodside, B., 152
Woodson, R., 247, 248
Woolverton, W. L., 205
Worling, D. E., 17
Wyckoff, L. B., Jr., **17**, 229

Xue, B. G., 74

Yamaguchi, T., 201
Yamamoto, J., 273
Yamamoto, T., 160
Yi, J. I., 274
Yoon, S., 277
Yoshida, S., 139
Young, K. R., 305, 308, 309

Zajonc, R. B., 244
Zarcone, J. R., 163
Zeiler, M. D., 98, 99, 115, 118
Zentall, T. R., 244, 246, 249
Zettle, R. D., xi, 260, 298
Ziegler, D. R., 115
Zilles, K., 250
Zillmann, D., 142
Zimmerman, J., 126
Zimmerman, R. R., 331
Zink, C. F., 62
Zirkel, P. A., 127

Subject Index

Page entries for headings with subheadings refer to general/introductory aspects of that topic.
Page entries in **bold** refer to figures/diagrams.
Biographical information about authors is listed in this Subject Index in addition to the Author Index.

ABA (Association for Behavior Analysis), 17
A–B–A–B reversal design, 30–2, 39
ABC (Applied Behavioral Consultants), 312
A–B–C (antecedent, behavior, consequence), 24
Absolute stimulus control, 181–2
Acquisition, respondent, 47–8, **47**
Activity anorexia, *see* Anorexia nervosa
Activity-induced taste aversion, 316
Addiction; *see also* Drugs
  behavioral economics of, 205–6
  neuroscience of, 160–1
  and second-order conditioning, 53–4, 62
  substitutes/partial substitutes, 178, 205
Adjunctive behavior, 162–4, **163**
Ad libitum weight, 80
Adolescence, 111–12
Adventitious reinforcement, 177
Adversarial relationships, 146
Advertising, 14, 260
Aggression, 127
  breeding aggression, 142–4
  imitative, 254–6, **255**
  operant, 141–2
  reflexive, 140–1, **141**
  and submissive behavior, 223–4
Ainslie–Rachlin principle, 207/**207**
Alcohol experiment, multiple schedules of reinforcement,
  178
American Psychological Association, Experimental Analysis
  of Behavior Division, 25, 17
American Sign Language, 270/**270**
Amygdala, 227–8
Analysis, behavior, *see* Behavior analysis;
  see also Experimental analysis; Functional analysis
The Analysis of Verbal Behavior (Journal), 271
Animal Education (Watson), 13–14
Animal behavior; *see also* Birds
  activity anorexia, 315–16, **315**
  avoidance responses, 134–5
  behavioral flexibility, 328–9, **329**
  behavioral rigidity, 326–8, **326**, **327**, **328**
  cultural taboos, 336–7
  ethics of animal experiments, 127
  imitation, 243–6, **245**, 250
  Japanese monkey, observational learning, 243
  symbolic communication in pigeons, 279–83, **280**, **282**
  token reinforcement in chimpanzees, 234–5, **234**
Anorexia nervosa/activity anorexia, 161–2, 164–5, 314–15

activity/food reduction cycle, 317
  in animals, 315–16, **315**
  assessment/treatment/prevention, 318
  behavioral economics of, 206
  biological context of eating/activity, 167
  conditioned overeating, 316–17
  excessive physical activity, 315
  in humans, 317–18
  reinforcement effectiveness of food, 166–7
  reinforcement effectiveness of physical activity, 165–6,
    165, **166**
  and taste aversion, 161–2
Antecedent, behavior, consequence (A–B–C), 24
Anticipatory contrast, 179
Antidepressant drugs, 140
Apes, 250
Applied behavior analysis, 3, 10, 295, 296–7, 320–1;
    see also Problem behavior; Research
  anorexia nervosa/activity anorexia, 314–18
  applications of behavior principles, 310
  autistic children, 311–14
  behavioral contracts, 298/**298**
  breast self-examination (BSE), 318, 319–20
  changing criterion experimental design, 310, **311**
  cigarette smoking, 112–13, **113**
  differential reinforcement of other behavior (DRO), 297
  drug use/abuse, 53–4, 62
  generalized imitation training, handicapped children,
    253–4
  generality of behavioral change, 299–300
  mother–child interaction, verbal, 289
  personalized system of instruction (PSI), 305–6, 320
  pigeons, use in quality control, 190–1, **190**
  precision teaching, 306–10, **307**, 320
  psychiatric patients, behavior modification programs,
    236–7
  self-control, training, 310–11, **311**
  self-injury, 210–11, **211**, 297
  side effects of punishment, 144–6
  smoking, moderation of excessive, 310–11, **311**
  social environmental focus, 300
  temper tantrums, extinction, 89/**89**
Applied Behavioral Consultants (ABC), 312
Association for Behavior Analysis (ABA), 17
Associations, 47
Associative strength, 59
Astrology, 1–2; *see also* Superstition
Attachment, to aggressors, 234

Attention, contingent on misbehavior, 233
Authority, obedience to, 260/**260**
Autistic children, 311
   applied behavior analysis, 312–14
   intensive behavioral intervention, 311, 312, 313, 314
   mirror neurons, 312
   observational learning, 250
Automaintenance, 167–8
Autonomic responses, operant conditioning of, 156–7
Autoshaping, 153–4, **153**, 167–9
Aversive control of behavior, 121–2, 146; *see also* Avoidance
     responses; Punishment
   aversive stimuli, 121–2
   contingencies of negative reinforcement, 129–31
   escape responses, 129, 130/**130**, 131/**131**
   long-term effects of negative reinforcement, 135
   negative reinforcers, 27, 129
Avoidance responses, 129, 130/**130**, 132
   analysis of avoidance behavior, 134
   discriminated avoidance, 132/**132**
   nondiscriminated (Sidman) avoidance, 133–4, **133**
   and shock frequency, animal experiment, 134–5

Baby in a box, 10; *see also* Children
Babbling, infant, 8, 24
Baboons, cultural taboos, 336–7
Backward
   chaining, 224–5
   conditioning, **51**, 52–3
Bad news, 229–30
Baer, Donald, **251**; *see also* Author Index
Bandura, Albert, 254/**254**; *see also* Author Index
Bartering in chimpanzees, 235
Baselines, experimental, 30, 32–3
Baseline sensitivity, 32
Baum, William, **214**; *see also* Author Index
BDNF (brain-derived neurotrophic factor), 140
Behavior
   analysis, *see below*; *see also* Experimental analysis;
     Functional analysis
   animal, *see* Animal behavior; Birds
   avoidance, *see* Avoidance responses
   biological context of, 6–7, 298; *see also* Conditioning;
     Culture; Genetic selection; Selection
   causality, 1, 5, 18
   contextualist viewpoint, 7
   definition, 1
   elicited, 24, 43, 66
   and feelings, 19–20
   imitative, *see* Observational learning
   impulsive, 207–8
   intraverbal, 276
   involved/apathetic, 236
   law of, 200
   maintenance, 299
   modification, 210–11, **211**
   moral, *see* Ethics
   mystical accounts of, 2; *see also* Superstition
   negative reinforcement, *see* Aversive control of behavior;
     Punishment
   neural basis of, *see* Neuroscience

   ontogenic, *see* Ontogenetic behavior
   operant, 4, 7–8, 10; *see also* Operant behavior,
     reinforcement/extinction
   perception as, 36–9
   phylogenetic, 41–2, 62
   precurrent behavior, 258/**258**
   problematic, *see* Applied behavior analysis; Problem
     behavior
   reflexive, *see* Reflexive behavior
   reoccurrence of, 88
   repertoire of, 77
   rule-governed, 257–8, 259, 270–1
   scientific approach, 2, 9–10; *see also* Behavior analysis;
    Experimental analysis
   selection of, *see* Selection, behavioral
   sequences, 42–3, **43**
   species-specific, 151–2
   systems, 155
   textual, 277
   theory, 2, 96–7
   thinking as, 18, 20–1
   trapping, 299
   verbal, *see* Speech; Verbal behavior
Behavior analysis, 3, 187; *see also* Experimental analysis;
    Functional analysis
   applied; *see* Applied behavior analysis
   and culture, 8–9
   history, 11–15
   and neuroscience, *see* Neuroscience
   rise of, 16–18
   and science, 96–7
Behavior Analysis and Learning (Pierce and Cheney), xiii–xv
The Behavior Analyst, 17
Behavior of Organisms (Skinner), xi, 7, 16, 17, 97, 221
Behavior and Social Issues: What Works in Education, 309
Behavioral
   change, assessment, 34–6
   contracts, 298/**298**
   contrast, 177–8
   dynamics, 118
   economics, *see* Economics, behavioral
   flexibility, 328–9, **329**
   measures, 47
   medicine, 314
   momentum, 109–10
   neuroscience, *see* Neuroscience
   persistence, 136–7
   pharmacology, 6
   rigidity, 326–8, **326**, **327**, **328**
   selection, *see* Selection, behavioral; *see also* Evolution
Behaviorism, 13, 14
Bettelheim, Bruno, 137
Beyond Freedom and Dignity (Skinner), xi
Biological level of selection, *see* Genetic selection
Birds
   begging reflex, robins, 41
   concept formation by pigeons, 188–9
   imitation, pigeons, 244–6, **245**
   imprinting, ducklings, 7
   nest building, robins, 42
   operant chambers, **194**

parrot "speech", 277
pecking of milk bottle tops, 243
perception, 173
pigeon discrimination, 175–7, **176**
pigeon quality control, 190–1, **190**
Project Pigeon, 88–9
snuggling, chicks, 155
spontaneous imitation, 244–6, **245**, 250
Bitonic functions, 163/**163**
Blaming the victim, 177
Block building experiment, 31/**31**
Blocked-response CEOs, 273
Blocking, 57–8, 61, 62
Blowfly (*Phormia regina*), 328–9, **329**
Bobo doll experiment, 254–6, **255**
Brain-derived neurotrophic factor (BDNF), 140
Brain hemispheres, 288; *see also* Neuroscience
Break-and-run pattern of responding, 97, 106
Breast cancer, 318–20
Breast self-examination (BSE), 318, 319–20
Breland experiments, species-specific behavior, 151–2; *see also* Author Index
BSE (Breast self-examination), 318, 319–20

Calorie-wise foods, 317
Cambridge Center for Behavioral Studies, 17
Cameron, Judy, 38, 69, 70/**70**, 146; *see also* Author Index
Cancer, breast, 318–20
Catholic taboos, 337
Cats
    imitation, 244
    trial-and-error learning, 15
Causation, immediate/remote, 5
Celeration, 306–7, **307**
CEOs (conditioned establishing operations), 28, 273
Chain schedules of reinforcement, 222–3, **223**, 229/**229**
    backward chaining, 224–5
    concurrent, 231–2, **231**
    heterogeneous/homogeneous, 224
Change in associative strength, 59
Changeover
    delay (COD), 197
    response, 196–7
    Changing criterion experimental design, 303, 310, **311**
Children; *see also* Humans; Schools
    autistic, *see* Autistic children
    baby in a box, 10
    block building experiment, 31/**31**
    delayed imitation by infants, 248–9, 250
    discipline, *see* Problem behavior; Schools
    handicapped, generalized imitation training, 253–4
    Little Albert experiment, 14
    lying behavior, 242
    nursing reaction chain, newborn babies, 43/**43**
    obesity, 316–17
    rooting response, newborn infants, 43
    speech, 8, 24, 289–90
    spontaneous imitation by infants, 246–8, **246**, **247**, 249
    temper tantrums, extinction, 89/**89**
Chimpanzees, token reinforcement, 234–5, **234**
Chinese taboos, 337

Choice, 193, 219; *see also* Behavioral economics; Matching law
    alternation/changeover response, 196–7
    changeover delay (COD), 197
    choice paradigm, 194–8
    experimental analysis, 193–4
    experimental study procedures, 197
    Findley procedure, 197–8, **197**
    foraging, optimal, 204–5
    interval schedules, concurrent, 195–6
    operant chambers, **194**, **195**
    ratio schedules, concurrent, 195/**195**
    two-key procedure, concurrent, 194/**194**, **195**, **197**
    variable-interval (VI) schedules, 196, 203–4
Cigarette smoking, *see* Smoking
Classroom discipline, *see* Schools; *see also* Problem behavior
Clicker training, 222
COD (changeover delay), 197
Coercion, 144–6
Coercion and Its Fallout (Sidman), 127, 133, 144
Cognition, Creativity and Behavior video, 99
Cognitions, *see* Thinking/thought
Cognitive dissonance theory, 241
Commands, 260
Commitment response, 207–8, **208**
Communication, *see* Speech; Symbolic behavior; Verbal behavior
Concept formation by pigeons, 188–9
Concurrent
    chain schedules, 231–2, **231**
    interval schedules, 195–6
    reinforcement schedules, 194
    superstition, 196
Conditional discrimination, 189–90
    laboratory analysis, 278–9, **278**
Conditioned
    aversive stimuli, 121
    establishing operations (CEOs), 28, 273
    overeating, 316–17
    punishing stimuli, 144
    reflexes, 12–13, 16
    reinforcers, 77, 221, 281; *see also below*
    responses, 46, 47, 48; *see also* Respondent/s
    stimulus (CS), 46
    stimulus function, 26
    suppression, 57, 135
    taste aversion (CTA), 316
Conditioned reinforcement, 221–2, 239–40
    delay reduction hypothesis, 230, 232, 237–9, **239**
    determinants of, 225–7
    discriminative-stimulus account, 227
    established response method, 226–7
    establishing operations, 226
    establishing, 226–7
    generalized conditioned reinforcement, 232–3;
    generalized social reinforcement, 233–4
    good/bad news, 229–30
    information content of stimuli, 228–30, **228**
    neuroscientific research, 227–8
    new-response method, 222, 226
    observing response, 229, 230

Conditioned reinforcement – (*Contd.*)
  pairing, 227
  quantification/delay reduction, 237–9, **239**
  schedules of reinforcement, 222–5, **223**, 229/**229**, 231–2, **231**
  stimulus–stimulus (S–S) account, 227
  tokens/money, 234–7, **234**
  unconditioned reinforcers/reinforcement, 221, 225–6
Conditioning
  biological context, *see below*
  fear (Little Albert experiment), 14
  operant, *see* Operant conditioning
  and problem behavior, 233, 297–8
  reflexive, 14, 16
  respondent, *see* Respondent conditioning
  second-order, 53–6, **55**, 62
  selection of, 6–8, 65, 72/**72**, 74–5, 329–30
  simultaneous, 51–2, **51**
Conditioning, biological context, 158, 170
  activity anorexia, 161–2, 164–7, **165**, **166**
  adjunctive behavior, 162–4, **163**
  displacement behavior, 164
  facultative behavior, 162
  genetic selection, 6, 328–9, **329**
  instinctive drift, 151–2, 154
  interim behavior, 162
  nature of autoshaped response, 167–9
  negative automaintenance experiment, 167–8
  neuroscience of addiction, 160–1
  omission procedures, 168–9, **168**
  schedule-induced behavior, 162
  species-specific behavior (Breland experiments), 151–2
  taste aversion learning, 158–62, **159**
  terminal behavior, 162
Conference, experimental analysis of behavior, 16, **17**
Consequences, selection by, 3–5, **4**, 8, 73, 323, **324**, 330, 335, 338; *see also* Culture; Genetic selection; Selection
Context
  of behavior, 27–8
  of conditioning, 158; *see also* Conditioning, biological context
Contingencies; *see also* Aversive control of behavior; Punishment
  attention contingent on misbehavior, 233
  contact with, 85–6
  interlocking, 280, 282
  limited-hold, 108
  natural, 98–9, 261
  reinforcement, 5, 6, 27, 32–3, 68/**68**, **122**
  reward, 70
  and reinforcement schedules, 97, 108
  social, 261
  survival, 324–5
  three-term, 67/**67**, 289
Contingency-shaped behavior, 259–61, **260**
Contingency-specifying stimuli, 258
Contingent response, 72
Continuous
  recording, 304
  reinforcement (CRF), 77, 80, 81, 85, 101–2, **101**, **102**
Contrast, behavioral, 177–9

Controlling stimulus, 171
Correspondence relations, 241–2, 265;
  see also Observational learning; Rules
Countercontrol, 234
CR (conditioned response), 46–8; *see also* Respondent
Craving/drug withdrawal, 54, 56
CRF (continuous reinforcement), 77, 80, 81, 85, 101–2, **101**, **102**
CS (conditioned stimulus), 46
CTA (conditioned taste aversion), 316
Culture/cultural
  and behavior analysis, 8–9
  behavioral norms, 1
  definition, 8
  evolution, 4–5, 9, 336–8
  metacontingencies, 336
  practices, origin/transmission/evolution, 4–5, 9, 335–7
  and selection, 4–5, 335
  taboos, 336–7
Cumulative record/recorders, 78–8, **78**, **81**

Darwin, Charles, **324**; *see also* Author Index
Darwinian selection, *see* Natural selection
Delay reduction hypothesis, 230, 232, 237–9, **239**
Delayed conditioning, 51/**51**
Delayed imitation, 243
  infants, 248–9, 250
  pigeons, 244–6, **245**
Delayed matching to sample, 186–8, **186**
Dependent variables, 29/**29**
Depression, 139, 140
Deprivation operation, 76
Diet foods, 317
Differential imitation, 256
Differential reinforcement, 66, 172–3, **172**
  of other behavior (DRO), 176, 297
Differential response, 172/**172**, 174
Differentiation, response, 84
Direct replication, experimental, 33
Discipline, classroom; *see* Problem behavior; *see also* Schools
Discrimination, 3
  conditional, 189–90, 278–9, **278**
  index, 174–5, **175**
  respondent, 50–1
  simultaneous, 182
  successive, 182
  training, breast self-examination, 319
Discriminated
  avoidance, 132/**132**
  extinction, 84–5
Discriminative
  functions, 26, 263
  stimuli, 26, 66–7, 86/**86**, 227
Displacement behavior, 164
Disruptive behavior, 34–6, **35**, 144; *see also* Problem behavior
Distal reinforcement contingencies, 6
Domestic violence, 141–2
Dopamine, role, 6, 74, 139, 140, 228
DRO (differential reinforcement of other behavior), 176, 297
Dropping out, 145

Drugs; *see also* Addiction
  antidepressant, 140
  behavioral pharmacology, 6
  cannabinoid, 74
  effect on brain/behavior, 32–3
  overdose, effects of context, 55–6, **55**
  tolerance, 54, 62
Dualism, 14
Ducklings, imprinting, 7
Duration recording, 304

EAB, *see* Experimental analysis of behavior
Eating disorders, *see* Anorexia nervosa
Echoic behavior, 276–7
Economics, behavioral, 205–6
  and activity anorexia, 206
  addiction, 205–6
  Ainslie-Rachlin principle, 207/**207**
  commitment response, 207–8, **208**
  self-control, 207–8
Economy, token, 236–7
Education, *see* Schools
Effect, law of, xi, 15, 73, 209
Eisenberger, Robert, 70/**70**; *see also* Author Index
Elephant experiment, 88
Elicited behavior, 24, 43, 66
Emitted behavior, 24, 25
Emotion/al; *see also* Feelings
  distress, and punishment, 127; *see also* Side effects of
    punishment
  responses, 4, 84
Empathy, 249, 250
Enjoy Old Age: A Program of Self-Management (Skinner &
    Vaughan), 11
Environment, 18, 25
Epling, Frank, **332**; *see also* Author Index
Epstein, Robert, **17**, **244**; *see also* Author Index
Errorless discrimination, 182–4, **183**
Escape responses, 129, 130/**130**, 131/**131**
Established response method, conditioned reinforcement,
    226–7
Establishing operations, 27–8, 273
Ethics, 133
  of animal experiments, 127
  of punishment, 126, 127, 128, 129
Evolution, 324; *see also* Genetic selection;
    Selection
  conditioning, 6, 7–8, 65, 72/**72**, 74–5, 329–30
  cultural, 4–5, 9, 336–7
  history, 323
  of learning, 6
  by natural selection, 4–6, 324; *see also* Genetic selection;
    Selection
  observational learning, 245–6, 250
  operant–respondent interrelationships, 150
  rule following, 261
  social signals, 332–3, **332**
  speaking/vocal tract, 268–9
  of vision, 173
Exercise, excessive, 315; *see also* Anorexia nervosa/activity
    anorexia

Experimental analysis of behavior (EAB), 2, 23, 39;
    see also Functional analysis; Research
  assessment of behavior change, 34–6
  baselines, 30, 32–3
  behavioral research tactics, 28–30
  children's block building experiment, 31/**31**
  dependent/independent variables, 29/**29**
  disruptive school child example, 34–6, **35**
  first conference, 16, **17**
  generality, 33–4
  hypothetical constructs, 36
  perceiving as behavior, 36–9
  rabbit urine experiment, 28–30, **30**
  replication, 33, 34
  reversal design, 30–2, 39
  single-subject research, 30, 33
  statistical groups design, 33
  Stroop effect, 36–7, **37**
  trends, 35
Extinction, behavioral, 82–3, 123, 229, 330–1
  behavioral effects, 83
  burst, 83, 297
  discriminated, 84–5
  and discriminative stimuli, 86/**86**
  emotional responses, 84
  force of response, 84
  and forgetting, 87
  operant variability, 83
  partial reinforcement effect (PRE), 85–6, 96
  resistance to, 85, 101–2
  respondent, **47**, 48, 61–2, **62**
  response differentiation, 84
  spontaneous recovery, 86–7
  stimulus, 171
  of temper tantrums, 89/**89**
Extraneous sources of reinforcement, 209

Facultative behavior, 162
Fading, 182, 184–5
Fantino, Edward, 238/**238**; *see also* Author Index
FAPs (fixed action patterns), 42, 326–8, **326**, **327**, **328**
Fear conditioning (Little Albert experiment), 14
Feelings and behavior, 19; *see also* Emotional responses
  reports of, 19–20
Ferster, Charles Bohris, 11, 94–5, **94**; *see also* Author Index
FI (fixed-interval) reinforcement schedules, **103**, 105–6, **105**,
    106, **107**
Financial reinforcement, *see* Tokens/financial reinforcement
Findley procedure, 197–8, **197**
Fixed action patterns (FAPs), 42, 326–8, **326**, **327**, **328**
Fixed-interval (FI) schedules, **103**, 105–6, **105**, **106**, **107**
Fixed-ratio (FR) schedules, 103–4, **103**, **104**, 235
Fixed time (FT) reinforcement schedules, 105, 116–18
Flexibility, behavioral, 328–9, **329**
Flexible action patterns, 42
Fluency, 308
fMRI imaging, 287
Food
  conditioned overeating, 316–17; *see also* Anorexia nervosa
  multiple schedules of reinforcement, 178
  reinforcement effectiveness, 166–7

Foraging
  model, xi, 318
  optimal, 204–5
Ford, Henry, 221
Forgetting, and extinction, 87
Formal similarity, 276
FR (fixed-ratio) schedules, 103–4, **103**, **104**, 235
Free operant
  avoidance, 133
  method, 75
FT (fixed time) reinforcement schedules, 105, 116–18
Function-altering events, 263
Functional analysis; *see also* Experimental analysis
  of behavior, 5, 23–5
  conditioned establishing operations (CEOs), 28
  context of behavior, 27–8
  of environment, 25–6
  establishing operations, 27–8
  stimulus classes, 26–7
  stimulus functions, 26, 36
Functional independence, 273

Galizio, Mark, **262**; *see also* Author Index
Generality
  assumption of generality, 106–8
  of behavioral change, 299–300
  experimental, 33–4
Generalization
  gradients, 50/**50**
  respondent, 49–50, **50**
  response, 299
  stimulus, 180, 299, 313; *see also below*
Generalization, stimulus control, 179–80, 313
  absolute stimulus control, 181–2
  gradients, 180–1, **180**, **181**
  relative stimulus control, 182
  simultaneous discrimination, 182
  successive discrimination, 182
Generalized
  conditioned reinforcement, *see* Conditioned
    reinforcement
  conditioned reinforcers, 232, 281
  imitation, 251–4, **252**
  matching law, xi, 200–1, 212–13, 214; *see also* Matching
    law
  obedience, 260/**260**
  reinforcement, 281
  social reinforcement, 233–4
Genetic selection, 323–4; *see also* Evolution; Phylogenetic
    behavior; Selection
  behavioral flexibility, 328–9, **329**
  behavioral rigidity/fixed action patterns, 326–8, **326**, **327**,
    328
  conditioning, 6, 328–9, **329**
  contingencies of survival, 324–5
  genetic regulation of behavior, 326–8, **328**
  mutation, 325
  phenotype, 325/**325**
  phylogeny, 323
  sources of genetic variation, 325
Genotype, 325/**325**

Gesturing, selection/evolution, 332–3, **332**; *see also* Symbolic
    behavior
Glenn, Sigrid, 336/**336**; *see also* Author Index
Golf, teaching, 225
Good news, 229–30
Gradients, generalization, 180–1, **180**, **181**

Habit formation, 13; *see also* Conditioning
Habituation, 44–5
Hedonic value of stimuli, 227
Helplessness, learned, 137–40
Heroin
  addiction, 205–6
  overdose, effects of context, 55–6, **55**
Herrnstein, Robert, 198/**198**; *see also* Author Index
  experiment, 198–9, **198**, **199**, **210**
  law of effect, 209
Heterogeneous chains, 224
Hindu taboos, 337
History
  of behavior analysis, 11–15
  ontogenetic, 46
  of reinforcement, 5, 24
Homeostasis, 54
Homogeneous chains, 224
Honeybee, 327–8, **327**
Humane punishment, 129; *see also* Ethics
Humans (*Homo sapiens*); *see also* Children
  aggression, 142
  communication, 201
  cultural transmission, 337
  delayed imitation, infants, 248–9, 250
  evolution of speech, 269
  operant chambers, **195**
  spontaneous imitation, 243–4, 246–8, **246**, **247**,
    249
  taboos, 337
Hypothetical constructs, 36
Hypertension, 299–300

Iconic signing, 334
Identity matching, 284, 285/**285**
Imitation, *see* Delayed imitation; Observational learning;
    Spontaneous imitation
Immediate causation, 5
Immunosuppression, conditioned, 56
Imprinting in ducklings, 7
Impulsive behavior, 207–8
Independent variables, 29/**29**
Index, discrimination, 174–5, **175**
Infants, *see* Children
Information content of stimuli, 228–30, **228**
  good/bad news, 229–30
  observing response, 229, 230
  schedules of reinforcement, 223, 229/**229**
Instinctive drift, 151–2, 154
Instructions, 261–3
Instrumental response, 72
Intensity–magnitude, law of, 44, 48
Intensive behavioral intervention, autistic children,
    311–14

Interim behavior, 162
Interlocking contingencies, 280, 282
Intermittent reinforcement, xi, 85–6, 96, 98–9, 101–2
Interreinforcement interval (IRI), 110
Interresponse time (IRT), 114
Interval recording, 304/**304**
Interval schedules, 103/**103**
    fixed-interval (FI), **103**, 105–6, **105**, **106**, **107**
    scalloping, 106/**106**, 126
    variable-interval (VI), **103**, 108–9, **108**, **109**, 196,
        203–4
Intraverbal behavior, 276
An Introduction to the Science of Human Behavior
    (Nurnberger, Ferster, & Brady), 95
An Introduction to the Study of Experimental Medicine
    (Bernard), 28
IRT (interresponse time), 114
Inverse scallop, 126
In vitro reinforcement (IVR), 74
IRI (interreinforcement interval), 110
Islamic taboos, 337

Jack and Jill experiment, 279–81, **280**
Japanese monkey, observational learning, 243
Jewish taboos, 337
Joint control, 264/**264**
Journal of Applied Behavior Analysis (JABA), 10, 17,
    296
Journal of the Experimental Analysis of Behavior (JEAB), 5,
    17, 118, 289

Keller, F. S., 16, 305–6; *see also* Author Index
Korperstellung (Magnus), 16

Language; *see also* Speech; Verbal behavior
    defining, 267–9
    of reference, 267
Latency, 73
    law of, 44, 48
Laws
    behavior, 200
    of effect, xi, 15, 73, 209
    of intensity–magnitude, 44, 48
    of latency, 44, 48
    matching, *see* Matching law
    optimal foraging, 204–5
    quantitative law of effect, 209
    of the threshold, 44
Learned helplessness, 137–40
Learning
    definition, 1
    evolution of, 6
    observational, *see* Observational learning
    and ontogenic behavior, 46
    visceral, 157
Level, respondent, 48
Limited-hold contingency, 108
Linguistics, 271; *see also* Speech; Verbal behavior
Lithium chloride, 159, 160
Little Albert experiment, 14
Local reinforcement contingencies, 6

Low calorie foods, 317
Lowe, F. C., 106–7, **107**; *see also* Author Index

Magazine training, 77
MammaCare program, 319–20
Manding/manding relations, 271–2, 273–4
    analysis of, 290–1, **291**
    autistic children, 313
    impure, 274
Marine snail (*Aplysia*), 326–7, 330, **326**
Matching equation, 200, 203, 212, 213
    estimating slope/intercept, 217–18
    log-linear representation, 214, **215**, **216**
    setting values of independent variable, 217/**217**
Matching law, xi, 198, 200, 219
    application, self-injury behavior modification, 210–11,
        211
    calculation of proportions, 199
    departures/exceptions, 201–2, **202**, 215
    experimental evidence, 209–10, **210**
    generalized matching law, xi, 200–1, 212–13, 214
    Herrnstein's experiment, 198–9, **198**, **199**, **210**
    human communication, 201
    more than two alternatives, 203
    neuroscientific study, 218–19
    overmatching, 201, **202**, 213
    practical implications, 203–4
    power law for matching, 212–13
    proportional matching, 198–200
    quantitative law of effect, 209
    ratios, 212
    reinforcement schedules, 203–4
    relative rates, response/reinforcement, 200, **210**
    response bias, 201, **202,**, 213, 214–16
    sensitivity, 213, 214–16, 218–19
    single-operant schedules of reinforcement, 208–11, **210**,
        211
    sources of error, 212
    time spent on alternatives, 202–3
    undermatching, 201, **202**, 213, 215, **216**
Matching to sample (MTS), 185–6, **185**, 287
    delayed, 186–8, **186**
Maximization, 204
Maximum associative strength, 59
McDowell, J. J., 210/**210**; *see also* Author Index
Mechner notation, 99–100, **100**, 103, **133**, **174**, **176**, **223**
Media influences, 254–6, **255**
Melioration (optimal foraging law), 204
Memory processes
    cognitive metaphor, 186
    forgetting, 87
    remembering/recalling, 87–9, **88**
Metacontingencies, 336
Methadone addiction, 205–6
Mirror neurons, 243, 249–50, 312
Mixed schedule of reinforcement, 229/**229**
Molar/molecular perspectives, 116, 117, 134
Momentum, behavioral, 109–10
Money, as generalized conditioned reinforcer, 235;
        see also Tokens
Monkeys, observational learning, 243, 244

Montserrat, island of, 45
Moral behavior, *see* Ethics
Morrow, Joe, **312**; *see also* Author Index
Mother–infant
    attachment, 331
    interaction, verbal, 289
Motivation, 69–70, **70**, 97
MTS, *see* Matching to sample
Multiple baseline designs, 301
    across behaviors, 302–3, **303**
    across stimulus conditions, 301–2, **301**
    across subjects, 302
Multiple functions, 291
Multiple schedules of reinforcement, 173–5, **174**, 223, 229/
    229
    anticipatory contrast, 179
    behavioral contrast, 177–8
    determinants of, 178–9, **179**
    discrimination index, 174–5, **175**
Mutation, 325; *see also* Evolution; Genetic selection
Mystical account of behavior, 2

Natural selection, 4–5, 6, 324; *see also* Evolution; Genetic
    selection; Selection
Nature-nurture debate, 152
Nazi concentration camps, 138
Negative; *see also* Aversive control of behavior; Punishment
    contrast, 177
    punishment, **68**, 69, **122**, 123, **123**
    reinforcement, 68/**68**, 141–2
    reinforcers, 27, 129
    Neuringer, Allen, 82/**82**
Neurons; *see also* Neuroscience
    mirror, 243, 249–50, 312
    operant conditioning of, 74–5
Neuroscience, xii, 5–6
    addiction, 160–1
    conditioned reinforcement, 227–8
    derived conceptual relations, 287–9
    matching law, 218–19
    neural basis of reward, 6
    observational learning, 249–50
    taste aversion, 160, 161
    New-response method, 222, 226
News, good/bad, 229–30
Nondiscriminated (Sidman) avoidance, 133–4, **133**
Notational systems, 24
    Mechner notation, 99–100, **100**, 103, **133**, **174**, **176**,
    223
Nursing reaction chain, newborn babies, 43/**43**

Obedience to authority study, 260/**260**
Obesity, childhood, 316–17
Object permanence, 23, 24
Observational learning, 242, 243, 265; *see also* Delayed
    imitation; Spontaneous imitation
    behavioral interpretation, 256
    behavioral neuroscientific perspective, 249–50
    bird pecking of milk bottle tops, 243
    Bobo doll experiment, 254–6, **255**
    complex observational learning, 254–6

differential imitation, 256
evolutionary basis, 245–6, 250
generalized imitation, 251–4, **252**
Japanese monkey food/sand separation, 243
laboratory studies of imitation, 244–50
operant imitation, 251
social cognitive interpretation, 256
training application, handicapped children,
    253–4
Observing response, 229, 230
Omission procedure, 168–9, **168** ; *see also* Negative
    punishment
Ontogenetic behavior, 46, 62; *see also* Respondent
    conditioning
    conditioned/unconditioned responses, 46, 47, 48
    and learning, 46
    respondent acquisition, 47–8, **47**
    respondent discrimination, 50–1
    respondent extinction, **47**, 48, 61–2
    respondent generalization, 49–50, **50**
    respondent level, 48
    spontaneous recovery, 49/**49**
Ontogenetic selection, 111
Operant/s, 24, 25, 65, 157
    aggression, 141–2
    behavior, 4, 7–8, 10, *see also below*
    chambers, 75–6, **76**, **79**, 79–80, **194**, **195**
    classes, 66, 77
    conditioning, *see below*
    functions, 271
    imitation, 251
    level, 77
    rate, 75
    regulation, marine snail, 330
    –respondent interrelationships, *see below*
    variability, 83
Operant behavior, reinforcement/extinction, 65–6, 90;
    see also Extinction
    contingencies of reinforcement, 67–9, **67**, **68**, 70
    definitions, 65
    differential reinforcement, 66
    discriminative stimuli, 66–7
    as emitted behavior, 65
    identification of reinforcing stimuli, 70–2, **72**
    operant classes, 66
    positive reinforcers, 66
    Premack principle, 71, 72
    response deprivation, 71–2
    rewards and intrinsic motivation, 69–70, **70**
    S-delta stimuli, 67
    topography, 66
Operant conditioning, 4/**4**, 16, 38, 72–3
    of autonomic responses, 156–7
    conditioned reinforcers, 77
    continuous reinforcement (CRF), 77, 80, 81, 85
    cumulative record/recorders, 78–8, **78**, **81**
    deprivation operation, 76
    evolution of, 329–30
    free operant method, 75
    magazine training, 77
    model experiment, **79**, 79–81, **80**, **81**

of neuron, 74–5
probability of response, 75
puzzle box example, 73/**73**
repertoire of behavior, 77
selection by consequences, 73
selection of, 7–8, 65, 72/**72**, 74–5, 329–30
shaping/successive approximation, 77–8
theory, 10
Operant–respondent interrelationships, 136–7, 149–51,
    169–70; *see also* Conditioning; Genetic selection;
    Selection
    autonomic responses, operant conditioning, 156–7
    autoshaping, 153–4, **153**
    behavior systems, 155
    and evolution/natural selection, 150
    instinctive drift, 151–2, 154
    operants/respondents, 157
    reinforcing reflexive behavior, 155–6
    sign tracking, 152–3, **152**, 154
    species-specific behavior, 151–2
    stimulus substitution hypothesis, 154–5
Optimal foraging law, 204–5
Orders/commands, 260
Overdose, heroin, effects of context, 55–6, **55**
Overeating, conditioned, 316–17
Overmatching, 201, **202**, 213
Overshadowing, 57, 58

Palpation, breast, 319
Parrot "speech", 277
Partial
    reinforcement effect (PRE), xi, 85–6, 96, 98–9, 101–2;
        see also Reinforcement schedules
    substitutes, 178, 205
Pavlov, Ivan Petrovich, 11, 12–13, **12**, 16; *see also* Author
    Index
    Pavlov's dogs experiment, 12–13, 66
Peak shift, 181/**181**
Pennypacker, Henry S., 319/**319**; *see also* Author Index
Perception
    as behavior, 36–9
    seeing as conditioned response, 38–9
    Stroop effect, 36–7, **37**
Perceptual set, 39
Personality traits, 97
Personalized system of instruction (PSI), 305–6,
    320
Pharmacology, behavioral, 6; *see also* Drugs
Phenotype, 325/**325**; *see also* Evolution; Selection
Phylogenetic behavior, 41–3, **43**, 62; *see also* Evolution;
    Genetic selection; Selection
    reflexive, *see* Reflexive behavior
Phylogeny, 323; *see also* Evolution; Genetic selection;
    Selection
Physical activity, reinforcement effectiveness, 165–6, **165**,
    166; *see also* Anorexia nervosa
Pierce, A. E., Chair in Psychology, 11
Pierce, David, **332**; *see also* Author Index
Pigeons
    imitative behavior, 244–6, **245**
    Project Pigeon, 88–9

quality control application, 190–1, **190**
    stimulus discrimination, 175–7, **176**
    symbolic communication, 279–83, **280**, **282**
Placebo effect, 56
Plasticity, neural, 75
Polydipsia, 162, 163
Positive
    contrast, 177
    punishment, 68–9, **68**, 122–3, **122**
    reinforcement, 10, 68/**68**, 127–9, **128**
    reinforcers, 27, 66, 70
Postreinforcement pause (PRP), 104, 106, 116–18
Power law for matching, 212–13
PRE (partial reinforcement effect), xi, 85–6, 96, 98–9, 101–2;
    see also Reinforcement schedules
Precision teaching, 306, 320
    applications, 309–10
    basic principles, 308–9
    celeration/charting behavior change, 306–7, **307**
    fluency, 308
Precurrent behavior, 258/**258**
Preference, 193; *see also* Choice
    reversal, 207
Premack principle, 71, 72, 123–4
Preparedness, 159
Preratio pause (PRP), 104
Primary aversive stimuli, 121
Principles of Psychology (James), 15
Principles of Psychology (Keller & Schoenfeld), xii
Principle of reinforcement, xi, 15
Private behavior, thinking as, 20–1
Private world, 18
Probability of response, 75
Problem behavior, *see also* Applied behavior analysis
    causes and prevention of, 314
    classroom discipline, 144, 233, 236
    differential reinforcement of other behavior (DRO), 297
    direct treatment of, 298
    disruptive school children, 34–6, **35**, 144
    temper tantrums, 89/**89**
    truancy, 145–6
    unintentional conditioning, 233, 297–8
Problem solving, 81–2, **81**, **82**
Progressive ratio schedules, 98, 110, 165
Project Pigeon, 88–9
Protozoan (*Spirostomum ambiguum*), 45
PRP (postreinforcement pause), 104, 106, 116–18
PRP (preratio pause), 104
PSI (Personalized system of instruction), 305–6, 320
Psychiatric patients, behavior modification programs, 236–7
Psychology Today, 17
Punishment, 1, 10, 122/**122**; *see also* Aversive control of
    behavior; Side effects
    abrupt introduction of, 124–5
    definitions, punisher/punishment, 122
    delayed, 125
    effect of drugs, 32–3
    effectiveness, 124
    humane, 129
    immediacy of, 125–6
    intensity of, 125

Punishment – (*Contd.*)
 moral issues, 126, 127, 128, 129
 negative, **68**, 69, **122**, 123, **123**
 positive, 68–9, **68**, 122–3, **122**
 and reinforcement schedules, 99
 relativity of (Premack principle), 71, 72, 123–4
 response alternatives, 129
 schedule of, 126
 use in treatment, 126–9
Puzzle box, 15, 73/**73**

Quantitative law of effect, 209

Rabbit urine experiment, 28–30, **30**
Radiation sickness, 159
Rate of response, 73
Ratio schedules, 103–5, **103**, **104**, **105**
 fixed-ratio (FR), 103–4, **103**, **104**, 235
 progressive, 98, 110, 165
 upcoming ratio requirement, 104
 variable ratio (VR), **103**, 104–5, **104**, **105**, 108
Ratio strain, 110
Rats, cultural transmission, 336
Reaction chains, 42–3, **43**
Recording/recorders, 78–8, **78**, **81**, 304/**304**
Recovery, spontaneous, 49/**49**
Reflex, 43
 conditioned, 12–13, 16
 response, 3
Reflexive behavior, 43–4, 62
 aggression, 140–1, **141**
 conditioning, 14, 16
 elicited, 43, 66
 habituation, 44–5
 primary laws of the reflex, 44, 48
 reinforcing, 155–6
 unconditioned response (UR), 43, 44
 unconditioned stimulus (US), 43, 44
Reflexivity, 284, 285/**285**
Reinforcement, 2; *see also* Conditioned reinforcement
 contingencies of, *see* Contingencies, reinforcement
 differential, 66, 172–3, **172**
 function, 26
 history of, 5, 24
 intermittent, xi, 85–6, 96, 98–9, 101–2
 negative, 68/**68**; *see also* Aversive control of behavior;
  Punishment
 nonspecific, 274
 positive, 10, 68/**68**, 127–9, **128**
 principle of, xi, 15
 and problem solving, 81–2, **81**, **82**
 rates, 109–10, 200, **210**
 schedules, *see below*
 selection by, *see* Selection, behavioral
 susceptibility to, 331–2
 time out from, 123
 values, eating/wheel running in rats, 316
Reinforcement schedules, 93, 119; *see also* Interval
  schedules; Ratio schedules
 assumption of generality, 106–8
 behavioral momentum, 109–10

break-and-run pattern of responding, 97, 106
 C. B. Ferster contribution, 94–5, **94**
 cigarette smoking application, 112–13, **113**
 contingency of reinforcement, 97, 108
 continuous reinforcement (CRF), 101–2, **101**, **102**
 dynamics of, 118
 fixed time (FT) schedules, 105, 116–18
 importance of, 93–4
 intermittent, 85, 96, 98–9, 101–2
 interresponse time (IRT), 114
 limited-hold contingency, 108
 mixed, 229/**229**
 molar perspective, 116, 117
 molecular perspective, 114–16, **114**, **115**, **117**, 117–18
 moment of reinforcement, 94
 natural contingencies, 98–9
 notational systems, 99–100, 103
 ongoing behavior and schedule effects, 99
 patterns of response, 97–8
 postreinforcement pause (PRP), 104, 106, 116–18
 progressive ratio schedules, 98, 165
 punishment, 99
 rate of reinforcement, 109–10
 rate of response, 114–16, **114**, **115**
 response-independent, 105
 run of responses, 118
 schedule-induced behaviors, 117
 schedule performance, 114–18
 single-operant schedules, 208–11, **210**, **211**
 steady-state performance, 97, 98, 110
 transition-state performance, 110–12
Reinforcers
 conditioned reinforcers, 77, 77, 221
 negative, 27, 129; *see also* Aversive control of behavior;
  Punishment
 positive, 27, 66, 70
Relationships, adversarial, 146
Relative stimulus control, 182
Relaxation, 299–300
Remembering, 87–9, **88**, 186–8
Remote causation, 5
Replication, experimental, 33–4
Rescorla–Wagner model of conditioning, 58–62, 226
 acquisition, 60–1, **60**
 associative strength, 59
 blocking, 61, 62
 equation, 59–60
 extinction, 61–2, **62**
Research, applied behavior analysis, 296, 300–1;
   see also Science of behavior
 changing criterion designs, 303, 310, **311**
 clarity/completeness, 304
 measurement issues, 303–4
 multiple baseline designs, 301–3, **301**, **303**
 objectivity, 303
 recording of behavior, 304/**304**
 reliability of observations, 305
Resistance to extinction, 85
Respondent/s, 24, 25, 46–8, 157
 acquisition, 47–8, **47**
 conditioning, *see below*

discrimination, 50–1
extinction, **47**, 48, 61–2, **62**
generalization, 49–50, **50**
level, 48
Respondent conditioning, 3–4, **4**, 16, 46–9, **46**, 62, 222
associative strength, 59
backward conditioning, **51**, 52–3
blocking, 57–8, 61, 62
complex conditioning, 56–8, 61, 62
compound stimuli, 56–7
conditioned response (CR), 46–8
conditioned stimulus (CS), 46
conditioned suppression, 57, 135
definition, 47
delayed conditioning, 51/**51**
equation, 59–60
extinction, 61–2
first-order, 53
homeostasis, 54
overshadowing, 57, 58
Rescorla–Wagner model, 58–62, **60**, **62**, 226
second-order, 53–6, **55**, 62
sensory preconditioning, 58
simultaneous conditioning, 51–2, **51**
temporal factors, 51–3, **51**, 62
trace conditioning, **51**, 52
Response
classes, 25
contingent, 72
deprivation, 71–2
differential, 172/**172**, 174
emotional, 4, 84; *see also* Feelings
equilibrium/homeostasis, 72
functions, 24–5
generalization, 299
hierarchies, 71
instrumental, 72
rates, 114–16, **114**, **115**, 200, **210**
shock interval, 130, 133
stereotypy, 81, 102/**102**
variability, 102
Resurgence, 102
Retention interval, 186, 187
Retirement, 112
Reversal
design, 30–2, 39
testing, 286
Reward
contingency, 70
and intrinsic motivation, 69–70, **70**
Rhesus monkeys, imitation behavior, 244
Rigidity, behavioral, 326–8, **326**, **327**, **328**
Robins (*Turdus americanis*), 41, 42
Rooting response, newborn infants, 43
Rules, 257, 265
construction/following rules, 258–9, **258**
contingency-shaped behavior, 259–61, **260**
contingency-specifying stimuli, 258
evolutionary basis, 261
as function-altering events, 263
generalized obedience, 260/**260**

instructions, 261–3
joint control, 264/**264**
orders/commands, 260
rule-governed behavior, 257–8, 259, 270–1
Run of responses, 118

Sales/advertising pitch, 14, 260
Salience, 60
Satiation, 80
Saying and doing, 241–2
Scalloping, 106/**106**, 126
Schedule
induced behavior, 162
of punishment, 126
of reinforcement, *see* Reinforcement schedules
Schedules of Reinforcement (Ferster & Skinner), 94–5
Schools, *see also* Problem behavior; Teaching
use of variable-interval schedules, 203–4
Schwartz, Barry, 81/**81**, 82; *see also* Author Index
Science of behavior, 1–2; *see also* Behavior analysis;
    Experimental analysis; Functional analysis; Research
basic assumptions, 18–21
biological context of behavior, 6–7
evolution of learning, 6
operant conditioning, 4/**4**
remembering, analysis, 187
respondent conditioning, 3–4, **4**
selection by consequences, 3–5, **4**, 8, 73, 323, **324**, 330, 335;
    see also Culture; Genetic selection; Selection
selection of operant behavior, 7–8
Science and Human Behavior (Skinner), xii, 10
Science Magazine, 279
S-delta stimuli, 67
Search image, 39
Secondary reinforcers, 221, *see also* Conditioned
    reinforcement
Second-order conditioning, 53–6, **55**, 62
Seeing/sight, *see* Vision
Selection, behavioral, 329; *see also* Culture; Evolution;
    Genetic selection
by consequences, 3–5, **4**, 8, 73, 323, **324**, 330, 338
extinction, behavioral, 330–1
ontogenetic selection, 111
operant processes, 7–8, 65, 72/**72**, 74–5, 329–30
operant regulation in marine snail *Aplysia*, 330
social signals, 332–3, **332**
Skinnerian paradigm, 8
susceptibility to reinforcement, 331–2
verbal behavior, 334–5
vocal sounds/speech, 333–4
Self-
control, *see below*
description, 281
determination, 9
efficacy, 257
examination, breast (BSE), 318, 319–20
harming, 210–11, **211**, 297
reference, 283
Self-control
behavior, 207–8
training, 310–11, **311**

Sensory preconditioning, 58
Sequences, behavioral, 42–3, **43**
Sesame Street (TV programme), 182, 251
The Shame of American Education, 310
Shaping/successive approximation, 77–8, 235
    autoshaping, 153–4, **153**, 167–9
Shock–shock interval, 130, 133
Side effects of punishment, 127, 128, 135–6
    aggression, 127, 140–4, **141**
    behavioral persistence, 136–7
    coercion, 144–6
    dropping out/truancy
    learned helplessness, 137–40
    social defeat/aversion to social contact, 139–40
    social disruption, 144
Sidman, Murray, **145**; *see also* Author Index
    Sidman avoidance, 133–4, **133**
Sight, *see* Vision
Sign tracking, 152–3, **152**, 154
Signal detection theory, xi, 39
Signing, iconic, 334
Simultaneous
    conditioning, 51–2, **51**
    discrimination, 182
Single-operant schedules of reinforcement, 208–11, **210**, **211**
    experimental evidence for, 209–10, **210**
Skinner, Burrhus Frederic, 9–11, **9**, **17**; *see also* Author Index
    on behavior analysis, 9, 16–18
    paradigm, 8
    B. F. Skinner: A Fresh Appraisal (film), 11
Smoking, moderation of excessive, 310–11, **311**
    reinforcement schedules, 112–13, **113**
Snail, marine (*Aplysia*), 326–7, 330, **326**
Social
    cognitive theory, 256
    contingencies/punishment, 261
    defeat/aversion to social contact, 139–40
    disruption, 144; *see also* Problem behavior
    episode, 280
    influence, generalized susceptibility to, 260
    reinforcement, 233–4
    relationships, 4
    signals, evolution, 332–3, **332**
Solving the Anorexia Puzzle: A Scientific Approach (Epling & Pierce), 318
Species-specific behavior (Breland experiments), 151–2
Speech, 8, 24; *see also* Verbal behavior
    development in infants, 289–90
    evolution of, 268–9
    matching, 201
    parrot "speech", 277
    selection/evolution, 332–3, **332**
Spider (*Cupiennius salei*), 42
Splinter skills, autistic children, 313
Spontaneous imitation, 243–4, 250
    human infants, 246–8, **246**, **247**, 249
    pigeons, 244–6, **245**
Spontaneous recovery, 49/**49**, 86–7
Sport, teaching, 225
Stalking the Wild Asparagus (Gibbons), 38

Statistical design, experimental analysis of behavior, 33
Steady-state performance, 32, 97, 98, 110, 195–6
Stimuli/stimulus
    class, 284, 285–6, **286**
    contingency-specifying, 258
    control, *see below*
    equivalence, 283, 287, 288
    generalization, 180, 299, 313; *see also* Generalization
    –stimulus (S–S) account of conditioned reinforcement, 227
    substitution hypothesis, 154–5
Stimulus control, 171–3, 191; *see also* Generalization; Multiple schedules
    bird perception, 173
    complex, 185–90
    concept formation by pigeons, 188–9
    conditional discrimination, 189–90
    controlling stimulus, 171
    delayed matching to sample, 186–8, **186**
    differential reinforcement, 172–3, **172**
    differential reinforcement of other behavior (DRO), 176
    differential response, 172/**172**, 174
    discrimination of identity, 185–6, **185**
    discriminative stimulus, 171, 172
    errorless discrimination, 182–4, **183**
    extinction stimulus, 171
    fading, 182, 184–5
    matching to sample, 185–6, **185**
    pigeon discrimination example, 175–7, **176**
    quality control application, 190–1, **190**
    relative rate of reinforcement, 177, 178
    remembering, 186–8
    retention interval, 186, 187
Stockholm syndrome, 234
Stroke, altered behavior management, 298
Stroop effect, 36–7, **37**
Structural approach (to behavioral classification), 23
Subliminal suggestion, 14
Submissive behavior, and aggression, 223–4
Substitutes, partial, 178, 205
Successive
    approximation, *see* Shaping
    discrimination, 182
Suicidal behavior, 297
Superstition, 168, 176
    concurrent, 196
Suppression, conditioned, 135
Survival, contingencies of, 324–5
Symbolic behavior, 283–4, 293; *see also* Speech; Verbal behavior
    communication in pigeons, 279–83, **280**, **282**
    derived conceptual relations, neuroscientific perspective, 287–9
    equivalence relations, 284
    experimental analysis, 284–6
    identity matching, 284, 285/**285**
    natural speech development, 289–90
    reflexivity, 284, 285/**285**
    reversal testing, 286

stimulus equivalence, 283, 287, 288
symmetry, stimulus class, 284, 285–6, **286**
three-term contingencies, 289
transitivity, 286–7, **287**
Symbolic matching, 284, **286**, **287**
Symmetry
stimulus class, 284, 285–6, **286**
stimulus equivalence, 235
Systematic replication, 33

Taboos, cultural, 336–7
Tacting/tacting relations, 271–2
analysis of, 291–2, **292**
Tandem schedules of reinforcement, 223/**223**, 229/**229**
Taste aversion learning, 158–62, **159**
conditioned (CTA), 316
Teaching, 11; *see also* Precision teaching; Problem behavior;
Schools
personalized system of instruction (PSI), 305–6, 320
sport, 225
The Technology of Teaching (Skinner), 11
Temper tantrums, 89/**89**
Teresa, Mother, 221
Terzich, Brenda, **312**; *see also* Author Index
Textual behavior, 277
Thinking/thought
as behavior, 18, 20–1
and behavior, causality, 18
concept formation by pigeons, 188–9
Thorndike, Edward Lee, 14–15, **15**, 16; *see also* Author
Index
Three-term contingencies, 67/**67**, 289
Threshold, law of, 44
Timberlake, W., 72/**72**, 154, 155; *see also* Author Index
Time sampling, 304
Tokens/financial reinforcement, 234–7, **234**
behavior improvement with tokens, 236
chimpanzees, 234–5, **234**
monetary schedule of reinforcement, 235–6
token economy, 236–7
Tolerance, drug, 54, 62
Topography
of response, 23, 66
of tact, 274
Trace conditioning, **51**, 52
Tranquilizers, 33
Transition-state performance, 110–12
Transitivity, 286–7, **287**
Trends, behavior change, 35
Trial-and-error learning, 14–15, 16, 73
Truancy, school, 145–6
Two-key procedure, concurrent, 194/**194**, **195**, **197**

Unconditioned
reinforcement, 225–6, *see also* Conditioned reinforcement
reinforcers, 221

response (UR), 43, 44
stimulus (US), 43, 44
Undermatching, 201, **202**, 213, 215, **216**
Upcoming ratio requirement, 104
UR (unconditioned response), 43, 44
US (unconditioned stimulus), 43, 44

Values, reinforcement, eating/wheel running in rats, 316
Variable-interval (VI) reinforcement schedules, **103**, 108–9,
108, **109**, 203–4
concurrent, 196
Variable ratio (VR), **103**, 104–5, **104**, **105**, 108
Verbal behavior, 267–70, 292–3; *see also* Speech; Symbolic
behavior
American Sign Language, 270/**270**
behavioral selection, 334–5
conditional discrimination, laboratory analysis, 278–9,
278
conditioned establishing operations (CEO), 28, 273
echoic behavior, 276–7
evolution of speaking/vocal tract, 268–9
formal similarity, 276
functional independence, 273
functional operant units, 271–2
generalized reinforcement, 281
intraverbal behavior, 276
language, defining, 267–9
manding/manding relations, 271–2, 273–4, 290–1,
291
multiple functions, 291
operant functions, 271
range, 270
rule-governed behavior, 270–1
tacting/tacting relations, 271–2, 274, 291–2, **292**
textual behavior, 277
Verbal Behavior (Skinner), 271, 290
Verbal community, xi, 271
VI, *see* Variable-interval reinforcement schedules
Violence, domestic, 141–2
Visceral learning, 157
Vision
as conditioned response, 38–9
evolution, 173
Vocal
sounds/speech, 333–4
tract evolution, 268–9
Volcanic eruption, habituation to, 45

Walden Two (Skinner), 9, 17, 295
Water misting, as aversive stimulus, 126
Watson, John Broadus, 7, 13–14, **13**, 16; *see also* Author
Index
Wheel running in rats, 316
Williams, Ben, 178/**178**, 179
Withdrawal, conditioned, 54, 56
Work-time, 118